The IABC Handbook
of Organizational
Communication

A Guide to Internal Communication,
Public Relations, Marketing,
and Leadership

Tamara L. Gillis

Editor

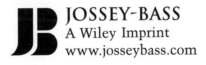

JOSSEY-BASS
A Wiley Imprint
www.josseybass.com

Published by Jossey-Bass
A Wiley Imprint
989 Market Street, San Francisco, CA 94103-1741
www.josseybass.com

Jossey-Bass books and products are available through most bookstores. To contact Jossey-Bass directly call our Customer Care Department within the U.S. at 800-956-7739, outside the U.S. at 317-572-3986, or fax 317-572-4002.

Jossey-Bass also publishes its books in a variety of electronic formats. Some content that appears in print may not be available in electronic books.

Library of Congress Cataloging-in-Publication Data

The IABC handbook of organizational communication: a guide for marketers, consultants, and communications professionals / Tamara Gillis, editor.
        p. cm.
"This handbook is the fourth edition of a project that began in 1981 as Inside Organizational Communication. It was published three times under that title (Ruess and Silvis, 1981 and 1985, and Wann, 1999). Here in 2006, the exhaustive collection of articles warranted a new title"—P.
    Includes bibliographical references and index.
    ISBN-13: 978-0-7879-8080-1 (cloth)
    ISBN-10: 0-7879-8080-3 (cloth)
    1. Communication in organizations—United States. I. Title: Handbook of organizational communication. II. Title: International Association of Business Communicators handbook of organizational communication. III. Gillis, Tamara L. IV. International Association of Business Communicators.
    V. Inside organizational communication.
    HD30.36.U5I56 2006
        658.4′5—dc22   2006007075

Printed in the United States of America
FIRST EDITION

HB Printing   10 9 8 7 6 5 4 3 2 1

A Joint Publication of
The Jossey-Bass Business &
Management Series
and
The International Association of Business Communicators

CONTENTS

FOREWORD

Although *business communication* is a relatively new term, finding its way into the common business lexicon about 2000, its roots go back much further than that, to the very beginning of commercial interactions, to the very beginning of recorded history as we know it. Along the way, communication has undergone dramatic change as humans discovered new and innovative ways to communicate.

Consider an innovation dating back to around 8,500 B.C., when early merchants discovered the wonderful portability of clay tokens with pictographs to record quantities of materials shipped and traded. What a dramatic shift from having to restrict such recordkeeping to the inside of a cave. Can you imagine the excitement over *that* discovery? Think of the time saved and increase in accuracy. It was no longer necessary to gather everyone in one location to review records or rely solely on verbal communication and possibly faulty memories. It was a communication explosion to be sure, and one that later led to the development of a series of alphabets and an evolution of written communication.

Massive communication shifts have been part of the business landscape since the beginning of economics and this change has continued for every generation since then. We are now in the middle of grappling with a global technology revolution that is continuing to unfold, the outcome of which is still being discovered. Though not always formally recognized as such, it is likely there has always been someone (or a group of someones) tasked with ensuring that these communication shifts were understood and accepted by the major stakeholders of the enterprise. These are the people described in this book as *business communicators.*

As business communication follows the path of innovation, the International Association of Business Communicators (IABC) has attempted to interpret, educate, and arm communicators with the information and tools needed to use communication to propel business forward. In 1970 a group of senior communication professionals formed an organization that addressed the needs of people who held the responsibility of ensuring effective organizational communication. The International Association of Business Communicators was then formed.

IABC's global network of thirteen thousand members in sixty-seven countries, representing ten thousand organizations, practice the disciplines of corporate communication, public relations, employee communication, marketing communication, media relations, community relations, public affairs, investor relations, and government relations. Its purpose is to ensure that members have the skills and resources to progress in their careers, develop and share best practices, set standards of excellence, build credibility and respect for the profession, and unite as a community.

In 2004, IABC joined forces with Jossey-Bass Publishers to develop a series of books that would enable all business professionals to take advantage of the lessons learned from business communication. The books draw on research from the IABC Research Foundation, including the groundbreaking "Excellence Study," and best practices from its programs, including an annual international conference, seminars, the Gold Quill Awards program, accreditation, Knowledge Centre reports, manuals, communication templates, the award-winning magazine, *Communication World,* and the monthly online supplement, *CW Bulletin.*

Since its inception, IABC has moved business communication forward, both as a profession and as a driving force that is critical to any organization's success. We are proud to be able to provide you with this information and hope that you will apply it to making your organization's communication more effective for the benefit of your customers, employees, and overall organizational excellence.

Learn more about the International Association of Business Communicators at www.iabc.com.

Natasha Spring
Vice President Publishing and Research
Executive Editor, *Communication World*

PREFACE

For more than thirty-five years, the International Association of Business Communicators (2005) and the IABC Research Foundation have endeavored to provide professional development programs and groundbreaking research that shares "best global communication practices, ideas and experiences that will enable communicators to develop highly ethical and effective performance standards." This book, as evidence of that mission, provides a substantial base of practical knowledge and insights about effective corporate communication and its impact on organizational success.

This handbook is the fourth edition of a project that began in 1981 as *Inside Organizational Communication*. It was published three times under that title (Reuss & Silvis, 1981, 1985; Wann, 1999). Each successive edition increased in content to reflect the changing concerns of organizational communication and its impact on organizations—large and small, public and private, for profit and not for profit. Here in 2006, the exhaustive collection of articles warranted a new title: *The IABC Handbook of Organizational Communication*.

The goal of this book is simple: to provide both conceptual understanding and practical applications of the elements of organizational communication. It presents a broad understanding of corporate communication, business communication, and organizational communication. Based on a survey of scholarly literature, we use these three terms—*organizational communication, corporate communication,* and *business communication*—interchangeably to describe these internal and external communication functions of an organization or company.

My sincere thanks to the chapter authors; their expertise and wisdom made this book possible. Special thanks go to the IABC Accreditation Council for their insights into the process of developing this collection. It is my hope that communication practitioners at all levels, educators, and those outside the communications field will find insights and understanding from this book that contribute to organizational success.

HOW THIS BOOK CAME ABOUT

Organizational communications is a vast, dynamic discipline, its practice affected by society and technology. To address every facet of organizational communication would fill many books of this size. Many periodicals and books are published every year giving new insights and highlighting research concerning its many facets. For these reasons, this book could not cover every facet. We instead address the most universal and pressing concerns in this edition of *The IABC Handbook of Organizational Communication,* as defined by an expert panel of professional communicators.

All sound communications projects begin with research. After reviewing the contents of the previous three editions of *Inside Organizational Communication* and the findings of a brief content analysis of current communication periodicals, I developed a list of potential topics for inclusion in this book. This list of topics was categorized, and an online survey addressing the topics was sent to an expert panel of communication professionals for review. The panel consisted of the members of the IABC Accreditation Council and a random selection of accredited business communicators from around the world. The results of the survey provided support for the framework and organization of the book. The respondents also asked that this edition reflect the international nature of business communication, new and traditional practical applications, and case studies and compelling research.

ASSUMPTIONS ABOUT THE READER

This book is designed and organized with a number of different readers in mind. If you are new to the world of corporate communication, the chapters in this book bring to the fore issues that are critical to understand and master in any organization. If you are a professional communicator, this book provides new insights on traditional and emerging issues in organizational communication. If you are a corporate executive outside the communication discipline, this book will help you understand the importance and reach of communication within your organization and with external stakeholders.

Understanding occurs when people ask questions and share information. This book follows suit. Like any other handbook, it may be read in a number of ways. First, it may be read from cover to cover. If you are interested in all facets of organizational communication, you will enjoy starting at the beginning of this book and reading through to the end. The book's organization builds from general topics to specialty interests. Predictions for the future conclude the collection.

Second, readers may choose to skim the book for topics of interest or topics related to a current challenge. This book touches on issues of interest to those new to the field of organizational communications as well as seasoned professionals.

HOW THIS BOOK IS ORGANIZED

When addressing the 2005 IABC International Conference, renowned political consultant James Carville used three adjectives to describe successful communication: *simple, relevant,* and *repetitive.* I use those same three adjectives to describe the content of this book. Much of the insight and advice about communication that is shared in these chapters seems *simple.* And complex concepts are outlined here in simple models to make them readily accessible. The topics addressed in this book represent what our panel of experts agreed was most *relevant* for communicators and other organization associates to understand about the process of organizational communication. Finally, many communication concepts overlap, and thus these elements are discussed directly and tangentially in a number of chapters. This *repetition* is necessary to fully appreciate the context of corporate communication.

This book is organized into six major parts. Part One serves as an introduction to business communication and addresses some universal premises concerning corporate communication. The chapters in this part introduce readers to the complexities and structures of corporate communication. The universal concepts of excellence, trust, culture, ethics, and measurement are reviewed to set the foundation for the role of corporate communicators today. These chapters provide fundamental axioms as well as testimonials.

Part Two, by far the largest part of this book, focuses on the current challenges of managing corporate communications and organizational communication. Cultivating a culture of communication is critical within any organization. The authors share insights into successful planning, implementation, and management of corporate communication. The strategies they review are fundamental to successful communication management.

Part Three contains six chapters that explore the common threads and evolving issues in the practice of employee communication and internal communication networks. At the heart of each excellent organization or corporation is a trusted and honored internal communication program. Integral issues of relationship building, employee engagement, change communication, and internal branding are highlighted here as key to developing that trusted internal program.

Part Four apprises readers of the role of public relations in the corporate communication program. A host of external publics await business communicators. These stakeholders will have an impact on the reputation and success of our organizations in reaching their goals. The chapters demonstrate the need for a strategic approach to managing external relationships.

Part Five addresses key concepts of marketing and brand management and its place in the corporate communication program. The chapters in this part, punctuated by testimonials and case studies, bring to life the internal impact and external challenges of marketing communications. Here, professionals share their insights and expertise for developing excellence in corporate performance through marketing communication programming.

Part Six reminds readers of the need to look to the future. The seven chapters that end the book challenge corporate communicators and their organizational colleagues to be prepared for new trends and issues that will continue to make an impact on successful organizational communication. The chapters here echo back to the issues presented in Part One. The issues of measurement, knowledge management, integration, technology, and emerging trends will continue to affect our organizations. Most notably, new values for the new workplace will ground new and seasoned communicators in the values that matter in our daily lives.

ACKNOWLEDGMENTS

The process of compiling a volume of knowledge like *The IABC Handbook of Organizational Communication* is an arduous one with many twists and turns along the way. I am grateful for the assistance and friendship that I received from Carol Gima, Ashley N. Miller, Natasha Spring, and Heather Turbeville. I will miss our virtual meetings and exchanges. I especially thank all the chapter authors who contributed their time and wisdom. Their expertise will help countless professionals make the right choices for their organizations. A special thank-you to the accredited business communicators who helped in the preliminary stages. And one big thank-you to Jeffrey for all his patience during this process.

February 2006

Tamara L. Gillis
Elizabethtown, Pennsylvania

References

International Association of Business Communicators. (2005). IABC's mission, vision and brand. Retrieved July 22, 2005, from http://www.iabc.com/info/about/aboutiab.htm.

Reuss, C. M., & Silvis, D. E. (Eds.). (1981). *Inside organizational communication*. New York: Longman.

Reuss, C. M., & Silvis, D. E. (Eds.). (1985). *Inside organizational communication* (2nd ed.). New York: Longman.

Wann, A. (Ed.). (1999). *Inside organizational communication* (3rd ed.). New York: Forbes Custom Publishing.

ABOUT THE AUTHORS

Jenifer Armand-Delille has shared her career in communications between the United States and France. She holds a bachelor in education and an M.A. in creative writing. Armand-Delille is professor of business communications for the M.B.A. program at the International Institute of Management, Paris. A corporate trainer for many years, she created and taught training sessions in multicultural communications for French executives at companies including Renault, Chanel, Bic, Merck, Mazda, and Loctite. Before that, she was associate travel editor at *Bride's* magazine, New York. She is currently membership chair of IABC's French chapter, a member of SHRM, and a freelance writer.

   Ayelet Baron is recognized as an expert in global business strategy and organizational change management. In her current role at Cisco Systems, she is responsible for Global Mobile Vertical's strategic initiatives and business planning. Prior to joining Cisco, she spent sixteen years as a consultant managing the development, implementation, and measurement of key initiatives and programs for global Fortune 50 companies embarking on major change initiatives. She was on the executive board of the Strategic Leadership Forum, international director at large for the IABC, and past president of IABC Toronto. Her articles

---

ABC = Accredited Business Communicator, International Association of Business Communicators. APR = Accredited Public Relations practitioner, Public Relations Society of America. IABC Fellow = This is the highest honor that IABC bestows on a member.

have been published in *Communication World, Strategic Communication Management,* and *Across the Board.* She holds a B.A. from York University, Toronto, and an M.A. from Hebrew University of Jerusalem.

Bill Carney is the author of *In the News: The Practice of Media Relations in Canada* and is a senior communicator with the government of Saskatchewan in Canada.

Gerard Castles is director of Gerard Castles & Associates, based in Hobart, Australia. He has nearly twenty years' experience in helping major organizations in Australasia, Asia, and the United Kingdom engage their people during times of major change. Prior to setting up his consultancy, he worked in the Sydney Office of McKinsey & Company.

R. Alan Crozier, ABC, formed Q^4 consulting in 2002 having previously been with Watson Wyatt Partners and before that Mercer. At Watson Wyatt, he was responsible for its human capital practice in Scotland and also for its strategic communication consulting capability throughout Europe. He has served on the steering board of the Corporate Identity Group, the professional advisory board of the M.Sc. in Corporate Communication Management at Salford University, and is currently on the U.K. Board of the IABC. He is a member of the Chartered Management Institute. Crozier has written for professional journals and presented at conferences in Europe and North America.

Elpi O. Cuna Jr., APR, is vice president and director for corporate communication for Manila Electric Company (Meralco). He is company spokesman for Meralco, a job he has held for twenty years, where he has led campaigns and handled issue management and crisis communication situations. A former Asia Pacific regional director of the IABC and past president of IABC Philippines, he is currently a member of the board of trustees. He is a past president and member of the board of advisers of the Public Relations Society of the Philippines, governor of the Manila Overseas Press Club, member of the National Press Club of the Philippines, governor of the Philippine National Red Cross Rizal Chapter, and member of the National Movement for Free Elections.

Roger D'Aprix, ABC, IABC Fellow, is an internationally known communication consultant, lecturer, and author; he has assisted many Fortune 500 companies in developing communication strategies and redesigning their communication training. He is managing director of his own consultancy in Rochester, New York. For fifteen years he held senior positions with two of the leading human resource consulting companies: Towers Perrin and Mercer. He has written six books on employee communication, the latest of which is *Communicating for Change: Connecting the Workplace with the Marketplace* (Jossey-Bass). He writes a monthly column for the *Ragan Report* on employee communication and is a regular contributor to the *Journal of Employee Communication Management.* He is a member of the advisory board of the U.K. publication *Strategic Communication Management* and serves on the board of ROI Communications.

Meryl David, ABC, internal communication manager at Zurich Financial Services Australia, has worked in communication for more than twenty years, managing her own business, coaching leaders in communication skills, and working as both consultant and in-house communication manager in the private and public sectors. She has served clients in Australia, New Zealand, South Africa, Singapore, the United States, and Japan. Now representing the Asia Pacific region on IABC's Accreditation Council, she has held voluntary offices within IABC continuously for eight years and is also on the advisory board of the Australian Centre for Public Communication.

Nick Durutta, ABC, is internal communications manager for the Capital Group Companies, a global investment management firm based in Los Angeles. Prior to joining Capital in 1996, he was a senior consultant with William M. Mercer, specializing in organizational communication. He received a bachelor's degree in communication from California State University at Fullerton. A member and a past director of the IABC, he has also served as a president of the Los Angeles chapter, as well as chair of the organization's international awards program.

Kathleen Ellis is an associate professor of Communication at the University of Colorado at Colorado Springs where she teaches undergraduate and graduate courses in organizational communication, research methods, and statistics. She specializes in instrument development and validation. Ellis has coauthored one book and several articles on organizational trust and has consulted in both private and public sector organizations. She received her B.A. and M.A. from the University of Colorado at Colorado Springs and her Ph.D. in communication at the University of Denver.

Merry Elrick founded DataDriven MarCom in 2003 to assist clients of Elrick Business Communications (EBC), the full-service, integrated marketing communications agency she founded in 1990. Her clients included major corporations, such as BP, GE, and Siemens. In 2005, she sold EBC and began to work exclusively on helping business-to-business marketers determine return on investment. An Addy, Tower, Pro-Comm, Tranny, Spectra, and Silver Quill Award winner, Elrick created the first nationwide broadcast and print campaigns for Wendy's Old-Fashioned Hamburgers. Elrick is a former member of the board of directors of U.S. District 4 of IABC, a past president of IABC Chicago, and a member of the Business Marketing Association and the American Marketing Association. She is a Certified Business Communicator through BMA.

Alison Rankin Frost is a communications strategist specializing in corporate reputation and brand management. In her career, she has covered all aspects of communication from advertising, public relations, and internal communications to change management, research, investor relations, and public affairs. She has worked in senior communications management roles in leading companies and consultancies. A member of IABC for over twelve years, she was director of communications for the Europe and Middle East Region, U.K. Chapter president, and vice president of professional development. She was chair of EuroComm twice and was instrumental in developing the EuroComm brand. She is the author of several reports on communications management.

Kellie Garrett, ABC, is senior vice president of strategy, knowledge and reputation at Farm Credit Canada (FCC). She is responsible for FCC's business strategy, knowledge management function, and all things in reputation, including brand management and corporate communication. Her team has won dozens of awards for innovative and best practice programs in diverse areas. She is a frequent speaker in her areas of expertise and a passionate volunteer for boards in the areas of palliative care, health care, and autism. Garrett is vice chairperson of IABC's Research Foundation Board in 2005–2006. She holds an M.A. in leadership and training.

Diane M. Gayeski is internationally recognized as a thought leader in organizational communication and learning. She leads Gayeski Analytics through which she has been engaged in over three hundred consulting and professional development projects by clients worldwide, such as General Electric, Johnson & Wales University, Metropolitan New York City Library System, Pitney Bowes, and Ernst and Young. In addition, she holds a full-time position as professor in the Roy H. Park School of Communications at Ithaca College in New York State. The author of thirteen books, she is a frequent speaker at conferences and private executive briefings.

Tamara L. Gillis, ABC, is associate professor and chairman of the Department of Communications at Elizabethtown College, Pennsylvania. Her research interests include change management, civic involvement, organizational design, and the impact of new media. She also serves as a communications consultant with Cooper Wright LLC. In her career, she has led communication programs for higher education institutions, associations, and a health care corporation. She has served as faculty in Swaziland, Namibia, and the Semester at Sea program. The IABC Research Foundation honored her with the 2004 Foundation Lifetime Friend Award. In 2001–2002 she chaired the IABC Research Foundation. She has held leadership positions at the district and international levels of IABC. The author of numerous articles and book chapters, she is also coauthor (with R. C. Moore) of a text on community media in Africa titled *Keeping your ear to the ground: A journalist's guide to citizen participation in the news* (The Polytechnic Press, Namibia, 2003).

Carol Kinsey Goman, president of Kinsey Consulting Services, specializes in the human side of organizational transformation, helping senior managers become more effective leaders of change, improving employees' change adeptness, and developing organizational cultures and management strategies that nurture creative collaboration. She offers seminars around the world and has authored over one hundred articles and nine books, including *"This Isn't the Company I Joined"—How to Lead in a Business Turned Upside Down.* She has served as adjunct faculty at John F. Kennedy University in the International M.B.A. program, the University of California in the Executive Education Department, and the Chamber of Commerce of the U.S. Institutes for Organization Management.

Rodney Gray is principal of Employee Communication & Surveys, based in Sydney, Australia. He is a forty-year veteran of senior corporate human resource roles and employee communication consulting. For the past twenty years, he has worked with clients in Australia and globally to improve internal communication processes and systems. He has been a member of committees for the IABC Research Foundation and has written for *Communication World* magazine.

James E. Grunig is professor emeritus in the Department of Communication at the University of Maryland. He has won three major awards in public relations: the Pathfinder Award for excellence in public relations research of the Institute for Public Relations Research and Education, the Outstanding Educator Award of the Public Relations Society of America (PRSA), and the Jackson, Jackson and Wagner Award for behavioral science research of the PRSA Foundation. He also won the most prestigious lifetime award of the Association for Education in Journalism and Mass Communication, the Paul J. Deutschmann Award for Excellence in Research.

Larissa A. Grunig is professor emerita in the Department of Communication at the University of Maryland. She served for more than two years as special assistant to the president of the university for women's issues. She has received the Pathfinder Award for excellence in public relations research sponsored by the U.S. Institute for Public Relations, the Outstanding Educator Award of the Public Relations Society of America (PRSA), and the Jackson, Jackson and Wagner Award for behavioral science research of the PRSA Foundation. She coauthored the first book on women in public relations.

Todd T. Hattori, ABC, is a director at large and ethics chair for the 2005–2006 IABC executive board. He directs employee communications, media relations, customer outreach, and Web communication programs for the Washington Department of Information Services. Hattori has provided strategic communication counsel for financial, technology, health care, and government organizations and taught undergraduate and graduate courses in design, writing, and communication planning. He earned a B.A. from the University of Utah in speech communication, with an emphasis on argumentation and negotiation, and an M.A. from Westminster College in technical writing.

Shel Holtz, ABC, IABC Fellow, is principal of Holtz Communication + Technology, a consultancy that helps organizations apply online technology to their organizational communications. He has spent nearly thirty years in the communications field as a director of corporate communications for two Fortune 500 companies and as a senior communications consultant for two human resource consulting firms. He is the author of *Public Relations on the Net* and *Corporate Conversations.*

Mary Ann McCauley, ABC, is president and principal of Catalyst Communications, located in the Twin Cities, a firm that provides strategic communication counsel. Prior to her corporate and consulting work, she was a journalist and owned and operated a community newspaper. She is a graduate of the University of Missouri School of Journalism. Active in IABC, McCauley chairs the IABC Accreditation Council. She was the 2000 recipient of the IABC Chairman's Award. She is an active contributor to the communities in which she has lived and worked and currently is a volunteer consultant with Minnesota Assistance Project.

Mark P. McElreath, ABC, APR, is a professor at Towson University in Maryland and has been a member of the IABC for more than thirty years. His areas of expertise include evaluative research, public relations, organizational communication, integrated communication, and ethics. He is the author of *Managing Systematic* *and Ethical Public Relations Campaigns.* In 2005 McElreath received a Lifetime Achievement Award from the Maryland Chapter of the Public Relations Society of America for his work in ethics and accreditation in the field of public relations. He is a member of the Commission on Public Relations Education and of the Universal Accreditation Board.

George McGrath is a partner and founder of McGrath Matter Associates, a public relations and public affairs consulting firm. Over the course of a twenty-five-year career in communications, McGrath has helped clients identify issues that are key to their success and develop business strategies and communication campaigns to influence the course of debates over public policy. He has worked with businesses, trade associations, and nonprofit organizations on a range of issues, including environmental protection, energy competition, health care delivery, and education. He served on the IABC international board between 1989 and 1994 and was IABC's international chairman between 1992 and 1993.

Adine Mees is cofounder, president, and CEO of the Canadian Business for Social Responsibility (CBSR). As a founding board member of CBSR, she facilitated the development of corporate Canada's first corporate social responsibility guidelines, CBSR's Good Company Guidelines. She is a cofounder of the Ethics in Action Awards; an appointed member of the Doctor of Business Administration Development Board with Royal Reeds University; a board director of the U.S.-based LightHawk, a conservation aviation organization; a board director of Metafore; and a past board director of the Canadian Social Investment Organization. Adine authored a chapter in the book *Global Profit and Global Justice.*

Paul Mlodzik, ABC, is vice president of Marketing, Agency and Call Centre for The Co-operators, the largest Canadian-owned multiline insurance company. His previous experience includes senior marketing and sales management roles with the Insurance Corporation of British Columbia, Coast Capital Credit Union, and the Prudential Assurance Company Limited. He is a frequent presenter at industry and professional association events on the topics of brand management, strategic communications planning, and making effective presentations. His work has been recognized with over fifty regional, national, and international awards. Mlodzik was presented with the 2004 Master Communicator Award (the highest honor given to an IABC member in Canada) by IABC Canada for his professional achievements, service to IABC and thought leadership. He holds a B.A. in economics from the University of British Columbia and an M.A. in communication studies from Concordia University. He has also earned several financial services designations, including Certified Financial Planner.

Christopher Nevill is a native South African who founded and continues to spearhead Foundation in Johannesburg, South Africa. His no-nonsense, practical, and often controversial outlook on issues has been forged in the crucible of South Africa, a country universally recognized as "the world in one nation." He has recently started a Ph.D., and his thesis is titled "Companies on the Couch." His sources of inspiration include the wisdom of writers and philosophers, both ancient and modern, and the great holy books of the world's religions.

J. David Pincus, APR, is a visiting professor in the Sam Walton College of Business at the University of Arkansas, Fayetteville. Before coming to Arkansas, he was professor of communications at California State University, Fullerton, and visiting professor in the Executive M.B.A. program at the University of Southern California. His primary research focus has been on the merger of communication and leadership/management in the workplace and in the education of future business and communication professionals. He is lead author (with J. N. DeBonis) of *Top Dog: A Different Kind of Book About Becoming an Excellent Leader.* He received his doctorate in organizational communication from the University of Maryland, College Park.

Lester R. Potter, ABC, IABC Fellow, is president of Les Potter Incorporated, an international consultancy he founded in 1998. His firm helps organizations worldwide use communication as a strategic management tool to boost organizational effectiveness. He is also visiting assistant professor (2004–2006) in the Department of Mass Communication and Communication Studies at Towson University, Maryland. He is currently a doctoral candidate in instructional technology at Towson. Potter is a past chairman of the IABC. He served on IABC's executive board, accreditation board, and as a trustee of the IABC Research Foundation. He is the author of *The Communication Plan: The Heart of Strategic Communication,* IABC's top-selling manual.

Vicci Rodgers established her firm, the Rodgers Group, in Chicago in 1987, after almost ten years in corporate communication positions with the Mead Corporation and Borg-Warner. The company provides clients with communication strategy, tactical support, research, and evaluation services. She served as on-site communication counsel for companies such as Borg-Warner, General Dynamics, Hallmark, Hobart Corporation, Asea Brown Boveri, and Whirlpool. She started her communication career as a journalist in the Washington, D.C., area. Rodgers served as a member of the international board of directors for

IABC, chairman of the Research Foundation, and in leadership positions for chapters in three states. She received IABC's Chairman's Award in 1998. Her firm's research expertise has been recognized with awards from the American Society for Health Care Marketing and Public Relations and IABC Gold and Silver Quill awards.

Paul M. Sanchez, ABC, APR, is practice leader for communication consulting with Mercer in the United Kingdom. He sits on the board of directors for Mercer's U.K. company and has been appointed a Mercer Worldwide Partner. Previously he was executive vice president and general manager for Stoorza Communications. His prior experience also includes fifteen years with Watson Wyatt Worldwide. He is the chair (2005–2006) of the IABC's Research Foundation. His past IABC activities include executive board member, executive committee finance director, Ethics Committee chairman, and board member of IABC's U.K. chapter. He has a B.Sc. in psychology and an M.Sc. in organizational communications. He has contributed to professional journals and publications and authored *Transformation Communications* published by IABC.

Hilary Scarlett is director of Scarlett Associates, a London-based communication and change management consultancy. Her work has spanned Europe, the United States, and Asia and concentrates on internal communication and the development of people-focused change management programs. She is accredited in the use of Organizational Culture Inventory, Organizational Effectiveness Inventory, and Leadership Impact. Her work also includes helping organizations to assess their current culture and the drivers of that culture, and helping managers to understand their leadership style and how it causes others to behave. She has an M.A. from King's College, Cambridge University, and is a member of the London IABC chapter.

Jeff Schmidt is responsible for leading sales programs and initiatives in the Europe, Middle East, and Africa (EMEA) region of Hewlett Packard, including an initiative to build better customer relationships: HP's Customer First Initiative. This pioneering work has helped focus the company on its most critical customer relationships, align all parts of the organization, and is fundamentally changing the way HP works with customers in all parts of the world. He was previously head of internal communications for HP EMEA and has more than twelve years' experience in various aspects of corporate communications, human resources, and marketing in both the United States and EMEA.

Mark Schumann, ABC, is a senior consultant and managing principal of the Towers Perrin office in Houston. From 1998 through 2004, he led the firm's global communication practice. He has over twenty-five years in corporate, employee, and human resource communication with extensive experience in change, mergers and acquisitions, and employer brands. He is the winner of IABC 13 Gold Quill Awards and is a past IABC Communicator of the Year of Houston and Dallas. He is a member of the IABC international executive board. Schumann holds a master's degree from the University of Denver and a bachelor's degree from Austin College in Sherman, Texas.

Pamela Shockley-Zalabak is chancellor and professor of communication at the University of Colorado at Colorado Springs. She also is president of CommuniCon, a consulting group that specializes in leadership development, conflict resolution, and development of team-based organizations. The author of six books and numerous articles, Shockley-Zalabak focuses on large-scale organizational assessment and planning. She received her B.A. and M.A. from Oklahoma State University and her Ph.D. in communication from the University of Colorado at Boulder.

Lorenzo Sierra, ABC, is an award-winning communicator. He is principal of LoSierra Communication Consulting. Sierra is past president of IABC Phoenix. The chapter was named International Chapter of the Year in 2004 for results achieved during the year he was president.

Brenda Siler, a seasoned communications consultant, has led communications programs at the American Speech-Language-Hearing Association, the Council on Competitiveness, AARP, the American Red Cross, and United Way. In 1998–1999, Siler was chair of IABC. In 1999, she was named by *PR Week* magazine as one of the top twelve African Americans in public relations. Siler is on the board of contributors for the *PR News* newsletter where she has been a guest columnist. She wrote the chapter "Research and Evaluation on a Shoestring" for the 2005 *PR News* guidebook, *Lesson Learned in the PR Trenches.* Siler is a graduate of Spelman College in Atlanta.

Jane Sparrow is general manager of employee communication and change at Sony Europe. She has been responsible for internal communication and change within Sony Europe since 2001. She travels extensively across Europe, working with local teams to plan and deliver internal and external communication. Prior to her current role, Sparrow was a senior management consultant for MCA Communicates, where she assisted board-level clients with marketing and communication challenges. She has also held marketing and communication management roles with IBM and is an adviser to many small businesses. She was the 2004–2005 region deputy director for IABC Europe.

Don W. Stacks is professor and director of the Advertising and Public Relations Program at the University of Miami's School of Communication. Stacks is the author of numerous articles, chapters, books, and professional papers dealing with public relations. He is a member of the Arthur W. Page Society, Commission on Public Relations Education, and Commission on Public Relations Measurement, and sits on the board of trustees for the Institute for Public Relations. He earned his doctorate from the University of Florida in 1978.

Sylvie Testard-Ramírez is head of Echo Research and director of research in France. She specializes in external and internal communication and coordinates several multicultural projects, as well as corporate social responsibility issues and is involved in the UN Global Compact Meetings and the Club Marketing and Sustainable Development of the French marketing association Adetem. She is a member of the International Committee of the French Association for Internal Communication. She trained at the Sorbonne Nouvelle University in Paris and the Centre of Journalism Studies in Cardiff (U.K.). She has spent more than ten years abroad, living and working in the United Kingdom, Spain, and Italy. She also lived in Mexico, where she worked as a freelance journalist and taught communication at the University Politecnico in Mexico City.

Karen Vahouny, ABC, is a founding partner of Qorvis Communications, one of the largest independent public relations firms in the United States. Prior to joining Qorvis, she was a partner at the Poretz Group, the first investor relations firm based in the Washington, D.C., area. Prior to joining the Poretz Group, Vahouny was vice president of corporate communications at PRC, a $750 million information technology company. Twice named Business Communicator of the Year for IABC/Washington, Vahouny served as a director on the IABC executive board, presented at several international conferences, authored articles for *Communication World,* chaired the IABC Think Tank, and chaired the investment committee in 2005. She is a trustee of the IABC Research Foundation and a member of the board of directors for the Capital Area Chapter of the National Investor Relations Institute. She holds a B.S. in marketing from the University of Virginia and an M.B.A. in finance and management from George Mason University.

Mark Weiner is the president of Delahaye, a division of Bacon's Information/ Observer AG. Delahaye measures organizational reputation and provides a complete range of marketing, communication, and PR activities in forty countries. He is a regular contributor to IABC's *Communications World,* PRSA's *Tactics, PR Week,* and *Ragan's Intelligence Report.* He sits on the editorial advisory boards of the *Strategist, PR News,* and Ragan Communications. Weiner is a member of the

Public Relations Society of America and is active in the Institute for Public Relations. He is the founder and past president of the Pubic Relations Service Council and a former board member of the Publicity Club of New York. He is the author of *Unleashing the Power of PR: A Contrarian's Guide to Marketing and Communication* (Jossey-Bass, 2006).

Patricia T. Whalen, APR, is an educator and consultant in the areas of organizational change, corporate crises, and integrated marketing communications. She is a faculty member in the Medill Integrated Marketing Communications graduate program at Northwestern University. In 2001, she authored a top-selling research study for the IABC, "How Communication Drives Merger Success." In 2005 she authored a book titled, *Corporate Communication from A to Z—An Encyclopedia for Public Relations and Marketing Professional.* Most recently she coauthored, with Thomas L. Harris, a new edition of his original book on integrating public relations into the marketing mix, *A Marketer's Guide to Public Relations in the Twenty-First Century.* Whalen holds a doctorate in mass media from Michigan State University, a master's of science degree in business administration from Indiana University at South Bend, and a bachelor's degree in English from the Ohio State University.

Brad Whitworth, ABC, IABC Fellow, is director of enterprise communication for the California State Automobile Association (CSAA), based in San Francisco. His work has earned him recognition as a thought leader in the field of internal communications. Before joining CSAA, he was director of internal communications for software maker PeopleSoft during one of the longest hostile takeovers in U.S. business history. Before that, he led internal and external communication teams in Hewlett-Packard's personal computing, enterprise systems, international sales, and corporate organizations. He developed the merger communications for the $20 billion HP-Compaq PC business and managed the company's Y2K communications program. He holds bachelor's degrees in both journalism and speech from the University of Missouri and an M.B.A. from Santa Clara University. He served as IABC chairman in 1989–1990 and has won six Gold Quill awards.

Stephen C. Wood is a professor of communication studies at the University of Rhode Island, where he teaches courses in argumentation, public discourse, interpersonal communication, media representations, and film studies. His major research interests include political rhetoric, the cultural intersection of baseball and film, and organizational leadership. He has published several works on communication and leadership, including a chapter (with J. David Pincus) titled "The CEO's Changing Communication Role: Precursor to Effective

Leadership" in the 1997 edition of the *Handbook of Administrative Communication.* He has worked as a professional negotiator and arbitrator in many union-management disputes. He earned his doctorate in public communication from the University of Maryland, College Park.

Katherine Woodall, APR, ABC, is a Towers Perrin principal based in the firm's Arlington, Virginia, office. She specializes in communications to drive organizational change. Before joining Towers Perrin, she worked for more than twenty years in corporate communications and marketing positions for Hewlett-Packard and Levi Strauss. She earned a bachelor's degree in English from Santa Clara University and completed graduate studies in comparative literature at the University of California at Berkeley. She teaches business communications in the English department at Santa Clara University. She is the coauthor of *Building Your Organization's Brand: A Practical Guide,* published by IABC.

PART ONE

BUSINESS COMMUNICATION IN THE EVOLVING CORPORATION

CHAPTER ONE

Characteristics of Excellent Communication

James E. Grunig, Larissa A. Grunig

In 2002, we published the last of three books (L. Grunig, J. Grunig, & Dozier) resulting from a $400,000 grant from the IABC Research Foundation for a research project to explain why communication has value to an organization and to identify the characteristics of an organizational communication function that increased its value.[1] This study, titled *Excellence in Public Relations and Communication Management,* generally is known as the Excellence study. In its request for proposals, the foundation asked for a study of "how, why, and to what extent communication affects the achievement of organizational objectives."

For many years, organizational communication professionals have expressed great interest in the third part of this research question: To what extent does communication affect the achievement of organizational objectives? These public relations professionals generally feel underappreciated by other managers or by their clients.[2] Often they believe they are disadvantaged in competing for organizational resources because they cannot explain the value of their work. As a result, communicators long have searched for a statistical model or other evidence to show that the public relations function has value to organizations.

In addition to explaining the extent to which the function has value, we were able to explain why it has value and how the public relations function should be organized to best provide this value. We collapsed these questions into two major research questions that guided the Excellence study:

- The effectiveness question incorporated the questions of why and to what extent communication increases organizational effectiveness. How does the public relations function improve the performance of an organization, and how much is that contribution worth economically?

- The excellence question asked how the public relations function should be organized and managed to increase the likelihood that it will make the contribution to organizational effectiveness identified in the answer to the effectiveness question: What are the characteristics of a communication function that are most likely to make an organization effective?

Based on our research related to the second question, we developed what Fleisher (1995) has called a generic benchmark of critical success factors and best practices in communication management. In most public relations benchmarking studies, a researcher compares a communication unit with other units in its own industry that are generally recognized as the best. The Excellence study, by contrast, identified best practices across different types of organizations: corporations, government agencies, nonprofit organizations, and associations. The generic benchmark produced by the study is a profile that we initially constructed from past research and by theoretical logic. Then we gathered empirical evidence from more than three hundred organizations in three countries to test whether this theoretical profile explains best actual practice as well as best practice in theory.

Generic benchmarking is more valuable than benchmarking a single case because it is unlikely that one organization will be, in Fleisher's words, "a world-class performer across the board" (1995, p. 29). In the Excellence study, we found that a few organizations exemplified most of the best practices, many exemplified some, and others had few of these characteristics. A generic benchmark does not provide an exact formula or detailed description of practices that a communication unit can copy to be excellent. Rather, it provides a set of principles that professionals can use to generate ideas for specific practices in their own organizations. In *Excellence in Public Relations and Communication Management*, Fred Repper (1992), the practitioner member of the Excellence team, explained how the theory of excellence can be used to audit communication programs: "One thing communicators never have been able to do is to compare our communication programs with a program that is considered the best and most effective. However, the normative theory provided in the book gives us an opportunity to measure the effectiveness of our communication programs against that of an ideal program. This comparison is the how to part of the book that each practitioner can use in planning his or her next communication program" (p. 112).

To explain why the best practices identified by the Excellence study make organizations effective, this chapter begins by establishing the value of communication to an organization. It then describes four categories into which the characteristics of best practice fall: (1) the relationship of communication to the management of the organization, (2) the organization and purpose of the communication function, (3) the management of individual communication programs, and (4) the organizational context that supports the best communication practices.

THE VALUE OF COMMUNICATION TO AN ORGANIZATION

In recent years, public relations professionals have searched for an explanation of the rate of return on an organization's investment in communication (its ROI). Research firms and other experts have responded with a deluge of papers, articles, seminars, and Web sites purporting to show how communication provides a financial return or contributes to organizational objectives. Most of the attempts to measure the value of public relations have suffered by confusing the different levels of analysis from which a researcher could address the value question.

Organizations must be effective at four increasingly higher levels of analysis: (1) the program level, (2) the functional level, (3) the organizational level, and (4) the societal level. Effectiveness at a lower level contributes to effectiveness at higher levels, but organizations cannot be said to be truly effective unless they have value at the highest of these levels.

The *program level* refers to individual communication programs such as media relations, community relations, investor relations, marketing communication, or employee relations that are components of the overall communication function of an organization. Communication programs at this level generally are effective when they meet specific objectives, such as affecting the cognitions, attitudes, and behaviors of publics or management, or both. However, we cannot say that these programs make the organization more effective unless we also can show that (1) they are directed at the most important publics of an organization and (2) their effects help to cultivate a good relationship with these strategic publics.

The *functional level* refers to evaluation of the overall public relations function of an organization, which typically includes several programs for different publics. Although individual communication programs successfully accomplish their objectives, the overall communication function might not be effective unless it is integrated into the overall management processes of an organization and has chosen appropriate publics and objectives for individual programs.

The public relations function as a whole can be audited, through self-review or peer review, by comparing its structure and processes with those of similar departments in other organizations or with theoretical principles derived from scholarly research, such as the generic benchmark provided by the Excellence study. The Excellence criteria require knowledge and professionalism by the communication unit. They also require understanding of and support for public relations by senior management. They can be used for both formative and evaluative analysis of the communication function as prior research that can be used to plan and organize the function and as a standard for reviewing the past structure and performance of the function.

The *organizational level* refers to the contribution that communication makes to the overall effectiveness of the organization. In the Excellence study, the review of the literature revealed that at a minimum, organizations must achieve their goals to be considered effective. However, typically there is much conflict within the organization and with outside constituencies about which goals are most important. Effective organizations are able to achieve their goals because they choose goals that are valued by their strategic constituencies both inside and outside the organization. Effective organizations choose and achieve appropriate goals because they develop relationships with their constituencies—their stakeholder "publics." Ineffective organizations cannot achieve their goals, at least in part, because their publics do not support and typically oppose management efforts to achieve what publics consider illegitimate goals. The public relations function helps make an organization more effective when it identifies the most strategic publics and conducts communication programs to develop effective long-term relationships with those publics. As a result, we concluded that the long-term value of communication could be estimated by measuring the quality of relationships with strategic publics.

The *societal level* refers to the contribution that organizations make to the overall welfare of a society. Organizations have an impact beyond their own boundaries. They also serve and affect individuals, publics, and other organizations that make up a society. As a result, organizations cannot be said to be effective unless they are socially responsible, and public relations adds value to society by contributing to the ethical behavior and social responsibility of organizations.

The concept of organization-public relationships emerged as the critical value provided by a public relations function to both the organization and society. Relationships are important because they connect the four levels of analysis. To be effective, communication programs should improve an organization's relationship with its strategic publics. Since society essentially consists of a web of relationships, the communication function contributes social value by improving these relationships one at a time. At the organizational level, relationships have secondary effects that organizations value: they improve the reputation of the organization and increase the likelihood of achieving organizational goals.

In recent years, organizations have evaluated their performance using a varied set of financial and nonfinancial indicators—a balanced scorecard (Kaplan & Norton, 1996, 2001). Relationships typically are referred to as intangible assets, whose value cannot be measured in financial terms (see Post, Preston, & Sachs, 2002, for a discussion of the total value of an organization to all of its stakeholders). Although relationships themselves are nonfinancial indicators, they also contribute to financial value. They can increase revenue, such as by increasing sales, but their greatest effects come from reducing the costs of conflicts with stakeholders and reducing the risks that stakeholders such as the government, the media, the community, or employees will oppose an organizational decision.[3]

Evaluation at the functional level therefore can be logically connected to these other levels by auditing the extent to which the communications function has a structure and conducts activities that are most likely to identify strategic publics and to result in high-quality, long-term relationships with them. In the rest of this chapter, we discuss what the Excellence study found to be the characteristics of such a function.

RELATIONSHIP OF COMMUNICATION TO THE MANAGEMENT OF THE ORGANIZATION

The communication function cannot provide value at the organizational level by identifying strategic publics and cultivating relationships with them unless the organization empowers senior communication executives. This logical necessity led to the first critical characteristic of an excellent communication function: the senior communication executive is a member of the dominant coalition of the organization or has a direct reporting relationship to senior managers who are part of the dominant coalition.

Economists coined the term *dominant coalition* in the 1960s to explain who makes decisions in large organizations. In small organizations, the owner or a single executive makes most decisions. In larger organizations, by contrast, a coalition of people who are most empowered by the organization makes these decisions. The dominant coalition should not be confused with an executive committee or with a list of managers in formal positions of power. Many of these senior managers are members of the dominant coalition, but some are not. In addition, many members of an organization, and some people outside the organization, are part of the dominant coalition even though they are not in formal positions of power. They influence important decisions informally.

In the Excellence study, the CEOs and senior communicators were asked to indicate whom they thought was in their organization's dominant coalition on a list of potential members, which included the senior communication officer. They also could suggest others who were not on this list from both inside and outside the organization. Nearly half of both the CEOs and senior communicators said the top communicator was in the dominant coalition (43 percent and 47 percent, respectively). The larger the dominant coalition was, the more likely it was that the top communicator was named as a member, suggesting that the more empowering an organization is of more of its members, the more likely it is to empower the top communicator. Most important, organizations in which the top communicator was in the dominant coalition had significantly higher scores on our total profile of communication excellence. Our in-depth follow-up interviews also showed that many top communicators who were not generally considered to be in the dominant coalition compensated by gaining informal access or reporting directly to the members of the coalition. Access to the dominant coalition also enhanced the excellence of the public relations function.

Being in the dominant coalition or having access to it increases the likelihood of a second characteristic of an excellent communication function: the senior communication executive is involved with the strategic management processes of the organization, and communication programs are developed for strategic publics identified as a part of this strategic management process.

The results of the Excellence study showed that participation in strategic management was the characteristic that statistically most defined an excellent public relations function. Communication executives are able to make contributions to strategic management that executives with other types of expertise usually cannot make. In organizations with excellent communication functions, a communication executive scans the environment to identify publics affected by the consequences of decisions or who might affect the outcome of decisions. An excellent public relations department communicates with these publics to bring their voices into strategic management, thus making it possible for publics to participate in organizational decisions that affect them.

Representatives of the public relations function who participate in the overall strategic management of the organization often use research to enhance environmental scanning, lead the process of issues management, provide counsel in crisis situations, identify activist groups and engage them in dialogue, construct scenarios of how publics might behave if certain decisions are made, and plan, organize, and evaluate communication programs to formally communicate with members of strategic publics.

A communication function seldom is excellent if it is isolated from strategic decision makers and cannot counsel them about the public relations implications of potential organizational decisions. Communicators in less excellent departments typically wait for orders from strategic decision makers on how to support decisions in which communicators played no role. As a result, they often are asked to develop communication programs to support a decision that they know will have negative consequences on publics and that publics will oppose.

A strategic top communicator therefore must have one foot in senior management circles and the other foot in the public relations department. The next set of Excellence criteria relates to that department.

ORGANIZATION AND PURPOSE OF THE PUBLIC RELATIONS FUNCTION

Scholars, communication professionals, and other organizational managers often view the communication function in different ways. Some see it as a department that provides communication services to other departments and as little more than a disseminator of information. The Excellence study, however, conceived of organizational communications more broadly: as a key management function that manages most organizational communication activities. The characteristics described in this section relate to roles and models of communication, the relationship of communication with other management functions, and its relationship with activist groups in the environment of the organization.

Communicator Roles

If at least one senior communicator in an organization plays a role in its strategic decision making, the organization will be more likely to think of public relations as a management function than as a department that provides technical support for other management functions. Scholars have conducted extensive research on two major roles that communicators play in organizations: the manager and technician (for a review, see Dozier, 1992, and L. Grunig et al., 2002). Communication technicians are essential to carry out most of the day-to-day communication activities of a public relations department. Managers, by contrast, are responsible for organizing and administering the communication function and participating in organizationwide decisions. Many practitioners play both roles. In less excellent departments, however, all of the communication practitioners, including the senior practitioner, are technicians. If the senior communicator is not a manager, public relations cannot be empowered as a management function.

The Excellence study found new information about the managerial role that previous research had only begun to discover. There actually are two types of communication managers: administrative managers and strategic managers. Administrative managers head public relations departments and manage day-to-day operations of the communication function, manage personnel, manage the budget, and monitor the activities of members of the department. For the most part, they are supervisors of technicians. Strategic managers do more: they step outside the communication department and participate in organizational decisions. They also do research and evaluation and think strategically about publics and how to build relationships with them.

Three characteristics of excellence in communication, are related to these roles:

- *The public relations unit is headed by a strategic manager rather than a technician or an administrative manager.* Excellent communication units must have at least one senior communication manager who conceptualizes and directs communication programs, or other members of the dominant coalition who have little knowledge of communication management or of relationship building will supply this direction. If the senior communication officer is a technician or an administrative manager rather than a strategic manager, the department usually will not be excellent.

- *The senior communication executive or others in the public relations unit must have the knowledge needed for the strategic manager role, or the communication function will not have the potential to become a managerial function* Excellent communication departments are staffed by professionals: practitioners who have gained the knowledge needed to carry out a strategic role through university education, continuing education, or self-study.

- *Both men and women must have equal opportunity to occupy the managerial role.* The majority of communication professionals are women. Research also has established that female practitioners are among the best educated in this field and most likely to take advantage of professional development opportunities. If women are excluded from the managerial role, the public relations function may be diminished because women are often among the most knowledgeable practitioners. When that is the case, the senior position in the public relations department typically is filled by a technician or a practitioner from another managerial function who has little knowledge of communication management.

Models of Public Relations

Public relations scholars have conducted extensive research on the extent to which organizations practice four models of public relations—four typical ways of conceptualizing and conducting communication activities (for a review, see J. Grunig & L. Grunig, 1992, and L. Grunig et al., 2002). This research has shown that excellent departments design more of their communication programs on the two-way symmetrical model of collaboration and public participation than on three other typical models: press agentry (emphasizing only favorable publicity), public information (disclosing accurate information but engaging in little research or other forms of two-way communication), or two-way asymmetrical (using research but emphasizing only the interests of the organization and not the interests of publics).

Two-way symmetrical communication is based on research and uses communication to enhance public participation and manage conflict with strategic publics. As a result, it produces better long-term relationships with publics than do the other models. Symmetrical programs generally are conducted more ethically than are other models and, as a result, produce effects that balance the interests of organizations and the publics in society.

The research for the Excellence study refined our understanding of the four models of public relations by identifying four dimensions that underlie the models: (1) the purpose of communication is symmetrical or asymmetrical, (2) the direction of communication is two way or one way, (3) communication activities can be mediated or interpersonal, and (4) communication follows or ignores rules of accountability and dialogue that make it ethical or unethical. The two-way symmetrical model embodies the most desirable of these characteristics: symmetrical, two way, both mediated and interpersonal, and ethical. The other models possess some but not all of these characteristics.

Three characteristics of an excellent communication function therefore are related to ideals exemplified in the two-way symmetrical model:

- The public relations department and the dominant coalition share the worldview that the department's goals and communication activities should be two-way, symmetrical, and ethical.

- Communication programs developed for specific publics are based on two-way symmetrical strategies for building and maintaining relationships.

- The senior communication executive and others in the public relations unit have the professional knowledge needed to practice the two-way symmetrical model.

Relationship to Other Management Functions

Many organizations have a single department devoted to all communication functions. Others have separate departments for programs aimed at different publics such as journalists, employees, consumers, donors, the local community, or the financial community. Still others place communication under another managerial function such as marketing, human resources, legal, or finance. Some organizations have multiple communication departments that combine several of these arrangements. Many also contract with or consult with outside firms for all or some of their communication programs or for such communication techniques as annual reports or newsletters.

Two characteristics of excellence are related to the organization of the function:

• *Public relations should be an integrated communication function.* An excellent communication function integrates all communication programs into a single department or provides a mechanism for coordinating programs managed by different departments. Only in an integrated system is it possible for public relations to develop new communication programs for changing strategic publics and move resources from outdated programs designed for formerly strategic publics to the new programs. If there are separate communication departments for each set of stakeholder publics and these departments are not integrated, the public relations professionals generally will find it difficult to identify and build relationships with a broad range of publics. The role of public relations in strategic management therefore will be limited.

• *Public relations should be a management function separate from other functions.* Even though the communication function is integrated in an excellent organization, the function should not be placed in another department whose primary responsibility is a management function other than communication. Many organizations splinter the communication function by making communication a supporting tool for other departments such as marketing. When the communication function is sublimated to other functions, it cannot be managed strategically because it cannot move communication resources from one strategic public to another as an integrated communication function can. In addition, it generally focuses on only one stakeholder category to the exclusion of other potentially strategic publics.

Response to Activism in the Environment

In the Excellence study, we paid special attention to how communication departments interact with the most active publics—those that typically evolve into activist groups. Our previous research had shown that most organizations, at least in the United States, experience pressure from activism (L. Grunig, 1992a). In addition, research on power in organizations suggested that organizations are most likely to empower the communication function when pressure from activists or crises produced by that pressure make public relations expertise valuable (L. Grunig, 1992b).

Our results confirmed that activism pushes organizations toward excellence. Many, but not all, of the organizations we studied seem to have responded to activists by developing excellent public relations departments. Organizations with excellent communication also were more likely to report success in dealing with activists than organizations with less excellent departments. Activists seemed to achieve some level of success regardless of how the organization responded; the difference provided by excellence was that the organization achieved success, as did the activists—a symmetrical outcome for the organization and the activists.

Our research on the ways in which organizations engage activists showed that excellent public relations departments respond to activists with two-way communication, symmetrical communication, involvement of activists in organizational decisions, and both formative and evaluative research on the activists.

That characteristic fit well with the rest of the Excellence theory: excellent public relations departments scan the environment and continuously bring the voices of publics, especially activist publics, into decision making. Then they develop programs to communicate symmetrically with activists and involve them with managers throughout the organization. Finally, they use both formative and evaluative research to manage their communication programs strategically.

These characteristics describe an excellent communication department at the functional level. These departments in turn translate their propensity for strategic, symmetrical communication into strategic and symmetrical programs aimed at specific categories of publics at the next level of management.

MANAGEMENT OF INDIVIDUAL COMMUNICATION PROGRAMS

The Excellence study examined the ongoing programs that excellent communication departments devise to develop and maintain relationships with their key publics. We asked the top communicators surveyed in the study to provide a detailed breakdown of the origins, management, and outcomes of communication programs for the three publics for which their organizations allocated the largest budgets. Top communicators most often mentioned seven publics: the media, employees, investors, the community, customers, government, and members. Any of these categories of publics might contain activist groups.

Our theory stated simply that communication programs organized by excellent departments should be managed strategically. We believed that communication programs in excellent departments would be more likely to have strategic origins and less likely to have historicist origins than those in less excellent departments. We also believed that excellent programs would be based on environmental scanning research and would use evaluation research to gather evidence that shows positive outcomes from the programs. Less excellent programs, by contrast, continue year after year with little or no research to identify new or changing publics without setting measurable objectives and without conducting evaluation research to determine whether these objectives have been met. Therefore, the next characteristic of excellence is that communication programs organized by excellent departments to communicate with strategic publics also are managed strategically.

Our results showed strong support for this characteristic. Excellent departments were more than the routine publicity mills of traditional departments.

Excellent programs arose from environmental scanning research, and they were assessed through all forms of evaluation (scientific, clip file, and informal). Managers of excellent departments also reported that evidence is available that their programs have positive outcomes, such as meeting their objectives, changing relationships, and avoiding conflict.

The last characteristics of excellent communication apply to the overall organization. Some organizations provide a more fertile context for excellent communication than others.

HOW THE NATURE OF THE ORGANIZATION AFFECTS COMMUNICATION

In the Excellence study and in previous research, we searched systematically for contextual conditions within an organization and in its environment that might explain why some public relations functions are more excellent than others. In general, our research has shown that characteristics of the public relations staff and of senior management explain best why communication is excellent. In particular, public relations is most excellent when communicators possess the knowledge to practice strategic, symmetrical communication and top management understands, supports, and even demands excellent communication.

Nevertheless, our research also has shown that the organizational characteristics of structure, culture, communication system, and treatment of men and women can provide a supportive context for excellent communication, especially for communication with employee publics. The Excellence study identified four characteristics of organizations that provide this supportive context:

- A participative rather than an authoritarian organizational culture

- A symmetrical system of internal communication

- An organic rather than a mechanical structure

- Programs to equalize opportunities for men and women and minorities

Although these conditions alone cannot produce excellent communication, they do provide a hospitable environment for it. Most important, these conditions provide a favorable context in which all employees work most effectively, but especially women and people of color. Within such an organization, employees are empowered to participate in decision making. As a result, they are more satisfied with the organization and are more likely to support than to oppose the goals of the organization. In addition, employees who are empowered to participate in decision making and engage in symmetrical internal communication are likely also to be effective symmetrical communicators with members of external as well as internal publics.

We found that the effective organization provides a hospitable environment for its increasingly diverse workforce. The CEOs, top communicators, and employees we surveyed seemed to agree on how women in particular are treated in their organizations. All three groups of participants clearly differentiated areas in which women are most and least supported. The survey data suggested that equitable treatment of women, as evidenced primarily by economic equity, and programs to foster their careers (such as policies against sexual harassment and efforts to encourage women's leadership abilities) are integral components of excellent organizations. Programs that provide a supportive work environment correlate especially highly with the other conditions found in excellent organizations. In addition, excellent organizations are beginning to offer some mentoring and advancement programs for women.

Our research showed that when the communication function was given the power to implement symmetrical programs of internal communication, the result was a more participative culture and greater employee satisfaction with the organization. However, we also found that symmetrical communication is not likely in an organization with a mechanical structure and authoritarian culture. A mechanical structure is characterized by centralized decision making, formal rules and procedures, perquisites and favors to distinguish management employees from subordinates, and limited participation in decision making by employees throughout the organization. An organic structure is decentralized, less formalized, and less stratified and allows most employees to participate in decision making.

Organic structure and symmetrical communication interact to produce a participative culture, and participative culture contributes strongly to employee satisfaction with the organization. An organic structure seems to be the key to an effective organization, triggering changes in culture, communication, and satisfaction. Symmetrical communication has a strong role in creating and implementing organic structure, but a communicator cannot step into any organization alone and establish an organic structure or symmetrical system of communication. The top communicator must work with the dominant coalition to develop an organic structure for the organization while he or she is developing a system of symmetrical communication. Our research on the internal context of an organization supported not only the need for symmetrical communication but also the need for the communication function to be represented in the dominant coalition to create the organic structural context that is necessary to create a participative culture and subsequent employee satisfaction.

HOW TO AUDIT COMMUNICATION EXCELLENCE

The members of the Excellence research team conducted formal and informal audits of the public relations functions of several organizations. The first audits were part of the research design of the Excellence study. After we identified the characteristics of excellent communication management for all organizations studied, we tabulated the scores on each characteristic for the nearly three hundred organizations that completed all three questionnaires: for the top communicator, the CEO, and employees. We then provided each organization with a report comparing its scores with the average organization, organizations in the top 10 percent of total excellence, and those in the bottom 10 percent. These reports made it possible for each organization to identify its strengths and weaknesses on the characteristics of excellence. For some organizations, members of the research team followed up the report with a personal presentation to the members of the communication staff.

The communication staff of any organization could follow the same procedure to audit its own communication function. The questionnaires used in the Excellence study are available in the appendixes of *Excellent Public Relations and Effective Organizations* (L. Grunig et al., 2002). The average scores on each of the characteristics of excellence can be found in tables throughout the book. In addition, we tabulated the average scores of these characteristics for the overall Excellence study sample, the top 10 percent of the organizations, and the bottom 10 percent. We will provide a table containing these scores on request. For several years, graduate students in the Seminar in Public Relations Management at the University of Maryland have audited the communication function of an organization of their choosing using these procedures. That process has been successful in continuing to define and validate the characteristics of excellence.

In addition to this quantitative approach to auditing the communication function, we have used the characteristics of excellence qualitatively to audit an organization's communication management. In particular, James Grunig has served on a communication advisory panel at the Brookhaven National Laboratory for a number of years. This panel evaluates the laboratory each year as part of a review by the Department of Energy. For each review, he, as a member of the panel, has informally used the characteristics of excellence as a template for evaluating the laboratory's communication function. Based in part on this experience, we prepared a white paper on evaluation of public relations for all Department of Energy laboratories, which is available online (J. Grunig & L. Grunig, 2001).

Any professional communicator or executive to whom the communication function reports could conduct a similar informal audit to compare that function with the generic benchmark we have developed. Professional communicators asked to serve as peer reviewers for other organizations could use the characteristics as a qualitative benchmark to frame their evaluation. The Excellence study has, in the words of Fred Repper, cited at the beginning of this chapter, provided the "opportunity to measure the effectiveness of our communication programs against that of an ideal program" (Repper, 1992, p. 112).

Notes

1. The first of these three books (J. Grunig, 1992) consisted of an extensive review of literature, conducted by the five members of the research team, which was used to design survey research of 327 organizations in the United States, Canada, and the United Kingdom. In these organizations, the senior communication executive, the CEO or other senior manager, and an average of fourteen employees completed questionnaires. The survey was followed by qualitative interviews with the senior communication officer, the CEO, and a second communication professional in twenty-five organizations scoring at the top or bottom of a scale of excellence that resulted from analysis of the survey data. A short summary of these results was published in the second book (Dozier, with L. Grunig & J. Grunig, 1995). The complete results were published in the third book (L. Grunig et al., 2002).

2. In this chapter, we treat the terms *public relations, organizational communication, communication,* and *communication management* as synonyms. We define *public relations* as the management of communication between an organization and its publics and view it as the management function through which an organization communicates with the publics found in different categories of stakeholders, such as employees, consumers, investors, government, the community, members, donors, and the media.

3. In the Excellence study, we estimated the value of an excellent communication function—one that is most likely to develop quality long-term relationships with a strategic public—by using compensating variation, a method of cost-benefit analysis. With compensating variation, the researcher asks the person most likely to benefit from having something or not having something, such as a good organization-public relationship, to estimate how much that something is worth. In the Excellence study, we asked CEOs to estimate the return produced by their communication function. We found that CEOs generally assigned higher values to communication when it met our criteria of excellence.

References

Dozier, D. M. (1992). The organizational roles of communication and public relations practitioners. In J. E. Grunig (Ed.), *Excellence in public relations and communication management.* Mahwah, NJ: Erlbaum.

Dozier, D. M., with Grunig, L. A., & Grunig, J. E. (1995). *Manager's guide to excellence in public relations and communication management.* Mahwah, NJ: Erlbaum.

Fleisher, C. S. (1995). *Public affairs benchmarking.* Washington, DC: Public Affairs Council.

Grunig, J. E. (Ed.). (1992). *Excellence in public relations and communication management.* Mahwah, NJ: Erlbaum.

Grunig, J. E., & Grunig, L. A. (1992). Models of public relations and communication. In J. E. Grunig (Ed.), *Excellence in public relations and communication management.* Mahwah, NJ: Erlbaum.

Grunig, J. E., & Grunig, L. A. (2001). *Guidelines for formative and evaluative research in public affairs: A report for the Department of Energy Office of Science.* Washington, DC: U.S. Department of Energy. http://www.instituteforpr.com/ measurement_and_evaluation. phtml?article_id = 2001_formative_eval_research.

Grunig, L. A. (1992a). Activism: How it limits the effectiveness of organizations and how excellent public relations departments respond. In J. E. Grunig (Ed.), *Excellence in public relations and communication management.* Mahwah, NJ: Erlbaum.

Grunig, L. A. (1992b). Power in the public relations department. In J. E. Grunig (Ed.), *Excellence in public relations and communication management.* Mahwah, NJ: Erlbaum.

Grunig, L. A., Grunig, J. E., & Dozier, D. M. (2002). *Excellent public relations and effective organizations: A study of communication management in three countries.* Mahwah, NJ: Erlbaum.

Kaplan, R. S., & Norton, D. P. (1996). *The balanced scorecard.* Boston: Harvard Business School Press.

Kaplan, R. S., & Norton, D. P. (2001). *The strategy-focused organization.* Boston: Harvard Business School Press.

Post, J. E., Preston, L. E., & Sachs, S. (2002). *Redefining the corporation: Stakeholder management and organizational wealth.* Stanford, Calif.: Stanford Business Books.

Repper, F. C. (1992). How communication managers can apply the theories of excellence and effectiveness. In J. E. Grunig (Ed.), *Excellence in public relations and communication management.* Mahwah, NJ: Erlbaum.

CHAPTER TWO

The Corporate Communicator

A Senior-Level Strategist

Nick Durutta

Corporations are subject to the same communication dynamics as any other human interactions. Whenever people get together—in a personal relationship, a social group, or a business venture—communication inevitably happens. The larger and more structured the group is, however, such as a corporation or nonprofit organization, the greater the need is for the communication to be managed in order for it to be effective.

Most corporations or large organizations acknowledge, sometimes grudgingly, that communication is important, yet it is a concept that is often misunderstood. "We need more communication!" is often heard in corporate boardrooms when things are going wrong; in fact, too much of the wrong kind of communication might be exactly the problem.

What those executives who are demanding more communication usually want is a more effective flow of information in their organization. This means seeing that the right information gets to the right people in the right way. But each of these elements can be challenging and complex. What is the "right" information? Who are the "right" people? What is the "right way" to communicate with them?

The corporate communicator is the individual who provides answers to these questions. To do this, he or she must be thoroughly integrated into the organization, working closely with senior and middle management, rank-and-file employees, and other key publics in the media, the community, and industry. The communicator needs to know and understand all of these audiences' information needs, concerns, and goals to devise a communication solution that meets the organization's greatest needs.

In this chapter, we examine the role of the corporate communicator as a strategist and adviser to the organization.

A STRATEGIC ROLE

To be most effective, corporate communicators must play a strategic role regardless of the type of organization or corporation in which they work. They must take a broad and in-depth look at the organization and assess where effective communication is most needed and develop a plan that makes it happens.

It is the responsibility of the corporate communicator to manage communication that:

- Supports organizational goals and objectives.

- Ensures a healthy flow of information in and among all levels of employees and management ("healthy" means that the most useful information is flowing to the people who need it).

- Is consistent throughout all of the organization's activities.

- Keeps the organization honest (ethical behavior is most effectively supported by open and honest communication).

- Avoids or mitigates potential crises.

To carry out these responsibilities most effectively, the communicator must be *proactive*, that is, anticipate needs rather than react when needs arise. This requires that corporate communicators be senior-level managers, working alongside the CEO or president and other senior corporate officers in discussing issues and making key business decisions. Communicators at this level are strategists rather than tacticians; they often manage others who perform specific tasks and execute tactics (Dozier, 1992).

Too often, however, communicators assume a tactician role, responding to dictated needs: to create a brochure, for example, or send out a news release. In this mode, communicators are reactive rather than proactive. This frequently prevents them from taking the broader view necessary to assess what communication approaches are truly needed.

At a senior strategist level, communicators are more likely to understand the organization's true communication needs. They know the organization's goals and objectives, even if these are not explicitly stated in a strategic planning document. They know the human dynamics of the organization, which usually are not explicitly stated anywhere. They are aware of issues among the organization's employees and within the organization's community that other senior managers may not, and they are able to identify potential opportunities to address them as well as obstacles that may stand in the way. They are able to identify, and head off, looming crises before they hit the front pages of the newspaper. They are able to address potential ethical breaches or conflicts.

A SENIOR-LEVEL ROLE

In a corporation, the president or chief executive officer oversees a dizzying array of factors that contribute to the well-being of the organization: research and production; customer and client service; marketing; employee relations; human resources; legal, safety, and security; facilities and asset planning; and many more. They usually have directors responsible for each of these areas who report directly to them. Communications is one of the primary needs a CEO must address, and the corporate communicator should be prominent among the senior adviser staff.

The corporate communicator should be one of the least isolated of any of the roles on the senior management team. While some roles, such as sales and marketing, might exist largely in their own silo, it is essential that communicators be in constant contact with all parts of the organization. That is the only way they can gain the knowledge to make strategic decisions.

A COMMUNICATOR'S PORTFOLIO OF SKILLS

Which skills does a corporate communicator need to bring to their role? I already mentioned the critical ability to strategically analyze an organization and recognize areas where more effective communication is needed.

But there are many other skills that must be in the communicator's tool kit. A corporate communicator must have basic communication skills, that is, be able to write and speak well. Yet there are senior-level communicators who may be effective on a strategic level but freeze up when making a speech or cannot write a well-crafted sentence. Because communicators never know what aspect of communication they might need to address, a repertoire of basic skills is essential:

• Writing. The ability to write well is perhaps the most necessary communication skill, especially in our global, electronic age. Writing well means more than understanding the basics of grammar, spelling, and punctuation. It means having the ability to present an issue or topic in a way that is understandable to a wide group of people with varying levels of education and background. It also means being able to gain an audience's attention, persuade and convince them, and trigger their emotions.

- Editing and design. Because most communicators will become involved with publications or Web sites, it is essential to understand the principles of editing and design. Good editing requires much of the same knowledge as good writing but is a distinct skill. (There are great editors who are not great writers, and vice versa.) Although a communicator need not be a designer, a basic understanding of design principles can be invaluable to planning and managing this function.

- Speaking. Sometimes the focus on written communications overshadows the importance of good oral communications. A communicator knows how to put words together for maximum understanding and effect in speech as well as in text. A communicator must be able to speak effectively, whether in a private conversation, addressing a roomful of people, or in an interview on national television.

- Listening. The ability to actively listen—to absorb not only the surface facts of a situation but to probe the many more subtle factors communicated by an individual or group—is an essential skill for communicators. Communication is often viewed as a one-way process: delivering information to a particular audience. But an equal part of the process is receiving feedback from the audience, both before the information or message is delivered, and after. In this regard, research and measurement become important tasks for a communicator.

Research involves collecting relevant information before crafting and delivering a message. The better that communicators can understand the factors influencing an issue, the better they can craft and deliver an effective message. If the issue is particularly complex or sensitive, the research can become quite extensive, to the point of involving professional research firms or specialists. Sometimes the necessary research has already been gathered and might be available from a private firm or a public database; at other times, the communicator may need to conduct independent research.

Measurement is the process of determining whether communication is meeting its goal or objective. This is a step that is often alarmingly overlooked, yet conducting communication without measurement is like buying a lottery ticket and never checking the winning numbers. Unlike other activities (such as sales or production), the results of communication can be challenging to measure, because it involves affecting the perceptions, opinions, and actions of groups of people. Yet it is possible; there are many effective measurement tools and resources available today to communicators.

- Planning. The ability to put it all together—to assess a business or organizational situation and develop a plan to implement the right combination of communication skills and tools at their disposal for maximum effectiveness—is possibly a communicator's greatest asset. Planning encompasses following a prescribed process of identifying goals, setting objectives, developing a solution, carrying it out, and measuring the results. It is through the planning process that communicators can truly establish their value as strategists rather than just tacticians who perform isolated tasks.

It is rare that a communication effort has a defined beginning and end, even if it appears that way. A public relations campaign for the opening of a new shopping center, for example, might appear to be over once the center is open for business. But the themes and messages of the campaign carry over into the continued communications for the center and incorporate lessons learned from the initial effort.

The most successful communicators understand that communication is an ongoing process, similar to a continuing conversation. It involves continually checking in with the audience to make sure the message is being received properly, and to be open to changing strategies and tactics accordingly if it is not.

WHAT CORPORATE COMMUNICATORS NEED
TO KNOW ABOUT THEIR ORGANIZATION

An effective corporate communicator must have thorough knowledge of his or her organization, with a good understanding of its industry, mission and strategic focus, management structure, products or services, customers and clients, community, history, employees (their demographics and issues), and culture.

There is typically a ramp-up period when a new communicator comes into an organization, during which he or she absorbs as many of the important particulars as possible before initiating communication. It helps, of course, if the communicator has previous experience in the organization's industry or in a related field, but this may not always be the case, particularly in today's increasingly global and mobile job market. It is not unusual for communicators to move from one industry, or even country and culture, to another many times within their career. As always, their basic communication skills and expertise should see them through these changes.

Communicators should realize that none of the key organizational elements listed above (with the possible exception of history) remains static. Most successful organizations reinvent themselves to some degree on a regular basis, shifting their business focus in response to competitive and environmental factors. Even something as seemingly constant as a corporation's industry may change significantly over time (think of large corporations such as General Electric or Philip Morris). The communicator must be able to adapt to these changes and develop communication strategies accordingly.

Understanding an Organization's Culture

Of all the key aspects of an organization or corporation, possibly the most challenging to understand is its culture, since often it is undefined. Even corporations that print their cultural values on wallet cards or lunchroom banners might not be fully communicating the nuances of their culture. Often such efforts touch on the culture in only vague, greeting-card terms, touting the organization's winning spirit, pride, initiative, employee loyalty, integrity, professionalism, and commitment. But what do these words really mean? How do they manifest themselves, and, most important, how are they rewarded and nurtured?

Understanding the hidden aspects of an organization's culture might be a communicator's most important task, since it may hold the key to effectively overcoming the obstacles and identifying the opportunities he or she will face. An organization that proudly and publicly proclaims integrity and ethics as cornerstones of its culture yet makes business decisions that appear to benefit only a few members of upper management rather than the organization overall is not one that is walking its talk. Similarly, a corporation that publicly applauds employee loyalty yet discards long-term employees approaching their fiftieth birthday in favor of bringing in younger employees (in lower pay grades) will quickly lose the trust of the workforce. It is one of a communicator's most important functions to identify for management when there is a disconnect between stated cultural values and the way the organization actually works, particularly when those practices might have severe legal and ethical ramifications.

An organization's culture also can have a profound influence on how a corporate communicator communicates. The style and tone used in communications is often an important, and typically unstated, part of a company's culture. This can translate to using or not using certain words or terms or even certain media.

Types of Corporate Cultures

Corporate cultures come in all styles, colors, and flavors. They often manifest themselves in subtle ways and can be very fluid. Some are formed and cultivated by design and intention; other cultures simply happen. Accordingly, not all cultures are effective; cultures can serve as an impediment to organizational effectiveness and success or a catalyst.

Corporate cultures are often defined by behaviors that are modeled and rewarded and are often demonstrated by the actions of senior management:

- Patriarchal: Top-down and autocratic; employees are told what to do; feedback and dialogue are discouraged; information is hoarded and dispensed on a strict need-to-know basis.

- Collegial: Information is shared without regard to levels or status and is considered an organizational resource shared with everyone.

- Formal: A culture governed by many rules and well-defined protocols; there is usually a "right way" and "wrong way" to do just about every-thing, with no deviation.

- Informal: A culture with very few protocols; communication is casual and at times unstructured; experimentation and risk taking are encouraged.

- Political: An arena for gamesmanship and hidden agendas; power plays and territorial squabbles and positioning are common. This type of culture is usually toxic to good communication.

A culture might be a pure example of any of the above, or a combination of two or more. Different cultures may even exist in different parts of the same organization. Such organizational schizophrenia, even in cases where it is effective, can be as confounding for a communicator as it can be living with someone who has multiple personalities.

Besides fully understanding the culture of their organization, communicators must realize that it cannot be created (or changed) with words—only through actions, and generally those modeled by senior management. An organization's employees will exhibit preferred behavior only if there is some benefit or reward attached, such as a bonus, chances for promotion, or even a kind word from the boss. A communicator cannot make these things happen. Communicators can reinforce and promote cultural values by showing them in action and making the benefits clear to managers and employees alike.

Types of Organizations

Another key factor in determining how a corporate, senior-level communicator performs this job is the nature or structure of the corporation or organization itself. Some primary distinguishing identifiers include:

- Privately owned versus publicly traded. Public companies have mandated communication responsibilities to their shareholders and the investment community, and the public perception of the company, and its products and services, can have a direct impact on the value of the stock. The communicator must be aware of any issues that could change this perception (such as through unwanted media attention) and develop plans for addressing these issues, preferably before they surface on the front page of the newspaper or on the nightly news broadcast.

- Small versus large. The larger the organization is, the greater the number of audiences that may be affected by its fortunes and activities. A small organization might be primarily concerned with its immediate customer and investor base and its employees. Larger organizations might be more concerned about publics within a larger sphere of influence: the community, government entities (at the local, state, federal or international level), and other diverse external audiences.

• For profit versus nonprofit. The communicator in a profit-making organization is focused largely on ensuring that the organization remains profitable and sustains its growth projections. This involves ensuring that customers and clients are aware of the organization's products and services and appreciate their quality, integrity, and value. They are often assisted in this effort by a marketing and advertising staff. In a nonprofit organization such as a charity or foundation, the communicator is often focused on fundraising, relying primarily on media exposure to convey the value of the organization's mission and activities to potential donors and volunteers. There are similarities to the two roles, but the tone and content of the communications will vary.

• Union versus nonunion. If a communicator's organization includes employees represented by a bargaining unit or employees who are considering organizing in this way, another level of complexity is added to the audience mix. Communication to employee groups must have the right tone and content.

• Local versus multinational. More and more corporate communicators are finding that their organizations are becoming global in reach. This brings in many issues relating to communicating among multiple cultures, multiple regulatory environments, and multiple languages.

The environments in which corporate communicators find themselves can be so varied that many specialize in working with certain types of organizations. There are corporate communicators, for example, whose career might consist of working only with health care nonprofit groups or multinational pharmaceutical companies. This helps them build a specialized knowledge base that can certainly be valuable, but not all communicators have the opportunity to be so specialized.

It is essential, therefore, that a communicator be a generalist—that is, fully familiar with the basic principles of effective communication—to be of value within nearly any type of organization, regardless of industry, location, or size. (Moreover, in a quickly shifting job market, a generalist communicator, with experience in many types of organizational environments, will be much more marketable.)

CORPORATE COMMUNICATOR ROLES

We have looked at the basic skills in a communicator's toolkit, but there are several roles in which a corporate communicator may apply these skills. During their career, communicators may find themselves in multiple roles. The nature of the organization will to a large extent help determine the roles for which a corporate communicator is responsible.

Public Relations

An organization's public profile—how it is perceived, regarded, and valued by the outside world—is often one of the most critical factors in its success. Regardless of the actual quality and integrity of a product or service, an unfavorable public image can destroy (and literally has destroyed) an organization. Similarly, a favorable public image can frequently boost an organization whose products and services may be of lesser quality, but usually not for long.

Gone are the days when public relations practitioners were fast-talking "flaks" who would do anything to get their organization's or client's name in print or on the air. In today's world, the communicator's responsibility is to represent the client or organization fairly and honestly, with the goal of cultivating a positive image or countering any unwarranted negative publicity as quickly as possible.

In this role, a communicator works closely with the entities that most influence the perception of the organization (and its products and services) among potential clients or customers. These can include the media, community groups, and other key audiences (publics). The communicator must build a relationship of responsiveness and trust with these publics, so they realize that the information they receive is accurate and honest.

Because of the importance of print, Web, and broadcast media to the public image of an organization, media relations is often a primary aspect of the public relations role and is frequently considered a discipline unto itself.

Investor Relations

Publicly traded companies must pay particular attention to the opinions of their organization held by the investment community, which includes financial analysts, brokers, and traders. It is to the organization's advantage that these audiences develop trust in the company's management and their ability to make good on the organization's business goals. That trust may lead to recommendations to purchase the company's stock. The communicator is their conduit to the organization, the person from whom they learn of developments, good or bad, that could influence the company's stock price. This role has become particularly critical in this age of greater transparency and mandated disclosure of financial information, where the slightest whiff of impropriety can trigger investor revolt, if not regulatory investigations.

Community and Government Relations

Hardly any organization is immune to oversight and regulation from a government entity, regardless of the scope or nature of its business. The company may work with local city planners when opening a new office or facility, a state review board when revising an employee pay policy, or a federal agency when introducing a new product. Cultivating a relationship of full and open communication with these entities is as important as doing so with any other key public. Of course, the more highly regulated the organization's industry (such as energy, financial services, or transportation) is, the more critical this role becomes. The communicator must not only have effective relationships with key government agencies, but also work closely with the organization's lobbyists who work to influence legislation.

Internal Communications

Often one of the most significant and challenging groups with whom communication must be managed are an organization's employees. An informed workforce that feels it is acknowledged and listened to is an invaluable asset. Building trust, dedication, and loyalty among employees should be a primary goal of all managers, of course. But the communicator occupies a special position. Quite often communicators become the catalyst, and the conduit, for communication between and among management and employees.

In this respect, the internal communications role is similar to that of working with any other audience or public. It is important that it not be a one-way effort, solely communicating the party line or canned management messages. Few people like to be fed information with no opportunity to respond or comment. As with the other roles, listening is an important part of the process.

Marketing Communications

How an organization's products or services are marketed—through advertising, promotions, branding and imagery, or sales campaigns—should have a direct link to the ways it communicates to other audiences. If a computer company's ads show it as hip, youth oriented, and innovative yet it portrays a stodgy, sluggish image when communicating to and interacting with key publics such as investors, employees, or community leaders, there can be a damaging misalignment. The consistency of a company's brand and its competitive values throughout all of its communications (and actions) is essential.

The way in which a corporation markets can also have a significant effect on many other business facets, including, significantly, its efforts to recruit new employees. Many potential job candidates know an employer from its public image, generally fostered through advertising. Is this the image you want your employees, both current and future, to have?

Corporate communicators may not be directly responsible for marketing communications activities, but because of the importance of this linkage, they should have a relationship with whoever does. Preferably the marketing communications manager should have at least a dotted-line relationship with the senior corporate communicator.

Additional Roles

There may be other roles that a corporate communicator may be called on to perform (benefits communications, events planning, or technical communications, for example). In most cases, the nature and size of the organization will dictate the corporate communicator's key responsibilities. It is not unusual for the communicator to be responsible for any or all of the above roles, in varying degrees and emphasis. But none should be considered or performed in isolation. Consistent organizational messages and cultural values should come across in all communications, to all audiences.

MANAGING COMMUNICATION DURING CHANGE AND CRISIS

One of the most critical situations for corporate communicators is a major change or crisis. It is during such periods of profound growth, downsizing, mergers, takeovers, changes in management, or a business crisis that the nature of an organization (its culture, values, business focus) is put to the test and can shift dramatically.

Corporate communicators prove their value at such times by helping the organization stay focused through ensuring the continued flow of well-targeted information. When situations or conditions are changing rapidly, the danger of miscommunication and wildfire rumors is at its greatest. The surest way to rein in escalating chaos is through responsive, thoughtful, and targeted communication.

It is not unusual for companies undergoing drastic change, particularly disruptive, unwelcome change such as an accounting scandal or a product recall, to cut back on communication. This can be either because the possibility of a business crisis has not been anticipated and planned for, or because organizations tend to pull back and remain quiet during an emergency, thinking that will help the situation blow over.

But it is during those times that well-coordinated communication is most needed. Corporate communicators who are part of the senior management team become one of the most important advisers in a period of crisis or major change. They need to advise senior management on the best communication strategies to employ—messages, sources, audiences, media—in order to begin to stabilize the situation.

Communication itself cannot correct a serious misstep such as the chief financial officer who has embezzled the funds of a company's pension plan. But it is an essential first step in turning around the situation. Without effective and well-thought-out communication, the chances are much greater for the situation to cause lasting and perhaps irreparable damage to the organization.

A CORPORATE COMMUNICATOR'S ULTIMATE RESPONSIBILITY

This chapter has shown the significance and breadth of the corporate communicator role and its importance within organizations. Clearly it is a role that requires broad-based strategic thinking and the ability to respond quickly to rapidly changing environments.

But how objective should corporate communicators be? To whom do they have responsibility? Are they advocates for senior management, employees, or the public at large? Is their role similar to that of an investigative reporter: telling the whole truth, no matter how raw or ugly?

The answer may seem obvious: the communicator's responsibility is to ensure the continued business health and integrity of the organization. But what if the communicator notes unethical or illegal behavior or, worse yet, is asked by management to be party to this behavior?

It is in such circumstances that the most important responsibility of the communicator takes precedence: to uphold the principles of ethical and honest communication and ensure the integrity of the profession. Here communicators can take guidance from the IABC Code of Ethics (2005) and work to ensure that they communicate legally, ethically, and in good taste.

Today's communicators work in an exciting and opportunity-filled time. Increasingly, their role is perceived as an essential, value-added senior-level one instead of a necessary evil that exists mostly to help the organization react to problems.

The burden of ensuring that this trend continues lies with communicators. They must challenge management and work to enact communication that is strategically focused and proactive. It is a responsibility that takes a certain degree of daring and risk taking. And it is one that will not only result in greater respect for organizational communication as a profession but in more effective organizations as well.

References

Dozier, D. M. (1992). The organizational roles of communication and public relations practitioners. In J. E. Grunig (Ed.), *Excellence in public relations and communication management*. Mahwah, NJ: Erlbaum.

International Association of Business Communicators. (2005). *International Association of Business Communicators Code of Ethics for Professional Communicators.* http://www.iabc.com/members/joining/code.htm.

CHAPTER THREE

Organizational Culture

Paul M. Sanchez

Organizations today operate in complex, interrelated, and ever changing environments where wave after wave of economic, social, demographic, technological, and regulatory change sweeps over them. To meet the challenges of these circumstances, leaders must understand the behaviors, beliefs, values, and working environments of their people, who ultimately determine how the missions of their organizations are accomplished. Leaders must be able to read the culture of their organizations and identify, understand, and apply the levers of change.

Most approaches to organization and management theory agree that culture is one of the key factors that can be used to explain organization results. But can culture be redirected to help achieve organization success? Is culture tangible? Is it a concept that translates into practical actions? Is it governable? Can culture willingly and consciously be shaped and managed? Can leaders and managers really change culture? These are the questions that weigh on the corporate mind and occupy those who study organization dynamics.

Louis V. Gerstner Jr. took over a failing IBM in 1993. In his book *Who Says Elephants Can't Dance?* (2002), he describes his data gathering and analysis of the IBM situation. He addresses the changes in strategy, structure, and process that were necessary to drive people to create a new IBM. He was convinced that above all the other changes he was putting in place, the deeply rooted culture of IBM had to change if it was going to survive. He says, "I came to see, in my time at IBM, that culture isn't just one aspect of the game—it *is* the game" (p. 182).

This chapter explores the concept of culture and its management by defining its effects and discussing techniques to assess an organization's culture in order to better allocate resources to achieve business success. It also examines the significance of communication as a reflection of, and as a force for change to, organizational culture.

WHAT IS CULTURE?

Culture, in its simplest meaning, is the sum total of how an organization accomplishes all that it has to do to fulfill its purpose or mission. It can be observed in the many ways that things get done—in the processes that everyone in the organization knows must be followed for work to be accomplished. Culture is embodied in the phrase, "This is the way we do things around here."

The management researcher and writer Fons Trompenaars defined culture as "the way in which a group of people solves problems and resolves dilemmas" (Trompenaars & Hampden-Turner, 1997, p. 6). This is a very hands-on, pragmatic approach. Geert Hofstede (1994) described culture in a somewhat more philosophical way: ". . . Culture is a deeply rooted value or shared norm, moral or aesthetic principles that guide action and serve as standards to evaluate one's own and others' behaviors" (p. 68).

Both of these definitions, and those of others who work in the management and behavioral sciences fields, leave one convinced that culture is indeed a first principle of organizational functioning. They demonstrate that although culture is not concrete, it is surely a potent force that either fosters and supports or impedes and frustrates.

If one accepts these definitions, then it can be seen that all the overt and subtle patterns of behavior in organizations do indeed weave themselves together to create an unmistakable personality or character of the organization. This personality endures over time and can be both a blessing and a curse as an attribute of organizational functioning. If the organization demonstrates long-term success, its abiding culture is identified as the cause of its capacity to not only cope in challenging times but to thrive and prosper. The organization's ability to resist forces that would sap its energy, distract it from its mission, or weaken its brand are all identified as positive cultural characteristics.

If an organization fails, its culture can be blamed for being change resistant: closed to new ideas, lacking an innovative spirit, and too slow to respond to fast-changing customer needs. Culture in this view is seen as closing the windows on life-saving information that would allow the organization to recognize and deal with environmental forces that have a material impact on its fate.

HOW CULTURE AFFECTS AN ORGANIZATION AND THE PEOPLE WITHIN IT

Culture has a pervasive influence on how an organization functions. It determines how an organization responds to its business environment, how it organizes its work, how it structures its day-to-day activities, and how it deploys and rewards its managers' and employees' skills and talents. Culture also determines the patterns of social interaction used to accomplish work and the nature of the relationship, or contract, between the organization and its employees. Equally important, it sets the tone of and orientation to customer or client service.

Because of this impact on an organization's practical behaviors, culture has enormous strategic significance. To be successful, an organization must ensure that it shapes its culture to its business, mission, and strategy. For example, work processes need to be aligned with the types of products or services offered and the human capital practices in place. Because of this, there is no one right or wrong culture. In fact, different organizations within the same industry can have very different cultures that work for them and their customers.

The question leaders need to ask is whether the current culture is keeping pace and supporting the organization's business strategy. The benefits of doing so can be significant. An aligned culture and business strategy enables effective processes and helps the organization deliver positive results to shareholders, customers, and employees. When there is misalignment, the organization may be profitable or successful in the short term, but over time fail to achieve its potential and be far distant from its maximal performance.

THE CULTURAL BLUEPRINT

Every organization—large or small, public or private, for profit or nonprofit—has only four basic elements with which to create a successful organization for its enterprise: strategy, structure, people, and process. These four elements flow from a clear statement of the organization's mission or purpose for being. These are the elements that leaders, managers, supervisors, and employees at all levels must formulate, shape, integrate, and manage. Thus, the organization's culture is formed, shaped, and reinforced through the interplay of these elements—for example:

- The strategy articulates how resources will be focused and applied to accomplish the organization's mission.
- The structure determines how the organization will arrange itself to carry out this strategy to ensure the mission is achieved.

- People are deployed within the structure to carry out the required work.
- The procedures, the "hows" of work and the way the organization actually functions, capture the meaning of process.

These four elements work together to enable mission accomplishment, and the interplay forges the culture. When they are in balance, there is harmonious operation and functioning. In such cases, the culture is positive and supports mission accomplishment. When there is an imbalance among these four elements, the organization's performance will be suboptimal. Poorly defined strategy; outdated, poorly designed structures; dysfunctional, inefficient processes of any sort; and a lack of the right people at critical levels and in the right positions will disappoint stakeholders and bring the organization to an untimely end.

ASSESSING AN ORGANIZATION'S CULTURE

There are many approaches to understanding and working with concepts surrounding organizational culture. Business and social science research provides models to explain and work with the concept and reality of culture, thus developing a workable model based on how people and organizations behave and believe. Working from that foundation, these models yield certain building blocks or dimensions that can become measurable components to create a picture of current culture, and when so focused, on a desired culture. A model developed by Mercer Human Resource Consulting, a global human resource consulting firm, can help leaders understand their organization's current culture by assessing that culture across five dimensions: achievement, environment, perspective, power, and risk.

Leaders can use this model or others as the basis for diagnostic instruments, such as employee and management audits, surveys, and assessment tools. Such instruments can reveal the nature of an organization's current culture and help leaders determine which aspects of the culture may be preventing it from achieving peak performance. These tools can also demonstrate how things are done within the organization and provide a frame of reference that leaders can use to compare their current organizational culture with their ideal.

The Mercer model is divided into eighteen subdimensions, each of which addresses specific attitudes, behaviors, and values within an organization. These subdimensions paint a picture of an organization's culture and identify potential areas for improvement.

Achievement

Achievement can be collective or individual. To understand an organization's culture, it is important to ascertain whether the organization places emphasis on rewarding group or individual accomplishment. The following subdimensions evaluate an organization's achievement priorities and behaviors:

- Accountability. Are responsibilities distributed to groups or individuals? Who is held accountable for successfully completing projects? How are mistakes or incomplete projects handled? Is there a sense of group or individual accountability?

- Rewards. Do rewards reinforce individual or group effort? Do rewards (financial and nonfinancial, formal and informal) emphasize individual contribution or team effort? In short, is teamwork or individual contribution encouraged and rewarded? Who gets credit for a job done well?

- Work. Is work done by teams or individuals? Are projects and processes oriented toward collaboration or independence? Do you get the cooperation you need to get the job done? Does teamwork facilitate or hinder work or project completion? Is work assigned to teams or individuals?

- Work-life balance. Are personal needs acknowledged? Does the organization accommodate individual members' needs to attend to their nonwork obligations? Do most people seem to be able to integrate their work life with their personal life? Does the organization provide specific programs geared to facilitating work-life balance?

Environment

An organization's environment can be process or outcome focused, depending on whether its managerial and production systems are structured to focus on procedures or results. The subdimensions that comprise environment are:

- Decision focus. Are members' perceptions of decision making and its correctness based on the decision process itself or the decision outcome? Is the fairness of process and correctness of decision perceived as the result of equitable outcomes or as the result of equitable processes? Do equitable decision-making attributes such as voice, participation, and full disclosure justify or ameliorate perceived inequitable or unfavorable outcomes? Do equitable outcomes make nonparticipative processes more acceptable?

- Managerial focus. Does management focus on completing tasks or facilitating relationships? Is emphasis placed on how tasks are done or on facilitating relationships? Do managers focus on the tasks or the human resources needed to complete projects? Do tasks get done at the expense of relationships? Is relationship building and management a recognized management technique?

- Pace. Is there a sense of urgency? Is pressure exerted to act and deliver results, or is time allowed for thoughtful consideration and consensus building? Is the pace slow or fast?

- Production focus. How is quality balanced against meeting deadlines and quotas? Is quality compromised in favor of getting things done? Is precision compromised in favor of meeting volume goals? Or is quality the all-purpose cover for missed production targets? To what extent is error tolerated? Is service considered a legitimate trade-off for production?

Perspective

Is the organization's perspective forward or backward thinking? The organization's prioritization of either innovation or steadfast continuity of practice and procedure is a key cultural indicator. The subdimensions of perspective are:

- Action. Is the organization prepared to meet future demands? Are actions taken in response to identified existing conditions or in anticipation of future challenges? Does senior management encourage a proactive or reactive approach? Does the organization anticipate and prepare for or wait and react to market changes?

- Time frame. Does the organization encourage a long-term perspective? Is success measured with short-term or long-term results? Are employees encouraged to plan ahead and set goals for the long term? Or is there a disposition to seek faster solutions? Is the organization oriented toward long-term accomplishments or short-term success?

Power

Within an organization, power can be shared or retained. The organization's use of differential power in interactions can be assessed through:

- Communication. How is information distributed and shared? Is information distributed based on position and role, or is it openly shared? Is there effective two-way communication? Do employees get the information they need to do their jobs? Do employees have the opportunity to voice their opinions, ideas, and concerns?

- Conflict. How are work disagreements handled? Are differences resolved through participatory process or preemptive judgment? Are conflicts ignored until they become serious? Do people feel comfortable disagreeing, or is there a reluctance to openly express contrary views?

- Decisions. How are plans made and carried out? Are decisions and policies made and directed on a local basis or by organization leadership? Are employees empowered to make their own decisions? Do employees share in establishing work rules? Do employees have authority to act on their own?

- Status. What prompts recognition and appreciation? How important are role, position, and people connections? Are they valued more than the quality of work? Are rewards and promotions based on status or performance? What is more important: doing a good job or knowing the right people?

- Structure. Are work rules strictly followed? In tasks and interactions, is priority placed on following established protocols or arriving at solutions? How formal is the organization? Is adherence to process more important than getting the job done? How centralized within the organization framework are the power centers and decision making?

Risk

Does the organization encourage risk taking over risk avoidance? An organization's risk tolerance can be examined through its attitudes and behaviors related to:

- Decisions. Are decisions permitted to include risk? Is taking risk acceptable when making decisions? Do those who make unsuccessful risky decisions bear some form of organization punishment? Does the organization encourage making calculated decisions that involve risk when all possible consequences cannot be explored? Are legitimate mistakes forgiven or institutionalized in the corporate memory?

- Innovation. Is creativity encouraged and reinforced? Are new ideas developed through incremental steps in a defined process? Or are leaps and experimentation in innovation fostered? Are people encouraged to come up with ideas and suggestions? Are they encouraged to try new ways of seeing things? Are people encouraged to go outside formal procedures to achieve organizational goals?

- Tradition. Are old practices and policies reevaluated? Is reliance placed on time-tested processes or on new ways of doing things and new systems? How tradition bound is the organization? Are new practices and ways of doing things attempted? Are old policies and procedures regularly evaluated for improvement?

MEASURING CULTURE AT THE SOURCE

It is best to assess and measure culture at the source: with those who work within the culture, including members at all levels of the organization. No single group of employees is likely to provide a complete picture of the culture. This applies across operational and functional areas, where differing groups within an organization may share common values but have different practices and procedures. Equally, people at various organizational levels, from senior executives and middle management to assembly line workers, may and often will experience the organization's culture differently.

With this in mind, it can be helpful to conduct a survey (based on one of the prevalent cultural models) for either all employees (a census) or a representative sample. This approach offers numerous benefits when developing a comprehensive view of organizational culture—for instance:

- A survey is one of the best ways to involve employees in the process of developing and enabling a new business strategy. The survey communicates to employees the issues that management feels are important for the future of the company and serves as a tool to manage employee expectations with respect to coming changes, particularly in how the research findings are communicated back to the workforce.
- Employees can provide perceptual information in a quantitative means on the way company policies and practices are actually working in an organization. A survey may probe beyond the examination of formal structures and processes to provide insights into how a company's work is accomplished. An employee survey also quantifies information on employees' view of their relationship with the company. Research limited to cataloguing formal policies cannot reveal whether employees believe they are being treated equitably, whether they trust management, or whether they feel pride in the company. Because employee perceptions drive their work behavior, it is essential to gather and understand this type of information.
- Employees are good reporters of workplace practices. Employee feedback can be more than expressions of employee morale; when analyzed professionally, feedback becomes essential information about the organization to be used by management in planning for the company's future and addressing near-term issues. While a comprehensive employee survey can be complex and time-consuming and require objectivity to ensure the integrity of results, it can be the first step in managing a culture shift in an organization.

CURRENT CULTURE VERSUS IDEAL CULTURE

Once an organization has a clear picture of its culture, leaders may find that the culture is not aligned with business strategy in ways that help achieve the mission and maximize performance. When this occurs, it can be helpful to begin the process of change by first defining the organization's ideal culture—that is, the culture that enables and facilitates business strategy. A clear picture of the ideal culture can then be used as a measuring stick against which leaders can assess the differences, or gaps, between where their organization is versus where it needs to be. It is this aspirational statement that often finds its way into vision statements.

An ideal culture should be driven by the organization's business strategy, so the employees who are closest to the business strategy—who know it the best—are truly in a position to define the ideal culture. By asking organization leaders about the desired culture and the rank-and-file employees about their perceptions of their real-life experiences at work, an organization can develop a panoramic view of the current culture and the ideal culture at a particular moment in time. Subsequently, an analysis of the gaps between the current and ideal cultures can pinpoint discrepancies and help leaders begin the arduous and detailed process of moving the current culture toward the aspirational culture that will help the organization to succeed in the future.

COLLECTING LEADERS' VIEWS ON CULTURE AND CULTURE GAPS

A cultural audit of an organization's senior leaders can complement the observations and insights gathered in the employee survey and provide a framework for discussion among decision makers about the impact of culture on an organization. In particular, it can also offer a view of the culture gaps that exist within the leadership team of an organization. Executives are able to see quickly how much agreement there is within their own ranks on what the ideal culture should be, how it is shaped through the various change levers, and their perception of the current culture in the organization.

For many organizations and executives, this usually leads to discussions about the implications of these gaps, what could change by closing the gaps, and which culture building blocks should have priority and which will have the biggest impact on the organization.

A cultural audit with senior leaders could be offered as part of an executive workshop or retreat. Coupled with employee survey results, the information gathered through the audit tells the story of the culture within the organization. Taken together, these results outline or highlight the organizational culture and show, in a tangible way, how culture manifests itself in the behaviors that people expect from each other in the organization. These results may also provide a high-level view of how differences in certain individual characteristics (such as tenure in the organization, level in the organization, or other demographics) affect people's perceptions about expected behaviors.

Finally, these diagnostic tools can be extremely insightful in identifying the cultural gaps between current and ideal culture, thus providing the foundation for a successful change program.

ANALYZING RESULTS AND EVALUATING GAPS

The results of the employee survey and the executive audit can be analyzed in a number of ways:

• Comparing the current culture as described by the employee survey with the current culture described by the executives in the executive audit. This enables organization leaders to determine the extent to which their perceptions match overall employee perceptions of the current culture of the organization.

• Evaluating employee survey results across different functional groups within the organization or even across such variables as organizational level. This helps to identify subcultures within an organization, which can be particularly valuable in revealing areas or groups within the organization that can be either change champions or barriers to change. To the extent that such subgroups can be identified early in a change process, attention and resources can be applied that will facilitate a smoother change process.

• Comparing culture assessment results in depth helps business leaders understand the culture gaps that exist across the organization. By probing the gaps, the effort it will take to align the gaps, and the potential payoff, business leaders can make the strategic decisions that map ways to change or shape the culture.

Of course, not all gaps need immediate attention. For instance, in an organization where attention to detail is particularly important (such as an accounting firm or a precision tool and die maker), gaps between the current and desired cultures around reward and recognition may be ignored in order to concentrate on more significant gaps—for example, in perceptions about work processes aimed at accuracy and reliability. Selecting which gaps to close can be as important as the methods employed to close them.

In addition, the gap analysis and selection process should lead to a discussion about change implementation and the practical issues surrounding it. Leaders may need to initiate further discussions to determine whether proposed changes have management buy-in, assess whether the organization is ready and prepared to embrace change, identify potential roadblocks to broad change, and decide which resources and tools will be required to achieve and sustain change that move the culture from point A to point B.

COMMUNICATIONS AND CULTURE

One of the clearest manifestations of culture is that of communication. Communication as a process, a function, and a result is both a reflection and cause of the organization's culture. How an organization conceives and manages communication does more to tell about its culture than any other single process element.

The manner in which an organization approaches communication policy, staffing, planning, and budgeting paints a clear picture of how it thinks of itself and how it wishes to relate to employees and its external constituencies: its shareholders, customers, and the public at large. One of the most important aspects in this regard is whether the values of the organization's external brand are communicated to, and reflected by, the internal behavior of its employees. Whether brand values are reflected in how employees are treated, how human resource programs are fashioned, and how they are communicated become a potent force for shaping the desired culture.

Openness, a willingness to actively gather perception and opinion, information sharing, communication planning, the integration and application of technology, and preparation and development of supervisors to communicate effectively with their people all paint a clear picture of the organization's culture. But what is often forgotten in discussions about culture is that these very tools also can help guide and shape a new culture.

COMMUNICATIONS AS A VEHICLE FOR CULTURAL CHANGE

Although culture is persistent, it is not necessarily permanent. Like a person's habits, with concerted effort an organization's culture can be changed.

Many process elements must be integrated to shape and develop culture. These elements range from the basics, such as the design of reward systems (including pay, benefits, performance management, and training and development) to the more strategic framing of vision and defining values. But all of these are ultimately dependent on the act of communicating them: of conveying their purpose and how to operationalize each program for management and employees throughout the enterprise. Thus, communication moves to center stage in the matter of cultural change.

The true power of communication as a force to implement and sustain a change of culture is its ability to win the hearts and minds of employees—to establish trust. This creates a value chain that can result in improved customer service, productivity, and mission accomplishment. To win hearts and minds, however, requires communication planning of the most strategic nature. It requires sustained and comprehensive activity across a spectrum of communication channels and stakeholders, from face-to-face to mass communication activity. It also demands interactivity and participation throughout the organization, from the boardroom to the mailroom. Only when corporate communications become an exchange of information, as opposed to the downward dissemination of information, can culture be shaped to serve the needs of the organization and its constituencies.

THE RELATIONSHIP BETWEEN ORGANIZATIONAL CULTURE AND NATIONAL CULTURE

One important aspect of culture concerns the interrelationship between organizational culture and national culture. Globalization is a fact of life, connecting markets across wider distances than ever before. This has led to an increase in offices, operations, and business activity, often far from an organization's traditional headquarters, thereby limiting its ability to control day-to-day decisions. Global organizations understand how to conduct business simultaneously in many different economic, social, and political environments. What can be learned from these successes?

When considering the fit between business strategy and culture, a multinational organization also must consider differing national values that may place constraints on organizational practices in its various national branch offices. As well, a culture that enables effective work processes in one country may not be easily transferable to another country, or may in fact suppress productivity.

Multinational organizations may be affected in two ways. First, organizations often reflect the national culture of their country of origin. A commonly cited example is Japanese businesses in comparison to U.S. businesses, where group behavior and performance is emphasized over individual performance. Thus, business strategies that require a high degree of teamwork will benefit from the Japanese model over the U.S. model.

Second, organizations doing business outside their home country need to adapt their organizational culture to interact productively with businesses based on different cultural values. For example, organization A from the United States believes in taking a fair amount of risk in expanding its lines of business. But its branch office abroad does business in an environment that does not value risk in financial dealings. To expand its lines of business in that country, the branch office may have to borrow money locally, but local banks may not consider that organization a good candidate for a loan because they perceive its behavior as too risky. Thus, multinational organizations need to be sensitive and consciously decide whether to modify their business practices to harmonize with local organizational practices, particularly those derived from national cultural values.

Modern trends in global communication and globalization of trade may ultimately lead to a relatively homogeneous global culture that will soften national differences that are relevant to the conduct of business. But currently it is important to recognize and understand the potential conflicts between national and organizational cultures.

References

Gerstner, L. V., Jr. (2002). *Who says elephants can't dance?* New York: HarperCollins.

Hofstede, G. (1994). *Uncommon sense about organizations: Case studies and field observations.* Thousand Oaks, CA: Sage.

Trompenaars, F., & Hampden-Turner, C. (1997). *Riding the waves of culture: Understanding diversity in global business.* New York: McGraw-Hill.

CHAPTER FOUR

The Communication of Trust

Pamela Shockley-Zalabak, Kathleen Ellis

Most of us know when we are trusted, and we consider it a good thing. We know when we do not trust others or are not trusted, and it is not a good thing. Yet while we know trust is desirable and important, it remains difficult to describe and even more difficult to build or rebuild. Most people agree to all of the above statements and then move on because there is not much understanding of what to do about this notion of trust. While trust is somehow everyone's responsibility, it is also no one's responsibility.

With globalization, scandals in all types of organizations, fast-paced change, and new pressures for innovation and changes in processes, forms, and relationships, the turbulence of organizational life places increasing importance on the somewhat elusive notion of organizational trust. Trust is considered pivotal for networks, alliances, uses of information technologies, workplace diversity, customer loyalty, decentralized decision making, and the list goes on. More confidence is placed in our understanding of trust in individual relationships than in what it means to trust an organization. Trust influences a wide range of employee and customer behaviors and is somehow linked to overall organizational performance. Yet few leaders and communication professionals regularly focus directly on trust.

This chapter argues that organizational trust is a fundamental leadership responsibility and a growing area of responsibility for communication professionals. We describe what organizational trust means and why it matters for effective organizations. Trust fundamentally influences communication and is in many ways a result of organizational communication. In other words, trust is primarily a communication-based concept. Leadership communication and its relationship to trust is presented. The influence of peer groups and corporate communication on organizational trust is described. Then a five-dimensional organizational trust model that is useful for building and rebuilding organizational trust is reviewed. Finally, the role of organizational leadership and the communication professional in developing trust is defined.

ORGANIZATIONAL TRUST

What does *trust* mean? The answer is simple: "Tell the truth." "Don't withhold information." "Do what you say you are going to do." Yet when we get right down to it, we know it is not simple. What I think is the truth may not be the truth for others. Perhaps I do not have the information you need or I cannot give it to you. Managers, workers, customers, and other stakeholders regularly disagree about whether the expectations each has of the other are met. So how can we describe this notion of trust?

Numerous definitions of trust focus on trust resulting from positive expectations about another's conduct, with distrust reflecting negative expectations of another's behavior. The key here is behavior. While everyone has individual intentions, the trust-distrust evaluation is determined not by what we intend but by what we do. There are many examples of when people have intended to deceive and have been successful because their behaviors were initially judged to be trustworthy. We can also remember entering a group and distrusting what might happen. When we contrast that experience with entering a group where trust levels were high, we quickly realize that past behaviors and experiences influence our expectations of future behaviors and experiences.

The organization structures for individuals and groups the relationships and environments subject to trust evaluations. It is hard enough to trust family and friends, let alone individuals we barely know or with whom we have little or no face-to-face contact. We usually do not get to choose our boss, team members, customers, or other stakeholders. In fact, the hierarchy and relationships defined by the organization chart can be described as a trust blueprint. By describing who has the right to decide and where the linkages are supposed to take place, the organization chart really is a complicated way of describing how organizational trust should work. If the rules are clear and the chart is followed, then personal behaviors are not so important. While at some level the organizational chart describes how trust flows, few with organizational experience will say that adhering to the chain of command is what generates a high-trust organization. And as networks, alliances, virtual groups, and other organizational forms replace older and more bureaucratic models, fewer and fewer organizations are operating as hierarchies. Thus, trust through control is replaced by trust through relationships.

It is fair to conclude that organizational trust encompasses a wide variety of organizational relationships. However, organizational trust is a more inclusive concept than simply integrating all organizational relationships. It encompasses relationships, but it also includes a variety of environmental influences and basic organizational competencies. These aspects of trust will be more fully described when the trust model is discussed for both leadership and communication professionals.

Although somewhat obvious, it is important to explicitly recognize at this point that perceptions of organizational trust both influence and result from human communication. Organizational trust cannot be separated from planned and informal organizational communication processes. It is for this reason that leaders and communication professionals are increasingly admonished to figure out how to build trust in uncertain and rapidly changing environments.

Why does trust matter? Trust affects virtually all that happens in the organization. Research studies over many years consider trust a foundation for cooperation and the basis for stability in both organizations and markets. Trust is related to diverse customer and stockholder behaviors. It has been consistently linked to employee perceptions of overall job and communication satisfaction. High trust levels in both face-to-face and virtual teams predict a higher level of performance than moderate and low trust levels. High trust levels contribute to more open communication, high-quality decision making, improved risk taking, low employee turnover, and more overall organizational commitment.

Prior to developing the organizational trust model presented later in this chapter, several hundred studies that relate multiple aspects of organization-wide performance to organizational trust were reviewed. We found that high levels of organizational trust have been associated with (1) more adaptive organizational forms and structures, (2) the ability to form strategic alliances, (3) effective crisis management, (4) reduced litigation costs, (5) reduced transaction costs, (6) product innovation, and (7) economic performance. The evidence is overwhelming. We need to work at organizational trust—understanding it, monitoring it, building it, and rebuilding it.

ORGANIZATIONAL COMMUNICATION AND TRUST

It is obvious that leadership needs to "walk the talk" in order to generate positive trust environments. However, it is not as easy as it sounds. It is hard to be open and consistent with competing stakeholders. Furthermore, many, if not most, leaders do not accurately understand their personal impact on others, let alone their impact on trust. Leaders know much better what they intend than what is understood. Unclear priorities confuse and breed diverse trust perceptions. The amount and type of information that leaders send to others is directly related to organizational trust. Trust levels are linked to how consistent leaders are, how they demonstrate integrity, what happens in the sharing and delegation of control, and whether concern for others is demonstrated. Trust in top management is often based on organizational policies, processes, programs, and perceptions of justice in dealing with employees and other stakeholders. In fact, our research (Ellis & Shockley-Zalabak, 2001) strongly suggests that trust in top management is more important than trust in immediate supervisors when it comes to overall employee perceptions of satisfaction and effectiveness. In addition, perceptions of trust in leadership as well as trust in peer groups are linked to perceptions of organizational competence. The intriguing reality is that employees may trust that management is honest with them, but if they do not trust that organizational members (including themselves) are competent to meet organizational challenges, they will have low trust levels.

Trust in peers and work teams is based on many of the same behaviors as trust in leadership. Peers and team members make trust evaluations of each other based on perceived honesty, quality of communication, and willingness to collaborate. These trust evaluations are directly related to group and team performance. The higher the trust is, the better is the performance on almost all measures of group output.

Leadership and peer trust are based on a variety of communication behaviors. It is also important to remember that the corporate communications and human resource and human relations functions also directly influence trust levels through the policies, procedures, and programs for which they have responsibility. It is important for leaders to develop inspiring visions and missions; however, it is equally important to think about how these statements of direction are communicated. What are the planned and informal means of transmitting key values and priorities? Does planned communication "walk the talk"? Do the Web site and the internal newsletter accurately reflect what organizational members experience from leadership? How are celebrations and reward programs handled? Are various stakeholders supportive of organizational values? How do the corporate communications and human resource and human relations functions learn about important trust gaps? Do external organizational messages reflect trust in customers and stakeholders? How do advertising and public relations messages represent trust to diverse publics? How is bad news communicated? Uncertainty? How does the crisis management plan contribute to or detract from trust? Planned messages and programs are directly linked to perceptions of organizational trust. As such, the communication of trust becomes a professional responsibility for a variety of organizational specialists.

DIMENSIONS OF ORGANIZATIONAL TRUST

We hope the argument for doing something about organizational trust has been convincing. Yet the obvious question remains: What can be done? How can trust building become more intentional and less elusive or accidental? There is no final answer, but we do think that identifying five critical dimensions of trust provides a framework for both leaders and communication professionals to begin to build trust consciously and intentionally.

In a 2000 International Association of Business Communicators Research Foundation research study (Shockley-Zalabak, Ellis, & Cesaria, 2000), a model of organizational trust with an accompanying measurement instrument was developed and tested on an international scale. Over thirty-five hundred research studies that described organizational trust were reviewed. We surveyed respondents from fifty-three organizations, translating our survey work into multiple languages. We used a very large database to develop normative comparisons. The comparison database contained data from the United States (twenty-five states), Italy (eleven cities), Sydney, Singapore, Hong Kong, Tokyo, Bombay, and Taiwan. The industries represented in the database included banking, telecommunications, manufacturing, computer software and hardware, education, and sales and customer service. Company sizes ranged from approximately 100 to 146,000 employees. That work resulted in an expansion of Aneil K. Mishra's four-dimensional model of trust (Mishra, 1996) to the five-dimensional model we present in Figure 4.1.

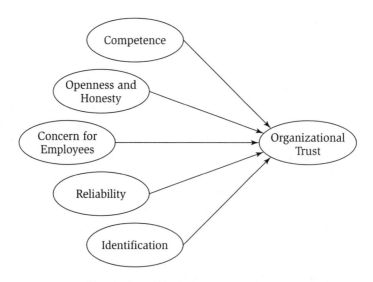

Figure 4.1. Path Model of the Five Dimensions of Organizational Trust

The general definitions of the five dimensions are as follows:

- Competence. As it relates to organizational trust, competence involves the extent to which we see not only our coworkers and leaders as being effective, but also our organization as a whole. Competence reflects how strongly we believe that our organization will compete and survive in the marketplace.
- Openness and honesty. *Openness* and *honesty* are the words people use most often when they are asked what contributes to organizational trust. This dimension involves not only the amount and accuracy of information that is shared but also how sincerely and appropriately it is communicated.
- Concern for employees. Concern for employees includes the feelings of caring, empathy, tolerance, and safety that are exhibited when we are vulnerable in business activities. Sincere efforts to understand feelings contribute to high trust levels in any relationship.
- Reliability. Reliability is determined by whether management, coworkers, teams, suppliers, or organizations act consistently and dependably. In other words, can we count on them to do what they say they will do? Does congruency exist between their words and actions?
- Identification. Identification reflects the extent to which we hold common goals, norms, values, and beliefs associated with our organization's culture. This dimension indicates how connected we feel to management and to coworkers.

As our model indicates, organizational trust has many faces. We therefore recommend that the following considerations be used to test the development of specific trust-building plans:

- Trust is multileveled. This means that trust interactions span leadership, coworker, team, organizational, and interorganizational levels. Trust building must address all interaction levels.
- Trust is culturally rooted. It is closely tied to the norms, values, and beliefs of the organization. It also relates to broader national and regional cultures. Trust building cannot ignore the culture of trust or distrust that exists.
- Trust is communication based. It influences and is the outcome of communication behaviors such as providing accurate information, giving explanations for decisions, and demonstrating sincere and appropriate openness. Trust is also linked to planned organizational communication.
- Trust is dynamic. Trust is constantly changing and can cycle through phases of building, stabilizing, and dissolving. Just as trust can range in degree from distrust to optimal trust, it can also vary from fragile to resilient. Fragile trust develops out of perceptions of short-term outcomes, while resilient trust usually is based on a long-term history of integrity.

- Trust is multidimensional. It is cognitive, based on facts and analysis. It is emotional, based on reactions to people and events. Finally, it is behavioral, based on what organizations collectively and individually do as a result of cognitive and emotional reactions to people, events, challenges, and opportunities.

BUILDING ORGANIZATIONAL TRUST

Organizational leadership and organizational communicators both contribute to the development and maintenance of organizational trust.

The Role of Organizational Leadership

Organizational leadership at all levels has responsibility for trust. While most in leadership positions would agree with this statement, few focus directly on their trust responsibilities. Leaders need to develop a more comprehensive understanding of what constitutes trust behaviors, with specific emphasis on the distinction between interpersonal and organizational trust. Many leaders rely on their personal integrity without understanding that the positions they occupy provide few within the organization the opportunity to interact with them on an interpersonal basis. Although integrity and intentions are critical, the impact of leadership is interpreted through multiple networks of relationships, behaviors, and events, making communication behaviors and decisions the currency of trust.

The use of the trust model can facilitate leaders' understanding and development. Given that those in leadership positions have developed a thorough understanding of trust, what else needs to be done?

Monitor Trust Levels. First, leaders need to develop an ongoing process for monitoring the trust levels within their organizations. Leaders regularly collect performance data for their organizations, yet few collect data that directly assess trust levels. Even organizations that conduct regular employee and customer satisfaction surveys usually do not include reliable and valid trust measures. Earlier in this chapter we described links between trust and organizational performance. A clear understanding of an organization's trust level can provide leadership with important data that may precede or forecast changes in performance outcomes.

Develop an Understanding of Trust in Particular Contexts. Second, leaders need personal development in (1) distinguishing between interpersonal and organizational trust, (2) understanding trust within particular organizational contexts, and (3) examining leadership activities within the organization for their contributions to the trust environment. This can usually be accomplished through training and developing the leadership communication plan. However, training and development are more likely to be effective if accountability systems acknowledge explicitly the importance of leadership communication for the trust climate of the organization.

Examine Organizational Decisions and Practices Using the Trust Model. Third, leaders should be challenged to examine their strategic directions, decisions, and communication plans within the framework of the trust model. How does the organization understand *competence* from the direction and decisions articulated by leadership? What do external stakeholders understand? In some respects, articulating competence is answering the "why" question. Why will our new direction help us compete, survive, lead, improve, and respond to challenges?

Does the organization believe leadership is open and honest? If full disclosure of information cannot be made for a variety of strategic reasons, how can leadership communicate directly what can and cannot be made known? How can leadership directly address the inevitable seeming contradictions brought about by changing circumstances? What can leadership do to remain open and honest when uncertainty is high and important decisions remain in a pending state? These are complex questions, yet research supports the perspective that leaders are more trusted when they increase communication messages during times of uncertainty and express the "I don't know" perspective with directness and a commitment to bring information forward when possible. Research also indicates that during times of uncertainty, leaders communicate less to constituent groups with the rationale that waiting for more definitive answers will better assure people. In reality, waiting protects leaders from their own uncertainty and generally lowers trust levels among stakeholders.

Leaders are responsible for the policies and processes that are interpreted as concern for employees. Organizational policies and practices should be regularly examined for how they express concern and for their implicit and explicit messages about trust. Performance evaluation systems, accounting and reporting practices, monitoring of employee behaviors (for example, use of time, telephone and computer use), access to information, involvement in decision making, reward programs, and a host of other practices and processes all are subject to trust evaluations.

Closely related to the assessment of concern for employees is the trust dimension of reliability. Are processes and practices consistent across employees and key stakeholders? Does leadership do what they say they are going to do? Does the organization regularly bring important information to those affected? Reliability should not be confused with sameness. Reliability as a trust dimension refers to consistent behaviors that exhibit competence, honesty, and concern, not necessarily unwavering support for past decisions.

Finally, leaders need to develop and articulate organizational goals, norms, values, and beliefs that form the basis of the desired organizational culture. This development and articulation is critical to the identification dimension of trust. Do goals, norms, and values include employees and key stakeholders? Can employees relate their own futures to the direction of the organization? Can vendors and customers see in these strategic directions their own desired connectedness to the organization? How does leadership know if identification is present or absent?

Structure the Organization for Trust Building. Fourth, leaders are responsible for the professional communication functions within the organization. Human relations, corporate communications, advertising, marketing, public relations, and other information functions are designed and staffed as a result of how top management views the importance of these operations. The leaders of communication functions shape trust levels by their own understanding of how the functions contribute to important organizational outcomes. The very design of the organization reflects assumptions about trust and who has responsibility for trust building. While no one design can be claimed to be innately superior to another, most high-trust organizations place communication professionals in critical line responsibilities. Leaders who take the notion of trust seriously examine their organizational structures for the centrality or lack thereof of functions responsible for trust building.

The Role of Communication Professionals

Communication professionals are organizational leaders in terms of both job function and the specific job knowledge they provide for other leaders. Nonetheless, until recently, the role of the communication professional has focused only indirectly on trust building. Increasingly, however, communication professionals are challenged to explicitly develop programs and processes that build organizational trust. The following discussion describes important professional areas that are linked to trust building. The list is not meant to be inclusive but points to key responsibilities for communication professionals.

Monitor Trust. For organizations to effectively develop high-trust environments, regular understanding of levels of organizational trust must be developed and interpreted for a host of planning decisions. This monitoring responsibility usually resides in human resources, internal communication, or corporate communications functions. Trends in trust levels, when related to trends in performance data, provide powerful information that is important to the evaluation of communication planning, training and development, appraisal systems, and other strategic initiatives. The communication professional becomes responsible for guiding top management in determining the type of data to be collected, who should collect the data, the assessment of the reliability and validity of the data, data interpretation, and the dissemination of data to be included in the planning processes of the organization. Instruments such as the one published by IABC (Shockley-Zalabak et al., 2000) provide psychometrically sound ways to begin measurement. Focus groups, organizational climate questionnaires, interviews, and other data also provide insight.

Review Policies and Practices. Policies, processes, and a host of organizational practices carry implicit and explicit messages about trust. Human resource and internal communication professionals are increasingly tasked with reviewing the policies and processes regularly used by the organization with employees and vendors for their impact on trust. Marketing and sales professionals often provide this same review with regard to customers. Policy and procedures manuals, employee benefits, disciplinary processes, supervision responsibilities, performance appraisals, and other processes can be evaluated in each of the dimensions of the trust model. For example, an employee orientation manual may effectively describe how employee contributions will be evaluated (competence), how communication exchanges among supervisors and work groups are to take place (openness and honesty), how equitable salary and benefits programs are to be administered (reliability), and what the core goals, values, and beliefs of the organization are (identification). A review of the orientation manual may reveal that while four of the five dimensions of the trust model can be identified in the manual, no messages that communicate real concern for employees are present. It is not that the organization does not want to express concern, but the preparation of an important document simply is not comprehensive in its expression of trust messages. Of course, at times it will be more than the messaging that needs to change. These comprehensive reviews may reveal policies and procedures that need to change or improve.

Develop Training and Awareness. Training is an important component of most effective trust-building efforts. Leaders usually do not understand the comprehensive nature of organizational trust. Leadership, management, and supervisory training should include development of an understanding of organizational trust and its importance to organizational performance. Next, training should address how individuals contribute to organizational trust with both their individual behaviors and their more strategic communication activities. Employees can also benefit from an awareness of the importance of organizational trust. Increased job satisfaction, the ability to innovate, and the ability to identify with a successful organization all are related to perceptions of trust. Both individual and team training can focus on how employees contribute to trust networks. Mandatory training is of particular importance. Management development, employee orientation, job training, team training, and process training (for example, performance appraisals, disciplinary reviews, legal responsibilities) all should incorporate comprehensive messages utilizing the basic dimensions of trust.

Plan Organizational Communication. Internal communications, corporate communications, public relations, advertising, marketing functions, and others literally plan how the organization describes itself to its various publics. Although planned organizational communication reflects strategic direction, change initiatives, new products or services, competitive positioning, or response to crisis determined by top leadership, planned organizational communication also becomes the reality of how diverse stakeholders come to know about and experience the organization. Message crafting and message delivery are critical responsibilities in the trust-building process. Of course, strategic direction must have integrity in order to build high trust with stakeholders. Nonetheless, integrity without communication that is trusted will not build a high-trust environment in and of itself. Communication professionals know this. However, most professionals have been trained to develop accurate and attractive messages with less awareness of what these messages communicate about trust.

One Fortune 500 employee relations and communication department provides an interesting example of how trust building has become an intentional department strategy. The vice president for employee relations and communication adopted the five-dimensional trust model described in this chapter as a framework for his department. He and his staff, with the assistance of an outside consulting firm, reviewed the mission and values of the organization, a year's worth of internal publications, and the annual responses to the employee satisfaction survey to determine which dimensions of the trust model were regularly present and where opportunities existed for improvement. They discovered that competence and identification were the least represented of the dimensions. Therefore, they developed a strategy to incorporate stories into their monthly newsletter that focused on employee achievements and advancement opportunities. They asked for and received commitment from the entire corporate leadership team to review all speeches for elements of the trust model. They added trust development to their mandatory supervisory training program. Finally, to measure trust, they incorporated new scales into their employee satisfaction survey. Within two years, the department was able to present to top management employee satisfaction survey improvements and reduced turnover rate data for several divisions of the company. We do not claim that their experience was directly related to their new emphasis on trust, but they believe, as do we, that trust played an important part in their performance.

In sum, it is fair to say that the communication professional has a core responsibility for trust building. That responsibility, however, cannot be executed without close collaboration with top leadership. With this collaboration, the communication of trust can be far more intentional than it has been in most organizations. The challenges are real, but the benefits are enormous.

CONCLUSION

Trust matters. Organizations with high trust levels have better results than those with low trust levels. Although this makes sense, not enough effort has been expended in intentionally trying to build trust. In the past, we have treated trust as too subjective to strategically direct our focus. That is a mistake. Trust influences communication and results from communication. We can build trust with competent people who have integrity and know the importance of strategically using a variety of effective communication processes. We can build trust by focusing on competency, openness and honesty, concern for employees, reliability, and identification. The communication of trust is both a primary leadership responsibility and a core competency for communication professionals.

References

Ellis, K., & Shockley-Zalabak, P. (2001). Trust in top management and immediate supervisor: The relationship to satisfaction, organizational effectiveness, and information receiving. *Communication Quarterly, 49,* 382–398.

Mishra, A. K. (1996). Organizational responses to crisis: The centrality of trust. In R. M. Kramer & T. R. Tyler (Eds.), *Trust in organizations: Frontiers of theory and research* (pp. 261–287). Thousand Oaks, CA: Sage.

Shockley-Zalabak, P., Ellis, K., & Cesaria, R. (2000). *Measuring organizational trust: A diagnostic survey and international indicator.* San Francisco: International Association of Business Communicators.

CHAPTER FIVE

Communication Ethics

Sorting Out What Is Right and Wrong

Mark P. McElreath

Like a firefighter who classifies fires according to what fuels them and their severity, like an emergency room nurse who identifies and treats various types of illnesses and injuries, a professional communicator should learn to perform triage when confronted with ethical choices.

All ethical choices are not the same. It is a waste of time to treat all alike. It pays off to know how to distinguish between ethical situations, problems, and dilemmas.

Ethical situations are fairly simple and straightforward, and to solve them, all a professional needs to do is to act professionally—to do what is right. There is not too much to be debated, although you may need to spend some time educating the misinformed or misguided. For example, someone asks a communicator to omit legally required information from a press release or to put an unsubstantiated statement in an advertisement. The professional knows what to do, because that is what a professional is expected to do. It may require educating and explaining to others what is required and why, but for the professional, it is a relatively simple matter of just doing it right the first time.

Ethical problems have a number of possible ethical solutions, and there can be a genuine debate among equally sincere, good people about what should be done. For example, an editor under deadline pressure wants to use a photograph taken in public of a public figure, but it shows the person in a bad light and might hold that person up for ridicule or embarrassment. It would be legal to publish the picture, but would it be ethical? There are a number of creative, ethical solutions to the problem, and the professional should take the time to engage in that discussion. The difficulty is learning how to frame the issue so that a genuine dialogue can occur without stirring up emotions and defensive reactions. The key to solving an ethical problem is seeking a win-win solution and allowing enough time to come up with a creative, ethical solution.

Ethical dilemmas create a "damned-if-you-do, damned-if-you-don't" situation for the decision maker who must choose the lesser of two evils. Regardless of what is done, someone will be hurt. For example, a senior executive is involved in a sex scandal that violates corporate policies and has the media calling for an official statement. No matter what the professional communicator does, the executive, the company, and others also may be hurt. But the facts are facts and need to be disclosed. The key is to limit the amount of harm to innocent individuals and lessen the negative impact on the corporation. Ethical dilemmas require crisis communications management skills.

Professionals need to be both legal and ethical in their communication activities. They need to recognize, as the corporate code of ethics of a major international firm states, "The law is a floor. Ethical business conduct should normally exist at a level well above the minimum required by law."

To be legal means to obey the law. But what if, for example, the law in one country allows bribery, or "facilitation fees," to be written off as a tax-deductible cost of doing business? Is it ethical to engage in or to condone bribery? *Merriam-Webster's Dictionary* defines *bribery* as corrupting or influencing someone with gifts or favors. Ethicists would posit that if the bribery harms someone, especially innocent people, then it is wrong. Because it is practically impossible to bribe someone without doing harm, especially to other stakeholders not aware of the bribery, condoning or engaging in bribery is another example of when you may be legally right in certain jurisdictions but ethically wrong wherever you are.

Ethical communicators accept and conform to professional standards. Professionals know about and help establish standards by which decisions are made about what is right and what is wrong. The best communicators engage in communication that not only is legal and ethical but also is in good taste. Professionals engage in communication activities that are sensitive to the cultural values and beliefs of their public and target audiences.

This chapter highlights factors that affect ethical situations, problems, and dilemmas for professional communicators. We begin with two key points:

- Basic assumptions and principles of ethical communication—to tell the truth, to be fair by treating others as you wish to be treated, and to do no harm to the innocent—apply throughout the world.

- From a personal and corporate point of view, it pays to think through ethical situations, problems, and dilemmas before they happen—to know in advance how you intend to ethically manage communication—and to recognize the many factors that influence ethical decision making.

Ethical issues for professional communicators can occur at a variety of levels. The legal environment that an organization faces at the local, regional, provincial, state, national, and international levels often identifies some of the ethical issues affecting the organization as well. But in practical terms, it is the people in an organization who make the ethical, and unethical, decisions. Consequently ethical dilemmas need to be analyzed at the small group, interpersonal, and intrapersonal levels. This chapter discusses ethical decision making at each of these levels.

FACTORS WITHIN THE INDIVIDUAL

Within each individual communicator, a number of characteristics affect how that person makes decisions about what is right and what is wrong:

- Maturity. Some people, even as children or teenagers, have more ethical maturity than others. Some individuals carefully consider issues before them, and, others do not. Maturity is not necessarily related to chronological age.
- Professional experience. The school of hard knocks teaches lessons that profoundly affect a person's ability to decide right from wrong. Making tough, ethical decisions is valuable experience. The less experience a person has with making ethical decisions, the more difficult those decisions are, and the more likely some of those decisions will be wrong.
- The ability to deal with uncertainty. Some people thrive on dealing with dilemmas. Others have difficulties processing information under time pressures and not having enough information. Some people become rattled and cannot think clearly when the pressure is on; others become focused and make good decisions under difficult circumstances.
- Formal education in ethics. Whether from hearing sermons, attending lectures, or reading, the more knowledge a person brings to bear on an ethical dilemma— that is, the more factors a person considers in making an ethical decision—the better. Thinking through ethical dilemmas prior to or after experiencing them is preparation for future decision making.
- Differences between men and women. Brain specialists, sociobiologists, and philosophers have explored the differences between men and women and their ways of thinking and making ethical decisions. One argument has it that men are more rule oriented, and women are more relationship oriented. Consequently men tend to focus on rule compliance and sanctions; women focus on fairness and equity. Certainly the sexes are equally suspicious of the other. Two studies

of U.S. college students found that women tend to think men are less ethical, while men tend to think women are less ethical (Kidwell, Stevens, & Bethke, 1988; McNichols & Zimmerrer, 1986).

INTERPERSONAL FACTORS

The relationship between two individuals affects ethical decision making. For example, superior-subordinate relationships in the workplace powerfully influence who says what to whom, and with what effect. Regardless of status differences, the level of trust between two individuals affects communication. With greater trust, colleagues are more likely to make ethical decisions. Lacking trust, they have more difficulty making innovative, ethical decisions.

The natural tension between a public relations professional and individual reporters and editors in the media—each depending on and needing the other, each working under different pressures and deadlines—can affect how ethical issues involving the media are resolved. The best media relations are built on mutual respect and trust between the communicator and media representatives. That trust can be established and maintained only if accurate information is the currency of the relationship.

SMALL GROUP FACTORS

Peer pressure is very apparent in small group meetings. Sometimes peer pressure can be positive, encouraging reason and fairness. At other times, especially when a group is tired and running out of time, peer pressure operates against creative, ethical considerations. Effective group leaders learn to be alert to these tendencies and avoid groupthink. Unethical leaders know how to manipulate groupthink to their advantage.

"Not enough information and not enough time" is one of the biggest excuses that individuals and small groups give for making decisions that later are judged to be unethical. Time pressures affect individuals, but they especially affect small group decision making. Too many deadlines are artificially imposed for ulterior purposes. While firm deadlines and a genuine lack of information may be unavoidable, in many situations it is the perception of a lack of time that adversely affects decision making. Ethical leaders know when to stress absolute deadlines and when to search for, and find, more time and information to make the best decision possible.

As one corporate code suggests, "When in doubt, don't." If you sense you are about to make an unethical decision, then stop the decision-making process. Give yourself and your colleagues more time to think through the issues. Ethical leaders know when and how to stop a rush to judgment.

ORGANIZATIONAL FACTORS

Organizational factors affect the quantity and quality of ethical decisions. The size of an organization makes a difference in a number of ways. Ethical issues in a firm with three employees are not the same as they would be if those same three individuals were part of an organization with thirty thousand employees. Not only would the ethical problems be different, the solutions to these problems would be different. Large organizations require a different set of management skills. For example, consider the potential solutions to the problem of a slanderous rumor spreading within an organization. A professional communicator in a relatively small organization, say, fewer than twenty employees, could deal with this situation quickly at one group meeting. It might take days, weeks, and even months to deal effectively with such a rumor within a much larger organization.

Certain types of technologies breed their own set of ethical situations, problems, and dilemmas. Consider, for example, nuclear power industries, hospitals, universities and school systems, grocery stores, and food processing firms. Professional communicators learn, too often the hard way, that the basic work of the organization carries with it certain ethical dilemmas.

The mind-set of senior management may be one of the biggest predictors of success or failure in dealing with ethical issues. If candor and honesty are the hallmarks of senior management, this set of attitudes and behaviors will spread throughout the organization. If the actions of senior management generate distrust, these negative attitudes will affect a wide range of decisions, especially those requiring a judgment about what is right and what is wrong.

Many organizations have developed specific processes for dealing with ethical issues. Some, especially organizations anxious to be in compliance with governmental regulations, have established training programs and departments dealing with ethics. Most mature organizations develop their own code of ethics and recognize that the process of developing and revising the code may be as important as the code itself.

Competitors help keep organizations honest. Misstate a fact about a competitor's product or service, and you will find out how closely your corporate statements are watched. The activist public scrutinizes a corporation's words and actions, as do regulators. Lots of people outside the control of an organization help keep it honest.

PROFESSIONAL CODES

Professional associations such as the International Association of Business Communicators (IABC) and the Public Relations Society of America, to name two of the largest in this field, are significant sources of pressure. The Global Alliance for Public Relations and Communication Management has information and resources for communicators to use to identify and resolve ethical issues. The Universal Accreditation Board is made up of a consortium of professional communication associations interested in accrediting its members, and ethics are a critical part of its accreditation examination and study materials.

One of the primary missions of a professional association is to encourage its members and others to engage in ethical activities. Because it is difficult for an association to sanction its members without raising libel and restraint-of-trade issues, most associations stress their educational efforts to encourage ethical behavior more than the sanctions that may be imposed on members who violate articles of the association's code of ethics.

There is a predictable amount of redundancy among the professional codes in this field. They offer guidelines that essentially encourage telling the truth and not engaging in harmful business practices. The IABC code clearly addresses the relatively universal nature of ethical corporate communication. The IABC code states it is

> . . . based on three different yet interrelated principles of professional communication that apply throughout the world.
>
> These principles assume that just societies are governed by a profound respect for human rights and the rule of law; that ethics, the criteria for determining what is right and wrong, can be agreed upon by members of an organization; and, that understanding matters of taste requires sensitivity to cultural norms.
>
> These principles are essential:
>
> - Professional communication is legal.
> - Professional communication is ethical.
> - Professional communication is in good taste [IABC, 2005, para. 2–4].

In certain jurisdictions around the world, governmental direct and indirect controls on media organizations and licensing of communication practitioners are major sources of pressure for ethical behavior. Even when licensing is not required, close governmental scrutiny of public communication has an effect on business communicators.

It is beyond the scope of this chapter to discuss legal issues affecting communicators. Most professional communicators are expected to be both legal and ethical. But it is possible for a professional communicator to be ethical yet not legal. An example is civil disobedience involving public communication, such as an animal rights campaign that deliberately violates the law in order to gain media attention, with members of the organization willing to pay the consequence of breaking the law.

Cultural values and beliefs strongly influence ethical decision making. Profound differences in cultures can be seen at the international level. But they also occur among small communities, for example, going from one proverbial side of the railroad tracks to the other in a small town. Ethical communicators take cultural values and beliefs of key stakeholders into consideration when developing campaigns. While these cultural differences are important, practically all cultures around the world agree to three basic concepts: telling the truth, treating others as you wish to be treated, and doing no harm to the innocent. Scholars, religious leaders, and ethicists have acknowledged that these ethical concepts are important in most cultures in the world, especially those where professional communicators are employed. For professional communicators, there are more similarities than differences among cultures when it comes to the right way to communicate.

CONCLUSIONS AND PRACTICAL SUGGESTIONS

A number of factors affect ethical decision making in public relations and business communication: factors that operate at the intrapersonal, interpersonal, small group, and organizational levels and factors outside the control of any one organization, such as competitors, professional associations, laws, public policies, and cultural values. Being aware of these factors may reduce some of the surprise and may clear up some of the uncertainty that happens when a communicator is confronted with an ethical dilemma.

Here are some practical suggestions for communicators who want to be ethical:

- Know yourself. Write your own personal code of ethics based on one of the professional codes. It will help you think through how you will deal with ethical dilemmas before they happen.

- Learn how to recognize and deal creatively and professionally with ethical situations, problems, and dilemmas.

- Know your colleagues and how they act in small groups, and understand the nature and characteristics of your client or employer. Help your client or organization develop its own corporate code of ethics. The process, if it is done right, raises strategic questions about the organization, positions the communicator in the middle of the process, and prepares you for crisis communication management.

- Know the law (or find someone who does), and be able to describe the legal issues and regulatory agencies that affect your business.

Respect the cultural values and beliefs of your stakeholders. Recognize that they too, if they are good people, share your values of telling the truth, being fair, and doing no harm to the innocent.

I recommend the following readings and Web sites:

- *Communication Ethics and Universal Values,* by Clifford Christians and Michael Traber (Thousand Oaks, CA: Sage, 1997).
- *Ethics Across Cultures,* by Michael C. Brannigan (New York: McGraw-Hill, 2005)
- The Ethics Resource Center in Washington, D.C., which offers practical suggestions for developing corporate codes of conduct and other useful state-of-the-art information (www.ethics.org).
- The Association for Practical and Professional Ethics has many useful resources (http://php.ucs.indiana.edu/ ~ appe/home.html).
- An extensive Web site for ethicists is maintained by Lawrence Hinman of San Diego State University (http://ethics.acusd.edu/).
- For practical suggestions for dealing with bribery and other "pay for play" schemes, see the Web site for Transparency International, an association of businesses fighting corruption worldwide (www.transparency.org).
- For resources and practical suggestions for dealing with communication ethics, see the Web site for the Global Alliance for Public Relations and Communications Management (www.globalpr.org).
- For information about the relatively universal accreditation examination that is administered for a large number of professional associations in public relations, go to the Web site of the Universal Accreditation Board (www.praccreditation.org).
- For more information about the IABC Code of Ethics for Professional Communicators, go to its Web site (www.iabc.com).

References

International Association of Business Communicators. (2005). *International Association of Business Communicators Code of Ethics for Professional Communicators.* http://www.iabc.com/members/joining/code.htm.

Kidwell, J. M., Stevens, R. E., & Bethke, A. L. (1988). Differences in ethical perceptions between male and female managers: Myth or reality? *Journal of Business Ethics, 6,* 487–493.

McNichols, C. W., & Zimmerrer, T. W. (1986). Situational ethics: An empirical study of differentiators of student attitudes. *Journal of Business Ethics, 4,* 175–180.

PART TWO

MANAGING COMMUNICATION

CHAPTER SIX

Strategic Approaches to Managing the Communications Function

Diane M. Gayeski

Communication activity in organizations happens all the time; it is a natural and necessary means for individuals to accomplish professional roles, coordinate activities with others, and forge relationships. People, for the most part, speak for themselves. But who speaks for the company? The formal aspects of communication—establishing and managing the voice of the company—are the responsibility of professional communicators. These functions include:

- External communication, such as investor relations, media relations, public relations, government and community affairs, philanthropy, corporate Web sites, and managing the corporate reputation

- Internal communication, such as employee newsletters, business update meetings, employee benefits and policy materials, intranets, collaboration systems, and electronic news displays

- Marketing communications, such as advertising and sales materials, trade shows, customer help and feedback functions, and e-commerce Web Sites

Each of these is a complex specialty, and their associated issues and activities are covered in detail in subsequent chapters. The purpose of this chapter is to explore some strategic decisions that affect how and where this work gets done:

- Where do professional communication functions reside organizationally?

- How do communicators align their messages with the organization's strategy and with each other?

- Do employees or external contractors perform the work?
- How do projects and staff get funded?
- How do communications managers demonstrate value?

WHERE DOES COMMUNICATIONS RESIDE ON THE ORGANIZATIONAL CHART?

Communication professionals can fill many different roles in organizations, and those jobs can reside in a variety of departments. Under the umbrella of business communicators are meeting planners, speechwriters, financial communicators, Web and graphic designers, advertising and public relations managers, and communication strategists. There is no one best way to construct their reporting structures, but the strategic decisions about how to design jobs and where to place them certainly do affect the daily work life of the communicators in these positions. In general, roles directed toward employee communication are placed within human resources, while external communication may reside in a corporate communication or marketing department. Larger and more complex companies usually employ many communications professionals who fill fairly specialized roles, while small organizations may have just one person who is a jack of all trades.

In small organizations, there is generally no one person whose total responsibility relates to communications. Employee communications, such as occasional recruiting, explaining company rules and benefits, and organizing some meetings, probably falls to the person in charge of human resources. Promotional communications, such as maintaining the Web site, developing brochures, and developing proposals and presentations, is done by marketing. The CEO takes charge of telling the company story to important customers, investors or donors, and employees.

Once an organization gets a bit larger, there may be one person designated to produce communications, usually having responsibility for both external and employee communication. To whom should this person report? Although this may seem like a small decision, it affects the way that communication projects are prioritized and measured. Typically, growing organizations feel the most pressing need is in communicating to potential customers or donors, so their first full-time communication professional typically resides within marketing or fundraising. In organizations in which an external advertising and public relations agency does most of the promotional work, the first full-time communicator may be in charge of employee communications. Perhaps the ideal place for the new communicator to reside is in a staff position reporting directly to the CEO. In this capacity, the communicator would provide counsel to the executive team, looking at long-term company strategies and selecting communication interventions that relate to this level of objectives. Most surveys of the communication profession report that more than half of the senior public relations and communication executives do report directly to the CEO (Likely, 1998). Where the position actually resides is important for several reasons:

- *The communicator's supervisor will bring his or her own lens into making decisions about funding and evaluating the work of the communicator.* Therefore, if a communicator reporting to a vice president of marketing wants to install plasma screens to provide news updates to employees, that idea may not carry as much weight as if a new opportunity to exhibit at a trade show were proposed. A vice president of human resources, for example, may not know how to evaluate a promotional campaign.
- *The career path of communicators depends somewhat on where that function resides.* If a person hired as a communication specialist within the human resource department wants to advance in the company, the logical choice would be to learn more about human resources and work up the ladder within that function. If the communication function resides within marketing, a different set of skills will be needed to advance within that professional field.
- *In order for the communicator to play a strategic role in improving business performance, it is necessary to have a seat at the table and have the inside track on organizational strategy and goals.* If communicators get buried under a bureaucratic department and do not have regular contact with executives, they become relegated to a role as order taker, simply designing publications or running meetings without having the opportunity to analyze and select the most powerful interventions. This very much plays into the question of whether communicators are business strategists or craftspeople and how they are viewed, valued, and supported by their executives.

In large organizations, professional communicators are likely to be placed within many different departments. For example, the company may have a chief spokesperson and speechwriter reporting directly to the CEO. Professionals in investor relations may work within the finance department. An entirely separate department of corporate communication may provide media relations, community relations, and philanthropy support. Employee communications and training for supervisory communication usually reside within human resources. Advertising and special events sponsorship typically are placed within marketing. And departments, divisions, or separate field offices all may have their own communication professionals. For instance, the information technology department of one of the world's largest hotel chains hires its own communication professionals who are responsible for communicating news and strategy to its own computer professionals and to communicate with all employees about issues related to information technologies.

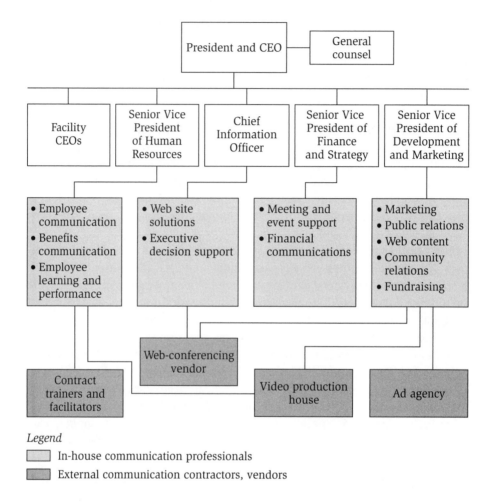

Figure 6.1. Typical Placement of Communications Functions in a Complex Nonprofit Organization

Figure 6.1 presents a fairly typical organizational chart for a complex non-profit organization such as a health care system. It shows that communicators reside in several places within the hierarchy, including both internal positions and as external contractors and agencies.

The landscape of communication departments changes rapidly, and such change should be welcomed. An international benchmarking study found that within the United States, communication departments that have not changed have dipped in importance in their organizations. In this survey, a majority of participants (around 80 percent) said they felt that the perception of the importance of communication had increased over the past year. The only group that dropped significantly below average response consisted of those working in departments that had not restructured in the previous twelve months (Barnfield, 2002).

BRIDGING THE ISLANDS OF COMMUNICATION

One of the challenges facing communicators when they are dispersed across the organizational chart is coordinating the flow, load, tone, and content of messages. Employee communications, investor relations, public relations, and supervisory and executive communications are often designed and managed in separation functional silos. Professionals in these areas often have little incentive to collaborate, and they actually may have many barriers to do so. This creates a situation that I call the "islands of communication" (see Figure 6.2).

When each of these areas creates messages and communication events, they tend to ignore the fact that their materials and meetings represent only a small fraction of the communication load for their target audiences. They may also inadvertently contradict the content or the tone of other items in the communication stream. What happens then? Audiences become overloaded in two ways and form their own filters to opt out and tune out. First, the sheer volume of information and demands on their time become overwhelming, and audiences

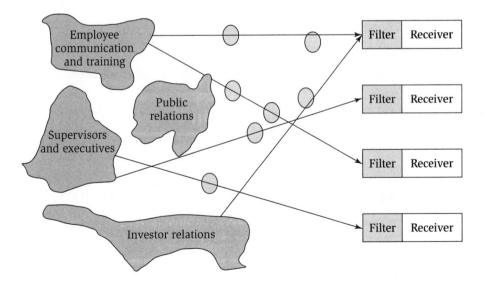

Figure 6.2. Islands of Communication

simply opt out. They either physically delete or throw out messages or they opt out of meetings. The other way is that the inconsistency of messages and tone causes cognitive dissonance. Employees and customers do not know what to believe and tune out. People are tired of hearing about some major initiative in the newsletter, being taught something a bit different in a required training class, and then having their supervisors tell them to ignore the whole thing because it was just a passing fad.

These situations cause poor performance because a lot of important messages are completely ignored; even worse, they cause cynicism, mistrust, misdirected efforts, and inconsistent brand messages. Here are some examples of these situations. In a large Canadian bank, my consulting firm did a study to document the communication load of key roles, such as branch managers and customer service representatives. We found that if they actually read, listened to, and attended to all the materials and meetings that were expected of them, they had have no time in the week left to do their jobs. At a nonprofit health care organization, human resources sent employees a notice that they would be receiving a less generous benefits package in the forthcoming year and that employees would now be responsible for paying a larger percentage of their insurance premiums. In employee mailboxes that same day was a letter from the CEO asking employees to contribute to the annual fundraising effort. Not only were both the benefits and fundraising messages unsuccessful and annoying, but the CEO came across as out of touch and uncaring, a trait that branded him and cut short his tenure (Gayeski, 2000).

One of the strategies for bridging the islands of communication is creating cross-functional project teams across human resource, marketing, public relations, employee communications, and training for major organizational initiatives such as quality programs, the introduction of new products or services, or company reorganizations.

Another is consolidating communications functions into fewer departments. In fact, in many organizations, employee communication, public relations, advertising, investor relations, executive communications, and community relations are all part of one department.

For example, Hewlett-Packard (HP) recently centralized its global internal communication function. Internal communication reports to the company's senior vice president for corporate marketing and the executive vice president for human resources. This dual reporting structure enables internal communication to help coordinate a myriad of internal messages within a framework consistent with HP's external messaging and branding. The Program Management Office (PMO) is a standing internal communication committee designed to unify messaging across regions, businesses, and functions. It is therefore a permanent version of the communication council, a central committee developing overarching guidelines around such issues as measurement and editorial message and building standard tools and templates to be used throughout internal communication worldwide (Shaw & Andrews, 2005).

In the late 1990s, a major breakdown in communication between managers and employees was the catalyst for a renewed focus on the role of internal communicators working within General Motor's plants. GM developed the role of business communication integrators whose job it is to engender consistency between the methods of communication in plants across the company by instituting five common processes for internal communication. They are also responsible for working with local leaders to improve their communication skills and develop their approach to people management (Grates, 2005).

Xerox's communication structure includes a mix of centralized and decentralized functions:

- Centralized: Corporate communications, marketing, and public relations
- Decentralized: Employee communications, which is placed within individual business units
- Formal councils in communications and marketing to ensure alignment of messages across the corporation
- Tightly linked informal networks among communicators to enable cross-functional information sharing and best practices swapping

OUTSOURCING THE COMMUNICATION FUNCTIONS

In large organizations, the complexity of communication tasks means that more communicators with increasingly specific roles and areas of expertise are hired. In these situations, a key strategic decision is whether to hire these communicators as employees or as external contractors. Over the past decades, the tides of outsourcing have shifted many times. In the 1980s, many organizations embraced new technologies such as videotape and videoconferencing for communicating with their employees and external audiences; in the 1990s, these technologies expanded to include desktop publishing, multimedia, and Internet and intranet sites. When corporate coffers were full, staffing levels in communications grew, along with large investments in communication technologies. When economic times grew harder and the new technologies were changing rapidly, the trend was to outsource these functions.

Today most organizations use a mix of internal and external communication professionals. Inside communicators generally handle strategy and project management; these people are close to the company, its executives, and its culture and know how to set guidelines and goals. They are easily accessible and fill key roles as spokespersons, planners, and communication coaches. However, it is difficult for any one communicator to be fluent in all the skills, crafts, and technologies of communication. That is where freelancers and contract consultants and producers come in. If an organization does not need full-time help in any one aspect of communication such as speechwriting, it is best to hire it out. Today most video production and a lot of Web programming is outsourced because it is difficult for organizations to keep up with the changes in technologies and to house sophisticated studios and editing space.

The advantages of in-house resources are that they can be counted on to be readily accessible and they become familiar with the organization's products and politics. Therefore, they can quickly write materials and react to changing organizational needs. When dealing with sensitive material, executives are likely to prefer to work with employees rather than outside contractors, who may also be working for the competition.

Outsiders have the advantage of being able to specialize in particular topics or skills such as Web programming, executive speechwriting, crisis management, photography, or evaluation methodologies. Most organizations employ one or more advertising and public relations agencies to develop and produce large-scale campaigns. External consultants can also provide a more unbiased assessment in some situations and are more protected from corporate politics when they need to deliver unpopular messages or recommendations. They also bring their knowledge of trends and approaches from their other engagements and clients. Finally, when large-scale corporate initiatives happen, such as a big change in benefits plans, a rebranding effort, or a merger, more people are needed to do the work, so it is likely that major parts of those projects will be turned over to an external communication vendor. Thus, it makes sense for most organizations to employ full-time communication strategists and project managers who can then supervise and coordinate a number of contractors or projects.

HOW COMMUNICATIONS GET FUNDED

Communication professionals and projects are funded in a variety of ways, and along with the organizational structure, this variable is one of the most significant strategies that has an impact on the role and function of communicators. The most traditional form of structure and funding is the service center model. In this strategy, there is one central communication department that is funded by an overall "tax" on each corporate unit. The communication department receives an annual budget and performs projects for internal clients on a first-come, first-served basis. At the other end of the continuum of funding is the profit center model, in which the communication department charges for its projects and even takes on clients outside the organization to make a profit. A number of communication departments with unique service offerings or technologies take this route, and by bringing in a profit, they are able to protect their own jobs in times of corporate downsizing and expand their staff beyond what might be needed only for internal clients. For example, in the 1990s, when a number of in-house video departments were about to be placed on the corporate chopping block, they turned themselves into profit centers (even separately incorporating as joint ventures between the organization and the employees of the video department) and were able to retain their jobs and facilities.

A number of funding and structure models lie between the two extremes of service centers and profit centers. Many communication departments operate as cost centers, where they charge their internal clients for services rendered. In full charge-back operations, the department charges enough to cover the cost of personnel, overhead, and out-of-pocket project expenses. For example, if the manager of quality decides to roll out a new Six Sigma initiative that includes employee meetings, executive presentations, a video, and periodic newsletter articles, the employee communication department estimates what personnel (either in-house or freelance or both) will be needed and for how many hours, and comes up with a budget for actual expenses such as printing and meeting refreshments. The client is then either charged a fixed fee or is billed for actual expenses. A less aggressive approach is for communication departments to charge clients only for out-of-pocket expenses, while personnel and overhead (such as their office space, equipment, and supplies) are covered in an annual budget funded by the organization.

Each of these approaches has advantages and disadvantages. In the traditional service center, clients do not have a cost barrier preventing them from working with their in-house communication professionals. The communication work emanates from a central department staffed by full-time employees. However, this ease is tempered by several problems. One is that executives often feel that communicators in such structures can become rather complacent because they have a captive client base. Also, it is difficult for an organization to predict how much money to budget for communications for an entire year; the budget could run out when one eager client proposes a huge project, leaving no resources for other worthy causes.

While profit centers seem like a great deal to executives and while entrepreneurial communicators may like the prospect of selling their services to outside clients, such relationships are tricky to navigate. In-house clients may feel that they are being squeezed out by external clients, and they may dislike having to pay a market rate for communication services. In such situations, internal clients will also have the option of using external services, so a profit center may actually lose its best and closest customers. There are also issues of confidentiality when external customers suddenly start showing up in communication offices and media facilities.

While the service, cost, and profit centers describe centralized models in which the communication department resides within the corporate headquarters, there are also variations in terms of decentralization. In organizations with multiple sites, communicators may report to a vice president or director whose office is at headquarters, but they may actually work at offices in other locations. For example, in a manufacturing company with several sites across the country or the globe, employee communicators will probably live and work in those locations in order to be closer to their customers. Some even have dual reporting relationships—to both employee communications at headquarters and to the local business division or plant manager.

In some organizations, individual departments or locations fund their own communication support. For example, instead of the staffing money coming from corporate headquarters to support an employee communication specialist at an individual manufacturing site, the site itself may fund and supervise that position. Shared services is a rapidly emerging model; in this approach, two or more departments or locations get together and jointly fund communication positions. For example, let us say that there are two hospitals in a national health care group that are located near each other. They may get together and fund their own media relations department to deal with the local market.

HOW COMMUNICATION FUNCTIONS DEMONSTRATE VALUE

While few executives need to be convinced of the value of a company's reputation and its relationship with internal and external stakeholders, when it comes time to compete for resources, the communication function often faces challenges. It is difficult to prove any direct relationship between most communication interventions and the bottom line because so many variables affect human performance and the impact of many projects may take years to show up. For example, an employee suggestion system may indeed garner some immediate ideas that reduce costs or increase profits. But beyond this, the effects of asking for employee input may raise morale and engagement, thereby making the organization a more attractive place to work. This can lower turnover and attract better candidates. However, those last factors would be almost impossible to prove in any statistical way since so many other factors go into decisions about where to work and how much commitment to put into one's job.

Typically communication projects are measured by satisfaction surveys or some type of use measure. For example, employee communication programs are usually assessed by communication audits that solicit employees' reactions to the overall climate and tools used (such as newsletters and meetings). Their opinions are gained through surveys, focus groups, and individual interviews. Use measures include counting the number of hits to various intranet pages, gauging attendance at meetings, or counting suggestions or responses to messages. While these measures certainly do give an overall indication of opinion, they do not get to the kind of bottom-line measurements that can provide a good basis for calculating return on investment.

Communications projects cannot be measured unless they start out having specific, measurable goals that influence organizational performance. For example, an intranet site that provides regulations, links to good travel bargains, and paperwork for filling out travel requests might reduce the costs of processing travel reimbursements by reducing staff time and gaining lower-cost travel arrangements. A communication manager could track before and after statistics about how much staff time is used in processing travel expenses and the average cost per trip. An employee suggestion system can track how many suggestions were implemented and what impact they had on costs or profits. A campaign to conserve energy can track electricity and heat costs.

But how does a communication manager measure the benefits of an electronic news system that posts the company press releases, stock price, and profiles of new employees? How does one know whether the intranet helps performance, or whether it is an attractive nuisance just taking people's valuable time away from their jobs? Does the annual open house and tour of the plant have a positive impact on the relationship to the community, and even if it does, how does that benefit the corporation?

These issues of measurement are central to the challenges and successful management of organizational communication. Nevertheless, there are ways to explain the value of a good communication system in terms that executives can understand. Two powerful concepts are intangible assets and human capital (see Figure 6.3). Intangible assets are organizational factors that are not on the books in terms of actual money in the bank or physical objects

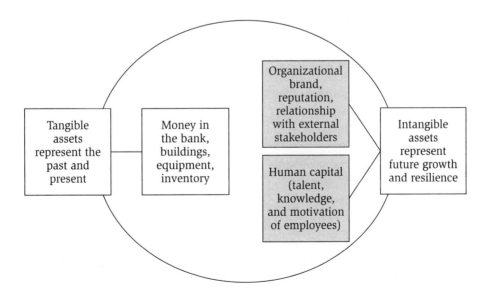

Figure 6.3. Tangible and Intangible Assets

such as buildings and inventory. Intangible assets include the brand, having good community and employee relations, having loyal customers, and having a smart and committed workforce. Analysts know that these factors are what drive future profitability, which has a direct bearing on stock price. Human capital is the collective willingness and ability to perform of the workforce. This is affected by motivation, knowledge of the business strategy, and training (Gayeski, 2005).

THE COMMUNICATOR AS PERFORMANCE CONSULTANT

In order to be a strategic asset, communications needs to be structured and run as a function that has a direct impact on organizational performance. This means that instead of taking on projects because an executive thinks it is a good idea or because other organizations are doing similar things, the communication manager needs to function as a performance consultant. To do this, the manager needs to:

- Maintain close relationships with management to stay on top of strategic goals and performance gaps.
- Identify as precisely as possible the cost of the current performance gaps or the potential gains of successfully implementing new strategies.
- Analyze the possible causes of substandard performance and the drivers of the desired goals.
- Understand what motivates each audience (customers, investors, employees, regulators), and design messages tailored to the needs and styles of each.
- Select communication interventions based on the probable impact in terms of significant goals and problems.
- Develop measurable and observable objectives for communication campaigns and projects.
- Estimate the return on investment for each communication project.
- Evaluate each project based on the stated measurable goals.
- Continually benchmark best practices in organizational communication as well as major research studies that link communication to performance.

The communication function (or more precisely, *functions*) is rapidly becoming managed as business drivers rather than corporate frills. By carefully selecting the right organizational design, staffing roles, relationships with constituencies, funding models, and evaluation strategies, professional communicators have unprecedented opportunities to move up the ranks of their companies and become major players in organizational strategy.

References

Barnfield, E. (2002). *Key benchmark data for communicators—2002/3.* London: Melcrum Publishing.

Gayeski, D. (2000). *Managing the communication function: Capturing mindshare for organizational performance.* San Francisco: International Association of Business Communicators.

Gayeski, D. (2005). *Managing organizational learning and communication as business assets.* Upper Saddle River, NJ: Pearson-Prentice Hall.

Grates, G. F. (2005). The role of communication integrators at General Motors. *Strategic communication management, 9*(2), 30–34.

Likely, F. (1998). Reorganize your communication function: Ten structural models for the new Look Organization. *Strategic communication management, 2*(5), 28–34.

Shaw, K., & Andrews, R. (2005). Introducing centralization in HP's global IC function. *Strategic communication management, 9*(1), 26–29.

CHAPTER SEVEN

Strategic Planning

Timeless Wisdom Still Shapes
Successful Communication Programs

Lester R. Potter

Some say that strategic planning reached its zenith in the 1960s. If so, then why is it so widely practiced today? Strategic planning remains popular for the same reason that classical music does. Classical music conforms to certain established standards of form, complexity, and musical literacy. Among the most popular classical works today are compositions dating from the 1600s and 1700s. Doubtless there were detractors of this timeless musical form who predicted its demise. Just as they have been proved wrong, so have the detractors of strategic planning. Strategic planning, which also conforms to certain established standards of form, content, and literacy, truly is timeless wisdom that continues to shape successful business.

My personal journey to become a strategic planner/communicator began in the mid-1970s. One of the first strategic thinkers I studied was William E. Rothschild, of General Electric and Harvard Business School. Rothschild summarized strategic planning this way: "Because of the scarcity of money and resources, most companies must become more selective and limit their investment to those companies which can provide an attractive payoff and in which they are strong. Furthermore, they must count on some business to finance the growth of others. Thus, they need a resource allocation system that will enable them to select their best prospects. This is the purpose of strategic planning" (Rothschild, 1979, p. 12). In thirty years of professional practice, I have facilitated strategic planning processes with for-profit organizations in many different industries, nonprofits large and small with a variety of missions, and a variety of government agencies. The common link is the value of strategic planning as a day-to-day guide on what to do to achieve organizational success. Business leaders, managers, or communicators who have no strategic plans as guides are at the mercy of what I call *crisis du jour.*

STRATEGIC PLANNING TODAY: WHAT IS HAPPENING?

Like many other business management practices, strategic planning has been transformed by technology. Yet like classical music, its essence remains the same. Business leaders rely on the strategic planning process to provide both the criteria for making day-to-day organizational decisions and a template against which all such decisions can be evaluated. Strategic planning answers three basic questions: First, where are we going? Second, what is the environment? And third, how do we get there? (Goodstein, Nolan, & Pfeiffer, 1993).

Strategic planning usually consists of four phases: an internal review, an external review, a strategy summary, and contingency plans. The first phase begins with a systematic process to determine exactly what the organization wants to achieve. After much group facilitation, these broad descriptions are usually captured in vision or mission statements. Many organizations have both, with the vision statement at the top of the hierarchy governing the big picture of achievement. The mission is far more relevant and useful to business managers, especially communication managers. A good mission statement answers the following questions: What function does the organization perform? For whom does the organization perform this function? How does the organization go about filling this function? Why does the organization exist (Goodstein et al., 1993)? It takes a great deal of organizational analysis, often called needs analysis or situational audit, to write these short, simple statements. An organization must analyze what businesses it is in, its customers, its markets, and its competition and then decide where it wants to go as an organization.

The next phase consists of making certain assumptions about the environment through which the organization must navigate in order to achieve its mission. In this phase, an organization studies external forces, in a process often called *environmental scanning,* that it assumes will have an impact on its ability to achieve its mission over the life of the strategic plan. I usually interject self-imposed restraints into this phase of planning. These restraints relate to the organization's values and corporate culture. An organization's values come from its corporate culture, defined as "a pattern of beliefs and expectations deeply held in common by members of the organization" (Goodstein et al., 1993, p. 60). Values, in turn, give rise to situational norms (the way we do things around here) that are manifested in observable behavior. All this is of enormous importance to the organizational communicator, especially behavior of publics.

The third phase usually consists of putting together all that the organization has learned in the internal review and the external environmental scan. To do this, an organization must conduct an internal performance audit. This includes the ubiquitous SWOT (strengths, weaknesses, opportunities, and threats) analysis. SWOT analysis looks at the recent performance of an organization in terms of some basic indexes, such as cash flow, growth, staffing, quality, technology, operations, service, profit, and return on investment, identified as critical to the strategic profile. The performance audit provides data for gap analysis, determining the degree to which the strategic business model is realistic and workable (Goodstein et al., 1993).

Then an organization is usually ready to formulate goals, objectives, strategies, and tactics. Goals describe future desired results toward which efforts are directed (Bedeian & Zammuto, 1991). They can be broad brush, such as "to maximize shareholder wealth." Goals should be achievable, but there have been those who urged business leaders to think big. Collins and Porras did just that in their book, *Built to Last: Successful Habits of Visionary Companies* (1995), when they urged organizations to have a long-term vision that is supposed to be so daring in its scope as to seem impossible (Reingold & Underwood, 2004). Goals that are achievable, even if considered stretch goals, work best today. For communicators, goals must be understood by members of the organization; therefore, the simpler and more achievable they are, the better.

Objectives must be specifically written so that those charged with implementation can clearly see how the objective will help manifest a goal into reality. A simple acronym to remember when formulating objectives is SMART (Potter, 2001, p. 52):

S = specific

M = measurable

A = attainable

R = relevant

T = time sensitive

Strategy is a curious little word with a big impact. Steiner (1979) observed that it originally was used by management to mean what you did to counter what a competitor did or intended to do. Sometimes the word *strategy* is used to cover every aspect of strategic planning, as with the balanced scorecard. Some speak of strategy as the answer to this question: "What should the organization be doing?" A strategy specifies general direction and priorities. The essence of strategy is choosing to perform activities differently from competitors so as to provide a unique value proposition (Kaplan & Norton, 2001).

Successful strategy is not a tool reserved for the for-profit sector. For-profits, nonprofits, and government agencies all have the same problem: it is not easy to determine strategy. Nonprofits and government agencies typically have considerable difficulty in defining clearly their strategy. Kaplan and Norton (2001) have seen "strategy" documents extending to fifty or more pages. Most of the document, once the vision and mission are articulated, consists of lists of programs and initiatives, not the outcomes the organization is trying to achieve. These organizations must understand that, as the highly regarded Harvard Business School's Michael Porter said, strategy is not only what the organization intends to do, but also what it decides not to do, a message that is particularly relevant for nonprofits and government departments (Kaplan et al., 2001).

Government and nonprofit organizations can be strategic and build competitive advantage in ways other than pure operational excellence. But it takes vision and leadership to move beyond improving existing processes to a strategy that highlights which processes and activities are the most important to implement (Kaplan et al., 2001).

Tactics are the step-by-step details that must happen to accomplish a strategy. Standing alone, they may be small things, but taken together, they have big impact on success of the plan. Most strategic plans fail due to lack of effective tactical execution. Conversely, all too often, organizational communicators focus only on tactical execution of various media rather than on an overall strategic communication plan for their work. In such situations, training in strategic planning and, subsequently, developing a strategic approach to communication management is extraordinarily valuable.

The fourth phase of the typical strategic planning process consists of contingency planning. This phase accounts for how the organization will anticipate the unexpected and still achieve its plans. What will the organization do if things do not go as planned?

Contingency planning involves the following (Goodstein et al., 1993, p. 32):

1. Identifying the most important internal and external threats to and opportunities for the organization, especially those involving other than the most-likely scenarios.

2. Developing trigger points to initiate action steps for each contingency.

3. Agreeing on which action steps will be taken for each of these trigger points

Strategic planning has helped many organizations achieve success. But what are planners and business leaders saying and doing today? According to *Fast Company* magazine (Lidsky, 2004), strategy is always perfect on paper. But when it has to be executed, failure can creep in. This suggests that it might be time to retire the sunny strategic visions and stop filling out the templates. Some successful companies such as "IBM and Philips are moving away from the empty practice of strategic planning and instead work to integrate strategy and execution" (p. 77).

Len Schlesinger, vice chairman and chief operating officer of Limited Brands, told *Fast Company* magazine: "My job has a large strategic component to it and a large tactical component to it. And what I've discovered is that it is extraordinarily difficult to operate in a tactical and strategic mode simultaneously. At some point," Schlesinger continued, "You have to be willing to trust your instincts without the benefit of a detailed plan. You can go through life aggregating numbers, getting analyses, and getting more data, but by the time you know the right answer, it's irrelevant. Sometimes you have to make decisions faster than arriving data. I've always trusted instincts" (Lidsky, 2004, p. 78).

But Amazon's CEO, Jeff Bezos, says when someone has a good idea, "We can measure that" (Deutschman, 2004, p. 57). Bezos is well known for relying heavily on intuition and insight. But even Bezos seems to adhere to the old bromide of what gets measured gets done.

At General Electric, which pioneered or perfected many of the strategic planning techniques in common use today, the process is still viewed favorably. A team working on a promising new technology explained why it does not get lost in the strategic shuffle at a "behemoth like GE with US$134 billion in annual sales." The answer lies in the company's yearly strategic planning process known as the S-1 (Underwood, 2004, p. 75).

In 1999 Ravine noted the following trends that would continue to influence strategic planning efforts:

- Strategic planning is moving down from the executive suite.
- Middle managers must have the ability to be aware of the climate and environment of a firm in order to accelerate rethinking of business practices.
- Firms are increasingly committing themselves to strategic planning.
- Game theory is hot.
- Customers are key to strategy.

Each year, there is some new innovation that touts itself as the newest, best way to manage. In 2003 alone, 5,301 books claiming to be about business were published, up 30 percent from just three years earlier. The business book market was projected to reach $828.6 million in 2004 (Lidsky, 2004). That is why I believe in the timeless wisdom of strategic planning as management fads come and go. The process makes you think and do research before you act, focus on the right things, and decide what you will and will not do within resource constraints. With this as a backdrop, it is time to discuss the communicator's role in strategic planning.

THE ROLE OF STRATEGIC PLANNING IN COMMUNICATION MANAGEMENT

To survive and prosper, organizational communicators must contribute significantly and measurably to strategic management. They must think, act, and manage communication programs strategically, recording measurable results that contribute to the accomplishment of the organization's mission. This fact transcends state and international borders, for-profit, nonprofit, and government organization types. It is relevant to the specialist as well as the generalist practice of communication. It is true of internal and external communication. The only reason organizational communication programs exist is to build and maintain good relationships with key publics, recording measurable results that help the organization realize its mission.

An organization's management relies on the strategic planning process to provide both the criteria for making day-to-day organizational decisions and a template against which all such decisions can be evaluated. The organization's mission, goals, objectives, strategies, and tactics are all developed in the strategic planning process. Enlightened senior leaders demand that communication programs contribute to achieving the organization's mission, goals, and objectives and that they facilitate the implementation of key strategies and tactics. That is what managing communication strategically means. It means that there is a causal relationship between the communication activities and the achievement of the organization's mission. It means that communication programs support successful completion of the organization's strategic activity in a measurable way. Anything less will not be tolerated. Communicators who do not practice communication strategically are often frozen out, replaced, or realigned under some other higher-valued functional area of the organization.

The heart of strategic communication management is the communication plan. It reconciles communication activity with the mission, goals, objectives, strategies, and tactics of the organization in a measurable way. For communicators, learning all they can about organizational strategic planning makes them better prepared to build and execute an effective, results-oriented communication plan, one that they can claim with all authority is strategic.

A communication plan is a written statement of what communication actions will be taken to support the accomplishment of specific organizational goals, the time frame for carrying out the plan, the budget, and the procedures for measuring the results of communication.

For decades, organizations have used strategic planning techniques to get where they want to go. Communication plans serve the same purpose: they guide the communicator to those right actions that will help the organization achieve its goals using communication as a strategic management tool. Strategic plans, marketing plans, and business plans are all similar. It follows, then, that to be considered strategic, communication plans must be structured in a similar way.

The typical strategic plan consists of four major sections, and each section may have as many as ten subsections. My model for an effective communication plan is similar, but the plan is structured somewhat differently:

1. *Executive summary.* Write this last. It is a summary of the plan that any busy decision maker can easily and quickly read to get the main points of your plan.

2. *The communication process.* This is an explanation of what strategic communication is, written for decision makers who may not understand this researched-based and business-oriented way of managing communication.

3. *Background.* This is a step-by-step listing, often written in paragraph and bullet point style, that brings the reader up-to-date on the main events that led the organization to the situation it currently faces and, accordingly, the need for the communication plan.

4. *Situation analysis.* The heart of my process of strategic communication planning, this section determines the real issues that an organization must address. Research is instrumental to this section, which seeks to separate cause from effect and disease from symptom. You can treat effects or symptoms, but until you do something about the cause, the effects will reappear. I find it helpful to list causes, or issues, followed by listing the facts about each one in bullet points under it. These facts form the basis of what actions to take to counter them or capitalize on them later in the implementation step.

5. *Message statement.* What is the major overall message your plan needs to share with publics, target audiences, and stakeholders? This depends on the type of plan you are developing. Is it an internal communication plan only? External only? Is it an integrated marketing communication plan that includes other communication components, such as advertising, product marketing, or community relations?

6. *Publics, target audiences, and stakeholders.* In this section, list in order of importance the publics, target audiences, and stakeholders that you must reach based on the intent of the plan. Break down publics into target audiences or stakeholder groups into the smallest segment possible. Publics can—and should—be segmented as markets are segmented in strategic and marketing planning. That way, you will not forget anyone, and you can target your communication much more efficiently. It is better to have too many segments than too few at first. Later, when you see that the same message, media, and method of receiving information apply to a number of target audiences or stakeholders, you can collapse them into one for more efficient treatment.

7. *Message to target audiences and stakeholders.* List a one- or two-sentence message you want to communicate to each target audience or stakeholder. Remember that the communication plan must incorporate ways of listening to target audiences and stakeholders as well as developing messages for them. The

plan should include goals that establish, maintain, and develop good relationships with target audiences and stakeholders. Rely on mediation, negotiation, and conflict resolution with target audiences and stakeholders, not just on getting the right message to the right people through the right channel.

8. *Implementation.* Now it is time to put it all together. What are you going to do about the problems or opportunities this communication plan addresses, using the information you have gathered? You are now ready to use your craft skills.

9. *Budget.* Just as in strategic planning, resource allocation is all important to the communicator. Budgets are always finite, and to be a successful communicator, you must accomplish your mission and stay within budget guidelines.

10. *Monitoring and evaluation.* This is not only research done prior to developing the plan, but research conducted during or after the plan to evaluate the success or failure of any aspect of implementation. Such monitoring and evaluation conducted during the plan allow you to make course corrections and maximize your chances for overall success.

Following is a summary of the relationships of each strategic communication planning element in this ten-step planning model. The list conforms to sound strategic planning methodology. Each of the seven headings is grouped under the major strategic planning headings (Potter, 2001, p. 135):

Problem or Opportunity
- From the situation analysis, which lists the issues the plan will address from the research.
- Publics, target audiences, and stakeholders that have some relationship to the issue. Building and maintaining good relationships with these groups is the reason for all communication and public relations programs.

Goals and Objectives
- List them as expected outcomes in the implementation step. If you do all the communication activities planned for each target audience or stakeholder for each issue that affects them, then what outcome do you expect to achieve?

Strategies and Tactics
- Messages
- Media and timing
- Cost

Measurement of Success or Failure
- Monitoring and evaluation

Effective strategic communication planning and management begin and end with research. Research is the communicator's firm foundation on which to build relevant, results-oriented communication plans. Practicing communication strategically, beginning with research, is relevant to the specialist as well as the generalist practice of communication. There are two types of formal research: primary and secondary. Primary research is data collected for the first time, specifically for the project on which you are working. Since you do everything from scratch, primary research is generally more expensive and time-consuming than secondary research. You can hire a research firm to do it or do it all yourself. But either way, the advantage of primary research is that it is completely relevant to your current situation. The tools of primary research are interviews, surveys and questionnaires, and focus groups.

Secondary research is data collected by others that you study and apply to your situation. It is generally less expensive and quicker to obtain, but it must be adapted to your situation. A visit to the library or the Internet can yield a wealth of data. Experts agree that a combination of primary and secondary research is best (Bivens, 2005).

Science provides a way of knowing. To the extent that communicators use the scientific method for decision making in communication and public relations management, the communicator elevates the function from the intuitive enterprise of the artist and makes it part of the organization's management system. At the core of this management system are the following aspects of research. First, research is conducted to define the problem (or issues) for the purpose of developing a communication or public relations program. Second, research is done to monitor program implementation for performance accountability and for strategic adjustments. Third, research is conducted to measure program impact or effectiveness with respect to goals and objectives (the expected outcomes) (Broom & Dozier, 1990).

Knowing how to conduct research is a fundamental strategic tool of successful communicators. With these skills, they are better able to compile a key step in the process of strategic communication planning: the situation analysis.

STRATEGIC PLANNING AND COMMUNICATION MANAGEMENT: A UNIFIED DISCIPLINE

It appears that communication is being given more respect in strategic management than in the past. Following is just a sample from recent business periodicals:

• Avon, the global cosmetics business, rebuilt its manufacturing and transportation infrastructure from top to bottom. The leaders of this transformation believe that communication is perhaps the single most critical success factor and the one they most underestimated (Cohen & Roussel, 2004).

• Michael Weissman and David Mosby, authors of *The Paradox of Excellence,* "believe the solution to managing ever-escalating expectations is all about communications [sic]—constantly reinforcing to customers, investors, and others exactly what it is that distinguishes you as valuable" (McGregor, 2005, p. 29). They emphasize the value of nurturing long-term relationships, a fundamental tenet of communication and public relations management.

• Teresa Amabile, who heads the Entrepreneurial Management Unit at Harvard Business School, studied creativity in organizations for eight years. Making the case against the belief that a streamlined organization is a creative organization, Amabile wrote, "Unfortunately, downsizing will remain a fact of life, which means that leaders need to focus on the things that get hit. Communication and collaboration decline significantly" (Breen, 2004, p. 75).

• IABC's EXCEL Award winner in 2003 was Edward Barnholt, president and CEO of Agilent Technologies. In an interview with IABC's *Communication World,* Barnholt said, "I see a direct link from morale to productivity to customer satisfaction and the bottom line. I think lots of studies have shown that higher employee satisfaction leads to higher customer satisfaction. And, ultimately, higher customer satisfaction leads to higher business levels and better results. . . . Communication is critical in accomplishing this" (Spring, 2003, p. 38).

This chapter is about strategic planning, strategic communication management, and what I believe is the unification of the disciplines. Strategic planning seeks to measure results of strategic activity. Strategic communication is built on that same premise: measuring results. Yet performance measurement in organizations remained a problem. In the early 1990s, Kaplan and Norton developed a process to solve the measurement problem: the balanced scorecard, which recognizes that an organization's ability to develop, nurture, and mobilize its intangible assets is critical to success. Financial metrics alone simply cannot capture the value-creating activities from an organization's intangible assets (Kaplan & Norton, 2001, pp. 2–3):

• The skills, competencies, and motivation of its employees

• Database and information technologies

• Efficient and responsive operating processes

• Innovation in products and services

• Customer loyalty and relationships

• Political, regulatory, and societal approval

Organizations that adopted Kaplan and Norton's balanced scorecard recognized that competitive advantage comes from the intangible assets listed above. It follows that strategy implementation requires that all strategic business units, support units, and employees be aligned and linked to strategy. These organizations realized that the formulation and implementation of strategy must be a continual and participative process. Organizations need a language for communicating strategy as well as processes and systems that help them to implement strategy and gain feedback about their strategy. The adopters of the balanced scorecard realized that success comes from having strategy become everyone's everyday job.

WHAT DOES THE FUTURE HOLD?

Consider the huge implications to communicators of the balanced scorecard. As more and more companies adopt the balanced scorecard and become what Kaplan and Norton call "strategy-focused organizations," such organizations require that all employees understand the strategy and conduct their day-to-day business in a way that contributes to the success of that strategy. This is not top-down direction but top-down communication. Executives use the balanced scorecard to help communicate and educate the organization about strategic matters. When executives clearly define strategy, communicate it consistently, and link it to the drivers of change, a performance-based culture emerges that links everyone and every unit to strategy (Kaplan & Norton, 2001).

For decades, communicators have been trying to explain to executives that they can help do this. There are numerous success stories; here are just a few:

• Mobil uses the balanced scorecard to communicate strategic objectives to employees, not to command them what to do. Mobil used a comprehensive and continuing communication process based on the balanced scorecard to make sure that everyone understood the strategy (Kaplan & Norton, 2001).

• The May Institute, a Massachusetts nonprofit institution, is one of the largest U.S. providers of high-quality behavioral health care. For May, the balanced scorecard communicated the role of human resources and personnel development, which fostered more balanced discussions at board meetings. Beyond the communication role, the balanced scorecard was used to highlight the importance of human resource processes, particularly retention and recruitment in a tight job market (Kaplan & Norton, 2001).

• New Profit, a Boston-based venture capital philanthropic fund, used balanced scorecard beyond its role in managing internal operations and relationships with portfolio organizations as the primary communication tool with its board of directors and donors (Kaplan & Norton, 2001).

Long gone are the days of simple jobs for simple people. Today over 50 percent of the work performed in industrialized countries is knowledge work (Kaplan & Norton, 2001). The challenge today as never before is to motivate the hearts and minds of employees at all levels of the organization to strive for continuous quality improvement, cost reduction, meeting customers' expectations, and countering the competition. The balanced scorecard provides organizations with a powerful tool beyond traditional strategic planning for communication and alignment. Yet Kaplan and Norton's own studies show that less than 5 percent of the typical workforce understands their organization's strategy. Organizational communicators are needed and add tremendous value to business management.

References

Bedeian, A. G., & Zammuto, R. F. (1991). *Organizations: Theory and design.* New York: Dryden Press.

Bivens, T. H. (2005). *Public relations writing: The essentials of style and format.* New York: McGraw-Hill.

Breen, B. (2004, December). The six myths of creativity. *Fast Company,* 89, pp. 75–78.

Broom, G. M., &, Dozier, D. M. (1990). *Using research in public relations: Applications to program management.* Upper Saddle River, NJ: Prentice Hall.

Cohen, S., & Roussel, J. (2004). Avon gets its (supply chain) makeover. *Fortune, 150*(9), 178–184.

Collins, J. C., & Porras, J. I. (1995). *Built to last: Successful habits of visionary companies.* New York: Harper Business.

Deutschman, A. (2004, August). Inside the mind of Jeff Bezos. *Fast Company,* 85, pp. 52–58.

Goodstein, L., Nolan, T., & Pfeiffer, J. W. (1993). *Applied strategic planning: How to develop a plan that really works.* New York: McGraw-Hill.

Kaplan, R. S., & Norton, D. P. (2001). *The strategy-focused organization.* Boston: Harvard Business School Press.

Lidsky, D. (2004, November). What's next? *Fast Company,* 88, pp. 69–85.

McGregor, J. (2005, April). The performance paradox. *Fast Company,* 93, pp. 29–30.

Mosby, D., & Weissman, M. (2005). *The paradox of excellence: How great performance can kill your business.* San Francisco: Jossey-Bass.

Potter, L. R. (2001). *The communication plan: The heart of strategic communication* (2nd ed.). San Francisco: International Association of Business Communicators.

Ravine, S. (1999). Facts and trends. http://www.careers-in-business.com/spjobs4.htm# Trends.

Reingold, J., & Underwood, R. (2004, November). Was built to last built to last? *Fast Company,* 88, 103–111.

Rothschild, W. S. (1979). *Strategic alternatives.* New York: AMACOM.

Spring, N. (2003). Communicating under pressure: Agilent Technologies CEO receives IABC 2003 EXCEL Award. *Communication World, 20*(5), 36–40.

Steiner, G. A. (1979). *Strategic planning: What every manager must know.* New York: Free Press.

Underwood, R. (2004, August). Lighting the GE way. *Fast Company,* 85, pp. 73–75.

CHAPTER EIGHT

Aligning Internal Employee Communication with Business Strategy

Ayelet Baron

The corporate world has changed dramatically over the past decade, and these changes have created a new environment in which we need to strategize and communicate. Not only has the fabric of organizations changed, but we have different generations in the workplace that prefer sending and receiving information in very distinct ways.

Employers are more and more focused on the bottom line, cutting costs and putting corporate survival above all else. Employees, who have experienced life-changing events like the terrorist attacks of September 11, 2001, and the Asian tsunami, are seeking more meaning in their lives, and at the same time, many are worried about keeping their jobs. Shaky economic confidence and a decline in corporate loyalty have created an employee base that operates with an increased need for a sense of control.

Many employees are experiencing a sense of disillusionment in the corporate world. According to over forty Gallup polls, approximately 75 percent of employees are disengaged from their jobs. Gallup estimates that "actively disengaged" workers are costing U.S. businesses $300 billion a year in productivity losses. What is causing seven out of ten workers to be totally disengaged by the workplace? According to Gallup, the main culprits are poor managers and a lack of leadership, which has a high transparent cost to the bottom line.

This new environment is the one we need to work within. We need to build solid business strategies that employees can buy in to and deliver. Employees want to be engaged and feel they are part of the process; they want to understand their role and what is in it for them. People who understand the big picture and how they fit into delivering it are far more likely to be motivated to do their part, which translates into implementing business strategies.

Employers must understand that creating their business strategy is the first step. Having employees understand their role in translating the strategy to action is what it is all about. Strategy is a guiding element to the extent that the strategy-making process enables managers to grasp the strategy and translate it to their employees.

What happens in many organizations today is that leaders communicate entirely opposite to employees' needs. They start their communication with sharing the big picture, while employees are focused on what is in it for them. Employees first want to know if this new or revised business strategy will allow them to keep their job and feed their families. Once they understand what is in it for them, they want to understand what role they can play in the strategy. Only then do they want to hear about the big picture (Figure 8.1). There needs to be better synergy between how leaders communicate and how employees want to receive information.

This does not mean that communicating about the marketplace and the competition is not important. It is critical; but the communication should not stop with the big picture. Managers need to play a significant role in helping their employees understand the implications and what it means for them.

Communication should be about providing employees with the information they need to be effective in their jobs. Senior management should view communicators as enablers of business strategy—facilitating the sharing of information so people can act on it.

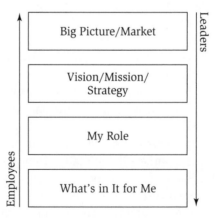

Figure 8.1. Better Alignment Is Needed Between Employees' Communication and Management

This chapter defines business strategy and presents an overview of how to build a communication strategy that delivers results. It also focuses on the most important aspect of an effective communication strategy, which is having a leadership communication approach—a clear definition of the role of leaders and managers in getting employees to deliver the strategy.

DEFINING BUSINESS STRATEGY

The increased focus on business strategy has emerged from companies' need to respond quickly to changing markets and increased competition. Competitive strategy is about being different and choosing a set of activities to create sustainable advantage and deliver a unique mix of value.

Strategy is about the basic value an organization delivers to its customer and how it plans to deliver it. The need for consistency and clarity is basic. Employees need to understand what the strategy is so they can implement it by showing customers what the organization stands for.

A good strategy is focused and clear. It is straightforward to communicate and provides employees with a road map. It can also be simplified by having a couple of short-term activities where success can be achieved. Management might have one group focus on one activity and another group focus on the other. Employees need to see short-term wins that demonstrate the validity of the vision. If the quick win is clear and visible, people will be more likely to play their part in making the strategy happen.

Business strategy needs to have a certain level of consistency; it cannot be reinvented every few months. It can evolve, but if it is introduced as yet another change that the company has to undergo, employees will start referring to business strategy as the "flavor of the month."

The challenge of developing or reestablishing a clear strategy is primarily an organizational one and depends on the leadership. Strong leaders who are willing to make decisions and prioritize key issues are an essential ingredient. A good strategy explains why an organization is different and sets limits on what is to be accomplished.

At the core of leadership is strategy. There is a strong correlation between strong leaders and solid strategies. A big part of senior executives' responsibilities is their ability to define and communicate the organization's unique strategic position, make key decisions, and prioritize activities. Strategy cannot be delegated; it must rest in the hands of leaders who are willing to make choices and define the trade-offs. A leader also has to make sure that everyone understands the strategy. Strategy cannot be a vision that is understood only by the executive team.

It is a popular belief that strategy needs constant innovation and creative thinking. Although this is true, it also requires constant discipline and clear communication. Having an explicit strategy provides employees with guidelines on how they make decisions and choices that arise as a result of trade-offs in their day-to-day activities. The bottom line is that a good internal communication strategy should support the business strategy and help the organization succeed.

USING STRATEGY TO DRIVE DAILY ACTION

Many organizations embark on the annual strategic planning process to provide their executive teams with answers to the question of shareholders, customers, suppliers, partners, analysts, the media, board members, and employees: "So what exactly is the organization's strategy?"

Traditional strategic planning processes are aimed at driving an organization's overall long-term strategy. It determines where an organization is going over the next year or more, how it is going to get there, and how it will know if it got there. Planning is traditionally considered to be one of the three major functions of management, along with managing people and leading.

Many organizations have an internal operations team that facilitates a review of the mission and vision, market and competitor analysis, threats and opportunity analysis, and the creation of a multiyear plan. This team is often responsible for the annual planning process that is driven by a predetermined calendar that outlines the business and financial milestones. In some organizations, the annual budgeting process determines the business plan.

Quite often the internal planning team already knows much of what needs to go into a strategic plan. However, joint development of the plan helps to clarify the organization's plans and ensure that key leaders are all on the same page. Far more important than the strategic plan document is the strategic planning process itself.

Do not make the common mistake of bringing together a large group of managers and asking them to define the direction. Managers and employees expect leaders to define the direction of the business.

Strategic planning serves a variety of purposes, including these:

- Clearly defines the key priorities of the organization and how they will be addressed.

- Ensures the most effective use is made of the organization's resources by focusing the resources on the key priorities.

- Establishes key success factors and metrics that can be tracked over time.

- Provides the strategic direction and agenda for the organization to which business units can align.

- Drives clear accountability for key initiatives and results.
- Provides a joint road map for execution.
- Incorporates mechanisms for review and course corrections as market and competitive landscapes shift.

Strategic planning matters only when the process supports continuous decision making and is owned by the executive team. The executive team needs to be driving the process and directly involved in every step. The end result needs to be a plan that is easy to implement and translate to the organization, not a two-hundred-page PowerPoint report that no one will look at until the next planning cycle. A business strategy cannot be a three-ring binder full of charts and budgets.

When people are led and not managed, their performance can be phenomenal. Tapping into the spiritual and mental capacities of people, rather than just the physical parts, is like striking gold for any organization. For employees to be committed, they must be involved and engaged, not merely viewed as a stakeholder.

The change adoption curve (Figure 8.2) is one of the most effective tools for building communication strategies as it shows the five phases every person goes through in becoming aware of a new business direction to implementing it in daily life. As people change the way they work to adopt new ways, they have to reorient themselves to the way things are now.

For the organization to succeed, the transition needs to be managed by taking into account how people change behavior and helping them make it a less painful and disruptive process. Table 8.1 outlines each stage that people go through in moving from being aware of a new strategy to internalizing it as how they work.

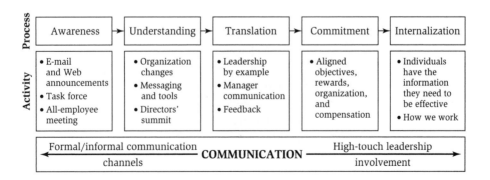

Figure 8.2. Translating Strategy to Action

Table 8.1. Applying the Stages of Behavioral Change to the Communication of Business Strategy

Stages of the Behavior Change	What's on People's Minds	Potential Outcomes of the Communication	
		Positive	Negative
Awareness: People are starting to become aware of the strategy but do not have the specifics and do not know the possible outcomes	• What is the business direction? • Do I play a role in implementing the strategy? • Will I be measured and rewarded differently? • How does this help our organization be more successful? • What are the potential outcomes?	Understanding	Confusion
Understanding: People who are aware of and understand the strategy and what it entails start to accept it	• Why is this strategy important? • How will this strategy be implemented? • Why should I care about this strategy? • Do I support this strategy?	Translation	Resistance
Translation: People have an understanding of their specific role in implementing the strategy and can translate it to their specific job	• How can I implement the strategy in my work? • How does it affect my day-to-day activities? • What stays the same and what changes? • What do I need to do differently? • What are everyone else's roles and responsibilities?	Commitment	Decision not to implement

Table 8.1. (*Continued*)

Stages of the Behavior Change	What's on People's Minds	Potential Outcomes of the Communication	
		Positive	Negative
Commitment: People focus on how to achieve the business strategy and start feeling a sense of commitment, which the organization cannot take for granted	• Is there consistency of purposes? • Are resources being invested and aligned? • How engaged are senior leaders and managers? • Are people at all levels of the organization passionate about the strategy? • What are some successes of the strategy? • Are there any visible outcomes? • What are the rewards?	Internalization	Aborted after implementation
Internalization: People own the business direction and are enthusiastic about it as it matches their goals, interests, and values	• What else can I do to help drive the strategy? • How can I help others? • How will we evolve the strategy? What's next?	It's how we work here— what's next?	

What is important to remember is that until people get to internationalization, they can revert to the way they used to work. That is why it is important to have communication strategies aligned with each stage of the process. At the awareness and understanding stages, formal communication methods are mostly used; face-to-face communication is needed to get from translation to internalization. An employee is not going to be able to translate her role in the strategy as a result of an e-mail or brochure she read.

Formal communication usually spans official announcements, major policies, processes, reporting, and high-level communication from senior executives. It helps create awareness, and when it is effective, it can build understanding. Informal communication builds commitment and helps employees translate the business direction to their own role—as it involves face-to-face communication between a manager and an employee. The more time and resources that are invested in making sure employees can translate the strategy to their own circumstances, the more likely the organization is to have a committed workforce who knows how to execute the plan.

LEVERAGING ORGANIZATIONAL SYSTEMS: CREATING SOLID COMMUNICATION STRATEGIES

Effectively communicating organizational strategies relies on the quality of communication skills on the part of leadership and the quality of information they have to share with their employees.

Leadership Communication Is Essential

A critical determinant of the ability to communicate an organization's strategy lies in senior management's capacity to create a culture of openness. Can problems be talked about openly? If the answer is no, then the organization will most likely fail in its ability to implement its strategy. An organization may have a brilliant strategy, but its success or failure lies in its ability to execute it.

Leaders must spend as much time on the action plan as they do on designing the strategic road map. Often this requires addressing organization issues and confronting the barriers blocking the successful implementation of a strategy.

Today, more than ever before, a leader's ability to communicate—through words and actions—is crucial. This is a critical factor in developing and maintaining organizational trust. A number of studies report that employees today show the following characteristics:

- Employees are increasingly questioning leaders' ability to manage their organizations.
- There is an increasing sense of fear in the workplace due to constant change initiatives and uncertainty.
- "Doing more with less" really means that employees are actually doing two or three jobs.
- Employees are more likely to stay longer in their jobs as a result of the economy and are feeling they are doing more with less in an environment that does not continue to challenge them.
- With pay freezes being the norm, many employees have not received a pay increase or promotion in a very long time.

- When employees get a challenging new opportunity that promises a certain level of job security, they move to the new job.

Many employee surveys, interviews by external consultants, 360-degree feedback, peer reviews, and similar tools have not been used effectively. Employees get their communication from how the organization acts: what gets noticed, who gets promoted, what gets senior management's attention, and so on. They are tired of posters with slogans and newsletters that tell them about the change initiative of the moment. Employees do get excited and motivated when they are part of the process and are truly engaged.

Organizations have a higher degree of success in implementing their strategy when senior management sets out a strategic direction and then spends time finding out what key individuals at all levels think about the new direction:

- Is this a distinctive business strategy that people believe will take the organization to the next level?
- Can we execute the strategy?
- What is getting in the way, and what is enabling it?
- Do we have the courage to deal with the obstacles?

The successful leader is a person who can take a complex strategy and translate it to statements that are readily comprehensible to the people who are going to have to make the changes work. The thing to remember is to say what you will do and do what you say. Leaders are paid to understand the organization's larger problems, but at most companies, the people under them are paid to do their jobs.

What does it mean to have strong leaders who drive the implementation of solid business strategies and communicate through their actions? First, good leaders inspire others. They create an open environment where people can communicate without the need for constant formal surveys and they do not send e-mails telling people they are empowered. Effective leaders and managers do their job so that others can be successful in theirs. Second, good leaders make decisions and prioritize activities. They spend their time trying to prevent problems. Finally, good leaders take into account the hearts and minds of their employees by realizing that their strategy can be successful only if employees understand what they need to do. They do not parachute the strategy down to the organization.

Effective leaders incorporate the strategy into the daily life of the organization so that all employees participate in the excitement of implementing the strategy. Good management is usually transparent and does not often make headlines, but it does work. Leadership is not about the leader; it is about how the leader builds the confidence of everyone else.

Organizations Are Held Together by Information

When I was consulting, I asked a senior executive what he thought was the biggest communication challenge in his organization. He looked at me and said,

"We told them the strategy once. Why do our employees not get it?" At that moment, I realized that *he* did not get it. Communication is ongoing hard work. If it is to be effective, it cannot be a one-time event.

Solid communication strategies consider how people in a specific organization prefer to get information, and it varies by company. Multiple communication channels must be used, and the messages must be simple, consistent, and relevant to an employee's situation. Communicating a business strategy to employees should not be executed like a massive advertising campaign. It must be targeted and segmented.

Here are my guidelines for aligning communication strategy with business strategy.

Do Not Make Assumptions About Your Organization. Go out and talk with senior executives, managers, and employees at all levels. Listening and assessing the current environment is a big part of your job. Ask questions about the strategy, and evaluate the most effective ways for people to get information in your organization and how they want to provide feedback. If everyone in the organization understands the company's vision and strategy, then this job will be easy. If they do not, you need to figure out the most effective ways to get them the information they need to be effective in their jobs. Employees do have preferences in terms of how they receive information about the company's strategy. Make sure you know what employees think is most effective. You will see the results of your investment over time. There is no one approach; it is all about taking the time to listen and understand the environment.

Make Sure Senior Management Identifies and Jointly Agrees on Who the Common Enemy Is. Too often instead of the common enemy being outside the company (like a competitor), conflicts arise between functional silos and corporate and business units. As a result, the organization spends most of its time trying to deal with internal issues and not on what counts—customers, the community, shareholders, and others. Its employee base will also be disengaged because they will not have a clear understanding of how their role fits into where the company is going. Employees seem far more engaged when the organization's "common enemy" is external.

Find Out How Senior Executives Spend Their Time. Ineffective top management meetings can create the perception that the leadership team sessions produce no visible results and critical decisions are not being made. Perception foretells reality: senior executives may choose to spend even less time together as a team, and the organization may be stymied in its ability to drive growth. Find out whether the senior executive team is doing its job in meeting employees' expectations. Are they:

- Setting the direction?
- Addressing and resolving conflicting views about priorities?
- Creating an environment for people to deliver results?

If this is not happening, you may need to look at ways to make their team meetings more effective and dedicate time on the agenda to address these issues. Organizations that effectively manage executive time have structure around top management meetings and experience more growth than their peers by:

- Separating meetings on operating performance and strategy.
- Increasing the total number of hours the executive team spends together addressing only key strategic issues.
- Pushing for decisions as the result of the meeting, not just discussion and general information sharing.
- Focusing only on the issues and opportunities, with the biggest impact on the long-term intrinsic value of the organization.
- Presenting viable strategy options for decision making.
- Linking resource allocation and accountabilities to strategy approval.
- Providing ongoing communication of key decisions, implementation plans, metrics, and actual outcomes.

Find Others Who Share Your Mission. Work with other groups in the organization that have similar business objectives. Make sure your communication strategy is in alignment by working with the right people in every organization.

Demystify Communication. Make sure everyone in the organization sees their role as sharing information about the strategy and how it is being implemented. There is no ownership when it comes to sharing information. Leaders need to set the direction and prioritize the activities so employees can achieve the goals. Consider new ways when it comes to two-way communication; conducting a survey is not the only way to get feedback from employees. Find out what opinion leaders (the people others tend to listen to and are influenced by) in different parts of the organization think about the strategy. Another approach is for senior management to set up a task force of its best managers to interview key people across the organization, which sends a message to employees that it is serious about getting input. The best managers are often the busiest managers, but these are the people who have credibility. They also tend to have the courage to tell the truth to executives. The observations and feedback should be shared in a facilitated session with task force members and senior management. Employees will judge management's ability to listen by watching to see if the changes they recommended are actually taken into consideration in the implementation.

Make One of Your Goals Helping Employees Understand the Business. Provide ongoing information on the industry, key customers, and competitors. Employees also want to learn more about what differentiates their organization in the marketplace.

Make It Simple. Do not view communicating the business strategy as yet another change initiative. If people in the organization do not understand how the company is supposed to be different and how it creates value compared to its competitors, then how can they make all of the choices they must? Those in marketing need to understand the strategy; otherwise they will not know what to market. Salespeople need to know the strategy, or they will not know which customers to call on.

Play a Facilitation and Leadership Role in Making Sure Everyone Understands Their Role. Communicators are often told that communicating the strategic plan is their responsibility. Make sure the executive team understands what the responsibility for creating clarity around what the strategy means at the business unit and individual levels, and ensure that it is implemented and shared by every manager. Part of every manager's job is communicating the strategy to his or her team and redefining it in a way that everyone understands. It is a manager's responsibility to make sure his or her employees' priorities and time are focused on achieving the strategy. This should not be delegated to the communication function.

Help the executive team distill your strategy to three to five simple themes. This process will allow you to create your key communication messages for your stakeholder community. In this way, you can create a powerful management tool that aligns behaviors and decision making at all levels of the organization. Communicators must work with their executive management to craft simple themes. The best strategic themes need to be:

- Distinctive—based on how the organization will be different from its competitors in a way that creates more value and stands out in the industry.

- Selective—have the same level of clarity on what the organization will not do as what it will do. Scarce resources—capital, time, and talent— must be focused on the most critical investment areas.

- Suggestive—a well-articulated corporate strategy needs to foster creativity at the business unit level. Strategic themes need to be constructively ambiguous to provide guidance while allowing the business units to create creative and distinctive strategies.

And always use the guideline that leaders serve as role models, leading through the power of personal example.

CONCLUSION

Many organizations may have sound strategies in place, but their ability to execute them effectively often falls short. High-performing organizations recognize that execution means working within the organizational culture to get results. It is more than simply knowing what to do; it is knowing how to do it—understanding how to implement the strategy and successfully execute when the circumstances change.

When communicating business strategy, follow these guidelines:

- Have a well-defined communication strategy that ties communication and business initiatives.

- Make sure managers are clear about their role in translating business strategy to their employees. Leaders need to understand that communication is more than just another meeting. The rewards and recognition systems must also be aligned.

- Provide communication training for managers to build their skill sets and become more effective communicators.

- Measure, reward, and recognize managers not only for their ability to communicate the big picture and vision to employees, but on their ability to translate the strategy to what each of their employees has to accomplish at work.

- Have senior management highlight best practices and individuals who are key to strategy execution.

- Consider how employees' work contributes to the business goals, what skills they need to be productive, and how their performance is measured.

- Keep it simple. Strategy is an ongoing process. Senior management must see the need to build a story that can easily be communicated internally and externally.

- Make sure feedback processes are in place—that the processes ensure that people understand the messages and can translate them to their own situation.

- Provide ongoing information on how the organization is doing in meeting its business objectives.

- Facilitate information sharing by driving an ongoing communication strategy that aligns the organization.

Ensuring that employees have the information they need to be effective in their jobs all the time is one of the most challenging tasks of any company. Communication is still one of the most undervalued contributors to high performance and competitive advantage.

Individual behaviors determine an organization's collective success over time. It is critical to understand how the organization influences each individual's behavior—in terms of structure, decision rights, motivators, and information—and affects their performance. Performance is the sum total of what every employee does every day across the organization.

When implementing a new business strategy, help senior executives put the right metrics in place to measure success. Bring data to management by conducting assessments that track how well information flows within the organization and whether employees believe they have access to timely, relevant, and accurate information.

If finding time for strategic decision making is a problem within your organization, do some research into how to develop a governance process that includes a communication methodology to help executive teams focus on the most critical business issues and make decisions within a set time frame. This could establish guidelines around who should be included in strategy meetings (fewer people can usually achieve more), how to define the business problem, and how much time can be spent at each step of the meeting before a recommendation or resolution must be agreed on. Ironically, some scarce time needs to be set aside for senior management to agree on the decision-making and escalation process.

Clear roles, accountabilities, and success metrics also need to be communicated to ensure successful implementation. As good business strategy is largely dependent on good cross-functional communication, it is important to build leadership communication plans as an integral part of internal communication strategy.

Make sure that decision making is clearly defined and people have a collective focus on common goals with the right information and incentives. Senior executives need to translate the strategies into action and be clear about how they expect people to execute it. It is more than just changing the organizational structure and hoping the changes result in sustained productivity improvements. Being able to organize and execute strategy is the secret recipe for success. Table 8.2 summarizes the critical success factors.

Table 8.2. Critical Success Factors

Focus on	Stay Away From
Ensuring senior executives recognize the importance of communications in achieving business results	Tactical and reactive communication programs
Facilitating strong leadership from senior management to create commitment and drive the implementation of the strategy—making sure their actions match their words	Business strategy that employees see as the "flavor of the month"
Building trust and strong relationships between management and employees	Thinking that sending an e-mail or making an announcement will ensure people understand the strategy
Establishing clear targets and metrics to ensure accountability—measuring managers at all levels on communication effectiveness	Not being able to know when the strategy is fully actualized
Driving an explicit commitment to ongoing and timely communication, relative at all levels, to ensure people have the information they need to meet the goals	Event-based communication
Having senior executives view the role of communications as a strategic business partner	Seeing this role as an implementer
Seeing your role as a facilitator of information that helps employees understand their role in implementing the business strategy	Focusing on the posters, balloons, and T-shirts as a way for people to understand their role in implementing the strategy

CHAPTER NINE

Issues Management

Linking Business and Communication Planning

George McGrath

Organizations today must navigate a turbulent, highly competitive, and fast-changing environment in pursuit of their business goals. Like mariners on a stormy sea, an organization's leaders must constantly scan the horizon for future threats and opportunities so they can avoid trouble and find the fastest, safest passage to their destination. Such forecasting is the basis of an organization's strategic planning process. Through the issues management discipline, it also becomes a key component of communication planning.

Issues management is a process that identifies the issues, trends, and stakeholder attitudes that can affect the organization for better or worse and develops strategies and tactics, including communication programs, to deal with them.

The *American Heritage Dictionary* (2000) defines an issue as "a point, matter of discussion, debate, or dispute." A discussion of an issue involves a debate between different points of view, which ideally leads to agreement or resolution. W. Howard Chase (1984), who pioneered the practice of issues management, further defined an issue as the gap between an organization's performance and the expectations of its stakeholders, such as customers, investors, employees, communities, elected official and regulators, or interest groups.

This gap can have implications for the organization's overall business strategy as well as communication. For example, the organization may be performing in line with shareholder expectations or even beyond expectations, but it has not told its side of the story. In this case, the issue can be resolved primarily through communication. But if the organization is performing below stakeholder expectations, the issue may require an adjustment to operating strategy.

HOW ISSUES DEVELOP, AND HOW ORGANIZATIONS CAN INFLUENCE THEM

Gaps between stakeholder expectations and an organization's or industry's performance evolve, driven by gains in human knowledge and demographic and social changes. Often these gaps are crystallized by a major newsmaking event that puts the issue front and center with the public—for example:

- Development of tools for modeling data on global climate trends has raised global warming as an issue of concern to governments, the public, and business, leading to mandates for reducing industrial emissions of greenhouse gases. Catastrophic hurricanes linked to global warming generate renewed calls for action to reduce emissions.
- Rapid expansion of cities and suburbs, and corresponding traffic congestion and environmental problems, create an issue on whether and how to limit or direct the growth of new communities and restrict the activities of real estate developers.
- Corporate accounting scandals, and the resulting multibillion-dollar losses for investors and employees, focused public attention on the issue of corporate ethics and resulted in more stringent financial reporting requirements for corporations and increased regulation of accounting firms.
- Aging populations and the increasing demand for health care have kept the issue of access and cost of health care front and center and have intensified pressure for health care providers and pharmaceutical companies to better manage the costs of their products and services.

In the early stages, the problem may be recognized by only a few experts who are closely studying the area, much like the scientists in the late 1970s with their global warming models. Over time these emerging issues can move from the fringes to the front page as more people become concerned about them and seek to pressure the organization to make changes or government to legislate remedies.

By the time an issue reaches the crisis stage, an organization's response will be limited largely to damage control. When the costs and damage to the company's reputation are tallied after the crisis is over, someone will inevitably observe, "We should have seen this one coming."

The issues management process helps organizations identify possible crisis situations before they occur. The earlier an organization gets involved in these issues, the more options it has for shaping the discussion, deflecting potential threats, or adapting its business practices to meet the needs of a changing world.

THE FIVE-STEP ISSUES MANAGEMENT PROCESS

The issues management process has five basic steps:

1. Identify potential issues. What business actions, social trends, legislative developments, or media topics create potential areas of concern or vulnerability for the organization?

2. Set priorities. On which issues should the organization focus its attention based on their potential impact and timeliness?

3. Establish a position on the issues. What is the organization's view of how each of its priority issues should be managed and ultimately resolved?

4. Develop the response. How should the organization adapt its business plans and policies to changing stakeholder expectations; or alternatively, how should the organization communicate with stakeholders to bridge the gaps in perception?

5. Monitor the issues. How should the organization track the ongoing development of priority issues and adjust the organization's position as needed to reflect changing circumstances.

ISSUES IDENTIFICATION

Issues identification involves looking both inside the organization, at its business strategies, operations, and behavior, and outside, at social, economic, or political trends and developments that may have implications for the future of the business and how key stakeholders view the organization.

The inquiry can be conducted informally by the communications manager, as part of the preparation of the annual communication planning process. Or it can be designed as a more comprehensive effort involving representatives of different staff and line business functions.

How far and wide should an organization scan for potential issues? That depends on its size, complexity, and amount of resources available. For example, global businesses will have to examine trends and developments in markets around the world. Organizations operating in one country or region can stick closer to home.

As a starting point, there are a few simple steps any communicator can take to identify the immediate, near-term issues facing the organization and the organization's readiness to deal with the issues:

1. Review the organization's business plan and current operations. Is the organization engaged in activities or considering changes that might create controversy, debate, or dissent? Are there similar implications for any products or services either currently offered or under consideration? Where is the organization most vulnerable to a shift in its operating environment, such as the emergence of new competitors; a change in attitudes among customers, investors, employees, or other constituents; or new social standards that will create a gap between company practice and social norms?

2. Evaluate stakeholder attitudes and concerns. Communicators are typically on the front line dealing with employees, journalists, investors, elected leaders, and communities, so this is an area where they can provide the organization with insights and added value. What subjects are generating the greatest number of inquiries, comments, or complaints from the press or public? Where are the greatest gaps between stakeholder expectations and the organization's performance?

3. Weigh senior management's concerns. What news stories pique senior management's interest and generate requests for more information? What competitors is the organization most concerned with? What trends or events are recurring subjects in formal or informal management gatherings?

4. Consult with in-house experts. What does the government affairs manager see as the major upcoming legislative and regulatory issues on the horizon? What technological developments is the chief information officer concerned about? What workforce trends is the human resource director following?

5. Scan the news media for social, political, economic, technological, or cultural trends and issues that have relevance and potential impact for the organization. What issues have recently made the jump from obscure trade journals to mainstream media? Where are leading commentators and pundits focusing their attention?

6. Understand the common concerns of your industry. What are the key issues being tracked by the trade or professional association? What are the leading topics being discussed at industry conferences, meetings, and seminars? Has a competitor had behavior problems that potentially affect the credibility or reputation of the industry as a whole or bring industry-wide practices under scrutiny?

Stretching the Boundaries of the Search

To identify issues that may still be emerging, you will have to reach out to a broader range of information sources and dig deeper for ideas, trends, and events that have implications for the organization's future. A number of approaches can be employed:

- Meet with influential academics, legislative and regulatory staff, and members of advocacy groups. In particular, look to leading authorities and advocates and leading organizations—people and groups that seem to be first in articulating an issue. These sources may be known through their actions, for example, an advocacy group with a history of promoting landmark legislation or a company known for its progressive work/life practices.
- Track the development of legislation and regulation in bellwether jurisdictions, which set the pace for their neighbors. These areas typically have heavily urbanized populations, high education levels, and progressive political attitudes. In the United States, for example, California has long been an early leader for the development of new environmental regulations, such as automotive emissions standards, energy conservation guidelines, and alternative energy, setting the stage for national policies that are later applied to all fifty states.
- Monitor publications of think tanks and trend watchers. Futurist organizations and public policy groups such as the Hudson Institute, the Discovery Institute, and the EastWest Center of Hawaii publish books and periodicals on issues, trends, and future scenarios. In addition, there are many professional trend watchers, such as Faith Popcorn on consumer trends and Nicholas Negroponte on technological developments, who extrapolate future developments based on what they see today.

Capturing Ideas and Information from the Issue Scan

Ideas, trends, and information from the issue scan must be captured in some form so they can be assembled, analyzed, and ultimately considered by senior management and policymakers within the organization.

If scanning is being conducted by an individual (for example, the communication manager), the information product could be a memo, report, or presentation to senior management that describes the trends and potential issues identified through the scan and their implications for the organization. The document should include a recommendation to continue to monitor the trends for further developments, conduct more in-depth research, or develop a position and response to the issue.

ISSUE PRIORITIZATION

This initial inquiry should generate many areas of potential concern for the organization. However, limited management time and resources as well as competing priorities will restrict the organization's ability to respond to every potential situation. Therefore, the next step in the issues management process is to establish priorities and create the short list of key issues.

The process for screening out the most critical issues is not complicated. It can be done with a few simple and direct questions about each potential issue that surfaced in the identification phase:

- What is the issue's current or potential impact on the organization's ability to do business or its reputation: high, moderate, or low?

- What is the probability that the impact will occur: high, moderate, or low?

- What is the likelihood it will have an impact now, in the next twelve months, or in the next thirty-six months?

Top-priority issues are those with a major and imminent impact on the organization. They require an immediate response: the development of a statement that summarizes the organization's position on the issue, likely questions and answers, and an action plan.

Medium-priority issues may require development of a position statement and supporting materials, such as responses to likely questions. Action plans can be longer term in nature. The only indicated action may be to keep monitoring the issue.

Low-priority issues can be put on a list for periodic reassessment or dropped from consideration.

To facilitate the evaluation, a numerical value can be assigned to each response—for example, a three-point scale: 1 (low), 2 (moderate), and 3 (high). This makes it easy to score the impact of each issue and create a short list of top-priority issues.

DEVELOPING THE ORGANIZATION'S POSITION ON THE ISSUE

Before the organization takes any action, it must determine its position on the issue: how it views the issue and how it believes it should be handled or resolved.

The process of building an issues statement goes beyond the communications or government relations department. It should involve the key decision makers inside the organization who are affected by the issue or will have a role in its resolution. For example, if the issue relates to product safety, the sales, marketing, product quality, and customer relations groups should be participants in the discussion. If the issue concerns the environmental impact of a manufacturing facility, the plant manager as well as the corporate health and safety officer should be engaged in the process.

To develop a position, participants will need to reach an agreement on several areas:

- How serious an impact could the issue have on the company's reputation or ability to achieve its business objectives?

- How is the issue likely to develop over time? Absent the company's involvement, is the likely outcome favorable, unfavorable, or neutral for us?

- Which groups have a stake in this issue? What stakeholders are on our side? What groups are firmly opposed to us?

- What can we do to change the development and resolution of the issue? How should we engage in the debate with activist groups, elected officials, or the media? Should we resist changing our policies or operations, or should we take actions to adapt?

- Most important, what impact can the organization have? Can we affect the resolution of the issue by taking an active role? Do we have the credibility and resources to win the argument? Or do we need to work with others who might be inclined to support us, so we can pool resources and engage others in the debate?

The process of assembling the facts and discussing their implications for the organization will identify weaknesses as well as strengths in the company's position and can indicate areas where company policies or procedures should be changed.

CRAFTING THE ISSUE STATEMENT

The end result of this process is the issue statement—a one- to two-page document that defines the issue and the organization's position on it, and the response—what the organization is doing or believes should be done. It contains the following components:

- Issue summary: A short description of background on the issue and its development, impact on the organization, and current and future activity, such as legislative or regulatory actions

- Issue position: The organization's position on the issue and actions taking place around it, including actions the organization may take on its own to deal with the matter

- Issue owners: Names and contact information for the individuals in the organization responsible for monitoring and managing the issue

The issue statement should be circulated internally to all groups that have a role in managing and resolving the issue. The organization's stated position should guide the development of talking points and statements for use in external communications with stakeholders.

The issue statement is more than a one-time opportunity to reach consensus and agreement on what to do. Issues evolve as new information is developed, actions are taken, and the debate takes new turns. The statement can and should be a living document that serves as the core of the issues tracking and management process.

STRATEGY DEVELOPMENT

The selection of specific strategies will be driven by the organization's response, its analysis of its own strengths and vulnerabilities on the issue, and how it prioritizes its stakeholders.

In some cases, a statement of the organization's position and response to the issue will suffice to deal with inquiries. Other issues, because of their immediacy, potential impact, complexity, or duration, will require detailed action plans.

Assembling the Issue Team

In the process of developing the issue position, the organization should identify a senior leader as the issue owner. He or she must have the authority to recruit a cross-functional issue management team, assemble resources to support the effort, and seek changes in corporate policy or operations if required.

The issue team's size and membership depend on the scope, complexity, and impact of the issue. The team should include participants who know the issue and the stakeholders involved and have subject matter expertise that can help develop a solution. For example, a team dealing with a potential product safety issue could include:

- The product manager responsible for sales and marketing of the product
- The quality assurance manager who deals with its manufacture
- The product development or technology manager who knows how the product was developed, its components, and how it works
- The communication manager who knows key external stakeholders such as the news media
- The customer relations manager who will have to handle inquiries or complaints from product users
- The legal affairs director who may have to deal with claims arising from product problems

Organizing the Planning Session

Once the issue team is formed, work can begin on developing the organization's action plan. An initial planning session can help start the effort by bringing the key players together to review the issue and brainstorm potential responses. The agenda for the kickoff meeting could include these components:

- A review of the issue, the organization's position, and the organization's response. The presenter could be the issue owner or a member of the group involved in developing the position. If the description, position, and response have not yet been developed, the issue team should prepare a draft as part of its action plan.

- Status of the issue. What is the issue's stage of development? Are any events imminent that will galvanize stakeholders or accelerate action?

- Identification and prioritization of stakeholders. What groups are involved in the debate or resolution of the issue, and what are their attitudes?

- Objectives. What should the organization seek to achieve with key stakeholders?

- Strategies. How should the organization marshal its resources or align with other groups to achieve the desired response?

- Tactics. What specific tools and techniques will be used to implement the strategies?

- Measurement. How will progress be tracked and evaluated?

- Timing, responsibilities, and budgets. Over what time frame will the plan be implemented, by whom, and at what cost?

Identification and Ranking of Stakeholders

Stakeholder analysis is a critical component of developing the action plan. Various stakeholder groups should be studied and ranked by attitudes and importance: who is for the organization's position, who is against, who is undecided, who is most or least influential in the debate. A product quality issue, for example, has implications for many stakeholder groups:

- Customers will be concerned if questions arise about quality and may seek alternative products, depressing sales.

- Employees could see employment prospects suffer if product sales decline; morale could be affected by attacks on the company's reputation.

- Shareholders have a financial stake in the company; declining product sales could hurt earnings and reduce the value of their investment.

- Interest groups such as consumer organizations or user groups will push solutions, which could range from calls to reformulate or redesign the product, to publication of consumer warnings, to demands that it be withdrawn from distribution.

- Elected officials may be drawn in if the issue becomes visible in the media or constituents or advocacy groups lobby for action. They may pursue legislation to regulate the way the product is manufactured and sold or hold hearings that generate more attention for the issue.

- Regulators charged with consumer protection could mandate the company take action to address the issue.

- News media will seek to guard the public interest and will educate or inform readers about the issue. They will gather positions from all parties in the debate and point the way toward a consensus position, if one exists. The media response will shape how many stakeholders view the matter.

The issue team should rank the stakeholders in order of importance. This will provide priorities and focus for the action steps.

Define Objectives

The organization's position and response to the issue will drive the definition of objectives for each critical stakeholder group. In the case of a product quality issue, the objectives could be:

- With consumers, maintain the perception that the product is effective and safe, and protect the company's reputation as a manufacturer of reliable, quality products.

- With regulators, obtain regulatory endorsement that the product meets or exceeds all quality standards.

- With interest groups, avoid calls for product recalls, and obtain product endorsement and support from major product user groups.

- With the media, vigorously defend the product, and ensure the company's position is included in news coverage.

Objectives must be measurable and specific. This may require baseline research (for example, opinion surveys to determine what consumers believe about product safety now), or content analysis of current media coverage to form a picture of how the issue and the company's position are currently being portrayed. The issue team can then discuss targets—for example, increasing the representation of the organization's position in major media covering the issue.

Determining the Proper Response

There are three modes of issue response: reactive, adaptive, or dynamic.

An organization in a reactive mode decides it is not going to change its policy, procedures, practices, or products in response to an issue. It instead seeks to deflect the issue through communication or lobbying campaigns that try to slow or stop the progress of outside action by elected officials or regulators.

An organization can take an adaptive response to an issue and voluntarily change its policies, practices, or products before changes are defined by other advocates and mandated by law. The organization gets credit for exercising leadership and may be able to institute a change on a more favorable basis than if the terms had been defined by outsiders.

In the dynamic response, the organization models how an issue will develop: what advocates will be attracted to it, what the likely arguments and counterarguments are, and what consensus solution is likely to be acceptable to the organization and society. Then the organization can lead the way in articulating the issue and a possible solution, attract advocates, and build public support for its desired outcome.

Which approach is best depends on the timing of the issue and what is at stake for the organization. Issues that have already made the front page or the legislative agenda are going to be dealt with in a reactive fashion: the best the organization may be able to do is raise enough questions to prolong the debate and postpone the outcome. It may not seem to be the most enlightened approach, but when the organization is in a crisis mode, with its business at stake, a defensive strategy may be the only alternative. In the early 1990s, U.S. health care providers and insurance companies conducted an aggressive campaign to successfully thwart federal government efforts to restructure the industry and expand health coverage to the uninsured. Of course, access to health care remains a critical issue to this day, awaiting another crisis to bring it back to the front pages.

Given enough time, an organization can adapt itself to changing stakeholder attitudes and shape the terms of the debate. Consider the efforts of the fast food restaurant industry to deal with the issue of obesity by adding more salads, low-fat yogurt, and "lean" options to their menus. At the same time, the industry has formed trade groups to carry the message that ultimately the debate is about freedom of choice, not regulating what people eat, and fast food menus offer a range of choices (and nutrition information) that enables consumers to responsibly exercise their right to choose.

Strategy Selection

The selection of specific strategies will be driven by the organization's chosen response, its analysis of its own strengths and vulnerabilities on the issue, and its stakeholder priorities.

For example, an organization may find that it lacks the credibility to advance its position given its past behavior or how the public perceives its self-interest. Its strategy in this case might include aligning with third parties, such as advocacy groups, that can take the lead in the debate. Or an organization may decide to change in response to an issue but may want to buy time so the costs can be staggered over a longer time frame. In this case, the organization may pursue a strategy in which it agrees with stakeholders on the need to change, but identifies gaps in current knowledge that require further research before the change is implemented.

Depending on the nature of the issue and the chosen response, potential strategies include:

- Conducting a communication campaign to educate stakeholders about the company's actual performance on the issue and close perception gaps. Communication activities use the full range of information and persuasion tools known to the field.

- Building a coalition with other organizations or stakeholders to develop a proposed solution, pool resources, coordinate activities, and communicate broad support for the position.

- Communicating the organization's position directly to elected officials and their staffs to influence the content or timing of legislation or regulatory actions.

- Mobilizing support for the organization's position from the grassroots— for example, by educating the organization's employees about the issue's importance to them and encouraging them to speak to friends and neighbors, write supportive letters to the editor, meet or write their elected leaders, and make their views otherwise known.

- Redesigning a product or developing new policies and procedures to adapt the organization to new or emerging stakeholder expectations.

MONITORING KEY ISSUES

Issues are not static. They continually evolve, branch out, and take new directions. Once an issue is identified, it should be tracked and periodically reassessed to determine if it remains relevant to the organization, if the fundamentals of the debate have changed in any way, and whether the organization's action plan needs to be modified to accommodate recent developments or new information. Issue monitoring tools include:

- Opinion research such as telephone polls or online surveys is used to determine attitudes of different stakeholder groups on the issue and track changes in attitudes over time as stakeholders receive new information about it.

- Monitoring of news media coverage on the issue helps track key developments, the level of media and public interest, the most quoted and most influential advocates, and the organization's effectiveness in communicating its views through the media.

- Monitoring Web sites and blogs on the issue can help determine the views of different advocacy groups, how the topic is being debated pro and con by proponents of different solutions, and what new arguments may be emerging on the fringes of public opinion.

- The development of legislation can be monitored through media coverage, tracking services such as LexisNexis, postings of proposed legislation or regulatory action on government Web sites, and meetings with legislative staff.

CONCLUSION

Communicators today are being challenged to be more productive, more efficient, and more effective with fewer resources. This challenge requires a focus on the areas that have the greatest impact on the health, well-being, and growth of the organization.

Issues management is a tool that identifies issues critical to the organization's current performance and future prospects. By surfacing and prioritizing these concerns, communicators are better able to focus, coordinate, and maximize their time and resources against the greatest areas of opportunity, or points of pain, for their organizations. The communicator can also play a critical coordinating role by facilitating the flow of issues information to those who can help the organization examine the matter, respond to it, and ultimately develop a solution.

Once initiated, issues management should become a continuous-loop process. An issue is identified and prioritized, the position and response are developed, the action plan is designed and implemented, the issue and the organization's response are tracked, new information and results are gathered and evaluated, the issue's status is compared with new issues surfaced through environmental scanning, priorities are reset, if necessary, and the process continues.

Communicators have the skills essential to resolving contentious issues and bridging gaps between the organization and its stakeholders. By seeking opportunities to create a dialogue with constituents early in the development of an issue, before battle lines are drawn, they can reduce the risk to the organization's reputation and operations, and help to reach a balanced resolution that is fair to all parties.

References

The American Heritage Dictionary of English Language: Fourth Edition. (2000). Boston: Houghton Mifflin Company.

Chase, W. H. (1984). *Issue management: Origins of the future.* Stamford, Conn.: Issue Action Publications.

CHAPTER TEN

Change Communication

Twelve Questions to Ask Before Communicating Change

Carol Kinsey Goman

In a recent survey by the Conference Board, 539 global CEOs were asked to list their top concerns. In Europe and Asia as well as in North America, organizational flexibility and adaptability to change consistently ranked at the top of the list. Only revenue growth was of higher concern.

Acknowledging this finding, communicators have a tremendous opportunity to provide leadership in the communication of change in organizations. Rapidly changing technologies make yesterday's choices obsolete. The turbulent economy increases pressure to do more with less. Companies swim in a shifting stream of relationships: they are competitors one day and partners the next, and sometimes both at the same time. Corporate restructuring is becoming an annual affair. Mergers and acquisitions are on the rise. Customers are demanding everything better, faster, and cheaper. Competition is fierce. The volume of information is overwhelming. The rate of change is accelerating. And employees are increasingly skeptical about committing to business strategies that are constantly being redefined.

Developing change-adept organizations will require an expanded definition of *change communication* from speech writing, intranet content development, e-mail messages, roll-out/cascade programs, and the rest of the current traditional approaches to a more strategic overview. This change must encompass leadership behavior, reward systems, organizational goal setting, recognition programs, work processes, workplace design, and organizational conversations within formal and informal networks.

It also means letting go of any preconceived notion of the right way to communicate change and giving up the myth of any expert's infallible advice. No transformation formula lasts forever, and by the time the guru's new book has been published, it is already obsolete. In fact, the best change communication techniques are not found in any single source or strategy. Instead, the most effective guidelines evolve in response to a series of questions.

QUESTION 1: WHAT IS THE EMPLOYEES' PERSPECTIVE?

Organizations do not change. People do . . . or they do not. Sometimes employees resist change (especially if it seems arbitrary and destined for a short life), but sometimes workers see the need for change before their management does.

Frontline employees deal regularly with customers and observe firsthand the issues, challenges, and successes of those they serve. The information technology department sees advances in technology before the rest of the organization has adapted to the most recent advance. Professionals throughout the company attend association meetings and have access to experts in their field.

Let us say that your organization has hired the best and the brightest, and your job is to tap their expertise, points of view, and concerns. The first question that you should ask is: "What do employees think?"

- What are the complaints you hear most often from customers? ("In what ways are we disappointing customers?")

- What are the compliments you hear most often from customers? ("In what ways do we please or delight customers?")

- What do you read in the newspapers or hear on the news that concerns you about the future of this company? ("What are the rumors or stories about our company or about the industry that worry you?")

- What organizational policies, procedures, or systems get in the way of your doing superior work? ("If you could throw out rules that interfere with your performance, what rules would go?")

- What do you like most about working in this organization that you would not want to change? ("What do you brag about to your friends and family?")

- What is the risk of trying to stay competitive in this dynamic business environment with the organizational status quo?

- What are you concerned that the leadership of this company might change?

- What are you concerned that the leadership of this company might *not* change?

Once you gather the collective insight of the workforce and give the entire organization access to it, you may find that the impetus for change already exists. At the very least, an understanding of the employees' perspective helps you identify where to build on existing alignment and how to address the gaps. A few follow-up questions can help with that analysis:

- In what ways does employee perception already align with that of leadership? Do they see the same organizational strengths, weaknesses, and challenges?

- How can you build on this alignment when communicating change? Just as in a negotiation, places of convergent agreement create a foundation: "We all agree that the customer is disappointed with our speed of delivery."

- Where are the gaps? If, for example, employees say they do not see the threat of international competition—and if this is an area of great importance to your leadership, you need to know early on that they will not accept competitive pressure as a reason for change unless they are given further evidence.

QUESTION 2: DID YOU SET THE STAGE FOR CHANGE?

The best time to discuss the forces of change is well in advance of an organization's response to them. Everyone in the organization should have a realistic appreciation of the precursors of change and transformation: the impact of globalization, market fluctuations, technological innovations, societal and demographic changes in the customer base, new offerings by competitors, new government and regulatory decisions. And here technology can be a great asset. Although it certainly should not be the only medium, the intranet can be a timely vehicle for competitive and industry information.

Above all, candor is a must. Candid communication goes beyond simply telling people the truth when it is advantageous. Preparing people for the marketplace reality of constant change takes an unprecedented openness and transparency: a proactive, even aggressive sharing of everything—financials, business strategies, risks and failures, as well as successes.

Here are some other ways to set the stage for change.

Interactive Workplace Experiences

When Rubbermaid held a product fair in its headquarters town, it displayed storage bins, kitchen items, and other plastic housewares, each with a label that detailed what it cost to make and what it sold for. It sounds like a run-of-the-mill corporate event except for two things: the fair was open only to Rubbermaid employees and the products were not Rubbermaid's but those of its competitors. Rubbermaid wanted its workers to see for themselves what they were competing against.

Outside Expertise

The commercial organizations of Bayer used an "IMS year in review" presentation in order to show Bayer's position, wins, and challenges in perspective with the industry. (IMS is a company that tracks information on the pharmaceutical industry and then sells it back to companies.) This gave employees an opportunity to see how they stacked up against the competition and to ask questions from an unbiased external source.

Business Literacy

When Jack Stack arrived at International Harvester's factory in Springfield, Missouri, the engine remanufacturing plant was losing $2 million a year on revenues of $26 million. Stack and the 119 employees of the now independent Springfield Remanufacturing Corporation initiated an amazing turnaround. Ten years after he bought the company, SRC had sales of $73 million, and the firm had hired almost six hundred additional workers. How did he do that? By increasing all employees' business literacy. Stack created a system called "The Great Game of Business," which was designed to teach every employee about the entire business, including the finances of the company.

Customer Feedback

At Ritz-Carlton Hotels, employees continually create change in order to solve customers' problems. Here is how it works: if a particular hotel has, as its primary customer complaint, a problem that room service takes too long, the manager informs employees in that department and asks for volunteers to form a committee to find the root of the problem in the room service system and to change the process or create a different one that solves the problem.

Looking Ahead

Companywide discussions around questions like the following can provide the stimulus for future thinking:

- What trends are going to affect the future of this organization?
- What government regulations could change the rules of this industry?
- What social issues could cause our customers to stop (or increase) buying our product or service?

- What kinds of technological innovation would most drastically affect our product or service?

- What changes in pricing, services, process, or other areas could the competition introduce that would cause us to rethink the way we do business?

- What companies that are not our competitors now could become competitors in the future?

- What current competitors could become partners in the future?

- What are the global forces that could most affect our market?

- Under what conditions could this industry become obsolete?

- What possible opportunities do you see that we are missing?

QUESTION 3: HOW WILL YOU TRACK EMPLOYEE PERCEPTIONS?

As important as it is to find out what employees are thinking before a change, it is just as crucial to have a system for monitoring employee perception throughout the change process.

Employee interaction and feedback loops help organizations track the level of workforce comprehension. The greatest advantages come when organizational feedback is gathered immediately after the delivery of every important message by asking these questions:

- What are the most important points we just covered?

- What did you not understand?

- With what do you disagree?

- With what do you agree?

- What else do you need to know?

Many communicators supply an e-mail box or a telephone number for individuals to ask questions about the change or to voice their concerns. Others use short online surveys to help determine which messages are getting through and which are not. Still others create a communication advisory team. The members of the team usually represent a vertical slice of the organization. Their primary function is to remark on the quality of communications: What are they hearing? What is their reaction to the message? What questions do they have? What would make the communication more effective?

QUESTION 4: DO YOU HAVE HONEST ANSWERS TO TOUGH QUESTIONS?

Not only can employees tolerate honest disclosure, they are increasingly demanding it. And when it comes to change, employees want straight answers to these tough questions:

- Will I keep my job?
- How will pay and benefits be affected?
- How will this affect my opportunities for advancement?
- Will I have a new boss?
- What new skills will I need?
- What will be expected of me?
- How will I be trained and supported for the new challenges?
- How will I be measured?
- What are the rewards or consequences?

Until these personal issues are resolved, employees are too preoccupied with their own situation to pay much attention to meeting the needs of the organization. It is advisable to take these sensitive issues head-on and to let people know where they stand. If these workplace concerns are not addressed, the company rumor mill will speculate, gossip, embellish, trade half-truths, and generally elevate the workforce's anxiety level.

QUESTION 5: CAN YOU ANSWER THE MOST IMPORTANT QUESTION: WHAT'S IN IT FOR THEM?

There are personal advantages to be found in almost every change, but people may need help discovering what the advantages are. Sometimes employees just need to be guided through a few questions: What are your career goals? What are the skills you would like to learn? What job-related experiences would you like to have? In what ways might this change help you to fulfill some of your personal objectives? (It might be the chance to learn how to use new technology, the experience of serving on a change task force, an opportunity to make suggestions for improvements outside their usual work area, a way to increase a personal network within the organization, or a chance to be cross-trained in needed skills.)

Another way to point out advantages is by using actual examples of others who benefited during a similar situation. If you implement an organizationwide change but begin it in one department or division, you can use the success stories of people who have found personal advantages—learning and growth opportunities, increase in self-confidence, more job satisfaction—in the process.

QUESTION 6: HAVE YOU NARROWED THE "SAY-DO" GAP?

Organizations send two concurrent sets of messages about change. One set of messages goes through formal channels of communications—speeches, newsletters, corporate videos, values statements, and so forth. The other set of messages is delivered informally through rewards and recognition programs, performance objectives, measurements, training, work processes, systems, promotions, and the leadership's off-the-record remarks and daily activities.

Formal communication is what companies say to employees about the organization and its goals. Informal communication is what the company does in terms of actions to demonstrate and support it. For change communication to be effective, the formal and informal channels must be aligned. Corporate communicators like David Moorcroft at the Royal Bank of Canada pioneered the use of research tools to measure (and then find ways to narrow) the "say-do" gap.

Senior managers are beginning to understand the importance of congruent, behavior-based communication as a requirement for leading change. In the words of Sue Swenson, president of Leap Wireless, "What I do in the hallway is more powerful than anything I say in the meeting room" (personal communication). Communicators who coach CEOs can begin by asking their executive two questions:

- What do you and your leadership team currently do that already supports the change?

- What do you have to do differently to align with the change? For today's skeptical employee audience, rhetoric without action quickly disintegrates into empty slogans and company propaganda.

QUESTION 7: CAN YOU PAINT THE BIG-LITTLE PICTURE?

Vision is the big picture, and it is crucial to the success of the enterprise. But along with the big picture, people also need the little picture. And here is where first-line supervisors are your greatest communication asset. Whether you provide talking points or discussion guidelines (to encourage interaction), supervisors are the vital link in turning an organizational vision into practical and meaningful actions. Here are some examples:

Big picture: Presenting the concept of transformation.

Little picture: What does this mean to us?

Big picture: Setting long-term corporate goals.

Little picture: What are some short-term goals we can set?

Big picture: Developing the overall objectives of the transformation.

Little picture: What are our priorities?

Big picture: Creating the mission of the organization.

Little picture: Where does our contribution fit in?

Big picture: Communicating organizational values.

Little picture: What does this mean in our daily work?

QUESTION 8: WHOSE VISION IS IT?

An organizational vision is not the same as long-range or even strategic planning. Planning is a linear process of progression toward a goal. Vision is more holistic—a sense of direction that combines a good business strategy with a comprehensive organizational purpose that declares its own importance. A vision describes a business as it could become over the long term and outlines a feasible way of achieving this goal.

Effective communicators understand the power of vision to imbue people with a sense of purpose, direction, and energy. A compelling vision of the future pulls people out of the seductive hold of the past and inspires them to set and reach ambitious corporate goals. But if the vision belongs only to top management, it will never be an effective force for transformation. The power of a vision comes truly into play only when employees themselves have had some part in its creation. So the crucial question becomes, "Whose vision is it?"

In the end, people have to feel that the vision belongs to them. What this means in practical terms for the communicator is that your job shifts from crafting executive messages to facilitating structured employee conversations and involvement.

One example is the way Planned Parenthood set its vision for the future by engaging everyone in that conversation. "Vision facilitators" guided the process for the national organization, at every affiliate and among the different constituents: medical directors, clinic directors, educators, and others. Although the organization's president's views were strongly represented, everyone's thoughts were considered, and the vision was formally ratified at their annual conference. The result is a cohesive vision for the future that is owned by the entire organization.

QUESTION 9: ARE YOU EMOTIONALLY LITERATE?

People have to understand the rationale for change: the business case, the marketplace reality. But change is more than just the logic behind it. Change is also an emotional process. With the insight that people skills (the soft stuff of business) hold the key to transformation, human emotions take on greater significance.

Large-scale organizational change almost invariably triggers the same sequence of emotional reactions: denial, negativity, a choice point, tentative acceptance, commitment. Communicators can either facilitate this emotional process—or ignore it at the peril of the transformation effort.

Denial

If the workforce has been insufficiently prepared for the reality of discontinuous change, people's initial reaction is usually shock and denial. People in shock are emotionally numb and refuse to believe that the change will take place.

In dealing with denial, communicators are faced with the challenge of making sure that all employees understand that the change is important, real, and imminent. The best way to ensure that is to involve people in the planning process from the beginning. The earlier you gather employee input, encourage discussion, and ask for ideas, the more it pays off in employee commitment and energy.

Negativity

When people have moved through the numbness of denial, they usually begin to have very negative feelings—self-doubt, fear, sadness, self-pity, depression, frustration, anger, grief, and even hostility.

It is counterproductive to ignore negative feelings or to attempt to cheer up people who are in obvious distress. What works best is to allow sufficient time for the reality of the situation to sink in and then to create safe places (face-to-face facilitation works best) for employees to express concerns and feelings.

It is almost always unproductive to tell people that they must change to correct past performance. It is also unrealistic to speak of correcting in cases where the past has been highly successful. But in any case, it is wise to assume that workers have done their best. Telling them it was not good enough—that, in effect, *they* were not good enough—is demoralizing and demotivating, and guaranteed to build resentment.

Instead of blaming the old ways, you can help employees detach from the past by allowing them to mourn it. To facilitate people through the mourning period, the past can be honored in a ritualistic sense. From pictorial displays on company walls to mock funerals to parties celebrating the history of the organization, rituals help people say good-bye and move on.

Choice

Next comes a period of vacillating emotions as people decide whether to support the transformation. There is a schism in organizations going through transition, as some employees move into new roles and relationships while others stand firm in their opposition—which leaves the undecided majority feeling much like the taffy in a taffy pull.

Communicators help employees through transition by giving them honest information about requirements for future success within the organization. It is important to discover and tell the stories of company "heroes"—those workers whose behaviors exemplify success under the new model. The benefits of communicating employee success stories are twofold. First, it is an opportunity to recognize and reward those who have already embraced transformation. Second, it provides all employees with real-life examples of theory moving into practice.

Acceptance

Once people have agreed to support the change, they are ready for action. Organizations in the early stages of the acceptance phase are characterized by abrupt increases of energy and enthusiasm. The communication challenge at this point is to focus all this energy by restating the overall vision, giving employees access to all information needed to understand the dynamics of the transformation, breaking the overall change into incremental steps with time lines and measurements, and emphasizing the need to collaborate with others and experiment with various solutions.

Commitment

In the final phase of the emotional process, workers emotionally invest themselves in the newly structured organization. Commitment is a time for celebration. To have transformed an enterprise *and* engaged the enthusiasm of the workforce is a tribute to both leadership and employees. This fact needs to be acknowledged and celebrated throughout the organization.

Commitment is also a time for rewards. Communicate the results the organization has achieved, and single out those individuals and teams whose achievements were outstanding, but find ways to acknowledge everyone's contribution. (And always set up a measurement system.)

Above all, commitment is a time for reflection and learning. The commitment phase offers a unique opportunity for the entire workforce to think back through the change and find the strategies, behaviors, and attitudes that were the most effective with this transition to prepare for the next one:

- How did you feel initially about the change?
- What helped you get through any negative feelings?
- Where did you go for support?
- What did leaders and communicators do exceptionally well?
- What do leaders and communicators need to improve for next time?
- What personal strategies, attitudes, and work practices served you best?
- What went better than you anticipated?
- What do you plan to do differently next time?

QUESTION 10: ARE YOU TELLING STORIES?

I am often introduced as a change management expert who is married to a man who refuses to change anything. During my speeches, I tell humorous stories about the resistance that Ray puts up and how I learned, from managers and communicators I had interviewed, different ways to handle his protests.

After every speech, audience members come up to me to comment on my husband. Many people recognize their coworkers or loved ones (or themselves!) in him, and some jokingly commiserate with me. What I find most intriguing about this phenomenon is that in my twenty-three years of professional speaking, no one has ever approached me after a program to say they most appreciated my "fifth point." That is because they do not remember what my fifth point was. But they *do* remember Ray and the lessons about handling change resistance that they learned through my stories.

Here lies a lesson for communicating change. Social scientists note that there are two modes of cognition: the paradigmatic mode and the narrative mode. The former is rooted in rational analysis; the latter is represented in fairy tales, myth, legends, metaphors, anecdotes, and stories. Good stories are always more powerful than plain facts.

This is not to reject the value in facts, of course, but simply to recognize their limits in influencing people. Facts are neutral. People make decisions based on what facts mean to them, not on the facts themselves. Facts are not influential until they mean something to someone. Stories give facts meaning.

Here is another difference. Trying to influence people through scientific analysis is a push strategy. It requires the speaker to convince the listener through cold, factual evidence. Storytelling is a pull strategy, in which the listener is invited to join the experience as a participant and to imagine acting on the mental stage that the storyteller creates. Stories resonate with adults in ways that can bring them back to a childlike open-mindedness and make them less resistant to experimentation and change.

QUESTION 11: DO YOU KNOW HOW CHANGE REALLY GETS COMMUNICATED?

Town hall meetings in which senior leaders speak candidly about change, great stories that embody the spirit of change, well-designed intranets filled with pertinent information about the forces and progress of change, interactive transformation sessions in which a cross-section of the organization cocreates a vision and develops the strategy, online employee surveys that query and monitor a workforce as it deals with the nuances of change, icons and symbols and signage that visually reinforce change, and (especially) first-line supervisors who are trained and prepared to engage their direct reports in a dialogue about what change means to them: these are and will remain vital tools for communicators. But as powerful as they are, these are formal communication channels operating within the organizational hierarchy. And a single informal channel, the company grapevine, can undermine them all.

An organization's social network—those ties among individuals that are based on mutual trust, shared work experiences, and common physical and virtual spaces—is in many ways its true structure. In the hallways, around the water cooler or coffee pot, over the telephone, as part of a blog, in rogue Web sites, and through e-mail messages, news is exchanged and candid opinions are offered. During these informal exchanges and daily conversations, people decide whether to support change.

Communicators looking to influence the grapevine are using a variety of approaches.

First, they are creating physical and virtual space for informal communication to take place. One example is Caterpillar's European headquarters in Geneva, Switzerland, where employees represent a mixture of nationalities from all over the world. While essential for a successful global operation, this diversity complicates communications.

A few years ago, employee communication manager Gottardo Bontagnali kept thinking about the role played by the central market square—*piazza* in Italian—in virtually all European villages. In addition to going there for necessities of daily life, villagers went there to exchange news, pick up gossip, pass on information, and socialize. It was, and still is in many places, the village's most efficient communications tool.

So Bontagnali decided to create a piazza at Caterpillar's Geneva headquarters, based on the village theme. Local artists were brought in to paint the walls of the top-floor cafeteria with large village scenes, dotted with bright yellow Cat machines, of course, as well as sights from multiple Cat locations. And the villagers portrayed in the panoramas were actual Cat employees.

Employees were then encouraged to use the "piazza" for informal meetings. "Let us discuss it over a cup of coffee in the piazza" has now become part of the Caterpillar's business culture in Geneva.

Second, they are enlisting employees as communicators in two-way communication strategies. Rob Hallam is vice president of employee communications at PitneyBowes. He is also in the somewhat unique position of reporting to a CEO (Mike Critelli) who has a deep understanding and appreciation of the importance of internal communications. While the company uses a full spectrum of communication models, methods, and media, it is not surprising to find that PB also has had a long-standing interest in the role of informal communication to socialize change.

"PB Voice" is a two-way communication strategy that provides a channel to share business priorities and gather opinions directly from the workforce. An employee interested in becoming a PB voice partner (the term for an employee-communicator) submits an application that is reviewed by a small group of managers and peers. Selected partners are then trained and given tools to create workplace discussions about important company happenings. The partner is given responsibility for building relationships with key business leaders to facilitate the flow of business-related communications and for making sure that the key concerns of the work group he or she represents are being addressed. A terrific development opportunity for employees with leadership potential and an organic way to introduce change from a grassroots level, the greatest value of PB Voice from Mike Critelli's perspective is "my exposure to all the insights and perspectives that I wouldn't normally get from formal channels."

Finally, they are identifying opinion leaders throughout the organization. Although a variety of selection processes are being used, perhaps the most sophisticated tool for identifying opinion leaders is social network analysis, which consists of a survey of the individuals in a "network" (a group or an organization) asking whom they most rely on for information and whose opinion they seek. Then social network analysis creates computer-generated maps of both the direct and indirect links in a given network. This approach provides a highly accurate evaluation of who influences opinions and behaviors throughout an employee population. Social network analysis also allows communicators to find the hidden influencers—those who may not have many direct connections but nevertheless strongly influence other opinion leaders.

QUESTION 12: ARE YOU POSITIONING CHANGE AS AN EVENT OR A CORPORATE MIND-SET?

Throughout the industrial age, the organization was orderly and stable; disorder, variation, and instability were viewed as counterproductive. When change was introduced, it was as an event, or series of events—a linear progression to some future (fixed) state. No wonder people still struggle to fully understand that stability is a thing of the past and that ongoing change is the new reality. The rhetoric and actions of their organizations have lulled them into understanding and accepting change as incremental and finite.

The omnipresent forces of change have made that mind-set obsolete. New technologies, shifting customer preferences, global challenges, and unexpected government decrees come seemingly from nowhere and totally transform some industries and make others obsolete. Because the world is uncertain and unpredictable, companies need to share that complex and ambiguous reality with their employees.

Communicators who continue to position the current strategy as the right answer to future challenges encourage employees to anticipate a spurious return to stability as soon as the correct structure, product mix, and staffing are in place. And when this state of permanence does not result—when the next "right answer" is announced and last year's strategy discarded—employees become more skeptical, more resistant, less trustful, and less willing to believe that the company leadership has any idea of what is going on.

If adaptable, change-adept organizations are what CEOs really want, then the only communication strategy that is going to produce the desired result is one that includes instability as a positive element—and ongoing change as business as usual. So my final question is this: Are you still referring to change as "the event," or are you positioning it as a constant corporate mind-set and vital component of organizational success?

CHAPTER ELEVEN

Current Realities in Crisis Communication

Elpi O. Cuna Jr.

Global communication and global interaction enable communicators to learn from each other and have a vicarious look into the other's crisis-handling models. Each situation and the variables in each situation are different. Yet common circumstances like environmental issues (such as water shortage, global warming, and forest denudation), natural calamities, and disease outbreaks that strike a common chord in peoples across all climates bring diverse peoples together in grief, outrage, or concern. Tragic accidents, human drama, and acts of violence bind us all. These touch the very core of being human—the basic needs of security, food, clothing, shelter, love, acceptance, the reason for being, and a feeling of belonging.

To cite an example, the passing away of prominent leaders is now an armchair activity of people the world over. The death of Pope John Paul II was an around-the-clock saga that kept television viewers, especially devout Catholics, riveted to their television sets, thanks to twenty-four-hour reporting by cable TV channels, Cable News Network, and the BBC. Not only did we get an update but also an in-depth look at church traditions and the origins of and reasons for its ceremonies.

The coverage of the final rites with religious leaders and heads of state gave a visual statement and confirmation of the ecumenism and acceptance of diversity of the late pontiff. This provided continuous coverage for the devotees, the curious, and the wanting-to-be-informed viewers alike. The election of a new pope, again telecast worldwide, lent a conclusion to the demise of a pontiff. It was a sad event, a loss of a leader, ending on a note of hope and continuity.

It exemplifies the reality that when an event is deemed important and newsworthy, the whole world can watch, nonstop. And when a crisis strikes, the whole world can watch and judge. Being unknown may not help one avoid this coverage. The novelty of obscurity can work for or against one in a crisis.

Thus, having a more involved and informed public, adds a new dimension to crisis handling. Suddenly we are not alone. A crisis is solved locally but can be watched and discussed globally. Web sites and blogs, and new electronic ways to come, add to the access and the speed.

Crisis situations bring out the best and the worst, the beginning of and the end of, the true worth of any person and of any company. Being "in flight" or "up against a wall" where corporate adrenaline keeps pumping is a situation that takes its toll on and challenges the company reputation, integrity, and credibility. And when the very core of a company is questioned, that hits close to the heart.

Communicators who work in public service and public utilities know that the company moves within the realm of regulations and laws. I work for a private electric distribution firm that serves over four million customers in Metro Manila, the seat of the national government, and nearby provinces where industrial estates are located on Luzon, the biggest island of the Philippines. That it is a publicly held company and the largest such private electric distribution firm adds to its being a high-profile corporation. Any development makes the headlines.

Controversies are not new, as the balance to stay viable within what is allowed by the law and serve customers, especially those in the lower economic classes, continues. Then there are the public issues and public figures who have to be managed to keep the company reputation intact and integrity unquestioned.

The power industry is undergoing deregulation; thus, implementation of new procedures and guidelines is ongoing as the company prepares itself for change. Added to these are regular consumer concerns, service needs, and new customer situations that arise due to new regulations.

As industry changes are implemented, communicators are challenged to keep alert and plan ahead, scanning for probable issues and handling crises if and when they arise. A lot of insights have come our way in the nearly twenty years that I have handled issues for the company. Advocating for a public utility has kept the corporate communicators on their toes.

This chapter seeks to go beyond the traditional models of crisis communication by acknowledging cultural differences that affect and influence communications with key stakeholders during the resolution of a crisis.

Traditional models of crisis communication have in common a number of guidelines and axioms for communications management:

- Be proactive, and have a crisis plan in place are expectations.
- Use a single-spokesperson model or a crisis team to deliver organizational messages.
- Identify priority stakeholders, and make immediate disclosures to reduce rumors and speculation about the crisis situation.
- Be accessible to stakeholder groups and the media.
- Offer assistance to those affected by the crisis, and follow up with corrective measures.

But each crisis is different, and different cultures may require adjustments to these traditional beliefs.

WHERE WE LEAST LOOK

Handling a crisis today still calls for the standard procedures experienced crisis managers know. We need even more sensitivity to people (both internal and external) in spite of and with all the mass means to communicate. Crisis communication and management require:

- Plenty of the sensitivity and emotional intelligence.
- Relationship management and alliance-building skills.
- Sensitivity to the culture, subcultures, and their nuances.
- Quick thinking and nontraditional ways (like community dialogues and other grassroots activities), especially when faced with limited resources.
- A firm grounding in the realities of the situation, especially when the variables affecting the situation, like regulations and court decisions, are beyond a communicator's control.
- The realization that media information cannot be manipulated or controlled. Media representatives have their own mind and reasons for seeing a position, event, or statement the way they do.

Other factors to consider that are posing more challenges today include balancing the interests and needs of stakeholders (who have been segmented more efficiently today for more personalized messages and motivations), acknowledging stakeholder importance, and recognizing more extraneous variables (like public opinion, economic conditions, political realities, and regulatory constraints) that can bear heavily on the crisis situation (or be the dark horse that can make or break a crisis or an impasse).

Seeing the Big Picture and Recognizing the Details

Sometimes the solutions are where the communicator least looks. For example, after a series of negative media stories about the company, a breakthrough can happen with a public and unsolicited testimony from beneficiaries of a community livelihood project funded by the company to debunk the press stories that the company is antipoor. That is why the skill of zooming in to see details that could break the case (for example, sloppy proofreading of a news release could change the company statement) is just as valued as the skill of "zooming out," or seeing the whole picture and the interconnection among different events, variables, audiences, or "flanks" to see down the road.

Strategic thinking is needed. Sometimes unknown adversaries are sources of media stories or opinion leaders that whip up a public opinion frenzy against the company. And when that happens in a regulated industry, legislative inquiries, filing and counterfiling of cases, and opposing views at regulatory body hearings or even the judiciary begin. The intricacies of rates and tariffs, implementing guidelines of new laws, and the like are difficult to explain, especially when what has to be implemented is not a popular course of action like a rate adjustment. The astute communicator must decipher if the matter giving the company negative press is that of the issue itself or a bigger socioeconomic concern.

For example, a mandated rate adjustment is difficult for the public to accept when a new tax has just been implemented. A crisis may occur when the company is perceived as anticonsumer and consumers become more demanding with the service or begin to question the company's projects and financial statements and its resource management.

The zooming-out skill keeps us from being so parochial or myopic and helps the crisis communicators take the offensive to address the problem. The communicator has to dissect the situation, the different forces at work, the audiences and their respective desire, and then match these with the resources at hand while thinking ahead.

When we drown in the many details and allow ourselves to be led by the details, we surrender our control and forward-thinking skills. Then we begin to simply react, which should never happen in a crisis.

Amid the many details that the crisis communicator has to pay attention to, the focused crisis communicator will be able to quickly isolate the message, see where the logic is going, and skillfully use basic communication skills of listening, organizing, and summarizing these messages and communicate simply and clearly.

Sometimes in trying to be transparent or comprehensive, too much might be said and too many details presented, which can confuse the publics. While these may be interesting to and necessary information for the internal audience, the detail overload can be confusing to the external audience. The communicator must be the source of that judgment. It is much more than having a good creative handle or an eye-catching ad campaign.

Prioritizing or Segmenting the Audiences

In wanting to explain the company stand, the focused communicator knows how to zero in on a single message. This single message can be varied and rewritten to match the needs of the diverse audiences. The more detailed the knowledge is that the communicator has of the different audiences that have to be prioritized, the better the message will be received. Of course, the message must not be oversimplified. This is one constant challenge when explaining rates and regulatory changes.

We cannot please everyone. So it has to be clear who is the major audience to address first and down the line. With priorities set, we are able to tailor messages for the stakeholder or audience, telling them both good and bad news.

Here are other important elements to consider:

- Strike a balance of each stakeholder group's interest.
- Masterfully communicate in all the different media available, and make each work at the right time and for the right audience and message.
- Transform the message for each of the different media.
- Make the crisis situation prove to the publics and other stakeholders that the company truly walks the talk in its social responsibility statements and commitments, especially under duress.

For example, the supreme court decision that my company is now implementing, that of making refunds to customers, made consumers happy. But it made banks and investors concerned about the viability problem it would cause. In this case, communicators worked with a cross-functional implementation task force, and each sector represented in the task force handled its respective stakeholder group. Each communicator had to weave in all the stakeholder concerns and come up with a plan in tandem with other specialists.

In good times, it is easy to churn out ads and messages of the company's support of certain groups or advocacies. When in crisis, the public remembers these advocacies and begins to see how truly committed the company is to what it said. If the company does walk its talk in hard times, then credibility and trust rise, and a positive relationship can develop. Otherwise the social advocacies of the company can be dismissed as mere propaganda. That is why, in good times, the communicator must be circumspect in crafting such statements of corporate commitments. The communicator must assess whether these statements can be sincerely supported in crisis. And when the crisis strikes, these statements of public advocacies must be revisited for any contradictions.

In a crisis, the organization and its employees should be primed to defend and advocate for the company. Before any crisis strikes, the procedures and roles should be clear and prepared. And when the crisis does strike, the employees hear about it first from management, get updated information, know and believe in it, and know what to do.

Employees belong to other social groups, their families, and their communities. People they interact with ask them about the crisis and what the company stand is. Retirees, contractors, and employees of subsidiaries and affiliates and their families also can advocate for the company, especially at family gatherings, community meetings, civic club meetings, sports events, and others.

THE EFFECT OF EMOTION ON CRISIS COMMUNICATION

Audiences can and will judge us when we handle a crisis because technology and mass media give them that power. But the ability to move them—whether they are our local audience, the global audience, or the different stakeholders whose support have a bearing on the companies we represent—is best studied and mastered by communicators. That may require using nontraditional and more personalized means of communication that give insight into the audiences' psyche, culture, and socioeconomic conditions.

Western studies are available, thanks to the pioneering works of research companies and foundations like that of the International Association of Business Communicators (IABC). But to complete the global picture, similar research and studies in other parts of the world are needed just as frequently. For example, an Asian audience will react differently to the same message or motivation especially when the crisis affects different peoples on various continents. The different countries in Asia all have their own cultures, subcultures, and regional differences. A study on interpersonal communication patterns in Asia could yield different results with different reasons for the results.

Thus, it is the sensitivity to the emotional side of crisis management that is interesting and best for us to look at more closely. In Asia, where I am from, the ways of the person, understanding his or her psyche, and knowing the groups or persons with whom one interacts are factors that can help resolve a crisis. Also your friends and organizations or those of your audience should be considered.

Relationships and Affiliations

Beyond a person is his or her family, clan, community, and allies. Extended family ties, including relationships by affiliations (like in-laws, godparents, province mates, fraternity brothers, schoolmates), are valued relationship networks.

A bond made by these affiliations or a common experience through these affiliations can be key to resolving a crisis. The go-between in an Eastern setting is a person imbued with diplomatic skills and negotiating experience who lays the groundwork for agreement or conciliatory talks.

The crisis communicator arranges for simultaneous talks with different groups of stakeholders led by a person or persons acceptable and credible to the groups. So while a group of executives are presenting before lawmakers, customer service representatives are meeting with consumers, and other company representatives are addressing civic groups and presenting the company stand on a television talk show or regular radio broadcast.

Thus, while the standard crisis-handling procedures continue (and should be in place), so-called nontraditional ways are also used to solve the crisis. More often these are interpersonal and group communications where sensitivity and discernment are most needed.

Culture and Grassroots

In the East, a person's dignity or stature in the community or groups to which he is a member is important. Saving face, respect for the pecking order in the family or organization, and respect for age, authority, experience, and seniority are revered and observed.

In the Philippines, there are over seven thousand islands of rich natural resources and with a people who are a blend of East and West. The Philippines is made up of Luzon, Visayas, and Mindanao islands. While we can be Western in our language, clothes, music, and so on, we are very Eastern in our manner of dealing with others, non-Filipinos included. For example, we address someone we hold in esteem or acknowledge for his age or stature by a title. A younger person addressing the older or more esteemed person by his name alone would be considered a rude breach of etiquette. The use of the proper title in addressing a person, regardless of age or stature, would be respectful, thus opening avenues to discuss problems and unpopular issues.

In public dialogues, "strutting one's stuff" when replying could be perceived as being too sassy, arrogant, pushy, or even hostile. This then creates barriers in winning public support or sympathy. Excessive assertiveness, especially on a cool medium like television, could make impassioned pleas sound like veiled threats.

As another example, in reassuring the public that electric power will be restored soon, the company spokesman says, *Patuloy po namin ginagampanan ang aming serbisyo upang maibalik po namin ang kuryente at makaaasa po kayo na hindi kami titigil hangga't hindi namin naibabalik ang serbisyo ng kuryente sa lahat ng aming customers na naaapektuhan ng bagyo* (We will continue to fulfill our commitment to serve you and assure you that line work will continue around the clock until electric service is restored to all our customers affected by the typhoon). In this example, combining the knowledge of the medium, choosing the right person to speak for the company, and couching the message in a clear and sincere manner acceptable to the audience yet with a sense of urgency helps the company win sympathy or acceptance, defuse hostility, gain public trust, and maintain its credibility.

Generally, sympathy goes to the underdog in unpopular situations. In a crisis, a company represented by someone who comes across as humble, honest, straightforward, concerned for fellow men, considerate and caring, or respectful can persuade an antagonistic public to be more understanding or accepting of the company position. Then there is the x-factor of the spokesman being charismatic. For radio, where the voice carries everything, the speaker must come across as sincere, believable, respectful, and knowledgeable to draw in the audience.

Intuition and Soul

Gut feelings and intuitive ways of finding solutions can help a crisis communicator. Also, it is being comfortable with "eureka" moments of sudden insight, unplanned solutions that pop up in the course of the crisis, and a feeling whether a person or a course of action is a risk. We need to be able to use both sides of our brains to resolve a crisis. To intuit also saves one from saying things that one will later regret or propels one to do things that will win public support as the crisis unfolds.

Others could call this "thinking out of the box" or street smartness. Gut feelings tend to come with experience and exposure to different problematic situations and different personalities: an outspoken consumerist, a cautious executive, an activist leader, a nitpicking writer, an impulsive speaker. Constant exposure and some setbacks here and there are good teachers.

Crises also can have a spiritual side. The Philippines, having the largest Christian populace in Asia, predominantly Catholic, has had crisis moments lifted up to divine intervention such as during the bloodless People Power Revolution of 1986 where Filipinos, regardless of religious sect and social strata, filled the streets challenging military might and firepower, going by prayers, rosaries, sheer number, and faith.

In times of crisis, Filipinos turn to their deep faith and find some comfort in silence. Silence, for meditation practitioners, is a steadying, grounding way to be attuned to the intuitive inner self, religious ways, reflection, and strength. This mystique slow a frenetic pace, calming one down to think clearly.

In dialogues with groups of opposing views, say, management and labor or company personnel and irate customers, what is left unsaid may be a breakthrough. Sometimes the unsaid is best left that way. What is between the lines matter, given away by nonverbal cues.

Nonverbal cues are culture bound too. For example, in the Philippines, people who go to mass usually stand with their hands crossed over their chest. It may not be that they are critical or shutting themselves off from the rites. It is just that most would not be comfortable with their hands at their sides. Then there is a use of pouted lips to point to an object or place with no need for words. It is a discreet way to call someone's attention, answer someone's raised eyebrows without disrupting the speaker, or signal where something is without making a sound.

Silence can also be a sign of respect in a hostile situation, in deference to the presence of an elder or an authority figure.

NONTRADITIONAL WAYS AND LIMITED RESOURCES

Today, everyone has had to learn to do more with less. Above-the-line efforts need budgets to match reach, frequency, and specifications. Below-the-line activities, like corporate theater, are used to build morale among employees; community-based immersion and civic group involvement by company officials sometimes do a better job of winning public trust. The more sustained and immersed the efforts are, the more sincere the company is perceived to be. A relationship of trust and friendship begins. And when crisis strikes, there is enough of a reservoir of goodwill to give the company a chance to explain its side or even for the recipients of the goodwill activities to stand by the company due to their personal experiences rather than media coverage.

Knowing which information channels of wide reach and low cost to use when a crisis hits in financially troubled times is a creative way to communicate. Public utilities especially have to be judicious and prudent in conducting information campaigns and other promotions so as not to incense the public or incur regulatory ire regarding where resources are being placed. Firms of basic services are in the public eye and are watched for signs of unnecessary spending that may be passed on as expenses to an unwary public.

Technology is changing the way information spreads within a country and between countries. The phenomenon of text messaging over cell phones is one example. Almost everyone, regardless of social or economic class, has a cellular phone to text a friend or relative anywhere in the country or reach relatives or friends abroad. Today, having a land line is not expected; having a cell phone is. It is an inexpensive way to keep in touch. Millions of text messages are exchanged daily. It is also one way to spread news at the press of the Send button.

With the popularity of the medium, it is one way to broadcast news and the company stand in succinct, compact messages. It is also one way customers can send feedback to the company. The use of prepaid cell phone cards is popular, and for the sender, it is economical and provides him or her anonymity when sharing feedback.

This is one way the company has replied to customers to update them when their electric service will be restored and why their service was interrupted during a thunderstorm. The company stand can also be sent out to employees with official cell phones. Beat reporters can send in their queries and clarifications to designated company officials.

REALITIES BEYOND US

Being creative while communicating during a crisis is as critical as understanding the many stakeholders affected by the crisis. Crisis communication needs to be grounded and realistic, especially when the variables affecting the situation are beyond our control, such as regulations and court decisions. Sometimes it can be a long and bitter struggle.

The judgment (much like the clinical eye for physicians) on whether to respond to negative stories—whether it would clear the issue and put the company in a position of strength or whether it would start an unproductive word war—is a discernment that comes over time.

Public utilities operate in a highly regulated environment. Staying viable and fulfilling social responsibilities is a balance that must be met. Without viability, there would be no resources for social responsibility. But not having social responsibility would affect viability. The balance has to be achieved, the company stance must be communicated, and the stakeholder support must be maintained.

Continuous relationship building with government and regulatory bodies, issue management and environmental scanning, and dedicated tracking and study of laws and regulations are needed. Strong ties and constant dialogue with regulatory bodies are activities to be nurtured. A history of compliance with regulations is the best way to nurture this relationship and prove the company's professionalism and responsibility as a business and good corporate citizen.

In a public service industry, balancing consumer advocacies and company viability is always a challenge to the regulators and to the company as well. Prevention, as much as can be done, is the goal, so as not to reach crisis level. And when a crisis happens, the gamut of crisis communication activities then begins, aiming for a quick resolution.

CHAPTER TWELVE

Corporate Social Responsibility

Adine Mees

In 1997 my CEO asked me to align and merge the company's marketing department with the newly emerged corporate social responsibility (CSR) team. I was working for Citizens Bank of Canada, a national online bank and a subsidiary of Vancity, a globally recognized leader in CSR. The response from both teams was interesting. The CSR team had serious doubts that the marketing staff understood the importance of walking the talk and were afraid their efforts would be watered down and exploited through slick public relations and advertising efforts. The marketing staff was frustrated with the snail-like pace of the CSR team and did not understand why they had to move so slowly and cautiously. Both saw each other as aliens from another world. Those were the early days. The staff was bright, dedicated, and creative, and it did not take long to build a strong department that was up to the task of infusing the company's brand with CSR and identifying the operational capacity needed to deliver on that promise. As a new bank in a mature market, we needed to be able to differentiate ourselves with a modest budget.

A company's brand and culture cannot change overnight. CSR and branding share some common characteristics, and change management is one of them. CSR and branding speak to the company's mission, vision, and values. For the execution to work well, they need to be infused into the company's DNA.

Information and action steps outlined in this chapter provide the basic tools and frameworks necessary to effectively demonstrate and communicate a company's CSR commitment. Customizing a CSR program and communications to suit your company's business reality, culture and brand will lead to CSR success.

DEFINING CSR: DOING WELL BY DOING GOOD

There are many definitions of CSR. Many business managers still make the mistake of seeing it simply as a form of progressive philanthropy. It is not. It is much more than that. Canadian Business for Social Responsibility (CBSR), a network of Canadian companies interested in CSR, defines it as "a company's commitment to operate in an economically and environmentally sustainable manner, while acknowledging the interests of all of its stakeholders" (2005, para. 2). At the United Nations Earth Summit in 1992, Secretary General Maurice Strong defined it as the ability to provide for the needs of the world's current population without damaging the ability of future generations to provide for themselves. These are lofty goals and are often intimidating for business management to grasp and act on. If a company's brand, product, or suppliers are under the critical lens of a church group, a nonprofit, or an active lobby group for its labor standards or environmental performance, it is vital that management understands CSR within these dimensions.

GETTING STARTED: CREATING A ROAD MAP FOR SUCCESS

When I was at Citizens Bank, the process began by revisiting the bank's vision, mission, and position statements. Together the executive team drafted language that incorporated a responsibility agenda and listed key performance competencies that they would need to be able to deliver. There already existed a solid list of more traditionally accepted core competencies like risk and reputation management; to this we added items like social and environmental issues management and stakeholder engagement. Then the marketing and CSR functions were merged to ensure that CSR was embedded in the company's products and communications. This was followed by the launch of an overarching ethical policy that governed the bank's investments, operations, and supplier relationships, a Canadian banking first. Later came a social audit: the Ethical Policy Compliance Review.

Ultimately work must occur on many fronts with many business tools simultaneously. While the random acts of goodness strategy (doing lots of good to great things without a strategic framework) may have worked for many of the early CSR adopters, it is quite likely that it will not work that well today. As more companies in the mainstream are adopting a CSR agenda, developing a clear plan of action and a corresponding business case is more the norm than the exception. Many best practice case studies have been developed and serve as examples of learning lessons the hard way. These examples can be found at Canadian Business for Social Responsibility (www.cbsr.ca), Business for Social Responsibility in the U.S. (www.bsr.org), and Business in the Community in the U.K. (www.bitc.org.uk). Benchmarking best practices in a sector is a good first step and one that will save time and money in the long term.

Once a benchmarking study has been completed, it is time to define the scope of work. This study will help streamline the process. Until you have set a stake in the ground and defined the impact for your company in terms of opportunity and risk, all ideas will sound interesting, and you will feel that you need to look at them all—an overwhelming and impossible task for someone just starting out.

When I joined CBSR, I documented my experience in the form of a road map. It uses a management systems approach to build a CSR plan and ultimately a culture. That plan is included here.

Building a Corporate Social Responsibility Plan: Using a Systems Approach

A business planning approach to CSR requires discipline and focus. Developing a CSR plan can feel a bit overwhelming. Since the definition of CSR and what it means at an operational level within business is still evolving, it is important to develop a disciplined planning approach to implementing and embedding CSR within the company.

CBSR developed, with its member companies, a step-by-step planning and assessment tool: the GoodCompany Guidelines for Corporate Social Performance (CBSR, 2001). These guidelines are organized into six main stakeholder groups: community, employees, customers, shareholders, suppliers, and the environment. According to CBSR (2001, p. 12), "A stakeholder is any person, group, or entity that is impacted directly or indirectly by a business' activities or that directly or indirectly impacts on the business' activities. This includes but is not limited to community members, employees and their families, customers, suppliers, shareholders, community and environment groups, politicians, professional and academic organizations, the biosphere, world population and future generations."

Typically, socially responsible initiatives are implemented along a continuum:

- Begin with an internal (and/or public) commitment to the initiative.
- Develop a policy to formalize and articulate the commitment.
- Create programs to implement the policy.
- Evaluate the success of the programs, and measure the progress.
- Involve key stakeholders in program development and evaluation.
- Become accountable for this commitment by reporting on the initiative.

Each of these points along the continuum represents a deeper level of commitment and a higher degree of sophistication. This is typically called a systems approach to implementing CSR. Within the system, there is a built-in process of continuous improvement. As the company works through the CSR continuum, its commitment deepens. Opportunities to strengthen a company's commitment will surface, and through the systems approach, internal policies, programs, and management systems can be revised and refreshed to ensure that corporate performance is improved.

A step-by-step approach will ensure realistic goals and outcomes:

- Step 1: Begin with a self-assessment. Do a quick self-assessment or gap analysis to determine what socially responsible initiatives your company has implemented and the depth of that commitment (for example, policy, program, or management system). This analysis can be completed using a tool like CBSR's GoodCompany Guidelines or by engaging an independent third-party social audit consultant.
- Step 2: Determine your priorities. Record your company's strengths and weaknesses, and prioritize them to meet your company's needs. This process may begin in a number of ways. A risk approach flags gaps that may cause risk to your reputation or financial enterprise. A cost-benefit approach to priority setting helps identify initiatives that are the most cost-effective to implement. Or you may want to build on strengths and take existing initiatives to a new level. A combination of the three may also be considered. Priority setting is a critical step in the process.
- Step 3: Establish a values statement. In a code of conduct, outline the basic CSR principles that will be used to inform all business decisions and actions. Write this commitment in simple language, and make it inspirational. This will become your north star as you work with staff, suppliers, community, customers, and other relevant stakeholders to ensure that everyone is moving in the same direction.

Things to Think About Before You Begin

Consider the big picture. From climate change to food security to international labor conditions and the imbalanced distribution of wealth, it is clear that our current habits are neither balanced nor sustainable.

Business has an opportunity and responsibility to be part of the solution. A systems approach to planning offers companies a step-by-step approach to CSR integration and improvement. For these actions to transform into significant and lasting change, it is important for company owners and leaders to ask themselves a few fundamental questions about their business:

- Does your company have a strategic vision that answers the following questions?
- How does your company affect the lives of the people it touches?

- How does your company help to create a fairer, more just, and compassionate world?

- Do you have a vision of your company as environmentally sustainable, and are you on track to achieve that vision?

Long-term success in this journey to sustainability is achieved when social and environmental criteria are embedded in the company's core business practices, its strategic vision and planning, and consequently its overall culture. This is a big step for most companies. It is challenging but both critical and possible. Understanding the overall impact of your company's product or service is something that must be considered at every step of the way.

The deepest level of corporate social responsibility occurs when a company leads by example, encouraging and supporting others to adopt social and environmental initiatives. It is this leadership that builds a culture and community of responsible businesses, setting new standards for future generations and framing the challenge for tomorrow's environmental and social innovators.

Putting It All Together to Communicate CSR Commitment

As reported by Collins and Porras (1995), companies that are consistently clear in their communications about their corporate values and company purpose and, more important, live by them, outperformed the U.S. stock market average by fifteen times. A clearly articulated set of corporate values and commitment to CSR brings together employees, directors, and other stakeholders to work toward a common goal. This can motivate employees more powerfully than compensation and other incentives.

Effective communications need to flow directly from your company's vision and mission statements. Here is an exercise to help you build on this concept:

- What does our company stand for? When you answer this question, do not be afraid to include an element of aspiration in your answer. This is the first step, and it needs to include innovation and leadership. Your task is to create an inspirational statement that captures people's hearts and imaginations while it expresses the unique personality of the company. This statement captures the company's purpose.

- How do we want to be perceived? What kinds of behaviors are you known for or want to become known for? This will capture the values that guide the way you conduct business and make decisions. This list will capture the company's values.

- What do we want to be? Your vision is where you want to end up—where you want to be. It needs to balance ambition (enough to make your heart race) with ability. This must be achievable by a certain future time. This will capture your company vision.

Statements of purpose, values, and vision become stronger and more meaningful when developed through a cooperative dialogue with as many of the people at work as possible. If well-articulated statements of purpose, values, and vision already exist, revisit them and understand how they support, encourage, and inspire a commitment to CSR.

Link Vision with Effective Communications. Lofty and aspirational statements serve an important purpose, but they are just one component of the overall CSR communications. Your company's identity must be explored to develop key messages that will inform all internal and external communications. Consistency is critical to the success of CSR communications efforts.

Begin by developing a position statement for the company. This is a statement about how your company is unique and different from its competition. It describes the company's position in the marketplace. One of the most successful positioning exercises was developed by 7-Up. It described itself and became known as the "uncola." How is your company special and different? Is CSR a part of this positioning? A positioning statement looks something like this:

> ABC provides [produce or service description] to [customer segmentation description] who want [the product or service at a minimum but here you may want to stretch and include an aspirational CSR element as well].

Once a position statement is developed, think about your customers' and other stakeholders' experiences. Describe how they will feel about doing business with your company. What will their experience be? This is called the *consumer end benefit.* A consumer end benefit can be as simple as: "I feel really good about where I buy . . . because . . ." You can do this exercise for your staff as well: "I feel really good about working at . . . because . . ."

Today, people have an incredible number of choices. If one company can provide a competitive option with an added benefit that makes people feel good about the product they are buying or the place they are working, they are developing a longer-term relationship built on trust and loyalty, two key elements companies spend millions of marketing dollars to secure.

Develop Key Messages. An essential component of effective communications is delivering strong key messages: compelling, consistent, and credible messages. Key messages must be relevant to the audience and provide clear and accurate statements of what the company stands for and what it brings to their lives. As the communication professional, you need to understand what your company delivers on the consumer end benefit: your core competencies. Companies have identified and fostered many traditional core competencies. As a CSR company, there are new ones to add to the list—for example:

- Building effective working partnerships with reputable organizations and associations that are advancing CSR, particularly those aspects that relate to your core business practices
- Excellent stakeholder engagement practices and processes
- Media relations and issues management
- Being sensitive to and understanding the complexities of CSR

At this point in the process, the series of documents that have been developed provide the list of three or four key messages that will be used in media interviews, collateral material, staff forums, annual general meetings, and advertising. What are the three or four most important points about your company's purpose and position that you want to get across?

Communicate Commitment Internally to the Board, Senior Executives, Management Team, and Employees. Each of these audiences requires a message customized to it. A best practice for reaching these stakeholders is anticipating their questions and concerns and then incorporating those messages into your communications. Typically a communication tailored to the board and senior executives addresses CSR from the perspectives or governance, risk management, and business and market opportunity.

Since communicating with these internal stakeholders often includes an address at a meeting, it is helpful to develop a PowerPoint presentation that answers the following questions:

- What does CSR mean to our company?
- What does it mean for our sector?
- What are the trends (corporate, government, society) in our country and our markets?
- What are the risks, and where are the opportunities?
- How will we manage our CSR initiatives, and how will performance be monitored and reported?

Communication to line managers needs to address CSR from the following perspectives:

- CSR 101: What is CSR?
- Business case: How does CSR add value to what I do on a day-to-day basis?
- CSR testimonials from your company's customers and suppliers.

- Where is the company performing well, and where does work need to be done?
- How is the company planning to roll out its CSR program? (How will this affect my workload?)

Communication to company employees needs to address CSR from the following perspective:

- CSR 101: What is CSR?
- Why does your direct manager or supervisor think CSR is important?
- Testimonials from employees in other companies on how CSR has made their work environment better.
- CSR testimonials from your company's customers and suppliers.
- Examples of CSR practices that are already in place at the company.
- Opportunities for employee engagement.
- Where is the company performing well, and where does work need to be done?
- How is the company planning to roll out its CSR program? (How will this affect my workload?)

Getting Everyone on Board. There is great value to be gained from engaging your board of directors and senior executives, as well as the management group, early on. Their continued involvement in the development of CSR policies and programs will give them a sense of ownership and pride in these new initiatives. An additional benefit may be that their contribution and commitment can secure CSR's longevity in your company, in that it is seen as an integrated, core part of the business, and not as a superfluous and expendable program that can be easily cancelled during periods of temporary revenue crisis.

To initiate their involvement, a formal communication should be addressed to the board of directors and executive as well as the management group. Exhibits 12.1 and 12.2 show sample text that may be used to invite these key stakeholders to a CSR presentation. The language and message need to be tailored to your company, its sector, and its reach. Your goal is to secure commitment and support. CBSR also recommends that the memos come from your CEO or the senior executive responsible for CSR.

Here is how some of CBSR's members are communicating their CSR messages:

"Make no mistake, as with all successful companies, Alcan operates to optimize financial returns. But this can only be achieved by ensuring customer satisfaction, hiring and retaining the best workforce, investing in the best technology and by being a valued partner to our stakeholders and the

Exhibit 12.1. Sample Memo to the Board and Executive

Corporate social responsibility is increasingly appearing on the radar of our customers, suppliers, and regulators. What is it all about? How will it affect us? How well are we performing? We would like to request your presence at a CSR presentation during which we will cover some of the basics as well as some of the specifics. Your opinion, insights, and experiences will be valuable components of this discussion.

We'll be looking at trends in those markets where we do business:

- Governance and compliance (board accountability)
- Growing number of codes of conduct and CSR standards
- Increasing demand for disclosure and transparency
- Growing controversy around environmental issues, human rights, and First Nations
- Increasing societal demands
- Heightened media interest
- Investment and market expectations

We'll also delve into the business benefits:

- The license to operate
- Safety and risk management
- Enhanced reputation and brand value
- Attracting and retaining top talent

The field of CSR is a broad subject that ranges from community relations to sustainable development. It deals with issues that affect most companies and sectors, such as product safety, energy consumption, workplace profile and safety, community development, voluntarism and fair labor practices, and those that are specific to our business [identify them here]. Because the field is evolving and society's expectations are growing, it is important that we take the time to understand what CSR means to our company and our future—what the challenges and opportunities are—and place our CSR stake in the ground.

---

communities where we operate" [Travis Engen, president and CEO, Alcan, 2005, personal communication]. "The license to operate is the license to grow. That's the business value of CSR" [Ashley Nixon, adviser on sustainable development, Shell Canada Ltd., 2005, personal communication].

"Suncor has generated total annual shareholder returns averaging more than 25 percent. The long-term growth of Suncor's share price is a reflection of investor confidence in our strategy to develop our business in a way that is both profitable and responsible" [Rick George, president and CEO, Suncor Canada Ltd., 2005, personal communication].

Exhibit 12.2. Sample Memo to the Management Group

Today, effective corporate leadership includes an ability to embed corporate social responsibility (CSR) into the core of a business's operations. Corporate social responsibility is increasingly appearing on the radar of our customers, suppliers, and regulators. What is it all about? How will it affect us? How well are we performing? We would like to request your presence at a CSR presentation at our next management meeting, during which we will cover some of the basics as well as some of the specifics. Your opinion, insights, and experiences will be valuable components of this discussion.

What is corporate social responsibility? We'll spend some time defining it and understanding it. Why is it important to our business success? We'll look at the business case for CSR and how it can add value to our bottom line. We'll be covering how it can build sales, build our workforce, and build trust in our company. We'll then spend some time looking at what our competition is doing and how we perform against them. This will be an interactive discussion with lots of time for questions and discussion.

CSR TODAY: FROM DOING GOOD TO THE INTEGRITY OF THE BOTTOM LINE

Over the past decade, the dialogue about corporate social responsibility within business has shifted from philanthropy to something much more comprehensive, difficult to measure, and challenging to master: the integrity of the bottom line. Although "doing the right thing" is still the principal motivator for many companies, risk and reputation management are driving initiatives far beyond the boundaries of doing good. Business managers have a growing awareness that they will be held accountable for their entire social and environmental footprint and that their actions will be examined and judged in a very public forum.

Acknowledging That Business Needs to Earn Its License to Operate

At Suncor, a constituent of the Dow Jones Sustainability Index (DJSI), corporate social responsibility is built into the company's "Core Purpose"—its operations are rooted in sustainability and stakeholder engagement. In a recent sustainability report, titled "What's at Stake?" the question is answered this way: "Suncor works with a large and diverse group of individuals and organizations—stakeholders who may be impacted by our operations or who could, through their actions, affect Suncor. Their interest in our social, environmental and economic performance covers every aspect of what we do as a company, from the goods and services we acquire to the people we employ and the products we produce and sell. So what is at stake? In a word: everything."

Large companies are also having a large impact within the retail sector. As perhaps befits one of Canada's first companies and one of today's largest retailers, it is Hbc that is leading the charge on ethical sourcing, and it is not just about doing good. Hbc's vulnerability to criticism was demonstrated when the human rights group Maquila Solidarity Network named it "sweatshop retailers of the year" in 2002. Hbc was already working to end supply chain labor issues, but its leaders realized that effort was not enough. In order to put an end to redundant efforts by various retailers and audit more factories, Hbc CEO George Heller used his leadership and influence within the industry to make tremendous gains in a relatively short period of time.

For company managers who have not yet made CSR a priority, the stakes are particularly high among publicly traded companies. With Moody's Investor Service, the credit ratings agency, and Goldman Sachs Global Investment Research in the United Kingdom now both taking a long, hard look at CSR performance, companies are being analyzed in a way that they have not been before: on their ability to operate in a responsible and sustainable manner and, perhaps equally as important, their ability to report openly and honestly on their performance.

When looking at CSR leadership today, business managers are developing their expertise in areas of strategic relevance to their business: their staff, customers, and investors. In fact, five critical issues or opportunities are facing today's corporate leaders:

- Good corporate governance and its impact on investor confidence
- Effective stakeholder engagement
- Clear and trusted CSR performance reporting and disclosure
- Strategic integration of sustainability values and principles through change management processes
- A shift of perspective from one that is primarily focused on risk management to one that incorporates a view to business opportunity

On the topic of stakeholder engagement, companies that are putting the time and effort into engagement are reaping the rewards. This approach takes time and is about building trust and awareness between the company's decision makers and its key constituents. On the topic of CSR reporting, many companies are still unclear who their primary audiences are, and readership and impact consequently are low, particularly for the resources expended.

On the topic of governance, we still have a long way to go to see corporate boards embrace the kind of diversity required to fully represent a diverse set of perspectives. Board mechanisms for greater accountability and transparency in management reporting now seem to be firmly on corporate Canada's radar screen. Some of the most exciting and interesting work is happening today on the topics of CSR integration into corporate culture and shifting the company's CSR perspective from one of managing risk to one of creating business opportunity. The attention of communications managers must be on those CSR priorities on which they can act and influence: stakeholder engagement and CSR reporting. This leads to the intersection between corporate social responsibility and company and product branding.

From Focus Groups to Stakeholder Consultation and Engagement

Typically key stakeholders are identified as staff, customers, investors, and communities. The list can grow and include entities like the environment and future generations. Fundamentally, a company's ability to listen to and earn the respect of its most valuable stakeholders will determine its ability to access raw materials, manufacture a product, and bring it to market. *Stakeholder engagement* is one of the new buzzwords in the business world. Regardless of whether it is trendy, companies will end up doing it in some form, either sitting around a table in conversation or staring at each other across a courtroom.

Building Trust Through CSR Reporting

CSR started making its first forays into corporate financial reports in the form of photos of staff and customers as a way to liven up what was a rather dull and one-dimensional piece of corporate communication. The next phase of early CSR reporting was revolutionary and came from the entrepreneurial efforts of Ben and Jerry's in the United States and the Body Shop in the United Kingdom. These reports were written by an author external to the company who had come up with a number of performance indicators to measure the company's performance against. Today we are seeing a formalization of CSR reporting with third-party verifiers (often large accounting firms) measuring performance against an internationally recognized reporting standard like the Global Reporting Initiative (GRI).

There are five components of an effective CSR report:

- Be genuine in your efforts and your language. Many reports are filled with platitudes and vague language, neither of which build up your "trust" account with stakeholders.

- Use simple clear and specific language in your report. Make it believable and easy to understand.

- Focus on impacts (what happened as a result of the company's effort) over outputs (how much money we donated).

- Shift away from using only lagging performance indicators (what we did) to adding some leading performance indicators (what we can do to improve on our business impacts).

- Start using an internationally recognized reporting standard like the Global Reporting Initiative.

Using Open and Honest Communications to Build Your Trust Account

Norske Canada published its second CSR report in 2005, "Real Measures." It is an excellent example of a company working the five components listed above. The report is well written and not too text heavy, and it is open and honest. In it CEO Russell Horner openly acknowledges a lapse in community engagement: "We made mistakes as well. Most notably, we learned that sound environmental science and regulator process is not a substitute for open communication and dialogue with the community. This oversight caused much anger, frustration and distrust with some neighbours of our Crofton mill . . ." The management of the company realized that they had embarked on a flawed community engagement process and outlined the steps that they took to correct it. Detailing the company's corrective actions in the report is not that unusual. Admitting to the error on the second page of the report is. Russell continues by saying that "there will be other contrasts between excellent and weak performance" in the pages of the report. He then lists a handful of "counseling" environmental and CSR nonprofits that the management at Norske consider to be among their closest and valued advisers because, he acknowledges, "like good friends, these institutions help us to celebrate our progress and confront us with our failures." These are powerful words to describe a progressive and smart approach to stakeholder engagement and reporting. Both are contributing significantly to building the company's reputation and corresponding brand value.

Finally, consider tailoring the report to specific audiences. The trend is moving toward producing multiple shorter reports targeted toward specific audiences to be distributed in a way that increases their reach and readability, such as intranets for employees and point-of-sale brochures for customers.

References

Canadian Business for Social Responsibility. (2001). *GoodCompany guidelines for corporate social performance.* www.cbsr.ca/cbsrsupport/goodcompanyguideline.htm.

Canadian Business for Social Responsibility. (2005). *What is CSR?* http://www.cbsr.ca/about/whatis.htm.

Collins, J. C., & Porras, J. I. (1995). *Built to last: Successful habits of visionary companies.* New York: HarperBusiness.

CHAPTER THIRTEEN

Communicating for a Merger or an Acquisition

Patricia T. Whalen

For nearly forty years, major corporations worldwide have been following the mantra that "bigger is better" and that "buying growth is easier than building growth." Hence the continuous wave of mergers and acquisitions (M&As) that began in the 1960s and seemed to peak by 2000 has seen a new resurgence starting in late 2004 and continuing throughout 2005 with such announced combinations as Procter & Gamble and Gillette, SBC and AT&T, Federated and May Department Stores, Symantec and Veritas, Bank of America and FleetBoston, Kmart and Sears, and the list goes on.

Despite all this activity, it is fairly well known from M&A history that the majority of these deals will fail to increase shareholder wealth and will not achieve their financial goal; as many as half of them will be "demerged" in full or in part within the next five years. These trends were noted among academics and such consulting firms as Bain, McKinsey, and A.T. Kearney more than twenty years ago, but it has been in just the past few years that the media have begun to issue warnings with such headlines as these:

Some of the findings discussed in this chapter are from a 2001 study by the author that was underwritten by the IABC Research Foundation. "How Communication Drives Merger Success" (2002) referred to as the Whalen IABC Merger Study throughout this chapter, summarizes the findings of an extensive online survey of more than four hundred communicators who had recently undergone a merger or acquisition and is available for purchase from the IABC.

"Why Mergers Don't Work" (*Barron's*, April 20, 1998)

"Mergers Test Investors' Patience—New Firms' Shares Often Don't Thrive After the Marriage" (*Chicago Tribune*, June 23, 2000)

"The Merger Hangover: How Most Big Acquisitions Have Destroyed Shareholder Value" (*Business Week*, October 14, 2002)

Today one needs only to read about Morgan Stanley's disastrous 1997 merging with Dean Witter, Hewlett-Packard's widely hyped 2002 merger with Compaq Computer that ultimately cost Carly Fiorina her job, the recent problems of such deals as AOL/TimeWarner and DaimlerChrysler, and the dismantling of such media empires as Clear Channel and Viacom to get a sense of the magnitude of the problems that massive M&As face.

A *CFO* magazine survey of Forbes 500 chief financial officers suggested that M&As fail because of people-related issues such as incompatible cultures, inability to manage the acquired company, inability to implement change, or clashing management styles and egos (Forbringer, 2002). These findings are a double-edged sword for corporate communications professionals. On the one hand, recognition of the importance of communication and integration activities can elevate communicators' role in the M&A process and get them invited to early strategy meetings from which they might otherwise be excluded. However, this emphasis on postmerger communication and integration may absolve the original deal makers from entering into a bad deal from the outset or, at least, overpaying for that deal and unfairly shifting responsibility for the deal's success to people who had little or nothing to say about it in the first place.

There is ample evidence to suggest that while poor communication and cultural integration activities can and do play an important role in M&A failure, a bigger cause for an M&A to be labeled a failure is its inability to recoup its purchase price or recover its stock price. These problems are typically due to a gross overestimation of the cost savings and revenue increases that can be achieved from the deal. While there is little that corporate communicators can do to affect those estimates or the purchase price, there are ways that corporate communicators can influence, including the M&A strategic planning process, identifying and addressing key targets, and creating communications tools to meet the needs of the M&A. These activities are the focus of this chapter.

UNDERSTANDING THE TERMINOLOGY

To be effective in developing powerful M&A strategies, corporate communicators should be familiar with some of the key terminology in the field.

Mergers and Acquisitions

For the purposes of this chapter, the terms *merger* and *acquisition* (M&A) are used as interchangeable concepts to describe a variety of combinations that, regardless of the specific method, all require some form of merging of firms' assets and personnel. Here are some of the legal definitions of the various ways firms can combine (Ozanich & Wirth, 1993):

Acquisition. Technically this is the direct purchase of assets of another company using cash, stock, or a note providing for payment at a specified rate and time. Usually the acquired firm continues to exist, but under new ownership.

Merger. A merger officially refers to the combination of two corporations' assets into a single existing entity. Typically, when a merger takes place, the acquired company ceases to exist, and it takes on the name and identity of the acquiring firm.

Consolidation. Similar to a merger, a consolidation is where both firms cease to exist as they were, and a new identity is created that incorporates both firms' identities.

Joint ventures. These deals involve two or more firms that invest in a new venture, but they continue to operate their parent firms as separate and independent organizations.

Merger of equals. This is an often misused term in M&As and occurs when firms publicly position a clear "acquisition" as a "merger of equals," thinking that this designation will help smooth the integration process.

A true merger of equals can occur in a merger or a consolidation when both firms play an equal role in deciding how the newly merged firm will be organized. When this happens, the integration process is typically smoother, because there is a greater chance for making the right decisions about the fate of the firms' operations and employees. In addition, those decisions will most likely be perceived as fairer when both firms have an equal opportunity to contribute to the process. However, this is rarely the case.

Typically there is a lead firm (usually the acquirer) that calls most of the shots in the deal, and it usually intends to install its processes and managers at the acquired firm. This was the case when Jurgen Schrempp, the chairman of Daimler-Benz, planned the 1998 merger with Chrysler Corporation to form the $40 billion DaimlerChrysler Corporation. He repeatedly used the term *merger of equals* when discussing the deal, and the characterization was widely believed by employees and the media, at least in the early stages. But shortly after the deal's completion, it became clear that the characterization was misleading. Schrempp admitted to the media that he intentionally mischaracterized the equality of the two firms to help the deal go through. This revelation caused a class-action lawsuit on behalf of Chrysler's shareholders and resulted in dozens of negative news stories. DaimlerChrysler's stock took an immediate nose-dive and has never fully recovered.

The lesson here is that while a merger of equals can be a sound approach to an M&A, if one firm is clearly the acquirer, it should take the lead in all of communications, both internally and externally, and be up front about its role in managing the deal. But that does not mean that an acquirer should convey an attitude of "to the victor go the spoils." Smart acquirers acknowledge the unique qualities of the acquired firm and show respect to its management team and workforce. After all, one assumes that the acquired firm has something to offer, or the deal would not have been made in the first place.

Synergy

An often misused and definitely overused term with regard to M&As is *synergy*. When an M&A announcement is made, the investors, the public, and employees are typically told that the combined firm will achieve great synergy, meaning that the two firms will achieve more as a combined operation than what they could achieve separately. This is the argument for paying more for a company than its market value.

A few years ago, the media seemed to buy any public statement about a deal's potential for synergy. But today there is a growing cynicism about M&As, and the public and the media now recognize that there are many less than synergistic reasons that firms are acquired or merged. They are often related to power issues such as getting even with an old rival, eliminating the competition, fulfilling the ego needs of a CEO, or just plain greed. When real synergies are provided, they tend to be in terms of increased revenues or reduced costs.

Revenue Synergies. Revenue synergies come from market growth, cross-selling opportunities, and improved competitive position due to the M&A, but they are particularly hard to predict because they require broad assumptions about these things. Indeed, a recent McKinsey study found that 70 percent of mergers do not achieve their revenue synergy targets. *CFO* magazine suggests that some acquirers, such as Eaton Corporation, have avoided the problem by forecasting only cost synergies and "[refuse] to be drawn into a game of guesswork" (Frieswick, 2005, p. 27).

Cost Synergies. Cost synergies are slightly more predictable and more likely to be reported than revenue synergies, although the McKinsey study found that 40 percent of those M&A targets are also missed. Most cost synergies fall into one of two categories: financial synergy and operating synergy.

Financial Synergy. This type of cost synergy is often sought when the focus of the deal is diversification and to merge the two firms' financial assets. This is often the motive for conglomerates that acquire firms in unrelated fields. But financial synergy is also a goal for most deals even if the firms are in related fields and the acquirer still plans to operate them independently. Some key cost savings through financial synergies include:

- An improved tax situation
- Eliminating duplicate accounting, legal, and computer systems within corporate headquarters
- A lower cost of money from lenders
- Reduced operating expenses from the sale of unneeded assets such as the second corporate office space
- Combining the merging organizations' insurance plans, employee benefits, and pension funds

Operating Synergy. The second, and more widely reported, type of cost synergy is operating synergy. This type of synergy is often sought when two firms are in a related field and are forming what is typically called a strategic merger, where there are a number of perceived similarities in markets and operations. Some of the most common operating synergies sought during strategic M&As are:

- Integration or reduction of production facilities
- Plant specialization
- Lower transportation costs
- Achieving economies of scale in purchasing and manufacturing
- Reductions in general selling, administrative, and overhead expenses

These types of synergies often come from head count reductions and plant closings and can be stressful for an organization and its employees. Interestingly, *CFO* reports that despite the predictability of cost synergies, some executives concentrate only on revenue synergies in their M&As. Dick Heckmann, CEO of Carlsbad, California–based K2 Corporation, was quoted as saying, "If you buy companies and start driving cost synergies, all you end up with is a pissed-off organization. That's why we never base a merger on cost synergies, [although] we go after them if we find them" (Frieswick, 2005, p. 2).

PREPARING FOR THE M&A

Every corporate communicator faces the possibility that he or she could be called into the CEO's office and asked to have a press release and communications plan ready to go by the next day to announce a major merger or acquisition to the world. Ideally, there would be many weeks advance notice, but because of disclosure rules and the risk of information leaking about the deal, most companies tend to keep all but a few insiders in the dark about the deal until the last possible moment. In this situation, there are three important things for the communicator to do:

- Ask a lot of questions about why the M&A is being undertaken and what it is trying to achieve, knowing the motive behind the deal will help shape the most appropriate communications strategy.

- Recognize that there are several keys stages to the M&A process (see Figure 13.1). The communicator should sketch out each of these and identify the key goals and targets for each phase. The three broad stages are:

     The preannouncement planning stage that ends once the deal is made public

     The premerger planning stage that focuses on obtaining regulatory approvals and creating excitement on Day One, the official first day of the newly merged entity

     The postmerger integration stage, where all the of functional plans now need to be put into place and the businesses are integrated and the promised synergies achieved

- Identify all of the firm's constituencies that will be affected by this M&A and ask the following questions as they relate to the deal:

     What do we want from them?

     What will they want from us?

     Who will be the most resistant to the deal and why?

     What must we do to overcome that resistance?

     Who influences the likely resisters and who do they influence?

     What messages will influence them?

DEVELOPING THE M&A PLAN

After identifying the motive, the key planning phases, and the key targets for the deal, the next step is to rough out a plan of attack. As Figure 13.1 demonstrates, the M&A plan can be complex. While the corporate communicator may likely develop the plan, its implementation will require the dedicated efforts of a sizable cross-functional integration team with members from both firms. In the early stages, when confidentiality is critical and the deal is not yet completed,

M&A Planning Overview

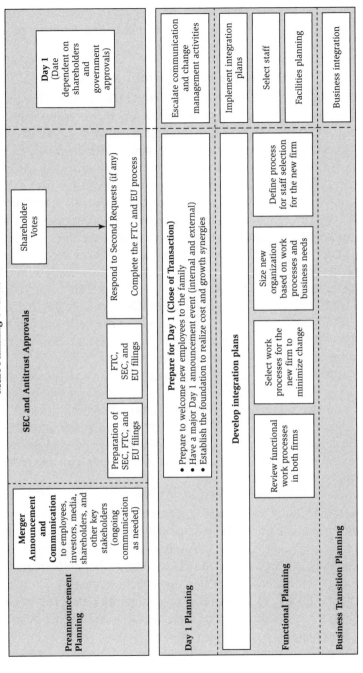

Figure 13.1. M&A Planning Overview

Note: SEC = Securities and Exchange Commission; FTC = Federal Trade Commission; EU = European Union.

Source: Adapted from Maxey (2001).

the team will be small, and there will much information that cannot be shared with the other firm. The size of the team and the information available should grow as time progresses and the deal is consummated.

Predeal Planning: Cultural Due Diligence

Despite all the M&A failures and the belief that cultural mismatches cause them, it is still relatively rare for M&A planners to conduct any type of cultural assessment prior to the public announcement of the deal. Granted, it is very difficult, if not impossible, to perform a cultural audit of a firm in secret before a deal is announced, but there is evidence that involving those with expertise in employee communications can be of great help in the early stages of the M&A planning. Cultural due diligence can point out some potential pitfalls for the deal in terms of organizational culture, management styles, employee reward systems, and work ethic. A survey conducted by Towers Perrin and the Society for Human Resource Management Foundation found that 72 percent of the successful M&As had substantial involvement of human resource executives during the due diligence phase of the M&A, while only 39 percent of those that failed had this level of involvement (CFO.com Staff, 2001). Despite this, due diligence continues to focus on the financial soundness of the deal, and communicators are often not brought into the loop until after the deal has been decided on by a small team of corporate finance and legal experts.

Once the deal has been announced, cultural compatibility assessments are somewhat easier to conduct, but arm's-length legal requirements will continue to keep firms from sharing certain confidential information until the deal has been approved. Sometimes firms use "clean teams," which are neutral third parties who can do some of these assessments independently and help the firms prepare for the deal without sharing confidential information with either firm.

Preannouncement Planning

If the communicator has not been asked to participate in the predeal cultural assessment, then the preannouncement stage will be his or her first involvement in the planning for the M&A. The most important activity in this stage is creating a compelling explanation for the M&A and translating the messages into the appropriate communication vehicles for specific audiences. These typically include a press release for the investment community, letters and intranet articles for employees, a brochure or flyer for customers, and frequently asked questions for managers.

When planning the communications tools and the messages conveyed in them, it is important to note that while investors may view the deal enthusiastically, there is a good chance that the employees of the target firm will view the news as disastrous. The communications plan and internal messages must address these issues and provide an honest and forthright discussion of the potential impact of the deal without terrorizing the employees and creating a mass exodus of key staff.

One of the biggest challenges in the preannouncement stage is to work on the communications materials while keeping the information secret until it is ready to go public. This may require the corporate communicator to do his or her own typing and copying of the materials to limit access to them. With today's new disclosure laws for publicly traded firms, rumors must be contained. While most firms take a position to never comment on rumors regardless of how correct or incorrect they may be, if a rumor appears to have gone public and people could potentially trade on the stock based on that rumor, most firms will move up the announcement to avoid the risk of selective disclosure. This means that the corporate communicator must be ready to make the announcement at a moment's notice.

Unless the deal is very controversial or meets with great resistance from certain quarters, as was the case in the HP-Compaq deal announcement, the most interest and media focus for the deal will take place around the initial announcement. This means any key messages the firms want to convey about the deal need to be incorporated into the early announcement, which has a high probability of making front-page news. After that, follow-up reports about the deal tend to slow down or are buried in the back section of the paper. The image management firm Lippimott & Margulies found that firms that planned a name change for the merged entity should provide it during the initial announcement or risk that it will be lost in obscurity if announced later (PR NewsBriefs, 2000).

Premerger Planning

Once the announcement is made and the initial media frenzy has dissipated, the corporate communicator moves into the premerger planning mode. In this stage, three key activities must be done simultaneously:

- Obtaining approvals from all of the government oversight groups, including any specific regulators in the firms' industries

- Planning for the official merger kick-off with a series of special Day One activities

- Developing the ongoing integration plans that will help the two organizations work as one

Before the deal can go through, the merging firms must obtain approvals from such government regulators as the Securities and Exchange Commission, the antitrust division of the U.S. Justice Department, the European Commission (if appropriate), and other regulatory bodies that may have a voice in the deal. In addition, the shareholders of both firms (if publicly traded) must approve the deal. While the primary communications activities for this are typically handled by the legal, government affairs, and finance departments, a coordinated effort is critical, since all public communication will likely enter into the review proceedings. Any negative headlines or comments from board members, key investors, employees, or customers will likely hinder the approval process. To speed the approval process, corporate communicators are sometimes asked to help generate support from customers and employees and may be asked to keep interest in the deal alive in the news media.

Planning for Day One

A key activity for corporate communicators during this premerger planning stage is developing materials and strategies to create interest and enthusiasm for the new entity on its first day in operation. Many firms see this day come and go with little or no public acknowledgment because the media have lost interest in it. But internally this is a critical day. It is Day One of the new organization, and most firms want to make as much of it as they can, especially with employees and customers. Dow Chemical Company certainly accomplished this with a wide array of internal and external communications activities.

By the time the Dow Chemical Company's $12 billion merger with Union Carbide Corporation was approved in 2001, making it the second largest chemical company in the world (it is now the largest), it had been languishing in the European Union regulatory system for nearly eighteen months. The media had lost interest, and it was difficult to keep employees enthusiastic about the deal. The good news about having this much time to plan was that by Day One, the company had put together some spectacular plans to make the world take notice of the deal. It held a "Dow Day" on Wall Street, with banners streaming from the New York Stock Exchange building, and greeters distributed Dow pens to traders as they entered the building. Dow's CEO rang the opening and closing bell for the first day of trading of the new Dow stock, held a press conference in New York, and granted dozens of print and electronic media interviews. Hundreds of news stories were generated about the event.

All of this was covered by a TV crew from Dow's in-house news department, which ran the story live at all Dow and Union Carbide facilities worldwide. At company headquarters in Midland, Michigan, employees watched the proceedings from an auditorium and then sat in on a live discussion with company executives about what the deal would mean for the two firms. Magazines were distributed to employees detailing the history of the two firms along with a package of materials that provided answers to many questions about benefits, timetables for integration, safety rules, and other matters. In addition, an elaborate package of materials for customers of both firms was distributed to the sales force and mailed to key customers.

CULTURAL INTEGRATION PLANNING: PRE- AND POSTMERGER

In addition to helping with the approval process and a big Day One kickoff, the corporate communicator is also typically a key player in an integration team that is trying to ensure a successful integration of all newly merged employees once all approvals have been received. The team continues to operate as long after the completion of the M&A as is deemed necessary.

The Whalen IABC Merger Study found that integration teams were used for 79 percent of the reported M&As, and for these firms, the corporate public relations department led the internal communications efforts 50 percent of the time, while human resources led the efforts 23 percent of the time. The remaining firms used departments such as finance, legal, or marketing to lead the internal communications efforts.

A 1999 study by management consulting firm A.T. Kearney (Howard, 1999) found that the four greatest barriers to integration were failure to achieve employee commitment, obstruction of middle management, cultural barriers, and lack of leadership commitment. The integration team needs to address each of these barriers and involve as many functions and levels from both organizations as possible to identify what resources and training will be necessary to overcome them.

How Much Cultural Integration Is Necessary for a Successful M&A?

A critical goal of the integration team is to figure out how much integration is necessary. Although there seems to be universal acceptance that the success of an M&A today is dependent on cultural integration, it should be clear from the discussion about synergy motives that not all M&As will require a consolidation of operations or the merging of employees and that cultural integration is not always necessary or even desirable. In fact, a forced integration could cause more problems than it solves if newly acquired employees are made to work within a cultural environment that is uncomfortable for them.

Interviews with a number of employees who had experienced mergers that were promised to be hands-off arrangements suggested that internal conflict increased when unwanted communication and centralized controls were put in place in the form of management memos and newsletters, imposed corporate procedures, and a change in incentives to take into account overall corporate performance. These findings were also supported by the Whalen IABC Merger Study, which showed that for firms seeking just financial synergy, higher levels of communication correlated with higher levels of conflict and lower assessments of the merger's success. Figure 13.2 shows how a mismatching of the synergy motive and communication strategy can lead to an increase in internal conflict.

Integration Strategy and Motive

	Autonomous Financial Synergy	Integrated Operating Synergy
Strong Communications Tactics	Mismatched Strategies High Conflict	Matched Strategies Low Conflict
Weak Communications Tactics	Matched Strategies Low Conflict	Mismatched Strategies High Conflict

Figure 13.2. Relationship Between Integration Strategy and Postmerger Communication

Conversely, many M&As are quite successful when they are left to operate independently from the parent. An example of this type of M&A was Cisco Systems' $7.2 billion acquisition of fiber-optics equipment maker Cerant Corporation in 2000. While it conducted a great deal of targeted communications to employees before the completion of the deal, it ultimately took a hands-off approach with the organization and kept formal communications to a minimum after the deal closed. Intel management also recognizes the need for these types of hands-off deals, referring to them as "green acquisitions," where they want the company to be nurtured and grow.

Developing the Communications Tools

Once the degree of integration has been determined, the communicator's role is to help develop the right communications tools to achieve the desired level of integration. In addition, the communications should keep employees informed of the deal's progress, answer questions, and address any misunderstandings or concerns that employees may have. A research study of 108 of the largest M&As of the 1990s that I undertook uncovered a long list of formal and informal communications tools that communicators typically use in the premerger and postmerger stages (Whalen, 2001). Figures 13.3 and 13.4 provide a list of which tools were used before the completion of these deals, which were used after, and which were used both before and after.

The Likelihood of Conflict

Another important factor for which the communicator should be prepared is the level of internal conflict. The Whalen IABC Merger Study found a higher level of conflict in firms pursuing strategic M&As. This makes sense, given that strategic mergers usually look to achieve operating synergy through employee

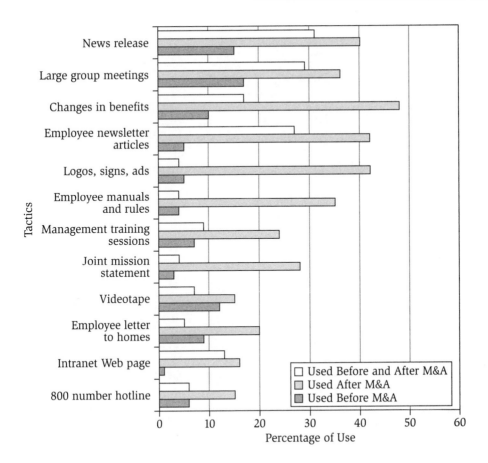

Figure 13.3. Formal Employee Communications Tactics Employed During M&As

Source: Whalen (2001).

layoffs and the consolidation of facilities. It stands to reason that employees in the merging firms will be nervous and suspicious from the moment the deal is announced, or even earlier if rumors surface prior to the announcement, and they will fight for positioning and scarce resources.

This fear and suspicion will only grow as headlines report more and more layoffs as the result of deals going bad or, worse, planned mass firings before the deal is even consummated. Consider what happened to sixteen hundred Crocker Bank managers who were fired on Day One of Wells Fargo's acquisition of the firm. According to Jim Collins's book, *Good to Great* (2001), Wells Fargo management decided that the Crocker managers were not compatible with the Wells Fargo culture because they had elegant offices and perks that the Wells

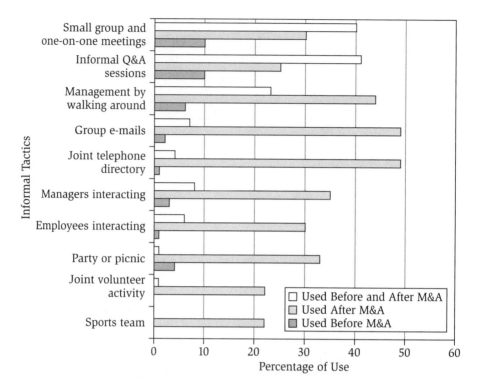

Figure 13.4. Informal Employee Communications Tactics Employed During M&As
Source: Whalen (2001).

Fargo managers did not have. Therefore, before the deal was even consummated, it was decided that "the average Crocker manager was just not the same caliber as the average Wells Fargo manager and would have failed in the Wells Fargo performance culture" (p. 53).

With such sweeping generalizations, is there any wonder that people become angry, defensive, secretive, and resistant to an announced deal when they hear that their firm is being acquired? Some employees go into a siege mentality as soon as the deal is announced. Marks and Mirvis (1997) called this reaction "the merger syndrome" and suggest that the best employees will begin to leave, while those who remain will experience physical and emotional stress that lowers their performance and organizational commitment (Marks and Mirvis, 1997).

Gerald Arbuckle looked at employee anxiety during a wave of health care mergers and labeled their reaction "culture shock." He suggests that employees in this type of M&A situation need to go through a grieving process: they need to grieve the loss of their firm's identity, the loss of their fellow coworkers, and the loss of their routines and comfort levels (Arbuckle, 2003). He also found that when the firms announced that synergies would be achieved through consolidation of facilities and the integration of people, the degree of conflict and culture shock that employees experienced rose significantly.

Reducing Culture Shock

An interesting finding from the Whalen IABC Merger Study was that firms that had lower levels of internal conflict and rated the deals a success were far more likely to have employed informal, face-to-face communication strategies than those who felt the merger was not a success. The respondents in the unsuccessful deals tended to use only traditional, formal communication tools that corporate communicators are trained to employ, such as newsletters, intranets, hot line numbers, and videotaped messages from the CEO. Communicators in the most successful M&As used formal tools to help create opportunities for members of the merging firms to interact with each other. These tools took the form of training opportunities that mixed people from both firms, managers walking around the acquired firm's facilities and meeting people, combined sports or volunteer activities, joint parties or other social occasions, as well as joint e-mail and telephone directories that helped employees find their counterparts in the sister firm.

The lesson from these findings is that both formal and informal communications are necessary during a strategic M&A. Employees will always need information in printed form or on the Internet to understand the reasons for the deal, as well as its timetable, the impact on product lines, changes in benefits, new shipping procedures, and other changes. But the research shows that this information will be trusted and relied on more if the merging firms also take the time to create informal interactions with members of their key constituencies to explain the strategy behind the M&A and answer questions in person. The informal interactions are much more time-consuming and the information is harder to control for corporate communicators, but the most successful firms put strong emphasis on management training and encourage face-to-face communications about their M&As. They also anticipate most of the questions that will be asked and try to have FAQs for managers and the sales force well in advance of the deal's completion so that their informal interactions are as useful as possible. The bottom line is that it is not the amount of communication but the type of communication that is most important to a successful M&A.

ADDRESSING THE NEEDS OF EXTERNAL AUDIENCES

Although the majority of the emphasis of this chapter is on internal audiences, other key groups are also affected by the deal and addressed in the communications plans. Three of the most important external audiences are investors, communities, and customers.

Investors

The investment community is the most important group to address at the outset of the deal, since the market's reaction can have a dramatic impact on both firms' stock prices. Since combining the firms adds no value in itself, economic theory predicts that the market reaction should be neutral, with the acquirer's stock price dropping slightly and the target firm's price rising to create a wash for investors. If the market perceives real synergy in the deal, the stock price for both firms will rise. If the market sees little strategic value in the deal, both prices will drop. When the payment for the deal is entirely in stock, a bad reaction can end the deal immediately, so corporate communicators typically work hard to explain the value of combining the firms.

One problem that often arises is that over time, investors hear very little about the deal and lose interest or confidence in it, putting the stock price at risk again. Sometimes so much effort is expended on planning for the combined firm that normal day-to-day public relations is ignored. Communicators need to find ways to keep interest alive by updating investors on the approval process and continuing to announce successes that occur at both firms.

Communities

Just as employees are concerned about the downside of the deal, so are the communities in which they reside. Plant closings and layoffs can have a disastrous effect on a community's tax base and can put schools and basic community services such as police and fire protection at risk. Enlightened firms include their communities in the communications plans, and many firms have found creative ways to help them recoup lost jobs by donating plant facilities and providing marketing expertise to help attract new businesses to the community. Maintaining community goodwill is critical throughout an M&A. A firm never knows when it may need to ask for a favor such as a waiver of a local ordinance to assist in its consolidation plans.

Customers

Customers often face a variety of problems after an M&A. A *BusinessWeek* survey showed that 50 percent of consumers say they are less satisfied with companies' service two years after a merger (Thornton, Arndt, & Weber, 2004). The problem is most acute in service industries that have direct impact on the quality of people's daily lives, such as oil companies, cable TV providers, and retail stores. A common problem occurs in billing and in a subsequent lack of customer service to try to fix those problems when accounts change hands.

Bank mergers are another area that has had a major impact on customer satisfaction. A Maritz Research study estimated that more than half of the 109 million U.S. households surveyed experienced a bank merger between 1999 and 2004. Many of these consumers found their bank services reduced as the banks tried to recoup some of the premium prices they paid for the M&A. The result for many of the banks was a double-digit customer defection rate. Recognizing the problem, many banks have rededicated themselves to focusing on customer service. "When First Union Corp. bought Wachovia in 2001 and then took its name, it made customer retention a top priority. . . . The result: Wachovia's customer-satisfaction score soared 10.6 percent two years after the deal" (Thornton et al., 2004, p. 63).

CONCLUSION AND RECOMMENDATIONS

There is a myth addressed in the Whalen IABC Merger Study that M&A communications can be reduced to a formula. Many books and articles on M&As outline a standard approach to achieving cultural integration and have preset ideas about how customers, investors, communities and government regulators should be handled. Although there are some clear stages in the planning cycle that are common to most M&As and some best practices for handling M&A communications, each deal is unique and needs its own set of strategies and tactics.

Best Practices

Many factors will influence the best combination of tools to use. Some of the most important factors are the motive for the deal, how much rivalry existed between the two firms prior to the deal, the size difference between the two firms, how much interaction will be necessary between the employees of the two firms, and the geographical separation between them. For some M&As, honest and open communication at the outset will be all that is necessary for a successful transaction. For others, a great deal of planning and implementation will be necessary from the moment the deal is conceived, and it will continue to be necessary throughout the life of the merged organization.

Probably the biggest factor that separates the successful from the less than successful deals is the use of experienced communicators who are involved in the planning early and have created an M&A action plan that allows them to learn from their own and others' past mistakes.

Worst Practices

The least successful M&As seem to occur in firms that discount the role of professional communicators and treat all M&As alike with cookie-cutter communications and very little customization. They tend to do financial due diligence only, with no cultural audits and no impact studies on marketing and customer service. They overuse formal communication in nonstrategic mergers and underuse informal communication in strategic mergers. They focus mainly on communicating to external media and the investment community, while ignoring employees' concerns. They often put too much emphasis on being fast and keeping the deal secret rather than giving themselves enough time to implement their plans effectively.

PARTING THOUGHTS

The research outlined in this chapter suggests that the conventional wisdom about cultural integration and the need for better M&A communication is only partly right. Certainly, good communications, especially honest and interactive communications, along with a well-designed integration strategy, will help a sound M&A reach its full potential by reducing the amount of nonproductive time spent in dealing with personality clashes and employee misunderstandings. But communications will not eliminate the conflict that will naturally arise when painful workforce reductions and the closing or consolidation of facilities are necessary. Communications also will not make up for a gross miscalculation of the synergies that can be achieved or the overpayment for those synergies.

Today's M&As face some of the toughest scrutiny in history. The media no longer give them a free pass. Customers have become suspicious of the motives behind them. And the investment community is no longer willing to carry the entire burden of the deals through stock-only transactions. Corporate communicators need to be part of the M&A planning process early on and need to ask the right questions and ring the alarm bell when the answers do not make sense.

References

Arbuckle, G. A. (2003, January–February). Nine axioms for success in mergers. *Health Progress, 84*(1), 38–42.

CFO.com Staff. (2001, June 27). HR function critical to successful M&A, survey finds. http://www.cfo.com.

Collins, J. C. (2001). *Good to great.* New York: HarperCollins.

Frieswick, K. (2005, February 1). Fool's gold. *CFO, 27.*

Forbringer, L. R. (2002). Making mergers work. Olin School of Business. http://www.olin.wustl.edu/discovery/.

Howard, L. (1999, August 23). Mergers won't mesh without people plan. *Property and Casualty/Risk and Benefits Management,* pp. 7, 12.

Marks, M., & Mirvis, P. (1997, May–June). Revisiting the merger syndrome: Dealing with stress. *Mergers and Acquisitions,* 21–27.

Maxey, C. (2001, April 10). *Dow and Union Carbide—Communications and change management in mergers and acquisitions: A case study.* Presented at Northwestern University, Evanston, IL.

Ozanich, G., & Wirth, M. (1993). Media mergers and acquisitions: An overview. In A. Alexander, J. Owers, & R. Carveth (Eds.), *Media economics: Theory and practice.* Mahwah, NJ: Erlbaum.

PR NewsBriefs. (2000, July 2). Name it now. *PR News*.

Thornton, E., Arndt, M., & Weber, J. (2004, December 6). Why consumers hate mergers. *Business Week,* 58–63.

Whalen, P. T. (2001). Well said: The role of communications in mergers and acquisitions. *Investor Relations Quarterly, 4*(2), 26–28.

Whalen, P. T. (2002). *How communication drives merger success.* San Francisco: IABC Research Foundation.

CHAPTER FOURTEEN

Managing and Communicating Cultural Diversity

Jenifer Armand-Delille

Our world is a cultural kaleidoscope, a tenuous mosaic of otherness—people, groups, and organizations with differing beliefs, values, lifestyles, and experience. Shake the kaleidoscope—change countries, jobs, or lifestyles—and the particles of culture instantly rearrange themselves into a different pattern. The variations of cultural diversity are as endless, fascinating, and potentially unstable as the patterns of the kaleidoscope.

Cultural diversity is generally seen as differences in race, ethnicity, language, age, nationality, and sexual orientation among various groups within a community, organization, or nation. A broader definition might include professional experience, job tenure, cognitive capacities, socioeconomic level, physical abilities and capacities, and sexual preferences. In short, diversity includes a large number of variables that make us different from each other.

Globalization and technological advances have simultaneously shrunk and expanded our horizons. Personal digital assistants, laptops, and cell phones have blurred workplace boundaries, while e-learning, artificial intelligence, and real-time speech recognition force us to interact faster than ever before. Global team members routinely hold virtual meetings in cyberspace, and it is not uncommon for a manager from Milwaukee or Milan to conduct business in Bangkok, Paris, and Los Angeles within a thirty-day period. However, for the most part, our understanding of cultural diversity has lagged far behind our jet trails. A major challenge of global business today is to span unfamiliar cultures and groups efficiently in order to work more productively.

WHERE CULTURE FITS IN

To understand diversity, we need to appreciate the vast resourcefulness and identification survival skills inherent in a culture. Who am I? How do I relate to others? How do I communicate? How do I make use of time? What is true for me? What is right or wrong? These are the universal questions cultures can answer.

A culture emerges whenever a set of basic assumptions is held in common by a group of people. Defined as a set of acquired characteristics that promote worldviews and behavioral norms within groups or nations, cultures develop to help individuals, groups, and nations organize to resolve universal life issues. Essentially conservative, self-protective, and resistant to change, cultures seek above all to ensure their own survival. Thus, when managing cultural diversity, we touch on deep fundamental values and ideals that are often unconscious and difficult to change.

In Europe and elsewhere, national and regional boundaries are in constant flux. Modern intercultural theory has also shifted from viewing individuals as monocultural beings to the concept of people as simultaneous carriers of multiple cultures (Boyacigiller, Kleinberg, Phillips, & Sackmann, 2004).

Take a thirty-eight-year-old unmarried Frenchman, who lives in the suburbs of Lyon and has worked for twelve years in financial management for a multinational in the aeronautics industry. Each of this employee's individual characteristics—gender, nationality, age, function, marital status, corporate identity, location, hierarchy—corresponds to a different cultural identity in which contradictory basic assumptions and rules may be held. These overlapping subcultures are in turn nested within this individual's visible cultural identity: French nationality.

Depending on circumstances, different cultures will come to the fore, especially if group values are shared or under threat or when there is homogeneity and empathy among the group. If our Frenchman's job performance were under attack, his professional culture would predominate, and he would instinctively call on his work culture references, network, and assumptions to resolve the crisis. If the issue at hand revolved around voting for or against a new shopping center in his home town, our Frenchman would instinctively slip into his local cultural identity, temporarily laying aside his professional culture. If he were the only Frenchman on a team of Chinese colleagues, he would probably react through his perceptions of the differences in national cultural identity.

Writer Anaïs Nin aptly summed up the essential dilemma of cultural understanding: "We don't see things as they are; we see things as *we* are." This common misperception, known as the transubstantiative error, consists of seeing the world through our own cultural and experiential filters. An important truth in understanding and managing diversity is that others are not like me and may not perceive and process information or act as I do or as I wish they would.

WHAT IS CULTURAL DIVERSITY MANAGEMENT?

"True diversity management begins and ends with individuals. It begins with each of us accepting our responsibility as actors in the diversity scenario" (Thomas & Woodruff, 1999, p. 9).

Diversity management is the task of recognizing, analyzing, and bridging differences between groups and individuals in order to maximize the value and creativity of each person as well as the synergistic benefits to the organization. Diversity management has come to the forefront in the past fifteen years. Today diversity includes a wide palette of business practices aimed at establishing trust, a stimulating work environment, and a diverse workforce. Developing policies and standards for treating employees with respect and dignity, diversity training, mentoring, apprenticeships, encouraging minority support groups, and linking compensation to diversity results are recognized best practices. Other positive initiatives are alternative work patterns, day care, diversity audits, good communication standards, and, above all, management accountability.

Diversity does *not* mean accepting others to the exclusion of our own values, and it does not imply browbeating a team into groupthink. True diversity management encourages freedom of expression while allowing ambiguity and some conflict between people and groups around the organization's common goals.

WHERE DOES DIVERSITY STAND TODAY?

The world is constantly changing. In 1995, the English language was second only to Mandarin Chinese as most commonly spoken in the world in terms of native speakers. It will likely drop to fourth place after Chinese, Hindi, and Arabic by 2050. The Spanish language is rapidly catching up. In the future, it is predicted that more people will speak more than one language; English will be one of those languages, and Chinese will probably become the next "must-learn" language, especially in Asia (Graddol, 2004).

In the European Union (EU) where geographical and cultural borders are progressively blurring, diversity efforts are a priority since the ratification of the EU Charter on Fundamental Rights in 2000. For the first time in Europe's history, common policy for human rights was defined in six key areas: dignity, freedoms, equality, solidarity, justice, and citizens' rights.

A 2004 European Commission green paper reported that 88 percent of respondents think the EU should step up its efforts to combat discrimination following the enlargement of Europe. Similar trends toward incorporating and legislating gender parity and diversity are slowly developing in Asia and Africa.

Things Are Not Like They Used to Be

According to the most recent study by the U.S. Bureau of Labor Statistics, minorities and women will make up 70 percent of the incoming U.S. workforce by 2008. The 2001 edition of *Women and Diversity Wow! Facts* states there are now 9.1 million women-owned businesses that continue to grow at twice the rate of all U.S. firms.

In the United States, single households now outnumber married couples with children. Demographic age groups include 52 million "veterans" born between 1922 and 1943, 76 million baby boomers (1946—1960), Gen-Xers (late 1960s–1980) representing 51 million people, and 70 million millennials (1982–2000) now coming into the workforce. In 2050, the worker-to-elderly ratio in the United States will be 3 to 1; only 2 to 1 in England, France, and Germany; and a scant 1.4 to 1 in Japan, Spain, and Italy (Schramm & Burke, 2004).

The Business Case for Diversity

In the 1990s, diversity management moved beyond the politically correct stance as the business case began to be proved. Promoting diversity is now high on management's priorities. When it is well implemented, it stimulates creative solutions, interpersonal performance, and the bottom line. An estimated $2.8 billion spent yearly on diversity management in the United States alone now includes stand-alone functions independent of human resource management, such as diversity officers, experts, coaches, and diversity councils. Today organizations adopt scorecards, benchmarks, and best practices; train managers in diversity conferences; and give diversity leadership seminars. But are results real and measurable?

DIVERSITY'S IMPACT ON PERFORMANCE

Elizabeth McArthur (2005), founder of Diversity at Work Ltd., paints a dire picture for companies that do not incorporate good diversity practices:

> Businesses that fail to successfully manage diversity will suffer economic and social consequences. A workplace culture that allows low morale, employee turnover, harassment, discrimination, absenteeism, and disruption to work teams results in a loss of productivity. When individuals are marginalized or isolated by their co-workers and/or managers because of cultural differences, the outcome is a poisoned work environment, contributing to employee absenteeism [p. 1].

In 1996, a group of social scientists at Business Opportunities for Leadership Diversity (BOLD) Institute launched a five-year study on how to leverage diversity for business performance. Although no firm data support a causal link, the study found that "a match between the demographic composition of the workforce and the firm's customer base will yield higher sales, thus enhancing organizational performance" (2003, p. 7).

Research by Joshi and Jackson (2003) suggests that diversity in teams has a positive effect on business outcomes because of increased diversity in social networks that enhance performance.

Laura Liswood, senior adviser on diversity issues to Goldman Sachs, is more prudent: "There is a connection between diversity and financial success, but typical profit-and-loss systems don't capture the benefits that diversity creates. A lot of the benefits are not quantifiable, but it's also true that we have not devoted the same level of resources to attempts to quantify diversity results. . . . Human resource metrics don't have the same analytical power as other business metrics" (Hansen, 2003a, p. 28).

Positive Corporate Image

Research (Wright, Ferris, Hiller, & Kroll, 1995) has shown that stock values temporarily increased in companies that received awards for exemplary affirmative action programs. Conversely, companies with discrimination lawsuits pending suffered losses in stock valuation. This finding suggests that companies that implement high-quality diversity programs benefit from positive publicity and public confidence, at least in the short term.

Recruiting and Retention

According to Elizabeth McArthur (2005, p. 1), "Businesses with an effective diversity strategy will have a leading edge in employee productivity and retention. At a time when the pending retirement of the baby boomers will strip the workforce of massive numbers of skilled workers, businesses will experience a shortage of workers to replace retirees. An inclusive work environment is simply good business. The loss of one employee due to poor management practices is too many!"

C. J. Prince (2005, para. 10) gives this caveat: "Exactly how to set goals becomes tricky, because to some CEOs, putting a specific number on hiring smacks of a quota system, which can undermine minority candidates and make them feel like token hires."

Increasing competition over top talent in the global business village has contributed to mobility and excellence of the candidate pool. The BOLD Institute study (2003, p. 7) confirms that "when HR practices support the creation of a workforce that has the skills needed to turn diversity into an advantage, diversity is more likely to lead to positive performance outcomes."

The Cost of Poor Practices

While good diversity management keeps turnover low, poor practices have the opposite effect. Accountability in diversity has come to the forefront with the increasing number of discrimination lawsuits that corporations have faced in the past decade. Jennifer Hicks (2005), a cultural diversity researcher, gives the following statistics:

- Sexual harassment charges increased 146 percent between 1992 and 2001. They have increased 150,000 percent since 1980.
- Pregnancy discrimination charges increased 126 percent between 1992 and 2001.
- Sexual discrimination charges increased 112 percent during the same period.
- Racial discrimination charges increased 484 percent between the 1980–1989 decade and the 1990–1999 decade.
- National origin charges increased 112 percent in the period 1992 to 2001.

In May 2005, Marc Thomas, chief executive of GE Aviation Materials LP, accused the parent company, General Electric, of discriminating against him and other black managers in awarding pay, promotions, and perks, claiming that GE refused to reward or promote him despite his excellent performance record. The lawsuit seeks $450 million in damages as well as back pay, increases in pay, benefits, and a broad change in General Electric's personnel practices. General Electric said it would seek dismissal of the lawsuit.

While the majority of discrimination suits are justified, some high-profit multinationals complain of being easy targets for discrimination lawsuits, saying they suffer from the supersized "Microsoft effect." Is the diversity movement suffering from an excess of judicial zeal? Sally Pipes, president and CEO of the Pacific Research Institute for Public Policy, a free market think tank, thinks so. "The lesson [of a recent class action suit against Wal-Mart] for successful companies is that if they want to treat people as individuals, and not members of a victim group or class, they could face a three-pronged attack of greed, feminism, and judicial activism. This, not competition, is what turns the marketplace into a hostile environment" (Pipes, 2004, para. 12). Justified or not, the negative fallout from a lawsuit for an organization can be devastating in terms of image and financial loss.

Diversity and Cost Control

Controlling operating costs is an area positively affected by implementing good diversity practices. According to its corporate Web site, the 3M Corporation (2005) is pursuing relationships with small, minority-owned, and woman-owned businesses as a diversity and growth strategy with many benefits to the bottom line.

A Right Response to Advocacy

Empowerment of minorities (defined as groups of people who differ racially or politically from a larger group of which they are a part) is a reality that has changed the business landscape forever. In addition to financial soundness, businesses are now ranked on diversity friendliness in hiring, promoting, and retaining. In 2004, the National Association for the Advancement of Colored People developed a methodology and ranking for assessing results in integration of "African-Americans and other people of color" among major industries including hospitality, telecommunications, banking, and automotive. In the 2004 NAACP Report Card for Lodging Industry, the Intercontinental group (formerly Six Continents) improved its ranking in 2003 from tenth place with a score of 2.39 (C average) to third place in 2004 with a score 2.88 (B−average) among thirteen hotels chains evaluated.

A Company That Has Managed Diversity Well

In July 2004, Bank of America was again named one of the "50 Best Companies for Minorities" in *Fortune* magazine's seventh annual listing. In a formerly male-dominated industry, Bank of America's labor pool of 143,000 employees is 70 percent female, underscoring the trend that women are fast becoming the majority in the financial world. Cited for seven straight years by *Working Mother* magazine as one of its "10 Best Companies for Working Mothers," this company is successful in addressing some of the critical issues of its labor pool.

WHAT IS NEW SINCE TITLE VII?

In the United States, Title VII of the 1964 Civil Rights Act provided the widest umbrella of protection for American workers of diverse origins, prohibiting employment decisions based on race, color, religion, sex, and national origin. Protected classes in the United States include African Americans, Asian Americans, Latinos, Native Americans, and women. In 1965, Executive Order 11246 required government contractors to make affirmative (corrective) actions regarding discrimination by promoting "good faith efforts to recruit, hire and promote women, minorities, veterans and people with disabilities." Legislation followed protecting workers against discrimination on the basis of age (1967), pregnancy (1978), citizenship status (1986), and disabilities (1990).

In 1972, the EOC created the Equal Employment Opportunity Commission as a watchdog institution for minority rights. In 1991, the Civil Rights Acts forbid minority quotas, placed the burden of proof on employers, and for the first time allowed monetary punitive damages for discrimination victims. Further equal employment opportunity legislation protected workers who choose to take unpaid absences (1993) or fulfill military obligations (1994).

Has Legislation Changed Anything?

The plethora of laws aimed at protecting the rights of women and minorities enacted over the past thirty years has forever changed the landscape of diversity management. Phenomenal sums have been awarded in discrimination settlements, such as a 2005 ruling against retail giant Wal-Mart. Patrick Brady, a twenty-one year old with cerebral palsy, was hired for a position in a pharmacy unit and claimed he was subsequently reassigned to other responsibilities, such as garbage collection. Brady, who quit Wal-Mart after four days, was awarded $5 million in punitive damages, a sum likely to be reduced to less than $1 million in appeal. Organizations today know that while implementing diversity is first and foremost a moral issue, failure to do so can seriously damage reputation, business solutions, and the bottom line.

Women and Diversity

Although the glass ceiling has cracked slightly, it is not yet shattered despite the handful of women CEOs running companies worldwide. In May 2005, the World Economic Forum's Global Competitiveness Programme published the first-ever study on the global gender gap. The survey analyzing fifty-eight nations according to economic participation, political and decision-making empowerment, educational attainment, and health and well-being shows that the slimmest overall gender gap exists among Norwegian, Icelandic, Danish, and Finnish nationals. According to the study's findings, Canada ranked seventh, followed by the United Kingdom, Germany, and Australia; the United States ranked seventeenth, Russia thirty-first, and Greece fiftieth; and Pakistan, Turkey, and Egypt scored lowest in gender parity. Saadia Zahidi (2005), economist at the World Economic Forum and coauthor of the ground-breaking study, commented in an interview, "Countries that do not fully take advantage of one-half of the talent in their population are misallocating their human resources" (Zahidi & Lopez-Claros, 2005, para. 9).

In 2005, only nine female CEOs ran Fortune 500 companies, including Anne Mulcahey of Xerox Corporation, Margaret C. Whitman of e-Bay, and Patricia Russo of Lucent Technologies. Two non-U.S. citizens rank in the *Wall Street Journal*'s Top Ten Women Executives: Rose Marie Bravo of Burberry's and Xie Qihua, chairwoman of Shanghai Baosteel, China's largest iron and steel producer. Anne Fudge, CEO of Young & Rubicam, is the only African American woman to run a global advertising firm. Other notable examples of women executives are Fumiko Hayashi, president of BMW Tokyo; Wu Xiaoling, deputy governor of the People's Bank of China; Naina Lal Kidwai, Indian deputy CEO of HSBC; and Ana Patricia Botin of the Banco Español de Credito.

African Americans and Ethnic Minorities

According to the American Community Report of the U.S. Census Bureau (2003), in 2003 approximately 12 percent of the population was composed of African Americans, 13 percent was Hispanic/Latino, 4 percent was Asian American, and Native Americans made up 1 percent of the population. Despite advances for minorities due to equal opportunity legislation and practices, the State of Working

America 2003 biennial report notes that 20 percent of whites work at very low-paid jobs, while African Americans account for 30 percent and Hispanics 39.4 percent of below-poverty-level workers. Diversity legislation is slowly changing these disparities.

An example of minority clout is the 2004 ruling against Abercrombie & Fitch, a U.S. retail apparel chain of seven hundred stores and twenty-two thousand employees. Judges awarded a $40 million class action settlement to Latino, African American, Asian American, and women plaintiffs after establishing inequalities in recruitment, hiring, job assignment, training, and promotion. The settlement required the company to institute verifiable diversity programs such as a new internal complaint system and benchmarks for hiring and promoting women and minority employees according to goals, not quotas. In the future, job ads will be posted in publications targeting minorities, and the company has hired twenty-five trained diversity recruiters.

Hispanics and Latinos

Hispanics come from the mainly white Iberian Peninsula of Spain and Portugal, while Latinos are indigenous people groups from Central and South America and Mexico, according to the Latino-Hispanic Historical Society in Los Angeles. The July 2005 U.S. Census Report revealed that one of every five Americans under age eighteen is Hispanic or Latino, and there are 41.3 million Hispanics and Latinos of a total U.S. population of 294 million. While this immigrant population has traditionally entered the job market at the low end, Rodolfo O. de la Garza, a political science professor at Columbia University, feels that the growing Hispanic population reflects a "powerful cultural transformation" as part of a blended culture that is "influencing and being influenced more openly" by mainstream American mores and attitudes (Files, 2005).

Monster.com Takes on the Minority Market

Monster.com, the leading global online career site, has put diversity communication into practice. According to a 2004 Monster Meter (online) poll, 65 percent of Americans do not think their company has taken an active role to promote diversity. To create a better match between job seekers and employers intent on building diverse workforce environments, Monster's Diversity and Inclusion launched a new product solution, the Strategic Partner Network. In January 2005, Monster created an alliance with CCI (Community Connect Inc.), operator of BlackPlanet.com, AsianAvenue.com, and MiGente.com. The new entity gives recruiters immediate access to the most popular online communities for African Americans, Asian Americans, and Latinos. Other partners include GayWork.com, NAACP, and ThirdAge. The site provides diversity job postings, a diversity résumé database, and targeted media placements designed to correlate brand image with being an employer of choice. Additional resources on the site are a free diversity newsletter (account creation required) and access to a list of diversity advisers. Monster announced that within months of the alliance with CCI, more than 400,000 new members had joined the network.

Age Discrimination

In Asia, India, and Africa, elderly people are respected and often honored, while in Western European and Anglo-Saxon cultures, the aging are too often viewed as less efficient workers who have outlived their usefulness. The rights to work past mandatory retirement age, obtain a loan, or even exist in the eyes of others are some of the issues older people face. Positive Aging, an advertising agency specializing in promoting older consumers, proclaims: "WARNING! Ignoring the New Consumer Majority (adults 40 +) could be hazardous to your business!" (www.positiveaging.com). While laws against age discrimination go back thirty years in the United States, twenty years in Canada, and ten in Australia, no such laws currently exist in the United Kingdom, although a project is slated for a vote in 2006.

In a 2005 decision, *Smith* v. *City of Jackson,* the U.S. Supreme Court made it easier for employees over age forty to allege age discrimination, ruling that employers can be held liable even if they did not "intend harm." This decision could cause backlash for the 75 million older American workers who make up almost half the active workforce, as employers may now fear legal reprisals from this group and be more hesitant to hire or keep them.

WHAT CAN (AND PROBABLY WILL) GO WRONG WITH DIVERSITY EFFORTS

Communications fail every day. Successful communication requires that the message and meaning intended by the sender are correctly received and decoded by the receiver. Dattner (2003) asserts that this is no mean feat. Even when words and nonverbal language are perfectly understood, additional information is necessary to communicate successfully across cultures. In general, cross-cultural miscommunication derives from the mistaken belief that words and actions have the same meaning across cultures. The closer the surface attributes of cultures appear to be, the more that communicators tend to rely on mistaken assumptions.

In one communication model, the ladder of inference, people select data to ignore or register and then interpret those data according to their values, contexts, and assumptions. They then draw selective conclusions, adopt beliefs based on those conclusions, and take action at the top of the ladder. However, people can and do reach different conclusions and beliefs, and when they disagree, they tend to shout their "obvious" conclusions from the tops of their respective ladders, making it difficult to resolve differences and share knowledge (Senge et al., 1994).

Ethnocentricity

Intercultural misunderstandings can occur when people make false assumptions based on their own culture. Managers should accept cultural differences in their employees and respect them for them; contradictions make people interesting.

Reacting in an ethnocentric manner is dubbed the "be like me" attitude by intercultural researchers Thomas and Inkson (2004), who give the following advice for successful intercultural negotiations:

- Gain the knowledge to anticipate differences by learning the codes and conventions of the groups you plan to deal with.
- Practice mindfulness. Observe the context as well as how the message is delivered.
- Develop adaptive skills. Some degree of adaptation seems to improve relationships; too much may cause suspicion.

Ethics and Diversity

Ethical issues can also be a source of cultural clashes due to diversity. The difference between ethics and values is not always clear. The SHRM Ethics Resource Center in Washington, D.C. (2003), found that the percentage of respondents who had occasionally observed ethical misconduct in the workplace rose from 33 percent in 1997 to 46 percent in 2003, while the increase in those who had often observed misconduct more than tripled from 2 percent in 1997 to 7 percent in 2003.

HOW TO IMPROVE DIVERSITY SKILLS

Managers who lack experience in diversity issues may fall into common traps. Diversity experts Thomas and Woodruff (1999) affirm:

> Diversity-mature companies adopt a framework and process to guide [their] diversity efforts. These keep them on track by identifying what will be required for success and how success will be measured. Companies with less diversity maturity lack such a framework and process. These companies often fall into diversity traps.
>
> - Activity trap. Managers measure success in terms of the number and magnitude of activities.
> - Public relations trap. Managers measure success by how well the media and other external entities speak of their efforts.

- Training trap. Managers measure success by the amount of training that has been completed.
- Awareness trap. Managers measure success by the degree of "awareness" that exists [pp. 223–224].

Managing diversity effectively, according to Hal Jones, chief consulting officer for Roosevelt Thomas Training and Consulting, requires a strategic diversity management process rather than one-off efforts. His suggestions include feedback and rewards functions for all groups and encouraging across-the-board mentoring and career development. Jones also recommends that roughly 25 percent of a manager's performance bonus be tied to measurable goals of hiring, retention, and promotion (Hadden & Catlette, 2001).

Benchmarking Diversity Results

Ryder System, a U.S. supply chain company with thirty thousand employees, uses metrics to evaluate litigation costs as well as minority hiring and promotion numbers. The company requires diversity training for all employees with additional emphasis for managers on "managing differences within heterogeneous groups and pushing employees toward quality performance. The program also teaches litigation avoidance by describing scenarios and behaviors that put the company at risk of lawsuits" (Hansen, 2003b, p. 31).

Core Skills for Managers

Cultural competency is achieved when managers are capable of incorporating ethnic and cultural considerations into all areas of the workplace environment. Three core skills can help, according to Thomas and Woodruff (1999, pp. 229–231): "The ability to identify diversity mixtures. . . . The ability to analyze the mixtures and related tensions. . . . The ability to select an appropriate response."

IMPLEMENTING AND COMMUNICATING DIVERSITY INITIATIVES

Once a diversity plan has been designed, managers and communicators face the challenge of implementing and communicating it to all stakeholders. A set of diversity practices labeled "best of the best" by the Federal Communications Commission (2004) recommends the following measures: (1) direct support from the CEO and top executives, (2) direct communication for diversity efforts throughout the organization, (3) specific goals and objectives and measurable evaluation criteria, (4) diversity goals and objectives in the performance appraisal and compensation processes, and (5) training and guidance to management and staff.

Among the vehicles recommended for educating employees about the benefits of diversity are employee newsletters, intranet Web site announcements, formal adoption of a diversity value statement, publicizing the appointment of senior (diversity) executives, face-to-face meetings, and focus group sessions.

As managers, if we take responsibility for understanding and respecting cultural differences, learn how they affect the process of business and professional communication, and deal with the problems and opportunities that occur along the way, we will acquire the core skills necessary to manage diversity in the twenty-first century.

References

Boyacigiller, N. A., Kleinberg, M. J., Phillips, M. E., & Sackmann, S. A. (2004). Conceptualizing culture: Elucidating the streams of research in international cross-cultural research. In B. J. Punnett & O. Shenkar (Eds.), *Handbook of international management research* (2nd ed.). Ann Arbor: University of Michigan Press.

Business Opportunities for Leadership Development Institute. (2003). *The effects of diversity on business performance: Report of the diversity research network.* Hoboken, NJ: Wiley.

Dattner, B. (2003). *A framework for understanding cross-cultural misunderstandings.* New York: Dattner Consulting LLC. http://www.dattnerconsulting.com/papercross.doc.

European Commission Green Paper. (2004). *EU approach to managing economic migration.* Brussels: European Union.

Federal Communications Commission, Subcommittee on Career Advancement. (2004, December). *Diversity: Best of the best practices.* Washington, DC: FCC Advisory Committee on Diversity for Communications in the Digital Age.

Files, J. (2005, June 10). Report describes immigrants as younger and more diverse. *New York Times,* A12.

Graddol, D. (2004, March 18). *Voice of America* [radio interview].

Hadden, R., & Catlette, B. (2001). *Contented cows give better milk.* Germantown, TN: Saltillo Press.

Hansen, F. (2003a, April). Diversity's business case doesn't add up. *Workforce Management,* 28–34.

Hansen, F. (2003b, April). Tracking the value of diversity programs. *Workforce Management,* 31.

Hicks, J. (2005). Number of discrimination suits soar. *IM Diversity.* http://www.imdiversity.com/Villages/Careers/articles/hicks_discrimination_suits_soar.asp.

Joshi, A., & Jackson, S. S. (2003). *Managing diversity to enhance cooperation in organizations.* Hoboken, NJ: Wiley.

McArthur, E. (2005, April). Managing diversity for success. *Link and Learn newsletter.* http://www.linkageinc.com/company/news_events/link_learn_enewsletter.

National Association for the Advancement of Colored People. (2004). *Score card 2004 NAACP Lodging Industry.* http://www.naacp.org/inc/docs/economy/economic_lodging_report_card-04.pdf.

Pipes, S. (2004, July 8). Discrimination suit against Wal-Mart obtains class-action status. *Contrarian: News and Comments on Women's Issues, 8*(9). http://www.pacificresearch.org/pub/con/2004/con_04–07.html.

Prince, C. J. (2005, April). Doing diversity, Chief Executive, no. 207. http://www.chiefexecutive.net/depts/management/207.htm.

Schramm, J., & Burke, M. E. (2004, June). *Workplace forecast: A strategic outlook, 2004–5.* Washington, DC: Author.

Senge, P., Kleiner, A., Roberts, C., Ross, R. B., & Smith, B. J. (1994). *Fifth discipline fieldbook: Strategies and tools for building a learning organization.* New York: Doubleday.

SHRM. (2003). *Ethics Resource Center 2003 business ethics survey.* Alexandria, VA: Author.

Smith v. *City of Jackson,* No. 03-1160. (March 30, 2005).

U.S. Census Bureau. (2003). *State of working America report.* Washington, DC: U.S. Government Printing Office.

U.S. Census Bureau. (2005). *State of working America report.* Washington, DC: U.S. Government Printing Office.

Thomas, D. C., & Inkson, K. (2004). *Cultural intelligence.* San Francisco: Berrett-Koehler.

Thomas, R. R. Jr., & Woodruff, M. I. (1999). *Building a house for diversity.* New York: Amacom.

3M Corporation. (2005). *Supplier diversity.* http://www.3m.com/about3m/diversity/supplier.html.

Women and Diversity Wow! Facts Report. (2001). Washington, DC: Business Women's Network.

Wright, P., Ferris, S. P., Hiller, J. S., & Kroll, M. (1995). Competitiveness through the management of diversity: Effects on stock price valuation. *Academy of Management Journal, 38*(1), 272–288.

Zahidi, S. (2005). *Interview.* World Economic Forum, Global Competitiveness Programme. http://www.weforum.org.

Zahidi, S., & Lopez-Claros, A. (2005). *Women's eEmpowerment: Measuring the global gender gap.* World Economic Forum, Global Competitiveness Programme. http://www.weforum.org.

CHAPTER FIFTEEN

Communication Counsel in Corporate Communication

The Care and Feeding of Leadership

Mark Schumann

A few years ago, my mother was trying to describe what I do for a living to the members of her bridge club.

"I thought your son was a reporter," one of her friends said, "because he studied journalism."

"No," my mother responded.

"I thought he was in business," another remarked.

"Sort of," my mother answered, "but he doesn't really run anything."

"I've got it," another commented. "He is a waiter at a restaurant," perhaps remembering one of my summer jobs.

Then my mother stopped for a moment, thought, and concluded, "Well, what he does *is* a lot like being a waiter. He makes sure people get fed."

While my mother may have oversimplified what we communicators do for a living, her well-intentioned description does capture the essence of our mission. As communicators within organizations, we are in the business of making sure people get fed, only the nutrition of our concern is the food for the soul to emotionally connect people with organizations . . . employees, customers, shareholders, members of the community, and other stakeholders.

It is a unique role. After all, we are not really journalists even though many of us studied journalism. We are not really marketers even though an organization's brand is a fundamental part of our work.

The most significant contribution we can make to an organization is to be its conscience. We orchestrate and influence how the organization provides a steady diet of authentic information to inspire, clarify, and connect stakeholders. That means we need to wake up each day and ask ourselves, "How are we helping people get the truth they hunger for?" That need for authenticity is important for any audience, and it is especially true for employees because they are the ones who deliver what the organization promises.

Certainly there is a fundamental need for truth. American workers are hungry for the truth but simply do not feel they are being fed. In a Towers Perrin study (2004), a thousand randomly selected employees from American companies revealed that American workers were increasingly cynical and suspicious of information they received from their employers, whether it was about a corporate strategy or the details of career opportunities. Just over half (51 percent) of the respondents believed their company generally told employees the truth, and almost a fifth (19 percent) disagreed. And 51 percent believed their companies tried too hard to spin the truth. Employees believed their companies were more truthful with shareholders (60 percent) and customers (58 percent) than with employees.

As communicators, we can do many things to make our organizations more credible. But it takes more than strong communication skills to influence an organization's commitment to truth. Our work must begin with how we counsel the leaders of organizations to support and nurture a transparent communication experience starting with how we help the organization find, keep, and motivate the right people in the right jobs at the right times. That requires a commitment of leadership to authentically engage employees in an ongoing dialogue. Communicators should be at the center of orchestrating this experience so employees ultimately will feel fed.

IT ALL BEGINS WITH LEADERSHIP

Behind every great leader is a communicator—or several. A leader is a brand, the bravado, the boss. A leader sets the tone for candor, simplicity, empathy. How we help capture what is inside a leader's mind and heart—the values, beliefs, commitments, and convictions—will make a difference in how employees emotionally connect with the organization.

It is not as simple as writing a speech or a news story. That is what separates this work from conventional reporting or marketing. A reporter looks for truth and reports facts without an emotional perspective. A marketer may on occasion convey the emotional dimension without necessarily focusing on the facts. We have to do both.

As counsel to leaders, we must position the leader to convey what is true within a realistic context and with a sincere conviction that carries emotional substance. This is a constant and consistent effort to project the soul of someone we need employees to trust. How we position and package, nurture, and leverage a leader to create this connection may be the most important contribution we can make. We can have more impact on an organization, its results, and the quality of the experience for employees the more effectively we provide this necessary counsel.

It is not easy. Leaders have egos and not always consistent communication skills. The egos can get in the way of making accurate assessments of the communication skills. A few years ago there was a CEO who fancied himself to be a strong communicator. We were making a videotape address to employees when all of a sudden, he stopped the camera to change the lighting. When we asked what he was doing, he said, "I want to shoot this the way I shot my grandson's birthday party last week." Another CEO once remarked, "I know how to write. I write letters to my kids every day." The very qualities that make someone an effective leader behind the screen may make the leader ultimately challenging to work with when it is time to appear in front of the screen.

As employees, we need leaders to inspire us to connect emotionally. That takes more than media. As communicators, we must reach beyond our command of tactics to be a counselor, a coach, a conscience. We must discover the authenticity of the leader before we can shape an image based on what the organization and the employees need and who the leader is.

THE FUNDAMENTAL EQUATION

A clear way to imagine how to counsel leaders is to think of our work as a basic equation:

Capture a leader's authenticity + Feed the employees what they need and want = Create the emotional connection to the organization

First, we use our insight and instinct to capture a leader's authenticity. Second, we use our communication skills to leverage that authenticity to feed the audience. The result is an emotional connection we create with the audience. Let us take a look at each part of this equation.

Capturing the Authenticity of the Leader

People often describe our work as corporate storytellers. We do help people in organizations share stories that make up lasting fabric. Stories capture interest, they are easy to remember and repeat, and they create legends. As we develop our stories about our organizations, we create characters for our leaders to play.

But this is real life, not fiction; a business, not an art colony, so we cannot create a character outside a person's authenticity. Our creative challenge is to take who a leader is and use our instinct, insight, and skill to shape that leader into what people need to experience: to capture this leader at his or her best; create a comfort zone in which the leader can most effectively connect; understand, as with any great athlete or artist, the importance of the warm-up, the necessity for practice or rehearsal, the most effective way to deliver feedback, and the necessity of reinforcement. In this way our work is similar to coaching a political candidate during a campaign. We are always in the middle of an election. Politicians face voters every few years. Our leaders face the voters every day.

Over the years I have worked with many leaders in their efforts to connect with employees. From the best of these leaders, I have learned a number of lessons for any leader who wants to connect. For any communication counsel committed to capturing a leader's authenticity, here are a few:

- A leader must look good from every angle. The crowd never views a leader from one dimension simply because there is not one dimension to a crowd. This stage is not a proscenium. It is in the round. There is no way to hide. A leader is always on. There is no "off the record."

- A leader must sound good every minute. There is no tolerance for fatigue, anger, or artificial humanity. There is a constant demand for energy, passion, curiosity, sincerity, and empathy. It is all in the tone of voice. That tone is remembered longer than the words said.

- A leader must understand that there is a limit to what people can remember. We remember simple phrases. The best leaders pay attention to the sound bite as a way to simplify even the most complex topics. They time their messages for the ever-shrinking attention span.

- The best leaders make anyone feel as if, for that moment, only two people exist: the employee and the leader. We worked with a CEO who was well known for connecting with employees. As years passed and his organization grew, that must have become quite a chore. But the legend continued because of how the CEO connected: one person at a time.

- A leader must project warmth, enthusiasm, and command. The best leaders demonstrate they are in charge. It is not that they do all the work, but they have a vision, a plan, and a clarity of purpose, and they care.

- A leader must say *we* more than *I*. The best leaders speak in the collective, whether news is good or bad. They never take individual credit and always refer to the team. They lead by inclusion, not exclusion. They never send the signal that people are lucky to see them. It is actually the leaders who are lucky to have the chance to connect.

- A leader must capitalize on defining moments. All leaders face situations that define how they connect with others. How we help leaders handle such situations can define the character we bring to the work. Such moments do not happen by accident. It is up to us to help shape how a leader responds. For example, we worked with a CEO at a moment his company faced a potential disaster. Because he was well rehearsed in the basics of how to communicate, he was willing to be coached on how to make the most of the moment and endeavor to turn a potentially negative situation into a positive one. By realizing this could be a defining moment and relying on the fundamental training he had received, this CEO maximized the opportunity and the connection.

• A leader must be willing to give us time. We cannot do the things we need to do if we cannot access the people we need. Without time with a leader, it is impossible for us to capture the leader's authenticity. We are not magicians. We must approach leaders with the conviction that we will get to know who they are, how they think, and how they work in order to help them make smart choices about what others see. We can capture a leader's authenticity only if we have an authentic relationship.

• A leader must be willing to speak from the heart. Communication with employees requires a glimpse into a leader's soul. Without approaching the inappropriate or contradicting the message of the moment, a leader must reveal something of the self each time he or she reports or responds. Employees have a fundamental need to know who is in charge, not simply to recognize the name on the e-mail.

Feeding Employees What They Need and Want

Feeding the audience is not as simple as delivering food from the kitchen. Our role as communication counsel is to lead the leader to the feeding. That is easier said than done. Time is limited, patience is limited, and results are expected. We need to choose what we can control and influence. Part of this is about the content and part about the delivery. Part is recognizing the simple ways we can help a leader offer what others need. Here are seven things we can do each day:

• We can help a leader balance the informal and the formal. We can carefully orchestrate a leader's movements, where a leader goes, whom a leader talks with. One CEO we worked with would give us two hours a week, to structure as we needed, whether he was in or out of town. We tailored his appearances for maximum opportunity to feed the grapevine positively. As we structured his time with employees, we carefully followed a four-to-one ratio, with four informal appearances to every formal one. How we perceive a leader is more effectively created by what appears to be spontaneous compared to what is obviously orchestrated. He spent most of his time simply walking around, saying hello, and engaging in informal conversations, and he connected.

- We can help a leader appear to be spontaneous. Virtually every moment we created for this CEO was planned and scripted, but he never looked or acted canned. That did not necessarily come naturally to him. He rehearsed, and he took a lot of pride in how natural he appeared. To make this happen, we led him through many practice sessions of how to be spontaneous. Essentially he rehearsed enough to be able to wing it naturally with employees.

- We can help a leader focus on captive moments. As we arranged the CEO's schedule, we paid careful attention to how, when, and where employees would be captive, such as where they would be waiting around and killing time. We would make sure, for example, that he was visible around the lunch hour when people were milling about and standing in line at the cafeteria. We made sure he was seen doing his "informal thing" by as many people as possible. We made sure that we scheduled his time so he could be in front of as many employees as possible without repeatedly seeing the same employees.

- We can help a leader offer substance, not just style. Never did we simply send this CEO out without a carefully constructed message. He always had something to say, so employees would tell each other about seeing him; they would pass on information he had offered. Such tidbits became his news flash, and we incorporated this element into every communication approach. To prepare him, we would place his key messages on note cards he kept in his pocket. That way we could vary the message by audience segment. We trained him to check the note card before reaching the next destination.

- We can help a leader believe in symbols. We worked with another CEO who made annual trips to company locations to conduct employee briefings. The subject of one round would be cost control. Like many other CEOs, this man did not like to fly commercial airlines. He preferred to travel by private jet. That probably would not be a problem for most companies, but this happened to be an airline experiencing financial challenges. The idea of a CEO flying a private plane because he did not like airports did not really work, but he insisted, so it was no surprise that he got some negative feedback when he arrived in the first city in a private jet to deliver a message about cost control. As his counsel, we helped him discover how people savor a symbol long after they remember the content. Fortunately, he learned how to board at the airport gate.

- We can help a leader remember that actions speak louder than words. We often talk about the say-do gap that can exist in organizations. My experience reinforces how real that can be. Part of the job as counsel is to help leaders realize when they are communicating and how much communicating they do without words. We must essentially protect them from undermining themselves in unguarded moments and give them enough understanding of the impact of what they do so they consider what they do in advance of their actions. Much of this is a collection of small actions in tiny moments: saying hello to someone, disciplining someone in a public place, being detected as arrogant or detached or insincere. It is up to us to help them recognize that what they do is as much a part of the story as what they say.

• We can help a leader measure the impact. We cannot simply counsel based on instinct. We must counsel based on fact. For the most part, we can easily collect all the facts we need. We can, and should, go to employees on a regular basis to ask them what information they are hungry for and how that affects their emotional commitment to the organization. We can, and should, go to them after each episode of a communication experience to determine its effectiveness. We can, and should, go to them with a pulse poll any time we need to quickly determine if a message or a messenger rings true. We can learn a lot from the polling of politicians as we counsel a leader to make smart choices about how to spend time and capital and remind the leader what a difference candid communication can create.

Creating an Emotional Connection Between the Employees and the Organization

If we capture a leader's authenticity and feed the audience in a transparent experience, we can create emotional connections within our organizations. That requires us to, in addition to keeping our fundamental communication skills sharp, approach our role as counsel with a great deal of sensitivity. This role as corporate conscience boils down to a few basic rules, honed over time, that are present every day we work:

• Be sensitive when developing the message. What we create for an internal audience is fundamentally different from what we develop externally. Outside the walls, the layering of the story may closely follow the traditional inverted pyramid we learned in journalism. Inside the walls, the story should closely follow a piece of literature, with a carefully planned opening, build, and ending. On the inside, our primary reason for creating an emotional connection is to help the organization recruit and retain the people it needs.

• Be sensitive when coaching the voice. It is not just the content or how the story develops. The key to the emotional connection is the clear voice that captures the essence of the leader—the tone. We have to decide how we want an audience to react and what tone is needed to generate that reaction. We worked with a CEO who was a down-to-earth, salt-of-the-earth leader, as engaging in person as any leader could be. But he was a chain smoker and a chain cougher. His cough got in the way of his ability to communicate in person. So we put him on video, cut the cough through sound editing, and created the authentic persona of an engaged leader.

• Be sensitive in selecting the platforms. The setting matters. Several years ago, a CEO had an important story to tell to retain key employees, but he was dull. We asked him where he went for inspiration, hoping to catch a glimpse into his soul. He began talking about his property in Wyoming, the hills he walked, and the lessons he learned about the long-term view of business strategy by observing nature. That is where we took our camera for him to tell his story because he was comfortable and authentic.

• Be sensitive how you coach a leader. It is possible for a leader to overrehearse. We must artfully coach around this. It is not easy because most leaders like to be prepared for everything and resist spontaneity. Our challenge is to help them see and trust what spontaneity can produce. We worked with a CEO who wanted to deliver a key message to her constituents. The message was eight minutes long, and she insisted on extensive rehearsal. By the end of the rehearsal period, there was not a spontaneous breath left. No one was happy. So after we finished the shoot, we asked her for a couple of minutes to grab some additional footage for a class we were teaching. We managed to ask her to deliver the same words for this other purpose. Without feeling the pressure of the moment, she was magic. So we used these shots in the final piece. When she viewed the tape later, she said, "Maybe we didn't need all that rehearsal after all."

• Be sensitive to how a leader tells the story. At the foundation of how we position a leader to communicate is what we orchestrate to convey truth. And we always acknowledge that a leader operating behind the screen must put on the public face before emerging in front of the screen. I worked with an authentic CEO who has total command over how he portrays himself. He realized that as a leader in a role, he needed to be carefully scripted and carefully rehearsed, yet had to remain within a zone of credibility. One time we shot a video of him in a parody of an early morning news show. To capture his magic, we said, "If this approach is to simulate an early morning news show, we want to shoot this early in the morning, so if we are pretending to be on the air at seven, we are going to shoot this at seven." The result was that he was believable, the setting was credible, and the message was delivered.

• Be sensitive to the authentic "food" people need to hear. In the end, all the counsel is only as worthwhile as the results we create. Emotional connections do not simply happen because communication is clear. They happen if the content and delivery hit the right balance to be relevant and if we feed the hunger that people experience. We can help people understand what the organization is, what it stands for, what the brand promises. This is what makes the difference for an employee between doing a job and delivering the brand. We can help people believe what the organization needs to accomplish and how critical individual contributions can be, how each person can make a difference to what the organization accomplishes, and how it feels to work for a place that succeeds. We can help motivate people and coach the organization to recognize and reward those who commit and contribute and answer the "what's in it for me" question to emotionally connect and consistently perform.

LESSONS FOR COMMUNICATORS IN COUNSELING

A few years ago, my mother asked me what it takes to do our work. I told her about the people I had worked with, the mentors who had shared, the tough moments and rewarding ones. In the end, we as communicators are grounded in what we bring to an organization and to leaders; that can help us see the light of day and turn on the light for others. Here are the final lessons for us as an organization's conscience, as counsel to leaders, as communicators working to create emotional connections:

• Imagine. To continuously project what impact we can have, what relationship we can build between the leader and the people. To avoid limiting our palate to the formal, to appreciate the power of the informal, and to protect the CEO from himself or herself.

• Listen. To focus intently on what we hear, without feeling, without ego, without feeling compelled to respond until a leader is ready for us to speak until we get that cue that the space is open. To let the orders, opinion, observation be given, and then respond.

• Borrow trouble. To always imagine the worst, to picture everything that can go wrong, no matter how simple or complicated. Years ago, one of our jobs for a CEO was to map his jogging course when we were on the road. So we worked with our folks in a particular town and gave the CEO a map. One morning the phone rang at 5:00 A.M., and it was the CEO: "It's snowing, and I am lost. What do I do?" We had a backup crew waiting to pick him up.

• Ask the question. To be willing to ask the question no one else will ask but many will want to ask. We worked with a CEO who had just fired perhaps the third or fourth highest person in the company. As we often do with CEOs who want to deliver a message, we asked him to dictate or actually write what he wanted to say. He wrote a message that had the warmth of a message to captors, gilded with the ultimate phrase of corporate speak: "leaving to pursue other interests." We asked, "Did you can him?" He looked at us, somewhat stunned, and we remarked, "You know, we can't get too far unless we start with the truth and edit," because everyone will be asking the question we just asked. Then we rewrote the statement.

• Build the skills. To always remember to focus on our craft. This is all about our role: how we develop the skills we need to become the counsel a leader needs; how we strengthen our capabilities as thinkers, writers, coaches, and facilitators; how we use the ability to tell a story and package a leader to influence policy and connection; and how we maximize our participation in professional associations, such as the International Association of Business Communicators, to continue to stretch ourselves.

- Protect our credibility. To realize in the end that our personal credibility is ours to protect. That is the bell we must listen to. When it rings, we must act in order to be true to ourselves. For us to authentically portray leaders, we must work with authenticity and protect the standards we bring to our work.

We will make our mothers proud.

Reference

Towers Perrin. (2004). *Is it time to take the "spin" out of employee communication?* www.towersperrin.com/hrservices/webcache/towers/United_States/publications/ Reports/2004_Enhance_Corp_Cred/Enhance_corp_cred.pdf.

PART THREE

INTERNAL COMMUNICATION

CHAPTER SIXTEEN

Internal Communication

Brad Whitworth

Organizations—whether they are community hospitals, nonprofit associations, or multinational oil companies—exist for one reason: we can accomplish more when we work together as teams than we can as individuals. But to create a truly effective team, each member of that team must understand the organization's vision, goals, and objectives and then be moving in that direction. That is relatively easy for small organizations to accomplish.

When an organization grows in size or complexity or spreads across borders and time zones, it needs an internal communications program to help keep its team in sync. Think of it this way: with a little practice, a pianist and a violinist can create magic as a two-person team. But a 107-person symphony orchestra will always need a director to reach its musical goals.

There are three fundamental building blocks to any internal communications program: hierarchical communication, where CEOs, vice presidents, directors, managers, and frontline supervisors play a key role in the communications process; mass media communications, where newsletters, e-mail, videos, blogs, and other vehicles reach broad employee audiences; and, most often overlooked, the nonformal networks of invisible communicators that exist in every organization.

STARTING AT THE TOP

The simplest internal communication programs historically relied on an organization's existing hierarchical structure to move information to employees. Patterned after military command-and-control structures, such programs started with top-down messages driven from the highest levels of the firm, typically the chairman, president, or CEO. Successive layers of executives, managers, and supervisors were expected to push or cascade the messages down until they reached every employee. The more levels of management there were, the more difficult it was to ensure timely and consistent delivery of information. This cascading practice still exists and can work effectively for some organizations, particularly smaller and simpler ones. However, far too many companies rely on managers as their only means of communicating with their workforce. For large, complex organizations with many layers of management and multiple sites, this approach is not very timely or efficient.

Over the years, many organizations have been removing extra management layers and flattening their hierarchical structures, largely as cost-cutting moves to be more competitive. An unintended benefit has been improved internal communication. A big drawback to this form of internal communications is that some managers do a far better job of communicating with their teams than do others.

The Manager's Communication Role

Studies have consistently shown that most employees expect their immediate managers to share important company information and put it in context.

Communicating Change: Winning Employee Support for New Business Goals (Larkin & Larkin, 1994) describes five decades of research that prove the importance of communicating change through frontline supervisors. The research shows that immediate supervisors are the preferred source of information and have more credibility with employees than do senior executives.

Yet organizations generally have done a poor job of telling supervisors about their communication responsibilities, training them to communicate effectively, measuring how well they communicate, and rewarding the ones who do it well. Some managers are natural communicators; others require lots more coaching and training. It is not an easy thing for many managers to do, particularly those who have been promoted for their technical expertise over their interpersonal and leadership skills. Communication professionals can help by providing messages, structure, training, and coaching for supervisors and managers to build their communications prowess and effectiveness.

Managers must make sure that information moves smoothly and quickly to their direct reports and ultimately to every frontline employee. But managers must do far more than "tell" today. They also own the responsibility of putting information into context for their employees. They need to help interpret top-down messages and engage their employees in dialogue about the relevance of the information. They need to ask all the members of their teams the right questions to learn what is going on.

It does not stop there. Managers are responsible for moving that information, good and bad, from the front line back up to top executives. An organization's senior-most managers must know what is happening throughout their organizations, particularly where frontline people work with customers.

The real goal of creating this two-way exchange is not merely to tell employees what their executives want them to do or inform executives what customers are saying. The ultimate prize is to engage all employees and turn them all into active advocates for the organization.

Managers and supervisors should continually engage in a dialogue that moves the organization closer to fulfilling all of its desired goals. It also means that it is just as important for managers and supervisors to know how to listen as it is to talk.

Managers must be skilled in all forms of interpersonal communication, starting with one-on-one conversations. The immediate manager is the only one who can explain changes to job assignments, set individual goals, recognize on-the-job performance, and deliver appropriate individual rewards. The immediate manager is also in the best position to hold one-to-many discussions with her team about the group's role, create aspirational goals, highlight team performance, and reward the team's accomplishments.

There are topics where the immediate supervisor is probably not the most credible person to lead some discussions. For example, the chief financial officer is probably the most credible person to describe corporate financial results, and a human resource manager is likely the best person to explain complex benefit changes.

A supervisor's one-to-one and one-to-many conversations are best done face-to-face. But as organizations grow and spread, employees often find themselves reporting to remote managers. That means that managers must be comfortable with electronic substitutes for face-to-face communications.

The Third Dimension

Diverse organizations must also find effective ways to move information across their business units, breaking down the structural silos that they unknowingly build around departments. For example, a nurse in a hospital's neonatal unit needs to know a lot about his own department's goals and processes. He may not need to know equivalent details about the hospital's intensive-care unit, but he should know something about what is going on there.

It is a natural desire of executives and communicators to have every employee know everything that is going on everywhere within an organization. Although this is certainly an admirable goal, it is also an unrealistic one in a large or complex organization. We cannot expect every employee to either know everything that is taking place or, more important, want to know everything. Everybody needs to know something, but nobody needs to know everything.

Senior Leaders as Communicators

It takes more than middle managers and frontline supervisors to create an effective communications environment for an organization. It also requires senior leaders who take communications seriously and are model communicators themselves. Employees expect their senior executives to share their vision for the organization and their ideas and perspectives with the entire team. Employees deserve to know that their contributions are valued by senior leaders. They expect open, honest, credible communication. They expect leaders who are visible, approachable, and conversational. They want leaders who can tell compelling stories.

That means that effective executive communication is not merely a CEO's monthly column or an occasional e-mail message to all staff. It also includes regular staff meetings, all-employee gatherings, informal meetings, brown-bag lunches, and many other communication opportunities. It means that the top executives practice MBWA (management by wandering around) to engage employees firsthand in two-way discussions. It is listening to employees' concerns and sharing observations. It is talking about work-related topics and getting to know employees as individuals. It is asking about an employee's sick child as well as discussing a competitor's latest product innovation.

MBWA should not be limited to the organization's chairman or CEO, though it needs to start at the top. All members of the senior leadership team must be active participants in creating the proper communications environment. They cannot afford to hide in meetings or wait in their offices for issues to show up on their doorsteps. They must be out and about—in sales offices and break rooms and on the factory floor—actively asking questions of employees and providing answers when asked. And they should demand the same behavior from their direct reports.

An important by-product of effective senior management communications is credibility. When a senior leader tells a story, it has to be believable. When a leader sets a direction, it has to be clear. And when a leader makes a decision, it must be in alignment with the words he or she has been saying. The old adage, "Actions speak louder than words," is certainly true in the corporate world. Communicators, who often help craft leaders' messages, must constantly check to make sure that their actions and words are in sync. If the messages delivered by top leaders are not matched by their actions, employees have little choice but to believe the actions. Credibility suffers as a result.

MASS MEDIA: FILLING THE GAP

Organizations realized decades ago that they could not rely solely on managers and senior leaders to communicate with the workforce. Some managers took to communications naturally, and many took their communications role seriously. But others never shared information with their employees. Still others left out key information or added unwanted detail. Many never received needed skills training in communications.

As a result of this managerial inconsistency, internal communicators began bolstering their companies' internal communication programs with newsletters, magazines, bulletin boards, and other mass media solutions. They started simply, with modest publications that were often called house organs. Organizations turned to communication professionals with journalism and mass communication experience to produce these publications. The introduction of mass media channels provided a tremendous amount of control over the timing of the message and the consistency of the wording. Over the years, these mass media channels have expanded from their humble beginnings of mimeographed newssheets and bulletin board programs to include the latest electronic delivery mechanisms: videos, satellite TV networks, e-mails, intranet sites, Webcasts, broadcast voice mails, blogs, and many more.

The content in an internal communications program has evolved over time too. Many early employee newsletters focused on company picnics, bowling leagues, employees' service anniversaries, and the birth of employees' children. Photos were often staged "grip-and-grin" poses with a senior company official handing a trophy to a proud employee while shaking hands and mugging at the camera. You would be hard-pressed from the earliest employee publications to determine anything about a company's products, services, strategic business direction, competitors, or industry news.

That has changed. Today's best company publications deal honestly with an organization's strengths and weaknesses, its market successes and failures. The best internal magazines and newsletters deliver good news and bad news. The reporting and writing are powerful. The stories are about employees and their accomplishments. The publications invite employees to freely discuss what is going on in the organization and suggest ways to make things better. Photojournalists provide strong images that make the stories compelling and effective.

The best internal communication programs go far beyond publications. They mirror the broad range of mass media available in the world outside work. Technology has had a major impact in shaping these channels over the years. Communicators have been able to introduce the latest technology into their organizations over time.

Technology's impact was extremely limited at first, initially focused at making the communicator's job easier. The reason was that technology was expensive, and its applications were limited to number-crunching back-office functions that could be automated easily. From the 1950s to the 1970s, electric typewriters replaced clunky manual models. Linotype machines disappeared when computer-set type arrived. In the 1980s and 1990s, industrial video shoved 16mm film aside. Fax machines moved documents around the world in minutes instead of days. Word processing, publishing software, and personal computers simplified and speeded up production processes for newsletters and magazines.

Employees felt the true impact of technology on their communications when it moved from back-office production to frontline delivery. Computers moved from their glass-enclosed rooms and ultimately onto every employee's desk and into their homes. When PCs were put in employees' hands for e-mails, Internet access, blogging, instant messaging, and more, the formula changed forever. Recipients could become participants in the communications process. The one-way push of information from management to employees was now technologically enabled to become a two-way dialogue. Producing a sophisticated employee newsletter became less important than providing the appropriate electronic forum for two-way interaction between employees and the organization's leadership.

Most employees entering the workforce today have grown up in a digital world surrounded by PCs, CDs, DVDs, cellular phones, and video games. That societal shift has also fundamentally changed the organization's communications formula. Participation in the communications process is a given for workers today and an important objective for communicators.

The authors of *The Cluetrain Manifesto: The End of Business as Usual* (Locke, Levine, Searls, & Weinberger, 2001) are right: it is all about the conversation. They explain that the Internet lets people invent new ways to share relevant knowledge at blazing speed. They explain how conversations taking place on Web sites and message boards, and in e-mail and chatrooms, give employees a voice that can radically alter traditional businesses by challenging top-down communications hierarchy.

While mass media channels have overcome many of the shortcomings of top-down managerial communications, they are not perfect either. Readership studies show that not all employees read publications, e-mail, or intranet content. Video programs face distribution challenges that limit employee viewership. The personal computer has given huge numbers of employees access to vast amounts of information via e-mail and intranet sites. However, certain groups of employees still do not have easy access to PCs because of the nature of their jobs. They do not sit at a desk eight hours each day. They are driving forklifts, teaching classes, or assembling automobiles. Even if they do have access to information with the PC, they may not have time or interest to do so.

NONFORMAL COMMUNICATION NETWORKS

A lot of company news does not move through mass media channels or the company's hierarchy. Instead, it flows naturally through a network of employees who give, take, shape, and accumulate information: the crowd of people who eat lunch together every day in the company cafeteria, the group of smokers from several departments who gather around the communal outdoor ashtray and compare notes about the latest executive promotion, and the company's softball team that chats about a new product over a couple of beers after the game. All of these groups share information that they have heard from their managers, read in a company newsletter, or seen on the local TV station. They discuss the messages they have heard and always uncover the inconsistencies.

These nonformal networks are usually dismissed by company executives and slapped with negative labels like "the rumor mill" or the "grapevine." They are seen as maverick communication factories that produce inaccurate information. However, smart communicators are tapping the power of these hidden communication links and making them the third side in their internal communications triangle. Because it does not cost anything to build these networks—they occur naturally in all organizations—the return on investment for using these networks is extraordinarily high. These nonformal networks are efficient, quick, and highly credible.

The study of these nonformal networks is an emerging practice that draws on anthropology, mathematics, chemistry, and subatomic physics. One of the leaders in the field is Karen Stephenson who teaches at Harvard and the University of London. Stephenson developed and now markets software that builds a visual map of an organization's social networks. The software uses algorithms to analyze data from employee surveys that basically ask people whom they communicate with the most. The graphic representation looks like a giant spider web of multicolored lines interconnecting every individual in an organization. Some people are extraordinarily well connected; others have only a few links outside their immediate work group. The network map spotlights the invisible influencers in an organization—people who carry quiet corporate clout but may not have an important job title.

Stephenson (2005) has dubbed people in those roles the "hubs" of the network, the best connectors among people and information. She labels other key roles as "gatekeepers" (the information bottlenecks who make themselves indispensable by controlling contact with the rest of the network) and "pulse-takers" (who carefully cultivate relationships to monitor the ongoing health of the organization).

New Yorker writer Malcolm Gladwell's *The Tipping Point: How Little Things Can Make a Big Difference* (2000) similarly describes three roles individuals play in social networks. "Connectors" are sociable people who bring people together. "Mavens" like to pass along knowledge. "Salesmen" are skilled at persuading the unenlightened. Although Gladwell uses different terms to define slightly different roles, his point is the same as Stephenson's: messages and behaviors spread like viruses through these social networks by word-of-mouth epidemics triggered with the help of those role players.

There are ways for communicators to tap the power of these social networks. For example, suppose you stage a monthly breakfast meeting for the CEO and a randomly selected group of employees from across that organization. If you sprinkle a few "mavens" and "hubs" into the mix, you are almost guaranteed that messages from the CEO will spread quickly and effectively through the network as soon as the breakfast is over. Or instead of designing and printing posters to invite employees to a town hall event, let the "salesmen" work their network magic using "word of mouse" to distribute a personal invitation by e-mail.

Used effectively, social networks are an excellent way for internal communicators to connect effectively and inexpensively with their employees.

EXACTLY WHO IS AN EMPLOYEE?

It used to be fairly simple to answer that question: either someone was an employee or was not. The person received a paycheck from the company or did not. He or she was invited to staff meetings, went to the company Christmas party, received the company newsletter, and bowled in the company's bowling league—or did not.

Today it is harder to define who belongs to an internal audience. Organizations have full-time employees, part-time employees, contractors, consultants, temporary employees, and just about every other kind of worker. Add to that mix all the workers in franchises, strategic partnerships, independent distributors, and other allied organizations that are not officially part of the corporate structure. All of these people have information needs, but their needs are as varied as their jobs. Some people who are near the fringe of the organization may actually need more information than a regular, full-time employee to be able to do their jobs effectively.

Individual employees may also have widely varying information needs. Think of two salespeople with identical job titles who sit side by side in the same office. One has been in a sales role for seventeen years and has been a top performer for the past five. The other has been selling for just three years. Their information needs will be very different.

Communication professionals must take these audience demographics into account as they develop internal communication plans. Employee communications are like bathing suits: one size does not fit all.

There is also an increasingly fuzzy line between internal and external communications. Consider a Microsoft engineer living in Redmond, Washington. Chances are very good that she uses Microsoft products (and receives Microsoft's customer communication), owns Microsoft stock (and receives shareholder communication), and reads a Seattle newspaper (and sees her company's media communications). It is critical that internal communication programs work in concert with media relations, investor, and customer communication, striving for consistency in messages and timing.

In addition, communicators recognize that information can easily ooze across these fuzzy boundaries. An e-mail intended for an employee-only audience can (and usually does) find its way beyond an organization's borders. While it has always been possible for a hard copy of an internal company document to be shared with outsiders, it is much simpler for digital information to move anywhere at the speed of light. Communicators must assume that any information they produce that is targeted at an employee audience is likely to be seen by competitors, regulators, retirees, and journalists.

RECOGNIZING LIMITATIONS

When we start an internal communications function in an organization, we discover that there are a few people and departments that completely ignore us. They do not seek our help to develop plans, they send out important messages without our input, and they even stage employee events without letting us know what they are doing. In an organization with unlimited resources, we could be involved in all of those activities in addition to managing employee portals, producing newsletters, writing executive announcements, and doing the thousands of other things on our never-ending to-do lists.

Communicators will recognize that there are finite limits to their capacity for involvement. Most of the communications that take place inside their organizations will not, and probably should not, pass through internal communication programs. We cannot stage every staff meeting or script every telephone call. We cannot review every e-mail message. But we can prepare strategic meetings about an impending change and craft key messages for an all-employee voice mail message. We can develop guidelines for e-mail etiquette and share them across the organization.

The key role any communicator can play is to create the environment in which employees at all levels of the organization can easily exchange the information they need to do their jobs. We can set the stage and provide critical information for the formal and informal conversations that take place between employees, supervisors, managers, senior leaders, customers, and stakeholders.

References

Gladwell, M. (2000). *The tipping point: How little things can make a big difference.* New York: Little, Brown.

Larkin, T. J., & Larkin, S. (1994). *Communicating change: Winning employee support for new business goals.* New York: McGraw-Hill.

Locke, C., Levine, R., Searls, D., & Weinberger, D. (2001). *The cluetrain manifesto: The end of business as usual.* Cambridge: Perseus.

Stephenson, K. (2005). *Network management.* Retrieved August 2005 from www.netform.com/html/netmanage.pdf.

CHAPTER SEVENTEEN

Manager-Employee Communication

Hilary Scarlett

As anyone who has been in employment for more than a few years will know, organizations have changed, and are changing, dramatically. Globalization means that organizations have to work across countries and cultures. The impact of technology has increased both the speed of bringing products to market and the copying of those products by competitors. Delayering has removed much of the structural hierarchy. The loss of long-term commitment between the organization and the employee means that employees are more questioning and challenging than in the past. As in Western society in general, there is less deference to authority. Many more women now go out to work. The days of command and control in most organizations have gone. All these mean that organizations are very different places to work in now than even ten years ago.

Obviously these changes have an impact on the people who work in those organizations, what they do, how they work, how they feel about their employer, what is valued. Not least, these changes are also reflected in the role of the manager.

The material in this chapter are based on over twenty years' experience of working with leaders and managers across a wide range of organizations. In addition, the following people accepted an invitation to be interviewed, and I thank them for sharing their experience and learning: Simone Niven, Smith & Nephew; Ian Wright and Charlotte Knight, Diageo; Hamish Haynes, Sky; Amanda Wooding, Smiths Group; Michael Croton, BP; Angela Blacklaw, Department for Environment Food and Rural Affairs, UK; Ken Young, Department for Work and Pensions, UK; and Victoria Gould, Morgan Crucible.

The manager can no longer rely on hierarchical power to get the employee to do what is required. Not only are employees less likely to tolerate an authoritarian boss, but leaders, managers, and all other employees are recognizing that getting work done by using power and control is rarely the most effective form of leading or managing. Using control and authority might lead to compliance but not to the employee's commitment. Compliance builds resentment from the employee and places a strain on the relationship. From the manager's perspective, in the long term it is not even an efficient use of time: getting people to do things through compliance often requires checking that the task has been done or that it has been done properly.

In addition, managing through authority is based on an assumption that the manager is the person best placed to make decisions. The concept of empowerment recognizes that many decisions are best made by those who are closest to the task or the customer: the employee rather than the supervisor. Empowerment requires a relationship of trust, not one of control.

Organizations are striving for more efficient methods of working with limited resources, so managers need to be able to get the best out of their teams. The relationship is shifting from one of telling people what to do to one where the manager's role is to identify how best to support the employee.

Many organizations have changed how they work: project teams come together for specific tasks and then disband. Matrix management also means that managers have to work with teams over whom they do not necessarily have formal authority. With organizations relying much more on networks and project teams, the ability to form relationships quickly has become essential. One of the key qualities organizations should look for in managers today is an ability to create strong, constructive, and collaborative relationships.

There are other compelling reasons for businesses to look long and hard at the relationships between managers and staff. Although employees join an organization, they leave their manager. No matter how large the pay packet, how generous the benefits, if employees do not get along with their manager, they will leave, and this is especially true of the more confident and able ones.

Another strong argument is the employee-customer-profit chain (Rucci, Kirn, & Quinn, 1998). There is a direct link between management behavior, how employees feel about the organization, and how the organization fares. Employees who feel they are treated well by the organization (that is, by their manager) are more likely to give the customer better service; this means the customer is more likely to spend more and return to the store.

Looking to the future, trends suggest that jobs that require direct interaction with customers will become increasingly important. Ensuring these interactions are positive and successful is the goal of every customer-oriented organization and the responsibility of each manager.

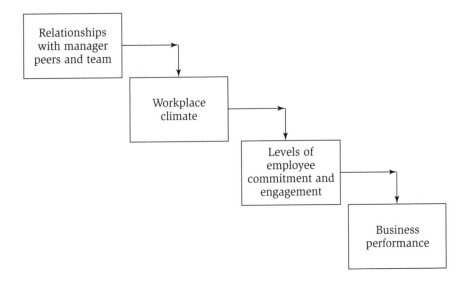

Figure 17.1. Relationships at Work and Business Performance: The Inextricable Link
Source: ©Scarlett Associates, 2005.

For managers to play their part in creating a workplace that enables employees to flourish and give their best, they need to understand three things:

- The importance of relationships and their impact on the workplace climate, the commitment of employees, and, in turn, the impact on business performance (see Figure 17.1)
- What creates a strong working relationship
- How to nurture their working relationships

THE MANAGER'S ABILITY TO DEVELOP WORKING RELATIONSHIPS

The key role of a manager today is to be able to build good, strong, constructive working relationships. Managers need to be able to engage employees and negotiate with them—not negotiate in the sense of industrial relationships and pay bargaining but in the sense of discussing issues and reaching a shared agreement with them to which ideally the employee feels fully committed. Good managers recognize that the relationship with their teams needs to be mutually supportive: both sides must feel they are benefiting, so that this is a win-win situation. The good manager enables employees to work together toward a common goal.

The following items, culled from my work with a range of clients and from interviews conducted for this chapter, are some of the qualities that organizations have identified as essential for being a good people manager. It is by no means a comprehensive list but it covers the main themes:

- Self-awareness. This encompasses recognizing and understanding your own emotions, knowing your tendencies and preferred style of managing and communicating, your strengths, and the areas that require further work.

- Good communications. Good managers understand the basics of good communication. They:

  Make sense of information for their teams. One of the important communication roles for managers is to take the information they receive and make it meaningful to their teams.

  Listen. Each manager should make it a priority to listen more to team members. Good managers know the value of listening, not only for their own benefit but for the benefit of the employee too. Feeling that we are listened to, and listened to well, makes us feel valued. Good ideas can come from any member of the team, and a manager who is a good listener is more likely to create a climate where employees feel inclined and encouraged to contribute ideas.

  Can vary their communication tone and style according to the situation. Great communicators have a repertoire and range of styles of communication. They think not only about what they want to say, but what they want their team members to feel and do as a consequence of the interaction; they can adapt their tone and style to suit the occasion and the desired outcome.

- Build trust. Trust is a fundamental dimension of interpersonal relationships. We trust people whom we feel have our interests at heart. This trust is based on the experience of the person. It is built over time and is based on a belief that this person will be honest with and loyal to us. Managers need to demonstrate a track record of being honest and of having both the organization's and the employee's interests at heart.

- Know your team members. Know what interests and motivates them.

- Practice empathy. The ability to put oneself in someone else's shoes and understand how that person might be thinking or feeling is crucial. Without this, misunderstandings can escalate. With so much change constantly affecting organizations and the employees who work for them, it is essential that managers have the ability to empathize with how an employee might feel about transitions.

- Respect coworkers. Good managers treat team members with respect and treat them as adults. Moreover the manager who makes it clear that he or she respects team members and has high expectations of them is more likely to get good performance from them.

- Gain commitment. People are sociable beings and want to belong and feel part of a team or the organization. As part of their communication skills, good managers have the ability to make people feel part of a team and understand where it is best to consult or involve teams in making decisions.

- Handle conflict. No matter how strong the working relationships are, conflicts will arise. Good managers know how to strike the right balance between being an empathetic manager while keeping enough distance that they can handle conflicts in a responsible and fair way that takes the interests of the organization, the team, and the individual into account.

Defra, the U.K.'s Department for Environment, Food and Rural Affairs, began with a lengthy list of behaviors that were expected from leaders and managers at all levels of the organization. Over time, it became clear that some behaviors were more valuable and relevant to Defra than others. Defra reduced the number of behaviors and clustered them under what are now informally known as "The Big 5":

- Taking personal responsibility. This includes behaviors such as demonstrating honesty and integrity, being aware of the power of throwaway remarks, and understanding the impact of your behaviors. It also means acting in a corporate way and not expecting others to take on your management responsibilities.
- Shaping and communicating a vision of the future. This touches on the ability to translate a general vision or direction into something clear and meaningful for the team, defining objectives and outcomes, and being able to persuade people of the benefits of trying new and more efficient ways of doing things.
- Putting diversity into practice. This requires managers to build and maintain complementary teams, encourage people to work in a way that suits them best, and encourage all team members to express their views. In policymaking, it also requires people to consult widely to reflect the world in which we live.
- Making things happen through others. Defra's ways of working have changed, and the size of the workforce has been reduced. This requires managers to be good leaders of their teams and to be able to work with external

organizations and agencies to get work done through and with them. Defra makes it clear to leaders and managers that there are times when others might be more skilled than the manager and therefore the role of the manager is to empower the employee and support him or her. Coaching becomes an important skill.

• Facing up to hard choices. This is particularly relevant to managers working in an environment that is constantly more demanding with fewer resources. Thus, managers must have honest and fair conversations about resources and performance; they will sometimes have to make unpopular decisions for the public good. They must face up to what might be unpleasant truths. This behavior recognizes that being a manager can be very tough.

IMPROVING MANAGERS' RELATIONSHIP-BUILDING SKILLS: WHAT IS WORKING

When developing managers' skills, many organizations historically have focused on training programs and coaching: that is, what people need to learn or to do differently. However, there is an important step before this (see Figure 17.2) that ensures that the learning is based on a firm foundation and helps to make sure that the learning will stick. This is *creating the need*: ensuring that managers who are about to embark on improving relationship-building skills see why they need to do this, that is, why the organization needs improved work relationships and why they as individuals will benefit, along with their teams.

The commitment to making changes is much stronger when managers can see and feel at a personal, team, and organizational level why they need to change. Enabling managers to perceive the need for change can be done in many ways and depends very much on the circumstances of each organization. An e-mail from the CEO telling all managers that they need training will not

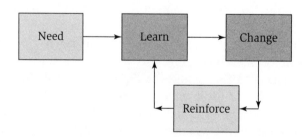

Figure 17.2. A Four-Step Process for Changing Behavior

suffice: it might lead to compliance but not to a deep commitment to changing behavior. One of the means to create a sense of personal need for development is getting feedback or self-assessment.

For one of the organizations interviewed, a recent history of difficult industrial relations led to the recognition of a need for change; for another, it was a change program that would be heavily dependent on each manager's leading his or her team through restructuring, downsizing, and greater customer focus. For the U.K. Department of Work and Pensions (DWP), there were several compelling reasons for improving line managers' communication ability. First, DWP is an organization formed from a merger of departments with differing but complementary aims. Under one DWP, these aims now need to be fully integrated. Second, the workforce is large (120,000 employees) and geographically scattered. And the strongest reason is that employees made it clear through the employee survey that, as in the vast majority of organizations, they trusted information given to them by their line manager more than any other source.

Continuing with the model, once the new skills have been explored and learned, managers need to have an opportunity to test them. Often it is only when the manager tries to put some of the new skills, approaches, or behaviors into practice that he or she will become aware of what is easy to do and what is more difficult. This is why one-off training modules are not sufficient to make a difference: managers need the ongoing support and reinforcement from their supervisor and peers.

What Organizations Are Doing

Here are practical examples of what organizations are doing to support managers in improving their relationship-building skills.

Being Clear About What Is Expected. Organizations cannot begin to help managers improve their relationship-building skills until they have clearly defined what is required. BP, the global oil company, had historically relied on an implicit understanding of its culture and way of doing things. Several mergers later, the company now has to be more explicit about what is required, and part of the challenge has been to do this in a way that fits with different cultures. The U.K. DWP started with the design of a competency framework so that it could show leaders and managers what good management looks like.

Recruiting and Promoting the Right People. Several of those interviewed reported that a manager's ability to communicate well and create good relationships at work had become one of the essential criteria of recruitment. When Diageo, the global drinks manufacturer, recruits managers, it looks for the ability to be inspirational leaders. The organization sees this ability as a significant differentiator.

Making Leaders and Managers More Self-Aware. The first step for managers to improve relationship-building skills is to become aware of their current management style. Intentionally or unintentionally, managers' behavior has an effect on their team, so they need to be aware of what they are doing and their impact on others.

For many organizations, once the competencies have been developed and articulated, using a 360-degree feedback tool is the next step. Options include using a tool that already exists (this usually offers the benefit of enabling managers to benchmark themselves against norms) or creating a tool specific to the organization that measures the manager against the competencies set out for that organization.

The main aim for Smiths Group, a global engineering company, in focusing on leadership development was its desire to make the most of the talent and ability already in the organization. A group that has grown globally through acquisition, it was aware of the need to define across the group what skills, attitudes, and behaviors are expected of leaders. Once the definition was understood, the group profiled senior leaders through an intensive day of whole-life interviews and self-completion questionnaires. The exercise was completely voluntary; Smiths Group emphasized that profiling should be in the best interests of both the group and the leader and that the output would be an individual development action plan focused on strengthening the leader's capabilities.

For each leader, what emerged was a picture of his or her strengths and preferences. This information allowed the leader and his or her boss to make better decisions about areas of development and where the talents of the leader would be best suited. From the group's point of view, the profiling enables it to make more robust decisions about appointments and succession planning as well as identify common development needs in leaders.

Providing Training. Training is often the first tool in helping managers develop relationship-building skills. Setting up a training course is relatively simple; creating one that makes a difference is a much greater challenge. Diageo was committed to creating a training program that was practical, useful, and engaging. The training course has been two years in the making. Part of its appeal is that it draws on real-life people in politics, business, sport, and the military: it looks at their communication skills and helps managers to see what they can learn from these models and apply to their own work.

The one-day workshop includes self-assessment so that managers can understand their style. To ensure the content of the course is closely aligned to real issues, participants are asked to bring along a case study or something they are working on, so that they can apply the learning during the day.

Because Diageo is a global company, there have been challenges in ensuring that the workshop fits all countries and cultures; one of the learnings has been to adapt the role models and examples to fit local culture. Proud of the quality of the training content, the communications team has kept a close eye on how the program is rolled out. To ensure quality is maintained, only people who really know the subject matter are allowed to facilitate. Diageo is exploring how it can keep the learning alive for participants once they go back to the workplace. A first step in this is using the intranet to provide reminders of course content and self-assessment tests.

Morgan Crucible, a global engineering firm, has been going through substantial changes, and as part of its plan to equip managers to handle the changes, it too created and rolled out communications skills training program that focuses on face-to-face and team-based communication. To ensure learnings are put into practice, course participants are invited to reconvene a month after the training to discuss what is working and where they need further help.

Rooting Training in the Business Need. The common problem reported by managers who have been to a training course is how to use the skills when they return to their place of work. They might have a new level of awareness or some new practices they want to try, but others around them have not changed. Unless the practices are quickly put into use, enthusiasm to use them fades.

One of the most effective ways of helping managers to develop their relationship-building and communication skills is to train the managers in the context of the real business challenges and goals faced by the management team. From the managers' perspective, they can see that they are developing communication and relationship skills because the skills are enablers to achieving their business goals.

For example, one management team needed to get employees to take greater responsibility. They needed to move, in transactional analysis terms, from Parent-Child to Adult-Adult relationships. A training session was arranged for the whole management team. The training session went well because the team was working toward a collective goal. Also, the training had a much more enduring impact because the team of managers had gone through the training together and with their manager. Together they discussed what they were trying to achieve as a department and as a management team, and together they discussed what they could do differently, collectively and individually, to achieve their objectives. After the training, all knew what the others had learned and committed to and could therefore support one another in trying to change their way of working with employees. This approach created ongoing reinforcement of the learning.

The aim for several of the organizations interviewed was to do less formal training and more learning on the job because this is where people are most receptive to learning. The aim is to get managers to be conscious learners, that is, constantly reflecting on what is working well and why, and what not so well, and then applying that learning to how they manage in the future.

Further Support. Based on the idea of peer support, some organizations, such as Morgan Crucible, have introduced learning sets and follow-up workshops for managers. Learning sets are small peer-learning groups. These provide a forum where managers can share ideas and get help on issues they are finding problematic.

Leading and Role Models. One of the key criteria for success is having a leader who fully supports the development of relationship-building skills in the organization. Several of the interviewees mentioned that if they had not had the full-hearted support of their CEO or leader, they would have achieved very little at all. Ken Young, head of corporate communications at DWP, mentioned the value of having a permanent secretary (head of the department) who regularly reminded his executive team that the communications team could create and support the communications but could not deliver the communications: it was up to each member of the executive team to set the example and communicate the vision and its implications.

Coaching and Mentoring. Several of those interviewed said that they are using coaching as part of their development program for leaders and managers. Some organizations allocated a certain number of hours with a coach for each leader or manager to ensure that all had at least some initial experience of coaching. As part of its approach to developing talent in the organization, Smiths Group is encouraging its leaders to participate in its mentoring program as a potential mentor or mentee. This helps those who are being mentored and means that their leaders are developing highly useful mentoring skills. Angela Blacklaw, head of people development at Defra, said, "By being exposed to some very skilled coaches, our leaders and managers have learned what good coaching looks like and it is a very useful skill to have. They have learned how to challenge one another in a constructive way."

Creating an Inclusive Culture: Breaking Down the Barriers. BSkyB, the British part of the television company Sky, has taken the view that in addition to some management training, its main focus should be the creation of a community that is inclusive. The approach is based on a view that all employees are good citizens who want to do well and want the company to do better; as Hamish Haynes, group head of internal communications, said, "It's based on a sense that we're all in this together."

The internal communications team plays an active part in creating this culture. In addition to all the usual media typical in an organization of thirteen thousand people who are geographically spread out, they create special events. These events are deliberately made open to all employees so that managers and staff at all levels can mix together. Events include hiring a local cinema and inviting employees and their families to previews of films. Not only does the invitation to a preview make all staff feel special, but it is a shared experience across all staff levels that helps to create a strong sense of one company.

One of its more recent initiatives is to create Sky Forum, a quarterly meeting to discuss issues raised by staff. Elected by their peers, the forum members, not the leadership team, decide the agenda. For the leaders, the forum provides a means by which they can hear directly from employees about issues that concern them and can address them before they turn into a significant crisis.

Evaluation

For all organizations, the ultimate test is whether helping managers to improve their working relationships has an impact on the business and on the bottom line in the short and longer terms.

There are various methods of evaluating the impact of development activities. Diageo uses an evaluation questionnaire at the end of the training session. Some organizations track shifts in 360-degree feedback to see if managers are getting more positive ratings over time. Self-assessment is also reviewed to see if managers feel they are improving and can demonstrate changes they have made. Some organizations, such as Morgan Crucible and BP, use their employee opinion and culture mapping surveys to see if ratings of managers are improving. Others look at specific business outcomes such as employee retention, customer feedback and behaviors, and relationships with external stakeholders.

Common Themes for Success

Improving relationships between managers and their teams is a goal that takes time and commitment to achieve. Given the link between the climate in the workplace and business performance, it is a goal for which organizations that want to succeed, and continue to succeed, must strive. There are some key criteria for success:

- Having genuine support from the CEO or leader
- Helping managers to become more self-aware of their management style and communication preferences
- Ensuring that leaders and managers see the link between relationship-building skills and personal, departmental, and corporate objectives
- Building peer support so that learning is reinforced and supported in the workplace
- Ensuring that any training or development activity fits with the local culture and business context
- Identifying and recognizing successes so that managers believe that they can make improvements
- Taking a long-term view because there is no quick fix

The Role of the Human Resources, Organization Development, and Communications Professionals

For many human resource (HR), organization development (OD), and communications professionals, there is still a battle to be fought to gain acceptance that relationship-building skills are an area that should be invested in. Several of the interviewees slowly influenced and created the moment when the organization was ready to focus on relationship skills.

Some recognized that they had had to get the basics in place first, such as building a communication infrastructure, before they could begin to have a conversation about skills development. As Michael Croton from BP said, "There are two key parts to communication: setting the context and having the conversations that lead to understanding and action amongst employees. A key role for communicators in the corporate centre is to provide people with context in a way that is meaningful to them. By meaningful, I mean that it stimulates the conversations or thinking that enable people to do a better job or feel a stronger connection with what the company is trying to do."

Whether the responsibility for skills development rests in HR, OD, or communications, most of the interviewees said there had been good cross-departmental collaboration and a recognition that people-focused functions need to work together and support one another. Since improving relationship-building skills requires a multifaceted approach, all of these functions will be called on to play a part.

For each of the organizations, real momentum was established once the leader or leadership team could see the link between relationships in the organization and business success. The challenge for the HR, OD, and communications professional is to help them see this link.

No matter how great the infrastructure or the communications media that the organization puts in place, communication is working well only when employees feel they have a manager they can talk to. Employees who feel they have a good working relationship with their manager are more likely to be committed to the organization. This creates a climate and culture that enables the organization to succeed. The role of the HR, OD, and communication managers is to enable people to see this link and provide the support to enable managers to create strong, positive relationships.

Reference

Rucci, A. J., Kirn, S. P., & Quinn, R. T. (1998, January–February). The employee-customer-profit chain at Sears. *Harvard Business Review, 76*(1), 82–97.

CHAPTER EIGHTEEN

Throwing Rocks at the Corporate Rhinoceros

The Challenges of Employee Engagement

Roger D'Aprix

The task of engagement—that is, unleashing the full energy and talents of people in the workplace—is today's most critical leadership challenge. It is also formidable. Despite all the talk to the contrary, we are still a society that struggles with the question of how to lead people effectively in institutional settings. For the most part, the history of human capital leadership both before and during the industrial revolution was a sad affair. It was largely characterized by a fondness for autocracy that was aided and abetted by bureaucratic management structures. The underlying but unspoken premise was that workers are untrustworthy, childlike creatures who need more than anything to be parented—rewarded when they conformed and punished when they rebelled.

Some years ago the psychologist and business critic Harry Levinson (1973) characterized this time-worn arrangement as "The Great Jackass Fallacy." His simple question was if we are so enamored with carrot-and-stick reward systems, we need to reflect on what we typically put between those two objects—namely, a jackass.

For most managements, the practices that grew up over the long history of the industrial revolution, which included both worker abuse and paternalism, stemmed from the belief that the workforce was nothing more than another cost of doing business. Global competition, the emergence over time of a large body of educated workers, and the massive application of technology that could be manipulated only by talented knowledge workers have together introduced a new set of realities. Nonetheless, too many organizational leaders have clung to the old views despite all the evidence to the contrary and have continued to treat the members of their workforce as interchangeable units of cost.

Witness the numbers of mindless workforce downsizings that continue to this day to cut costs or meet arbitrary profit targets. Tally up the costs of not appreciating and recognizing the contribution of key performers, who quit in disgust. Consider the numbers of talented people who leave organizations because they can no longer tolerate a martinet of a boss. The waste in talent and dollars is appalling.

David Sirota, one of the coauthors of *The Enthusiastic Employee* . . . (Sirota, Mischkind, & Metzler, 2005), says, "Usually starting about six months after being hired, something happens to the great masses of employees who begin work enthusiastically. We find significant declines in morale in 9 out of 10 companies after 'the honeymoon period.' It is not just that the novelty wears off; the decline—and its deleterious impact on performance—is a consequence of management practice. In fact, one can say that, often it is *management* that kills enthusiasm" (pp. xxix–xxx).

In this chapter we define employee engagement and the organizational factors that encourage, and more often discourage, engagement. A simple process to begin to address employee engagement organizationwide is also reviewed.

ENGAGEMENT AS A SOFT ISSUE

Those of us who think and talk in depth about issues like engagement are often frustrated by the tendency to label them as soft, as though they were not worth discussing or so squishy that they were practically impossible to define or manage.

The word *soft* in the corporate lexicon is usually a derogatory term. We tend to think of *soft* people as weaklings. We speak of the soft-hearted, for example, as opposed to the "hard-nosed" or the "tough-minded" among us. Or we talk of *soft* numbers when we really mean numbers that are hard to come by or difficult to manage. Or we talk of someone who speaks softly. It is usually not a compliment. The connotation is timidity or uncertainty—qualities that in corporate life are generally not admired. Even Teddy Roosevelt added to the bias with his admonition to "speak softly but carry a big stick."

The author Umberto Eco (2005) uses a wonderfully vivid phrase to describe one of his characters in a short story titled "The Gorge." The character is a kind man who blames God for the evil around him. Eco writes, "He had it in only for God, and that must have been a real chore, because it was like throwing rocks at a rhinoceros—the rhinoceros never notices a thing and continues going about its rhino business, and meanwhile you are red with rage and ripe for a heart attack" (p. 66).

Communication professionals face a "rhinoceros" of their own. Metaphorically, it is that self-satisfied body of business leaders who devalue any initiative or process designed to improve human leadership. Their knee-jerk reaction is dismissive. In their view, such efforts are doomed to failure, too time-consuming, too expensive, or too much to add to the everyday workload of those charged to manage people in an organization. In their view, leadership is an extracurricular activity.

I will go to my grave wondering why such people resist the simple proposition that treating people with respect and concern is somehow counterproductive to business results. As a veteran of many of those discussions over my long career as a corporate executive and consultant, I believe that this virtual rhinoceros is the natural enemy not only of engagement but of any leadership initiatives that cannot be tied unequivocally to the bottom line.

Seriously addressing issues like employee engagement in many organizations is a lot like throwing rocks at a rhinoceros. Anyone who has ever given a sweaty-palmed presentation of a fragile new idea to a skeptical audience knows what I mean. Anyone who has ever been confronted by the dubious raised eyebrow or folded arms of an audience of one understands the simile. Anyone who has seen her proposal reviewed, trashed, and modified beyond recognition knows the pain of watching the rhino aroused and ready to charge. Anyone who has been patronized by a boss who withholds praise but is anxious to criticize knows about the presence of this virtual beast.

I am inclined to give these behaviors the form of a rhino because those who demonstrate them tend to camouflage the rhino at the same time they show many of the same thick-skinned behaviors as the genuine article. Rhinos tend to attack without warning. They like to blend into the landscape and depend on surprise. They are unpredictably aroused by seemingly innocent stimuli, and like their African cousins that can see only about thirty-five feet in front of them, they are terribly nearsighted.

Much of this behavior is instinctive rather than calculated. It is a product of years of living with a mythology that says you can be tough and ruthless and get results *or* you can be soft and indulgent and watch the business decline. In reality, it is all a matter of balance. Former CEO Jack Welch at General Electric used to differentiate among four types of manager/leaders:

- The ruthless, who focused on the numbers regardless of the people costs
- The people managers, who thought people and their needs were infinitely more important than any numbers
- The incompetent, who achieved neither the financial nor the people goals
- And then the only managers he wanted to keep: the ones who met the numbers through excellent people leadership

THE ROCK THROWERS

Tolerance of autocratic management behavior, the tendency to layer organizations with unnecessary levels of approvals, and the inclination not to trust or value human assets have all given birth to this virtual beast that charges ahead oblivious to the rocks that are hurled at it by a multitude of persistent researchers, enlightened management thinkers, human resource professionals, and countless consultants. The rhino has managed for years to go about its nasty and costly business while the rest of us marvel at its capacity to ignore the forces aiming to tame it or end its mindless run.

Still, at the dawn of the information revolution today, there is great hope. Current pressures and realities seem to suggest that the days of the dominance of the corporate rhino are numbered. The various rock throwers are finally having an impact on those who have acted out their belief that the soft management issues were not worth the effort to address them.

One of the most persistent rock throwers has been the Gallup Organization. Another has been David Sirota, the noted researcher and author. Still another has been author and consultant Frederick Reichheld. Towers Perrin, the well-known human resource consulting firm, has added the considerable weight of its research and reputation as a well-placed rock aimed at the thick head of the corporate rhino. Let us take them one at a time.

Gallup, under the leadership of consultant Marcus Buckingham, has been a leading advocate and popularizer of the notion of engagement. In fact, Gallup may well be the first organization to use the term. Writing in their best-seller *First, Break All the Rules* (Buckingham & Coffman, 1999), Buckingham and Coffman note the difficulty of guessing how well one company or one manager is doing in eliciting employee engagement. They emphasize that the real pressure for increased engagement is coming from institutional investors, who command billions of dollars in company stock. Describing this group as "the ultimate numbers guys," they assert that in years past, they did not concern themselves with issues like culture and employee satisfaction or engagement, seeing them as fundamentally irrelevant.

They have done an about-face in recent years, says Buckingham and Coffman, and have started to pay much closer attention to how companies treat and lead their people. The California Public Employees Retirement System oversees $260 billion worth of stocks; the Council of Institutional Investors manages over $1 trillion in investments. The reason for their attention to enlightened leadership and corporate governance, according to Buckingham and Coffman, is that a good deal of the value of a company resides between "the ears of its employees."

Thomas Stewart (1998, p. 199) writes in his classic book *Intellectual Capital* that the most valuable aspects of jobs are now "sensing, judging, creating, and building relationships." That means, says Stewart, that when someone leaves a company, he or she takes part of its value along, often straight to the competition. Adds Buckingham and Coffman, a company that is bleeding people is also bleeding value.

Along with the loss of people, an equally compelling reason for paying attention to the level of engagement in a company is the desire for capturing discretionary effort. In short, every employee, regardless of the nature of his or her work, has a reserve of discretionary effort that he or she can choose to contribute or quietly withhold. To the extent that such employees truly feel engaged in the vision, mission, and goals of the organization, they are much more likely to expend that discretionary effort to achieve them. Such is the power of engagement.

The business case for engagement is clear to anyone who cares to look. Practically all companies today are engaged in a kind of pit bull battle in their respective industries. Globalization and the advantages enjoyed by such low-wage countries as China and those who comprise the so-called Third World make innovation one of the most prized qualities of any workforce. And clearly it is engaged workers who are most likely to be the innovators.

Recognizing all of this, the Gallup Organization has spent the past twenty-five years or so gathering engagement data from millions of people in hundreds of companies. Buckingham and Coffman note that searching for the drivers of engagement in this stack of data was like looking for the proverbial needle in the haystack. The search was to identify the core elements that help attract, focus, and keep the most talented employees. The end result of this huge research effort was what Gallup finally termed the Q12 survey items—the twelve questions that tended to identify which organizations had the greatest percentages of engaged people.

The twelve questions, not surprisingly, are heavily slanted toward an individual's personal relationship with the organization. Equipped with that understanding, Gallup has been able to determine the degree of engagement in any particular work organization. The items in question link to such critical issues as productivity, profitability, retention, and customer satisfaction.

Ten of the twelve questions in the research linked consistently with the organization's level of productivity. Eight are linked to profitability. Five are linked to employee retention. Of the twelve questions, Buckingham says that six were the most powerful predictors of an engaged workforce: an understanding of job expectations, the availability of the materials and equipment to do the job, the opportunity to contribute one's best at work, recognition or praise for a job well done, whether their supervisor cared about them as a person, and whether there was someone at work encouraging their development.

It was clear in all the data that supervisors, team leaders, and managers were powerful influencers of whether people were or were not engaged. All of that

is entirely consistent with the research findings through the years in other studies that people quit bad bosses rather than companies. And it emphasizes the
conclusion that the most powerful communication experience of any employee
is that day-to-day interchange with authority figures—particularly his or her
immediate supervisor.

The remaining Q12 questions have to do with whether employees perceive
that opinions are listened to, if the company mission creates individual pride,
whether coworkers are perceived as committed to quality work, and if people
had a best friend at work. As Figure 18.1 shows, the degrees of engagement and
of disengagement in the companies in the database were roughly equal. The
group that was neither engaged nor disengaged was by far the largest at 69 percent, so the opportunity to do better is huge. The implication for communication professionals is clear: to have an impact on engagement, concentrate a
significant part of your strategy on improving the typical line manager's efforts.

Researcher David Sirota comes to a remarkably similar set of conclusions
after reviewing the most recent employee data he gathered from 1994 to 2003.
His database since 1994 includes 2.5 million employees in 237 diverse public
and private organizations in eighty-nine countries.

Here is what Sirota and his coauthors (2005) claim are finally the key drivers
of engagement—what he defines as "the three primary goals of people at work."
In no particular rank order they are achievement, equity, and camaraderie. By

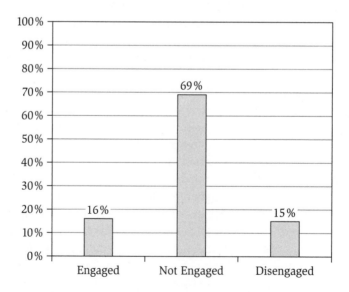

Figure 18.1. Gallup Data on the Degree of Engagement in Typical Companies
Source: The Gallup Organization.

achievement, they mean the pride one takes in doing well things that matter and receiving the recognition that creates pride in the organization's accomplishments. The components of achievement sound very much like some of the elements of the Q12—the challenge of the work itself, the ability to acquire new skills, the training and the resources needed to do the job, the perceived importance of the job, recognition for performance, and working for a company in which one can feel pride.

Sirota et al. say that a second element of the three primary goals of people at work is *equity,* the need to be treated justly in relation to the conditions of employment. The basic conditions they describe as physiological (a safe working environment, an equitable workload, and comfortable physical working conditions), economic (a reasonable degree of job security with satisfactory pay and benefits), and psychological (being treated respectfully with credible and consistent leadership). Again the echoes of the Q12 can be clearly heard.

The third element is *camaraderie*—"having warm, interesting and cooperative relations with others in the workplace." The closest of the Gallup Q12 questions to this element is, "I have a best friend at work." In both cases, the researchers are pointing out the importance of the workplace as a social community where people can derive satisfaction from the day-to-day interchanges with coworkers. It is not surprising that the stimulation that comes from working with like-minded and compatible people is an important element in determining engagement.

Both Frederick Reichheld and Towers Perrin approach the subject of engagement in similar fashion by showing its impact on performance. In *The Loyalty Effect,* Reichheld (1996) reports studies showing that customer loyalty is often dependent on employee loyalty (that is, commitment). In other words, committed employees are much more likely to create loyal customers who provide the repeat business that every organization depends on. The power of this relationship lies in Reichheld's finding that a 5 percent improvement in customer retention yields a 25 to 95 percent increase in profits, depending on the industry. The performance link is both clear and powerful.

Towers Perrin (2003), in an outstanding report on employee engagement, presents the results of a survey of forty thousand employees in medium and large organizations in North America. One of the primary interests of the study was to determine what factors most influence employee engagement. In rank order of importance the study determined these ten:

- Senior management interest in employees' well-being
- Challenging work
- Decision-making authority
- Evidence that the company is focused on customers

- Career advancement opportunities
- Company reputation as a good employer
- A collaborative work environment
- Resources to get the job done
- Input on decision making
- A clear vision from senior management about future success

Once again you can hear the echoes of both Gallup's and Sirota's research in their findings. Achievement, equity, autonomy, pride, resources, camaraderie, caring leadership—all of these qualities resound through their collective findings, as does the assertion that attention to these matters profoundly affects the performance of the individual and therefore the organization. Here is what Towers Perrin concludes about the linkage between employee engagement and business performance:

> The notion is deceptively simple. Employee behavior influences customer behavior (think of the last time you walked out of a store without making a purchase because of an ill-informed, rude or poorly trained salesperson). Customer behavior directly affects revenue growth and profitability, among other things. So it is critical to shape the behavior of the individuals at the beginning of the chain: employees. *That means creating an overall work experience, and developing and managing a series of workplace programs and practices, that directly support desired behaviors and high levels of engagement* [italics added p. 9].

THE ENGAGEMENT POWER OF THE BOSS

So the rhinoceros and its handlers are an anachronism. But the important question remains: How do you create that overall work experience that supports high levels of engagement? The answer lies in aligning a number of key influencers from management behavior to what gets inspected and rewarded in an organization. Towers Perrin says that the answer can be found in paying attention to the ten drivers of engagement.

They boil down to two key concerns: challenging and satisfying work and influence and control over one's work environment. In the words of Towers Perrin (2003), "Employees need to believe that some authority and autonomy come along with the increased responsibility and risk they are being asked to bear in various ways in the workplace" (p. 10).

The one word that sums up the need most directly is *leadership*—not just leadership from the top but leadership at all levels of the organization, and particularly leadership at the level closest to the employee. Undeniably one of the most critical influencers of employee behavior is the behavior of the boss. *Boss* is an unfortunate word because it conjures up all of those negative images of arbitrary behavior, unmerited privilege, checking up, and "because I said so." A more accurate term is *line manager leadership.*

I once consulted with an organization that changed all of the management titles in its company from *supervisor, manager,* and the like to *leader.* The new business cards read "leader of [fill in the blank]." That simple action did not change behavior overnight in that company, but it certainly sent a powerful message about the company's expectations of the people it had appointed to lead its workforce.

In its report, Towers Perrin (2003) spelled out the challenging process that any company that was serious about employee engagement had to subject itself to. The focus was on the first five of the ten engagement drivers. Senior management is told to communicate a clear vision for long-term success and to do so with integrity so that words and actions match. It is also advised to communicate openly and honestly.

The human resource consultancy advises employers to do everything possible to provide a challenging work environment, including encouraging initiative, coaching and developing people, and holding them accountable for performance. While supervisors tended to score more favorably than senior leaders in the eyes of the employees responding to the research, supervisors were also advised to become more accessible and open and supportive of change. Giving people autonomy to make decisions, communicating career opportunities, and advancing high performers were also cited as important needs.

TRANSLATING IT ALL INTO PRACTICAL ACTIONS

For the communication professional, all of this information presents an important set of challenges. The first is to reexamine the traditional way in which he or she has performed the employee communication task. This will require a reinvention of the role. In the past, the communication professional has been a tactician charged with delivering organizational messages as efficiently as possible. That meant essentially the task of "sending out stuff." Top-down communication that reacted to events and that required a high degree of reportorial skill was what was required.

The new competitive environment calls for much more than journalistic or electronic skills geared to the efficient dissemination of information. What is now required is the ability to size up employee communication needs, collect relevant data, and use this information as the basis for strategy. What is required is strong analytical skills, deep knowledge of the organization's business and marketplace, the ability to synthesize volumes of information and turn it into suitable communication strategies, and the ability to counsel a preoccupied and pressured leadership.

It is not a role for the faint-hearted. For years, the traditional employee communicator has focused on media and mass communication of clear messages. Those who are truly interested in the issue of engaging employees to improve organizational performance are going to have to think through what this new role requires of them.

One clear need is to improve leadership communication at all levels of the organization. Working with the senior leadership will require the communication professional to acquire strong consulting skills. That means being comfortable in the role of influencer rather than simply program designer and implementer. Influencers also need to be strong collaborators. This task of engagement is so broad and diverse that no one organizational specialty can own it. It will have to be a collaborative effort of everyone who has a stake in the game.

In specific terms for communication professionals, there is no doubt that it will require attention to the communication role that has been most ignored in the past. This refers to the task of supporting the line manager's communication and leadership role. What does that entail? I can best answer that with the model set out in Figure 18.2.

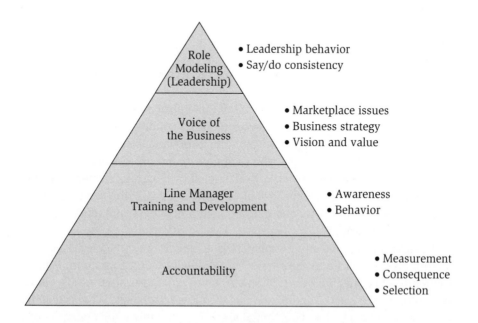

Figure 18.2. Elements of a Successful Line Manager Communication Strategy

Any line manager communication initiative must be based on a clearly understood and executed strategy. Working from the conviction that engagement is a critical need of the organization, that strategy has to take into account a number of basic issues. First, there must be a willingness to impose accountability on line managers for leading people in such a way that they are more likely to feel engaged. That requires awareness, training, and some sort of performance management to be certain that the required behavior is leading to results.

In my view and experience, the training is much less a matter of skills training than it is teaching people the importance of engagement and giving them a model to emulate. The model that I have found to be the most effective is based on addressing an employee's engagement needs from the most basic questions: What is my job? How can I help? It assumes that people's engagement needs begin with a focus on the performance issues closest to them and then progress to the larger issues of how they fit into a team and then into the larger organization before they can determine how much discretionary effort they are willing to expend for that organization. It is a dynamic, almost day-to-day, minute-by-minute decision-making process having much to do with how they are treated over time. And it is profoundly affected by the nature of the work they are doing.

In all of this, the immediate manager or supervisor plays a critical role by answering the six questions of the model through his or her words and actions (Figure 18.3). Coaching, listening, providing performance feedback, recognizing accomplishments: all of these are the basics of eliciting lasting engagement. This is the role of the contemporary manager in today's competitive work organizations, but it will not happen without accountability for the behavior.

In addition to training managers and holding them accountable, any line manager initiative must take into account the need for senior managers to provide the proper role modeling and prodding that is essential to sustained performance. That means consistent leadership behavior to reinforce the kind of engagement culture the organization has deemed critical to performance and business results.

That same initiative requires a selection process in place that accurately identifies leadership talent and puts only those in leadership positions with the basic instincts and people skills to make it happen. The simple reality is that in this process as in so many others, you cannot make a silk purse out of a sow's ear. An executive of Inter-Continental Hotels once put this selection issue in crystal clear terms for me: "If you want people in my business who smile and greet guests hospitably, hire people who are friendly and smile and then teach them the hotel business." Similarly if you want real leaders in place in an organization, select people with people skills, and then teach them the other things they need to know.

Figure 18.3. A Model of the Employee Questions Line Managers Must Answer

Finally, line managers cannot make engagement work without support and without information. There is a need to ensure that they are fully educated in the marketplace issues of the business and provided the information and tools necessary for effective communication and leadership.

DRIVING THE RHINOCEROS AWAY

Clearly engagement is not a simple matter. It is a complex human process that is vital to an organization's competitiveness and business success. That means that it requires a collaborative effort by all concerned parties to attack the fundamental causes of disengagement. Those causes are deeply rooted in the psyches and dysfunctional behavior of many institutional organizations, from corporations to governmental and nonprofit agencies. Like the charging rhinoceros, they do not go quietly into the night. Those causes must be carefully identified through a deliberate data-gathering effort to demonstrate the harm they cause. And then they must be addressed one by one with carefully integrated actions.

Communication professionals by virtue of their interests and backgrounds need to be a vital part of that collaborative effort of helping to make the business case, collecting the data that show the root causes of disengagement, lobbying for the necessary training and development, and consulting with senior leaders on corrective action.

The task is formidable. It is also essential.

References

Buckingham, M., & Coffman, C. (1999). *First, break all the rules.* New York: Simon & Schuster.

Eco, U. (2005, March 7). The gorge (G. Brock, Trans.). *New Yorker,* 62–73.

Levinson, H. (1973). *The great jackass fallacy.* Boston: Harvard Business School Publications.

Reichheld, F. (1996). *The loyalty effect.* Boston: Harvard Business School Press.

Sirota, D., Mischkind, L., & Metzler, I. (2005). *The enthusiastic employee:* How companies profit by giving workers what they want. Indianapolis: Wharton School Publishing.

Stewart, T. (1998). *Intellectual capital: The new wealth of organizations.* New York: Doubleday.

Towers Perrin. (2003). *Working today: Understanding what drives employee engagement.* www.towersperrin.com/hrservices/webcache/towers/United_States/ publications/Reports/Talent_Report_2003/Talent_2003.pdf.

CHAPTER NINETEEN

Communicating Major Change Within the Organization

Rodney Gray, Gerard Castles

M ost communicators from time to time manage projects to communicate major changes in their organizations: mergers, acquisitions, divestments, restructuring, downsizing, outsourcing, major changes to work or processes, vision, mission or values, or formal attempts to change the organization's culture. In the first half of this chapter, Rodney Gray outlines the findings of a recent research project on change communication and the key drivers of successful change. In the second half, Gerard Castles presents a proven process for managing the communication aspects of major change projects.

WHAT WE KNOW ABOUT MAJOR CHANGE

A research project conducted by Rodney Gray in 2003 (for Australian and New Zealand clients of a leading corporate affairs consultancy, the Allen Consulting Group) revealed much about what is needed for the successful communication and implementation of major change in organizations (Lindsay, 2004).

A key objective of the research project was to identify statistically the key drivers of satisfaction with major change, and in particular to ascertain the communication practices associated with employee satisfaction with major change. A lengthy survey was designed with items on a wide variety of factors that an extensive literature search found might possibly have an impact on satisfaction with change. Specifically, the study was designed to measure the extent to which many different factors correlated with employees' perceptions that major change "appeared to be well planned" and "implementation was well handled."

Significant Findings

The survey items that correlated most strongly with change management fell into thirteen core issues that clustered into three main areas (see Figure 19.1):

- *Change communication*—the extent to which formal communication about change was well handled (consistent, timely, and adequate). Strongly related were survey items to do with information sufficiency and cross-area communication.

- *Upward communication*—the extent to which it is easy for employees to raise issues freely and get their ideas and opinions listened to. Strongly related to this were survey items to do with change consultation, job authority, and recognition.

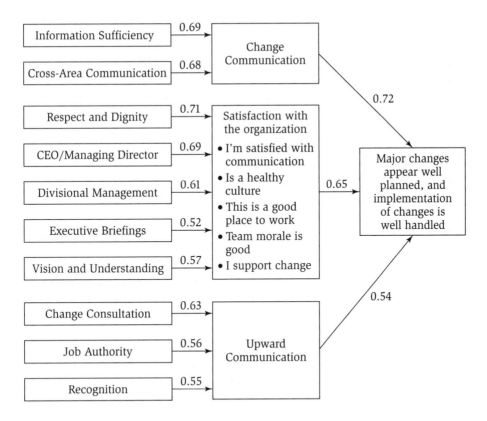

Figure 19.1. Key Drivers of Change Management

Source: Research conducted by Rodney Gray for the Allen Consulting Group, Oct. 2003.

- *Satisfaction with the organization.* Strongly related to this cluster of items were survey items on respect and dignity, CEO communication, divisional management communication, executive briefings, and communication and understanding of vision.

Employees are likely to believe change is well planned and implementation well handled if they are satisfied with the organization overall; the organization's culture is a healthy one; they would recommend this to others as a good place to work; morale in their work area or team is good; and they support most changes the organization makes.

Clearly these are outcomes that communicators cannot directly influence. But it does confirm that change efforts are likely to be more successful where there are satisfied employees, healthy cultures, and high morale.

Note that correlation by itself measures only association and does not indicate which is cause and effect. However, we are probably safe to assume that the strong correlations mean that communication about change and upward communication are important factors in the successful implementation of change. With the items about satisfaction with the organization in general, it may be a two-way street in that poorly implemented change may cause dissatisfaction among employees, and an organization or business unit with poor morale may resist well-intentioned change.

This research suggests ten critical factors in regard to change communication (see Figure 19.2).

Change Communication. It is not surprising that communication specifically about the major change itself was the key driver of satisfaction with change management. As a minimum, the survey showed communication about change must be adequate and well handled, timely notice of changes must be given to those who are affected, employees must be informed through formal channels before they hear it through the grapevine, and various messages from different sources must be consistent.

Information Sufficiency. People must get sufficient information about what is going on in the organization. Also, there must be more than enough information available about what is going on if employees want it.

Cross-Area Communication. Also referred to as cross-functional, horizontal, or lateral communication, it is clear that communication across the organization is critical to success in communicating major change.

Given all the effort that has gone into process mapping since Total Quality Management became popular a couple of decades ago, it is surprising that most organizations have real issues here. In one leading organization, only 15 percent of employees were satisfied with communication across various functions.

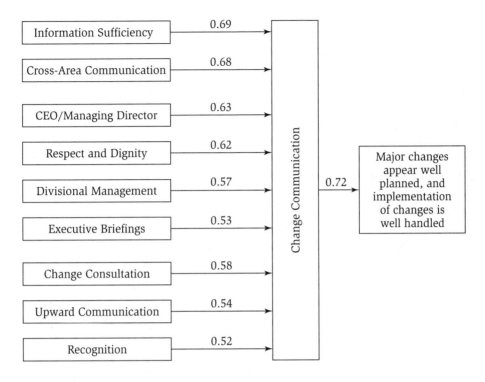

Figure 19.2. Key Drivers of Change Communication

Source: Research conducted by Rodney Gray for the Allen Consulting Group, Oct. 2003.

It is also notable that in countless communication audits, employees report that they provide excellent information to those who depend on them but do not get this from others they rely on.

The survey items suggest that different areas communicate well with each other when there are changes in the way things are done; when project teams are involved in change efforts, they communicate well; and teams receive good communication from others they depend on to do their jobs well.

Upward Communication. This cluster of issues has to do with management's ability to listen. The survey items here were that people can get their ideas listened to by the right people; it is easy for employees to raise issues with management; people are asked to give their opinions on changes, problems, and how to improve things; and people are comfortable expressing their opinions freely, even if they disagree with their managers.

Consultation About Change. In focus groups, participants often comment about the extent to which they are involved in or consulted about changes in the workplace. They do not expect to be consulted about major changes or market-sensitive issues. But they do expect to be consulted about the implementation of changes that affect them, their jobs, or work areas.

Recognition. Employees are likely to believe change is well planned and implementation well handled if they are satisfied with the amount and frequency of informal praise and appreciation provided, and sufficient effort is made to recognize the individuals or teams that make good progress implementing change.

Respect and Dignity. Survey items concerning employees being treated with respect and dignity, especially when they are retrenched, were key drivers of satisfaction with change communication and also satisfaction with the organization. It is difficult to imagine that anyone could be successful in the management of major changes without treating others with respect and dignity at all times.

Chief Executive Communication. There is overwhelming research evidence that most organizations have a blind spot in regard to communication from the top of the organization. Research shows that typically only about a third of employees are likely to be satisfied with CEO communication (compared with two-thirds with immediate manager communication).

Not only does CEO communication correlate strongly with change communication (see Figure 19.2), it strongly affects "satisfaction with the organization," which affects "change management" (see Figure 19.1). The survey items comprising this factor were (in order of significance) that the chief executive:

- Does a good job of communicating with the workforce in general
- Takes account of the concerns of people at all levels
- Understands the needs of people in all areas
- Lives the organization's values and is a good role model
- Keeps people informed about future plans and directions
- Is credible, frank, and honest
- Is sufficiently visible

Divisional Management Communication. The survey items regarding the divisional head were the same as listed for the CEO. However, it is expected that divisional heads will have a better understanding of the needs and concerns of the division's workforce than would a more remote CEO. Employees expect that managers will get out more and will primarily communicate "big picture" issues concerning the impact of major changes on the people of the division.

Executive Briefings. The findings about executive briefings are somewhat ambiguous. On one hand, the research showed that employees like briefings, and at least in regard to major change, briefings do correlate moderately with effective change communication. But on the other hand, executive briefings have not previously correlated strongly with employee satisfaction with communication in the organization.

The message from survey findings (and qualitative research conducted over the years) is that executives should conduct briefings with groups of employees that are small or intimate enough that meaningful discussion can take place. While employees may like large "town hall" meetings, these usually do not provide effective, two-way interaction. But an executive visit and discussion with about forty or fifty employees is likely to be effective if handled well.

Less Significant Factors

There were also a number of core issues that correlated less strongly with change management:

- One-on-one and team meetings and quality of team interaction
- Immediate manager and supervisor communication
- Electronic communication and access to electronic technology
- Other communication approaches (including publications)

These findings do not necessarily mean these are not important and can be neglected. It may be that they may apply more at a local level (teams or immediate managers) or are support tools rather than success drivers (electronic communication or publications).

What Organizations That Communicate Change More Effectively Do Differently

In this project, three organizations were shown to be handling change better than the others, at least in the opinion of employees. That is not to say that employees thought they were handling change well. Far from it. The scores indicate that they were handling change better. Their positive scores were 24 percent higher, and their negative scores were 30 percent lower.

By segmenting the survey results from all organizations into two groups (see Table 19.1)—Group A, "Change Handled Well" (39 percent positive, 30 percent negative), and Group B, "Change Not Handled Well" (15 percent positive, 60 percent negative)—and comparing the findings of the two, we can see where the big differences are and identify what the better organizations are doing differently such that employees perceive that change is handled better.

In write-in comments, respondents commented on communication efforts that they felt contributed to a change that was well handled. Assigning the comments made in the "change handled better" and "change not well handled"

Table 19.1. Differences in "Change Well Handled" versus "Change Not Well Handled" Organizations

Key Drivers	Group A Better Than Group B
Respect and dignity	26%
Change communication	25
Satisfaction with organization	25
CEO communication	23
Sufficiency of information	22
Executive briefings and road shows	20
Recognition	19
Divisional management communication	18
Employees understanding of vision	16
Communication upwards; management listening	15
Communication across different areas	14
Change consultation	10

Note: Group A = change handled well; Group B = change not handled well.

organizations to various categories revealed some interesting comparisons. Table 19.2 shows the percentage of comments made in each grouping of organizations that relate to the core issues.

In the organizations that are handling change better:

- There were more favorable comments relating to specific change communication efforts (22 percent versus 16 percent).

- There were twice as many mentions of the CEO (6 percent versus 3 percent).

- There were twice as many mentions of divisional managers' communication efforts (11 percent versus 5 percent).

- There were half as many mentions of electronic communication approaches (13 percent versus 26 percent).

- There were fewer mentions of the immediate manager or supervisor (2 percent versus 7 percent).

Many other aspects scored similar percentage of comments, including openness and honesty, team meetings, training, information packs, and publications of various kinds.

Specific communication about change, and the communication implied by the leadership and behavior of management, are key factors influencing employee perceptions; communicators need to be aware of both.

The lower scores for "electronic communication" most likely mean it is a tool, not a driver. Seen in that light, it can have an important role, but the

Table 19.2. Percentages of Comments Made About Issues

Issues Comments Were Made About	Group A: Change Handled Better	Group B: Change Not Well Handled
Change communication	22%	16%
Electronic communication	13	26
Divisional management communication	11	5
Team interaction, meetings	9	9
Published information	8	5
Chief executive communication	6	3
Training	5	5
Respect and dignity	5	3
Consultation and involvement	4	7
Information packs	3	2
Open communication	3	2
Immediate manager/supervisor	2	7
Executive road shows	2	5
Project team communication	2	3
Communication upward (ability to raise issues, express opinions)	1	2

medium is not a replacement for key messages, specifically about change, and messages conveyed by the decisions and behavior of the organization's management.

The research indicates that concentrating on these top ten factors will help ensure that change communication efforts are successful. In addition you should follow a proven methodology to manage the entire process.

ENGAGING PEOPLE ON THE TRANSFORMATION JOURNEY: A PRACTICAL GUIDE

Shifting agendas, uncertainty, anger, and fear are the norm. Each employee is preoccupied with his or her own fate. Meanwhile, senior management has lost touch with the real issues that frontline staff are worried about and are fearful of communicating before they have all the answers. The rumor mill runs rampant, uncertainty thrives, trust diminishes, the change process gets undermined, and shareholder value destroyed.

This scenario is played regularly around the world as organizations attempt to transform themselves in the face of increased competition or changing market pressures.

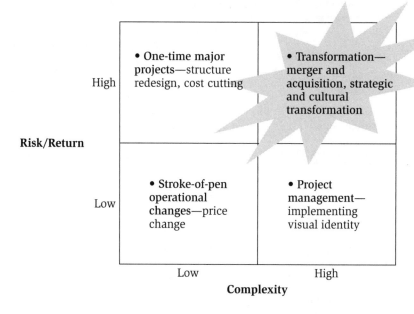

Figure 19.3. Transformation: High Stakes and High Complexity

It does not have to be that way. If leaders and communicators understand the journey they are undertaking and recognize and execute a simple plan to deeply engage stakeholders, they will not only survive, they will truly transform their organizations.

Know It When You See It

Transformation is about change in hyperdrive. It is when the stakes are high and the task is complex. Knowing this is important (Figure 19.3). Trying to manage a transformation effort without the needed resources or focus can cause major damage.

Transformation usually involves multiple parallel shifts in areas such as strategy, structure, culture, and systems over a period of several years. Transformations are by their nature messy, evolving, and chaotic processes, with intense spikes of activity and rapid shifts in direction as opportunities or issues arise.

The challenge is to engage stakeholders on the whole transformation journey, avoiding the starburst syndrome where heat and light are generated early but then fall away.

Creating a Flexible and Robust Engagement Strategy

The answer is not to hope that "these problems won't happen to us," but to design a flexible and robust engagement strategy that will cope with the inevitable stresses of transformation. The process is not complex, but execution requires courage, agility, and perseverance. A practical three-step guide can be used to develop and execute an engagement strategy to support transformation. Each step is summarized briefly.

Step 1: Getting the Lay of the Land: The Quick Diagnostic. This is not about a large and cumbersome research project. A quick diagnostic can tell you almost everything you need to know. It can take anything from a few hours to a few weeks, but the objective is the same: to get a sense of the lay of the land. Here are some key questions that must be asked and answered before you can move forward.

- Identify a sponsor. Who has the clout to make it happen? Communication and engagement is a strategic issue that must be driven from the top. The first step is to identify a sponsor for the project with the skill and will to drive a robust engagement strategy that addresses controversial and difficult issues like leadership commitment, really involving people, taking on board concerns, and telling the truth about what is happening even when the news is bad. If sponsorship for the strategy is pushed down the line into human resources, marketing, or corporate communication, it will likely fail. Ultimately the issues that are fundamental will be decided around the leadership table. You need to ensure the person driving engagement has a seat at that table.
- Identify outcomes. What is the prize, and how will it be achieved? Too many communication professionals complain of being ignored and not having a seat at the leadership table. The reason is simple: too many communicators are seen as peripheral to delivering bottom-line performance. They are seen as delivering outputs, such as newsletters, Web sites, and speeches, not performance outcomes.

Therefore, a critical early step is defining performance outcomes: the prize that will be delivered through strong engagement of stakeholders. These outcomes may be cost savings, revenue growth, sustained service levels, avoiding lost time due to strikes, reduced employee churn, stakeholder buy-in to a change, or a heightened level of trust needed for the new organization to operate.

These must be identified in tangible ways, such as percentage improvement or financial measures that are aligned with key result areas or key performance indicators for the business. Align communication and engagement strategies against these, and management will take notice.

The outcomes are one part of this puzzle, and they do not remain static. You need to identify changing needs at each stage of the transformation process: prelaunch, launch, early-stage wave one implementation, and longer-term second wave change.

Once performance outcomes are agreed for the project overall and each stage of the process, the next step is to identify who is critical to delivering these outcomes.

• Identify the stakeholders. Who are the players? It is not enough to just list who has a stake in the transformation process. You must identify and map the relative importance of stakeholders based on criteria, such as when they are affected, their relative power and importance, and whether they are for, against, or neutral about the transformation process. You will need to map where the leadership team, various levels of management, team leaders, unions, key influencers in the business, people in hot spots, and other stakeholders are placed against these criteria, and from that prioritize where you devote time and effort.

Once that map has been completed, you then need to analyze stakeholders to identify the specific change objective with each, the issues and beliefs they have, and also their ability and willingness to get on board (see Figure 19.4).

• Analyze previous experience: What can we learn from history? It is more than likely that the organization as a whole, or some part of it, has attempted or been through something similar to the change you are contemplating. It may not have been of the breadth of what is being undertaken now, but it needs to be understood.

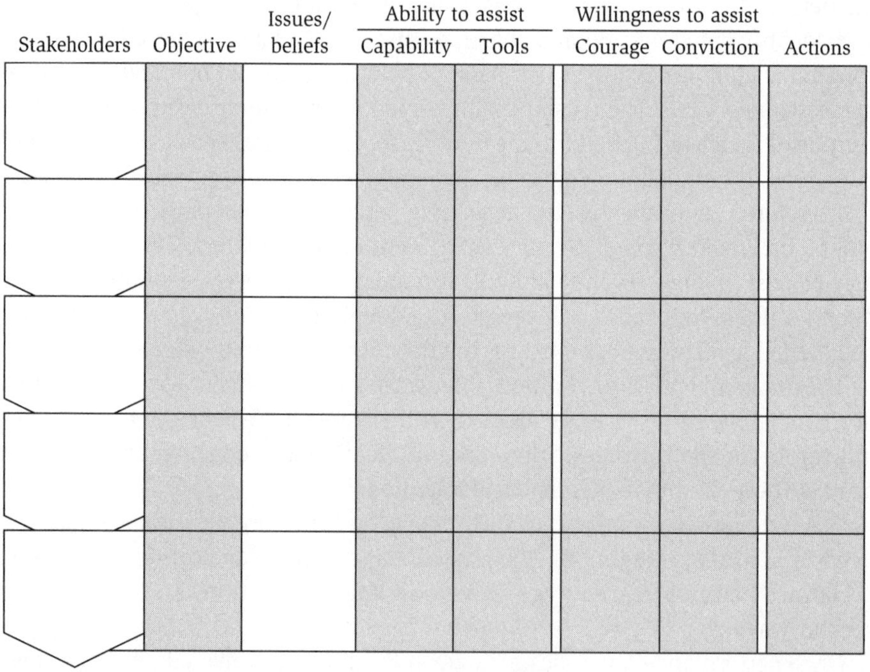

| Stakeholders | Objective | Issues/ beliefs | Ability to assist | | Willingness to assist | | Actions |
			Capability	Tools	Courage	Conviction	

Figure 19.4. Stakeholder Analysis

Take time to talk to people: previous change leaders, union officials, people who have left the organization who carry organizational intelligence. Find out what has worked and failed and why, what achievements people are proud of, and what causes them angst. Also, scan any previous research for clues about organizational strengths and weaknesses. These insights must be factored into your strategy.

• Diagnose readiness: Where is the organization at today? Are people tired, excited, overwhelmed? Janssen (1996) provides a useful framework for this analysis with his Four-Room Apartment (Figure 19.5). Understanding the change readiness of the organization is critical to shaping the engagement strategy. Organizations that are content need to be woken from their slumber. Organizations in denial have to face the harsh facts of reality. Organizations in confusion need direction, and organizations in renewal need to see the next horizon.

Figure 19.5. Diagnose Readiness: The Four-Room Apartment

Source: Richardson & MacNeish (1993). Acknowledgment to Claes Janssen.

- Lock in commitment. What will it take to get senior management committed? The senior leadership team must agree explicitly to the engagement plan. Like anyone else, they are more likely to support something they help create. That means going through the diagnosis in detail with them on their own and as a group so they can start to put their fingerprints on the engagement strategy.

Step 2: Build a Plan. Once you have completed the diagnostic and have a picture of the lay of the land, you can then start to build the foundations of the engagement strategy:

- Create a story. A friend of mine who is an author recently said that two things are profoundly important to shaping human existence: stories and symbols. Stories are being rediscovered in the corporate world. They were always there but lost in a sea of PowerPoint slides and boring speeches.

Stories are fundamental to a corporate transformation. People need a story that provides meaning in what can be a turbulent time, explaining the past, the present, and, as far as possible, the future. The transformational story must be honest, simple, relevant to the organization's current situation, and straightforward. Like any other good story, the transformation story must be based on fact, have heroes and villains, and have an emotional edge. Most important, people need to be able to see themselves in the story and identify with the characters. Stories must be told often, shared widely, and personalized. There is no one size fits all.

These stories can take many forms. I have seen a CEO write a twenty-page document describing the journey the organization had been on, the forces buffeting it, and the future. All the communication professionals, including me, advised him against it. It was a raging success filling an information vacuum that had been there for a year or more.

The story should be tested with some frontline managers and key influencers to make sure it addresses the issues staff are worried about as well as what senior managers want to say.

Some are blunt and spell out why an organization is in the mess it is in. Some stories are inspirational, talking about the "the light on the hill" and how it can be reached.

There are many ways to develop the story. For some it is a matter of the leader's spelling out his or her version of the transformation story and then fine-tuning it with the executive team. Other leadership teams develop them together in working sessions where the headlines, details, and nuances are thrashed out over days, weeks, or even months. Finally they need to be brought to life. We need to help leaders decide what symbols and significant acts can be used to make these stories real and stick in the minds of people who hear them.

• Lock in the principles that guide what you do and how you do it—the engagement compass. It is impossible to know what issues you will need to address once a transformation process starts, only that they will be many, complex, and often unexpected. An agreed set of principles provides clarity around how leaders will communicate with and engage their people. They provide a compass along with the flexibility to respond to situations as they arise.

These principles should be based on leading practice, but must be shaped to meet the needs of each particular situation and fleshed out to describe what these principles will mean.

• Create a road map. Organization transformation programs come in all shapes and sizes. They all have different phases—prelaunch (where the focus is on strategy development), launch, and implementation—which may involve multiple waves of change.

An engagement road map describes the major phases of the transformation journey, the engagement objectives and pivotal stakeholders for each stage, what we want to talk about, key actions and red flags, and those things that if they occur are show stoppers for that stage. This is a critical document and should be able to be reduced to one page that the leadership team constantly uses and refines.

• Develop and lock in ongoing systems to ensure people are engaged, not just told. In each stage four basic systems must be put in place to deliver real engagement. At each stage of the program you need to inspire, inform, listen, and deeply involve (Hutchison, 2001).

Inspire means providing a clear direction and inspiring people to act. People will be watching for hints of the future. You will need to work with the CEO and senior team to develop a plan of action they will take to signal the new direction. Through the symbolic power of the decisions they make, where they spend their time, and what they recognize and reward, they will shape perceptions. The key is to manage this, not leave it to chance.

Systems to make this happen could include site visits, a phased program of major announcements, or big events where leaders are given the chance to articulate their vision with broad groups of people. Monitor what people in the organization are thinking and saying, and eliminate any negative signals.

Inform refers to building understanding and awareness. This is where organizations have been traditionally strongest. The problem is, however, that too much has been output focused on Web sites, briefings, and information cascades that have little, if any, impact on the bottom line.

The challenge here is threefold. First, decide where and when to target communication to achieve outcomes. Second is to decide what communication content is needed to drive increased productivity, better service, or awareness of the "burning platform." Third is to determine the right balance between broadband and narrowband communication.

Larkin and Larkin (1994) created a minor revolution when they announced that change communication had been failing to deliver and that what was needed was communication delivered face-to-face, by frontline managers about real performance. They were largely right, with one major proviso: there is no one-size-fits-all approach, and leaders play a crucial role in transformational change. People do look to their immediate supervisors for interpretation, but direction comes from the top.

Communication ideas are still evolving on the right balance between broadband and narrowband. Broadband communication (briefings, Web sites, newspapers, and the like) reaches everyone and plays a role in creating basic awareness and context. However, it is narrowband communication (targeted briefings for select stakeholders, inquiry conversations, issues-based communication, and, increasingly, "viral communication") that is designed explicitly to flow through informal networks in organizations and is being recognized as crucial in transformation.

For years, communicators have fought against the grapevine, bemoaning its speed and accuracy. Now the role of viral communication through not just one but multiple grapevines is becoming increasingly powerful in organization transformation, particularly as a way of spreading ideas.

Popularized by Gladwell (2002) and built from buzz marketing ideas, viral communication is about using informal networks and cleverly packaged ideas to spread ideas like viruses. Organizations are now learning to spread ideas through "secret" Web sites on corporate intranets, "pirate" video clips, and blogs of CEOs saying what they really think, text messaging to employees, producing comic-book-based surveys, appreciative inquiry conversations that are seeded and then spread through networks, corporate blogs, and clever branding of change initiatives.

One corporate transformation team even partnered with a local coffee shop to rename coffees and food after key themes of the transformation program just to get people talking. All these initiatives follow a similar formula. They have a real strategic outcome in mind; they package ideas in ways that make them irresistible and use informal networks to take them across organization boundaries.

Listen is about understanding and addressing concerns. It is easy for leaders to go into "tell" mode and forget what people are really worried about. Systems must be in place to gather intelligence from managers and staff on a continual basis. If you do not know the top three issues being discussed daily in the cafeteria or at home after work, then you are not listening.

Feedback can take two forms: qualitative and quantitative. Qualitative feedback is the lifeblood of transformation. You need to have systems and processes that constantly scan for employee concerns, hot spots where performance has dropped off, or issues that might seem insignificant to managers but are about to flare up, like roster changes, food choices or quality in the canteen, and not seeing managers out on the floor.

This feedback can be gathered by having designated people on the team call half a dozen key contacts weekly to check up on progress. One bank CEO ran sessions to which surrounding branch offices sent people in pairs to have a quick update on the program and then spend 80 percent of the time discussing with the CEO questions that were being raised in their areas. The results of the conversations were summarized on the spot and sent back with the people who attended. Importantly, the CEO was on top of issues across the organization that were holding up transformation.

Quantitative feedback is also important. Some organizations have built quick surveys of about five or six questions that are asked monthly of a random sample of people to track ongoing levels of awareness, understanding, and buy-in to change.

Deeply involve means that people will engage only when they feel they are genuinely being involved. This is about leaders' making safe opportunities where people down the line and from across boundaries can shape solutions. By their nature, organization transformations involve complex system changes that cut across boundaries.

Key stakeholders must be involved in shaping the journey. Some organizations use search conferences or GE-style Work Outs to bring a cross section of stakeholders together to find common ground on the future and develop action plans to get there. Others create online or real-time forums where frontline managers or staff review what is happening and participate in decision making or the transformation process.

• Define performance indicators. You need to know if communication processes are working and performance outcomes are being delivered. You should agree to process benchmarks at the outset (for example, at least 90 percent of all shift employees must have been briefed within seventy-two hours). To check process, measure awareness in different parts of the business, and determine the number of people briefed.

Performance impact must be the key measure of communication effectiveness. Measure performance impact on productivity, lost time, safety, market share, employee churn, or trust. If performance is headed in the wrong direction, change your engagement strategy. Report to the senior team regularly, and take strong action with people who fail to deliver their part of the plan.

• Put a team in place to drive the engagement strategy. More often than not, existing structures and systems will not cope with the added pressure of transformation. You will need to create an engagement task force with representatives from the project team, the leadership team, and key people from across the business to help shape the engagement strategy, drive implementation, and support managers. Forming this team in itself sends a signal that engagement is important and cannot be imposed as a top-down exercise.

The design of the team will vary according to the needs of the situation. Sometimes what is required is a small task force; in others a broader representative team is needed.

Forming the team itself is a first step; processes must be built around it, including regular meetings at least weekly in the early stages and a formal reporting process at the senior team meetings.

Step 3: Implement and Learn. Implementation must be tightly managed. Transformation requires the same heightened level of awareness, flexibility, and attention to detail and activity that you would expect during an organizational crisis. During implementation, a cycle begins of:

- Rigorous implementation of agreed systems to inform, listen, involve, and inspire
- Tracking key performance indicators
- Regular interactions of the engagement team to fine-tune the ongoing strategy
- Creating strategies for specific issues or hot spots

Learning is also important. Without the focus and energy provided by change, engagement performance can slip away. Lessons from the transformation process must be assessed and built into the ongoing life of the organization.

Engaged people are critical to the success of all organizational transformations. Bring together a great business strategy, strong and wise leaders, plus switched-on people, and success will inevitably follow.

References

Gladwell, M. (2002). *The tipping point: How little things can make a big difference.* Boston: Back Bay Books.

Hutchison, S. (2001, February-March). Communicating in times of change: Contributing to the success of business transformation. *Strategic Communication Management, 5*(2), 28–31.

Janssen, C. (1996). *The four rooms of change.* Stockholm: Wahlström & Widstrand. http://www.claesjanssen.com/four-rooms/index.shtml.

Larkin, T. J., & Larkin, S. (1994). *Communicating change: Winning employee support for new business goals.* New York: McGraw-Hill.

Lindsay, A. (2004). Public affairs, reputation and organizational culture: Closing the gap between performance and behavior. *Corporate Public Affairs, 14*(2), 1. http://www.accpa.com.au.

Richardson, T., & MacNeish, J. (1993). *The choice.* Melbourne: Don't Press.

CHAPTER TWENTY

Internal Communication Media

Tamara L. Gillis

Corporate populations are their most diverse today due to globalization and innovative organizational structures. This diversity within organizations requires corporate communicators to employ a variety of dynamic communication media to reach today's internal audiences. Internal communication media provide the means for educating and coordinating hundreds or thousands of geographically and culturally diverse individuals within an organization to work as a team toward organizational goals.

According to Horton (1995), as a business process, internal corporate communication transfers information from the business environment into the organization, which directs specific activities that result in employee-driven economic transactions for the company. If the goal of internal communication is to share information essential to the competitiveness of the organization, then the goal of internal communication media selection is the improvement of the information sharing that facilitates relationships between the organization leadership and its employees in an effort to advance the company toward reaching its organizational goals.

Aligning internal communication plans with organizational goals and objectives is a key step in developing and strengthening corporate performance.

AN AUDIENCE-CENTERED APPROACH

Designing successful internal communication media as part of an internal communication program hinges on making an honest and meaningful connection between the organization's business plan, management, and employees. To that end, the media selected to deliver the messages must ultimately meet the information needs and preferences of the end users: the internal audience members. Internal audience members can be the employees of a company or members of an organization. For the discussion here, I will refer to employees or members and internal audience interchangeably.

Internal media that are readily accessible, reliable, and universal throughout an organization can be successful in keeping information flowing to those who depend on it. However, the audiences must see the information as useful, meaningful, and valuable. Otherwise they will find ways to discredit it, which leads to a breakdown in the relationship between the audience and the organization.

DEFINING OBJECTIVES OF INTERNAL COMMUNICATION MEDIA

Internal communication media are conduits to share with employees information about the company's business strategy, business environment, and financial situation and build relationships. More important from the employees' perspective, they want and need to know information about how they contribute to the company as well as the business plan: information about pay and benefits, career development and career opportunities, what the company needs from employees to reach organizational goals, and what employees get in return for doing what the company needs (Towers Perrin, 2004). With this in mind, objectives for developing internal communication media and its content may include the following:

- To inform and reinforce the company's business plan, that is, organizational goals and objectives
- To inform employees about organizational activities, problems, accomplishments, and the employees' role in these
- To encourage employees to provide feedback to management concerning organizational issues
- To provide a regular, frequent, and trusted forum for discussing positive and negative issues related to the success of the organization
- To establish a culture of information sharing for the improvement of individuals and the organization
- To reinforce the employee's role in the organization and in meeting organizational goals and to educate employees about one another's roles in the organization

- To provide a forum for clarifying company policies and procedures
- To recognize employee achievements and accomplishments

A coordinated internal communication program will develop a culture of communication that will benefit the organization especially during times of change. If employees know they receive accurate, timely, and honest information from a number of trusted internal media, they will look to these same media during times of change. As a result, these media will be most valuable in preparing and nurturing employees through major change initiatives and times of uncertainty. In a Towers Perrin survey (2004) of a thousand working Americans, "internal company media are viewed as more credible than the external media, the Internet or labor unions" when it comes to credible information on company issues (p. 8). In order of priority, participants reported that they were most likely to rely on the following sources for credible information on company issues: supervisor or manager, employee meetings, coworkers, print media, the company's Web site, external media, Internet search, and the union.

Research (Rauch, 2005; Business Communicator, 2005; Morrison, 2004) indicates a direct relationship between employee job satisfaction and the amount of communication they receive from their employer. Job satisfaction was highest in populations that received regular and trusted communication from their company about their contributions to corporate performance.

CRITERIA FOR MEDIA SELECTION

Based on the objectives and messages to be shared with the internal audiences, media selection is a critical consideration. Continuing with the audience-centered approach, the criteria for evaluating media selection should include the audience's needs for social presence and the media richness (Modaff & DeWine, 2002). These two criteria will affect audience reception of the messages. Social presence refers to the sociability of the medium, that is, its warmth and sensitivity. It may also include its ease of use. Face-to-face communication has a higher degree of social presence than, say, a corporate memo. When messages are sensitive in nature or require interpretation, a medium of high social presence is recommended. Media richness refers to the density of the information. Interactivity, responsiveness, and immediacy, as well as the formal use of language, are issues associated with media richness. Face-to-face communication also has a higher degree of media richness than a corporate memo.

Media may be categorized as formal and informal or controlled and uncontrolled. A combination of these traits is necessary to satisfy the needs and preferences of a variety of internal audiences. Formal media are often described as those that are mandated by the organization and used to send messages from management to employees; these are determined by the organization's structure. Informal media are described as exchanges of information on a peer-to-peer or anecdotal level.

We can also describe internal media as controlled and uncontrolled media. In controlled media, the content and distribution are dictated by the company. In uncontrolled media, the content and distribution are not dictated by the company. Some media, like some forms of electronic media, appear to fall into both categories. For example, an e-mail listserv on the company network may be used to distribute information that the company has not sanctioned. Consequently, these categories of media are not mutually exclusive. Harnessing the information power of uncontrolled and an informal media is a challenge. At one time, the grapevine or rumor mill, an uncontrolled and informal communication channel, was considered a nonviable network of information. Today it is the challenge of corporate communicators to use these peer-to-peer networks to enhance organizational information delivery and ultimately organizational performance.

Other considerations when developing internal communication media are developing two-way communication components, managing the external effects of internal communication, and managing the resources of the organization. Two-way communication is necessary for employees to feel satisfied with the information they receive about the company and to feel they contribute to the success of their work environment. Since employees are ambassadors of the company when they leave the corporate campus and rejoin the community each day, employee communication has a direct impact on external relationships with customers and the public. The better informed employees are about company policies and news and events, the less likely they are to spread damaging misinformation within the organization and externally through family and friends. Finally, the media an organization uses to reach its internal audiences will be affected by the size of the organization and the resources dedicated to internal communication.

SELECTING THE MEDIA

An organization must decide what combination of internal media will best meet its needs based on the objectives, the needs and preferences of the audiences it is trying to reach, and the available resources. As organizational conditions change, the audience's need for internal media may also change. For example, the frequency of publication and the method of distribution should be determined by evaluating the needs and preferences of the audience members as well as the messages being shared. Some media may be created and used for a specific campaign, such as a change initiative, and then eliminated once the change has been fully integrated into the organization.

As we consider the variety of media at our disposal, we also need to consider the planning process associated with the introduction of the media. Here are a few basic considerations when planning for the use of internal communication media: (1) audience needs and preferences (social presence), (2) resources, and (3) speed of delivery (media richness). Internal media must meet the information needs of the internal audience. But this must be balanced with the available resources and the need for interactivity and speed of response.

Audience Needs and Preferences

Whether a new medium is being proposed or an existing medium is being evaluated or reinvented, researching the communication needs and preferences of the intended audience will ensure that the medium and its content satisfy its organizational goals. The diversity of today's workforce may demand a combination of media to satisfy their information needs. A geographically dispersed workforce will also require more complex and coordinated internal communication programming. Surveying the intended audience (as a whole or in segments, depending on the size of the population) will help determine the best media to use and the type of content to convey the organization's messages. Some content is dictated by the organization's management; some may be dictated by the audience (employee or member). This audience research will help define these selections as well as provide a benchmark for future internal media measurement.

Available Resources

The resources available to meet the organization's and audience's needs and preferences include time, talent, and funds. As in any other organizational function, an operational process must be determined. This encompasses developing a budget to produce the media and a plan that outlines the collection and preparation of the information (writing, editing, and fact checking), production of the media (print, live, or electronic), and evaluation of its effectiveness. This is an important step in developing a consistent approach. It is at this point that the corporate communicator may evaluate whether the production can be accomplished in-house or whether it should be outsourced to an agency. Purpose, content, and frequency of each medium should be examined on a regular basis to determine whether it continues to meet the objectives set for it. Surveys and questionnaires are simple evaluation measures. (Additional information on internal communication measurement can be found in Williams, 2003, and Sinickas, 2005.) "Companies that periodically audit their communication processes and media do a better job of managing the key messages and information delivered to employees. With the proliferation of communication channels (e.g., print, electronic, face to face), there's growing opportunity for organizational communications to become out of sync and even contradictory" (Towers Perrin, 2004, p. 9).

Media Richness

What type of interactivity is necessary for the communication to be successful? How formal or informal should the language be? How quickly does the information change and need to be conveyed to the audience? These issues of delivery go hand in hand with the resources planning stage. These will also have an impact on the effect and success of the communication transmission, as well as communication satisfaction level of the audience.

The media selected and the way they are produced and delivered convey meaning and authority. This is a matter of perception on the part of the audience. Even the tone of one's voice and body language convey meaning. So does the choice of paper in a print publication and the graphics on a Web page.

Corporate communicators in multinational organizations also need to address the issue of multilingualism within their internal population. Failure to address the language needs of internal audiences sends an unintended message of authority and apathy to their communication needs and preferences.

Having a variety of coordinated media as part of an internal communication program will ensure greater success at meeting the varied needs of the organization and the audience. For example, a monthly employee magazine or newsletter provides a regular forum for insightful discussion of organizational issues and employee accomplishments. The annual report to employees provides the annual organizational progress and financial overview. Monthly or weekly unit meetings with supervisors provide opportunities to discuss organizational issues and encourage creative problem solving and team building that show the direct connection between employee engagement and organizational success. An active electronic presence in the form of a dynamic intranet with employee listservs, chatrooms, and blogs, as well as e-newsletters with formal organizational information, provides a forum for immediate discussion and resolution of a misunderstanding.

A SAMPLING OF MEDIA

For our discussion here, I have categorized internal media into four categories: live, print, broadcast, and electronic. This is not an inclusive list of all media; it is a sampling of them.

Live and in Person

Research studies and our daily workplace activities provide evidence that face-to-face communication rates the highest in social presence and media richness. Individual meetings, group meetings, and town hall meetings with the CEO delivering a message directly to employees provide an opportunity for internal audiences to personally evaluate credibility and completeness of an organizational message. Body language, facial expression, vocal tone, and the opportunity for interactivity make face-to-face communication compelling. Where large, geographically dispersed audiences are involved, this can be achieved through videoconferencing the large meeting forum. It can also be simulated through real-time conferencing Internet technology or even the rather informal chatroom format. The online media may reduce the ability for audience members to discern nonverbal cues, and the immediate interactivity provides the necessary information reinforcement.

Unit meetings with managers and frequent visits by executive management are regular components of most organizations. Research suggests that this is the most trusted and preferred means for employees to learn about their role in the organization (Towers Perrin, 2004). Large group meetings and town hall meetings with executive management are used with less frequency and to share news with all employees at the same time. Choosing one medium over another will send a message to audience members about the nature of the information or the importance of the audience members to the organization. Live media also include uncontrolled and informal media like the grapevine.

Print Media

The most traditional forms of internal communications are print media. In this category we include all print products, from a memo from the desk of the corporate executive, to human resource materials like brochures and policy handbooks, to the employee magazine and the formal annual report. When time is of the essence, traditional print media are slow to meet the demand of internal audiences. Print media are best at delivering information that is static (at least for the period of time between publications).

Corporate memos and letters take time to construct and may appear calculated due to the formal language, the formal presentation on company letterhead, and archival quality. Social presence and media richness are both low. There is no room for interaction, and interpretation of the message may vary from member to member.

Employee handbooks and orientation materials are formal and controlled media. Because of the expense of printing and the legal nature of the material contained in these publications, employee handbooks and manuals are designed to be read and saved as archival and ready reference material. The greatest complaint about these official publications is that of information overload. There is so much information in the employee handbook that it is often difficult to locate particular information, and it is mired in legal language; employees often forgo the policy manual and defer to peer networks or meetings with their supervisors. Organizing information should be a primary concern in developing a user-friendly employee handbook to help eliminate miscommunication and increase communication satisfaction.

Employee publications like magazines and newsletters are another fundamental form of internal communication and are more dynamic than handbooks and brochures due to the frequency of the circulation. Company publications vary in size, use of color, graphics, photos, and frequency of publication, depending on the size of the budget and the audience that management seeks to reach. The internal audience, whether they are employees, members, or retirees, makes judgments about the company or organization based on the production qualities of a publication, as well as the information contained in it. Slick, flashy publications may give the impression of sophistication to one audience while offending an audience that perceives the costly production values as a waste of organizational resources. Large organizations often publish several periodicals, each designed for a different audience.

Employee publications may focus on company policies and business news, as well as more human interest issues about employees and retirees (depending on the objectives set out for the publication). Typical objectives for employee publications include increasing employee understanding and support for the company's operations, objectives, plans, and activities; recognizing employee accomplishments on and off the job as a means for developing employee morale and community relations; and educating employees about the operations of the company and their role in meeting its strategic goals. Employee publications are typically distributed to retirees of the company as well as ambassadors of the organizations and its goals. Large corporations with a large retiree population may include profiles on retired members and information about retiree reunions and activities.

Many companies produce annual reports specifically for employees. These reports share financial data like the investor version of the publication, in addition to information about employee contributions to the organization's success and future direction.

Other miscellaneous print media include posters and flyers posted on bulletin boards in high-traffic areas of the company facility. Of course, this type of medium is effective only for organizations where employees work in one location or at least congregate in a communal location on a regular basis. While this communication channel may seem very low tech in today's age of electronic media, this can be an effective way of reaching an internal audience with short, timely pieces of information. To ensure credibility, bulletin boards should be monitored for current and reliable information. Old materials should be removed promptly and rogue information removed.

Audiovisual Programs and Broadcast Media

These media have become necessities for organizations with large, geographically dispersed populations who value sharing information simultaneously with internal audiences. Closed circuit broadcasts and educational videos and interactive CD-ROMs and DVDs are just a few of the ways that organizations can reach internal audiences.

Closed circuit broadcasting facilities provide organizations with an in-house television station for their own programming. Programs may include preproduced educational segments as well as live and recorded broadcasts of presentations by executive management and teleconferences. Since the company programs the channel, it can control the content and the frequency of delivery, making programs available to internal audiences at different times of the day and repeating for different shifts of employees, and it can update and rebroadcast material as necessary to meet audience and organizational demands. Program production can be outsourced to a production house, or an in-house studio may be developed. This can be a costly venture.

Educational videos, CD-ROMs, and DVDs may also be an option for providing information and educational materials to internal audiences. Similar production processes are shared with the broadcasting option.

Electronic Media

Much traditional live, print, and broadcast media are duplicated or simulated in electronic media. Face-to-face meetings can be simulated through online video technology and the immediacy of chatroom conversations. The content from print publications from the company policy manual to newsletters and magazines can be loaded to the company Web site and intranet. Video and audio programs can be made available online for download so employees can use them at their convenience. (With that said, it is important to note that new technology is not always a solution to improving the delivery on the message. While many employees may view a company intranet site, many may print out the information for later reading to avoid the eyestrain of reading from the computer screen.)

Perhaps the most popular electronic medium, e-mail is an immediate medium that is easy to distribute and virtually cost free (with the exception of the time element of creating the message and the distribution lists). In many organizations, it is quickly replacing traditional formal print media like letters and memos. An advantage of e-mail and e-mail newsletters is that they can reach a widely dispersed population simultaneously. E-mail also has the disadvantage of being perceived as capricious and informal. Often messages are written so quickly that the context and impact are not calculated. Recipients may feel that it is a one-way impersonal delivery when more personal communication is required. E-mail is suitable for sending routine information, broadcasting information to a large group of people simultaneously, and conducting transactions that do not require a high level of social presence. It is safe to say that e-mail is not appropriate for sharing personal or confidential information, since company e-mail is the property of the organization.

Intranets provide a controlled medium complete with graphics and sound capabilities that provide another immediate vehicle for internal communications. Since intranets are contained and maintained by the organization, employees or members can feel some security in discussing organizational issues. The Web environment also accommodates streaming video and podcasting of employee information programming. This can provide an extension and personalization of traditional audiovisual media like educational and informational video or closed circuit broadcast programming. Employees can download programming and view it at their leisure.

Other Web opportunities for individual discussion of organizational issues are chatrooms, blogs, and listservs. Employees or members of a multinational organization can meet in real time to discuss organizational issues. Company leaders can host these online activities, thus giving employees access to leadership in a more personal way. Although electronic media are often described as impersonal due to the control of the end user, they can also be described as personal media if used to unite geographically disparate populations in a real-time discussion of organizational issues. These discussions can be captured for archival purposes or for distribution in more traditional means at a later date.

A FEW PARTING THOUGHTS

Many of the media addressed in this chapter represent traditional, controlled, formal downward-communication media. A challenge for corporate communication programs is to develop more upward communications opportunities for internal audiences to make an impact on the organization and their own communication satisfaction. Two-way feedback components provide upward communication channels but are still driven by management. More employee-driven formal upward communication programs will be necessary as organizations survive environmental and economic forces. Consequently, corporate cultures must be accepting and prepare for unflattering employee communication as well.

There is no one right mix of internal media or one-size-fits-all solution to the use of internal communication media. Often the messages being delivered and the need for personal contact and immediate two-way responses will trump the best-developed and most trusted organizational media. In the end, this is an audience-centered process, and meeting the audience's communication and information needs will ensure communication satisfaction. These are important considerations for the corporate communicator who is developing a dynamic internal communications program.

References

Business Communicator. (2005, March). News in brief. *Business Communicator, 5*(9), 3.

Horton, J. L. (1995). *Integrating corporate communications: The cost-effective use of message and medium.* Westport, CT: Quorum Books.

Modaff, D. P., & DeWine, S. (2002). *Organizational communication: Foundations, challenges, and misunderstandings.* Los Angeles: Roxbury Publishing Co.

Morrison, R. (2004, November). Informal relationships in the workplace: Associations with job satisfaction, organizational commitment and turnover intentions. *New Zealand Journal of Psychology, 33*(3), 114–128.

Rauch, M. (2005, April). Survey says . . . *Incentive, 179*(4), 7.

Sinickas, A. (2005). *How to measure your communication programs* (3rd ed.). San Francisco: IABC Knowledge Centre.

Towers Perrin. (2004). *Is it time to take the "spin" out of employee communication?* www.towersperrin.com/hrservices/webcache/towers/United_States/publications/Reports/2004_Enhance_Corp_Cred/Enhance_corp_cred.pdf.

Williams, L. C. Jr. (2003). *Communication research, measurement and evaluation: A practical guide for communicators.* San Francisco: IABC Knowledge Centre.

CHAPTER TWENTY-ONE

Internal Branding

Employer Branding

R. Alan Crozier

There was a time in living memory when you could have a job for life. If you were loyal, worked hard, and did as you were told, your employer would provide a secure job, award regular pay increases, and provide a degree of financial security, even in retirement. Problems arose when the pace of change accelerated. New players from emerging economies entered the market, competition became much stiffer, the rules of engagement were changing, and traditional companies struggled with the speed of this process. These companies and their people were not prepared for what was happening.

What followed was a period of reengineering where businesses were restructured, refocused, downsized, or right-sized, and people were expected to "work smarter, not harder." Those who were not laid off were expected to stay, do as they were told, and do at least part of someone else's job as well as their own. In return, their employer would provide employment (while it could), pay them the same as before, but make gestures that it cared about them as employees. Perhaps not surprisingly with hindsight, people did not always stay with their employer; they started to look for ways to take charge of their own careers and sought better opportunities and better employers, whatever that meant. Companies not coming to terms with this new reality would lose talent.

The employer-employee relationship has now evolved from the parent-child state to an adult-adult state in which the new employment deal is more of a strategic partnership. Companies expect their people to develop the skills that they need and apply them in ways that help the business, meanwhile displaying behavioral competencies that are consistent with those of the company. In return, they will provide challenging work, support personal development, reward individual contribution, and treat people like adults.

In most advanced economies, regardless of the unemployment statistics, there is a skills shortage of some description. There are not enough highly skilled and talented people to go around. Recognizing that people as key talent are core drivers of value, organizations have to develop the ability to attract, fully engage, and retain that talent.

I first came across the phrase *employer brand* in this context when a client mentioned it in conversation in 1995. Every organization has one, and therefore it is worthy of definition, management, and nurturing, particularly if it can play a role in helping the organization mobilize the talent it requires for success.

What follows is a pragmatic view of employer branding based on developing and testing a hypothesis, practicing the principles with organizations, and testing employee and employer opinion on what is working for them. It is a practical process that can be started at any point and followed through to drive real benefits for any organization. This is a mixture of theory, practice, fact, and opinion; it is not intended to be an academic treatise.

THE PHILOSOPHICAL PERSPECTIVE

The philosophical basis for arriving at the employer-branding construct is built on three related tenets.

The Company Does Not Exist

At the practical, social, and emotional levels, organizations exist in the minds of people. Certainly they are legal entities with their own personality in law, but for all practical purposes, it is about people. The word *company* comes from the Latin *com panis,* literally referring to people sharing bread. Companies therefore are about people sharing common goals. Ensuring that all people in the organization are aligned with and committed to goals is not necessarily as easy as it sounds (Figure 21.1).

You will see from Figure 21.1 that there is no direct link between corporate objectives, strategies, and their achievement. The people responsible for the objective setting and the strategies to achieve them have to work with and through the others in the enterprise to ensure that they understand, accept, and act on these plans in their respective roles to drive their achievement. This can involve a complex cognitive and attitudinal system as well as having to deal with potentially differing agendas.

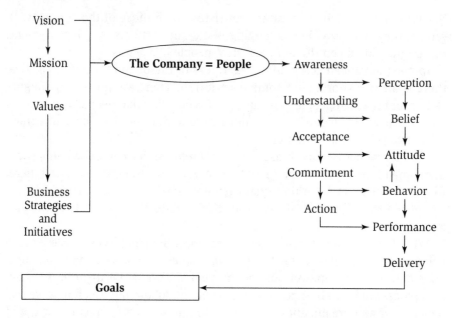

Figure 21.1. The Company Does Not Exist Without a Link Between Strategies and Achievement

Source: © R. Alan Crozier, 1995.

Organizations Are Systems

Organizations are dynamically complex open systems, continually changing yet persisting. Systems possess emergent properties that are not found in their component parts. Consider an orchestra. You could examine each instrument in detail, but it would not prepare you for what is created when all the instruments play together from the same score. So it is with organizations. The whole is greater than the sum of its parts. But in that type of system, it is very difficult to predict what the feedback will be to a particular intervention. There is not always a direct link between the cause of something and the effect it might have. In an organizational system, the effect can become the cause of something else. Feedback and effects are not limited by time and can be quite unpredictable. Systems have a way of self-sustaining, and so any intervention will be met by either feedback that reinforces the intention (and this may be found anywhere in the system) or feedback that tries to balance the momentum for the change by resisting it. Stability and resistance are two sides of the same coin. This means that it is impossible to do just one thing in an organization. Any new initiative has to be introduced and supported at critical points elsewhere in the system if it is to have a chance of becoming a lasting change. This is one reason that most change initiatives do not deliver on their intentions. This point will become clearer when we review some of the practicalities in organizational life.

Employees Are a Dynamic Asset

Employees' value can go down as well as up. That has a lot to do with the employer-employee relationship. Many factors affect that, and the extent to which any one or a number of factors affect employee commitment and performance will vary from business to business—and probably from one group of employees to another in the same business. It is potentially dangerous to assume that employees are a single amorphous group and deploy a one-size-fits-all solution across the board. This is where it is particularly useful to learn about employees' interests, issues, and concerns, as well as the extent to which they are aligned with and committed to the business objectives.

Many studies, like *Work 2002* by Watson Wyatt Worldwide, have shown that companies whose employees are truly engaged drive greater returns to shareholders than those where engagement is lower. Others have found links between employee attitudes and shareholder value; companies considered "best to work for" drive increases in shareholder value. It seems like common sense, but the hard numbers are needed to support the soft impressions, because that is what gets attention in the boardroom.

Around the time competition for talent was on the increase, the phrase *employer of choice* emerged. This struck a chord with many companies, and it became a popular strap line or tag line in recruitment materials as companies sought to differentiate themselves in that market. While the sense of the phrase is immediately understood, what it meant in practice is less clear. To many companies, it meant simply being flexible with total reward or being creative with personal development opportunities. What was clear was that the currency and effectiveness of the line decreased in inverse proportion to its popularity. It was not effective enough to say, "We are an employer of choice"; companies had to *be* an employer of choice without stating it in that way. This requires a more robust and holistic approach.

DEFINING EMPLOYER BRANDING

Employer branding is the process of creating an identity and managing the image of a company or organization in its role as an employer. This process has to take into account and manage the synergistic relationship between the values, systems, policies, and behaviors deployed by the company or organization in pursuit of its objectives through its people.

This hypothesis requires a holistic or systemic approach, which means that organizations have to take care of the total employment experience, not just part of it. Consideration has to be given to all of the ways in which the enterprise, in its various pursuits, interacts with its people. Ideally that starts before the recruitment process and does not necessarily end as the period of employment ends. In today's market, it should be feasible for the parties to work together again at some point for mutual benefit, assuming, of course, that the employment experience was conducive to that.

Although there may be few written definitions of employer branding, there are more interpretations in practice. Perhaps not surprisingly, as this notion emerged, businesses promoted their particular view of what it meant. The recruitment sector saw it as an opportunity to reenergize advertising and promote clients as valid destinations for talent. This is a perfectly legitimate thing to do but runs the risk of creating a gap between rhetoric and reality if the employment experience does not live up to the promise. This was effectively branding the employment proposition, not the employment experience.

Some practitioners in the employee benefits business sought to get involved in what they called employment branding; in effect it was packaging the employment deal, which concentrated on extrinsic and intrinsic reward. In itself this is a vital function, as people have to appreciate and value what they have in employment if companies are going to drive value from their investment.

One worrying manifestation is companies referring to the employee brand. Do they seriously want to create a population of automatons who so obviously belong to their organization? Are they trying to confer some attributes of the corporate or product brand on their employees? If this is being done in the name of alignment between corporate, product, and employer brands, then let us describe it appropriately. I cannot in my wildest imagination see a situation where today's employees would wish to think that they were being branded (like livestock)!

With the exception of the last point, the foregoing are all legitimate activities that increasingly are being carried out well and form an important part of the employer branding process. However, in and of themselves, they are not employer branding based on the hypothesis. Does the hypothesis have to change to a definition that suits what is common in the market, or is there still a place for the more challenging holistic view?

MANAGING THE EMPLOYER BRAND

First, it is important to visualize what it is we are trying to comprehend so that we can start to think about how it can be managed. Figure 21.2 shows the drivers and facilitators of the employment experience. The drivers are market forces, vision, and mission; all of the other elements are facilitators.

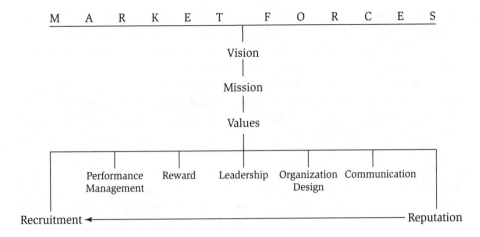

Figure 21.2. Drivers and Facilitators of the Employer-Employee Relationship
Source: © R. Alan Crozier, 1996.

Everything that happens inside the organization is influenced by something happening outside the organization. Competitive activity, customer expectation, regulation, and political and economic drivers influence the way the company responds to its environment. It is vital that this is positioned with employees as context for the internal policies and processes. Employees tolerate management's logic but will act on their own conclusions. If they can see a market-based rationale for the company's actions, they are much more likely to support it.

The vision sets the strategic goals for the organization; it should be simple and appealing to people at an emotional level. The mission is more specifically a performance tool, setting out the strategic purpose or the logical steps needed to achieve the vision. As such, it should appeal to the rational mind, and its relevance to the business plan should be made obvious.

Of the facilitators, values are the most important. Values provide the link between goals and purpose and the means of achieving them. They are the organization's guiding principles; they help condition behaviors and provide the "rules" to help employees take action. Values should underpin all other processes, policies, and, significantly, observable behaviors in the system.

Reductionism versus Systems Thinking

Typically, at least in Western society, a reductionism approach has been adopted: breaking issues down into their components and dealing with each in isolation. This is business as usual, stable, predictable, and able to be planned (even change). This assumption puts stress on the separate working parts (as do interventions) and can lead to fragmentation and an either-or mentality because what is valued is certainty and predictability. Organizations are structured in functions, which are then subdivided into departments. Each department and function has a budget and projects to complete, so a lot of work in organizations can be done in comparative isolation.

A systemic approach looks at the bigger picture and critically dependent issues. While this puts more emphasis on relationships and integration, it can also foster team working and experimentation; it can generate a both-and rather than an either-or mentality. It should produce a whole that is greater than the sum of its parts.

What can this mean in practice? A regional bank with around five thousand employees, part of a much larger group, wanted to introduce a new bonus plan in keeping with the rest of its group, thereby reinforcing its pay-for-performance philosophy. Rather than charge ahead and develop a communication strategy to do that, it conducted some research. Focus groups with junior staff and supervisors told us that any new bonus arrangement would be considered insulting and patronizing since they were acutely aware that salary levels had fallen well below those of their competitors. The bank knew that there were salary anomalies among more junior staff and had in fact been working on a solution, but this response caused them to pause and rethink the strategy.

The bonus arrangements were put on hold while the bank concentrated on pay policy. Once that had been designed and agreed, they launched their new remuneration strategy, which was visibly aligned to the market and the staff appraisal system. Then they introduced the new bonus arrangements that were linked to performance (team and individual), followed by their policy and programs on career development. Finally, they realigned their staff banking benefits.

This integrated roll-out took only one year and was very successful, as evidenced by the annual employee opinion survey results. The critical step was involving people at the outset. That effectively reordered the process, forcing us to step back from the presenting issue and deal with the other critical dependencies in the system. This approach brought success where others may have found costly failure. The initial single-intervention strategy may have resulted in industrial action.

Where Do You Start?

This whole issue needs not just support but a champion from the top of the organization. It affects all areas of business, and so someone who is able to take a functionally dispassionate but organizationally very passionate view of the desired outcomes is required. That could be the CEO. After all, this is about driving value.

Figure 21.3 shows a logical sequence for building the desired employer brand. This process will help to construct a coherent, congruent proposition for key stakeholders. It is in rare circumstances that a clean sheet will be available to

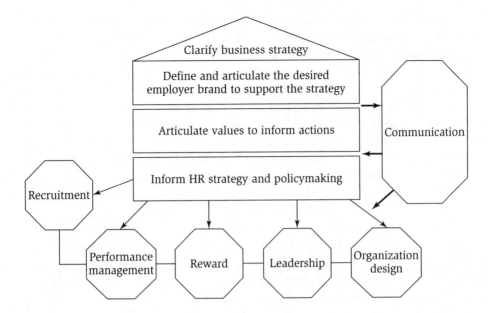

Figure 21.3. An Employer Branding Construct

Source: © Q⁴ Consulting, 2002.

afford that luxury. A new start-up (for example, General Motors setting up Saturn) would be a good example of the clean sheet scenario where senior management, employees, and their union representatives built the business and culture from the ground up. In most cases, you have to start from where you are, and one of two things can provide the springboard.

First, is there a pressing issue? From time to time companies have issues that must be addressed. Like the bank in the example, investigate what the real causes of the problem are, deal with them, and then support them elsewhere in the system. It can be dangerous to assume that because the issue has been addressed, the box can be checked off. For example, if you had identified a need for your managers to acquire better interpersonal communication skills to improve relationships and ultimately productivity on the shop floor, you might organize for them to attend a course on the subject. Is this item checked off? Probably not. Remember that systems have a way of self-sustaining, and so if on their return from the course, managers experienced balancing feedback from peers along the lines of, "We don't work like that around here," then there will be no improvement.

If, however, the context and desired outcomes are properly explained, new relevant objectives are framed in the performance management system, and commensurate reward or recognition systems are put in place, then the benefits could well outstrip the investment.

While this is really just joined-up thinking and the human resource department has many of the levers to pull in aligning the brand proposition, there is a massive role for organizational communication here. The need for communication input pervades all of this situation and is implicit in the success of any corporate initiative. Unfortunately, even when the need for communication is recognized, it is more often than not at a tactical level. Communication is not simply a management tool to be plugged into the back of an issue to give it energy. This misapprehension comes about from confusing information and communication. Information is the raw material; communication is the process applied to it to give it relevance and value. Yet although information and communication are different, they are inextricably related. Communication is not simply a tool to aid business. Business *is* communication.

In the absence of a pressing issue, it is important to find out what the leverage point might be to start the branding process. Finding the right starting point can mean desirable results with comparatively little effort. Guessing at it can lead to major resistance or at best apathy, with the next "great idea" consigned to the ranks of canteen or water cooler humor.

Design a simple tool that helps you identify what is working as intended in the employer-employee relationship and what is in need of further action. What motivates and engages people? What, if not addressed, may cause employees to look elsewhere? It is often better to have this work done independently.

A few years ago, this research became an imperative for some clients, and so we set about designing a tool to do the job. Working with BlackRock International and Oki Europe as peer reviewers and early pilot groups, we designed what is known as the Q^4 Profiler. This proprietary diagnostic tool looks at the employer-employee relationship in twelve dimensions. It can chart the employer's aspirational state as well as its view of the current state. It can, at the same time, take into consideration employee views on how the business is performing in those twelve dimensions (Figure 21.4). In addition, it examines the factors that attract, motivate, and retain talent; it examines how familiar people were with the organization before joining and how favorable their impression was at that time and currently; it tests advocacy; and, significantly, it can plot the company's position on an alignment and commitment matrix, which is a strong indicator of performance. Armed with this information, it is easier to plan the initial leverage point, what has to be done to support any intervention elsewhere in the system, and, critically, what the things are that will be likely to improve performance over time.

THE FINANCIAL PERSPECTIVE

There are two major components in putting a value on a business today: the value of the tangible assets and the value put on intellectual capital. Intellectual capital can be subdivided into three parts: customer capital (the value

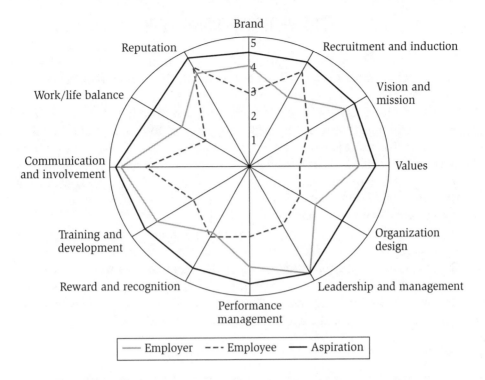

Figure 21.4. Q^4 Profiler

Source: © Q^4 Consulting, 2002.

of the company's customer relationships), structural capital (the ability of the business to manage and institutionalize its knowledge), and human capital (the value of the skills, knowledge, and competencies of its people). Typically the value of intellectual capital outstrips the value of tangible assets. This is usually expressed as a ratio, for example, 2.5:1. This ratio is known as Tobin's Q.

The elements making up the intellectual capital part of that equation are all heavily dependent on people. This begins to explain why looking after the people-focused aspects of the business are increasingly important from the perspective of financial performance. All of the big human resource consultancies have researched this area to identify the drivers of value. Although they have different ways of presenting their findings, the overarching theme is the same: focused, congruent people practices drive value. The nature of the measures used may differ among quoted companies, partnerships, or nonprofit, but the principles still apply.

THE PEOPLE PERSPECTIVE

If you were to review what companies require from employees and what employees look for from employment, you will find a remarkable synergy. Again, much research has been done in this area, and the results have been consistent over time. Generally people want to be able to do their best, have interesting and important work, have the opportunity to develop, and be fairly rewarded. The exact length, rank order, and nature of such a list will vary from business to business. That is why it is important to recognize what matters to your company's people. An organization is made up of individuals who have different roles, responsibilities, and interests but in their own way are ambassadors of the employer brand.

The power and influence of the employer brand may be underestimated in many cases (Figure 21.5). Crucially people inside the organization experience the drivers and facilitators of the brand as these components work in harmony to drive the desired behaviors and, ultimately, performance. This could be described as first-party experience. Third-party experience occurs when employees interact with other stakeholder groups.

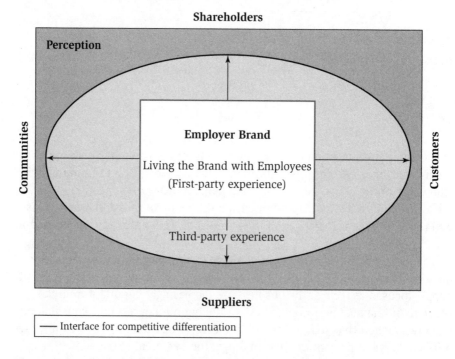

Figure 21.5. The Power and Influence of the Employer Brand

Source: © Q⁴ Consulting, 2002.

In order of frequency of contact with your employees, they could be customers, suppliers, the community, and shareholders. The potential impact and importance of these interactions may be put in the same order. Where third-party experience is less evident, perception plays a greater part in how the business is viewed; this is particularly true in the case of communities and shareholders. The point at which the business interacts with stakeholder groups is critically important, as that is where competitive differentiation takes place. These behaviors and interactions directly or indirectly affect the company's ability to attract and retain business, talent, investment, as well as supplier and community support.

The benefits of this approach are many and varied. Building a strong employer brand systemically from inside the organization enables the company to build something sustainable, flexible, and relevant. Through the creation of an aligned and committed workforce, you can drive performance and value. In the process, you will be able to attract, engage, and retain talent, and by enabling that talent to be empowered to give their best, you will be able to delight customers and keep shareholders happy. This way you get the employer branding "product" right. Then you can apply the graphic symbolism, nomenclature, and strap lines to promote it.

The process never ends. As the business imperatives change, the system has to change to support the new objectives. We must continually take a dispassionate view of the total employment experience so that we may accurately assess whether all of the components and elements are working synergistically to support the overall corporate objectives for performance.

The employer brand may have evolved, but it is not a given. Like any other corporate asset, that brand requires evaluation, planning, investment, and careful stewardship. Ultimately you can drive sustainable competitive advantage and leverage the most precious of corporate assets: reputation.

It is a *virtuous* cycle.

Reference

Watson Wyatt Worldwide. (2002). *WorkCanada 2002—Restoring confidence, regaining competitiveness.* Watson Wyatt Worldwide. www.watsonwyatt.com/research/resrender.asp?id=w-591&page=1.

PART FOUR

PUBLIC RELATIONS

CHAPTER TWENTY-TWO

Public Relations Research and Planning

Don W. Stacks

The role of research and planning is essential to any public relations campaign or program. Until recently, this aspect of public relations practice has suffered from what has been described as a lack of measurable outcomes. That is, public relations has been seen as a soft practice (one that focuses primarily on outputs) or "publicity," most often an in-house organ or media relations unit that produced press releases, newsletters, and other promotional materials. As such, much of public relations planning was focused on getting a message out to as many constituents as possible, often without much thought to the outcomes that these materials were seeking to influence. Today, public relations practice has evolved from producing clip books to a planned campaign, complete with a research base and public relations objectives that mirror those of the company's business objectives.

This chapter reviews the research and planning process involved in successful public relations campaigns that cross various corporate communication needs. It examines the research process and focuses on the goals and objectives that drive the campaign. The chapter is rounded out by an overview of the measurement process and a review of the research methods employed in both gathering data and providing indicators of program success.

PUBLIC RELATIONS RESEARCH AND PLANNING

Public relations research is no different from any other type of corporate research and should strive to meet several ends. First, it should be driven by the same general organizational research assumptions that drive other organizational areas. Second, public relations research must address achievable and measurable goals. Third, research has specific uses that should match those goals. Fourth, public relations research should be programmatic rather than one-shot case-by-case instance driven. Finally, public relations departments need to have the budget and resources to carry out this research.

Research is the controlled, objective, and systematic gathering of data. It seeks to describe, understand, predict, and control phenomena. Basic research begins by describing what it is that the public relations action is and what it seeks to do. Once described, the research can then be used to understand the concern or problem and establish a baseline against which the public relations campaign can be measured and evaluated. Research serves to provide reliable and valid data from which to answer questions of import to the organization. The keys to how well the questions are answered, however, depend on the research methods employed, the type of data gathered, the reliability and validity of those data, and the systematic collection of the data. This is how social science and business research should be conducted.

There are seven basic uses of public relations research. First, public relations research monitors developments and trends as part of the department's environmental scanning function. Second, it examines the current public relations position on an issue or problem. Third, it serves to assess communication activities and functions, such as messaging and corporate image, trust, relationships, and reputation. Fourth, it continuously and systematically measures communication effectiveness. Fifth, it tracks audience perceptions over time. Sixth, it looks for gaps in the current research that need filling. And, seventh, it evaluates over time the progress made in achieving organizational goals and objectives.

Based on this, it should be clear that public relations research and planning should be no different from other kinds of organizational research. Research should be planned based on the same decision-making process found in the organization. It should set measurable objectives and then determine the strategies to meet them—strategies that implement specific tactics or outputs that bring them to life. This process is typically divided into three phases: development, refinement, and evaluation, each having its own particular objectives in the overall campaign goal.

To be effective, public relations research planning needs to be behavior-driven and knowledge-based. Research objectives should focus on overall business objectives and goals in such a way to correlate with actual behavior, that is, change as demonstrated through reliable and valid measures. Planning should produce strategies based on public relations theory and practice conducted within the organization and industry. What public relations measurement and evaluation must be factored into planning and research? Public relations activities typically focus on driving mechanisms and falls into two general areas: providing people with information about something and using that information to motivate them to action. Hence, public relations research often indicates which actual behavior can be predicted.

BEST PRACTICES IN PUBLIC RELATIONS RESEARCH AND PLANNING

Research planning requires first an understanding of the problem for which the public relations research is being conducted and second a basic understanding of what surrounds that problem. In other words, research must be done to plan for public relations planning. This process of continuous research is called *environmental scanning:* the public relations department maintains a constant vigil for problems or new objectives to be addressed in the future. Once a problem or objective has been defined, most planning is conducted using a management by objectives program, which is dependent on a working knowledge of the factors influencing the problem or objective, strategy, and programming of the public relations work plan, carrying out that plan as an integrated campaign or program within the organization, and evaluating it on completion.

Effective public relations planning is accomplished through the following steps:

1. Reviewing secondary research and establishing benchmarks
2. Establishing achievable goals
3. Stating measurable objectives
4. Asking appropriate research questions
5. Employing appropriate research methodologies
6. Conducting programmatic research
7. Having the resources in place and the budget necessary

Secondary Research/and Benchmarking

No planning can begin until the problem is understood and the strategic options are known. Planning without first understanding the problem or the internal client cannot be done effectively unless previous research or research carried out by other organizations has been first examined.

Secondary/and Historical Research. All organizational research must begin with a thorough understanding of what has been done previously. Furthermore, to better understand what has been done and why it was done, secondary and historical research is both necessary and an antecedent to any research planning. Secondary research is research that has already been conducted or data reported. It can take a variety of forms, some public and some proprietary to the organization or to other organizations. Researching public or association databases may be required to understand the problem; academic and public libraries accessible both physically and by Internet provide a rich understanding of the campaign at hand. Bibliographies, case studies, and position papers such as those found at the Institute for Public Relations can be reviewed to provide background. Some secondary research is proprietary to the organization itself and may be found in other departments such as marketing, human resources, or general council. A review of secondary and historical material provides a window to both theory and past practices. It also reduces the costs associated with data collection as it often provides answers to questions without requiring additional and possibly expensive research.

Benchmarking. Secondary research also provides possible benchmarks against which to gauge progress in a public relations campaign. Without something to gauge against, a campaign cannot be evaluated during or afterward with any degree of precision. If secondary and historical data are not available, then data must be gathered prior to kicking off a campaign and must be planned for within the campaign time line. This is accomplished during the run-up to kick-off, that is, the developmental phase of the campaign. A good public relations department will constantly scan the organization for data that can be used to benchmark a public relations problem, thus reducing both research costs and time required to work up to the project.

Establishing Achievable Goals and Stating Measurable Objectives

Before objectives can be stated, goals must be established. A goal is a general outcome expected by the end of a campaign. All public relations goals should reflect the goals of the organization. Thus, a goal statement should have two components: one that clearly indicates the organizational goal and one that includes the public relations goal in meeting the larger organizational goal. Thus, if the organizational goal is to increase productivity, the public relations goal will be to provide the communication strategy and tools to help meet increased productivity. As such, the goal might be stated as: "To help meet organizational goals to increase productivity by establishing effective communication vehicles between management and labor." This goal establishes a relationship between the public relations department and the organization and helps the department become an important member of the management team.

Goals may be subdivided into the various tasks that must be planned during a campaign. Subgoals typically focus on specifics. During the developmental phase, subgoals include getting the right people on the problem, finding secondary and historical research, and establishing benchmarks. During the program phase, subgoals include monitoring and evaluating campaign strategies, as well as ensuring that the program's time line is met and that specific objectives have been met. During the evaluation phase, subgoals include meeting deadlines and budgetary concerns, whether the public relations goals effectively and efficiently were met and affected the organization's goals, and providing feedback on the current campaign and establishing a benchmark for future campaigns.

Once the public relations goal has been established, the objectives can be stated. While stating a goal is quite easy, stating objectives is much more difficult and something that most public relations departments or researchers do not do well. It is one thing to say that you want to get something done (a goal); it is much more difficult to state how you will do it (strategy and tactics), with what results (outcomes), and by what date. Thus, an objective is almost always written in the form of cause and effect with outcome. An objective might be, "To increase employee contributions to the annual giving campaign from 56 percent to 78 percent through an intranet e-mail push campaign by August 15." The objective clearly states what the problem is (employee contributions to the annual giving campaign), what the current giving and target are, what strategy is being employed (intranet e-mail push), and the date by which the objective is to be reached. To be this specific, the planning must rely on reliable and valid secondary or benchmark data and a realistic target. For example, stating that the campaign will increase attendance at an event by 20 percent is quite different if attendance has been low to begin with. A credible objective is one that mirrors organizational objectives, is stated in precise measurable ways, and is measurable.

Public relations objectives can be further broken into functional objectives that must be met or evaluated as a campaign progresses. From a logical perspective, the information or messages to be employed in the campaign must first get to the targeted audience and be both understood and accepted. Behavior without a reason is not dependable and is easily countered (what many do not understand in a public relations campaign is that there are other, competing messages that may interfere or produce behavior counter to what is wanted). Thus, we have an informational objective that has to be measured and evaluated. Once the information has been received and understood, one must ask if it motivated the target audience to do what is being requested (Have they had their attitudes or beliefs reinforced or changed?). Thus, we have a motivational objective that has to be measured and evaluated. Third, assuming that the target audience has received, understood, agreed with the message, and been motivated toward our request, we need to find out if they are planning on

Figure 22.1. Public Relations Objectives
Source: Stacks (2004). Used with permission.

doing what we asked (Will they actually commit to doing the requested action?). Thus, we have a behavioral objective that has to be measured and evaluated. (See Figure 22.1.)

As noted in Figure 22.1, there is a loop of sorts between the informational and motivational objectives. If the motivational objectives are not being met, an evaluation of the informational objectives must be undertaken to find out why the target audience's attitudes and beliefs have not been changed or reinforced. Obviously what is being measured during most of the public relations campaign deals with things that cannot be directly observed, with the exception of some informational objectives, such as whether the message is actually available to the target public (by employing clip books or Internet hits, for example). Thus, measurement, and particularly the measurement of attitudes and beliefs, will become an integral part of planning a public relations campaign and will be covered later in this chapter. Figure 22.1 shows the planning flow for evaluation, from informational to behavioral objectives, and then ends with an evaluation of whether the public relations campaign had an impact on the business or organizational objectives. Figure 22.2 demonstrates how the research should be planned during the campaign. Note that multiple evaluations are conducted that overlap to provide a viable time line and multiple benchmarks. This allows for strategy or tactic refinement throughout the campaign and provides additional data for comparing against business objectives and goals.

Asking Appropriate Research Questions

Research is driven by the kinds of questions asked. In general, there are four basic questions addressed by research: (1) questions of definition (What is it?), (2) questions of fact (Once defined, does it exist and in what quantity?),

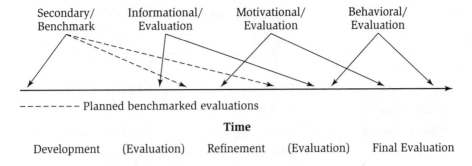

Figure 22.2. Programmatic Research and Public Relations Objectives
Source: Stacks (2004). Used with permission.

(3) questions of value (If it exists, how good or bad is it or was it?), and (4) questions of policy (What should be done?). All research must begin with the question of definition. What exactly are we researching? How is it defined or operationalized in terms of both business and public relations objectives? Once we have defined the problem or objective in such a way as to examine it as factual, do we have the quantitative information necessary to establish differences or changes over time—a baseline of sorts through either secondary or historical research, or should new research be commissioned? Next, the facts need to be established: How well have we done or, in terms of goodness or badness, what specifically was done well or poorly? Finally, the question comes down to, "What should we do?" based on our answers to the first three questions. This is the recommendation that the public relations department takes to the management table for action.

Employing Appropriate Research Methodologies

Choosing an appropriate research methodology depends on the type of questions being asked (Table 22.1). When problem solving or attempting to identify goals and objectives, the questions deal with definition. What is it? How does it exist? How might it be best approached? Secondary or historical research is often the best method to employ and may consist of field observation (knowledge gained from communicating with potential audiences or publics or from continuous environmental scanning), previously published research, or case studies. This is an important part of the developmental stage of any public relations campaign. Second, the facts must be gathered and benchmarks established against which the results can be evaluated. This requires quantitative methodology to run throughout the campaign: surveys, polls, communication audits, and in the more advanced departments, experiments or simulations that

Table 22.1. Research Methods

Secondary/Historical	Qualitative	Quantitative
Case studies	In-depth interviews	Surveys
Industry studies	Focus groups	Polls
Annual reports	Field observation	Delphi studies
Organizational files	Content analysis[a]	Content analysis[a]
	Informal observation	Experiments/simulations

[a]May be either qualitative or quantitative depending on how the content analysis is conducted.

deal with questions of fact. At times it is necessary to conduct qualitative methodology to establish how well the particular tactics are working by using focus groups, in-depth interviewing, or content analyses that deal with questions of value.

In general, we can break the actual research being conducted into three types. Secondary and historical methods consist of analyses of existing data, most often in the form of published documents. Quantitative or formal methods (which are best for questions of fact and at times definition) are scientific, employ large groups of participants or respondents, and with appropriate procedures can be generalized to larger groups through representative sampling. Qualitative or informal methods (which are best for questions of value and at times definition) are more concerned with an in-depth knowledge of a few participants or respondents. While quantitative methods seek to establish normative responses that can be generalized to a larger population, qualitative methods seek to better understand how problems came about or how well tactics were being received.

Before turning to the qualitative and quantitative methodologies used in public relations research, it is necessary to note that well-planned public relations campaigns should employ all three methodologies. This triangulation provides the information necessary to drive the "should" question or critically evaluate that question at campaign end. Obviously, planning for triangulated research costs more; employing the old saying, "You get what you pay for," the more formal and informal data that are collected, the better you will be at understanding what is occurring as the campaign progresses and the better you will be at making refinements when results indicate objectives that are not being met.

Qualitative Methods. There are five basic qualitative methodologies found in public relations research. Each provides a wealth of in-depth research but has limited to no generalizability to larger audiences. A way of establishing which method to choose may be a function of the degree of control required in the research. Generally, observation is the least controlled and in-depth interviews the most controlled. Observation can be of two types: informal, where no particular notes are taken, and formal, where the observations are noted and analyzed. Environmental scanning in an organization is often undertaken through observation. Focus group research asks small groups of volunteers to talk about particular questions through a moderator-controlled discussion that allows participants to tag on to others' statements by employing a schedule of questions and possible follow-up questions. In-depth interviews are one-on-one interactions where the interviewer asks questions of an individual through well-thought-out questions and possible follow-ups. Content analysis can have both qualitative and quantitative aspects. From the qualitative, a content analysis takes the messages that have been sent and evaluates them for their impact. That is, a press release may have been sent to the local media and published. A qualitative content analysis would look to see how the press release was positioned and whether it was used as desired.

Quantitative Methods. As a quantitative method, content analysis can be used to establish the fact that a message got out. This often is found in the ubiquitous clip book. But a content analysis can also tell a lot about the message itself: its readability, the number of times a product is mentioned in the media, and other things—for instance, "This paragraph consists of 116 words, 50 percent are passive, and it has a readability index of 12.0." (The readability index, calculated as a Flesch-Kincaid Grade Level, indicates that a reader needs at least twelve years of formal schooling to be able to understand the paragraph.) In other words, the content analysis becomes a quantitative method when its use is to establish some form of numeric measure. When we think of quantitative methods in public relations, however, the methods that come immediately to mind are surveys and polls.

A poll is a quick, factually based, and often behaviorally focused questionnaire that asks people to react to questions or statements on some metric such as "yes or no"; "strongly agree, agree, neither agree nor disagree, disagree, or strongly disagree"; or "on a 0 to 10 scale, how do you feel about X." The poll provides a way to quickly seek limited information; if representative sampling is used, it may be generalized to a larger audience. A survey is much longer and consists of both metric-based questions and open-ended questions that often seek to better understand attitudes. Thus, a question might be phrased in a "yes-no" format and then followed with a "Why do you say this?" question. Surveys often seek respondent attitudes about the information received, what that information has motivated them to do, and whether they think they will actually do what has been requested (thus seeking answers to the three basic public relations objectives). Surveys, when conducted with representative sampling, may be generalized to a larger audience. A Delphi study is usually a survey where the researcher tries to forecast the future based on successive waves of surveys with a panel of experts in a given field as a means of building a consensus of expert opinion and thought relating to particular topics or issues. Delphi studies are not generalizable.

Finally, the experiment or simulation is a carefully controlled, scientifically oriented methodology that seeks to find answers to basic questions or test hypotheses. Experiments and simulations are few and far between in public relations, partially because of lack of training in the social sciences and partially because they take time to set up and conduct. An experiment or simulation carefully controls the influence of independent variables (things that will cause change in predictable ways) on dependent variables (outcomes of relevance). For instance, the independent variable communication channel used (verbal, printed, Internet) to get a message out and the dependent variables might be the actions taken by the targeted audience or morale indicators.

Quantifying Using Measurement. When planning to conduct public relations research, it is important to think of how that research will be used over the long haul, whether it is for a specific problem or campaign. Hence, the more information that is gathered, the better the prognosis is for success. Part of this will be dependent on the type of data gathered. Public relations research seeks to gather information on what people believe or think—that is, attitudes and beliefs and if they have been created, reinforced, or changed. Attitudes and beliefs are the drivers behind behavior, and public relations has a demonstrated impact on both. The question, however, is how to measure something that by definition cannot be seen. The answer is through carefully created measurement systems.

Measurement systems are designed to create quantitative data that can be used to evaluate how people think. There are four kinds or levels of data: nominal, ordinal, interval, and ratio. Nominal data differentiate units, such as "yes" or "no" or "cars," "trains," or "airplanes." These data are quantified as simple counts (the number of each category) and are expressed as frequencies, percentages, and proportions. Ordinal data are data that have a planned ordering effect based on some principle (for autos, for example, compact, sedan, SUV in terms of size; income is often requested as an ordinal variable and set in increments) and are quantified the same way as nominal data. Both nominal and ordinal data are called categorical data because the quantification places each observation into planned categories.

Interval data are found on a continuum whereby the intervals between data points are assumed to be equal. While "yes" and "no" categorical responses are often quantified as 1 or 2, there is no assumption that the distance between the two categories is equal; they are just two different categories. With interval data, the distance between 1 and 2 is the same as between 2 and 3, which is the same as between 3 and 4, and so on. Interval data are quantified as means or averages, dispersions around the mean or average, and statistically standardized units allowing comparison of seemingly different metric systems. Interval data provide a wealth of information that nominal or ordinal data cannot. Statistically, interval data are more powerful than either form of categorical data (that is, they explain much more).

A special form of interval data is found when the research is trying to assess attitudes or beliefs. Attitudes and beliefs are generally obtained by asking respondents questions or statements on an "agree to disagree" continuum. This continuum has a requirement that some form of neutrality be assessed; hence there must be some way for the respondent to say, "I'm not sure." "I'm not sure" is not the same as "I don't know" or "I refuse to answer." Hence, we find that scalar (attitudinal or belief) data are found on a negative through neutral (arbitrary zero) to positive continuum. It could be negative $= -1$, neutral $= 0$, and positive $= +1$ or it could be 1, 2, and 3, respectively. Typically, attitudinal and belief measures consist of continuums ranging from five to seven equally appearing units. The most often employed attitudinal measure found in public relations research is the Likert-type measure, which asks respondents to respond to two or more statements (which reflect at a minimum the negative and positive statements associated with the particular attitude). A full-scale attitude measure would have several statements assessing each objective (informational, motivational, behavioral), although current practice is to focus primarily on the behavioral, which often assumes that informational and motivational objectives have been met, an assumption that may not be valid.

Finally, ratio data not only meet the equal interval criterion, but also have an absolute zero point (unlike the arbitrary zero in interval, scalar data). Monetary data are ratio in nature in that they can range from negative through zero to positive amounts, such as found in statements of trade balances or departmental budgets. Ratio data other than monetary or product production figures are not usually found in public relations; instead the focus is on interval or scalar data.

Finally, always try to gather data at the most powerful level when conducting research. You cannot take nominal data and redefine this material as ordinal or interval or ratio. You can, however, take ratio and reduce it to interval, interval to ordinal, and ordinal to nominal. Planning ahead—looking at what data are already available and their types—allows multiple uses of the data, especially when presenting the information to nonresearch or statistical audiences (such as upper management). Always keep in mind who you will be reporting to as well as who you are gathering data from.

Conducting Programmatic Research

All research should become programmatic over time. That is, the research a public relations department conducts should be based on previous research and lead to research down the line. Progressive and responsive public relations departments plan their research for the long term. Even during a particular public relations campaign, planning should be divided into the three stages or phases: development, refinement, and evaluation. At the development stage, both the communication and research goals and objectives should be developed. The goals must reflect the overall organization's goals and the objectives should be actionable and measurable. At this stage a SWOT (strengths, weaknesses, opportunities, and threats) analysis may provide information regarding circumstances, target audiences and their characteristics, and communication strategies and tactics. During the refinement stage, research is conducted at planned intervals that validate earlier decisions and provide for corrective action when decisions are found to be off-base through focus group, survey, interview, or observation research. Finally, evaluation research determines if the overall goals of the organization and public relations were met and to what degree. Evaluation research is based largely on performance effectiveness in terms of strategy, outputs from tactics, and behavioral outcomes.

Having Resources in Place and the Budget Necessary

By now it should be clear that planning and research are necessary for effective public relations. In addition, more than one research method, conducted at more than one time (often, unfortunately, only at campaign's end), is necessary to assess progress adequately. Research costs, in terms of resources and budgets, are something that both external and internal customers often fail to understand a need for. Educating the "customer" about research costs generally falls into five areas. First, what are the circumstances that require the research? Are secondary or historical data available? If so, costs may be significantly reduced. Second, can the research be conducted with in-house personnel and resources? If this is the case, costs may be significantly reduced. Third, who is available commercially to conduct the research, what are the costs, and what benefits will they bring to the research? Fourth, is the research planned, or is it a budget item? And, finally, what are the research questions asked? For purposes here, consider the following costs associated with research methods: focus groups can run $1,000 to $4,000 per group; one-to-one interviews $350 to $2,000 per interview; telephone surveys from $3,500 to more than $100,000 per telephone survey; and mail or Internet surveys, $5,000 to more than $100,000 per survey. Effective planning requires budgeting and in-house resources to be taken into consideration as early as possible, with an eye to establishing a programmatic approach to research.

CONCLUSION

Effective public relations research and planning require a mind-set that focuses on research as an integral part of departmental budgets and the programmatic and continual collection of data. All research planned in public relations should have clearly defined and achievable goals that mirror those of the organization and objectives stated in both actionable and measurable ways. Research should be triangulated and aimed at addressing the research questions appropriate for the problem or opportunity. Finally, effective public relations must have the necessary resources allocated to research.

Reference

Stacks, D. W. (2004). *Best practices in public relations research. Institute for Public Relations.* www.instituteforpr.com/bestpractices_ppt_files/v3_document.htm.

CHAPTER TWENTY-THREE

The CEO-Leader as Relationship Builder

Convinced But Unengaged

J. David Pincus, Stephen C. Wood

Becoming CEO, *the* organizational leader, is every business professional's dream job. An early 1990s "Pepper . . . and Salt" cartoon captured what may be the roiling ambition driving most business neophytes. A dapper young man is seated across a desk from a balding human resource executive, who asks the up-and-comer about his long-range career goal. Grinning confidently, the interviewee says, "Eventually, I'd like to get into CEOing."

We wonder whether he would say the same thing today.

Clearly, life at the top is not what it used to be. "CEOing" today is more public, perilous, and short-lived. Increasing numbers of chiefs are being pushed out by embarrassed and angry boards; others are seeing their job descriptions rewritten and curtailed by aggressive regulators and prosecutors. The corporate landscape is littered with a fraternity of recently disgraced CEOs, their publicized dismissals ravaging the credibility of the institution of business and all its captains. Their names ring out as part of an ominous public lexicon: Enron's Ken Lay, Tyco's Dennis Kozlowski, Martha Stewart, Boeing's Harry Stonecipher, AIG's Maurice "Hank" Greenberg, Arthur Andersen, Disney's Michael Eisner, Fannie Mae's Franklin Raines, Hewlett-Packard's Carly Fiorina, WorldCom's Bernie Ebbers, HealthSouth's Richard Scrushy, and on and on they go.

The backlash—the cost in dollars to investors and employees and in goodwill to the reputation of business—is incalculable. The backlash is exacerbated by insensitive, avaricious top executives who gave themselves gigantic compensation packages and golden parachutes while exhibiting little empathy for those affected by their greed and the cover-ups that destroyed pensions, slashed health benefits, and purged jobs. Corporate leadership today carries substantial social and cultural responsibilities that reach beyond the traditional financial and operations obligations. The recent string of scandals has shaken Americans' faith in business and its leadership and poses a serious threat to CEOs' and their organizations' prime asset: credibility. The need to confront the arduous challenge of restoring lost corporate credibility is at the heart of the evolutionary process that is redefining the CEO's job as leader.

In this chapter, we probe the impetus behind the CEO's emerging role as a "transformational" leader,[1] and what can be done to better prepare future corporate leaders for an arduous role that eschews coerced obedience and embraces negotiation, consensus, and understanding. In addition, we examine why and how the CEO's changing duties are triggering ripple effect challenges for the top professional communicator who advises the CEO.

WHAT IS THIS THING CALLED COMMUNICATION?

Before proceeding, we should address the elusive term underlying our analysis, because *communication* holds so many, often confusing, meanings to business and communication professionals. Such confusion, however unintentional, often results in raising walls of conflict between business and communication aficionados instead of building bridges of understanding that come from effective communication.

Defining communication is not simple. Literally hundreds of divergent definitions exist, each with its own merit.[2] Historically, business minds have conceived communication in exclusively informational terms—primarily message and data distribution. Although this is an oversimplification, most managers think of communication as writing memos and making presentations. An information-driven definition, no matter how broadly interpreted, fails to address the complex idiosyncrasies inherent in every form of interaction between people, be they CEOs and employees, their advisers, or their critics. Missing from the informational notion is the relational dimension of communication—the psychological, emotional and behavioral factors—that is absolutely crucial to bringing minds and hearts together. Communication at its best involves both informational and relational dimensions (for example, source credibility, audience response, and message interpretation). The role played by relational and informational factors in any communicative situation will vary with circumstances and players; however, ignoring one at the expense of the other invariably weakens the overall communication (not to mention the human relationship).

Communicating in myriad business settings, regardless of job, title, or role, entails a multitude of types of communication, ranging from one-on-one conversations to speeches in public forums, from small group meetings to mediated broadcasts, from motivating employees to understanding multinational and international dynamics, from fashioning strategies for employee newsletters to designing annual reports. CEOs need to possess a mix of communication competencies, from interpersonal to mass, that they can apply on a moment's notice (Exhibit 23.1).

THE CEO'S ROLE: BROADER, MORE COMPLEX

Years ago, CEOs were mysterious, nameless, faceless figures who worked behind closed doors, stayed out of sight and range of friends and foes, and dealt mostly with members of the organization's inner sanctum. That all changed in the tumultuous 1970s and 1980s as business became the target of critical stockholders, antiestablishment advocacy groups, and government regulators. With Chrysler CEO Lee Iacocca's emergence as a public personality in rescuing the beleaguered automaker from bankruptcy, appearing before Congress and in company ads, the door opened for CEOs to take on more visible, vulnerable leadership roles. Over time, the job progressively expanded in scope and complexity; CEOs became the public face of their organizations, operating from glass offices, and juggling multiple, varying organizational roles: reputation manager, spokesperson, relationship builder, change agent, and public figure, to note a few. (For a comprehensive review of the CEO's emergence as communication-driven leader, see Pincus & Wood, 1997.)

As the literal and figurative embodiment of their organizations, CEOs became the focus of competing, and sometimes conflicting, efforts by internal and external constituencies to gain their attention, each wanting larger chunks of the CEO's time and favor. That competition eventually forced chiefs to straddle the murky boundary line separating organizations (internal stakeholders) and the marketplace (outside constituencies). This so-called boundary spanner position compelled CEOs to play multiple allied roles—for example, filter, connector, gatekeeper, translator, arbiter—designed to link interests and parties in order to build, bolster or repair the corporate reputation, while developing lasting relationships with constituencies on both sides of the boundary line. (See Figure 23.1.)

The upshot of this redefining process is that CEOs have become public figures—lightning rods for all issues and interests. No longer can they hide behind the facade of assigned authority or title. To stakeholders and others inside and outside the corporate castle, the CEO is, in essence, *the* organization. As the

Exhibit 23.1. Ideal Attributes for Leaders and Communicators

Ideal Behavioral Attributes of a CEO-Leader

- Credible (by far most important)
  - — Trustworthy, believable
  - — Consistent (words and actions)
- Articulate
  - — Clarity (message)
- Persuasive
  - — Advocate, negotiator
  - — Aggressive sales mentality (ideas, organization, issues)
- Change agent/shepherd of change process
  - — Manager of relationships
  - — Architect of coalitions
- Compassionate
  - — Empathetic, caring
  - — Listener, seeker/user of feedback

Ideal Attributes of a Top Communicator-Adviser

- Business savvy and knowledgeable
- Big-picture perspective
- Communication/business strategist mentality
- Candid, direct, devil's advocate
- Understands CEO's priorities, preferences, strengths, and weaknesses
- Knows organization (its history, culture, marketplace trends)
- "Coaching" bent/expertise

The CEO as Communicator

In *Top Dog* (1994), Pincus and DeBonis profiled in depth the CEO as communicator. Among their findings were the four principles behind their argument that CEOs are "CCOs" (chief communication officers):

- Consistency—aligning words and actions, constantly; heart and soul of credibility
- Compassion—caring, being empathetic; listening; seeking and using feedback
- Organization—coordinating the CEO's communication with other managers' communication; matching sources, messages, and media
- Selectivity—strategic, limited role of CEO as communicator; role that supports and reinforces other managers' communication roles

Figure 23.1. The CEO as Boundary Spanner

public persona of their organizations, top dogs occupy the hot seat, forcing them to live with unrelenting scrutiny and second-guessing. Wall Street, media, investors, employees, government regulators, and especially reignited boards of directors are all vital constituencies quick to train judgmental gazes on a CEO's every move and word.

BUSINESS TODAY: ALL ABOUT RELATIONSHIPS

After an exacting review of the management, leadership, persuasion and communication, organizational behavior, and psychology literature of the past twenty years, our conclusion, and the premise underlying this chapter, is that most ruined CEOs and disastrous company situations can be traced to one or more failed relationships with essential stakeholder groups: alienating customers, losing investor confidence, sidestepping board members, duping employees, misleading media, angering legislators and regulators, lying to donors and volunteers, arousing splinter groups, underestimating communities, and disaffecting vendors. The souring of a company's relationship with any one of its key constituencies can, given boards of directors' intensifying vigilance in the wake of Enron and WorldCom (for example, Sarbanes-Oxley corporate governance legislation), spell disaster to a CEO and his or her organization.

Nurturing and strengthening healthy relationships underlies business success today. Organizational leaders spend the bulk of their time cultivating mutually productive connections with core groups inside and outside their boundaries, and their effectiveness in developing these relationships determines in large measure their and their organizations' relative success. "Almost everything in leadership comes back to relationships," says Mike Krzyzewiski, the ultrasuccessful Duke basketball coach (Krzyzewiski, 2000, p. 26). The better the relationships are among an organization's constituents, the better off the organization is, argues Max DePree, former CEO of furniture maker Herman Miller. "Leaders need to foster environments and work processes within which people can develop high-quality relationships—relationships with each other, within work groups, and with clients and customers" (DePree, 1989, p. 25).

More and more companies are going beyond talking the relationships game to playing it for keeps—UPS (employees) and Wal-Mart (vendors), among them. The reason is simple: strong relationships are the engine behind sustained, superlative performance. That was the central finding of a 2001 study of Fortune 1000 companies conducted by consultant Booz Allen Hamilton and Northwestern University's Kellogg School of Management. And no other company better exemplifies this emerging phenomenon than Starbucks, the international coffee specialist. Starting with CEO Howard Schulz, Starbucks views its relationships, dubbed *relational capital*, with key "partners," namely, customers, employees, suppliers, and alliance partners (such as coffee growers), as the bedrock of its decentralized culture and sustained success. "The culture is very relationship-oriented," said Michelle Gass, vice president of beverage. "It's built on trust. We talk about partnerships and mean it in every sense of the word" (Gulati, Huffman, & Neilson, 2002, p. 61).

Relationship-building competencies (that is, communication-oriented and critical thinking skills) hold the key to a reconfigured CEO role that is, and must be, increasingly dependent for its effectiveness on the support of decisive internal and external constituencies. The professional communicator's role as business adviser and counselor to the CEO has never been more vital or timely. If the recent disturbing examples of toppled CEOs have taught us anything, it is that crafting truly trusting relationships, able to endure traumatic and controversial times, is far easier to claim than achieve. Absent credibility, businesses' lifeblood, CEOs and their organizations, are virtually powerless to influence others.

CREDIBILITY: THE CEO'S BEST FRIEND

With credibility, all is possible; without it, nothing is. For over two thousand years, scholars and philosophers have underscored credibility's primacy in human interaction. Every leader needs it to be effective. But how does one "get" credibility? Research reveals two ways, closely related. *Presumed* credibility is inherent in the position. New CEOs, by bent of title and built-in authority, are presumed to be credible for a time. Sadly, too many leaders assume that title and the mantle of power make credibility permanent, impossible to lose. Nothing could be less true in today's hypercritical business environment.

However, whatever the level of presumed credibility, *earned* credibility trumps. That is, if top executives' actions prove untrustworthy or manipulative or even egalitarian, their credibility, and with it their effectiveness, vanishes like a magician's coin, often fatally. From Disney to Hewlett Packard, the lessons of diminished or lost credibility are indisputable: if constituents stop trusting or believing in a top executive, he or she is finished as the organization's leader. Forging healthy, credible relationships with primary stakeholders, those whose allegiance an organization must have, is not an indulgence of leadership, as perhaps once thought; it is its beating heart.

CEOS: EVERYTHING TO EVERYBODY?

CEOs today need to possess both pecuniary and persuasive capabilities if they are to win, and keep, increasingly prickly and reactive constituencies in the fold. It is little wonder that the average tenure of CEOs has been dropping steadily for years (Lucier et al., 2005). Top executives find themselves caught in a crossfire of pressures so volatile and instantaneous that those who lose a vital constituency's backing might not survive the next board meeting.

Being in charge is tougher than ever before. No CEO can hope to handle the job alone. It requires one person to wear too many hats, regardless of the breadth of his or her talents. Few things in corporate life are as they were even a generation ago; thus, top executives have had to adapt to a reconfigured environment, one filled with pressures unlike many faced by their predecessors, or die trying. "By and large, chief executives are still in charge," *BusinessWeek* observed in early 2005, "but their power is much more limited. The downsizing of the CEO has led, to a certain extent, to the supersizing of the advisers. That is not necessarily a cure for everything that ails Corporate America. It is a clue that successful CEOs will have to be *consensus builders* in the future. And should be a warning to CEOs everywhere: The age of the absolute corporate monarch is over" (Henry, France, & Lavelle, 2005, p. 96).

Unfortunately, most who make it to the corner office are absent the polished persuasive and interpersonal skills demanded by the job—skills not typically developed through education, experience, or professional training. Nevertheless, no right-thinking executive today would publicly deny the need for diverse communicative skills that fall under the relationships umbrella. An example of the tangible value of relationships is described by Jack Matlock Jr., former U.S. ambassador to the Soviet Union, in his book, *Reagan and Gorbachev: How the Cold War Ended* (2004). He analyzed how Secretary of State of George Shultz and Soviet Foreign Minister Eduard Shevardnadze created over time a personal relationship that bolstered their professional relationship and how their example influenced others to follow suit. "Neither was so naive to think that difficult issues could be solved by sociability," Matlock writes. "But both understood they were much more likely to find solutions to problems if they had confidence in each other. The personal relationship both cultivated and helped them weather potential crises without losing touch with each other. . . . Gradually, the stand-off, shout-at-the-enemy debating style that had plagued U.S.-Soviet relations since World War II was supplanted by personal networking" (pp. 264–265). This lesson in international diplomacy is equally applicable to business settings.

BELIEVING IS NOT NECESSARILY DOING

In their 1994 book, Pincus and DeBonis told the story of the CEO's changing role as organizational leader and how it underwent dramatic changes during the tumultuous political and economic upheaval of the 1970s and 1980s. As top managers reacted to fast-shifting marketplace and workplace conditions, marked by disaffected and increasingly vocal employees and customers demanding participation, the concept of CEOs as CCOs (chief communication officers) surfaced, symbolizing a new reality, which prompted mixed reactions by most CEOs. They suggested that "new" CEOs should be remade into communication-fortified leaders who understand the value of integrating business and communication strategies for constructing stable relationships with groups whose support organizations cannot live without (see Exhibit 23.1). "Contemporary CEOs are expected to be more than financial or operations wizards who make wise decisions behind closed doors. They're also expected to be able to sell those decisions to diverse organizational stakeholders and gain their buy-in. The job has shifted from one emphasizing technical skills to one stressing a mix of technical *and* human relations talents" (Pincus & DeBonis, 1994, p. 81).

Merely pointing out the need to change how they used to do their jobs did not necessarily convince CEOs to change their thinking or their behavior. Over the years, a few tried to be more communicative, but most held back or outright resisted. The stuff of communication was outside their comfort zone. But as calls for CEOs to step out of the shadows grew more insistent, top executives eventually could not ignore the case for change. Much of what was being asked of these corporate high priests—thinking of communication as an essential strategic business tool *and* as a set of tactical skills—was uncharted territory. To those chiefs whose interpersonal and persuasive communication capabilities are underdeveloped, the uncertainty in taking on an unfamiliar role can be intimidating and prompt those reluctant to adapt to instead cling to the traditional top-down role they know.

TIME TO WALK THE TALK

Nevertheless, in the years since *Top Dog*'s (Pincus & DeBonis, 1994) call for a new breed of CEO-leader, many books, articles, and studies have reinforced the call for top-echelon executives to expand their knowledge of human behavior and ability to shape others' attitudes and actions. Much attention has focused on convincing the nation's business schools, particularly M.B.A. programs, to revise their staid, numbers-driven curricula and make room for leadership, human behavior, and communication-oriented subjects. That point was hammered home in April 2002 when the Management Education Task Force of the Association to Advance Collegiate Schools of Business, the major business school accrediting body, issued a report questioning the relevance of business school courses and recommended more emphasis on "basic management skills, such as communications . . . leadership development and change management" (Andrews and D'Andrea Tyson, 2004, p. 63).

The case for change has been embraced rhetorically but not often in practice. Today few business executives or business school deans would dare dismiss or question communication's theoretical value to organizational effectiveness. Not only is such criticism politically insensitive, but it defies the popular notion that communication is not a luxury but something no leader or organization can do without. They say the right words and probably believe them. But identifying CEOs whose beliefs and words regarding communication are reflected in leadership strategy and behavior is akin to finding the proverbial needle in a haystack.

Reality reveals relatively few CEOs who have integrated communication-oriented principles into their everyday leader conduct. Understanding why is not hard. Executives were taught from business school through on-the-job experience to believe that true leadership is about the leader's making decisions and then issuing edicts. The emerging model of executive leadership, relying on slow-brewing, interactive processes like negotiation and feedback and relationship crafting, is admittedly harder to integrate into practice. But mastering the modern CEO role can pay off handsomely in a collection of value-added factors that have an impact on the unforgiving bottom line of customer loyalty, employee morale, stockholder support, and media perceptions.

Changing another person's long-held philosophy or attitude or behavior is almost always incremental and requires time, patience, and trial and error. The need to change may be compelling, yet resistance to an unpredictable future is equally compelling. The pull to stay on the road already traveled as long as possible is a basic tenet of human nature. Realizing that people invariably resist change allows enlightened executives to shepherd organizational change in ways that confront people's fear of uncertainty and minimize unavoidable trauma and disruption.

The tortoise-like pace that business schools exhibit in revising outdated and unrealistic education strategies illustrates this point. For well over a decade, most business school administrators and M.B.A. faculty were aware of the behavioral deficiencies in their programs, yet deterred by the many hurdles and angst that accompany curricular revisions, they held off doing what they knew was needed. Only recently have some of the leading M.B.A. programs stepped forward and signaled a serious inclination to reshape their rusty curricula.

EVERY CEO'S WISH: A BIZ-SAVVY COMMUNICATION ADVISER

While every CEO surrounds himself or herself with an array of specialist-advisers, communication counselors too often are relegated to subordinate roles. No CEO, however adept, is likely to possess all the communication competencies required of leadership today. Indeed, the enlightened leader knows his or her limitations and correspondingly knows to whom to turn for help. The organizational communication expert, if viewed as business credible by the CEO, works hand-in-hand with the boss to form strategies, analyze target audiences, shape messages, select the best source and media, and evaluate feedback on the effectiveness of the communication. The communicator-adviser may at times also act as the CEO's personal coach, teacher, and sounding board (see Exhibit 23.1).

The reality, though, is this: most CEOs are not strong communicators by proclivity, education, or training. They know little about how communication works or what it can do for them or their companies. Often top executives believe communication is best left to those who know that "stuff." But the current generation of chiefs increasingly seems to realize that communication cannot be ignored and should not be delegated. Unfortunately, it is the rare CEO—Chrysler's Lee Iacocca, GE's Jack Welch, IBM's Lou Gerstner, Intel's Andy Grove—who understands the central importance of communication in business life. Top dogs need help, and they know it; indeed, what they need is a helper, a counselor with expertise and experience they lack. More precisely, they need someone—maybe several someones—who understands the organization's culture and the marketplace encompassing it, and above all appreciates the nuances of merging communication and business issues into integrated strategies that benefit organization and stakeholders.

The top communicator-executive can be personal adviser to the CEO, professional confidant, live-in devil's advocate, tough-minded coach, junior psychologist, and master communication strategist. Ideally, this person is much more than a proficient communication technician; he or she can be a savvy business adviser whose specialty just happens to be communications and human behavior. CEOs have long lamented, openly and in a string of studies, that ideal communication advisers—those with business and communication acumen—are as unusual as a profitable airline. "More CEOs want to give their communication executives a seat at the table," observed Paul Argenti of Dartmouth's Tuck School of Business, "but to have that seat, they need to speak the same language and have a deep understanding of all areas of the business" (Alsop, 2005, p. B4).

"We can't stress enough the importance of CEOs having advisors who understand communication, leadership, and the organization's priorities and culture," noted Pincus and DeBonis. "But even all that isn't enough. The best counselors also identify the CEO's strengths and weaknesses, and aren't afraid to give blunt and candid advice, even if it means puncturing the CEO's ego or pointing out faults" (1994, p. 233).

For years, CEOs have been disappointed in their top communicators' weak business acumen and limited big-picture view. Such limitations tend to explain why most communication executives are not invited into the inner circle: they are perceived as narrow specialists, not as credible business thinkers and decision makers. Prototypical communication consultants are lightweights on hardcore business subjects like finance, accounting, and economics, a deficiency that curtails their credibility as advisers to CEOs and other managers throughout the organization. That kind of subpar business IQ makes CEOs skeptical of their top communicators' recommendations and thus, by association, less confident in the contributions of the organizational communication function.

Again, the CEO's views of communication have been shaped in large part by the top communicator's counsel, behavior, and effectiveness, or lack thereof. The occasional chiefs who do perceive their number one communicator as a bonafide business adviser believe them anomalies and exceptions—and thereby easy to underestimate, underuse, and undersupport them, and communication in general. Too many CEOs remain unconvinced of communication's potential to positively influence business outcomes.

THE CHALLENGE: PREPARE BETTER, INTEGRATE MORE

The current reality is that chief executive officers now accept communication's efficacy and necessity (conceptually, anyway) as a fact of business life, yet that acceptance has not found its way into their strategic thinking or leader behavior. This gap between belief and action needs to be narrowed and eventually closed if CEOs are to embrace their behavioral responsibilities as leaders, relationship builders, and role models. The challenge for CEOs is made more difficult because they are not getting the business—not just communication— counsel from their top communication professionals they know they need.

So what is to be done to fortify CEOs as communicators and communicators as business advisers? Ironically, the answer is the same for each: alter how they are educated and trained, and do so before would-be professionals' attitudes and behaviors are hardened and are still open to untraditional notions of a leader's transformative capabilities and responsibilities. This implies a pressing need to overhaul long-entrenched, outdated college curricula, never easy in a culture that honors the status quo. Having taught in communication and M.B.A. programs, we know of academia's disinclination to restructure long-stable curricula.

Business schools, M.B.A. programs especially, need an infusion of communication and relationship-building-type content and critical thinking experiences; communication schools need a potent injection of basic business concepts, principles, and processes into their curricula and internships. "A lot of deans don't realize the level of sophistication communication has reached and how it is being managed at a very high level within the corporation," notes James Rubin of the University of Virginia's Darden School of Business Administration (Alsop, 2005, p. B4). If we could reshape the future to our belief and preference, business schools and communication schools would, to the extent practical, merge into one school. Where business and communication would be perceived and presented as a singular, integrated major (for example, as constituent relations). As such, business and behavioral subjects would be equal in importance and emphasis—indivisible, indistinguishable, and interdependent. Perhaps this is a pipe dream, yet it may not be so far-fetched, considering the recent "wave of MBA redesign" examples dotting the United States (Bisoux, 2005, p. 27), and new calls by respected business school insiders to "rebalance" M.B.A. curricula "in order to link hard and soft skills" (Bennis & O'Toole, 2005, p. 104).

Similar encouraging, albeit sporadic, signs have surfaced in the communication community in recent years, including the Public Relations Society of America's national campaign to prod business school deans to incorporate communication into M.B.A. programs and increase dialogue between business and communication schools; Syracuse University's Newhouse School of Public Communications master's degree in communication management, a program that integrates courses from communication and business schools; and the San Francisco Academy, an intensive year-long program begun by Bay Area top communicators designed to bolster future top communicators' business depth.

The M.B.A. environment in particular appears to be on the cusp of transforming its belief in the need for change into revamped curricula. But the pace of remodeling programs is uneven. For some business schools, borrowing a communication professor to teach memo writing or speech delivery is the equivalent of "giving in" to the growing pressure. Most communication schools offer only an occasional elective course in some aspect of business communication. This is progress, but if communication and business programs are to bridge the divide and merge, then integrating the disciplines in meaningful educational ways is paramount.

In spite of a few upbeat examples of colleges that are integrating the teaching of business and communication topics, typical business school curricula focus almost solely on traditional business subjects and give only a passing nod, if that, to allied content and skills. Courses in public speaking, small group communication, interpersonal communication, intercultural communication, mass media, and business communication are highly salient to would-be business executives, but unfortunately they seldom fit into their business curricula what they regard as peripheral courses. Many premier companies, General Electric and 3M among them, are unhappy with business school graduates' deficiencies and are doing something about it. Rather than merely criticize, they are taking on the strenuous task of educating and training themselves by creating "corporate universities" that offer customized courses designed to fill gaps in employees' knowledge and skill sets.

A FINAL WORD

The need for and value of the communication component of organizational leadership is no longer doubted, as it was for most of the twentieth century. However, that intellectual acceptance has not yet translated into how CEOs think about and play their increasingly complicated "perceptions management" role or how they are trained to handle the expanding human demands of the multifaceted job. Given such demands, opportunity exists for professional communicators—but only those with the business savvy and intelligence—to influence the extent to which CEOs embrace their role as chief communicator and relationship builder.

Only when CEOs and their top communicators start working together as equal business partners will they begin meeting their collective obligation to create and carry out business and communication strategies. Strategies that aim to span boundaries, bolster stakeholder relationships, and escalate the organization's credibility are all essential requirements of those brave souls wanting to get into "CEOing."

Notes

1. A useful distinction between leadership approaches discussed in the management literature is transformational versus transactional leaders. Transformational leaders motivate others, employees especially, to "transform" their individual interests to

align with the organization's interests. Transactional leaders, in contrast, view employees and others as needing direction to perform "transactional" steps to do their jobs. Transformational leaders tend toward give-and-take and open communication, whereas transactional leaders rely more on their status and power to direct and control others.

2. Definitions of communication and its many allied terms, such as public relations, cover the gamut, beginning with the Comm 101 S-M-C-R (Source-Message-Channel-Receiver) linear definition. As communication became the object of increased study, the definitions and models grew more complex, interactive, and transactive. We refer the insatiably curious to Frank Dance and Carl Larson's still-classic *The Function of Human Communication: A Theoretical Approach* (1976) and its 126 definitions of communication.

References

Alsop, R. (2005, February 8). M.B.A. track. *Wall Street Journal,* B4.

Andrews, N., & D'Andrea Tyson, L. (2004, Fall). The upwardly global MBA. *strategy + business,* 60–69.

Bennis, W., & O'Toole, J. (2005, May). How business schools lost their way. *Harvard Business Review, 83*(5), 96–104.

Bisoux, T. (2005, May–June). The extreme MBA makeover. *BizEd,* 26–33.

Dance, E.X.F., & Larson, C. E. (1976). *The functions of human communication: A theoretical approach.* New York: Holt.

DePree, M. (1989). *Leadership is an art.* New York: Bantam Doubleday Dell.

Gulati, R., Huffman, S. & Neilson, G. (2002, Fall). The Barista principle: Starbucks and the rise of relational capital. *strategy + business,* 58–69.

Henry, D., France, M., & Lavelle, L. (2005, April. 25). The boss on the sidelines. *BusinessWeek,* 86–96.

Krzyzewiski, M., with Phillips, D. (2000). *Leading with the heart.* New York: Warner Business Books.

Lucier, C., Schuyt, R., & Tse, E. (2005, Summer). The world's most prominent temp workers. *strategy + business,* 29–43.

Matlock, J. Jr. (2004). *Reagan and Gorbachev: How the cold war ended.* New York: Random House.

Pincus, J. D., & DeBonis, J. N. (1994). *Top dog: A different kind of book about becoming an excellent leader.* New York: McGraw-Hill.

Pincus, J. D., & Wood, S. C. (1997). The CEO's changing communication role: Precursor to effective leadership. In J. L. Garnett & A. Kouzmin (Eds.), *Handbook of administrative communication.* New York: Marcel Dekker.

CHAPTER TWENTY-FOUR

Successful Media Relations

Brenda Siler

After years of practicing media relations, the same question still exists: "How do you get good media coverage?" And the answer is still the same: "Have a good story to tell."

What makes a good story? Just ask yourself a few commonsense questions: "Will it lead to change?" "Is it new?" "Does it have local, regional, national, or international implications?" "Does it involve a well-known personality?" Think about those things that interest you, and you have the answer as to whether you have something newsworthy to pitch to the media.

ONE GOOD STORY, SO MANY OPPORTUNITIES

The communications discipline of media relations has always been exciting to me. Today the opportunities to pitch a good story are endless. With a twenty-four-hour news cycle and many more news outlets, one can use quite a bit of creativity in framing a newsworthy issue for news media consumption.

Take the example of a local or regional news story of a hurricane threatening to hit along the Florida coast and you are a media relations staffer with an electrical power company in Atlanta or with the American Red Cross in Atlanta. What is the opportunity for your organization in Atlanta? Hurricane coverage has now become a national news opportunity. When a hurricane hits, there is always the threat of power outages and the need to bring in crews from other states. A Florida hurricane or a hurricane hitting any other southern state means that power crews will be called in from neighboring states. If you are doing media relations for a power company in Atlanta, chances are that you would be able to pitch a story about your company's crews being on standby for hurricane relief. You have a local angle to what probably will be a national story.

The same would follow for an American Red Cross angle. The Red Cross is known for its disaster relief efforts. When it comes to hurricanes, tornadoes, or floods, the Red Cross dispatches disaster volunteers to many locations nationwide. Again, there is an opportunity to put a local face on a national story. Such examples demonstrate that one knows how to deliver on a newsworthy story. If a similar opportunity comes around again, the news media will call you before you get a chance to pitch them a story.

A key lesson in media relations is to take the time to learn about the range of media outlets and the types of issues covered by those media outlets. You want to know a reporter's beat and be aware of the many specialty media that may be interested in your organization's issues. There are a number of pieces to the puzzle of successful media placement. All of these media placement opportunities feed into the twenty-four-hour news cycle. Here are a few of the major categories of news media outlets to be considered in developing your media strategy:

- Print media: daily newspapers, weekly newspapers, community newspapers, magazines, and newsletters
- Radio: syndicated news networks, local news and talk stations, and local stations with news readers that pull copy from wire reports (versus reporters who go out and cover news)
- Television: local network affiliates, local all-news channels, national networks, cable news channels, and local cable public access channels
- Online media: specialty Web sites (for example, health, public policy), online entity of local news media, and online entity of national media
- News groups and blogs
- Miscellaneous: Web sites or newsletters from organizations interested in your issues; includes wire services like the Associated Press that serve as feeds to other print and broadcast news outlets

YOUR MEDIA RELATIONS OPERATION

Whether you are a one-person or sixty-person communications shop, there are a few basics to the media relations function.

Media Lists

You can create a database using a wide range of directories, or you can subscribe to a database that can be accessed online from your computer. Depending on your organization's issues, maintaining a media database on your own can be a daunting task but nevertheless cost-effective. Subscribing to a media database service can be expensive but less labor intensive. Regardless of the method, the key is keeping the media list updated. Subscriber database services lure you by stating that they automatically update media contact information. My experience has been that as the subscriber, you still need to feed any updated media contacts to the media database service. These services miss many vital updates and media contact information.

Staffing

Staffing needs depend on the size of your organization, the range of issues, and the range of media placement opportunities. A one-person operation works if your organization has a limited, targeted focus. A larger media relations operation can include a media relations director responsible for assigning in-house media relations staff with beats, managing the online newsroom, managing the media relations evaluation and measurement duties, and leading media training activities.

Media Distribution

Distributing news releases and media advisories can be done the old-fashioned way: by mail. Today there are other mechanisms for distributing media materials. These include broadcast fax, media distribution services, and news wire services. Many of these methods give a price break with an annual membership fee. Determine the appropriate contract for your organization based on how many times you anticipate sending out a news release and the size of your media list.

Online Newsroom

If your organization has a Web site, you should have an online newsroom with basic media materials. Those basics include recent news releases, fact sheets (for example, on organizational purpose, structure, and key issues), and a listing of key organizational leaders (staff, board, and committees). A more in-depth online newsroom can have more layered topic areas, which include further details on key issues, a news release archive, leadership biographies, plus much more. Some organizational Web sites require reporters to sign in. Some offer reporters an opportunity to be added to an electronic mailing list for regular updates. Remember that when a reporter calls you, chances are that he or she has visited your company Web site and the online newsroom in advance. Make sure you keep this important media relations tool up-to-date.

Evaluation Process

Compiling news clips is a basic component of media evaluation. You can do this in-house or use a clipping service. How you evaluate those clips is subject to a wide range of opinions. Do you compare the size of the placement to advertising rates? Do you engage in another type of assessment that takes a look at the size, location, and quality of the story placement as the basis for rating the value? Did the placement cause a flood of calls or Web hits? The bottom line to evaluation is to start off with clearly identified goals and objectives. What is your wish for visibility through media placement? Who is your primary target audience? What mechanisms exist to tell you that your target audience was reached? Many of these questions require you to engage organizational leaders in a discussion about their wishes. You will find their expectations of media placement to be unrealistic. Tap into research about the practice of media relations to help make a case for the important factors to consider when evaluating media placement success.

POSITIONING THE VALUE OF MEDIA RELATIONS INSIDE YOUR ORGANIZATION

This section could be titled "Justifying Your Existence," because getting stakeholders to truly understand what is possible in media relations is rooted in your ability to chart a realistic media relations course. That usually means having many conversations with your organization's leadership about their vision. This vision becomes an assessment that should include who the leadership wants to talk to (audience determination), their assessment of key organizational assets that would interest those audiences (prioritizing issues), and what success would look like (part of the evaluation component). Once the vision assessment is complete, long-term and short-term media relations goals and objectives can be established. Working closely with your organization's leadership on these goals and objectives should result in buy-in for your media relations approach.

The next step in the process of gaining support is meeting with department heads and managers. These colleagues hold the key to ensuring that you and your media relations staff can understand details related to your organization's key issues so that media queries are handled with knowledge, support development of fact sheets and news releases that are vital media relations tools, and effectively identify and evaluate colleagues who can serve as issue experts with reporters. In fact, everyone in your organization is a potential media ambassador or publicist. By engaging the directors and managers within your organization, you are working toward creating a better understanding among colleagues about the inner workings of media relations while achieving buy-in for the role they play in executing a successful media relations strategy.

A STAR IS BORN: THE MEDIA SPOKESPERSON

Now you have your colleagues engaged. It is time to identify those individuals who will serve as your organization's key media spokespersons. My philosophy has always been that the head of public relations or media relations should not be quoted or at the microphone, though I understand that this sometimes cannot be avoided. Your job is to handle the media query and background facts and ensure accuracy and positioning. When it is time for the official organization statement, that is the time when your spokesperson is out front.

Whether it is the CEO or the issue expert, these individuals will require media training. They may be knowledgeable about their specialty, but articulating a well-crafted response in less than thirty seconds or dodging a tricky question from a reporter takes training and practice.

As the lead media relations staffer, if your background includes work as a reporter (in particular, broadcast news), you can probably conduct media training for your spokespersons. But you are better off getting an outside media training consultant to train your spokespersons to be "prime time" ready. In whatever manner you approach media training, be sure to include a videotape component of your spokespersons. The spokespersons should be able to see themselves in an actual interview scenario. The training will be enlightening to them and you.

Once the training is complete, prepare a list of tips that your spokesperson can quickly review prior to future interviews. When your spokespersons are scheduled for a media interview, you should always be in the room during the interview. If it is a telephone interview, use a speaker phone. Have a recorder to tape the interview. This recording can come in handy if you feel your spokesperson was misquoted. The tape can also be used for a postinterview critique with your spokesperson.

AT THE HEART, THE RELATIONSHIP WITH THE MEDIA

There is always a question of when the best time is to call a reporter. Before the twenty-four-hour news cycle became the norm, the answer to that question was easy. For daily newspapers, there were three key deadlines during a day. For television news, it was pretty much "do not call within the hour leading up to the broadcast." For all-news radio stations, you could try your luck and call just about any time. Yet even now, my philosophy about when to call a reporter remains the same: call when you are not pitching a thing.

It is important to develop a relationship with key reporters when you have nothing to lose. This allows you the time to understand the short-term and long-term interests of the reporter, so that you can appropriately match your pitch to their interests. This less stressful approach to building media relationships will also allow you to educate reporters about your organization, clarifying issues on which you can serve as a resource. By laying this foundation, you should be able to tailor your organization's issues to the reporter's interests. Another benefit will be that the reporter remembers to call you first when something is brewing in your industry.

When you need to make a hard sell with your issues because the media climate requires it, have that "thirty-second elevator speech" ready. This term is commonly used when marketing for career advancement. But it is also applicable to making a media pitch. This type of pitch takes practice. It helps to write out your facts before making the call. Whatever you do, prepare to offer the complete package, which may include e-mailing or faxing key facts immediately following the pitch and ensuring your spokesperson is waiting in the wings.

GETTING OUT YOUR MESSAGE

It is time to address the focus of your media pitch. First, who is the right reporter, and what is the correct media outlet? Take time to study the media closely. In addition to pitching mainstream media, learn about specialty media that may be interested in your organization's issues for the audiences you have identified.

What media relations tool should be used to spotlight your issue? Usually if you have an event for which you desire "day of" coverage, a media advisory, organized in a "who, what, where, why" format is an effective tool. This advisory should be sent to wire service daybooks, assignment editors, photo desk editors, beat reporters, and columnists specializing in the issue associated with the event.

At the event, whether it is a media briefing, a grand opening, or celebratory observances, make sure you have your organization's logo splashed everywhere. Something I learned while working for the American Red Cross is the "four-wall" policy when it comes to logo placement. When you go into a room where your event is being held, a large posting of your logo should be visible on each wall. Whenever a camera pans the room, your organization's identification is always there. The four-wall policy is in addition to the use of podium signs and a microphone logo clips.

News releases are usually produced to announce information that is more static (such as a position announcement or financial statements) or can be used in media kits that are distributed at your event or posted on your Web site.

Always create fact sheets to distribute or post on your Web newsroom that provide details supporting issues you are positioning.

When working on pitching a bigger, sprawling issue that would be better suited for an in-depth coverage, think through all of the opportunities for media pitching. For example, how would a children's health issue be positioned with the media? There are health and science reporters who would be an obvious pitch. Decisions about a child's health are made by parents; therefore, parenting magazines and Web sites could be another option. Among parents, it is usually the mother taking a lead role regarding the child's health care, so women's media such as *Working Mother* might be an option. Pediatricians are often tapped to do special features with both broadcast and print media. Add those individuals to your media list. Dig deep and peel back all of the layers of possibility.

Whenever you pitch, be patient. If your issue is not time sensitive, it may take weeks to a month to see a placement success. The instant gratification received from that "day of" coverage is hard to beat, but often the placement that takes a little longer yields better, more thorough coverage.

WORKING WITH PHOTOGRAPHERS

There are two angles to think about when working with photographers. If you are pitching an event where there is a possible photo opportunity, then media coverage can take place in the form of a photo story versus a story written by a reporter. Sometimes a print reporter who is assigned to cover your event may request a photojournalist. Cover your bets by sending the event's media advisory to the photo assignment desk as well. We often forget to include the photojournalist in our media mix.

There are publications and Web sites that will accept a photo along with a cutline (caption) that you provide. If you want to attempt to submit a photo to a media outlet, hire a professional photographer who knows press photography standards. Today's photojournalism standards require digital capability so that a photo can be electronically transmitted. There are many former print media photojournalists who freelance. To meet your needs, check with colleagues in other organizations for recommendations.

SPECIALTY MEDIA

As we have learned to embrace a global range of cultures, a bonus for the practice of media relations has been the growth of media outlets targeted to a variety of cultures. Check your media database for media outlets targeted toward ethnic-, religious-, political-, gender-, disability-, age-, and sexual orientation–specific audiences. Do not view these targeted media outlets as an afterthought. Instead include specialty media as part of your overall media strategy. Just like mainstream media, specialty media opportunities are available through print, broadcast, cable, and online outlets. Consumers seek information from sources that relate directly to their lives.

Working with specialty media requires you to be interested, sensitive, and ready to learn. Ask staff or volunteers in your organization about media outlets they like. Make a face-to-face media call to these outlets. Reaching out to diverse media outlets may also help your organization check its "diversity meter." Do your organizational business strategies and media objectives demonstrate a desire to reach out to a wide range of consumers? Do you have media spokespersons who can address issues of concern to diverse audiences? Be prepared, and avoid getting your organization in a bind. As the communicator, you can offer your leadership the perspective from a consumer's point of view. I call it the "outside-the-building" perspective.

CRISIS COMMUNICATIONS PLANNING

Every organization needs to have a crisis communications plan as a key component to the organization's crisis management plan. Because Chapter Eleven in this book is devoted to crisis communications, I include only a few key concepts.

First, find out if your organization has a plan to handle various types of emergencies, such as power outages, injuries, vandalism, or break-ins. From this foundation, you can begin to introduce the concept of other types of emergencies, such as improper behavior resulting in a scandal, sudden death of key staff or board leadership, lawsuits, protests by outside groups, or natural disasters. The discussion about emergencies can then move to a fuller conversation about crisis management planning and the communication component.

If you have not done a crisis communications plan, do your research by reading manuals and trade publications or by contacting colleagues who may be willing to share at least an outline for their crisis communications plan. Work with your media relations staff to draft a plan, and then present this to the organization's senior management team. By positioning a crisis communications plan as an essential component of good business practices, senior management can be better prepared. Senior management and department leaders can help in the preparation of the crisis communications plan by identifying key staff and their assigned roles during the crisis. The plan should include telephone numbers for those key staff along with step-by-step guidelines about how the plan will be executed based on the nature of the crisis.

In the event of a crisis, it is "all hands on deck." Assuming it is a crisis that will garner media attention, you and your staff will need to collect the facts, develop key messages, prepare statements for the spokespersons, craft news releases, and put into action a process by which regular updates will be provided to the media. The process for managing all of these should be outlined in your crisis communications plan.

To prepare for regular updates to the media during a crisis, work with your Web team to create "ghost" pages for your online newsroom. The ghost page is a template where you can plug in key facts, contact information, and a schedule for when regular updates will be provided to the media. If the crisis is such that a lot of media queries are anticipated, you should put into effect a special telephone line where the incoming message will provide basic information and a time for regularly scheduled updates to the media.

Again, these are just a few basic tips to consider when developing and implementing a crisis communications plan. There are many resources that can be accessed to help you develop a comprehensive crisis communications plan. Take the time to create a plan that makes sense for your organization.

THE EVALUATION QUOTIENT

The evaluation and measurement of media relations can be approached from a couple of angles. Before getting into a debate about column inches or number of clippings, let us look at soft types of evaluation considerations to consider within the world of hard-core measurement techniques:

- Assess how effective you were in engaging colleagues outside the media relations staff in the issue development and message strategy processes.

- If your spokesperson did a broadcast interview and you taped the on-air coverage, meet with your spokesperson and review the tape to evaluate the performance. Review some basic media interview tips with your spokesperson.

- Listen to the opinions of various stakeholders as they relate to your media coverage. This process can be eye opening as to whether message strategies and ideas about what success looks like hold true. Seeing results on air or in print may not have the appearance as originally imagined. This can serve as a reality check.

Other media measurements can also contribute to effective statistics in written reports and in oral presentations to senior management and board leaders:

- Media clippings: The appeal of a thick stack of media clippings can never be underestimated. Such a display can overshadow the fact that original media objectives may not have been met. But more can be done with a stack of media clippings and a composite videotape of television coverage. Some clipping services electronically store and categorize clippings. A drawback to using clipping services is that the service may not be able to access all of the media covering your issues. This is usually the case when attempting to document coverage in some trade publications where you have had successful media placement. Also, there is not a sure-fire way to capture broadcast clips. Television clips are easier, but accessing radio clips is still a challenge. A complete picture of media placement success can be illusive.

- Column inch comparison: This is an often-used technique for illustrating media placement success by applying advertising rates as a measurement indicator of value. This measurement technique attempts to make a statement about how much the publicity is worth if the space or time had been purchased. There are a number of variables that are considered, such as the amount of space or time devoted to the story. An ad rate is calculated for that space or time. If your organization receives a great deal of media coverage, then working with a media evaluation service may be necessary to calculate the total monetary value.

- Quality measurement: There are other evaluation methods that take the advertising rate process a step further to look at quality of placement. These techniques offered by a number of media measurement services look at quality factors such as placement of a story within a media outlet, placement of the organization's name within a story, and the number of times your organization's spokesperson is quoted, along with other factors. This information is taken and used to configure a report that may be more meaningful for measuring against media relations objectives than a report that measures based on advertising rates.

- Benchmarking reports: This type of report compares your coverage to that of your competitors. Showing that your placement success is better than that of a competitor on an issue-by-issue basis is another good type of evaluation report. You can also benchmark how effective your media placements are from year to year. Are you better or worse than the year before? Has your approach to pitching changed? If so, how does this affect placement success?

CONCLUSION

These media relations basics should get you started. Ensure your media relations approach is always based on the long-range and short-range goals of your organization. Once the strategic business direction of your organization is understood, development of media relations objectives that help drive business success can begin.

As you move forward with managing your media relations plan, include periodic check points or informal updates to senior management. Knowledgeable leadership maintains support turning key stakeholders into advocates for your efforts.

CHAPTER TWENTY-FIVE

Investor Relations and Financial Communication

Karen Vahouny

You are evaluating two corporations whose stock is traded on one of the public stock exchanges. They generate similar revenues and produce comparable earnings. They are in the same industry and have similar historical growth rates. Yet one company's stock's price has been steadily moving up and is viewed as fairly priced, while the other trades at erratic prices and is generally regarded as a risky investment. Why?

The answer to this question should be an integral part of an investor relations (IR) program. The investor relations function combines a number of disciplines, including finance and communication, in order to effectively counsel management and provide valuable information to the investment community. One part of the information mix involves the numbers, which is reflected in the company's financial statements and trends. The other part of the mix is nonfinancial, and this is also important in determining the value of a company's stock. The nonfinancial factors include the quality of management, competitive advantages of the products and services, success of research and development efforts, the company's position in the market, the prospective growth of the market, and diversification and types of customers, among others. An investor relations professional blends an understanding of the company operations and financial performance with the ability to communicate effectively with investors. Included in an IR officer's role is counseling management on the issues of public disclosure and regulation, providing market intelligence to management and the board of directors, monitoring the valuation of the company and those of its peers, and targeting and cultivating prospective investors. The effectiveness of an IR program is tied to the basic principles of good communication: audience identification and understanding, development of a well-researched plan, the selection and development of appropriate tools and tactics, strong execution, and evaluation and fine-tuning.

According to *The Standards of Practice for Investor Relations* (National Investor Relations Institute, 2004), investor relations can be defined as "a strategic management responsibility that integrates finance, communication, marketing and securities law compliance to enable the most effective two-way communication between a company and the financial community and other constituencies, which ultimately contributes to a company's securities achieving fair valuation." The roots of investor relations can be traced to General Electric Company (GE), a widely accepted model for the best practices across many business disciplines.

This chapter provides an overview of investor relations, including its origins and the role of IR professionals and key concepts for successful practice today.

IN THE BEGINNING

It is generally acknowledged that the genesis of investor relations was in 1953, when GE's chairman, Ralph Cordiner, began a process to formalize the company's relationship with its shareholders. According to the National Investor Relations Institute (NIRI), the result of this process was the formation of a new department and the coining of the term *investor relations.* The department's initial efforts centered on identifying the share owners, determining their needs, and then implementing the best process for achieving two-way communication.

WHY INVESTOR RELATIONS?

Investor relations is focused on helping companies achieve a realistic and fair market value for their stock. A successful investor relations program can help reduce the cost of capital for the company and ensure that shareholder interests are recognized and served.

If a company has 50 million shares outstanding that are trading at $10, the company's market value, or market capitalization, is $500 million. If the share price increases to $12, the company's market value has increased by $100 million to $600 million. The ultimate goal is to increase enterprise value and decrease the cost of capital. Here are two examples illustrating the benefits of a reduced cost of capital:

- A company may want to use its stock, rather than cash or debt financing, to fund an acquisition.
- A company wants to raise additional capital through a secondary public offering and use the proceeds for product development and marketing.

The role of investor relations today has changed very little from its original focus in the 1950s, although the tools are more sophisticated. Glenn Saxon, one of the original members of the GE investor relations department, as well as cofounder and the first president of NIRI, explained, "Our role is to keep the marketplace informed about the developments and activities of a public company, so that people who are interested in buying or selling its stock can get a fair price."

Although GE's chairman believed that reducing the company's cost of capital was a major goal of investor relations, Saxon said that he stressed that the needs of its share owners must always be kept in mind. Saxon noted that once an owner of several hundred shares scribbled a short note on a proxy card to thank Cordiner for doing a good job in running the company. Afterward, Cordiner carried the card in his pocket and would pull it out from time to time to show that his boss—an owner—thought he was doing a good job.

SHAKEN INVESTOR CONFIDENCE

The collapse among technology stocks following the NASDAQ stock market peak in March 2000 was the first in a number of troubling developments that shattered the confidence of investors. The technology stock implosion stemmed from a buildup of investor expectations that were not backed with financial results. Also uncovered was the unsettling practice of financial analysts who had publicly touted certain stocks but had private reservations or even skepticism about those same investments. Adding to the growing wave of investor distrust was the recognition that analyst compensation was tied directly to business generated for their firm's investment bankers—a "you scratch my back and I'll scratch yours" relationship.

This represented just the initial wave of investor disappointment. Unfortunately, there was more to come. Headlines of corporate malfeasance dominated the business news and later the general press as the impact hit individuals and their pocketbooks: Enron, its clouding of financial information, and the downward spiral of its stock; Tyco's senior executives accused of fraud, larceny, and the falsification of business records related to stock sales and bonuses; and the list goes on to include WorldCom, Global Crossing, and Parmalat, to name just a few, plus some of the investment banks and accounting firms involved in these cases.

These situations touched scores of investors who lost all or much of their wealth and employees whose retirement savings were wiped out. The Sarbanes-Oxley Act passed in 2002 was designed to improve the clarity of financial reporting and strengthen corporate governance, among other purposes. With increased regulation and the scrutiny of public company management, accounting, and reporting practices, investor relations has become increasingly important.

THE NUMBERS

Investors typically use a variety of quantitative tools to determine a valuation, or appropriate market worth, of a company's stock. Investors carefully study a company's fundamentals—the income statement (a summary of revenues, costs, and earnings during a specific time period), the balance sheet (a financial report that shows a company's assets, liabilities, and owners' equity on a given date), and the cash flow statements (reports that analyze changes in the company's cash position). In reviewing these reports, investors make an assessment of the company's financial history and track record, as well as a determination of positive or negative trends that may be emerging. A company's revenues and net income may be growing, for example, but its profit margin (its gross profit divided by sales) may be declining, and investors will question this trend and make a determination as to whether the investments being made will generate a higher return in the future.

Ratios, such as price/earnings ratio (the price of one share of stock divided by its earnings per share) and price/book ratio (the stock price divided by the book value per share, which relates to the value of its assets), are typically used in assessing valuation, but there are a host of other methodologies. Essentially, in applying these valuation tools, an investor is trying to determine whether a company's stock price appears to be fairly valued or whether it is under- or overvalued in relation to its future prospects and to similar companies.

"THE STORY"

The quantitative information is an important part of the process to determine whether to invest in a company. But there is another important nonquantitative factor that goes into the evaluation mix as well. In investor relations vernacular, this is called "the story." Investors will make a subjective judgment about a company on the basis of its story.

Research initiated by a professor at the University of Western Ontario concluded that on average, 35 percent of the investment decision is based on nonfinancial factors. Important performance characteristics revealed in the survey included the quality of products and services, strength of the company's market position, the effectiveness of compensation policies, the quality of investor communications, level of customer satisfaction, and strength of corporate culture (Mavrinac, 1997).

A common theme that spans all the components of a company's story is growth. Whether it is growth of the market, products, or services or the company's position in relation to its competitors, the core question being asked by the investor is whether the company has the potential to grow. The premium that an investor places on a company's stock will largely be related to his or her belief in the prospects for growth. Hence, identifying the issues that may have an impact on your company's growth prospects and what interests your target investor should be an important driver of your investor relations program.

Understanding the importance of the quantitative and qualitative aspects of the valuation process is critical to investor relations. If, for example, your company's price-to-earnings (P/E) ratio is 10 and all of the firms that would be considered comparable, in terms of industry, product or service niche, and size, have P/E ratios that are between 20 and 25, you would want to uncover the reasons for your below-average valuation and subsequently develop a strategy to increase your value. Perhaps in discussions with some of the people who have invested in your company, as well as those who have invested in one or more of the comparable companies you are evaluating, you learn that your organization's product capabilities are viewed as having limited potential. Or you may find that your company's vision appears to be too narrow, or there has been weakness on the part of management to successfully execute the corporate strategy. Another possibility is that your company is not being proactive in communicating its strategy and accomplishments to the investment community.

INFORMATION CENTRAL: THE IR FUNCTION AND ROLES

If an investor relations program is on track, it should serve two important constituencies: the investment community and corporate management. The IR professional or staff should function as "information central," delivering meaningful information on a regular basis to investors and serving as a clearinghouse for their questions and feedback. The other key role involves providing professional counsel to management on a variety of issues relating to the needs and concerns of the investment community (see Figure 25.1). In fact, an investor relations function maintains a delicate balancing act in supporting the needs and interests of both constituencies. You are employed by and provide counsel

Figure 25.1. Key Activities in Investor Relations

and direction to management, while also maintaining relationships with the investment community. There may be times you believe that management's interests may compromise your role of maintaining credibility with the investment community. These are times when investor relations professionals do battle with management, asserting that short-term needs should be put aside in favor of the long-term interests (and institutional memory) of the investment community. For example, management may want to delay revealing an operational problem to its investors or may want to present some information in a much more positive light than the investor relations person feels comfortable with. Although there are times when companies are legally required to disclose certain types of information, there are many situations in the investor relations domain that fall into a gray area, which forces IR professionals to balance their responsibilities to their two constituencies.

Clearinghouse for Investors

Investor relations professionals wear several hats in their dealings with the investment community:

• Providing their company's investors with information about the company. This can range from a brief telephone call, to a multipage document that explains the significance of a recent news item, to a full-day meeting for analysts and portfolio managers at the company's headquarters (and a range of other tools and forums in between).

• Identifying and working with reporters in cultivating positive financial coverage and responding to their questions about the company and its performance. News media coverage can be especially important in reinforcing a company's position with the investors who read an article or see the coverage on television and in reaching people who are not current shareholders.

• Identifying institutions and individuals who might be interested in purchasing stock of the company and developing appropriate means to communicate with these investors. Sophisticated screening criteria and online database tools can be used to target investors who may be interested in your company's stock, based on a number of criteria, such as investment style, market capitalization emphasis, geographical region, or industry focus.

• Building positive relationships with current and potential investors. This takes time and effort, but it can pay dividends in the form of increased shareholder support and loyalty. Investors cite a number of attributes of a successful IR department: responding quickly and accurately to investors' requests for information; maintaining a high degree of knowledge about the company and its financial performance; anticipating questions in advance and trying to ensure that as many as possible are answered in the investor materials and meetings; making the IR function and management accessible to the investment community; being candid and straightforward in communications; and setting realistic expectations—and meeting them.

• Actively soliciting feedback about the company from the investment community. The information from current investors sheds light on how the company's story is being perceived. Information from prospective investors can be extremely useful in strategizing the company's discussion points.

Counsel to Management

In addition to building relationships with and communicating with the financial community, the investor relations function has another equally important role in an organization: the role as counselor and sounding board to senior management. This valuable activity spans a number of areas:

• Synthesizing investor feedback and prioritizing the issues that require increased management emphasis or clarification in investor communications.

• Compiling data on the company's existing shareholders and their patterns of buying and holding (how long they hold the stock before selling it), which can be useful in structuring the ongoing investor communications program.

• Seeking out investor feedback and assimilating their concerns relating to the overall valuation of the company. A strong investor relations practitioner will help management view the company from an objective investor's point of view, which means raising and discussing the difficult issues. This uncovering of a company's negatives, accompanied by both qualitative and quantitative data whenever possible, helps ensure that management has a clear sense of how the company is evaluated by the investment community.

- Raising the issues that affect valuation not only for management discussion but optimally for closure. Thus, the investor relations function serves as an impetus for change in the organization. For example, a company may have a strong reputation and an exciting core business, but one of its divisions is viewed as a negative and nonessential to its strategy, therefore reducing the company's overall valuation. The investor relations professional can reinforce this issue to management; perhaps the answer is the sale of the one division and a renewed emphasis on the core business. The articulation of a plan to sell the division, or, more subtly, to deemphasize it, followed at some point in the near future by its divestiture, would likely boost the price of the stock, remove an obstacle for new investors, and result in increased shareholder value.

- Assessing the potential impact of an event on the price of the stock and, in the case of negative news, working to minimize the damage through the communication process. Let us say that a company determines that its upcoming quarterly financial results will be below analysts' published expectations. If it immediately discloses the expected level of shortfall and subsequently holds an investor conference call, this could reduce their concerns and lessen the potential negative impact. Company management can explain in straightforward terms the reason for the shortfall, what the company has done or is doing to correct the problem, and how long it expects the issue to affect financial performance. If the company shows a regular pattern of disappointing investors and falling short of expectations, the impact of any damage control will most likely be minimal, because the company's credibility is in question.

- Providing guidance to senior management—those responsible for speaking with investors—on the public disclosure of information. The Securities Exchange Act of 1934 requires that companies promptly disclose "material" information to the press, that is, events or developments that may affect an investor's decision to buy or sell the stock or may affect the price of the stock. Material information includes such news as the decision to effect a stock split, a change in top management, major borrowings, significant new products, or the closing of a major plant or facility.

- Providing valuable information, based on reviews and analysis of comparable companies, to other corporate departments. IR professionals may learn from investor conferences and conversations with analysts about industry trends or developments in their competitor community—valuable information that can be shared with the strategic planning, marketing, and sales departments. Figure 25.2 represents the two roles of investor relations, with the right portion displaying the role as clearinghouse for investors and the left side reinforcing the role as counselor to management.

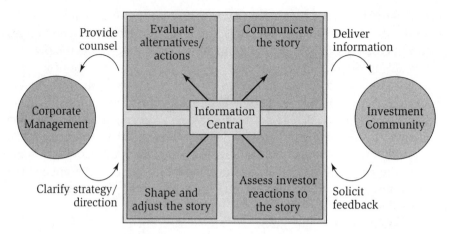

Figure 25.2. The Two Roles of Investor Relations

Research and Evaluation

Using information gathered from formal and informal research of investor attitudes and of buying and selling data, adjustments should continually be made to the investor relations program. Is the company changing its strategy, hence resulting in a different type of investor who might be attracted to the new focus? Have its acquisitions generated the results that investors anticipated? Do investors understand why the company is using a portion of its profit to invest heavily in sales and marketing? Do they understand and believe that the payoff will outweigh the cost? Does the company want to test the water on a new concept or potential product offering with investors, to determine how they would react before the step is taken?

These are just a few examples illustrating the ongoing nature of investor relations and the need to reevaluate, refocus, and constantly communicate with investors about the company's direction. Just as companies are constantly making changes to their strategy and operations, the IR program needs to be equally nimble. Figure 25.3 demonstrates the dynamic nature of investor relations and the consideration of such factors as internal and external developments, formal research and evaluation, and investor feedback and expectations.

Credibility Is King

Even if a company has outstanding financial results and a compelling story, there is one thing that can derail even the strongest investor relations program: a lack of credibility. Investors must believe that the company is going to execute the strategy and deliver results in the future. They need accurate information,

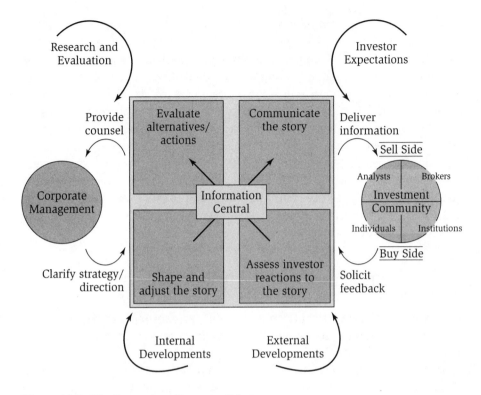

Figure 25.3. The Dynamics of Investor Relations

and they need it to be updated regularly. They use this information to make edu-cated guesses about how the company will perform in the future. Investors who work for financial institutions—for example, analysts who write reports for their firm's clients, portfolio managers who are managing their client's investments, or fund managers who are selecting stocks for their firm's funds—can be responsible for millions and even billions of dollars, and they rely on complete, candid information from the companies they follow. If they are basing their deci-sions on incorrect or outdated information, the quality of their investment decisions will be at risk.

Here is an example. Let us say a company has been telling its investors for eighteen months that it plans to introduce a new product on March 1. This prod-uct, based on a great deal of market intelligence and internal analysis, has enor-mous market potential and should generate a strong future revenue and earnings stream for the company. When the company tells investors that it has delayed the product launch by two months, investors immediately want to understand the reasons for the delay. If they are convinced that there are good reasons for the delay and they believe that another competitor will not introduce a similar product during the two-month period, then they most likely will continue to support the company, recommend it to their clients, and continue to hold the stock or possibly purchase additional shares. After the two-month delay, the company announces that it has postponed the launch for several more months. Would you expect investors to have the same commitment? Not likely, because the company has damaged its credibility, and investors will be much less likely to believe that company management is telling them the truth.

In investor relations, the "no-surprises" rule prevails. No one expects companies to execute perfectly or to perform exactly according to expectations every quarter. However, investors prefer that these surprises be kept to a minimum, and when they do occur, a company should carefully explain the problem and what it plans to do to correct it.

NOT ALL INVESTORS ARE CREATED EQUAL

Understanding the investment community—their investment criteria, communication needs, and so on—should be at the cornerstone of an IR professional's activities.

Your financial audience will be evaluating a number of factors that you, as an IR practitioner, cannot immediately change. For instance, they will consider what business you are in, as well as your income statement and balance sheet highlights. They also will review your stock's trading characteristics, such as:

- Number of shares outstanding. Institutional investors generally look for more liquid investments so that their trading activity will not have as much impact on the stock price.

- The float, or number of shares that can be traded by the public (the number of shares outstanding minus the number of shares held by company directors or management). A smaller float means that a company's stock will probably be more volatile, since a large transaction will most likely have an influence on the price of the stock.

- The number of shares held by management (insiders) and the amount of insider buying and selling (particularly with smaller companies). A company whose management owns relatively few shares or whose management is regularly selling shares will not be perceived favorably, since this sends a signal that management does not believe that the stock is a good investment.

- The volume, or total number of stock traded in a particular period.

Many investors focus on companies with certain market capitalizations (or "caps"). Another important consideration is their investment style. Many investments fall into three main categories: growth, value, or income. Growth investors look for strong projected growth in revenues and earnings. Value investors seek companies that are undervalued in relation to comparable firms. Income investors concentrate on cash flow and dividend payouts.

Investors can be part of the sell side, which means their orientation is to sell the stock to their institutional and individual clients, or the buy side, which include portfolio and fund managers who buy stock on behalf of their clients or funds.

Analysts and brokers are part of the sell-side audience:

- Analysts. Sell-side analysts produce research reports that a number of different investors use. In the case of larger firms, analysts provide their research to their firm's retail and institutional sales staffs, who use the reports in their discussions with individuals (in the case of retail sales) and with portfolio and fund managers (institutional sales). A company that has worked hard to build a strong and open relationship with its analyst will have a much easier time relying on that analyst's support during difficult times than a company that does not have credibility with its analyst. Even in the post-Enron era, an analyst can exert enormous influence on the price of the stock.
- Brokers (also known as registered representatives). Brokerage firms can range from the large national or multinational firms with huge numbers of brokers to regional and small, local firms. Brokers use analyst reports and their own data to provide clients with information about companies and whether to buy, hold, or sell the stock.

Investors on the buy side include individuals and institutions:

- Individuals. Although some individuals rely on stockbrokers to guide their investments, a growing number have turned to the many online, investor-oriented services available today. These include content providers, such as Microsoft and America On-Line, search engines like Yahoo! news services such as Bloomberg and Dow Jones, the stock exchanges, company financial filings (such as the Securities and Exchange Commission's EDGAR, in the United States), individual company Web sites, and online message boards and chatrooms. These investors, armed with a wealth of data on companies they are researching, can then turn to discount brokerages or the Internet to purchase or sell their stock and reduce the cost of their commission charges.
- Institutions. Institutional investors, who include portfolio managers and fund managers, rely on information supplied by a range of sources, including analysts and investor relations professionals. Portfolio managers purchase stock for their clients' accounts and oversee their clients' stock portfolios. Fund managers include those who select investments for various funds, including mutual funds and pension funds. Buy-side institutions can manage funds ranging from

millions of dollars to hundreds of billions of dollars. Given the potential size of an institutional investor's holdings, this audience can represent an important part of the investor relations program's target audience.

In targeting investors, you will want to carefully match investor requirements with the characteristics of your company. If your company is undervalued and has a market capitalization of $500 million (which is considered small), you would not want to target a fund manager who invests only in growth stocks with large market caps. There is a wealth of information available to help locate investors who might be interested in your company, including directories and online services. In addition, you can collect the names of people who may be interested in purchasing your stock through a variety of sources:

- Investors who call your company to request an investor information package or those who participate in your quarterly investor conference calls or Webcasts

- Industry conferences or trade shows

- Buy- or sell-side investors who follow similar companies and are quoted in the business or financial pages of newspapers

- Networking—at meetings of industry groups or trade associations or at investor meetings or conferences

- Your Web site, which may have an investor relations section offering an opportunity for investors to enter their name, address, and other information so they can receive information on the company

You should weigh the various positive and negative attributes of your audience and look at the existing mix of your shareholder base. Let us say your current shareholder base is almost entirely composed of individuals and you want to increase the number of institutional holders. You can identify institutional investors who might be interested and measure the results of your efforts over time. But you should also consider that as you increase your institutional ownership, a typical result is that they will hold your stock for shorter periods of time than individuals, will be less loyal than individuals, and will require much more time on your part and on the part of your management.

Also investors are pressed for time and many companies are competing for their attention. After identifying a list of target investors, you will need to decide how to proceed with introducing them to your company. Some investor relations practitioners add these names to their broadcast fax or e-mail distribution lists. Others may make a telephone call or send a short letter of introduction, followed by the mailing of an investor information package, which includes the company's annual and quarterly reports, a fact sheet or corporate profile, and perhaps trade or business press reprints. But you will want to do your homework on each potential investor so that you can effectively find what interests them and how your company might be a candidate for investment.

THE IMPORTANCE OF COMMUNICATION

One of the basic rules that applies in the investor relations world is to develop a consistent message and tell it simply, compellingly, and through a variety of channels.

Some companies may view investor relations as an obligation as opposed to an opportunity. The government agency in a given country, such as the Securities and Exchange Commission (SEC) in the United States, imposes requirements on public companies, and companies must meet those obligations. These include the Form 10-K report (which includes an annual summary of financial results, along with recent historical data), Form 10-Q reports (quarterly financial summaries), Form 8K reports (which report important events that could have a material impact on value of the stock), annual shareholders' meetings, and news releases that disclose material events or information. Companies that are truly focused on building shareholder value will go far beyond the communication required by law. An active investor communication program can increase shareholder wealth. An *Investor Relations Magazine* survey of twelve hundred analysts and portfolio managers concluded that companies with the best communication programs recorded above-average shareholder returns.

THE TOOLS OF THE TRADE

There is a wide range of communication tools at your disposal, and you can choose the ones that work most effectively based on informal and formal research of your investors.

Creativity in your communication materials and effective targeting of potential investors are critical, since you are trying to cut through the clutter and catch an investor's attention. You do not necessarily need to use all of these tools (with the exception of those required by law), but this list is a starting point in developing a plan. In addition to considering your audience's preferences, you will want to factor in management goals, the priorities of your investor relations program, your staff talents and resources, and your budget. Here is a list of some of the tools that are commonly used in financial communication.

Annual Reports

Many companies view annual reports as an opportunity to go beyond the information mandated in the Form 10-K, the legally required annual report for public companies filing with the SEC. Their goal is to create a report that integrates the corporate themes and strategy, highlights for the year and plans for the future, along with the business and financial information that summarizes the annual results and gives investors a clear picture of the organization's health. Sid Cato (2005), editor and publisher of the *Newsletter on Annual Reports*, noted, "The annual report to shareholders is the number one corporate communiqué" (p. 1). For many companies, the annual report is the single most important vehicle for communicating the company's vision, strategy, progress, and future plans, and significant time and resources are dedicated to producing a report that reflects this belief.

Some experts, however, would argue that annual reports have become less important in the communications arsenal, particularly with the speed and popularity of electronic channels. Investors also have criticized the time and cost involved with producing elaborate annual reports. Against this background, many companies have opted for the use of the 10-K "wrap," which combines a chairman's letter, perhaps a few charts or graphs, and the 10-K report, under one cover.

In its fourth annual report survey, NIRI noted that 2004 was the first time the number of companies producing 10-K wraps exceeded the number producing traditional annual reports. The NIRI survey said that 90 percent of the respondents cited cost cutting, and 63 percent noted ease of production for their decision.

The Form 10-K has been evolving as well, most notably the importance of the section known as the MD&A (Management's Discussion and Analysis of Financial Condition and Results of Operations). This has become a more prominent and expansive section of the Form 10-K following the problems that led to the adoption of Sarbanes-Oxley regulation, with investors and regulators demanding more clarity and straightforward language to better communicate the issues that have affected the company's financial results.

Marge Wyrwas, senior managing director of corporate communications and investor relations for Knight Trading Group in New Jersey, has created a model that she believes works well for her company's investor base. Knight's annual report combines the themes and highlights of a traditional report with only the MD&A section of the 10-K, as opposed to the full Form 10-K report. Although her company's 10-K is available electronically, she does not produce a separate printed version of that document.

Regardless of the format, investor relations practitioners agree that the report should meet the needs of the number one audience: current and prospective investors. Wyrwas notes that the report is used by other constituencies and that it is important to consider the needs of the secondary audiences (such as employees and customers) as well.

Quarterly Reports

Although Form 10-Q reports are required by the SEC, some companies create more expansive quarterly reports that are designed to complement the annual report. These may include a brief letter to shareholders, operating highlights from the quarter, financial statements, news, and photography. Many companies have decided to eliminate comprehensive quarterly reports in favor of using a combination of their 10-Q reports and quarterly financial news releases.

Annual Meeting

The purpose of the annual shareholders' meeting is to conduct necessary business matters, such as voting on by-laws changes, the board of directors, the issuance of new stock, and other matters. Prior to the meeting, shareholders are sent a copy of the proxy statement, and many choose to vote by proxy rather than in person. Companies also can use the annual meeting to project a core theme or message about the company, review accomplishments for the year, demonstrate or showcase products or services, and encourage shareholder questions about the company.

Internet

There is a growing trend for investors to rely on company Web pages as a starting point for their investment decisions. Many companies include a separate section of their Web site specifically devoted to investors and potential investors, allowing them options to download Form 10-K, 10-Q, and other filings, as well as to easily locate information on company management, recent news releases, historical financial results, and a host of other data. In addition, many Web sites offer investors the ability to ask questions electronically; to request information that could be e-mailed, faxed, or mailed; and to enter their name, address, and other information in order to receive regular updates from the company.

Investor Presentations

Many companies develop their presentation in PowerPoint format, with executives combining prepared comments with the computer-based presentation to deliver their message in a small group, larger conference, or Webcast format (which allows people to listen to the live presentation and follow along with the slides). The investor presentation has become a critical way for companies to try to condense and communicate their corporate story to the investment community. Many companies organize these presentations both to communicate key messages and deliver compelling investor themes. The presentation should address the question, "What's exciting about this company and its future, and why should I want to invest?"

One-on-One and Group Meetings

One-on-one and small group meetings are an essential part of the outreach effort, both to maintain regular, more personal communication with major shareholders and introduce the company management to prospective investors. Although financial data are important, many institutional investors, such as analysts, fund managers, and portfolio managers, look for personal interaction with the chief executive officer and chief financial officer. They rely on these opportunities to get a clearer picture of the company, its persona, the executives' commitment to growth and shareholder value, and their excitement and enthusiasm about the company's prospects. Investors also use these events to probe deeply into what is driving the financial results and assess management's command of their operations and their position in the industry. These meetings can range from one-on-one, informal discussions in an investor's office to breakfast, lunch, or dinner presentations for larger audiences at broker forums.

Investor Conferences and Analyst Tours

Companies often have the opportunity to present at conferences sponsored by brokerage firms, particularly if the analyst from that firm has included them or plans to include them in written coverage. These conferences can include the firm's institutional clients, their own brokers, and high-net-worth individuals. In addition, there are independent conferences that showcase firms in a given industry group or market capitalization range.

Analyst tours and analyst days are often used by larger companies with a number of analysts and institutional owners. It may be more cost- and time-efficient to host a larger group of analysts rather than traveling to meet individually with each one, particularly if a company wants to communicate something more immediately and consistently.

With the passage of Regulation FD (Fair Disclosure) and the requirement to avoid selective disclosure (giving information to one set of investors and not others), many companies broadcast their investor meetings and analyst days live on the Web (and make it available via replay). According to NIRI's 2004 Trends Survey Report (Thompson, 2005, p. 3), 57 percent of the survey respondents presenting at analyst conferences insist that their presentations be Webcast.

Investor Kits

These kits are used to introduce prospective investors to the company and can be sent by mail or obtained electronically over the company Web site. Investor kits could include one or more of the following: a short introductory letter, annual and quarterly reports (and/or Form 10-Ks and 10-Qs), proxy statement, advertising reprints or trade or business article reprints, and a fact sheet that includes a compilation of the major financial data, stock characteristics, and corporate strategy information.

Fact Books

These are used to present the same type of information in a fact sheet but in much more detail. Fact books are primarily used to give analysts and institutional investors expanded information on the company, compiled in a summary form. Given the growth in the use of computer-generated presentations, some companies have replaced the fact book with a hard-copy booklet of their investor presentation.

News Releases

A company's news releases that summarize the quarterly financial results are an essential ingredient of the investor communication program. These releases are issued prior to or at the same time as the quarterly filings and are used as a basis for the discussion in investor conference calls. Generally financial news releases include a summary of financial highlights, as well as charts that compare the current period's income statement, balance sheet, and cash flow data with comparable prior periods. Some companies use the financial news releases as an opportunity to include a summary of the business, quotations from the chairman or chief executive officer, and a discussion of trends demonstrated by the financial results. The investor relations or media spokesperson must be prepared to explain financial details and provide background to financial reporters immediately after dissemination of the release. Being able to respond to the reporter's deadline, perhaps well into the evening, is essential. News releases are a relatively low-cost vehicle to give investors regular updates about the company, helping to connect the ongoing milestones with the overall goals and strategy.

Conference Calls

The majority of public companies host conference calls with their investors immediately after the quarterly financial results are announced. According to the 2004 Trends Survey Report by NIRI, 95 percent of the members surveyed hold quarterly conference calls. Telephone conferences can be held after a major news event, such as an acquisition or divestiture, a major stock restructuring, or a product launch. These conference calls allow management the opportunity to summarize the events and financial summary and, perhaps more important, allow investors to ask questions. In addition to providing a telephone dial-in number, many companies also broadcast their quarterly calls through live Webcasts. Regular telephone and e-mail contact with current or prospective investors is also an essential part of the investor relations program.

Advertising

Advertising is another communication opportunity, ranging from corporate image advertisements in national or business media to more targeted, investor-oriented advertisements or "advertorials." Some companies reprint their advertisements and use them in mailings to investors, at investor presentations, or at their annual shareholders' meeting.

Media Relations

Companies have found that a strong media relations program can support the investor relations effort. You also want to build relationships with appropriate reporters and editors who cover your industry or geographical area. And you will want to try to initiate coverage, through a telephone call or media pitch letter, on the aspects of your company that communicate your strategy and strengths and also meet the reporter's interests.

Do not neglect the value of strong trade press coverage in your investor relations efforts, particularly if you are a smaller, less well-known firm. A strong trade press article often can attract visibility with a more targeted core audience for your industry. Sending a copy of a positive reprint, by mail or e-mail, to investors and including media articles in your investor kits is often used to supplement the investor relations efforts.

A BEST PRACTICE IR FUNCTION

GE has long been viewed as a best practice investor relations function and is a recurring winner in *IR Magazine*'s annual awards program. In 2005, the company was selected as the U.S. grand prize winner for best overall investor relations in the mega-cap category. Joanna Morris, GE's director of corporate investor relations, who has held this role for fifteen years, shares some of her views on GE's best practices:

- The role of the vice president of investor relations at GE is deliberately rotated every two to three years. This reflects the priority on having the chief IR officer well connected to the company's operating units and giving senior management the valuable experience of being on the front lines with investors.

- The priority on shareholder relations has long been cultivated and nurtured at the top, permeating all levels of the organization.

- "One of the best things we do is to be proactive about issues and news," she says. "We don't want one of the analysts who follows GE to be blindsided by a piece of news that comes to their attention from one of their portfolio managers/institutional clients." This requires Morris and her team to be on top of all corporate news and industry developments, assessing what needs to be communicated with the investment community and through what channels.

- "GE has placed an enormous priority on transparency [clarity and completeness of financial reporting], and we're now increasing our focus on corporate governance," she says. This also includes having the IR executive meet independently (without management) with the board of directors twice a year.

- Regardless of who an investor speaks with, they should get the same level of information. "We believe every question deserves an answer back, and we respond to every call, regardless of whether it's an individual investor with a small amount of stock or a large institutional holder."

- The company believes that face-to-face meetings with its investors are extremely important, with management participating in investment banking conferences, holding "road shows" in different parts of world, and hosting monthly in-depth meetings to give investors exposure to a different business unit and its management team.

INTEGRATING IR AND CORPORATE COMMUNICATION

Integrated communication has been a major professional development priority in recent years. It is clearly in the corporation's best interest for both IR and corporate communications professionals, regardless of organizational structure, to be as knowledgeable and as versatile as possible. Many companies have integrated investor relations and corporate communication into one central department to ensure that the corporate brand is leveraged among all constituents, as well as to maximize the skills and resources of all the staff involved in these functions.

Wyrwas believes that a centralized communications department that integrates both investor and public relations staff enables the company to communicate with all audiences more effectively.

Although investors represent one stakeholder group with certain specific information needs, a company can develop and use the same underlying messages, customizing and personalizing them to meet specific audience needs. Integrated messaging (the use of consistent messages across various constituents) can reinforce and help ensure that they are heard and understood. One way to accomplish this is by having the key communications and IR people work together to develop and update the key corporate messages.

Integrated communication can be managed effectively even when participants work in separate departments. Jeanie Herbert, director of investor relations for Beckman Coulter in California, says that although she reports to the chief financial officer and the corporate communication department reports to the vice president of human resources, they work to ensure consistent messaging and cross-fertilization. "IR, PR and marketing communication work closely together. It's critical that messages for an event for investment analysts are consistent with the story we present at a press conference and the exhibit we use at a trade show," she adds.

Mark Aaron, vice president of investor relations at Tiffany & Co. in New York, agrees. At Tiffany, reporting relationships do not interfere with the daily focus of both the IR and PR units, who report to different executives. "Collaboration is key," he says.

Linking the investor relations and communication activities can result in:

- Developing and communicating consistent overall themes and messages.
- Reaching investors through events and activities typically falling in the market or marketing communications' domain such as trade shows.
- Enhancing communications with employees, who may own company stock through stock purchase or retirement savings programs.
- Developing products for one audience (such as a video to kick off a sales meeting) that could potentially be used effectively with investors.
- Sharing information to enhance each function. For instance, data that IR gathers on competitors could be shared with the in-house sales/marketing organization, and data and anecdotes on customer reactions to a new product could be relayed to investors.
- Ensuring that there is a formal well-defined process for the dissemination of news and information that is considered material, and having an established crisis team to manage negative news and its potential impact on the value of the stock.

GLOBAL TRENDS

Investor relations practices outside the United States vary significantly. Stock listing requirements, disclosure policies, targeting and communicating with investors, regulatory oversight, and reporting frequency and format are among the various aspects of investor relations that can be affected by the legal, regulatory, and cultural practices of a given country.

Many companies, particularly larger multinationals, have expanded their IR focus to reflect the needs and interests of shareholders and prospective investors outside the country where they are based. This includes, for example, traveling to and initiating meetings in different countries and producing investor materials in different languages. Using local professionals to supplement the IR activities is a common practice.

According to Adrienne Baker, editor in chief of *IR Magazine,* major trends affecting investor relations include these:

- In Canada, corporate governance has become a much greater priority, with greater emphasis on disclosure, more in-depth MD&A sections in annual reports, and increasing investor relations interactions with the boards of directors.

- In Europe, hedge funds have become more influential investors, and at the same time, investor relations officers are asking for more transparency in how hedge funds are investing their capital.

- In Asia, many firms are looking to attract investors from outside their region, which is driving a greater number to list their stock on foreign exchanges and augment their disclosure, corporate governance, and reporting practices.

- In Latin America, Vanessa Theiss, assistant editor of *IR Magazine,* whose focus is on the emerging Latin America market, notes that Mexico and Brazil are viewed as having the most sophisticated IR programs, particularly with the rising number of initial public offerings. She also notes that the convergence of IR and PR, an issue in the United States, has received growing attention, as has the increased number of retail investors.

THE END RESULT OF A STRONG IR PROGRAM

A successful IR program can be characterized by less volatility in the price of the stock, a value that increases with performance, the respect of the investment community, and the ability of the company to return to the market for additional capital. Some of the desired results, which can be used for benchmarking and evaluation purposes, include:

- A changing shareholder base: getting the investors you want
- Analytical coverage by analysts who have intimate knowledge of the company and actively support the stock
- Lower volatility, with the stock price moving up steadily with minimum of fluctuation
- Positive coverage in the media that is read or seen by your investors
- A fair valuation of the stock
- Ultimately, a lower cost of capital

References

Cato, S. (2005). *Sid Cato's official annual report Web site.* Cato Communications. http://www.sidcato.com.

Mavrinac, S. C. (1997). Estimating the value of IR: What's it really worth? *Investor Relations Quarterly, 1*(1), 24–39.

National Investor Relations Institute. (2004). *Standards of Practice for Investor Relations.* Vienna, VA: Author.

Thompson, L. M., Jr. (2005, January 21). NIRI releases 2004 trend survey report. *NIRI's Executive Alert.*

CHAPTER TWENTY-SIX

Government Relations

Bill Carney

G overnment relations is the art and science of convincing governments to move to an organization's point of view.

This chapter will be of interest to communicators working in organizations that need government cooperation to operate (for example, oil and gas industries, which are taxed and regulated by government and receive government incentives to encourage drilling); industry associations that lobby government on behalf of groups of businesses or nonprofits (such as the National Association of Manufacturers and Canadian National Institutes for the Blind); advocacy groups calling for social change (such as Greenpeace, Mothers Against Drunk Driving, and the Cancer Society); and registered lobby groups that advocate on behalf of their clients with governments. These groups, if large enough, usually have both communications branches and government relations branches. As well, communicators in government will find this chapter of interest, since they often deal with government relations experts from the government perspective. Government relations can be practiced by business and by nonprofit advocacy groups.

In this chapter, *government* will mean a democratic, elected government, though not necessarily on the Western model. Singapore, Israel, and countries in Eastern Europe, for example, have democracies that follow different practices from the Westminster or Washington model. The hallmark of a democratic government is that the citizens have a voice in choosing their governments.

Within this overall principle, there are many types of governments. Canada, Germany, Australia, the United States, and South Africa are federations, having three levels of government: federal, state or provincial, and municipal governments, each with different powers according to the national constitutions. Nonfederal, or unitary, governments, have only federal and municipal levels of government; examples are England and France. There are also blended levels of government, which may be legislated by state or provincial bodies but carry out work at the municipal level, with appointed or elected boards, like school boards, public hospitals, and library boards.

Finally, there are quasi-judicial bodies, established and funded by government but operating at arm's length from it. Most countries, for example, have a national telecommunications regulator that sets rates and determines which telephony companies can provide what kind of telecommunications service, which may include telephones, cable television, Internet, and voice over Internet protocol. Bodies like these are established because the subject area is highly technical and because politicians want to delegate authority so they are not put into a position of being perceived as being in conflict of interest. Most state and provincial governments will establish a labor relations board to help resolve labor-management disputes and relieve government of having to intervene directly into every labor-management dispute. In such cases, governments set up enabling legislation outlining the power and limitations on the quasi-judicial body and may fund it. After that, appeals to such boards may be made to government or the courts.

For the communicator, it is essential to know which governments your organization needs to be dealing with and how they interrelate. In federal systems, three levels of government are often involved in legislating, funding, and delivering a public service. The communicator needs to know how they work and how they fit together. Even with only one level of government (for example, municipal), there can be many different departments that have to approve an application to develop a property (such as finance, zoning, environment, police and fire, and perhaps the city council itself).

WHO IS GOVERNMENT?

Most practitioners of government relations need to be able to relate to and work with both the administrative and political levels of government. *Political* refers to the elected members—those politicians who have run in a democratic election and won on a platform that appeals to more voters than any other politician in the campaign. *Administrative* refers to the employees of government, or public servants, who have the power to propose policy for political approval and develop programs to reach that policy. Politicians both direct administration and receive advice from administration. Politicians have direct accountability to their constituents. The administration is responsible to the chief administrator, who is in turn responsible to the political level. Most cities, for example, have a city manager who manages the administration and to whom all other administrators report. The city manager in turn reports to the elected city council.

There is usually a fair amount of turnover at the elected and senior administrator levels. Middle management takes the long-term perspective and has corporate memory. Often middle managers can be more helpful in understanding why decisions and policies were made and can certainly be more helpful in briefing an organization wanting to deal with government. Middle management in government and business is often the glue that keeps the organization together.

In working with politicians and administrators, it is vital that government relations understand and demonstrate two key principles of communications: know your audience, and respect your audience. The practitioner of government relations who takes the apocryphal view of H. L. Mencken that "the only way to look at a politician is down" is most likely to fail. While it takes considerable ego to be a politician (their starting point is quite literally that they are the best person in the constituency to be elected), nevertheless they work very hard to stay elected and usually have a notion of wanting to make social change in the manner that they and their supporters view as being positive. Usually civil servants have a sense of public duty that to them is in itself an honor. Both politician and public servant, particularly at the more senior levels, work harder than the private sector understands and have great pressure on their time. The practitioner of government relations is advised to use government time carefully and wisely, in a manner that stays focused on the issue and the solution to the issue.

STYLES OF GOVERNMENT RELATIONS

Organizations having or wanting to deal with government need to give some thought to their philosophical and tactical approach to government. Broadly, several different styles of government relations can be identified.

Confrontational/Cooperative

Some organizations, notably the right to life and prochoice factions on abortion, believe they are absolutely right and want governments to comply with their wishes. Others, like trade or industry associations, form closer ties with government and work quietly with government to protect their interests over the long run on a variety of issues. Some, like Greenpeace, can manage both, often working cooperatively on broad national issues but more confrontationally at the local level on local issues.

Radical/Reformer

Mothers Against Drunk Driving (MADD) is an organization that began as a radical group but ultimately moved into the mainstream. MADD started as a few outraged mothers of youth killed by drunk drivers who in the early days could express that outrage and get public attention only through free media. As they built support and the notion of driving while drunk became more socially unacceptable, MADD evolved into a more mature, sophisticated, and better-funded advocacy group, using a variety of government relations techniques to achieve legislative and social change. The radicals often blaze a trail through the forest, but it is the reformers who build the road. The questions for the communicator are, "At what stage is your organization?" and "What attitude does it take toward change in society and toward government?"

One-Time Cause/Ongoing Relationship

Sometimes, particularly at the local level, a group decides to develop a public advocacy program because of a single issue, such as a new road being built through the neighborhood or a new landfill too close to the neighborhood. Typically, once their issue is resolved, the group dissolves. Others, like medical and dental associations, have been government relations practitioners from the outset and view it as part of their mandate.

Single Issue/Multi-Issue

Some groups work under one main theme, like the National Rifle Association and Greenpeace, though within that theme may be many issues. Others, like the United Way, have many causes. Generally single-theme government relations is simpler to manage, in part because the message is single and simple.

Single Government/Multigovernment

Dealing with one branch of one government is easier than dealing with several branches at three levels of government. Again, the key is to understand your governments, their legislation, their responsibility areas, and their interrelationships.

Give some thought to the philosophical approach your organization wants to take to government. A one-time issue affecting a neighborhood, like a zoning change, may allow the neighborhood to be very aggressive with local government in its cause. A large corporation or industry/nonprofit umbrella group may have many issues at many levels of government, and likely will take a more conciliatory approach so as not to jeopardize concurrent and future issues.

GOVERNMENT RELATIONS AS A TEAM APPROACH

Government relations is often practiced as a team, which in a large organization may include a dedicated government relations branch, a dedicated communications branch, program and policy expertise, research, legal advice, and budget advice. It is important for the communicator in this group to have a good grasp of program and policy and a better grasp on how the public and key stakeholders react to that program and policy.

In smaller organizations, this team may be one person, contracting out technical advice when needed.

THE PRACTICE OF GOVERNMENT RELATIONS

The practice is not dissimilar to any communications approach, although with some unique aspects that will be discussed later. Factors of government relations may include:

- Issues identification and determination of a need in which government action is part or whole of the solution

- Audience and key stakeholder identification

- Research on both policy matters and public and stakeholder opinion on the issue

- A communications plan, which may include advertising, media relations, stakeholder relations, direct mail, and direct contact to move the public and key stakeholders to move governments to the position the organization wants

- Evaluation and modification of the plan if necessary

The key underlying any government relations exercise is moving public opinion to where it supports the organization's point of view. Governments in general, and politicians in particular, are moved by public opinion. This is one of the hallmarks of democracies: governments respond to what the people demand. While governments and politicians may be moved in other ways, generally it is moving public opinion that underlies most government relations efforts.

Case Study: The Louisiana Physical Therapy Association Campaign for Direct Access

This case is taken from a 2004 IABC Gold Quill winner (Deveney, 2004). The Louisiana Physical Therapy Association (LPTA) lobbied for a change in state law that forbade patients to have direct access to a physical therapist. Instead, they had to be referred to a physical therapist (PT) by another health care professional, such as a doctor. The state medical association opposed direct access, as did members of LPTA itself.

LPTA identified key target audiences (legislators, media, and the public being prominent); set goals and objectives, the goal being to get legislation to support direct access and objectives relating to moving media and the public to support direct access; developed a budget of seventy-five thousand dollars; and hired a lobbyist. Tactically they developed an award for legislators who supported direct access and used that as media hooks to get media attention. They targeted all state media by geography and had public speakers and media contact people for each area. LPTA received key endorsements from medical, allied health, and patient advocate organizations to counter the opposition from established health groups. Most important, it centered the campaign on its home page, which contained a full briefing on the subject. It then conducted an e-mail blitz, starting with those on its own lists and encouraging them to contact friends and family who had heard of the issue and directing them to the home page.

In terms of objectives, LPTA achieved what it determined as $313,065 in targeted media coverage in all Louisiana markets, as well as a 44 to 55 percent response to the e-mail solicitation. The goal was achieved. The state legislature passed legislation allowing the public direct access to PTs, and the governor, while opposing the legislation, did not veto it, recognizing from e-mails to his office how strongly the public supported it.

A successful, focused government relations exercise based on strategic and tactical communications achieved in one year what twenty years of previous lobbying had failed to do: gain direct access to PTs in Louisiana.

SPECIAL ELEMENTS OF GOVERNMENT RELATIONS

A number of elements should be considered when planning government relations programming. Selecting the best communication approach, being prepared by researching the situation, and knowing the players will help simplify this process.

Public Communications Is Not Mandatory

Sometimes a well-written position paper directed at a key middle manager, outlining an affordable, efficient, logical, and win-win situation, will be far more effective than a noisy media campaign. In fact, both politicians and administrators are sensitive to public attacks in the media. Administrators especially take the view that having to respond to noisy high-profile public campaigns is a distraction to their main job. For example, the public health boards in the equally sized Alberta cities of Edmonton and Calgary had one board with a budget from the province significantly higher than the other. One large reason for this was that the lower-budgeted health board had a CEO who was constantly in the media, while the CEO from the other board preferred making discrete telephone calls to key middle managers at the province and being helpful to the province whenever he could. The lower-key approach in this case proved far more helpful in moving the provincial government than the high-profile approach. In the case study, it should be noted that LPTA became more aggressive publicly only after trying the more traditional approach for several years without success. Often this kind of high-profile public lobby effort is a last resort, not the first tactic.

The Value of Research

Governments can be moved by public opinion. Research on public and key stakeholder attitudes and understandings to public policy is the lifeblood of government relations. It is also high risk; you may find out that the public is not on your side and as a result may have to find a way to move it there before you can approach governments. Focus groups and polling are key elements of government relations, and research should be included in every government relations program.

The Value of Coalitions

Governments respond best when there is broad public and stakeholder consensus on an issue. When there is no consensus within stakeholder groups, as in the Louisiana case, governments will not respond. Coalition building is a complex art, often putting competitors in the same lobby group. This is where the value of an industry or advocacy association comes in: they can work with the industry to develop points of view that the majority of members can support. Sometimes, however, it is necessary to speak against the majority view, which the Louisiana case demonstrates can be a successful enterprise.

The Role of the Lobbyist

Lobbyists or lobbying firms claim to have special expertise in dealing with government. That may relate to having worked for government or to simply being a professional who has dedicated his or her career to this particular element of communications and advocacy. There are no clear qualifications for a lobbyist; they may come from law, media, communications, business, or politics. While most countries require lobbyists to be registered, this does not mean that a lobbyist will be good or efficient, only that he or she has registered to do business with government.

There are some qualifications and expertise that organizations should look for in a professional lobbyist. First, they must genuinely like and respect politicians, administrators, and the political process. Second, lobbyists need good knowledge of how governments work, both philosophically and tactically. Third, they need to be able to network and keep in close contact with the administration and government. Fourth, they, like most other communicators, have to be able to juggle several complex files and issues simultaneously, providing all their clients with top-quality service. Finally, they need to be discrete. They will learn much about government and much about their clients; in order for them to have credibility, they need to be able to keep confidential information confidential.

Lobbyists are particularly good for small or new organizations that do not have a lot of expertise or experience with government; they may be necessary only from time to time with larger organizations with their own in-house government relations capacity. When hiring a lobbyist, do as you would do when hiring any important contractor, like a lawyer, ad agency, or researcher: check references, interview key management, discuss the budget, and determine their experience or understanding with your organization's values and policies. The reference check should include representatives from government as well as key clients. In interviewing potential lobbyists, lay out your expectations and your budget clearly, so that the lobbyists can determine whether they can support them (they usually will not if another of their clients has hired them to promote a different view). You want to hire a firm that can provide access or service that your organization lacks and that has a proven, verifiable record in your industry or area of concern.

Ethical and Practical Issues

Both elected officials and administrators often have conflict-of-interest guidelines that do not allow them to receive gifts or favors. Practitioners need to know these guidelines so as not to embarrass government contacts or put them into a potential conflict of interest. Bribery is a criminal offense in all democracies. These laws exist to ensure that public policy is created in the public's interest, and not because of personal favoritism.

Elected officials are extremely busy and have a lot of demands on their time, including family demands. They are far more responsive to a well-researched and well-argued position that has public or key stakeholder support than they are to being schmoozed at a barbecue that cuts into their personal or work time. Administrators also do not like to be "politicked"; they too would rather have a business meeting to discuss business, with a carefully laid out agenda so that they can prepare for the meeting. Government relations, as with any other type of communications, need to be practiced ethically, within the context of the law, and with some sensitivity and sympathy to the unique issues that their audience faces.

Researching Governments

A government communications branch is often a good place to start learning about a government and is usually more reliable than media coverage, which is more focused on the political horse race than on the policy being discussed.

Government communications branches should direct you to public documents such as legislation, annual reports, policy manuals, special reports, and home pages. From there, the practitioner can move to middle management for more detailed information and complex briefings. They can delve into how government programs work, their success, and the reasons they were established.

The Greatest Mistake Ever Made in Government Relations

Government relations can be successful and governments, and publics moved to support an organization's view. Too often, though, organizations will snatch defeat from the jaws of victory by either belittling the government or stating publicly that the policy change is not enough. This causes administrative walls to go up and political doors to shut. If an organization is that simple-minded, it loses the respect of governments at both levels.

The biggest mistake an organization can make is not properly thanking and recognizing the government when it makes changes in the organization's interest. Particularly if the practitioner, on behalf of the organization, is looking to develop a long-term, positive relationship with government, he or she should recognize the government when it takes actions in the organization's favor. Key players in the organization (typically board chairs or elected representatives from the organization deal with the political level, executive management of the organizations with executive management of government, and organizational communicator with government communicator) should call their government counterparts personally. Letters of thanks can be sent (they will be very carefully logged), and even a news release thanking the government can be sent out. Media will rarely use such a release, but it is not intended for them. It is intended to build a stronger relationship with a key stakeholder; government representatives will notice the news release even if the media do not. If necessary, the organization can always include language—like "we hope we can be as successful on other issues as we were on this"—in order to protect other files and keep negotiations ongoing with them. But thanking government is rarely done and is a tremendously powerful way to establish a positive and successful relationship with government, as appropriate thanks and recognition do in any other relationship.

Reference

Deveney, J. (2004). Louisiana Physical Therapy Association Campaign for Direct Access. In R. B. Barger (Ed.), *Best practices in communication planning and implementation: The 2004 collection of Gold Quill award-winning case studies.* San Francisco: IABC.

CHAPTER TWENTY-SEVEN

Taking a Leadership Position in the Community

It Is About More Than Writing a Check

Mary Ann McCauley

Community relations is an integral part of many businesses worldwide. It takes the form of financial contributions, employee volunteerism, in-kind services, and a variety of partnerships with community organizations. Although the implementation varies from country to country, involvement in the communities where they do business is increasingly a strategic business focus.

In 2001 the United Nations Volunteers (2004) and the New Academy of Business embarked on a project that looked at business-community partners in seven countries: Brazil, Ghana, India, Lebanon, Nigeria, Philippines, and South Africa. In all seven countries, it was found that corporate philanthropy and social investment are common practices.

A Home Office survey in 2001 in the United Kingdom revealed that during a twelve-month period, about one in five employees worked for companies that supported employee volunteerism. The survey estimated that the volunteered time was worth approximately 1.1 billion pounds sterling at the average national wage (Hardy, 2004).

A survey in 2004 by the Center for Corporate Citizenship at Boston College and the Hitachi Foundation of more than five hundred U.S. companies of all sizes determined that many of the businesses consider corporate citizenship a business essential. The two key factors driving corporate citizenship among those surveyed were internal corporate values (75 percent) and customer feedback (53 percent). The survey also revealed that company size was not a factor in commitments to corporate citizenship.

In this chapter, approaches to community relationship building and corporate citizenship are addressed. We examine community relations in terms of the benefits to both the company and the community.

TAKING A LEADERSHIP ROLE IN THE COMMUNITY

Community relations brings value to the community and business when an organization's values, expertise, and resources are aligned with the community's needs. This involves giving time, money, materials, and people in the right places at the right times.

The value derived by a business is realized in several ways:

- Providing a forum for leadership and skill development of employees through volunteerism
- Enhancing visibility in the community for the company, which helps increase morale and loyalty among existing employees and makes it easier to recruit employees
- Generating leads or sales of products and services by providing a venue for potential buyers to see the benefits of using specific products or services
- Enhancing brand identity, particularly for consumer products, in key markets through sponsorship of events that attract potential buyers
- Increasing the company's image as a socially responsible member of the communities in which it has a presence

Adobe is one example of a corporation that gains these benefits on a global scale: it supports community relations in countries where it has a presence. It has matching grants and employee volunteer programs that encourage employees to become engaged in their communities. The in-kind program brings products and support to schools in the United States, the United Kingdom, France, Canada, and Germany.

The value to the community also comes in many forms:

- Bolstering resources available to serve a specific population that is underserved
- Bringing expertise to an issue that otherwise would not be affordable by the agency or population in need
- Mentoring future community leaders through volunteerism
- Enhancing the image of a community through the visibility gained by corporate support of community initiatives
- Reducing the dependence of nonprofits on government support

DEVELOPING AND NURTURING EMPLOYEE ENGAGEMENT

Businesses have a great deal to gain by creating strong employee volunteer programs. These programs can range from providing time off to participate in corporate-endorsed community activities to providing matching financial gifts for specific amounts of time volunteered by the employee.

The African Oxygen (Pty) Ltd. (Afrox) program in South Africa demonstrates the individual empowerment that comes when community relations is a part of an organization's strategic plan (Niyonzima, 2003). Afrox has been running a community involvement program since 1995 that encourages employees to develop and maintain ongoing relationships as volunteers with community child care institutions, such as orphanages and centers for abused and abandoned children. The program has excellent management support, but employee participation is voluntary. In 2001 Afrox donated 28 percent of its net profits to its communities.

In 2003 employees supported 120 child care centers, hospices, children's hospital wards, and shelters. Between 50 and 60 percent of the sixteen thousand employees are involved. Each September Afrox employees celebrate their community support with Bumbanani Day, a day of activities, entertainment, food, and fun for underprivileged children.

Many volunteer opportunities give employees a forum in which to strengthen existing skills or hone little-used skills. Such activities benefit nonprofits since they get assistance at all levels, from entry level to senior management, that they could not otherwise afford. Employees get involved in a wide range of activities based on their interests and skills. Some initiatives that have global applications for companies doing business internationally include:

- Literacy programs
- Tutoring students at all levels of education
- Mentoring programs for youths
- Hunger-fighting programs
- Health care projects for the poor
- Housing programs for the poor or disaster victims

Inviting employees from a variety of business units and skill levels to sit on the contributions committee allows an organization to align its contributions goals with the interests of its employees and needs of the community. It is a morale builder to ask a representative group of employees to participate in this important decision-making process. It also is an opportunity for an employee to develop leadership skills, learn more about his or her community's needs, and get a firsthand look at what being a socially responsible company means to the company and to the community.

Managing an employee volunteer program is a time-consuming but rewarding endeavor. Managing these programs usually requires a combination of staff and employee volunteers. Many companies have committees established to plan, implement, and evaluate employee volunteer efforts. But these committees are not without a staff link back to the department accountable for community relations.

Retiree volunteer programs also have grown. These generally have some corporate support but are largely managed by the retirees. Support may consist of providing office space and use of telephones and copiers to assist with the administrative side. Many companies recruit or appoint volunteers to represent them on committees, boards, and task forces of organizations, which the company supports through grants, sponsorships, or in-kind services. Choosing the organization is just one step in building relationships within the community. The next key step, and just as critical, is selecting the right individual to represent your company on the community board.

Often this happens by serendipity, in that the organization is receiving support from your company because a key individual in the company has a special interest in the organization's mission. When the organization does not come with such an easily identified tie, it is essential that the relationship be assigned to the most appropriate person. This means approaching that board position no differently than you would when selecting the right candidate to fill a position in your company.

It is important to match the organization's personality with the personality of the corporate representative as closely as possible. An aggressive, no-nonsense person may not be the best choice for a grassroots, "do-it-by-consensus" board. And the reticent person who is not likely to contribute to board discussions does not belong on a board that expects its members to be actively involved in policy decisions. Before appointing someone to represent your company, learn as much as you can about the potential candidates and the community organization by:

- Interviewing potential candidates within the company, evaluating their strengths against the organization's needs and expectations

- Interviewing the organization's executive director to learn about his or her management style

- Interviewing a current board member (other than or in addition to the chairperson) and asking about board processes and culture

- Interviewing a long-time volunteer about his or her perceptions of the organization

- Reviewing clips and other printed materials about the organization

MAKING THE RIGHT CHOICES

Companies without specific criteria can find themselves involved with social, community, and civic organizations by chance rather than by design. Involvement by chance comes from the choices made by employees or senior management to support the programs and organizations in which they have an interest or a connection. These usually portray the company in a positive light, especially if the company offers support beyond the employees' volunteered time through in-kind services or matching contributions. However, they do not necessarily present a consistent image within the community. Without written criteria, they also present potential problems when tough decisions about denying support have to be made.

Businesses that fund nonprofit foundations or have written corporate giving criteria tend to be focused in their giving programs. It is important for the communication professionals in those businesses to establish close working relationships with their foundation colleagues so that the foundation's good work does not go unrecognized by the communities they serve and employee volunteer programs are integrated into the foundation's vision.

Criteria need to be established to guide the planning of a community relations program. The criteria should reflect the company's values and be tied to business goals. The full value of community relations initiatives will be easier to track and evaluate if specific criteria exist. For example, a high-technology company may sponsor grants and scholarships in math and science while supporting a local science museum or math competition.

Swinerton, a 117-year-old U.S.-based construction company, established a foundation in 2002 to better channel its community relations initiatives. In its 2003 foundation annual report, Swinerton describes its first year as highly successful because it was able to make contributions to more than seventy organizations largely recommended by employees. In keeping with its core competencies and core values, the community relations programs focus on five areas: health, community, construction education, arts and culture, and human sciences.

Regular surveys of community involvement by employees will provide a sense of the issues important to employees and allow you to see trends and identify commonalities. This is important information as you plan your community relations programs, especially if one goal is to gain employee support for your initiatives. You also may find an existing connection through an employee's involvement in an organization, which gives your firm the opportunity for a special initiative that will benefit both the community and your company. In establishing criteria, consider these questions:

- Where are the greatest unmet needs in our community?
- In what ways do those needs match our strategic business goals?

- What values do these organizations have in common with us?
- What are some benefits to the company and our employees if we support an organization?
- In what ways are we able and willing to contribute?

A change in leadership at SAFECO Insurance Companies prompted the assistant vice president for public relations to recommend that the company evaluate its community relations program to determine if it was addressing the appropriate needs and to determine how the program might evolve under the new corporate management. In 2001 SAFECO engaged Walker Information to conduct a measurement study to determine the value of corporate philanthropy to the business (Eaton, 2002).

One outcome based on the findings is that a program to develop leadership skills through volunteerism was created. The study gives SAFECO a benchmark against which to measure its philanthropic programs on an ongoing basis.

While a contributions committee may be making decisions about how resources are allocated, there is much more that needs to be accomplished in a well-managed program. The community relations manager will have a budget to track and will be expected to make recommendations to senior management about the annual levels of funding to be budgeted.

The contributions committee needs guidelines addressing the size and frequency of contributions. Many organizations have set amounts that can be contributed by branch offices and remote locations without first coming to the committee. They also may have ceilings on individual grants.

Considerations such as multiyear funding (how much and how long) are important. One school of thought advocates multiyear funding as being the most effective type of program. The rationale is that funding during a three- to five-year period gives the organization being funded and your company the greatest opportunity to see long-term benefits. This assumes that there is a strategic vision with clearly defined goals.

Finally, the overall community relations program needs to be evaluated regularly against its goals and desired outcomes. This can include an annual evaluation of individual initiatives, usually involving site visits, interviews with employee volunteers, and a review of the agency's balance sheet. Holding an agency accountable is increasingly an expectation of most funders.

INTEGRATING WITH MARKETING AND CORPORATE COMMUNICATIONS

Strategic planning is as critical to community relations as it is to any other initiative. The key is to align the community relations plan with the business, corporate communication, and marketing plans.

Community relations is another component of communication management. It can no longer be separated from other corporate communication initiatives. It should be considered one of the many elements used in positioning a company and its products or services.

There is a natural overlap between a company's charitable goals and its business goals that makes isolating community relations risky. The opportunities to leverage a company's community support are too beneficial to miss.

Depending on the size of your program, community relations may need a dedicated person or staff to manage it. If this is the case, it is important to keep this effort integrated with other public relations strategies and activities. If the public relations or corporate communication department is not directly responsible for the community relations effort, it is the responsibility of the communication professional to establish the link between the two initiatives.

Being integrated through a planning or structural organization will make the task of managing community relations more effective since many of the initiatives, including contributions, have the potential for external visibility. Internally there is much to be gained by keeping employees in the loop.

As you plan, keep in mind that some community relations initiatives may need tailoring to work well in other communities, requiring innovativeness and flexibility. Companies demonstrating the best community relations tend to focus on a single initiative, such as serving children or supporting technological education, and then localize the programs to each community.

Community relations programs offer companies a wealth of opportunities to be visible. Publicity and advertising strategies should consider community relations initiatives when plans are being drawn to market the company and its products or services. One of the reasons cause-related marketing is seen as valuable is that it creates an opportunity to advertise in a way that speaks to a common interest.

For the company that has a business-to-business product or service, gaining visibility in the community can be difficult, since the average reader of the local paper or viewer of local newscasts has no direct interest in what you market. Visibility through your community relations efforts can be a great asset. Enabling your key audiences to see your company active in local charity events, meet employees volunteering on board and committees, and see your company's name among contributors to nonprofits all help to create a positive image of your company.

Visibility can include publicity resulting from special events, news releases announcing board appointments, gifts, equipment or product or service donations, and sponsorships.

If you are considering cause-related marketing initiatives as part of your community relations effort, there are additional criteria to consider:

- Is there a logical tie between our products and services and the proposed sponsorship?

- What do we expect from this relationship? Leads? Selling product or services directly? Higher visibility? Volunteer opportunities?

- What is the probability this organization can meet our expectations?

- What does the organization expect from us? Product or services? Higher visibility? In-kind support? Financial support? Volunteers?

- What will it cost us to affiliate with this organization? Time? Money? Inventory?

For the company with a consumer product or service, being visible about community relations efforts can help create brand identity, and even sell products or services, while it reassures customers that you are striving to meet their expectations of being a socially responsible company. This is one key reason that auto manufacturers sponsor race teams and beverage companies sponsor amateur sports events.

Two companies have taken cause-related marketing to a different level in that their focus is on not only brand recognition and market share but also on economic development of a community. Figaro Coffee in the Philippines and Ben & Jerry's ice cream in the United States have implemented programs that foster economic development.

Figaro formed the Figaro Coffee Foundation in 1998 to boost coffee production, especially Barako, the generic name for a coffee grown and roasted in the Batangas region north of Manila. For a variety of reasons, Barako had lost market share over the years and was nearing extinction. Figaro's goal was to rebuild the demand for Barako and assist struggling coffee farmers (Nuguid-Anden, 2003). Its strategies included creating greater local demand for Barako through a variety of activities, including art exhibits and seminars about the coffee industry. It has created the City Blends brand, which uses specially designed packaging depicting the cities where charities are supported by the foundation. A development project began a campaign to help farmers plant Barako trees through an "adopt-a-farm" program. Although this initiative has not been without challenges, Figaro estimates that more than thirty thousand trees will be planted.

At Ben & Jerry's, the approach also has multiple facets. In its 2003 annual report, the company reported that it adopted a requirement of its franchisees in 2003 requiring them to hire and provide job training for disadvantaged young people under the firm's PartnerShops program. PartnerShops identifies nonprofit groups skilled in job training as partners. In 2003 the first PartnerShops was opened in Europe along with fifty-five U.S. shops. Ben & Jerry's ties its economic, social, and environmental missions into a single corporate mission, believing that all three must thrive equally for the company to be successful.

CONCLUSION

Community relations has proven to be a valuable business asset worldwide. Studies also show that volunteerism is a key part of any community relations program. One study conducted in the United States by the Center for Corporate Citizenship at Boston College (2004) found that the internal motivating factors for community social responsibility were:

- Traditions and values (75 percent)
- Reputation and image (59 percent)
- Business strategy (52 percent)
- Recruit and retain employees (38 percent)

The European Foundation Centre (2005), which was founded in 1989, has grown to more than two hundred foundations and corporate funders that serve forty-eight thousand organizations through networking centers in thirty-seven countries demonstrating the support businesses worldwide provide to the communities.

The Home Office survey in 2001 of U.K. workers revealed that during a twelve-month period, employees interviewed volunteered an equivalent of sixty-eight hours through employer-supported programs (Hardy, 2004).

As a strategic element of business, community relations needs to be planned, measured, and evaluated regularly to make certain an organization manages this valuable asset.

References

Center for Corporate Citizenship at Boston College. (2004). *The state of corporate citizenship in the U.S.: A view from inside 2003–2004.* Boston: Author.

Eaton, F. (2002). *Measuring the business value of corporate philanthropy: SAFECO Insurance Companies.* http://www.cof.org/files/Documents/Corporate_ Grantmaking/Measurement/Safeco_Case_Study.pdf?RETURNTO=%252FSearch%2 52FSearchResults%252Ecfm%253FAVAILABLEAFTER%253D%2526 AVAILABLEBEFORE%253D%2526CATEGORYIDS%253D%2526DOMAINIDS%253D %2526KEYWORDS%253DSAFECO%2526X%253D0%2526Y%253D0.

European Foundation Centre. (2005). *About the EFC.* http://www.efc.be/about/

Hardy, R. (2004, October). *Home Office research study 280: Employer-supported volunteering and giving: Findings from the 2001 Home Office Citizenship Survey.* London: Home Office Research, Development and Statistics Directorate.

Niyonzima, J. (2003, September). *Enhancing business-community relations: African Oxygen (Pty) Ltd Case Study.* http://www.worldvolunteerweb.org/fileadmin/docs/old/pdf/2003/031201_EBCR_ZAF_africaoxygen.pdf.

Nuguid-Anden, C. (2003, September). *Enhancing business-community relations: Figaro Coffee Company case study.* http://www.worldvolunteerweb.org/fileadmin/docs/old/pdf/2003/031201_EBCR_PHL_figaro.pdf.

United Nations Volunteers. (2004, April 29). *Enhancing business-community relations.* http://www.worldvolunteerweb.org/research/studies/ nab_unv/index.htm.

CHAPTER TWENTY-EIGHT

Public Relations and Ethical Conduct

Meryl David, Todd T. Hattori

In today's workplace, communicators regularly face ethical dilemmas. They need to make choices sometimes between a strong set of personal values and the values of the organization for which they are working, whether as an employee or a paid consultant. Making a conscious choice involves going into situations with eyes wide open and understanding what options are available. This chapter aims to outline some of these options and provide helpful guidelines for making the right choices for the right reasons.

Extensive research has been conducted to help explain the disconnect between recognizing and understanding what constitutes ethical standards and demonstrating sound ethical decision making. Although the following samples by no means represent the depth and breadth of available data, they reinforce the importance of looking at the perceptions behind the behaviors.

The 2003 National Business Ethics Survey (Ethics Resource Center, 2003) aims to yield answers on how employees distinguish right from wrong behavior in their work, the availability of resources to aid in making appropriate decisions, and the general practice of values like honesty and respect in the workplace. One of the findings was that some employee groups and organizations might be more at risk for ethics-related problems—for example: "Employees in transitioning organizations (undergoing mergers, acquisitions or restructurings) observe misconduct and feel pressure at rates that are nearly double those in more stable organizations" (para. 8). Also, "compared with other employees, younger managers (under age 30) with low tenure in their organizations (less than 3 years) are twice as likely to feel pressure to compromise ethics standards (21% versus 10%)" (para. 8).

The study found that in many areas, opinions about ethics remain "rosier at the top": senior and middle managers have less fear of reporting misconduct and are more satisfied with the ways in which their organizations respond to report of misconduct. "They also feel that honesty and respect are practiced more frequently than do lower level employees" (Ethics Resource Center, 2003, para. 8).

Research involving Australia's largest businesses in 2004 (KPMG Corporate Citizenship and Business Ethics Survey, 2004) showed that the top six ethical issues identified by management and employees were both similar and different:

Top Six Ethical Issues Identified by Management

- Personal use of corporate assets
- Falsifying sick leave or absenteeism
- Disclosure of confidential information
- Sexual harassment
- Conducting private business during working hours
- Conflicts of interest

Top Six Ethical Issues Identified by Employees

- Personal use of corporate assets
- Falsifying sick leave or absenteeism
- Conducting private business during working hours
- Sexual harassment
- Disclosure of confidential information
- Conflicts of interest

In a 1997 study of U.S. workers, sponsored by the American Society of Chartered Life Underwriters and Chartered Financial Consultants and the Ethics Officer Association, more than half (56 percent) of the respondents indicated some pressure to act unethically or illegally on the job. Better communication and open dialogue was cited by 73 percent of the respondents as one of the best solutions for reducing this pressure (Lynn, 1998, p. 85).

The study explored the link between workplace pressure and illegal or unethical behavior and also found that 48 percent of the respondents had engaged in one or more unethical or illegal actions during the past year as a result of pressure. The top actions were:

- Cutting corners on quality control (16 percent)
- Covering up incidents (14 percent)
- Lying to or deceiving customers (9 percent)
- Putting inappropriate pressure on others (7 percent)

A relatively small number—15 percent of the respondents—agreed that "ethical dilemmas are an unavoidable consequence of business and cannot be reduced."

Finally, in the 2005 IABC Research Foundation study (Bowen, Heath, Lee, Painter, & Agraz, 2005) of professional communicators, roughly half the participants were against the public relations practitioner's enacting a role of ethical conscience. This study investigated the opinions of a wide range of public relations professionals and recently retired executive practitioners in the United States, New Zealand, Israel, and Australia on ethical responsibility. The findings indicated the following themes:

- *Amoral and antiethical conscience:* Business has no connection to ethics or social responsibility and should have no such connection.
- *Legalism:* An analysis of ethics is not necessary if the organization follows legal requirements and seeks to do no harm.
- *Access denied:* The ability to act as ethical advisers to management or clients is hindered or fully restricted.
- *Little role for ethics counsel:* Public relations is a profession for hire, in which communicators act as managers and liaisons to management, but not as counselors or advisers to management on matters of philosophy, ethics, or right and wrong.

Ethics plays an important role in the success of organizations; communication seems to play an important role in facilitating ethical behavior in organizations, but the communication role is not always properly responsible for it. How can public relations professionals help organizations behave responsibly?

ROLE OF CODES OF ETHICS

Many employer organizations and professional associations have addressed ethics in conventional ways by issuing "codes of ethics generally requiring conduct 'in accordance with the highest ethical standards.' The codes state the obvious: people ought to behave themselves. Sometimes codes go even further and state the impossible; for example, that conflicts of interest should be avoided. But ethical dilemmas and conflicts of interest are part of the very fabric of life" (Davis, 2003, p. 29).

Conflicts of interest are at the heart of ethical dilemmas. A conflict of interest is a situation in which the decision maker has two or more competing interests. Public relations professionals, as employees or paid counselors, in particular regularly face conflicts of interest when they advise their clients on what and how much information should be given.

Taking ethics seriously requires more than simply doing good and avoiding evil. Even when you resolve to do the right thing, challenges remain. You often face right-versus-right situations. Such ethical problems require a choice between two equally correct courses of action. A clear code of ethics provides clarity for decision making when faced with right-versus-right dilemmas rather than presenting additional dilemmas.

Before we look at one model for ethical decision making, recognize that you should not have to confront ethical conflicts alone. The organizations that provide ethical codes of conduct should also provide policies that encourage, if not require, peers to bring dilemmas to one another's attention. Dilemmas are most easily seen when they affect someone else. "Rationalization can prevent even the noblest person from recognizing his or her own conflicts of interest" (Davis, 2003, p. 28).

Here is one model for dealing with ethical dilemmas and conflicts of interest.

CHECKLIST FOR ANALYZING AND RESOLVING ETHICAL DILEMMAS

The issue is not whether conflicts will exist but how to deal with them when they arise. Chris MacDonald (2002), of the Department of Philosophy, Saint Mary's University, Halifax, Nova Scotia, Canada, offers a model that can be used to consider and resolve ethical dilemmas:

- *Is this really a dilemma?* "The first step is recognizing the decision as one that has moral importance. Clues include conflicts between two or more values or ideals" (MacDonald, 2002, p. 1).
- *"Who are the interested parties? What are their relationships?* Carefully identify who has a stake in the decision, be imaginative and sympathetic. Often, there are more parties whose interests should be taken into consideration than is immediately obvious" (MacDonald, 2002, p. 1).
- *"What values are involved?* Think through the shared values that are at stake in making this decision" (MacDonald, 2002, p. 1). Which of those values are dear to the one making the decision and which to his or her organization?
- *What are the benefits and the burdens?* "Benefits—broadly defined—might include such things as the production of goods (physical, emotional, financial, social, etc.) for various parties, the satisfaction of preferences, and acting in

accordance with relevant values (such as fairness). Burdens might include causing physical or emotional pain to other parties, imposing financial costs, and ignoring relevant values" (MacDonald, 2002, p. 1). Patience might be one simple solution. If no one is being seriously harmed by the situation, might the passage of time satisfactorily resolve the dilemma?

• *How is this case analogous to others?* Most ethical dilemmas have been faced before. Professionals would be well served by keeping a careful record of ethical decision making within the organization. What are the similarities and differences? What course of action was taken? Was the decision good (MacDonald, 2002)?

• *With whom can you share your preferred solution?* "The only way to compensate for our inherent subjectivity is to seek the opinion of an independent party" (Davis, 2003, p. 29). Discuss your preferred solution with an ethically savvy person who is not directly involved in the situation. The other party may also be affected by his or her situation, "but it will not be the same situation as that of the primary decision maker. By consulting with others, . . . [you] benefit from a variety of perspectives. That's the next best thing to complete objectivity" (Davis, 2003, p. 29).

• *"Does this decision [comply] with legal and organizational rules?* Some decisions are appropriately made based on legal considerations. . . . [They] may also be affected by rules set by . . . [your] organization" (MacDonald, 2002, p. 2). Always remember that just because something is legal, it does not mean it is ethical.

• *Are you comfortable with this decision?* Rely on intuition as a check on your analytical decision making. Consider these questions:

1. If I carry out this decision, would I be comfortable telling my family, . . . [spiritual leader, or mentors] about it?

2. Would I want children to take my behavior as an example?

3. Is this decision one which a wise, informed, virtuous person would make?

4. Can I live with this decision [MacDonald, 2002, p. 2]?

BUILDING AN ORGANIZATIONAL CULTURE THAT SUPPORT ETHICS COMPLIANCE

Here are suggestions that can help organizations reduce workplace pressures and clarify ethics roles and responsibilities. Professional communicators can provide guidance and counsel to help make ethics an intuitive part of their organizations:

- *"Decide what ethics is and what ethics is not"* (Davis, 2003, p. 30). Diversity values, cultures, and situations sometimes complicate our ability to determine what is the ethical thing to do. "Many people mistake legality for ethical propriety" (Davis, 2003, p. 30). However, an action can be legal yet unethical and vice versa. When ethical issues arise, we often seek legal counsel first. If legal counsel advises that the actions in question are not illegal, you should then ask, "Are the actions ethical?" Ethics and ethical thinking are broader than legal issues and legal thinking. "Laws grow out of the ethical convictions of the people who enact them. Rather than being an extension of the law, ethics is the law's root or foundation" (Davis, 2003, p. 31).

- *"Ethical behavior often exacts a high price and requires a change in behavior"* (Davis, 2003, p. 31). Make sure your organization addresses such questions as, "Are we prepared to pay the price?" "Do we have the will to act accordingly?" "What will I do when others fail to recognize or reward a commitment to principle?" (Davis, 2003, p. 31). Although the values of an organization can help employees develop pride and self-respect, ethical behavior cannot necessarily be expected to produce measurable, positive, bottom-line results for the organization.

- *"Ethics is partly a matter of getting the facts straight"* (Davis, 2003, p. 31). Ethical and moral disasters can result when employees fail to comprehend the situation or circumstances fully or misapply strong values.

- *"Ethics is more than everyone doing his or her best"* (Davis, 2003, p. 31). Ethical conduct is about doing your best for the right reasons, which may include acting for the good of the organization and because you feel right doing it and can commit to the decisions made. Authenticity is perhaps the greatest dilemma. You have to decide whether to take a course of action to be true to yourself or for the right and proper reasons.

- *Support ethics guidelines with a system and process.* Ethical issues cannot be resolved without the right systems and processes that help clarify choices for individuals. Help senior management focus on the organization's structure and address questions such as these: How do we assign responsibility? Are the responsible parties held accountable? Do we regularly reexamine our own structures? Do we look for ways to safeguard fairness, honesty, caring, and other commonly prized values? Are employees challenged to live up to a high standard? Does our organizational system pass ethical muster? Are work rules fair, and do we communicate them clearly to those they affect (Davis, 2003)?

- *"Gain the commitment of the entire organization"* (Davis, 2003, p. 31). Commitment is difficult to obtain. Employees are more willing to commit if their executives encourage ethical discussions that help everyone develop an appreciation of who they are and how their values relate to the ethics of the organization. The threat and discomfort of talking about ethics can be reduced by letting employees know that they will not be targeted. Admitting that the subject may be threatening can enhance the productivity of ethical discussions. "Ethics is intensely personal, and no one is comfortable being . . . [judged by others]. On the other hand, human performance is rooted in self-concept and understanding. Everyone would like others to understand their values and deepest longings" (Davis, 2003, pp. 31–32). This is how communication professionals can play a significant role in helping build a culture of ethics within an organization.

• *Teach employees to recognize and resolve ethical issues.* One way to help employees understand how to recognize and resolve ethical issues is to create an internal forum for discussion. This might be a scenario-based training program, regularly scheduled meetings, or a specific event such as an ethics retreat (Davis, 2003). During the forum, employees can "review the high stakes of organizational behavior, fine-tune organizational values, and discuss ethical issues they may face" (Davis, 2003, p. 32). By deliberating case studies, employees will gain knowledge and develop skills that will help them resolve their ethical dilemmas. Helping employees gain this understanding, supported by clear policies and processes, will demonstrate the organization's commitment to taking positive steps toward ethical compliance and build trust among employees.

• *Ensure the rewards and consequences system support the right kind of decision making.* When it is clear to employees that unethical behavior is not condoned or overlooked, messages about the organization's code of ethics become more than just words on paper. Public relations professionals can play a unique and key role in helping management align rewards for ethical compliance and consequences for ethics violations.

• *Provide leadership in ethics from the top.* Senior management and other leaders within an organization play a critical role in establishing a culture of ethics. Make sure your organization invests in resources to develop leadership skills in managers and leaders. Learning about and developing an understanding of the ethics of the organizations and supporting systems and processes will lead to better and more consistent decision making among managers and leaders within your organization.

FACING ETHICAL DILEMMAS

Have you ever been asked to develop a publicity campaign based on a slogan that you know to be a false claim or to write a press release that contains information you know to be inaccurate? You would not be alone. Many communicators have faced dilemmas like this from time to time, and the situation becomes particularly challenging when offering your resignation is an option that will cause serious pain to people who depend on you.

Most everyday ethical dilemmas are far less dramatic. Consider this one: you are a public relations executive working for a nonprofit organization. You have produced all of your public relations brochures using one print company. One day the company account manager for your organization turns up at your desk with the latest in televisions with a DVD player built in as a gift. The representative explains that it had been running a special promotion for the quarter and, as the top client for the quarter, you had won this gift. What would you do?

This happened to an IABC member; although she was young and relatively inexperienced, she knew she was facing an ethical dilemma and had to make the right choice for the right reasons. She asked the representative to take the television (still packed in its box) to the reception area. Then she called her boss from his office and explained that the organization had won a promotional contest with a company that had won our business fair and square through the official bidding process. She suggested that this gift be used in the organization's library for watching training videos and other educational programming. There it would be a benefit to everyone in the organization. Her boss agreed with her suggestion.

The options that passed fleetingly through her mind included taking the television home after hours when no one could see her or saying "no thanks" outright to the vendor and giving it back (and potentially damaging a vendor relationship). Or she could have raffled it at the next big organizational event to raise funds for the organization.

Often there is not only one right choice. The important thing is to collect all the information, consider the interests and sensitivities for all stakeholders, work out the alternatives, consult with colleagues or managers to develop your understanding of the situation, and then make a decision that is legal and also that you feel comfortable defending if called on to do so.

DOING WHAT IS RIGHT

Many participants of the IABC Research Foundation ethics study (Bowen et al., 2005) identified the following opinions in support of senior-level public relations professionals acting as ethical counsel to their chief executives and organizational decision makers:

- *Reputation and ethics: Natural partners.* Ethical counsel is a natural activity in public relations given that practitioners are usually involved in research to understand the ideas and values of significant stakeholders and activities to maintain relationships with them.

- *Moral reasoning preferred over legalism.* Ethical and moral analysis is the preferred method of examining the potential consequences of decisions on significant stakeholders and maintaining effective relationships with them.

- *Access granted: Playing the role of ethical conscience.* Public relations professionals already act as ethics counselor or ethical conscience in organizations in an era in which greater corporate accountability and transparency appears to be in increasing demand.

- *Expansive normative role for ethics in public relations.* Public relations professionals are responsible for advising on behavior that is unethical or could be perceived as unethical by significant stakeholders holding different values from those of the organization or client.

Given that the buck stops with the board in organizations and that each organization is unique in its purpose, structure, values, and activities, the public relations function alone cannot be responsible for ethics. But as the title of a well-known book suggests, the fish rots from the head. So effective public relations executives need a healthy dose of courage to bring to the attention of senior management, the board, or even the authorities actions they are being asked to take that they do not feel are right.

Naturally, the organization that hires the individual has the right to instruct employees to do whatever is within the scope of his or her contractual agreement with the organization. When all is said and done, ethics is largely a matter of individual conscience and professionalism. Only you can know that you are doing what is right and for the right reasons.

References

Bowen, S. A., Heath, R. L., Lee, J., Painter, G., & Agraz, F. (2005, June). *An interim report of PR practitioners' ethical rules and values: Executive summary.* San Francisco: IABC Research Foundation.

Davis, G. W. (2003, October). Digging into ethics. *Association Management, 55*(10), 26–33.

Ethics Resource Center. (2003, May 21). *2003 National Business Ethics Survey executive summary.* http://www.ethics.org/nbes2003/2003nbes_summary.html.

KPMG Australia. (2004). *KPMG Corporate Citizenship and Business Ethics Survey, 2004 Forensic Fraud Survey.* Author.

Lynn, J. (1998, August). Do the right thing: Putting your business on the ethical up and up. *Entrepreneur Magazine, 26*(8), 85.

MacDonald, C. (2002, March 15). *A guide to moral decision making.* http://www.ethicsweb.ca/guide/guide.pdf.

CHAPTER TWENTY-NINE

Measuring Public Relations Programming

Mark Weiner

Every day, the imperatives of business affect public relations investment decisions as bottom-line thinking is here to stay. While some organizations and public relations (PR) executives thrive in this new environment of accountability, most perform in the range of "normative failure." In other words, one is just as bad as the next.

What we find as a result is a shared state of anxiety and uncertainty: senior management does not know enough about PR to provide guidance, and PR executives do not know enough about measuring PR's return on investment to help. The result is stasis, which is to say that nothing changes: timid, conventional approaches yield predictable, unspectacular results. It is a place where the margin of one's accomplishments is measured in inches instead of light-years, and rather than explosive success, one aspires to be the best of a mediocre breed.

So we hear the refrain: "For years, we have needed to more scientifically plan and measure our public relations . . . and I want to. Our executives are beginning to require it. But what is the best way to proceed? Will the results prove the value of PR? And what if the research shows that PR is not performing?" Questions exist, but this much is certain: without the proper research-based underpinnings, you may never fully comprehend the extent of your accomplishments so that success can be reinforced and merchandised. And without a measurable, systematic approach to public relations objectives setting, strategy development, and evaluation, you may never know enough about your

371

performance for improvements to be introduced when needed. And finally, without a scientific approach toward understanding and applying what is learned toward future endeavors, success will be fleeting rather than sustainable, and failures are bound to be repeated.

The inevitable outcome of being in such an indeterminate state is that while you are there, the world accelerates without you. Just as pain is your body's way of signaling itself to do everything possible to help make you well again, the same holds true for business. It is better to feel "the pain" at the onset (and for only a short time) so that the process for improvement can begin. Unfortunately, most PR professionals seek to mute their symptoms or, worse, ignore them.

Much can be gained when the rigor of science is married to the art of public relations: meaningful and positive business outcomes, market supremacy, and professional advancement. Companies that dominate do so because they understand and master their environment. The world's most admired companies did not earn their reputations without carefully studying themselves in the mirror and then acting on what they saw—the ugly as well as the beautiful. The only passage out of uncertainty is a direct one.

Companies and public relations professionals who enjoy the benefits of PR research and evaluation begin by embracing the process fully: they relish their victories because their wins are validated and can be merchandised more credibly. They also understand that uncovering shortfalls is a natural result of the process and allows course correction. As a result, they lead with confidence and certainty.

THE SCIENCE OF PR

Traditionally, public relations is rooted in the social sciences. Edward Bernays, often cited as the father of public relations, pioneered PR's use of psychology and other social sciences to design campaigns of public persuasion. He called this scientific technique of opinion molding the "engineering of consent" and described the PR counselor as a practicing social scientist. To assist clients, PR counselors would use research, and evaluation is a primary facet of PR.

Professional PR associations emphasize research and measurement in their credos and mission statements. The International Association of Business Communicators (IABC), for example, defines itself as an organization whose mission it is to help members to "make business sense of communication. Think strategically about communication. Measure and clarify the value of communication. Build better relationships with stakeholders" (2005, para. 2).

As part of its definition of public relations, the Public Relations Society of America (PRSA) identifies PR as follows:

As a management function, public relations encompasses the following:

- Anticipating, analyzing and interpreting public opinion, attitudes, and issues that might impact, for good or ill, the operations and plans of the organization.

- Counseling management at all levels in the organization with regard to policy decisions, courses of action, and communications, taking into account their and the organization's social or citizenship responsibilities.

- Researching, conducting, and evaluating, on a continuing basis, programs of action and communication to achieve the informed public understanding necessary to success of an organization's aims. These may include marketing, financial, fund raising, employee, community or government relations, and other programs.

- Planning and implementing the organization's efforts to influence or change public policy. Setting objectives, planning, budgeting, recruiting and training staff, developing facilities—in short, managing the resources needed to perform all of the above [2005, para. 4].

The examples of Bernays, IABC, and PRSA would suggest that scientific measurement is a critical component of public relations. Unfortunately, PR as it is routinely practiced regards formal research and measurement as afterthoughts. According to the 2005 Annual Measurement Survey conducted by *PRWeek*, less than 2 percent of budgets go toward research and evaluation, and it is not quite clear whether what respondents consider research and evaluation would be considered to be statistically reliable and directionally meaningful, or just a pile of press clippings.

Given the magnitude of the opportunities and the enormity of the challenge facing business today, there has to be a better way. The good news is that there are alternatives within the reach of almost every PR person: they can be just as often simple as they may be sophisticated, and they may be inexpensive just as often as they may be expensive. The test will come when it is realized that "the better way" will almost certainly require a change to the way public relations is being practiced in most organizations.

ELEVEN QUESTIONS YOU MUST ASK BEFORE STARTING A PR PROGRAM

The practice of measurable, scientific public relations cannot take place in a vacuum. You must have a practical understanding of your situation. Before beginning the process, you must answer the following questions, some of which may require formal research:

- What are your organization's objectives?
- What are your department's objectives?

- What other programs are currently underway?
- What other departments will be affected?
- How will you use the research findings?
- What are your key messages?
- Who is your target audience?
- Who influences that audience?
- Which media do they read, watch, or listen to?
- Who are your internal audiences?
- Who are your internal clients?

WHAT YOU NEED TO KNOW ABOUT PR RESEARCH

There are three forms of research in public relations: primary research, which centers on conducting original research; secondary research, which is based on the mining of preexisting data and information; and statistical modeling, which seeks to create some greater learning through the unified statistical analysis of disparate sources of data, both primary and secondary.

Primary research usually involves a process of questioning of respondents in order to gain a greater insight. The type of primary research that yields objective, statistically reliable results is known as quantitative research. When quantitative research is done properly, the findings can be projected to a larger population. Quantitative research gathers data in a variety of ways, but the most common methods are telephone surveys, Web site, mail, and e-mail surveys, each of which offers distinct advantages and disadvantages in terms of speed, cost, flexibility, and levels of audience participation.

The other form of primary research is known as qualitative research, which is most commonly conducted in the form of focus groups. Focus groups are small collections of a dozen people or so who are encouraged, under the direction of a facilitator, to share their opinions, frustrations, likes, and dislikes relating to the subject under discussion. Focus groups are useful for ideation, but their results cannot be projected to a larger population. For this reason, they are often abused as organizations in search of some quick, inexpensive feedback substitute focus group results for quantitative research. When properly used, qualitative research is staged as a precursor to quantitative research so that the survey can be that much more effective.

Statistical modeling is a process used in marketing and PR analytics to mathematically explain historical results and predict future outcomes. These analytics focus on probabilities and trends based on a number of variables that are likely to influence future behavior. In marketing, for example, a customer's gender, age, and purchase history might predict the likelihood of a future sale. To create a predictive model, data are collected for the relevant predictors, a statistical model is formulated, predictions are made, and the model is validated (or revised) as additional data become available. In PR, statistical models are most often used to uncover the effect of PR and its interaction with other marketing and communication agents, as well as such external factors as the weather and population, on sales or some other behavioral outcome. Models of this type, known as marketing mix models, seek to provide insight into what drives purchase behavior.

RESEARCH TOOLS FOR EFFECTIVE PUBLIC RELATIONS MEASUREMENT

While there is an array of research applications for public relations, we will focus on three fundamental tools for scientific measurement and evaluation of public relations: news content analysis, surveys, and statistical modeling.

Content Analysis

One popular application of secondary research is news content analysis, a method for tracking the activities or outputs of a PR program. Outputs might be defined as press conferences, special events, press releases, and speeches. According to *Webster's New World Dictionary of Media and Communications,* "News content analyses are a research technique of studying media in order to systematically and objectively identify the characteristics of the messages" (Weiner, 1990, p. 110).

Content analysis begins with gathering print, broadcast, and Internet content through the use of a media monitoring service, like Romeike in the United Kingdom or Bacon's in the United States; a news retrieval database like Lexis-Nexis or Factiva; an online monitoring service like Moreover; or by just combing the Web or hard copy media yourself. The content usually contains a variety of themes and messages, which are coded for references to a particular organization. Once coded, the resulting data are analyzed to determine trends and opinions. For example, in the case of a new car introduction, PR researchers scan consumer and trade press clippings, broadcast transcripts, and online car-buff discussion groups for references to a campaign in which the new model is promoted as being safe, luxurious, and fun to drive. They catalogue and analyze the intended references along with any unintended or negative references to determine trends and perceptions relevant to that model car, its brand, and its manufacturer.

In practical terms and in its most common form, content analysis is used as a means to report on the volume and quality of news coverage during a specified period of time. The resulting data are presented at consistent intervals. Typically these reports include information such as the name of the publication or program, the date the story ran, the circulation or audience, and a register of the messages contained in the story and its overall tone. Like all of the other research tools discussed here, the content analysis is used to prove and improve the return on your investment in PR.

Media Tabulations

As shown in Figure 29.1, even simple forms of news content analysis can be used to provide insight. In this example, which shows frequency and reach from one quarter to another, we can glean some indication of the direction of the PR program.

As simple as these data are, we can see at a glance if the program is trending up or down, and we might also be able to attach the timing of certain outputs to the corresponding results. The second quarter saw an increase of almost 100 percent over the prior quarter. Was there a publicity campaign or a special event underway during that period of time? Another simple measure is tracking by media type. In Figure 29.2, the pie chart indicates that almost 50 percent of the news generated on this subject came from daily newspapers. If newspapers were the focus of this campaign, that might reaffirm the plan. However, if most of the campaign's resources were directed toward magazines, you might need to review and adjust.

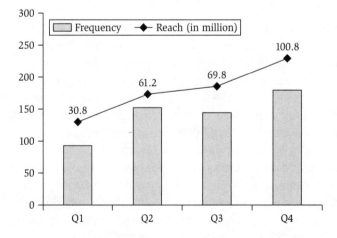

Figure 29.1. Quarterly News Content Analysis Provides Comparisons of Frequency and Reach

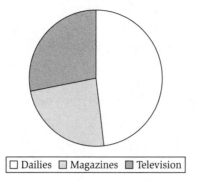

Figure 29.2. Media Tracking Provides Comparison Data of Media Coverage

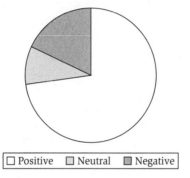

Figure 29.3. Measuring Impact on a Three-Point Scale

This sort of simple media analysis is well within reach of anyone in PR who has access to spreadsheet and charting software. Simply create a spreadsheet with column headings such as *date of coverage, circulation,* and *media type.* It is worth mentioning here two forms of PR measurement that are highly debated and therefore questionable. The first is the use of an advertising equivalency, in which case a dollar figure is applied to news coverage on an "if-purchased" basis, and the second is the use of a PR multiplier, wherein circulation or ad value is factored or multiplied by an arbitrary number to reflect the added impact of PR.

Up to now, examples have focused more on the quantity of coverage than the quality, so we cannot yet say whether the program was successful. The first step toward measuring the quality of coverage is to introduce the assessment of tone. Tone can be measured by using a three-point scale of *positive-neutral-negative* (see Figure 29.3). Although the illustration exemplifies a three-point scale, we would suggest a five-point scale since most articles are not either totally positive or totally negative. The five-point scale offers a higher level of granularity, using a scale ranging from *totally negative* (−2) to *somewhat negative* (−1) to *neutral* (0) to *somewhat positive* (+1) to *totally positive* (+2). At this stage, you would know whether the high volume of widely seen coverage is a good thing or a bad thing. This level of content analysis requires a true reading and interpretation of the content rather than simply pasting data from a clip tab.

Message Tracking

A still more advanced level of analysis tracks the presence and the tone of individual messages contained within a news item. In this case, you can see the extent to which the organization's key messages are being delivered as well as the tone of the messages delivered. Figure 29.4 shows five messages that might be used to describe any organization: large or small, for-profit and nonprofit. At Delahaye, we call these messages "core messages" for that reason.

Of the five messages shown, a mix of messages appears to be working according to plan, and some messages warrant improvement: *Quality Products and Services* is a theme that is being delivered in the highest proportion of positive-to-negative (about three-to-one), but the volume of coverage is only fourth out of five. If messages about the quality of products and services are important, these results suggest that the PR team reinforce these good results to generate even higher volumes of positive coverage. Conversely, *Stakeholder Relations* is a message in need of help, as negative coverage outpaces positive at a rate of almost two to one. On the positive side, *Organizational Integrity* is a solid performer, as is *Financial Management*. The theme of *Organizational Strength* is doing well but not as well as it could.

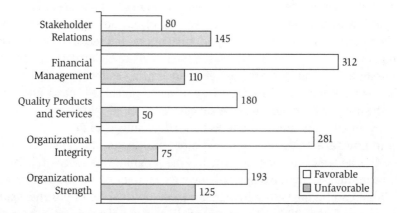

Figure 29.4. Tracking the Tone of Messages

While this level of message analysis can be done in-house, it requires a degree of involvement and objectivity that most organizations find difficult to undertake. At this level, it becomes easier to see where the possibilities for truly strategic, research-based public relations become available.

Public Relations Gross Rating Point. For years, there has been a growing desire to represent media coverage as something more than just hits. The understanding among those who fund PR programs is that clippings are just an incremental goal toward something more meaningful, such as recall, awareness, preference, and behavior. With such measures in place, public relations can be more easily integrated with and compared to other forms of marketing and communication.

Any discussion of PR's relationship and interaction with other forms of marketing must begin with an understanding of how various forms of marketing work. There are three forms of marketing and communication: controlled, semicontrolled, and uncontrolled. Public relations is only semicontrollable at best. Output activities are undertaken, and they make the news or not depending on the editor's judgment. Advertising and direct marketing are 100 percent controllable since you pay a dollar, and you can control frequency, reach, and positioning.

In managing controllable forms of marketing communication, advertisers use copy and advertising testing to make sure that the ads they eventually run will be proven in tests to be compelling, involving, and persuasive to the mass market. Once the visuals and content are finalized, advertisers plan and evaluate their ad spend using an industry measure known as a gross rating point (GRP), which represents the reach and the frequency of the ad campaign. Since the communication is controlled, the only variance left to consider is how many GRPs the campaign will put against their level of spending within a particular time frame and a given market.

Since public relations is only semicontrollable, copy and advertising testing in their traditional forms do not apply, since there is no way to know in advance if the magazine will use the product photograph or if the TV program will feature the product name in the lead story. Therefore, a new form of measurement had to be created. This measure would accurately represent PR's unique role within the marketing mix and foster the true integration of PR with other forms of marketing and communication: a PR-GRP.

The key consideration for creating a PR-GRP was the degree to which PR is controllable. PR-GRP has to not only represent reach and frequency, as in advertising's GRP, it also has to represent the quality or impact of news coverage. Finally, again reflecting PR's semicontrollable nature, the PR-GRP has to be applied after a story appears rather than before.

Creating the Impact Score: PR's GRP. Advertising has its GRP system. Television has its Nielsen ratings point system. Until the impact score, public relations did not have an equivalent distilled measure for the purposes of planning and evaluating media activity. The formula would look something like this: *Frequency* × *Reach* × *Quality.* The challenge became how to define quality and then how to distill these three measures into a single number.

The initial research into creating the impact score had three objectives:

- Identify the attributes that denote quality in media coverage.

- Assess their relative weight in influencing the likelihood that someone would be exposed to and remember the news coverage (awareness and recall).

- Integrate these factors into an easy-to-use, integrated performance measure.

For the first phase of the analysis, Delahaye focused on print media (although the research has since been extended to broadcast and Web-based media). It began by creating a list of possible attributes thought to indicate quality in news story. The list contained over forty attributes, such as "a story reporting news exclusively about one company" rather than "a roundup story mentioning several companies."

A representative sample of coverage was gathered from a variety of news sources. Stories were selected and then coded by expert media analysts. Some attributes were rated on a scale of 1 to 5 (where 1 indicated "a roundup story mentioning several companies" and 5 "a story reporting news exclusively about one company"), while other attributes were binary, that is, the attribute was either present or not (the presence of a visual, for example) representing the company. Each of the attributes was scored for each of the articles. The tone of the article (the editorial "attitude" conveyed toward the company) was also assessed; it was applied as an overall factor by which the attributes were multiplied, so that "an exclusive story with a photo" in a positive article was just as good as "an exclusive story with a photo" in a negative article would be bad. In this way, a content analysis of each of the news stories was completed based on each of the forty attributes.

The second phase was designed to reveal the extent to which each of the forty possible attributes drove awareness and recall among a representative group of a thousand people. Copies of each article were distributed in a controlled environment, and the participants were asked first to read each news item and then asked later the extent to which they remembered specific stories and story themes. After the data collection and analysis were complete, certain stories emerged as the most memorable, and these stories each contained common story attributes or key drivers of awareness and recall. These factors (now called *Prominence*) form the basis for Delahaye's impact score and net effect measure of media performance. The formula is proprietary, but the prominence factors include news item placement, headline, initial mention, extent of mention, dominance, and visuals, and these can be used to measure news coverage in any situation.

Impact score is a composite of prominence and tone that becomes a quality score on a scale of +100 percent to −100 percent. (Tone determines whether the score is a positive or negative number.) Prominence is a research-based estimation of the likelihood that someone will be exposed to and remember news about a company. Prominence factors are weighted based on their relative contribution to news item quality.

Net effect is the result of the reach of an individual news item multiplied by its impact score. Results are combined to determine an overall net effect for a specific period of time or surrounding a particular issue or event. Net effect can be positive or negative. It would be impossible to replicate the exact formula for duplicating the impact score and net effect scoring system as it is proprietary and the formula is a trade secret. However, the elements are presented above. and a do-it-yourself version of the process, as described here using the attributes in Exhibit 29.1, would give an approximation of the quality of news coverage you are generating.

The impact score is continually and uniquely validated during dozens of rigorous statistical analyses each year and has been shown to be a reliable and consistent distilled score for representing PR's presence within the marketing mix (see Table 29.1). What is more, it has been used to demonstrate PR's ability to drive meaningful business outcomes such as recall, awareness, and behavior. Although the actual weighting is proprietary, it is important that all PR

Exhibit 29.1. Elements of an Impact Score and Net Effect Scoring System

- Reach
- Frequency
- Impact

    Front page/cover

    Headline/lead

    Initial mention

    Extent of mention

    Dominance

    Visuals

- Presence of key messages
- Tone

Table 29.1. Analyzing the Impact Score Factors to Drive Business Outcomes

Impact Score Factors	Frequency	Percentage of Total Clips
Front page	10	11%
Headline	21	21
Exclusive mention	5	8
Significant mention	6	8
Lead mention	5	8
Visual/graphic	2	5
Percentage positive or neutral tone	120	95

persons know quantifiably what they have always believed to be true: public relations can deliver incremental sales and profits to an organization.

Competitive Tracking. To take the content analysis to another level, add competitors to the mix. This is a point at which complexity and cost may become considerations, so we recommend two ways to reduce the volume of clips and the time required to analyze them. First, identify the media that matter. Rather than tracking every publication and TV show, select only those that are known to be the most important among the target audience. Second, identify just those competitors are worth tracking; that usually reduces the list to two or three: your company, the market share leader (if it is not you), and the market innovator, or the company that may be responsible for changing the landscape of your category. An example in the automobile area might be Buick, Mercury, and Scion, respectively.

As the complexity increases, so does the capacity of the analysis to drive learning and insight. At this point, a process known as *message engineering* becomes possible. The theory is that if a message is important, frequently seen, and positive, then one simply reinforces the effort. If a message is important, frequently seen, and generating negative tone, then one must fix the situation.

Survey Research

Surveys are a quantified assessment of a person or a group toward a subject, developed as a result of previous influences. Most survey research involves questioning and probing among a representative sample of individuals. Carefully designed questionnaires are usually administered in a structured manner to uncover attitudes, needs, or preferences.

While there are many types of surveys, here are three that you can begin using today:

- The executive audit: A survey instrument for building consensus among those who fund or influence PR programs
- The media demographic audit: A database of media habits and lifestyle characteristics based on the results of a syndicated survey
- The journalist audit: A survey among key journalists to uncover the means to improve media relationships

The Executive Audit. The first requirement for proving value in terms of generating a return on expectation is met through the application of an executive audit of the senior executives who underwrite public relations programs. The audit is a clean-slate approach to uncover what PR underwriters seek from public relations—delivering key messages to target media, increased awareness, or even increased sales—matched with the executives' assessment of current PR performance. Delahaye conducts thousands of executive interviews each year, and the results indicate that PR investors have a good understanding of what measures are reasonable, meaningful, and measurable. Interestingly, executive assessments of current PR practices indicate that public relations departments tend to overdeliver on what PR underwriters value least (press clippings) while underdelivering on what they value most: raising awareness and delivering key messages to target media. Once these preferences and assessments are discussed and understood, more formal standards may be established against which value can be clearly demonstrated.

The executive audit, a form of qualitative research, is a brief telephone survey of internal public relations clients who have a primary impact on PR strategy, goal setting, and evaluation. The purpose of the survey is to provide the feedback needed by PR professionals to continually improve departmental and personal performance in meeting the needs of key executives. Reports are used to open up and formalize dialogue between PR professionals and their internal clients.

The executive audit measures the attitudes, preferences, needs, and expectations of top management when working with their PR departments. The survey concentrates on such issues as how internal clients feel about the role of public relations in achieving *their* objectives, what they feel are the most and least important PR activities, tactics, outcomes, and measures. Another battery of questions addresses the current performance of the PR department on each element, how PR success is best evaluated, and how they rate your efforts against what they know of competitors.

The executive audit results are used to accurately assess client attitudes, preferences, needs, and expectations for public relations effort in terms of:

- Professional attributes such as good writing and media skills
- Activities and tactics such as media relations and strategic PR guidance

- Achievement of client and companywide objectives
- Media considered most credible or most important
- Messages considered most credible or most compelling
- Helping to define the standards by which public relations effectiveness is measured (and what drives success in the opinion of this key audience)
- Determining the extent to which public relations now satisfies these preferences, needs, and expectations
- Setting the stage for ongoing dialogue in terms that are meaningful, educational, and consensus building

Media Audit. One of the most critical steps in any marketing and communication endeavor is that of targeting: the process of identifying and reaching the audience that is considered the optimal subject of your communication and marketing effort. Targeting should be considered in terms of the audience primarily and the media secondarily. Most PR targeting falls under the categories of either "Rolodex" targeting, which is calling the journalists who are in your Rolodex, or "coffee-table" targeting, a purely intuitive process based on what the publicist determines must be on the coffee table of the target.

The media audit is a form of secondary research that provides detailed analysis of national and local print and broadcast media viewership, listenership, and readership. Rather than simple circulation, the audit provides detailed information regarding targeted audience reach:

- Demographics, geographics, and psychographics
- Products and services owned and planning to purchase (including brand names)
- Leisure activities
- Media involvement

The media audit is used by PR professionals to manage their media relations plan more strategically in terms of targeting, positioning and return on investment. Since the media audit has detailed information about *your* target audience, you can make the most of your limited PR resources by targeting only the most productive print and broadcast media.

The value of public relations is also more meaningfully and easily communicated within the marketing mix because the audit goes beyond conventional PR wisdom to provide customer-driven planning and evaluation. For example, a luxury car manufacturer may use the audit to target just luxury car owners but only those expressing intent to purchase a new luxury car within the next twelve months. The car manufacturer can target by a number of criteria: brand, price range, domestic or import, and intent to purchase within the next twelve months. Further refinement comes by indexing versus age, income, and other variables.

Journalist Audit. The journalist audit, a form of qualitative research, is a brief telephone survey of journalists at your "media that matter" who have a primary impact on the success of your PR programs. The purpose of the survey is to provide the feedback that PR professionals need to continually improve the quality and quantity of media coverage by meeting the needs of key journalists.

The journalist audit measures the attitudes, preferences, needs, and expectations key journalists have for working with PR departments. The survey concentrates on such issues as what PR activities and attributes are important to journalists and how you are doing in the light of what they say is important and in comparison to competitors and peers. Another battery of questions addresses journalist preferences for notification, communications, press conferences, and special events.

The journalist audit results are used to accurately assess journalists' attitudes, preferences, needs, and expectations for your public relations effort in terms of:

- Professional attributes (for example, responsive, accessible)

- Activities and tactics (pitch calls, releases, events)

- Which of your competitive set is best, what they do that makes them best, and how you compare to the best on a variety of attributes

- Helping to define the standards by which public relations effectiveness is measured (and what drives success in the opinion of this key audience)

- Determining the extent to which your public relations efforts now satisfy these preferences, needs, and expectations versus competitors

- Setting the stage for continual improvement as evidenced in how the journalists treat your organization editorially and how your organization performs in the next annual journalists audit

Marketing Mix Modeling

Marketing mix modeling is an analysis that draws data from disparate sources and then integrates them to provide insight into the ongoing process of marketing. Using traditional databases like sales, advertising GRPs, or content analysis, researchers merge these data to create more complete views of the marketplace and estimate the impact of advertising, PR, pricing, merchandising, competitive activity, seasonality, and other factors on sales. Given an understanding of what drives sales, we can explain past results and influence future sales.

As new approaches and more powerful technologies become available, our ability to properly assess and accurately forecast marketing performance has never been greater. It is in this new environment that the line is being drawn through management's use of two words—*prove it*—and soon you may have no other choice but to do so.

The need for and the increased access to marketing intelligence has not led to a sea-change for marketers yet. Television advertising . . ., promotions . . ., and direct marketing continue to command significant spending, and their need to demonstrate and generate a positive return on investment (ROI) is scaled to the level of investment. As such, the day is coming when each of these marketing functions will be judged on its ability to deliver value. Those consuming the greatest resources will feel the most pressure first.

On the basis of relative spending, public relations may seem like a lower priority. But in terms of ROI, PR may be the most critical: marketing mix modeling analyses have repeatedly demonstrated that PR delivers a superior ROI, and an investment in PR often delivers a lift to other forms of marketing.

PR has the most to gain in this new environment. But in order to achieve some higher level of primacy, PR departments have to change the way they work. Success will be contingent on PR's willingness to work in a more integrated fashion with other marketing agents and use proven research techniques to demonstrate clearly a positive and meaningful ROI. In this setting, marketing decisions will be based on what drives results rather than on outmoded ideas of "what we have always done," and PR strategies based on empty goals such as "generate significant buzz" will go by the wayside.

The first contingency, the problem of integration within the marketing mix, is not confined to PR as traditional marketing communications relationships do not allow for easy marketing optimization either: mass market advertising, specialty advertising, and direct marketing, for example, are not traditionally aligned with marketing public relations, event sponsorships, and trade shows; there is little or no integration or alignment across groups. Even at the brand level, where brand managers oversee advertising, promotions, and PR, traditional views of each marketing agent often disallow the type of integration that yields meaningful leveraging and scale. The key to better integration is revealed in the second contingency, which speaks to the need for proven research techniques to manage programs smarter and to prove ROI.

Companies whose names you would recognize in categories as diverse as retail, automotive, telecom, consumer package goods, financial services, and motion pictures are feeding advanced news content analysis into sophisticated marketing mix models to make the PR-to-sales connection. In its own right, the content analysis gives PR people the feedback they need to do a better job in delivering a high quantity of quality media coverage. But when content analysis results are fed into a statistical model along with other marketing data, in order to tweak out the relative power of advertising, direct marketing, telemarketing, and trade marketing, the result is an ROI road map based on a common lexicon. Data points are the common thread interwoven throughout the marketing fabric. These savvy companies apply what they learn by shifting their emphasis within the marketing mix to drive the optimal combination of marketing-for-sales. It will not be long before PR is planned on the basis of what drives sales rather than what drives buzz. You had better prepare for it.

WRAP-UP

Clearly understanding the value and ROI of public relations holds huge promise for marketers in general and public relations professionals in particular. While the result of this type of analysis often brings with it increased budgets and staffing, it also has provided companies with opportunities to focus their precious resources on those programs that deliver. The savings derived from cutting nonperforming programs means that human and financial resources can be reallocated in ways that have helped PR departments to reduce budgets while generating even better results.

If it has not happened to you already, the day is soon coming when you will be asked to "prove it." Public relations research and evaluation methods have reached a point where PR pros can feel confident not just in being able to respond, but in taking the initiative to uncover new opportunities for savings, value, and a positive return on investment.

References

International Association of Business Communicators. (2005). *Information: Vision, mission and structure: How IABC can help you.* Retrieved July 6, 2005, from http://www.iabc.com/info/about/vision_mission_structure.htm.

PRWeek. (2005, June 27). Corporate comms funds up, reveals PRWeek's survey, pp. 1, 15.

Public Relations Society of America. (2005). *About public relations: Official PRSA definition: What it does.* Retrieved July 6, 2005, from http://www.prsa. org/_Resources/Profession/index.asp?ident = prof1.

Weiner, R. (1990). *Webster's new world dictionary of media and communications.* Upper Saddle River, NJ: Prentice Hall.

PART FIVE

MARKETING COMMUNICATION

CHAPTER THIRTY

Marketing Communication Today

Lorenzo Sierra

Growing up in Tucson, Arizona, in the 1970s and 1980s, I was a member of Tucson's burgeoning Latino American community. Like most other consumers of that era, I marveled as more and more product choices became available to me.

Although there were more choices, marketing approaches remained in the 1950s. That is, marketers continued to deliver their messages to me using the same tactics that made America's post-World War II economy the strongest on the planet. The faces and messages were largely Anglo. In essence, marketers of that day did not see me as "special."

In the early 1990s, I noticed that marketing messages were beginning to feature faces and places that looked like mine. I was learning about products and services in the language (Spanglish, a colloquial version of English and Spanish) my friends and I were speaking.

In my youthful naiveté, I figured marketers were specifically addressing American Latinos out of the goodness of their hearts. Little did I know that it was not compassion or enlightenment that led to culturally relevant messages; it was survival.

Welcome to marketing today.

In this chapter, marketing communication is defined and popular strategies for delivering marketing communication are explained.

MARKETING TODAY

Let us ask the fundamental question, "What is marketing communication?" The definition of marketing communication often depends on who you are talking to, and sometimes that person may even change his or her definition. But for purposes of this chapter, let us say that marketing communication is all communication activities an organization undertakes to promote its agenda to its audiences. It might be advertising, public relations, or a coordinated face-to-face campaign. The medium is irrelevant. The point is that your organization has something to say to someone, and you want the audience to take some sort of action.

Marketing communication is many things to many people. It is sometimes difficult to say what it is not. One need only review the International Association of Business Communicators Code of Ethics (2005) to determine what marketing communication is not. For example, marketing communication is not:

- Spin. Communication professionals engaged in marketing communication have truth as the foundation for all communication. Using falsehoods or half-truths in order to spin an event goes against everything professional marketing communicators stand for.

- Illegal. Marketing communication professionals will not use their messages to advance illegal activities.

- Unethical. Marketing communication professionals must adhere to the highest ethical standards. We are the voice of our organizations and must be sensitive to cultural values and beliefs.

There are many activities and media that fall under the marketing communication umbrella, each with advantages and disadvantages. The choice is yours on when and how to use each medium. The best foundation for all media is your creativity and your honesty.

CONDUITS OF THE INFORMATION AGE

Marketing communication professionals have more ways to get their message to their audiences than ever before. As recently as the late 1980s, professional communicators did not have their current suite of communication devices. One has to wonder how we got things done without cell phones, personal digital assistants, e-mail, wireless Internet access, personal computers, and all the other devices that have promised to make us more efficient. But things did get done. And to talk to some of the old-timers, they got done well: products were sold, minds were changed, and hearts were captured . . . without a single emoticon to be found.

Marketing communication professionals still make good use of traditional media like print, audio, and video. Over the past few years, many companies have introduced intranets as a means of informing employees about company happenings and policies, making Web site technology a standard medium.

Obviously the greatest advances for marketing communication professionals have been in the field of technology. Rarely does a fiscal quarter go by without the introduction of new or upgraded technology that allows people to communicate more effectively with one another.

Angelo Fernando, author of IABC *Communication World*'s "Technology Update" column, spends a great deal of his time tinkering, researching, and evaluating the latest and greatest technological toys. Fernando provided his unique perspectives on each of the technologies discussed next. (The following technologies may be legacy technology by the time the next edition of this book is released. At the time of this writing, the following technologies were emerging and evolving.)

Wiki

A wiki is a Web-based tool that allows any user to edit the content of a Web site or page. The word *wiki* comes from the Hawaiian word for "quick" or "informal." The most prevalent example of a wiki is http://en.wikipedia.org/wiki, or Wikipedia, a free content encyclopedia written exclusively by volunteers. In fact, if you want to create a new entry or edit an existing entry, you are free to do so, assuming you become a registered user.

From an organizational perspective, a wiki allows cross-functional teams, regardless of location, to collaborate on a knowledge project. Marketers can use this knowledge to gain unique perspectives in a real-time environment.

"It's not the best marketing tool," said Fernando. "But it does allow companies to collaborate more effectively than ever before" (personal communication, May 2005).

Text Messaging

As of this writing, text messaging is mostly a cell phone technology. With text messaging, a sender can deliver messages directly to a subscriber's cell phone. Think of it as the twenty-first-century fax blast.

Fernando believes that cell phones will not be the only bastion of text messaging. Portable communication devices, that is, devices with phone capabilities as well as wireless PC capabilities, will become more prevalent. This will give direct marketing a whole new dimension. Moreover, Fernando believes that text messaging technology will allow marketers to directly reach customers as they enter a place of business.

"As you enter a store, sensors will detect your portable communication device," Fernando said. "The store will transmit information about products or coupons to your device."

Companies will be able to instantly reach multiple employees who have portable communication devices. Employees, in turn will be able to respond to the message either directly to the sender or to the whole distribution list.

RSS

With RSS (rich site summary), Web users can receive new content from their preferred sources. For example, if you are keeping tabs on your competitors, you can go to a mainstream news site that covers your industry and select the RSS feed for your competitor. When the outlet posts a story about your competitor, you receive an e-mail that lets you know about the story when it is released. For marketers, RSS allows them to instantly announce to subscribers the organization's most recent news. "Very soon, RSS feeds will be available through portable communication devices of the future," Fernando said.

Organizations can use RSS delivery for internal purposes only. In an organization with a large and dispersed population, RSS technology allows employees to keep abreast of the organizational news they prefer.

Podcasting

Podcasting is so new that its ultimate direction is not yet set. It is akin to a radio program. It is an audio program sent via the Internet. Podcasting uses RSS protocol to notify subscribers of new content.

Organizations can create and deliver business-related audio messages to its audiences via applicable personal communication devices.

A Technology Caveat

Keep in mind that technology is just a way to get a message to your audience. Without a credible message that contains information valuable to the receiver, it does not matter what method of delivery you use. Once the novelty of a technology has worn off, all you have is your messages.

The technologies reviewed here have one thing in common: they are all one-way deliveries of messages. This leads to the marketing communication professional's most valuable tool: the ear.

SPEAK THE WORD

In an increasingly competitive global marketplace, an organization's ability to listen is often the determining factor between success and oblivion. Marketing communication professionals must take the time to truly listen to the wants and needs of its audiences.

Bolívar José Bueno is a marketing communication prodigy. In his early twenties, Bueno has established himself as one of the brightest minds in the profession. He coined the term *cult branding* in his book *The Power of Cult Branding: How Nine Magnetic Brands Turned Customers into Loyal Followers (and Yours Can, Too)* (Bueno & Ragas, 2002). In our technology-driven era, Bueno knows exactly where marketing communication power lies: with the customer. "The customer is totally in control," he says. "Marketers need to realize that customers *are* the brand" (personal communication, May 2005).

Customers in this sense are not only consumers but organizational stakeholders as well. Each customer has his or her perception of an organization. Each experience that person has with the organization has an impact on the customer's perception of the brand.

The marketing communication professional's task is to understand the elements of a positive brand experience for all customers. Once you understand the audience's expectations, you must develop messages that will resonate with each customer segment.

"The process now is to allow the customer to coauthor [your branding] with you," Bueno said. "Companies that listen to the customer—with a creative experience that is driven by the customer—end up creating very powerful brands."

Bueno (2002) cites nine brands that have transcended traditional brand loyalty to develop a cultlike following among customers and employees. These organizations, through their brands, make extraordinary efforts to listen to the customer, something Bueno says most organizations are not willing to do.

"This presents a problem for lazy companies, to be honest with you," Bueno said. "Listening is an active process. We're [marketing communication professionals] are going to have to develop better ways of listening to our customers" (personal communication, May 2005).

To increase the desirability of their brand, marketing communication professionals must develop ways of engaging internal and external customers in the messaging process. "The modern marketer has to bring the customer into the boardroom," Bueno said. "They have to bring an advocate of the consumer inside."

One of the cult brands featured in Bueno's book is Apple. Bueno cites the maker of Macintosh computers as one of the first to bring consumers into the brand-building process.

Customers mentioned in this section refer to internal and external customers. But it is absolutely vital that marketing communication professionals not only have a firm grasp on the pulse of the consumer, but also have a firm grasp on the pulse of the internal constituent.

"To me, selling in is more important than selling out," Bueno said. "You can read a hundred business books on what makes a company successful and no one has ever listed managing people as one of the factors that makes a company successful. Guess why? No one likes to be managed. No one wakes up and says 'I can't wait to get to work to be manipulated by my boss.'"

Bueno goes on to say that employees will give maximum effort when they feel as though they are part of something bigger than themselves. This is especially true if the employee can see how his or her contribution fits into the bigger picture.

"When your employees buy in, your customers buy in too," Bueno said. "You can have the greatest marketing program. You can have the best product. You can have the best displays and everything else. It comes down to the person who is in direct contact with the customer. If they do not treat the customer the way the customer wants to be treated based on your industry, you have blown the whole program."

But how do you develop messages that result in desired action? Most marketing communication professionals enter the profession through the creative end of the skill spectrum. That is, at their core, many marketing communication professionals are writers. Good writing is the foundational skill that all marketing communication professionals must possess. But it is growing increasingly difficult to get and keep the attention of the countless audiences. To develop effective messages, marketing communication professionals must look outside the profession for assistance.

THE SCIENCE OF PERSUASION

Like any other good marketing communication professional, Bueno takes his professional development seriously. As a busy professional, he makes time to continually learn. But you will not find Bueno at marketing communication seminars or conferences. "I spend my time going to conferences on quantum mechanics and physics and psychology," he said.

Nevertheless, you do not have to sign up for the closest seminar on Newtonian dynamics. But it is definitely worth your time to study disciplines outside traditional marketing communication. Marketing communication professionals who glean useful information from sociology, psychology, anthropology, and other disciplines will be able to differentiate themselves from other professionals.

Marketing communication professionals are quite familiar with the basic communication model: Sender ⟶ Message ⟶ Receiver ⟶ Feedback. Another model that should be in every professional's toolbox was created by Abraham Maslow. Maslow's (1954) hierarchy of human needs is a pyramid of motivational elements that lead a person to self-fulfillment. The base block of the pyramid is physiological needs. These are the biological needs of eating, sleeping, and drinking that keep us alive. Once physiological needs are met, the person seeks to achieve safety needs. Humans crave security. Next are love and belonging, and followed by esteem needs. The peak of the pyramid is self-actualization, which happens when a person attains a level where he or she seeks to become self-fulfilled. In other words, he or she has a purpose for being.

For marketing communication professionals, this model presents the ideal methodology for developing messages. One can develop truth-based messages that describe the essence of his or her organization based on levels of the pyramid.

For example, an employee's safety needs can be communicated by showing how the organization takes great strides to ensure safety. This is done by communicating policies that show how the company will not tolerate any form of abusive behavior. Of course, the organization must adhere to those policies to establish and maintain credibility.

According to Bueno and Ragas (2002), the foundation of *The Power of Cult Branding* is derived from Maslow's hierarchy of needs. From it, they developed the Seven Golden Rules of Cult Branding. Based in extensive research, the seven rules lay the groundwork for any organization to develop a cult brand:

1. Consumers want to be part of a group that is different.
2. Cult brand inventors show daring and determination.
3. Cult brands sell lifestyles.
4. Listen to the choir and create cult brand evangelists.
5. Cult brands always create customer communities.
6. Cult brands are inclusive.
7. Cult brands promote personal freedom and draw power from their enemies [Bueno & Ragas, 2002, p. 17.]

Despite the simplicity of the seven rules, most companies are unable to implement the rules in a manner that would take their brand to cult status.

As we embrace more scientific ways of developing messages, there are long-standing hurdles to overcome. Marketing communication professionals are often seen as the "newsletter editors" or "PR people." We use our art to craft messages that persuade our audiences to action. But over the years, researchers have proven that persuasion is not just the tool of the charismatic or charming. There is science behind persuasion.

Persuasion, it appears, can be empirically described by six principles developed by Arizona State University psychology professor Robert B. Cialdini (2001). Cialdini says that one does not need to be born with a world of charisma to be a persuasive person. All you have to do is understand and practice his six principles:

1. Liking. Do you have the type of disposition that makes people naturally like you?
2. Reciprocity. Do you give the way you would like to receive?
3. Social proof. Can you rally people (preferably influencers) to your cause?
4. Consistency. Do you ask others to be accountable for their commitments?

5. Authority. Do you have the expertise to be credible?

6. Scarcity. Can you make people feel as though they are "in the know"?

As with all other communication, the persuasive tactics should be used with the highest ethical standards. Far too often, especially in political campaigns, professionals use persuasive tactics to mislead or misinform.

NO DAY BUT TODAY

In the third edition of *Inside Organizational Communication* (Wann, 1999), the term *marketing communication* was not to be found in the title of any of the eighteen chapters. This book features an entire section with five chapters devoted to marketing communication, branding, reputation management, and customer loyalty. At one time these practices may have been seen as fads or buzzwords. They are now well-defined specialties within the organizational communication field.

To be most effective, all elements of marketing communication must by in synchronization with each other. Gone are the days when the advertising, public relations, internal communication, and marketing departments operate independently. Customers today have neither the time nor the patience to figure out what an organization is and stands for.

Marketing communication professionals have the opportunity to become increasingly valuable to their organizations. The first step is to understand that the creative disciplines cannot thrive in a vacuum. They cannot meaningfully exist if they are not perfectly aligned with the organization's raison d'être.

More and more marketing efforts have been launched to American Latinos. Every day I read about companies that are "addressing the Hispanic market." Such is marketing communication today.

As we refine and evolve marketing communication, we must always understand that no matter how advanced our delivery systems are or how much audience research we do, no one will listen if we have nothing to say, regardless of how loud we speak.

References

Bueno, B. J., & Ragas, M. W. (2002). *The power of cult branding: How nine magnetic brands turned customers into loyal followers (and yours can, too)*. Roseville, Calif.: Prima.

Cialdini, R. B. (2001, October). Harnessing the science of persuasion. *Harvard Business Review, 79*(9), 72–79.

International Association of Business Communicators. (2005). *International Associa-tion of Business Communicators Code of Ethics for Professional Communicators.* http://www.iabc.com/members/joining/code.htm.

Maslow, A. H. (1954). *Motivation and personality.* New York: Harper.

Wann, A. (Ed.). (1999). *Inside organizational communications* (3rd ed.). San Francisco: International Association of Business Communicators.

CHAPTER THIRTY-ONE

Branding and Brand Management

Integration and Innovation

Paul Mlodzik

Within the field of business communication is a series of disciplines, many of which are examined in this book. Marketing communications is a discipline that focuses on the end client. Whether the client is a consumer, another business, or a member of an association, marketing communications is primarily concerned with communicating the organization's unique value proposition (UVP) to the client with the goal of making a sale. This direct connection to the bottom line makes marketing communications practitioners very interested in measurable information, including client research, unit costs, distribution costs, marketing expenditures, and client satisfaction. As the saying goes, "Nothing really happens until a sale is made."

The goal of the marketing communications professional is to articulate the UVP clearly, concisely, and consistently. What value does our product or service deliver to the client? Why choose us over our competitors? What can or will we offer that no one else can duplicate? What unique experience can we deliver to our clients? The organization that can communicate and deliver on the best UVP usually wins.

TWIN THEMES: INTEGRATION AND INNOVATION

The past ten years have seen tremendous advancements in the art and science of marketing communications. However, few of these changes have been revolutionary; most have evolved as the result of advances in strategic focus, technology, and demographics. Yet despite the complex web of factors involved, two distinct themes have emerged.

Discussion about the integration of various communications disciplines has been a hot topic for many years. The proponents of this view referred to the subject as "integrated communications," "total branding" or "integrated marketing communications." Unfortunately, much of the hype around the subject has not lived up to its billing. Most efforts to integrate the communication disciplines within organizations have come up against internal and external barriers that defeated the key objectives of the exercise: focus, efficiency, and effectiveness in delivering on the UVP. Nevertheless, many organizations have succeeded in their integration efforts, and the results have benefited all stakeholders involved.

Innovation may be one of the most used (and least understood) words in business today. It has become synonymous with "the big idea that changes everything." However, experts on the topic are quick to point out that there is a spectrum of innovation that ranges from small increases in efficiency all the way to the revolutionary concept that changes a whole industry. Most innovations are more evolutionary, but they nevertheless are vitally important to improving organizational performance. Over the past decade, innovative advances in the field of marketing communications have changed the way we bring products and services to market, and they point the way to the future. As you review this chapter, consider the following questions:

- Do your marketing communications efforts have a clear client focus rather than an organizational bias or product or service orientation?

- Does your organization have a clear, unique value proposition that is central to its marketing communication efforts and reflected in its brand?

- Are your organization's communications disciplines structured to take advantage of the benefits of integration?

- Does your organization understand the spectrum of innovation and encourage innovation in its marketing communication efforts?

- Is marketing communications considered a key partner in the development and delivery of products and services to clients?

INTEGRATION

It was not long ago that the integration of various communications disciplines was identified as a revolutionary concept. After all, it seemed intuitively obvious that these disciplines must align their efforts for maximum impact. However, most organizations have found the path to integration full of obstacles. For those who have made the journey, the benefits have been worth the work.

Benefits of Integration

Why is integration desirable? The short answer is: efficiency and effectiveness. The ultimate goal of any marketing communications function is to optimize the use of resources (human and financial) to obtain the intended response from the target audience. If communication efforts are aligned and integrated across disciplines, then this goal can be better achieved through these avenues:

- A streamlined planning and development process involving all disciplines
- Sharing of research and insight regarding the target audience
- A consistent look, feel, and messaging
- Obtaining the same result with fewer resources or obtaining greater results with the same resources
- Increased leverage with internal support services and external suppliers
- Consistency of approach to the organization's brand identity and brand promise
- Staff who are focused on business objectives, not organizational turf

The greatest killer of marketing communications efforts is inconsistency. A lack of integration is guaranteed to create inconsistent messages both inside and outside the organization. How can it be otherwise? If there is little or no integration of communications disciplines, programs and messages are created in virtual isolation. For example, even if the marketing communications and public relations departments are presented with the same organizational objectives, they will develop different approaches if their efforts are not coordinated.

Inconsistency creates a disconnect with the client. If multiple messages are coming from an organization, which one is the true focus? Is brand promise going to be consistent with the client experience? What is the organization's real UVP?

Integration leads to consistency. It fosters a collaborative approach to delivering client value and addressing business issues and focuses resources for maximum efficiency and effectiveness. In short, integration of communication disciplines makes business sense.

Obstacles to Integration

The benefits of communication integration are many. Why have organizations had difficulty putting this theory into practice? The sources of opposition are the usual suspects:

- The silo approach to communications is well entrenched in many organizations.
- Managers of various disciplines do not want to share or diminish their authority.
- External stakeholders (for example ad agencies, consultants) introduce their own bias.
- Integration does not receive the appropriate level of focus or resources.
- Marketing communications begins too far down the value chain to be effective.
- Senior management is not sold on the benefits of the approach.

These issues are not unique. All organizations have an innate resistance to change. There is a natural fear of loss: loss of control, status, routine, and others. Some of these issues sound all too familiar. Support from senior management and a voice at the table are perennial complaints. None of these obstacles is insurmountable with the right combination of organizational analysis and a sound business plan.

Driving Integration in Your Organization

The concept that was before its time has finally arrived—but only for those willing to fight their way through the initial barriers. For the organizations that have made the journey to integration, the pain has been worth the gain. The journey has taken different paths for different organizations, depending on their size, culture, and market focus. Highly diverse organizations have made it work and experienced the benefits.

Here are some recommendations for driving integration in your organization.

Get a Mandate. This is perhaps the most direct route to full integration but also the most difficult. This approach involves building a sound business case around the benefits outlined above. (Facts and figures are essential.) Demonstrate the efficiency and effectiveness gains by outlining the structure and operating principles of an integrated communications function. Show senior management a plan. This direct approach works best in smaller organizations (with less complexity) or in organizations that have a senior executive with responsibility for most or all of the communications functions. This approach also works best if most or all of the communications leaders are involved in the creation and presentation of the plan.

Create a Communications Committee. In some organizations, full integration may not be possible due to structural, political, or other considerations. This does not mean that you cannot realize most of the benefits of integration. Many organizations have been able to establish a committee of representative leaders from the various communications disciplines that facilitates strategic planning and direction. While this does not necessarily have the maximum impact on efficiency, it can have a tremendous impact on effectiveness. This approach gets at the key issue of consistency. Arriving at a consensus approach to the market can be more difficult and time-consuming than a fully integrated approach, but the key benefits are still there.

Clarify Roles and Responsibilities. Whether or not all the communication disciplines are unified under a common organizational structure, all the key players must understand their roles and responsibilities. Lack of consistency often springs from a lack of clarity. Over the years, the lines have blurred among the various communications disciplines. For instance, where does marketing communications end and public relations start? If the leaders of the disciplines can agree on roles and responsibilities, then consistency has a fighting chance. Among the key questions that need to be answered are these:

- Who owns the look and feel of the brand?
- Who defines and articulates the unique value proposition for clients?
- Who creates the key messages? For which audiences?
- Who is accountable for achieving specific, measurable results related to communications?
- Who arbitrates any disagreements on communication issues?

Take the Lead. While a fully integrated structure with defined roles and responsibilities is the ideal scenario, there are some situations where this is not appropriate. In smaller organizations where contact is frequent and trust is high, structure is less important. Simply take an integrated approach to your communication planning, and ensure that the key concepts are discussed and applied.

Summing Up

If you are a consultant, it may not be appropriate to suggest some of the strategies outlined above. In these cases, you can still make an impact by showing leadership. Whether by example or education, you can introduce the principles of integrated communications management and demonstrate how they can benefit the organization. Make yourself the resident expert on the topic, and introduce new strategies on a timetable that makes sense to you and your colleagues.

The benefits of integration are related to planning, structure, process, and consistency. They speak to efficiency and effectiveness.

INNOVATION

To remain relevant and viable, all organizational functions must strive for continuous improvement. Continuous improvement requires innovation. Elaine Dundon (2002, p. 6), defines innovation as "the introduction of a new idea in profitable way." While this may seem like a narrow definition, Dundon goes on to discuss how "new" and "profitable" actually have wide applicability.

First, *new* can work on several levels. It can mean new to the individual, department, organization, or industry or even new to the world. If the idea has not been applied in that context before, it is considered "new." Second, *profitable* simply means that the idea results in strengthening the business. For instance, a new idea may not lead directly to increased sales, but it may lower the cost of acquisition, improve client retention, or increase client satisfaction. All of these factors lead to a more profitable enterprise.

Dundon stresses another key point, which addresses one of the key misconceptions about innovation. There is a spectrum of innovation, ranging from simple improvement in efficiency or effectiveness through evolutionary changes all the way to revolutionary concepts. Do not be trapped into thinking that innovation has to be "the big idea." Innovations come in all shapes and sizes.

Examples of Innovation

Innovation in marketing communications can be found in organizational design, application of technology, brand management, and almost every other facet of the discipline. Here are some innovations related to application of technology:

- Efficiency or effectiveness—the digitization and central storage of all communication plans and promotional materials for easy access by all team members
- Evolutionary—the use of e-mail as a marketing communications tool as the vast majority of consumers become e-mail users
- Revolutionary—redefining a business category by using the Internet as the primary marketing and distribution vehicle for products

Of course, the vast majority of innovations fall toward the efficiency or effectiveness side of the spectrum. All innovations ultimately build value for both the client and the organization. A number of small innovations could cumulatively build a competitive advantage for one organization over another. Occasionally the field of marketing communications innovates in bigger ways, with significant impacts on the underlying business.

The following examples demonstrate how marketing communications can play a leading role in the development of innovative business strategies.

Volvo. When you think of a Volvo automobile, what word springs to mind? You probably thought of *safety.* Most consumers agree. Volvo has become synonymous with automobile safety and has translated this into tremendous international success. In their well-publicized book, *The Twenty-Two Immutable Laws of Branding,* Ries and Ries (2002) discuss "The Law of the Word." They argue that "a brand should strive to own a word in the mind of the consumer" (p. 22). Volvo owns the word *safety* and achieved this through a long-term, consistent approach to integrated marketing communications. This was part of an overall corporate strategy involving innovations in the fields of engineering and manufacturing, but the key to the strategy was in marketing communications.

Nike. Before Nike reinvented the category of running shoes (and, later, sports apparel), the market was relatively quiet and good running shoes cost about $25 a pair. Today Nike is the undisputed market leader, and high-end running shoes can easily cost over $150. All it took was an innovative strategy and three little words: "Just Do It." Nike is not about running shoes; it is about competing and winning. It is about lifestyle and self-confidence. Nike started a relentless and highly consistent campaign that used every communications discipline, every distribution channel, and every media tool. Nike is now one of the world's most recognizable brands and a multibillion-dollar enterprise.

Disney. Disney ranks seventh on the list of the world's most valuable brands (Interbrand, 2005). It is a multimedia conglomerate without peer that has been able to extend its brand successfully into a multitude of businesses because it has focus. There is no more consistent and ubiquitous brand than Disney, and it all hinges on marketing communications and its ability to deliver on the brand promise. Disney is probably the best company in the world at marrying brand promise with experience. Every aspect of its operations, from use of the logo to customer service training, is rigorously controlled for quality.

Driving Innovation in Your Organization

Volvo, Nike, and Disney are all huge household names. However, the lessons they teach are instructive for any organization when considering innovation in the field of marketing communications. They have effectively employed both integration and innovation in their strategy and execution. For every brainwave like "Just Do It," there were a hundred smaller innovations at Nike to ensure efficiency, effectiveness, consistency, and client focus in marketing communications.

Here are some ideas for encouraging innovation within your marketing communications team:

• *Get on the same page.* Discuss innovation with your team. Share a common definition, and provide examples of the whole spectrum of innovative ideas. To create a culture of innovation, everybody must share the same concepts and language and feel free to openly discuss their ideas.

- *Celebrate your successes.* There is an excellent chance that your team or your organization has already been innovative, and you may or may not have noticed. If you use the definition of innovation offered above, you may find several examples in your own back yard. These successes should be celebrated and built on.
- *Throw away "the box."* People are always being encouraged to "think outside the box" when it comes to idea generation and innovation. This can be both intimidating and counterproductive. People are creative in different ways and should not feel less valuable if they are not of the "big idea" variety. Some people know their area of responsibility exceptionally well and may already have innovative ideas on how to improve existing products or processes. They may consider this "inside the box" and therefore not really innovation.
- *Focus on the client.* Many attempts to innovate are perverted by a lack of client focus. An idea that generates loads of money by reducing quality or cutting client benefits is not truly innovative. In the long term, such ideas are not profitable. Real innovation creates value for both the organization and the client.
- *Make time to innovate.* Most employees feel overwhelmed over 50 percent of their working hours, not a conducive environment for innovation. Managers need to create space and time for staff to be innovative. This is not a call for brainstorming or off-the-wall ideas. Innovation sessions need to review specific business issues or processes and often are most productive when facilitated.

We have now tied together the structure and consistency of integration with the continuous improvement and creativity of innovation. It is now time to package marketing communications efforts into a competitive advantage.

THE ROLE OF BRANDING

No examination of marketing communications can be complete without a sound understanding of the critical role of the brand. The brand is where all of the research, planning, integration, and innovation come together.

What Is a Brand?

For our discussion here, a *brand* is made up of the tangible and intangible associations consumers form about a company and its products or services. The key to this definition is reference to tangible and intangible associations. The importance of this reference becomes apparent when you consider the different ways in which clients (and potential clients) come into contact with a brand:

- Audiovisual: The most common form of brand contact is through sight or hearing. Most people experience hundreds of brand images and sounds every day in the form of advertising, logo and product placement, retail signage, packaging, and other avenues.

Exhibit 31.1. Branding Definitions

Brand: The tangible and intangible associations consumers form about a company and its products or services.

Brand promise: The implicit or explicit understanding of the value delivered by the organization (the unique value proposition).

Brand attributes: Adjectives positive or negative that stakeholders use to describe the organization.

Brand differentiation: Setting yourself apart from organizations with similar products or services (and often similar prices).

Brand equity: The value (in terms of money and loyalty) that a brand builds with its stakeholders over time, either positive or negative.

- Emotional: When people encounter advertising or have a direct interaction with a brand (by investigating or using the product or service), they necessarily have an emotional reaction.
- Cultural: People who regularly interact with the brand as clients eventually form a cultural opinion about the brand and organization. They form opinions about the values, client service philosophy, and spirit of the organization.

All of these brand interactions converge to form an overall impression of the brand. They also create expectations, also known as a "brand promise." (This brand promise is closely related to the unique value proposition discussed earlier.) A successful brand, and successful organization, is able to deliver on the brand promise that has been created through this series of tangible and intangible associations. (See Exhibit 31.1 for some additional branding definitions.)

The Importance of a Strong Brand

Organizations that have been able to build strong, well-differentiated brands have consistently proven to have higher levels of profit and client satisfaction (Interbrand, 2004). Independent research also shows that both clients and the general public are able to cite key brand attributes—that is, the ones that the organization wants them to repeat. This all leads to an accumulation of positive brand equity that can be used to gain market share, overcome mistakes, and expand into new markets.

Here are some of the main benefits of a strong brand:

- Creates meaning beyond the features of the product or service. Think Nike. Marketing communications for Nike rarely focus on running shoes. They focus on the competitive spirit that exists in all athletes, even armchair athletes.

- Reduces the need to compete on price. Think Starbucks. No major chain of coffee houses has more expensive products than Starbucks . . . , and loyal clients could not care less. Paying five dollars for a latté is worth the "Starbucks experience." Consumers pay a premium to have a gourmet coffee prepared by a "barista" in an impeccably clean, well-designed, and extensively merchandised space (Interbrand, 2004).

- Builds a relationship based on meeting expectations. Think McDonald's. The fast food giant built an empire on replicating the food, as well as the environment and customer service experience, in every location. You know what to expect, and you get it.

- Enhances the efficiency of marketing and sales efforts. Think Toyota. Toyota's cars and trucks are so well built and reliable that people take it for granted. When the company introduces a new vehicle to its line-up, it instantly becomes a big seller purely on reputation. Advertising and marketing expenses can be significantly reduced.

- Creates and enhances loyalty. Think Apple Computers or Harley-Davidson. People who buy these products join a community.

- Helps mask weaknesses and aids recovery. Think Tylenol. When some-one tampered with Tylenol bottles (resulting in a number of deaths), the company voluntarily recalled its entire product line. Tylenol was a trusted medication and a leading brand. By handling the crisis with integrity, Tylenol increased its market share against other leading brands.

- Builds a barrier to competition. Think Amazon.com. This original dot-com player redefined the book-selling industry with a new business model and new technology. It continues to innovate by customizing the online experience for every client. In fact, it is so far ahead of the pack that there have been no new entrants to the market in years.

- Extendible to products in new categories. Think Nike or Disney. Both established a solid brand based on a core competency. After they domi-nated their respective markets, they extended their brands into related businesses with stunning success.

It Is All About the Experience

Branding is much more than a cute tagline, a flashy TV ad, or even a quality product or service. It is about aligning a compelling brand promise with an experience that lives up to the billing. Few organizations are able to master both sides of this equation. That is why most brands fail.

The most common reason for failure is disconnection between the stated value proposition and the actual experience. How many times have you tried out a new product or service based on an implicit or explicit promise delivered through marketing communications, only to be disappointed with the end result? Many brands do not even get this far. They do not even get noticed because they fail to capture the public's imagination with fragmented and inconsistent messaging.

They need to follow a simple, two-step process: (1) communicate the brand promise to the target audience in a compelling way, and (2) deliver on that promise with a satisfying client experience.

The Concept of Authenticity

Most brands fail because of a disconnect between the brand promise and the actual client experience. This misalignment can be masked by confusing sales practices or products or services that are good enough to get by. In other cases, unscrupulous companies do not care if the brand promise is false as long as they get their money up front.

Fortunately, for reputable organizations, clients are becoming both more demanding and more savvy. They do research. They consult consumer Web sites. They talk to friends. Most consumers today can spot a value proposition that sounds too good to be true. And if they have a bad experience, they not only will take their business elsewhere, they will tell everyone they know about the experience.

This is where the key concept of brand authenticity comes in. The most powerful brands are the most authentic, as defined by the following criteria:

- Consumers can trust them to follow through on their brand promise.
- Consumers can believe the information they present through all media.
- Consumers can get a quick and accurate answer to their questions.
- A consumer who has a problem can expect to be listened to, treated respectfully, and have the issue resolved in a mutually agreed-on time frame.
- They are genuinely interested in meeting consumer needs and expectations.

Driving a Strong Brand

Outstanding brands are not the sole domain of international organizations with millions of marketing dollars at their disposal. You can probably think of a local or regional organization in your area that has an outstanding reputation for quality and service. Do not worry about the size of your organization or the nature of your business. Focus on the key concepts, and try some of the following best practices.

Champion the UVP. A clear, concise, and consistent UVP is essential to a strong brand and successful marketing communications. To be truly effective, the UVP should be understood and repeatable by every member of an organization. You can play a key role in making the UVP visible by using every medium and opportunity to discuss and promote it. "Brand ambassadors" are created when members of an organization truly understand and embrace the UVP.

Get Involved in the Value Chain. An organization is made up of departments and individuals with specialized skills. Each unit is a link in a chain starting with the development of products and services through to the front lines of sales and service. This value chain is only as strong as its weakest link. As the keepers of the UVP, marketing communicators should seek to understand and strengthen each link in the chain, so that the best possible value is delivered to clients. This means staying in regular contact with people throughout the organization.

Live the Brand. Branding is not solely the responsibility of the marketing department. An organization's brand resides in its people and their ability to deliver value to clients every day. The brand is literally everybody's business. The challenge is getting everyone to live the brand as they interact with both internal clients (their colleagues) and external clients. In order to act appropriately, employees must understand the brand promise and brand attributes and be offered concrete examples of brand-centered behavior. Each manager and staff member should be encouraged to think about how they can exhibit values consistent with the brand in their work unit.

Case in Point: Living the Brand
The Co-operators is the largest multiline insurance company in Canada. In 2004, the company launched a major brand revitalization campaign with a media plan that included national television ads. Two months prior to the media launch, an internal launch of the campaign was conducted for staff and key stakeholders including board members. Launch events were held across the country featuring senior management, marketing communications staff who worked on the campaign, and special guests who spoke to the power of branding. Staff were treated to popcorn and soda in a movie theater atmosphere and enjoyed a multimedia presentation, including:

- An introduction by the CEO or a senior vice president
- Presentations on "Branding 101" and "The Power of Branding"
- A behind-the-scenes video on the creation and filming of the new TV ads
- A primer on the company's UVP and key brand attributes
- Debut of the new TV and print ads
- A Q&A discussion on how staff could live the brand

Each manager received a specially designed folder that included the branding presentations, background information, media schedules, and a video/DVD of the new TV ads. Also included was a discussion guide for use with staff on how they could live the brand in their jobs every day. The ideas from these sessions were collected and posted on the company's intranet.

By involving staff well in advance, they fully understood and supported the brand campaign when it was publicly launched two months later. The Co-operators created a whole company of brand ambassadors who added value to the launch and felt pride in their organization.

A Note About Measurement

Measurement is an essential part of any marketing communications program. A sound (that is, statistically valid) measurement program has the dual benefits of providing valuable data on how to improve your UVP and the communications program you use to promote it and validating the investment of human and financial resources in the marketing communication program.

In the past few years, many quantitative and qualitative methods of measuring marketing communications have been proven to be accurate and affordable. Depending on your organization's goals and information needs, there are techniques to measure:

- Brand awareness and brand attributes
- The direct impact of marketing communications efforts on sales
- Loyalty of current clients and the factors that would cause them to defect
- The level of employee engagement: the extent to which employees say positive things about the organization, want to stay with the organization, and strive to do more than is required by their jobs

These measures and many others can provide vital insight and professional credibility.

A FINAL WORD

In the end, we are all selling something. We want our target clients to take some action, usually with a financial outcome. Organizations have business objectives; marketing communications must help achieve those objectives by producing measurable results with the resources they have invested in communications. Our leaders expect nothing less, and we should encourage these expectations.

There is a big difference between working "in" the business and working "on" the business. Communicators who work in the business are simply an expense, that is, corporate overhead. You are a spectator. Assets that are viewed as nonproductive are easily discarded.

If you are working "on" the business, you are a partner in the larger enterprise. You understand the organization's goals, and your plans and activities are specifically tied to achieving those goals. You are a player.

References

Dundon, E. (2002). *The seeds of innovation: Cultivating the synergy that fosters new ideas.* New York: Amacom.

Interbrand. (2004, August 2). Special report: Cult brands. *BusinessWeek, 64.*

Interbrand. (2005, August 1). Global brands. *BusinessWeek,* 86.

Ries, A., & Ries, L. (2002). *The 22 immutable laws of branding.* New York: HarperCollins.

CHAPTER THIRTY-TWO

Building and Sustaining a Dynamic Corporate Reputation

Alison Rankin Frost

The concept of corporate reputation has become increasingly important in recent years with more and more boards recognizing that a sound reputation is required to achieve business success. Consequently, the discipline of reputation management as part of a business's communications strategy has grown as rapidly in size and importance.

The way an organization manages its reputation can determine its ability to attain and sustain competitive advantage. In an environment where there is increasing competition, greater corporate responsibility, higher media exposure, and stronger customer awareness and expectations, businesses and organizations must be aware of their reputation, must understand the motivations of their different stakeholders, and must be able to adapt to take advantage of opportunities.

CORPORATE REPUTATION: WHAT IS IT?

First impressions count, but it is the long-term relationship that is important in corporate reputation.

We make immediate assumptions about people based on how they look, how they speak, or what they say. We use our past contacts and experiences as reference points to associate new contacts with brands. We can then make assumptions about them. For example, you see a youth running down a street. Is he

414

Exhibit 32.1. What Corporate Reputation Is

What people say (for example, word of mouth, print, or Web)

What they think (for example, assumptions, prejudice, hope)

How they feel (for example, emotions)

How they behave (for example, interaction with product or service)

---

running away from a crime? Is he running to save someone from an unforeseen accident? Or is he late for school or work? We make assumptions of his guilt or innocence based on the reputation of the group known as "young men." It may or may not be fair. Alternately we see a young mother with a stroller and a toddler. We think, "Ahh. How sweet." It may be accurate, or it may not be.

We make immediate assumptions about a business based on first contact. Visual image is important, so businesses spend time and money on getting first impressions right. They use pictures, colors, language, and content to associate themselves with similar brands so that they may get an immediate reputation association (we like the others so we will like them). Products need to live up to this image too. Customer service is also important. Lots of time, energy, and money are spent on getting these things right.

Sometimes things are done differently in each part of the business. The marketing department might focus on special offers to customers. Human resources could be focusing on personal development for staff. And the investor relations department may be focusing on protecting the business from analysts' commentaries simply because the sector in which the business operates has fallen out of favor.

Corporate reputation is a strange chameleon. At its core, it must be consistent, yet to stakeholder groups it must be adaptable. Reputation is both an objective and an outcome: we desire a specific reputation and plan how to achieve it; we must know how we are perceived now in order to initiate a change.

Corporate reputation is what stakeholders think or feel about the business or organization (see Exhibit 32.1). Sometimes they can externalize their thoughts and feelings and give tangible reasons for the positive or negative reputation. Sometimes they cannot: "I just know I like it" or "I just don't trust them." The nature of the corporate reputation affects stakeholder behavior.

WHY IS CORPORATE REPUTATION IMPORTANT?

The financial institutions of the City of London used to operate on the principle that one's word is one's bond, and their reputation for being true to their word was sufficient to seal the deal on word alone. Over time, this principle eroded; it has been replaced with a vast array of rules, legal documentation, and supervisory bodies.

The growth of white-collar crime and scandals, such as at WorldCom, has undermined the reputation of professionals in many industries. Shell got its oil reserves wrong and took action, but it has since had to restructure. How badly has the whole incident damaged its reputation not just with investors but also with regulators or present and potential employees? Arthur Andersen completely disappeared because of its handling of the Enron situation. Shareholders and regulators are watching companies more closely than ever before and have introduced a raft of regulations and legislation to protect us from corrupt, dishonest, or incompetent management.

So too has the growth of the Internet contributed to a fall in reputation of scientists and medical professionals, not because they are being dishonest but because laypeople have discovered that there is more than one scientific truth. The Internet has made it possible for all of us to research the many different ideas and best practices for our treatments. Even global warming, AIDS, and genetically modified foods have scientists supporting the many different views on each of these subjects, all with fully researched scientific evidence.

Politicians are forfeiting our trust and provoking cynicism and apathy by appearing to be economical with the truth. This is reflected in poor voter turnout.

Multiple financial, food, health care, and industrial scandals have made the issue of reputation more urgent and central in contemporary societies. As more knowledge and information are made accessible for individuals, we now know more than our parents and grandparents knew in their entire lives.

This flow of information has made us question and be skeptical about things we once took for granted. Many examples can be mentioned, including the Enron lawsuit, the U.S. telecom fraud, Global Crossing, Tyco, Xerox, Qwest, and Merrill Lynch.

The actions of these businesses are affecting the reputations of others who deal with them or operate in the same markets. As a result, the concepts of corporate reputation and reputation management are becoming important and valuable intangible assets at every company's foundation. Stakeholders will consider the reputation of an organization before they choose to interact with it.

REPUTATION: THE BASICS

The basic principles of corporate reputation (see Exhibit 32.2) provide a framework for developing a reputation management strategy.

Exhibit 32.2. Basic Principles of Corporate Reputation

- Every business or organization has a reputation. You cannot choose not to have one.

- It is not enough simply for a reputation to be good. It is more important that the reputation is clear. Clarity leads to strength and resilience.

- Reputation is not an offer of one-size-fits-all stakeholders.

- Corporate reputation needs to have a core set of values or principles.

- Reputation cannot be created overnight (but an image can).

- Reputation can be destroyed overnight (but only if it was not resilient in the first place).

- Reputation can be destroyed over a long period of time too.

- Reputation resilience is the reservoir of goodwill.

- Managing reputation is a process based on analysis of information and facts. Never just guess.

Every Business or Organization Has a Reputation

A business cannot choose not to have a reputation. Even if it tried to do this by not having a Web site or not speaking to the media, it would still have a reputation—in this case, a reputation for being secretive. If it chose not to interact with customers, it would have none. In these scenarios, the organization has a reputation but probably not the one it wants.

It Is Not Enough Simply for a Reputation to Be Good

It is more important that the reputation is clear because clarity leads to strength and resilience. Stakeholders should know what they are getting. For example, if an employee is expecting to join a low-pay, low-esteem company, he will not be surprised once he begins work. There will be no dissonance. However, if he was expecting fun and good pay, he will be disappointed. Management consulting firms have a reputation for hiring the best, working them hard, and then spitting them out if they do not continue to make the grade. Nevertheless, people are thrilled and proud to be chosen for this chew-'em-up, spit-'em-out world. We have no-frills airlines that sell cheap tickets at the airplane door followed by a fight for the seat you want. Yet passengers are happy about this because it is clear to them that is what they are buying.

Your business does not have to be the best, brightest, and nicest. It does not have to be the cheapest, cleanest, and kindest. You just have to make sure that what you promise, you deliver on. Be clear, and then there are no disappointments. Your reputation will remain intact.

Reputation Is Not an Offer of One-Size-Fits-All Stakeholders

Stakeholders have different wants, needs, and expectations. An investor wants good financial performance. Staff need to feel pride in their job. Customers expect the product or service they have been promised. Regulators expect compliance with their standards.

There are many different stakeholder groups and subgroups. How many and what they are will depend on your organization and the nature of its business. In managing corporate reputation, it is vital to know what these stakeholder groups are and what their motivations are for interacting with your organization.

It helps to think of your stakeholders as people who may fall into a number of stakeholder groups. In doing this, there is less chance of becoming blinkered by focusing on the stakeholder group to the detriment of seeing each stakeholder as an individual.

Corporate Reputation Needs a Core Set of Values or Principles

Stakeholders are a tricky bunch. They have a tendency not to stick to their stakeholder group. For example, your employees can be customers or shareholders. A journalist may also be a customer. And an investor's mother (or, worse, a hedge fund manager's mother) could have had a bad experience with your business. The point is that they will notice if you try to have one reputation with one group and a different reputation with another. It is hard to be "ruthless" with shareholders and "caring" with customers.

Stakeholders move between groups and often are simultaneously in several stakeholder groups. (For example, I have worked for a chocolate company while simultaneously being a consumer of its products.)

A set of core values or principles will provide a focus for all the organization's activities. They must be carefully developed, based on research and involvement of all stakeholder groupings, and will be the heart of the reputation management strategy. It is important that the expression of these values through corporate and individual behaviors is consistent.

Reputation Cannot Be Created Overnight (But an Image Can)

Imagine you are growing a field of corn. Everyone knows it is a field of corn and will be expecting corncobs. How big and tasty each ear of corn will be once picked and eaten will depend on which part of the field the seed fell into, how the corn plant was tended, and whether the corn was cooked properly.

Now translate this to creating a new business. Let us say it is a university. Stakeholders will be academic and nonacademic staff, students, donors, businesses (which may have an interest in research or in employing graduates), university regulators, alumni, and others.

The first influence on reputation of your university (the seed) will be the reputation of the sector (the field). What is the reputation of universities as a whole? Reputation can be influenced by the image chosen for your university (perhaps, top-flight academic wanting the best students). The image can be created and communicated from inception of the business.

Next, the reputation is tended and nurtured. In reality, this is a never-ending process when it comes to managing corporate reputation. It is this process that creates a reputation to distinguish your university from the rest of the pack. Image alone is not reputation; it is simply an expression of how the organization wishes to be seen by its stakeholders. Image needs to be backed up by the performance of the organization against the subliminal promises made by the image.

Reputation Can Be Destroyed Overnight

Shortly after Enron filed for bankruptcy in November 2001, a few employees of Arthur Andersen (its auditors) in Texas were discovered shredding documents. By March 2002 Arthur Andersen realized that there was no hope of the firm's surviving when it was indicted on criminal charges. Ten years earlier in the United Kingdom, Gerald Ratner, speaking to the Institute of Directors, joked that his Ratner's High Street chain "sold a pair of earrings for under a pound, which is cheaper than a prawn sandwich from Marks & Spencer, but probably wouldn't last as long" (Wilson, 2003, para. 8). This verbal gaffe instantly wiped an estimated 500 million pounds sterling from the stock price, and the stores had to be rebranded.

Reputation Can Be Destroyed over a Long Period of Time

Corporate reputation may be vulnerable to sudden impacts, but what is far more insidious (and far more common) is the gradual and imperceptible hits on corporate reputation. These little changes cause gradual and terminal decline—for example, failure to keep up with fashions, failure to build relationships with financiers, failure to act promptly to poor customer service.

We do not really notice the organizations or companies that slip away quietly over a long period of time. However, we do notice the ones that seem poorly and then suffer a series of mild reputation impacts, with a final nail in the coffin being an incident or event that may not have brought down a business with a stronger, more resilient reputation.

A number of years ago, I worked on a corporate takeover. The hostile takeover came out of the blue; the company had not been expecting it. It had grown from a family business to a large, multinational one, but the family still ran it as its own without taking account of the shareholders. Management had become complacent, the product was not keeping up to date, and everything generally was getting a bit sloppy. In the end, they lost their takeover battle because the company bosses had failed to build relationships with their investors. The investors wanted management they could work with.

Reputation Resilience Is the Reservoir of Goodwill

Effective management of reputation leads to greater resilience. If you invest in it, it will become stronger and able to resist either self-inflicted impacts or external impacts.

In October 2003, Matt Barrett, chief executive of Barclays Bank, was giving evidence to the U.K. Parliament's Treasury Select Committee. He was being questioned about interest rates on credit cards. Members of Parliament took a dim view of the fact that interest rates on Barclaycard had not fallen in line with U.K. interest rates. Barrett happened to mention that borrowing money on a credit card was not the wisest way to borrow. His comments were taken out of context and reported in the media as, "I do not borrow on credit cards." This comment could have had the same effect as Gerald Ratner's had had on his company, but Barclays had invested in its reservoir of goodwill over many years.

Think of a reservoir, but instead of being filled with water, it is filled with consistent brand experiences, positive interactions, and clear messages (Figure 32.1). Reservoirs are designed to store water and to enable a consistent supply. In a similar way, the reservoir of goodwill stores all the positive thoughts, feelings, beliefs and past experiences of the organization for times when the stock price goes down, or a member of staff is rude to a customer, or there is a crisis.

When something goes wrong and the media are all over your organization, you do not want your mother to think you work for a useless or incompetent business. Similarly, your stakeholders' mothers will write it off as a blip in an otherwise exemplary organization—an organization that does what it says it is going to do, in the way it says it is going to do it.

The reservoir of goodwill is more than simply ensuring that your business has positive media coverage, places good advertising, and sponsors the right sort of events.

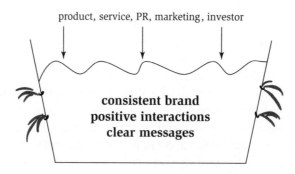

Figure 32.1. The Reservoir of Goodwill

Managing Reputation Is a Process Based on Analysis of Information and Facts

Many of us work for organizations that we did not choose to join. Perhaps there was a merger, acquisition, or restructuring. It is not uncommon for business to reorganize every eighteen months. I have even known people who have gone through a selection process and on the day they started work, the company had changed its name and the job they joined for had changed to something different.

It is not often that any of us would be starting a business from scratch and have a clean sheet to work with on developing corporate reputation. Usually we inherit a reputation and have to work with what we have.

Managing reputation is complex because it takes in all aspects of operations and all relationships with stakeholders. No one person in a company is called the head of reputation; that would be too simple. Management of corporate reputation requires great diplomatic skill in telling those responsible for specific stakeholder relationships that reputation of the whole business may not necessarily benefit from their great plan to sponsor the World Multi-Colored Hula Hooping Championship. Sometimes what seems to work for one stakeholder grouping does not work for others and leads to dissonance in the expression of the organization as a whole.

Arm yourself with facts and information about the current reputation of the business and the reputation of the sector in which it operates. Analysis of competitors' reputations is good too. Make sure that the stakeholder groups are segmented down to their subgroups. It is always useful to see how consistent or how different reputation is from group to group.

Guessing is useless and valueless. If you are serious about managing corporate reputation, there is a process to follow and facts to be gathered and analyzed.

MANAGING CORPORATE REPUTATION

There are five key stages to building and sustaining the reputation you want for your organization (not just the one that happens to be the current reputation).

Do Your Research

Find out what your current reputation is, and work out what you want your reputation to be. Obviously this will involve a number of different aspects of the business. You need to build a 360-degree view. How close is your reputation to what you want it to be? Where are the gaps? Where are the surprises?

Figure 32.2 shows an analysis of the reputation of a long-established business. Its customers are other businesses. In the diagram you can see the attitudes of five stakeholders to the organization. The comments in the speech bubbles are actual quotations and are representative of the views in each of the stakeholder

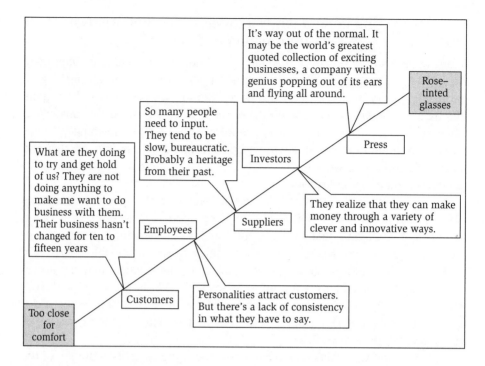

Figure 32.2. A Corporate Reputation Spectrum

groupings. The customers are closest to the business. They have close relationships with their account managers and feel that they know the business well. They do not see any changes. As we go along the line, we move toward the more distant relationships and the higher reputation.

In the case of this organization, the reputation is not consistent and therefore is at risk. There are no common core values and behaviors that bind the brand and reputation together.

Analyze the Relationships with Stakeholders

All stakeholders are not equal. Understanding the different stakeholders and their relationships with the organization is the next step. For example, you may find that there is one person who can decide the fate of your organization. It could be the regulator in a regulated industry, a major donor to a charity, a customer who buys 80 percent of your turnover, or a key manager who influences part of your workforce. Or it might be a large number of people: members of a pressure group or a segment of your customers, for example.

Know what influences the stakeholders, and understand what motivates them to deal with your organization. Then work out where the strengths and weaknesses are. Be aware too that if your organization is a multinational company, the culture of the different countries and regions in which it operates will be different. This will add a further dimension to the analysis of stakeholder relationships.

Coordinate Management of Communications

Stakeholders are exposed to a number of influences. For example, employees are not just influenced by employee communications; they are also influenced by what they read in the newspaper or see on television and by what customers say to them. Consumers (customers or members) will be influenced by employee behaviors when they use your product or service. Investors may be concerned by legislators' decisions. Legislators will be influenced by their electorate.

Therefore, while each individual function communicates with its target audience as and when required, they need to think about how what they are communicating will have an impact on other audiences that are out of their direct control. A reputation manager will be the focal point and guardian of the outcome (the reputation). Although it is often not practical to contribute to communications for each stakeholder group, the reputation manager can provide inputs in the form of information and advice and can protect the reputation by highlighting risk factors.

Integrate Other Points of Interaction

A good communications plan is the basis of effective reputation management; it is not enough on its own. Much of corporate reputation is a result of interactions by stakeholders with the organization—for example, a telephone call, using the product or service, dealing with a regular account manager, the state of the buildings, the cleanliness of motor vehicles bearing your brand, the attitude of staff, the manufacturing process of your product. All have an impact on corporate reputation.

Marketing and communications can build and reinforce the corporate image. The various types of interactions will provide stakeholders with an experience with your organization. Will their experience match the promise made by your communications? If it does, it reinforces the strength of the brand and reputation, making your corporate reputation more resilient. If they do not match (if there is dissonance), this depletes the reservoir of goodwill and makes your organization vulnerable.

Be Adaptable

Corporate reputation is never fixed once and for all when you follow these steps. The reservoir must be monitored (researched and analyzed) and tended (by communication and other interactions) to keep it topped up and ready. The circumstances in which your business or organization operates may change: new competitors may arise, fashions may change, new technology could appear.

Ability to change so that reputation can become increasingly resilient is a skill and an art. It is certainly not a matter of good luck.

Reference

Wilson, B. (2003, October 17). Barclay chief's gaffe recalls Ratner howler. *BBC News.* Retrieved July 20, 2005, from http://newswww.bbc.net.uk/1/hi/ business/3199822.stm.

CHAPTER THIRTY-THREE

Communication for Customer Satisfaction and Loyalty

Jeff Schmidt

Communicators are not the best explorers. There is something in the nature of the profession, and the temperament of the people who choose it, that gravitates to the things in business life that are safe, certain, and clear. We often find ourselves in the role of steady counselor, clarifiers of language or sorters of strategy, so perhaps personal risk taking becomes a natural victim, a characteristic seen as counter to our success.

Yet all around us, people are talking about the new world of business: the convergence of technology, the transparency of the enterprise, boundaryless decision making, globalization, acceleration, risk, growth, and change.

To keep up with all of these changes, this new world of business demands new leaders: strong men and women behind the wheel, visionaries who can map out the right route while also keeping the car under control. Their fuel is new ideas, better ways of working, and more efficient processes and practices. Their engine? Customers.

No matter how the business world changes, without satisfied customers lining up to buy what our companies sell, every communicator should be prepared to visit the hairdresser and dust off the resumé or CV. It is a simple equation, but one that begs a fundamental question be asked of our profession: If customers will always be the engine of the business world, then why do corporate communicators ignore them?

Perhaps you do not ignore them but have purposely decided to leave them in the care of your marketing group, or your sales team, or even your senior leaders and business executives. It is the safe approach, the certain outcome, and that clarity of responsibility we seem to drift toward as communicators. If the satisfaction and loyalty of our customers provide us with jobs and careers, then we can no longer afford to remain on the outside. It is time to move from content shapers to change leaders. It is time to explore.

Customer satisfaction and loyalty are built only through strong customer relationships. This chapter provides an overview of the opportunities that exist in the customer relationship space, an argument for why you should volunteer to lead some of the needed changes, and a basic framework for creating a pragmatic plan that helps your organization achieve better results. It does not rehash basic formulas, proven vehicles, or tested methods of effective communications. It will encourage you to break new ground and explore roads where traditional communicators rarely travel.

THE NEW FRONTIER

You will find that whether a company deals primarily with enterprise customers, small and medium businesses, or consumers, strong customer relationships are the main driver of satisfaction and loyalty. To be successful, those relationships have to be built and maintained in spite of increasing competition. That means your company has to communicate regularly with both potential and existing customers, and do it effectively, over a long period of time. This is difficult and getting harder.

Building good relationships without good communications is impossible, and many of the changes in the business world also provide the potential to disrupt your company's communication flow to customers. Increased globalization means more brands and more choices for customers. New technology lowers the barriers for competitors to communicate with your installed base in a personalized way. Accelerating decision cycles means that you have less time to establish a solid rapport with all the people who might influence a purchase. The challenges are increasing, and your company has to navigate all the potential disruptions while still finding ways to compete and grow.

That is why the time is ripe for corporate communicators. These challenges for your business are opportunities for you. To be more specific, working with customers represents an opportunity for corporate communicators *to* lead, not follow. Leading projects that touch customers, improve your company's relationship with them, and drive them to spend more with you instead of the competition is a wide-open field for our profession. In the past, we have left that job to others, but helping build better customer relationships is the next important frontier for corporate communicators.

Most corporate communicators today focus on four main pillars: employee communications, executive communications, analyst relations, and media and public relations. There are variations on these themes—human resources communications, business or strategic communications, shareholder or community relations and many others—and all of these are the foundation of our profession. Over the past few decades, we have seen steady progress and solid successes serving these stakeholder groups, but it is time we added a fifth pillar: the pillar of customer communications.

Just like the four existing pillars, working with customers can take many forms. You could focus on integrating and simplifying customer communications in partnership with marketing groups. You could lead strategic initiatives that improve relationship building and directly support your sales teams. If your organization is complex and requires heavy navigation, you can serve as a coordinating team that pulls together all the tools, messages, processes, and people into one master strategy. It is important to remember that communicating with customers and helping build better relationships with them is something that is done every day at your company, but the part that is optional and needs definition is your role. The possibilities are limited only by your ability to break new ground, lead your organization, and change old ways of thinking and working.

It does represent a risk, but the rewards for exploring this new frontier are significant. You can become more relevant to the success of your business, build stronger partnerships across organizational boundaries, and lead a wider range of projects that could take your career in unforeseen directions. If you have found that executives often do not care about good corporate communications, you will find a refreshing change when you begin to work on these types of issues: senior leaders always care about keeping customers satisfied and loyal. You could also find that working to build stronger customer relationships could be the key not only to earning your permanent seat at the management table, but also to having a greater impact at every stage of your career.

UNDERSTANDING CUSTOMER SATISFACTION AND LOYALTY

Many factors contribute to overall customer satisfaction and anything can play a role—from same-day service, production capacity, competitive pricing and global delivery—to your company's brand buzz, environmental policies, community involvement, or corporate culture. Building productive, long-standing customer relationships is the most critical factor and does not depend solely on effective marketing campaigns, regular sales calls, or the latest customer relationship management system from your information technology department. It is not about generating demand, meeting quotas, building the brand, or relying on technology. Customer relationships are built during every interaction, complemented with every telephone call, strengthened with each marketing event, and usually tied together by—no one.

Most companies lack a smart strategy that is comprehensive enough to span each stage of the relationship cycle and build bridges across organizational boundaries and geographies. No one really seems to be in charge, and if they are, you will find that they often do not reach out to all the groups in your company that can help them be successful. This is the biggest gap most companies have today.

If having a solid, smart customer relationship-building strategy is a primary factor that contributes to satisfaction and loyalty, that is also the place for communicators to start their exploration. You can begin by asking a lot of questions about your company:

- If an overall relationship strategy does not exist, which specific teams have the primary responsibility for finding customers, working with them, and keeping them happy?

- How are your customers segmented, and which customers have the highest value to your company? Do you make more money from new or existing customers? What resources are focused on those customers versus other segments? Which segment is your company targeting for growth in the next few years?

- What other teams already support customer relationship building, and what role do they play? What tools do they provide, or what processes do they manage?

- What is the most effective set of current activities being used for building relationships? Where are the biggest gaps? What has been effective in the past but is no longer being done?

- How often do face-to-face interactions with customers take place? Who manages them? What information do you gather from those sessions, and who manages the collection and dissemination of it? What insights are pulled from the information and communicated?

- How do things fit together today? Is it loosely coupled and left to the end user to sort it all out, or is it seamlessly integrated and efficient?

- How do you measure satisfaction and loyalty? Who communicates these measurements to all the relevant groups in your company?

These are questions that should provide a solid starting point for further discoveries about how customer relationships are built in your company, but a picture should also start to emerge about cracks in the wall, areas of opportunity where you could add value and apply your skills. Do not limit your thinking at this stage or get into the habit of saying, "That's not what a corporate communications team should be doing." Think of customer relationships as the engine of your business. Everyone has a responsibility for making that engine run. Everyone can contribute to creating a better experience for customers and improving their satisfaction. Start capturing all of the strengths, weaknesses, and ideas you uncover, and worry about the full solutions once you learn more and have spent some time exploring.

FIVE FUNDAMENTALS OF CUSTOMER COMMUNICATIONS

As you work through this discovery phase, keep in mind a few fundamentals about good customer communications. Relationships are built on the foundation of solid communications, and you should evaluate how well your company performs in each area. Those five fundamentals are consistency, applicability, visibility, clarity, and brevity.

Consistency

Consistency in communications is almost a cliché. Yet it is one of the most poorly executed activities in many organizations, particularly in how companies communicate to their customers. This is perhaps the largest area of opportunity for corporate communications to begin leading and worth a lot of exploration. Three ideas are:

- Unifying content and messages across organizational boundaries by identifying where breakdowns are occurring and putting simple processes in place to fix them.

- Leading a prioritization project where ongoing communications to a pilot group of your highest-value customers is tightly controlled across all teams for twelve months to ensure consistency. Share the lessons with senior management, marketing, and sales.

- Measuring the understanding of messages and content by customer-facing employees and comparing the results across different teams that are communicating with the same customers.

Applicability

Another fundamental of good customer communications is applicability. That includes timing, delivery mechanisms, and how the messages fit with the needs of potential or existing customers. A lot of this work is traditionally handled by marketing teams, but there is still an opportunity for corporate communicators to initiate a wide range of projects that add value. To be applicable, you have to understand your customers and uncover the things that are most important to them—for example:

- Do you fully use the research of your analyst relations function by sharing customer buying considerations, market trends, and competitive dynamics with your relevant internal teams? Creating a simple strategy to do this could have a big return on investment.

- Are your customer references up to date and covering your whole port-folio? Are they effectively communicated to your sales teams and being used regularly? Evaluating the use and effectiveness of customer refer-ences can help determine if some of your most fundamental sales tools remain applicable to the changing dynamics of your market and most important customers.

Visibility

Visibility is being active and exerting the effort required to be creative and cap-turing mind share at every opportunity. Usually this means executing well on a comprehensive, cross-functional strategy. You should:

- Explore your company's relationship-building strategy. Is it end-to-end, and does it include all the corporate communications stakeholder groups? Visibility can be generated through the press, the analyst com-munity, with executive keynote speeches, through community activism, and with employee ambassadors.

- Analyze the marketing portfolio. Where are the gaps that corporate communications could fill? What are the reach and effectiveness of your company's marketing efforts, and how can you supplement those efforts with your tool kit or stakeholder groups? The marketing partnership will remain essential throughout your work with customers.

- Understand the sales tool kit. Where are the most powerful tools? Are they being used consistently in each of your territories and by your teams? Where are the biggest gaps? What tools need to be more effective? Some basic employee research with your sales force could uncover many projects worth your time and energy.

Clarity

Another basic tenet of good communications is clarity. Too often the basic mes-sages of your company get lost in all the noise, the technical detail, the negoti-ation, or the jargon, and that is when you start losing customers. Be clear about essential points, and make sure they are understood. A couple of areas to inves-tigate are:

- Clarity over time and location. Is your company being clear with all of its audiences? Do nontraditional audiences such as analysts, employees, and the press fundamentally understand the value of your company's portfolio? Are messages clear over time and across locations? Do employees hear the same messages as customers? A simple audit that asks questions such as these can help determine if you are contributing to clear communication.

- Clarity about actions. Does your company's communication to customers contain a clear call to action? Are those actions being completed? A small project that asks both of those questions and analyzes root causes behind the answers might be worthwhile for your corporate communications team

Brevity

A critically important characteristic of customer communications is brevity. It is vital to get to the point fast. This does not mean that a longer, more in-depth interaction cannot occur, but it does mean that most communications have to be clear, with quickly digested bits of information. A couple of considerations:

- Are your messages able to be read and understood in less than fifteen or twenty seconds? Do they have an impact in this time frame? One idea is to volunteer to measure the retention of messages to customer groups and suggest ways to improve that retention.
- Are sales managers coaching their teams to be brief and clear? Offering some ongoing coaching or basic training from the corporate communications team could have an immediate impact. Also, consider teaching the basic skills behind public relations spokesperson training or effective speechwriting to small groups of sales employees.

Using the Fundamentals

Overall, these five areas are just starting points. They should open the door to further exploration of the value that you can add in your company and in your current situation. Since there is no magic formula, it is this process of discovery and engagement that is critical. Whether you are a senior communicator or a newcomer, it is up to you to judge which boundaries you are going to push, but you have seen that this is a journey where taking the first step is possible. Making up your mind and confidently taking that first step will be what is important. Just remember that this can be explored within your current remit, with your existing skills, and built through your established partnerships. It can be done as an exploratory pilot, a formal part of your communications plan, or by seizing the initiative and offering your services to customer-facing teams. Only you know the best way to proceed. Every organization has opportunities for leadership at any level, and it is the individual leader who creates new value, initiates breakthrough projects, and drives change.

CHANGE LEADERSHIP AND WHAT IT MEANS FOR YOU

The new role of the corporate communicator should be as a leader of change. Too often in the past, the communications function has been relegated to the role of supporting change. Opportunities exist for the communications team to lead change by helping other functions, serving as navigators and integrators in their companies, or breaking out on their own. This allows communicators to minimize risk by working within a predefined set of boundaries, probably using their current skills, resources, and remit. For those ready to take the leap, other opportunities may also exist.

Once you have finished the discovery phase and better understand what your company does today, there is a good chance you came up with a few ideas for strategic initiatives that would improve relationship building and help you directly support your sales teams and customers. What can you do with those ideas, and how do you take them forward? A simple five-step process, the DRIVE methodology, can help you begin charting a course for the future:

Discover and design

Review and rework

Implement and innovate

Validate and verify

Evaluate and educate

In a nutshell, DRIVE is a process for creating and executing simple plans. It is a commonsense approach that combines the fundamentals of strategy creation with some basics from change management.

The discover and design phase requires uncovering the opportunities for change that exist in your organization, examining those for relevance and impact and then designing the basics of a strategy that addresses those opportunities. This is the exploration and thinking covered in earlier parts of this chapter, followed by putting on paper the basics of a plan. In designing your plan, the key is simplicity. You should have no more than three goals, set out in simple language. Start with fewer deliverables and add more if needed, and your measurements should be clear. A good plan can be understood at a glance; no one should need to have you explain it.

The review and rework phase covers the review of your basic strategy to make sure it meets the needs of your organization and addresses the challenges you have discovered. For areas new to you, it is also the logical step for tapping the expertise of others, challenging any assumptions that you have made, and finding new allies who can help guide your work. Rework your plans based on what you hear during this phase.

The implement and innovate phase remains the most critical. It is often better to act fast rather than wait for all the parts to come together seamlessly. By taking action, you will learn more about what works, where roadblocks exist, and where you need to make changes. This should be viewed as an "innovate as you go" step.

The validate and verify phase often gets skipped once implementation begins. It requires consistently validating assumptions to ensure that situations have not changed. Combine this with regular verification that activities are on track, you have ongoing support, and the fundamental goals are actually being achieved.

The evaluate and educate phase calls for an accurate assessment of your progress and a strong communication flow back to key stakeholders. This seems basic, but the repeated education of participants and leaders provides both momentum and ongoing proof of your strong leadership, both essential requirements for success.

APPLYING DRIVE TO CUSTOMER RELATIONSHIP BUILDING

Specific application of this process will vary widely depending on your situation, but there are probably three main areas where it can be applied within your company: organizational navigation, knowledge building, and customer value measurements.

Helping your sales teams navigate the complexities of your organization maximizes productivity. This helps them increase the time spent building good customer relationships instead of searching the organization for information or support.

During the discovery phase, you should explore what keeps your sales teams busy and away from serving your customers. Start with a basic analysis of how salespeople spend their time, uncovered through interviews or surveys; once this is understood, it is simply a matter of putting a plan in place that reduces the complexity and distractions that are pulling your teams away from their primary charter. Some potential goals you could consider are:

- Help the sales team find the right subject matter experts within forty-eight hours.
- Put all tools that assist relationship building into one repository, and fill any major gaps.
- Evaluate all current relationship-building activities, and centralize them into one program.
- Document all complex processes where sales teams spend time, and work with owners to simplify those processes.

Building unique knowledge is another area of opportunity. Are you helping different teams understand your customers? Is your company capturing important information about customers, and is that information being reused? Most organizations have poor structures for building, retaining, and reusing knowledge about customers, and this is an opportunity for corporate communicators to position themselves as experts with valuable knowledge about customers and their priorities. Examples of goals are:

- Create a central repository of customer intelligence that all functions and teams can use.

- Design a press roundtable that builds better knowledge about the company's customers, its market challenges, and the successes you have seen working together.

- Capture employee ideas for building stronger customer knowledge, and have management recognize the best ideas every quarter.

Measuring customer value is another way to apply the DRIVE process and prompt changes that increase service and satisfaction. Does your company measure value by revenue and margin, by the volume of units purchased, or through repeat buying? Are firm metrics in place? Who owns them, and how are they communicated to the entire organization? All of these are areas where the skills of the corporate communications team can come in useful. Some potential goals are:

- Ensure quality and customer survey data are widely understood across every part of the organization and that every employee's role for improving scores is clear.

- Recommend improvements for measuring market growth or total available market by integrating all major internal and external data sources and compare with analyst reports.

- Develop a measurement for calculating lifetime customer value, and establish it as a common metric for all customer relationship-building work.

All of these are ideas that may or may not apply to your individual situation, but all are worth exploring for the potential value they could add to your organization. Using the steps of the DRIVE process, you can uncover new projects in these areas, put a plan in place, and deliver solid results.

WHAT THE FUTURE HOLDS

The future for communicators remains bright. With our current skill sets, we can increase customer satisfaction and build loyalty. We can help target the customer of highest value to the firm, understand what experiences the company provides to these customers, and build better relationships with them over time. It is this customer centricity, with everyone focused on the needs and requirements of good customer relationships, that will be the new differentiator for companies. Those able to mobilize all of their employees to this banner will succeed while others struggle.

For customers, their overall experience with your company will determine their buying behaviors. This includes how you communicate with them at every interaction point. That is why it is increasingly important for corporate communicators to play a role in building this experience and increasing satisfaction. It does not matter whether you build this experience directly or in support of other teams. Communicators just need to show that they are linked to customers, supporting the revenue growth of their companies, and building value for new parts of their organizations. Communicators are an essential part of the team and have the opportunity to prove it in new ways.

This means a new value proposition for corporate communications. It requires new ways of thinking and practicing the function. It will require stretching and discomfort, growth and strength, leadership, change, and willpower. It will mean that communicators must become explorers and find the new frontiers. They are definitely out there, waiting for us to arrive.

CHAPTER THIRTY-FOUR

Measuring Marketing Communication

Merry Elrick

If we are going to measure marketing communication, we should begin by defining the term. Most people in the business think of marketing communication as synonymous with integrated marketing communication (IMC), a concept that began to take hold in the United States in the late 1980s. There are probably as many definitions of IMC as communicators who practice it.

My definition is that it is a communication whole that is greater than the sum of its parts by virtue of strategic planning, which is based on knowledge gleaned from an information-rich database.

IMC is relatively easy to achieve on the superficial level—what I call fashion coordination. Your ensemble works together, colors coordinate, and you are not wearing high-top sneakers with a sparkly gold evening gown. That is the equivalent of following a graphic standards manual and policing the use of your logo.

Most communicators have mastered that level, and many have achieved the level after that: integration. The watch you wear and the car you drive all say something about who you are in a unified way. In IMC, it means you are using some mix of tactics—the Internet, advertising, PR, direct mail, sales promotion, trade shows—and making them work together synergistically to deliver a cohesive message.

If you have achieved integration, you will have the problem of trying to determine what tactics in your mix are working for you and what are not. By "working," I mean helping you achieve your communication objectives. Since the very definition of *integration* implies a multipronged approach, you have a number of tactics working simultaneously. How do you know what is the most efficacious mix of tactics unless you measure? To do that, a database is usually required, which takes us to the ultimate and final level of IMC: enlightenment.

Enlightenment takes place when the food you eat, the exercise you perform, the books you read, and the thoughts you think all serve to enhance your well-being. This level of IMC involves understanding prospects and customers and communicating with them—interactively—on an individual basis, or at least in very segmented groups according to their interests. You can know what their interests are only if you have captured and maintained that information in a database.

For example, if a customer's contract or lease is about to expire, you will communicate with him differently than you would if he just signed up. Where is a particular customer in the selling cycle? Has he purchased your widgets recently? Then perhaps he needs a video demonstrating how to use the widget. If he has had your widget for years, maybe he needs to learn about your new, improved widgets.

MEASURING BY OBJECTIVES

Objectives must be quantifiable. Your metrics must show that you actually measured how well you achieved your objectives, not how many column inches of PR you generated, not how many ads you ran, not how many positive comments you got from the sales team. While those may be desired outcomes, they are seldom valid objectives for a marketing communications program. What are valid objectives?

Aligning Communication Objectives with Business Objectives

This is where communicators must step outside their departments, and often their comfort zones, to work with the C-level suite. There is really only one basic question: How can marketing communication support the organization's business goals? Those goals are almost always related in some way to bringing in revenue, adding value, or increasing profitability. Even if your organization is nonprofit, there will be some bottom-line goal, such as increasing membership.

Communicators need to align their goals with their organizations' goals, which are usually about maximizing profitability. Basically short-term profits are required to stay in business, so communications that generate leads that turn into sales are contributing to short-term cash flows. When you create lead-generating communications efficaciously, you help maximize profitability.

To build and maintain the business over time, company executives often look beyond immediate profitability, with a vision of anything from producing the highest-quality widget to providing the best customer service in the business. However the vision is articulated, it is about increasing the long-term value of the company. Communicators can contribute to that value by building long-term equity in the brand.

Contributing to Short-Term Cash Flows and Long-Term Value

How will your organization increase its profitability and value? Does it need to increase share to get more leverage in the marketplace? How much more? If it retained more customers, could it reduce costs? By how much? When you have a specific problem, think how communication can help solve it and how you can quantify your solution.

One of my clients recently determined that his company should win back lost customers. These were small-volume customers who were allowed to fade. My client determined that as a whole, these small customers amounted to significant revenue and were worth wooing back. To do that, my client made seven organizational changes to make the company more attractive to smaller customers.

To get the word out, first we took the lost customer list—by definition, old and inaccurate—and telemarketed to scrub it clean. We then created a seven-part direct mail program highlighting each change and sent it out in two-week intervals. We offered the recipient multiple ways of responding, all trackable. Before we were into our third mailing, we had lured back enough business to pay for the campaign, and then some. That was our goal: to take in more money than we spent. It was not a flashy solution, just effective.

Thinking in Financial Terms

Whether supporting short- or long-term goals, communicators need to think about everything they do in financial terms, from developing a strategic plan to crafting a creative campaign and measuring results.

If we are not contributing to profitability in some way, we have to ask ourselves why we do what we do. I once worked with the president of a Fortune 500 firm who thought advertising was just a means to gratify the egos of those who created it. You can see his point if you think about awe-inspiring Web sites or gee-whiz brochures that are designed to look cool but ultimately have no relationship to the bottom line.

Our job as communicators is to develop that relationship. If our company's goals are to increase value and profitability, then we must manage our budget as an investment and measure the return on that investment—(ROI). The bonus is that when we achieve a positive return on investment, our budget is far less likely to be cut.

GENERATING LEADS AND SALES

If your goal is to create communication that generates leads that convert to sales, then you must demonstrate that the sale is tied directly to your marketing effort. We all know that many variables influence sales, such as brand awareness campaigns that are not designed to be lead generating. But when a lead comes in that can eventually be tracked to a sale, that is tangible evidence that marketing communication is doing something right. When you know the cost of the communication that generated the lead that became a sale and you know the amount of the sale, you can begin to calculate ROI.

ROI Defined

ROI is a financial term that must be expressed as a percentage of your initial investment. To calculate ROI at its most basic level, determine gross margin— the total contribution made to your company's profits—and subtract that from the total communication investment. Here is the formula:

$$\text{ROI} = \frac{\text{Gross margin} - \text{Communication investment}}{\text{Communication investment}} = \%$$

Remember that your return is a financial gain, not an increase in awareness, market share, leads, click-throughs, or even the revenue generated from marketing communication. It is the profits generated over and above the initial investment and expressed as a percentage of the investment. While marketers rightfully measure everything from message impact to brand preference, these measures do not demonstrate ROI (Elrick, 2003).

Adhering to Consistent Standards

The ROI formula is basic and just the beginning of what you need to take into consideration to measure ROI. You should find out what the standards are for calculating ROI at your company, and then maintain those standards rigorously. You will need to apply consistent definitions of the following terms:

- *Gross margin.* This is gross income divided by net sales, expressed as a percentage. Your company's gross margin shows how much it earns, taking into account the costs it incurs for producing the products or services you sell. What costs are included in this definition at your company? Will you need to take net present value into consideration in this calculation?

- *Communication investment.* What comprises your investment? Do you include the salaries of the people in your communication department? Your overhead? Even the cost of measuring your campaign may be included.

- *Lifetime value of the customer.* Suppose your campaign brings in a new customer and that customer reorders through the years. Make sure you include that revenue in your calculation. If you do not want to wait for years to capture those data, you may estimate the lifetime value of the customer according to your company's standards.

- *Net present value (NPV).* NPV reflects the time value of money. Your marketing investment may be made over time, and your profits may come in the future. Those future profits are not as valuable as profits that come in today, so future profits must be discounted according to the value your company determines would be equitable if profits were received today. When you are calculating gross margin, if your income and expenses occur over time, you will need to convert that into NVP.

- *Sales cycle.* How long do you wait after a campaign is complete before you declare that all the data are in your database and you can calculate ROI? If you have a long sales cycle, it may take years, because you will want to make sure you get every response attributed to your campaign. This may also require vigilance in following up with salespeople and distributors.

- *ROI threshold.* Sometimes called the "hurdle rate," this is the minimum ROI level for which a company will make an investment. If your company's hurdle rate is 25 percent, then your ROI must be 25 percent or higher (Lenskold, 2003).

It is critical to go beyond these definitions, because every company has different criteria. Get to know your chief financial officer, and determine how your company calculates ROI. Then adhere to your company's standards consistently over time to ensure you are comparing apples to apples as you progress.

Gathering the Data Required to Calculate ROI

In order to measure ROI, you need to make a link between the investment and the return; that is, link your communication to the lead, then to the sale, and back to the communication again (Figure 34.1). To do that, you must create a way for the customer or prospect to respond to your communication.

Build Response Mechanisms into Everything. Every tactic in your marketing communication mix—ads, releases, brochures, direct mail, newsletters, trade shows, e-mails, Web sites—should have at least one mechanism by which

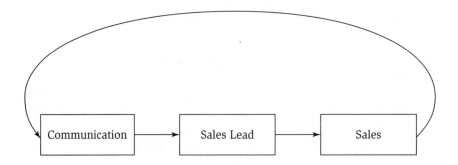

Figure 34.1. Linking the Investment and Return

customers and prospects can contact you. Each one should be coded. If you print a brochure with a unique 800 number, then you know that any calls to that number are a direct result of that brochure. If you want to drive prospects to your Web site, make a unique URL that is prominent in your brochure.

Make Capturing and Recording Systemic to Your Organization. This is sometimes the most difficult part of determining ROI: creating a process within your organization to ensure that all leads are captured, recorded, and reported. You may need to include the cost of a call center in your communications budget, with personnel to answer the telephones and record responses. You may need to work with your information technology department to add a portal with a new URL to your Web site to ensure that online responses are tracked. Or investigate some of the many companies that track click-throughs and online inquiries.

If the Internet is only part of your marketing communication strategy, you will need to make sure you capture all the leads your communication generates—online and off. This requires thinking early in the planning stages about how to capture leads. Save room in the budget for training customer service people to ask callers how they have heard about your company.

Plan Interactive Communication. The communication you plan to create should support your objectives. When your communication encourages customer and prospect interaction, so much the better. An e-newsletter, for example, containing links that invite the reader to get more information about a specific topic, will tell you about the level of interest in a particular product or service and what prospects your salespeople should contact, for example.

Other ways to induce responses are offers that are hard to refuse, like free white papers, guarantees, or coupons. The idea is to design communication that will generate leads and fill your database with as many targeted prospective customers as possible.

Develop Information Request Forms. Whether it is a business reply card or an online form, make sure prospects give you the data you need before you fulfill their request. There are two schools of thought about screening inquiries to your company: brief and comprehensive. The brief theory holds that it is critical to capture the essential information only: name, title, company, telephone number, and e-mail address. Ask for any more, and the prospect may slip away uncaptured.

The comprehensive theory holds that if a prospect is serious, you might as well qualify him or her upfront and save some telemarketing later. These forms might ask the responder to identify his or her area of responsibility, budget, plans to purchase within a given time frame, or whatever else you need to know. It is helpful to discuss this form and information-gathering objective with your salespeople, distributors, or the recipient of the leads you generate.

Establish a Lead Qualification Program. If your leads are not qualified through an information request form—and often only Internet leads are qualified this way—then establish a formal process. What happens once you capture the raw lead data? If you have already established criteria for what constitutes a hot lead, you can begin sorting. A hot lead is probably someone with buying authority or serious influence, an adequate budget, and a need for your product or service yesterday. A warm lead might be the same, with a need in the next month. Criteria will be different with every company. The way you categorize leads will vary too, but usually you will have groups of immediate, future, and non-prospects. Hot leads, and probably warm ones too, go immediately to the appropriate salesperson or distributor. Future prospects should be nurtured in a database, with multiple follow-ups to see if you can nudge them into immediate prospects.

Close the Loop Between Marketing and Sales

It is amazing how many companies provide fertile battlegrounds for marketing versus sales. When these two departments are not fighting, they are often not talking at all. But in order to measure ROI, marketers must know what sales result from their leads; that usually means talking to sales to find out. When marketers do not track their leads all the way through to sales, they have a communication program that looks like the one in Figure 34.2. Communicators may generate leads and get reports about those leads, but they are left hanging without knowledge of sales.

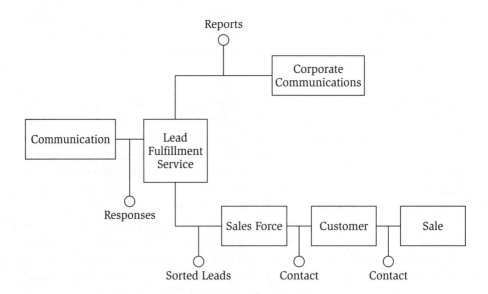

Figure 34.2. The Communication Process Before the Loop Is Closed

It is to everyone's advantage to cooperate. Salespeople and distributors are more likely to do so when they consistently receive leads that are well qualified, which is just one reason that lead qualification is a critical. It also makes the entire process more effective and efficient.

When communicators see which leads turn into sales and even where the most profitable sales originate, they can adjust their programs to create better, more targeted communication. That provides salespeople with better, more targeted leads. When that happens, the loop between marketing and sales is closed, and the communication process looks like the one in Figure 34.3.

Notice that a database is the foundation of this closed-loop process. Developing a database is often a stumbling block for communicators who want to demonstrate ROI. But unless your program is simple and could be tracked with a spreadsheet, a database is critical.

Develop a Relevant Database

Many of the enterprisewide systems companies install customer relationship management programs that include lead-tracking modules. But most are not designed with communicators in mind and do not tie the communication to the sale. They are no help, and sometimes even a hindrance, to marketers who want to show ROI. That is because salespeople have already entered the sales data in one system and will not enter it in another.

Marketers must find a way to import sales data into a database relevant to their needs—one that ties communication tactics to leads and sales. Such a database yields rich information that will help you compare your budget to actual costs, provide a solid rationale for upcoming budgets, give you the data you need to show ROI for each component of your IMC program, and, over time, help you increase the return on your marketing investment—(ROMI).

That is how powerful a database can be. But it takes time, commitment, a hefty budget, and a good rapport with the IT department to develop your own database. Alternately, there are some emerging companies that offer database technology to communicators, so you can outsource this function. However you do it, when you control the information you need to invest your budget wisely, your IMC process will look like the process in Figure 34.4.

This kind of planning based on hard data does more than justify your budget to the C-suite. It helps you find ways to get even larger returns and increase your ROMI on an ongoing basis.

BUILDING BRAND EQUITY

Before you can measure it, you have to know how *brand equity* is defined and, before that, how *brand* is defined. *Brand* has been a big buzzword in the last few years, and recent definitions are justifiably customer-centric. A sample

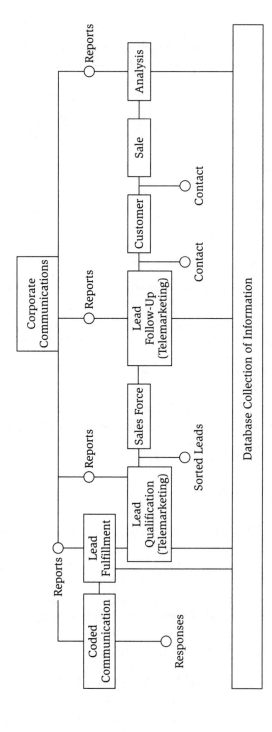

Figure 34.3. The Communication Process After the Loop Is Closed

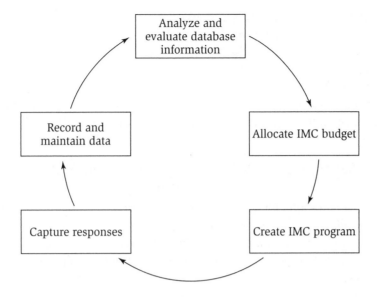

Figure 34.4. The IMC Process

definition is that *brand* is the sum of a customer's experience with a company, product, or service—how a customer perceives the company as a result of all his or her points of contact.

Customer perceptions are based on an amalgam of experiences, many of which are beyond the planned communication program. A customer at a cocktail party may hear an employee gossiping about the company; or talk to a receptionist whose tone is frosty; or see a repair truck on the highway with "wash me" written in grime. These experiences are hard to measure, and there is not a lot communicators can do about some of these contact points. At minimum, communicators should research what customer perceptions are and make sure those perceptions are in sync with what they want their brand to be.

Defining Brand Equity

It is vital to protect your brand because of its worth: "it is a set of assets, such as name awareness, loyal customers, perceived quality and associations that are linked to the brand (its name and symbol) and add (or subtract) to the value of the product or service being offered" (Aaker, 1991, p. 4).

If your objective is to build brand equity—to create long-term value—then your communication, in accordance with Aaker's definition, will be designed to create name awareness, loyal customers, and perceived quality. And maybe you will create associations that will enhance how a customer receives information about your brand, just like a Tiffany blue box is shorthand for, "Wow! There's going to be something really great inside this box!!" Associations like that make your marketing efforts more efficient and effective.

According to Schultz and Walters (1997, p. 143), a "brand-building communication investment is that which is expected, planned, developed and adequately sustained to have longer-term or longer-lasting effects and impact on customer, consumers and the marketplace than those identified as business-building."

Separating Lead-Generating from Brand-Building Communication

While admittedly difficult, and certainly imperfect, separating lead-generating communication from brand-building communication must take place for measurement purposes. It makes sense to identify each group by objective. If the goal is to build short-term business, then that communication should be put to the ROI test. If the goal is to build long-term value, then other measures are in order. Certainly there will be overlap, but this is an imperfect process. Compounding the issue is the time frame of measurement and making sure it corresponds with your company's accounting practices, something you must address individually in your organization.

Measuring Brand Equity: More Problems

Measuring components of brand equity—brand awareness, customer loyalty, and perceived quality—can certainly be accomplished. But if you want to prove ROI of your brand-building communications, then you have a more difficult, if not impossible, task. According to Lenskold (2003, p. 63), "While some forms of mass advertising are intended to generate immediate sales, a level of brand advertising can create emotional connections and brand preferences that last over a very long period of time and may even have implications on how the stock market values the company. It is not realistic to force investment decisions for this type of branding into a standard marketing ROI equation, since the incremental value will be impossible to identify for each investment." However, as technology evolves, there are more and more opportunities for meaningful measures. Schultz and Walters (1997) suggest a complex process based on the value of a customer. The idea is to establish a baseline of customer value and measure the change in that value as a result of brand communication programs.

Also emerging is econometrics, a complex statistical measuring technique. A recent article in the *Wall Street Journal* describes econometrics as the holy grail of advertising: "Econometrics uses statistical analysis to measure the relationship between different sets of events, such as the effect of educational qualifications on wage levels. To determine an advertisement's effectiveness, econometricians write an equation to measure the effect on sales of different factors, including the weather, price cuts and advertising. For the advertiser, the purpose is to help decide which ads to run" (Patrick, 2005, p. B8).

The Hierarchy of Effects

Historically, marketers have depended on measuring changes in attitude and awareness to gauge their effectiveness, and this may still be the most practical methodology for many. In 1961, Robert Lavidge and Gary Steiner, of the market research firm Elrick and Lavidge (coincidentally founded by my father, Robert F. Elrick, in the 1950s), hypothesized that consumers go through a number of attitudinal changes on their way to a purchase decision. Their model, the hierarchy of effects, is based on the premise that promotion or advertising is the force that moves people from one stage to another in the purchase process.

The process begins with potential customers who are unaware of the brand and move to an awareness of the brand as a result of advertising. More promotion increases their knowledge of what the brand or product is all about. Once they get to know the brand, they develop favorable attitudes to the point where they prefer the brand over others (known as *liking*). They then develop a conviction that this is the brand they should buy and make a purchase decision.

The premise behind this model is that advertising and promotion should not always be measured by sales. In fact, advertising helps build awareness and creates changes in attitudes, ultimately resulting in a purchase. Therefore, it is the change in attitudes and awareness that should be measured. This requires a benchmark study before the brand campaign begins and another study after it has been in effect. However, difficulties arise when trying to assign financial value to the increase in attitudes and awareness.

Assessing Customer Loyalty

In addition to measuring an increase in awareness, we can measure customer loyalty, another hallmark of brand equity. There are numerous ways to measure, but one of the easiest is to look at whether customer retention increases from one period—say, a fiscal year—to another. Another good indicator is tracking customer referrals. As the percentage of referrals increases and the volume of sales by these referrals goes up, so does loyalty. Again, it is measurable by comparing time frames. Another good indicator of loyalty is how much you can increase the price of your product or service without customer defection. If you create a brand from which it is difficult to defect—say, software that takes time and energy to extricate yourself from and duplicate elsewhere—you may create a kind of forced loyalty.

Whatever way you measure loyalty, the key is to determine the value of that loyalty. For example, if you can charge a premium price for your brand, what is the value in actual dollars of that brand advantage? Or what is the cost of acquiring new customers versus retaining them? With these kinds of hard data, you can quantify your brand communication results.

Other Ways to Assign Brand Value

There are all kinds of advantages to building brand equity. The question is whether you can quantify them. For example, a strong brand may allow you to reduce your marketing costs, enjoy leverage in the marketplace, attract new customers inexpensively, and enjoy a competitive advantage—all possibly quantifiable. The challenge is to determine how you will assign brand value in your organization, and it can be met successfully only by consensus between marketing, finance, and possibly sales.

U.K. Versus U.S. Balance Sheets

When it comes to reporting to shareholders, brand equity has no official value in the United States. It is an intangible asset that is lumped with other items under "goodwill," or maybe not even mentioned at all. In the United Kingdom, brand equity is added to the balance sheet, sometimes in the millions or billions of dollars. This makes it easier for companies to invest in brand building that will not pay off in the short term, while still giving their shareholders adequate information.

MORE THAN WE KNEW BEFORE

There is no question that whether assessing communication's contribution to short-term cash flows or long-term value, measurement is a difficult and trying business, and certainly imperfect. It requires judgment, especially in evaluating and analyzing the results of measurement efforts. But without measurement, we have no way of knowing if we are achieving our goals. We have no facts on which to base future marketing communications decisions. We have no way to determine if our budget is spent—or invested—wisely. We must measure with discipline, integrity, and consistency as best we can. As one client said about his new measurement program, "It's not perfect. But it's 100 percent more than we knew before."

References

Aaker, D. A. (1991). *Managing brand equity: Capitalizing on the value of a brand name.* New York: Free Press.

Elrick, M. K. (2003, April). *More on measurement.* http://www.datadrivenmarcom. com/moreonmeasurement.html.

Lavidge, R. J., & Steiner, G. A. (1961). A model for predictive measurement of advertising effectiveness. *Journal of Marketing, 25*(6), 59–62.

Lenskold, J. D. (2003). *Marketing ROI: The path to campaign, customer, and corporate profitability.* New York: McGraw-Hill.

Patrick, A. O. (2005, August 16). Econometrics buzzes ad world as a way of measuring results. *Wall Street Journal,* p. B8.

Schultz, D. E., & Walters, J. S. (1997). *Measuring brand communication ROI.* New York: Association of National Advertisers.

PART SIX

THE FUTURE OF BUSINESS COMMUNICATION

CHAPTER THIRTY-FIVE

The Future of Measurement in Corporate Communication

Vicci Rodgers

Measurement is key to successful communication in any organization. No matter where you work, volunteer, or participate, the delivery and interpretation of messages drive action. To direct action in a way that works best for your cause requires the right knowledge about the audiences you are trying to influence. This is quite basic. It is also the insight and direction that a rapidly growing group of successful managers expect their communication experts to help provide.

Business schools have been placing greater emphasis on skills that make good managers and great leaders. Some of this training falls into what used to be considered the softer areas of human resources and communication. If you look closely, you will find that the individuals leading these functions at many organizations did not climb the traditional ladders. Some are strategically placed as part of their management development path. Others are there to bring the functions in line by adding more business know-how and an ability to drive the bottom line. And a growing percentage of communicators are part of the senior management team. They have earned that elusive seat at the table because the function has proven its value or someone at the top believes in this powerful strategic resource.

According to a communication contractor to a major branch of the U.S. military,

We're led by one of the most effective communicators I know. He's a former infantry officer, not a public affairs officer. He sees things from the operators' perspective. He wants to know how to win battles. He wants intelligence about

453

how we're doing as an organization. And he's ready to make adjustments to the game plan as we go along. Metrics and measurement are a big deal for him. He asks the right questions. He has foresight and understanding about just how powerful a weapon communication can be in our arsenal. He makes sure we're using it properly. Success is measured by return on investment, not on press clippings [communication contractor to major branch of the U.S. military].

True leaders understand the value of communication and become better leaders because of it. They have found that it pays off. And this new breed of manager may be better equipped than we are willing to give him or her credit for when it comes to understanding the value of communication. As communicators, we have worked hard over the past twenty-five years or more to educate leaders in our organizations about the role communication can play. We have pounded on the boardroom door trying to get our voices heard. We have preached about the important role managers play in the communication process. We have been there to help our organizations through various crises and new product launches. The stage has been set.

Respected management journals now regularly carry articles about leveraging communication strategies, building communication skills, or measuring how key audiences receive messages. The doors are opening, and we had best be ready to respond in terms that will be understood, respected, and endorsed as part of a strategy for success. Management's increased awareness that communication can have an impact on the bottom line brings with it expectations that need to be managed. Because we can measure just about anything using an ever-growing number of evaluation tools, the future of measurement in corporate communication demands that we guide the process so that we are working within parameters that can result in actionable findings.

A SURVEY OF PROFESSIONAL COMMUNICATORS

To find out what communicators around the world think about the future of measurement, the Rodgers Group, working through International Association of Business Communicators (IABC), conducted an online survey in May 2005.

Of the 275 respondents, 60 percent have more than ten years of experience in the profession. The majority (89 percent) are not entrepreneurs; they work for corporations (56 percent), nonprofit organizations (13 percent), and a variety of other businesses, health care entities, associations, government agencies, and military institutions. Only 38 percent say they spend most of their time on employee communication issues. When it comes to scope of responsibility, 63 percent have countrywide, multicountry, or worldwide responsibility for communication. Almost half of the participants state that they serve an audience of more than twenty-five thousand.

The majority of our survey respondents work in North America, with 60 percent from the United States and 33 percent from Canada. The rest work in Australia, the United Kingdom, South Africa, and India.

Although our respondent group was senior in terms of years of experience and current position within their organizations, 80 percent stated they had responsibility for research for only ten years or less (almost 50 percent for five years or less). Most predict that measurement responsibilities will continue to move inside their organizations, especially as it pertains to internal communication.

While 52 percent have undergraduate degrees, another 38 percent of the respondents have obtained postgraduate degrees or sought continuing educational opportunities. Additional training in various areas of research methodology, metrics, and strategic planning is desired by most, with 59 percent seeking more expertise analyzing results and findings, 56 percent in setting measurable objectives, 51 percent in how to select and use online tools, and 34 percent in writing surveys and research questions.

Despite how far we have come professionally, we need to continue to obtain appropriate training to make the most of an increasing variety of measurement tools, as well as to interpret results and implement strategies that reflect what we have learned from our audiences.

SCIENCE OR SENSE?

Most communicators claim they have a good sense about what is needed when it comes to a communication challenge. Although this skill is a real component of what we do, it cannot stand alone, and it is highly unlikely now or in the future that recommendations based on gut feelings will help increase budget, resources, or credibility in any organization. That is not to say that gut feelings are not often accurate, but more than ever before, we are being expected to have quantifiable data to support the business value of communication expenditures. Another challenge for the future is to strengthen our ability to balance the quantitative with the qualitative.

Our survey respondents addressed the issue of balance in a variety of ways:

> The great thing about the numbers, the research, and the data is that it usually confirms our gut instinct. My gut has gotten better because of the numbers. When I say I think that this is the right way to go, I have done the research and data gathering—it then validates my gut. Makes me more sure that I'm right. Communicators have the ability to look long range. We're always looking at the next best way to do something.

> There's been a dramatic shift toward a focus on metrics. We need to gather quantitative data and have it available whether it's actually used or not. One manager may ask for the numbers while another one won't.

If you want to be a strategic player in the forward movement of a business, then you have to learn how to talk their language. Portray communication as a science instead of merely an art form. Apply scientific principles.

We have more capabilities for measurement, but it remains an endemic shortcoming in many organizations. The scientific part of it doesn't come naturally to most professional communicators. Let's face it, a large percentage of our group didn't go into communication because they love math. When you do it and do it well, it buys you credibility and influence. Those who get it, and do it, tend to be more successful overall.

It has been my experience that communicators generally have the ability to look behind the strategy and the numbers to the human perspective. This skill makes us better at understanding what communication can do. It may not come as easily to our counterparts in finance, legal, and other functional areas. We can create the balance between the research, the data, and the people we are trying to reach or hear. Our challenge moving forward is to keep that balance intact for our organizations. This requires the right mix of quantitative and qualitative research and the ability to analyze the results in terms that multiple groups can understand.

The director of communication for a pension corporation in Canada explains it like this: "If you're serious about the communication profession and want to move up the ranks, take time to learn about research and measurement. Take some business classes. Arm yourself with the knowledge and education to prove your value to the business." This senior communicator has helped establish a center for excellence focused on measurement services within the corporate communication function. Functional area managers from throughout the organization now turn to this internal research expertise for measurement that helps them plan and evaluate their efforts.

Some would argue that the research function does not really belong in corporate communications. But it is worth arguing. The two functions can and probably should be more closely aligned. How many times have you found yourself frustrated because you need a member of the research team to interpret the way a survey is written or to decode findings? Imagine the benefits of having communication experts working with research specialists.

We have more professional communicators joining the academic ranks every year, but we need more. Whether it is a university setting, online courses, seminars, or conferences, we need to continue to share our knowledge with our peers but also with those in other fields. We should be playing a bigger role in setting curriculum, teaming students with practitioners, and serving as guest speakers in schools of business and science. Harvard University's School of Arts and Sciences encompasses Harvard College, the Graduate School of Arts and Sciences, the Division of Engineering and Applied Sciences, and the Division of

Continuing Education. If communicators have a stronger understanding of business and scientific principles and business majors become equipped with a better understanding of communication, we would have a more ambassadors for strategic planning and measurement of communication in our businesses of tomorrow.

DO THEY UNDERSTAND WHAT YOU MEAN? DO YOU UNDERSTAND WHAT THEY ARE SAYING?

One survey respondent said it succinctly: "Words translate; meaning often doesn't."

We need to prepare research questions, present communication campaigns, and analyze feedback with a clear understanding of how our audience is influenced by language (including slang), culture, education (literacy levels), economics, and more. Determining how to segment, understand, communicate with, and influence audiences remain major challenges as we move forward. Here is what our survey respondents had to say:

> Language is not so much the issue as translations. The problem with multiple languages is the cross-cultural element of the questions and answers themselves that can cause interpretation of results to be skewed.

> Because we don't have expertise about every language and cultural scenario on staff, we conduct a survey and then use focus groups for additional clarification. We want to ensure that what we build is what they want and need.

> We need to do a better job adjusting for the more casual use of the language; the slang.

> Straight translation of existing English material doesn't address cultural differences, nor does it really talk to the Hispanic population as they would like to hear it. We are not stepping into their world and selling to them in the best way possible.

> We will be looking to increase our knowledge of first-nations audiences, and surveys in Cree/Dene/Inuit may become important.

An associate professor in the journalism department of a top-tier university explained, "Audience segmentation is so very important. This is the biggest issue we try to get students to understand. We can't bring in preconceived notions about audiences. We train them how to recognize diversity, whether it's ethnic, cultural, gender-based or even geographic. Ideally, we could really use more bi- and multilingual communicators."

As a group, we need to be careful when designing any type of research to make certain we have the information we need about who is responding and to look closely at the demographics before racing to any conclusions about troubling trends.

Designing the research questions, determining the necessary demographics, properly segmenting our audiences, finding ways to better understand our audiences and accurately interpreting research findings all remain challenges around the globe.

THE TOOLBOX

Our toolbox is exploding. We can survey, sense, observe, track, compare, contrast, and converse, and these are just a few approaches we can use to help determine how our audiences will respond to situations and information.

We asked communicators what they most often seek in the research they conduct. Nearly half (49 percent) say they are looking for ongoing feedback from key audiences, for example, through pulse surveys. Another 34 percent say that measuring the role of communications in meeting objectives is their key reason for doing research, while 30 percent say they use research to evaluate the effectiveness of a specific tool.

We then asked the survey participants what tools they have used most often in the past year to conduct research with internal and external audiences. Perhaps not surprisingly, online surveys proved most popular, followed by more traditional tools such as individual interviews, focus groups, and written surveys.

The following measurement tools and techniques that were used most often in the past year to conduct research with internal audiences were (respondents could list up to three responses):

- Online surveys: 62 percent
- Individual interviews: 39 percent
- Focus groups: 34 percent
- Face-to-face: 34 percent
- Written surveys: 34 percent

The following measurement tools and techniques most often used in the past year to conduct research with external audiences were (respondents could list up to three responses):

- Online surveys: 23 percent
- Online use: 20 percent (hits)
- Written surveys: 20 percent
- Focus groups: 20 percent

Using the research process to shape opinions is more effective than ever before. Audience polling during face-to-face or virtual classroom focus group work, or even through online resources, allows participants to see immediate trends and opinions of the larger group. The researcher can address concerns or take discussions forward while the audience is engaged. Throughout this experience, participants are gaining knowledge and shaping additional opinions.

There is a growing use of virtual focus groups to reach audience members in multiple locations and time zones. Online exchanges between groups of people with similar interests (for example, in blogs), purchasing information (such as sales over the Internet), or response to online offers (for example, Webinars or marketing information) provide a huge reservoir of opinions and information. (Learning how to tap into this network and knowing how to interpret these data is something you can read more about in Chapter Forty.)

THE BALANCING ACT

There is no turning back. We have to leverage communication measurement for our organizations, or be prepared for someone else to step in and do it. This may mean gaining additional training and knowledge through a variety of ongoing educational opportunities. It means accessing the help that is always available from fellow IABC members. It also means building critical alliances within your organization and helping to make communication and measurement part of the overall strategy for success.

The manager of communication for multiple real estate boards in Canada explains that the board of directors creates forward-thinking statements, and then it is up to the communication department to test those statements with internal and external audiences: "We measure internal movement as well as comparative data externally. We do research through the year in addition to annual surveys . . . but in bites that we can handle. The global marketplace and speed of change have outpaced the ability of many organizations to define, measure, analyze, improve, and control."

The technology allows us to gather regular, timely information from and about our audiences. This will become more efficient in the coming years, but it will only be as effective as we make it, based on how we design the research, engage audiences to participate, and properly interpret and act on the findings. We may have the ability to reach around the globe to gather data, but understanding what that information means and how best to use it will remain a constant challenge.

The communication director for a large privately held software company explained her company's approach to measuring communication success. She says that her team, which includes communicators and other managers, started with a clear goal: to understand what the media were saying about the company. "We made determinations and set strategies on what we wanted them to say when they reported on us," she says. "We started sending out key messages, then tracked trends and analyzed our share of the voice. We wanted to know what percentage of coverage in desired media included our key messages. We were able to state our position and get our new messages placed without losing ground on other key messages."

In this case, much of the measurement work was completed by an outside vendor, but the internal communication and management team makes the strategic decisions up front and is involved in the analysis.

This communicator added that the organization also has spent significant time educating employees about the messages being sent to the marketplace: "The more successful we are at pushing our message internally, the more successful we will be externally in creating the buzz we want in the marketplace. Everyone needs to understand the value." Her challenge to other communicators is to leverage what is available to you. Find resources, and find ways to associate your successes (or lack of them) with business return levels, whether it is legitimate revenue return or something else you want to measure.

A communication director for a major financial services institution emphasized the importance of getting a frontline sense of where the audience is prior to going into a measurement or feedback session: "Know how they feel prior to the conversation. Then you can throw more specific questions out during the actual session. We use a lot of tracking groups." On the flip side, this same director comments on the use of a 360-degree review process approach to measuring the effectiveness of managers when to comes to communication: "We need to be cautious. We may attempt to measure too much and miss the most important feedback. We need to find the best ways to measure communication effectiveness in our own organizations."

Does the future find us comparing the attitudes of our employees with those of our competitors or other similar companies? Or will we find management teams that are more interested in measuring how far they have moved the needle in their own organizations? We are seeing both. We also are seeing an increased connection between research that tracks and compares employee and customer satisfaction.

Managing the measurement process will be an ongoing opportunity. Our survey participants confirmed that while there is more demand for measurement, budget dollars are not pouring in. There appears to be some reallocation of funds as they move away from outside consultants and vendors and toward increased development of internal resources. But make sure you do not take on more than you can handle. Management is seeing the credible impact that communication research has on the bottom line. Funding will come as long as the expectations are realistic and the results have value.

It is not about counting clips or opinions. It is about measuring audience reception, retention, and reaction to key messages. How will your audiences' future actions make a difference to your business or organization's performance? That is the question that needs to be answered by communication measurement today and in the future.

CHAPTER THIRTY-SIX

Navigating the Infinite Nature of Knowledge

Kellie Garrett

"If the Industrial Age was built on people's backs, and the Information Age on people's left hemispheres, the Conceptual Age is being built on people's right hemispheres. We've progressed . . . to a society of knowledge workers. And now we're progressing yet again—to a society of creators and empathizers, pattern recognizers, and meaning makers," said Dan Pink (2005, para. 10)

Gen X and Y, blogs, social network analysis, storytelling, umbilical cord technology that enables communication anytime, anywhere: these are the elements of knowledge management (KM). They are at once futuristic science fiction as well as ancient human social practice.

Knowledge management matters because the volume of information generated is growing exponentially. We have much more sophisticated and speedy ways of sharing information from an almost infinite number of sources. Ironically, this information explosion, spawned by state-of-the-art technologies, cannot be leveraged without traditional human practices of transferring knowledge. Thousands of years ago, our ancestors used storytelling to transfer knowledge, adding context, color, and meaning to anchor learnings in community brains.

As we move from the information age to the dawning of the conceptual age (Pink, 2005), the communications profession will experience great opportunity and monumental challenges. Conceptual thinking requires the ability to make meaning out of seemingly unrelated thoughts, theories, events, and intangible feelings. The common saying that "knowledge is power" has never been more true, and yet it is the propensity to share, build on, and synthesize knowledge that will differentiate leaders, innovators, and thought leaders in the future. Why? Because it is the application of relevant, credible, and useful knowledge and advice that counts, not the mere possession of it. Conceptual thinking requires the ability to rapidly sift the wheat of knowledge nuggets from the chaff of information overload, and those who hoard their knowledge cannot increase it effectively. Humans are reciprocal creatures. If you share knowledge with me, I am more likely to help you with what I know. We also share our knowledge of our own free will. Understanding who knows what is more valuable than attempting the impossible feat of omniscience. This requires relying extensively on others, because the act of condensing information to produce knowledge and then using it wisely is an inherently social activity. Thus, those who hoard their own knowledge cannot increase it effectively. It takes the engagement of others, wide consultation, and the curiosity to ask questions (many questions) and rethink our own assumptions when faced with new information to develop our knowledge effectively.

As communicators, we now have an almost moral obligation to help with the collection, organization, distribution, and retrieval of knowledge that resides in the minds and experiences of vast social networks. In other words, we have become knowledge managers in the conceptual age. And make no mistake, knowledge management matters.

Knowledge management is a discipline that fosters practices to develop and access knowledge. Some organizations have business units devoted to KM, whereas others manage it less formally. No matter what methodology is used, KM is by definition complex due to its nature and vast scope:

> Knowledge is much more than what can be written down; it is a mix of experiences, contextual information and insight that can be captured in writing, but resides more richly in people's minds as manifested in thoughts and conversations. Knowledge management practitioners describe two forms of knowledge:
>
> Tacit or Implicit knowledge = knowledge that exists in the mind of the knower
>
> Codified or Explicit knowledge = knowledge that has been captured in documents
>
> Tacit knowledge is of greater value than explicit knowledge. It is much faster to obtain knowledge from an expert than by attempting to research a topic, as these attempts often entail wading through irrelevant content before an answer is found. An expert can easily provide the essential context needed to understand the content, or alternatively, he or she can connect the requestor to someone else who can provide the knowledge.

> All organizations have substantially more tacit knowledge than explicit knowledge. The shelf life of explicit knowledge is shortening dramatically. Content quickly can become outdated even when someone is responsible for updating information in document databases. People are not inclined to regularly document what they know as this is time consuming and does not benefit the "knower" [Garrett & Patterson, 2002, p. 3].

In other words, I know what I know. I feel no need to write down what I know as I can retrieve it without effort from my own brain.

A well-known organizational knowledge creation model was created by Nonaka (as cited in Beu and Leonard, 2004, pp. 1228–1231) and his colleagues. Called the spiral of knowledge, it "illustrates how knowledge moves from the individual level to organizational level knowledge. . . . Knowledge emerges from the combination of disparate perspectives and moves from the individual level to higher levels as it spirals through a process of socialization (tacit/tacit exchange), externalization (tacit/explicit exchange), combination (explicit/explicit exchange) and internalization (explicit/tacit exchange). . . . [An idea] must be discussed and shared with others, expanded through the development and testing of related hypotheses, results shared with others, and findings implemented in practice in order for the [knowledge] spiral to continue."

KM initiatives within organizations have primarily focused on capturing explicit knowledge, for example, in documents, data repositories, and Web content. Increasingly, it is recognized that developing tacit knowledge needs more emphasis because it provides greater value than explicit knowledge and because all organizations have substantially more tacit than explicit knowledge. Enhancing the focus on tacit knowledge exchange does not mean that explicit knowledge practices should be abandoned. Both are valuable; however, each requires very different strategies.

To return to a question fundamental to the communications profession, How do we make sense of mounds of information? How do we encourage individuals to tap into tacit knowledge? How do we create a culture of trust within organizations where knowledge sharing is the norm? The challenges are many, and here is just a sampling of them:

- Formal communication channels are the tip of the iceberg when it comes to reaching employees.
- The amount of information to manage is, well . . . , unmanageable.
- The goal-oriented focus of many employees and leaders leaves little room for tacit knowledge exploration.
- We do not know the breadth of what others know.
- We do not know what we do not know.

COMMON KM TOOLS

Fortunately, we have much to learn from KM practitioners, whose best practices can help communicators in the quest to leverage knowledge and enhance dialogue to surface tacit knowledge. Outlined here are four common KM tools: communities of practice, after-action learning, storytelling, and measurement.

Communities of Practice

The community of practice concept is a pillar to realize KM strategy. A community of practice is an informal group of members who come together on a voluntary basis to share knowledge about a particular industry, profession, or area of expertise and to share common activities, best practices, ideas, and emerging trends. Community members generally meet on a regular basis (virtually, face to face, or by teleconference). The community may create a shared library, publish a newsletter, host an intranet page or external Web site, invite guest speakers, develop tools, or undertake special projects. Communities serve as a forum for raising issues and resolving problems, where lessons learned and best practices are shared and group expertise is developed. Much has been written on the organic and sensitive nature of communities of practice. Since they are voluntary groups, experts highly advise that they decide and self-direct the projects they tackle.

A vital component of KM is less formal online connections between individuals facilitated by technology, such as chatrooms, instant messaging (IM), threaded discussion, and bulletin boards. Free-flowing dialogue usually characterizes these communities, creating an environment in which creativity and innovation can flourish. The downside within a corporate setting is that chat cannot be controlled, introducing risk for the participants if the culture is hierarchical and controlling.

After-Action Learning

Operational excellence and innovation are partially derived from an organization's ability to learn quickly from mistakes or failures. A formal after-action learning process, undertaken in a climate of discovery and curiosity rather than of blame, enables the dissection of a project or process once it is complete. The purpose of the discussion is to determine what went well versus what needs to be omitted or altered and to brainstorm what should be introduced in the future. The learnings are documented and disseminated to future leaders of the project or process in question. After-action learning is a way of continuously evaluating the effectiveness of work activities, with an emphasis on identifying, sharing, and implementing opportunities for improvement.

Storytelling

The ancient art of storytelling—is recognized by modern KM practitioners as one of the most effective ways to capture an experience, repeat it so that its lessons can become entrenched, build organizational culture, and contribute to corporate memory. Storytelling involves tapping into people's own experiences using their own words. There is no requirement for the story to be about best practice. The person's reputation, trustworthiness, and recognized expertise qualify the story as worth attending to or not.

Measurement

Although organizational knowledge (and in particular, individual tacit knowledge) is almost impossible to measure, measurement is one of the most important aspects of knowledge management. KM literature shares accounts of companies that use highly complex and costly metrics and models or rely on success stories to prove a return on KM investment. It is difficult to measure intangible benefits, the very reason it is important to do so. Organizations successful at implementing KM typically develop a set of quantitative proxies and qualitative indicators that measure KM initiatives and demonstrate their relationship to business results. These include the monitoring of activities and performance that manifest increased existence of knowledge and sharing of knowledge. This approach is similar to the type of measurement commonly used in quantifying the results of communication initiatives.

WHY KNOWLEDGE MANAGEMENT MATTERS TO COMMUNICATORS

These are some examples of how KM can operate within an organization. Communicators should be naturals at KM, even if they are fuzzy about the discipline. Most have an extensive list of contacts and notes at their fingertips because "you just never know" who can help you with a story, where that quote might come in handy, how that nugget of information from a peer will help crystallize a strategy or an opinion.

The fundamental reason KM matters to this profession is that knowledge cannot be retrieved or exchanged without communication. Without context, meaning, and nuances, information cannot be transformed into knowledge. In an era of information overload, communicators already work as sense makers. They also serve as intermediaries who connect knowledge seekers with knowledge possessors. In fact, Gladwell's description of mavens (2002) summarizes this role: "The word Maven comes from the Yiddish, and it means one who accumulates knowledge. . . . The critical thing about Mavens is that they aren't passive collectors of information . . . they want to tell you about it too" (p. 62). He goes on to say that mavens are "almost pathologically helpful. . . . Mavens have the knowledge and the social skills to start word-of-mouth epidemics" (pp. 66–67). If they are not mavens innately, the type of work most communicators perform within organizations automatically puts them in the know.

The world needs those who can cut through the waves of knowledge and swiftly share contextually what matters to the audience—be that one person or many. It requires people who can tap into both organizational and individual forms of knowledge. There are additional compelling reasons that communicators should pay attention to the principles of KM, and they ultimately have an impact on the bottom line. Well-executed KM principles simultaneously leverage knowledge, understanding, and innovation across companies (and even industries), while at the same time fostering employee engagement. An organization that seeks employee contributions in terms of knowledge, ideas, and after-action reviews is implicitly telling employees they are valued. When a human being's opinion is sought, he or she feels validated and more confident that he or she is seen as making worthwhile contributions. People become more daring, more innovative, more expressive . . . , and ultimately more engaged. Research shows that engaged employees are far more likely to provide excellent service and create an exceptional customer experience. This is the real return on investment (ROI) for most companies.

CREATING A BETTER BOTTOM LINE
THROUGH KNOWLEDGE SHARING

Companies that rely on innovation or customer service to succeed need, by definition, to develop cultures of open communication and rampant knowledge sharing. Top employers are working at deliberately creating internal cultures that mesh with their value propositions in order to increase customer satisfaction and loyalty. Cultures characterized by trust tend to have employees who share more knowledge and are more innovative. The more employees are trusted, the more they want to warrant such trust, going beyond the call of duty to prove so. Trust engenders a more relaxed feeling in which open communication, authenticity, respect, and a sense that one's contributions are valued. This leads to a sense of safety and openness, which has been shown to foster the sharing and growth of tacit knowledge. Finally, these organizational culture traits lead to higher productivity, innovation, employee and customer loyalty, and profit. After all, it is the employee who deals with the customer, and it stands to reason that a perennially dissatisfied employee is not likely to deliver the type of customer service touted by the company. Research has shown that highly engaged employees are more loyal and more productive and serve as better ambassadors of their companies.

Companies can be thwarted in the quest to improve employee engagement by a number of significant challenges. First, today's workers are more demanding of companies than their older predecessors were. They demand a degree of openness and the supply of meaningful context and development opportunities that have never before been seen. They also demand reasons for the work they are doing. (Older workers wanted that too but did not dare ask for it!) Second, service-oriented organizations need to provide their employees with the ability to resolve customer issues when they happen, without a chain of hierarchy that just sounds like stonewalling to a customer. Unfortunately, those chains of hierarchies are often deeply entrenched as rules, policies, roles, and standards of conduct, even in companies trying to be nonhierarchical.

Third, Krackhardt and Hanson (1993) conducted research that shows that companies are composed of both formal and informal communication networks and that the informal networks are usually networks predicated on trust that provide advice to members. They found that truly effective internal communication required that executives understand and engage all of these networks. This is because a key characteristic of informal networks is that their influencers are always leaders but not necessarily managers. Yet across many organizations, the only recipients of key messages are those in formal management positions. Thus, while effective communication presupposes the existence of the correct audiences, many critical conduits of knowledge often are left out of the communication loop because they do not occupy formal leadership posts. That does not make for effective communication.

The significance of senior management having access to such networks cannot be overstated. Not only does it allow the dissemination of knowledge, it also creates the opportunity to derive value from everybody in an organization and provide the chance for all employees to feel valued, whether in a formal management position or not.

THE COMMUNICATOR'S ROLE

Communicators have a major role to play in shaping positive organizational cultures. Working in concert with human resources, we can help to identify the organizational cultural traits required to produce business results and influence senior management to close the gap between the current and desired state. This is easier than it sounds, because the typical employee's experience is not characterized by empowerment, open communication, or a culture of knowledge sharing. O'Dell and Grayson (1997) state that people's "natural desire to learn, to share what they know, and to make things better . . . is thwarted by a variety of logistical, structural, and cultural hurdles and deterrents we erect in our organizations . . . these barriers include: silo thinking . . . a culture that values personal technical expertise and knowledge creation over knowledge sharing" (p. 6).

It is up to the communication experts to change these patterns and convince senior management teams that open lines of communication make for happier, more productive, and knowledgeable employees who value their greater freedom to share, learn, develop, and know more. Knowledge management is vital in this culture, as is a superb internal communication function. While it may be difficult to influence executives attuned to quantifiable business results to care about intangible areas such as knowledge management, communication, and culture, the research demonstrates the return on investment that results from paying attention to these areas. According to the Center for Creative Leadership (2004), "Effective leaders pay attention to the patterns of connectivity that are part of the organization. Connectivity—or inter-relatedness of the members of an organization—either strengthens or weakens the organization" (p. 2).

So here is how you as a communicator can thrive in such a knowledge-rich and conceptual era:

- Foster good personal knowledge habits. Read widely and be curious. Talk to others about learnings.

- Model stellar knowledge management practices: share what you know without reserve.

- Trust first. Model rampant knowledge sharing and trust that it will be used for the common good. Remember, "He who does not trust enough will not be trusted" (Lao-Tzu, 1997).

- Develop your social networks

- Ensure that your organization possesses a corporate content management strategy—the required taxonomy, documentation, archiving, and searchability structure to house explicit knowledge.

- Create processes to update vital explicit knowledge, for example, leveraging intranets and external Web sites.

- Create tools to encourage knowledge exchange: threaded discussions, meetings, or events with cross-divisional employees to create forums for person-to-person knowledge exchange.

- Make it easy for employees and customers to navigate your organization's knowledge, with directories that have more than tombstone data (who is an expert in what).

- Partner with human resources to work on culture definition.

- Organize communities of practice (start small if your organization has no formal program).

- Conduct after-action reviews after major projects. This is a great way to capture knowledge with lessons learned.

- Use storytelling in the workplace, and not just in feature stories and speeches. Encourage employees and leaders to share their experiences in their own words in a narrative style rather than a dry presentation as a way to share learnings.

- Measure the results of knowledge sharing and open communication.

- Develop templates that others can easily populate.

- Online chats or teleconferencing on hot topics are good ways to share knowledge before it has jelled enough to be codified (that is, written down).

Perhaps the most compelling reason for communicators to care about knowledge management skills is summarized by Pink (2005), who argues that the future conceptual age will mean the "revenge of the right brains": "The future no longer belongs to people who can reason with computer-like logic, speed, and precision. . . . In a world up-ended by outsourcing, deluged with data, and choked with choices, the abilities that matter most are now closer in spirit to the specialties of the right hemisphere—artistry, empathy, seeing the big picture, and pursuing the transcendent."

It sounds as if communicators are going to rule the planet—if they get that knowledge piece right.

References

Beu, D. S., & Leonard, N. H. (2004). Evangelism of great works in management: How the gospel is spread. *Management Decision, 42*(10), 1226–1239.

Center for Creative Leadership. (2004, April). *The new work of leadership: Connectivity, creativity and continuity.* www.ccl.org/leadership/enewsletter/2004/APRissue.aspx?pageId = 501.

Garrett, K., & Patterson, K. (2002). *FCC knowledge management strategy: Knowing and growing what we know.* Regina, Saskatchewan, Canada: Farm Credit Canada.

Gladwell, M. (2002). *The tipping point.* New York: Time Warner.

Krackhardt, D., & Hanson, J. R. (1993). Informal networks: The company behind the chart, *Harvard Business Review, 71*(4), 104–111.

Lao-Tzu. (1997). *Tao te ching* (Gia-Fu Feng & J. English, Trans.). New York: Vintage Books.

O'Dell, C., & Grayson, C. J. (1997). *If only we knew what we know: Identification and transfer of internal best practices.* Houston: American Productivity and Quality Center.

Pink, D. H. (2005, February). Revenge of the right brain. *Wired.* Retrieved May 30, 2005, from http://www.wired.com/wired/archive/13.02/brain.html.

CHAPTER THIRTY-SEVEN

New Values for a New Workplace

Christopher Nevill

In many serious forums in many parts of the world, many serious people are discussing and indulging in much earnest hand-wringing about the rape of our planetary resources, the disappearance of the ozone layer, and the overall failure of and blame that business carries in these areas. Politicians pontificate about the cutting down of the forests, the pollution of the oceans, and even the disappearance of the frog population. With the right touch of grandstanding and manipulation, all this obfuscation can even result in someone being elected to the most powerful political office on the planet.

In the final analysis, what actually happens after the hand wringing and pontificating? Not much. It is very much business as usual. By and large the standard of values applied is, "If you can get away with it, go for it!" Too many corporations employ very large teams of lawyers whose sole purpose is to determine what can be gotten away with.

The first question that needs to be asked in our search for new values is where our sense of outrage is. Just how far will we allow ourselves to be pushed before we react? Do we really have to take to the barricades and storm our Bastille to get something done? Do we have to turn everything on its head violently in order to effect change? The cost of that kind of violent change has always been too high. Is this what we must do: Destroy what we have, and much of it so wonderfully fine, in order to create the greater good? Or are there new values—very ancient values—that if we teach them again, could pull us back from the abyss that gapes before us? I know, with a deep visceral knowing, that there are such values and I know with equal certainty that if we simply apply them, everything can and will change. However, we are running out of time. We march steadily toward the brink, and unless we so something, and do something fast, I shudder to think what the results will be.

It is an ancient principle that nothing happens to us that is without point. The point of the event may escape us in the moment. The point of it on analysis and further assimilation may turn out to be quite small and not all that relevant. It will serve us well to remember that size or relevance is merely a point of view, not an absolute. The point of whatever happens to us may equally have huge implications for us; it may be life changing and perhaps even life shattering. If all of us can simply come to grips with this principle, this has vast implications. It means that nothing happens and nothing that we do is without meaning. It means that it is time to learn to tread lightly and with great caution and to pay particular attention to all that we say and do and all that happens as a result of our saying and doing. The other side of this ancient coin is perhaps a little more obscure. It is not what happens that is the important thing. What is important is how our society and we react to the event. It is this reaction that sets in motion a whole series of events that will make the event either opportunity or catastrophe. Hence the need for very particular attention.

A number of recent events are generally regarded as catastrophes. The terrorist attacks of September 11, 2001, and the tsunami wave that struck the Bay of Bengal area are very much in the forefront of such events. Some would argue that the invasion of Iraq is in the same league. And there are others. Without minimizing in any way the human scale of all these events, we need to ask with a vast outrage—and outrage not at the event but rather at the feebleness of our reactions—what we are doing with these events? What radical shift has there been in the way we talk to one another and the way in which we deal both with one another and the planet? There is a point in these events, but if we are to get it and turn them from catastrophe to opportunity, then we need to look at the set of values we apply as a knee-jerk reaction.

There is an odd South African expression. As George Bernard Shaw once lamented, we in South Africa also do funny things to the English language. We have an expression, a word that comes from one of our several languages, Afrikaans. The word is *klap*. It can be either noun or verb depending on context. The "k" is pronounced as in "kinetic" and the "ap" as in the English "up" so, phonetically, you would either give someone a "klup" or you would "klup" them.

A klap is a flat hand to the side of the head, intended to make teeth rattle and eyeballs roll. The idea is to bring the person to a state of consciousness so that he or she can grasp what is going on and what is actually happening. For the person getting the klap, it is not likely to be pleasant. It is not meant to be pleasant. Here is the question: How many more klaps do we need? What is it going to take for us to sit up, wake up, and start to do things differently? For how much longer are we going to stay where we are?

As human beings we are incredibly resilient and can absorb an enormous amount of physical punishment. There is doubt that we share this characteristic with what we call Mother Nature or Planet Earth. It too appears capable of absorbing huge blows. But there are limits that are not easy to discern. The human body can be pushed and pushed and then quite suddenly, a limit is reached; it becomes too much, and we expire. Much the same applies to our psychic fortitude. When we are pushed too far psychically, we often take refuge in madness of one kind or another. There is good evidence for the belief that Mother Nature is also dangerously close to these limits.

The complacency that appears to prevail—the idea that somehow it will all work out in the end regardless of what we do—can no longer be sensibly sustained. What was usual, what was acceptable, or what was the norm will no longer serve. We must look for what are called *new values* so that we can create a new workplace and a new way of living. The wonderful thing is that the new values are not new at all. These new values are as ancient as humankind. It has been said that the universe is filled with wonderful things, just waiting for our wits to grow sharper. What this implies is that it is up to us, not the universe or some other mysterious agency, to make these things happen. The stuff we are so desperately seeking is there and always has been. All we have to do is sharpen the wits and open our eyes.

REDISCOVERING THE ANCIENT WAYS

That is where we have to go: into the ancient ways of thinking and rediscover what has actually been available to us all along. This is both terrifying and at the same time hugely reassuring. It has also been said that it is we who are the enemy. It is us and our attitudes that keep us stuck where we are. It is us who prevents us from changing. It is us who invites what we call disasters into our lives. This is cause for great optimism, not despair. It gives us the ability to do it different. We are standing on the edge of an abyss. There is an ancient tale told by an ancient teacher. He said to his pupils:

"Come to the edge" and they replied: "We will not; we are afraid."

And he said: "Come" and again they replied: "We will not; we are afraid."

And again he said: "Come. There is no other way."

And they came, and they jumped and they flew.

It is time to jump. We have to jump with the absolute certainty that there is a safe place for us. There is nothing out there that is beyond our capacity.

And I dream.

I dream that one day business will no longer be the playground of egocentric, power-hungry bosses who care for none other than themselves and their cronies.

I dream that one day business will come to the realization that if we destroy the planet, we destroy ourselves.

I dream that one day business will realize that if it wishes to make profit, and that after all, is the legitimate object of business, then it must operate with healthy people in a healthy society.

I dream of the day when business will come to realize that in its own interests, it must actively facilitate the creation of such a society and such healthy people.

I dream of a day when business will realize that producing profit for shareholders is not the only responsibility that it has.

I dream of the day that business will make it possible for its employees to find meaning in the work they do.

I dream that one day all employees will see their workplace as a good place to go to and not some place they must endure from Monday to Friday and escape from at weekends and the annual holiday.

I dream that one day business will unlock the huge reservoirs of talent, knowledge, skill, and wealth that it guards so jealously for shareholders, so that these can also contribute to the commonweal of society.

And I dream that one day business will take its rightful place in society and not sit like some spectator and occasionally make some gesture provided that the gesture yields a return.

These dreams can no longer remain in the realm of dreams. Can you imagine such a world where what I have outlined above was a reality? Utopian? Why? You and I created the world that we have. Why can we not create another that is more to our liking? Simplistic? Hence, my own sense of outrage as I recognize how many times I have stepped back from the brink, how many times I have not gone forward and taken the risk, and how many times I have refused to jump because of my own fears and self-deprecation. We cannot afford do that any longer. In our own interests, we must start to make the dreams a reality.

MAKING DREAMS A REALITY

We can no longer rely on government. Government has neither the will nor skills, nor resources, nor wealth needed to provide the basic building blocks required for a healthy, vibrant society. Politicians pull the forelock in deference to both the wishes and power of business. Implicit in this is the recognition that the real power does in fact lie with business. This places the responsibility for making effective change a reality firmly in the hands of business, and business is in our hands. Like it or not, in its own interests, we—business—must grasp this nettle. There are encouraging signs that at least some of the large corporations are willing to do this. However, we cannot leave it to just a few. Hopefully, the process will be uncomfortable. As long as the process is comfortable, it will mean that we are simply doing the same old thing in a different way. What is now required is a radical movement away from the old ways, a stepping outside of what is regarded as safe and normal. It is precisely what has become the safe and normal way of doing things that has brought us to the present pass. Comfort is unlikely to be part of the deal. If you are comfortable in what you are doing, look hard because we may not allow the fear of the inevitable change, the inevitable pain of change, to stop us.

Business can, of course, say: "Why should we get involved in this? Our object is to make profits, profits for shareholders. What you are talking about is the realm of government and society." This very reasonable attitude is also a remarkably stupid one. It is truly time for business to stop shooting itself in the foot. Business cannot, in its own interests, refuse to immerse itself in the society in which it operates. The first change of attitude that business needs to make is for it to abandon the odd idea that somehow it is apart from society—that society and government are here and business is over there.

There is a story of the student who was invited to become part of a learned society. He was asked to present himself a few days early and on arrival was shown to his room and asked to make himself at home. After settling in, he proceeded to explore. As he was walking down one of many corridors, he came across, up against the wall, a pile of dirt, a bucket, and a broom. Until this moment, all that he had seen was immaculate. He looked at it with raised eyebrows and continued on his way. Later he came back to his room by the same route and the dirt had moved away from the edge of the wall and a little more to the center. The bucket and the broom were still there. He went past that same corridor later even, and the pile of dirt had moved even more away from the wall and even farther toward the center of the corridor. He resolved to speak to the relevant authorities at the first available opportunity. He deliberately chose the same corridor the next morning and the dirt was, firmly and inescapably, in the middle of the corridor. And it was then that the penny dropped. The dirt of course was his.

The dirt we all complain about at such length, as we go about our daily business, is ours. For how much longer can we wait for someone else to clean it up? Let us get busy. We must start to seek the new values and seek them in the ancient places.

WHAT ARE THESE SO-CALLED NEW VALUES?

All I can do in a short chapter of this nature is place some beacons that will indicate areas for future examination and consideration. It may be that some of you will become angry as you read. That would be very good indeed because very little happens on this planet without it being driven by anger or outrage. If you become angry, it means that you have been touched in some way; this means that there is an energy that can be used. We can take this anger and make it the driving force for what needs to be accomplished, and accomplished quickly.

One of the first, and perhaps the most important, is for us all to do what is necessary to develop an awareness of who and what we are. One of the things we all are is a teacher. Some of us are better at this than others, but all of us are teachers. There are many ways of teaching, and they all seem to boil down to two distinct methods. The one is to pass on facts and ideas. The other is to teach by our own example. Both are important, and it would seem that for truly valid teaching, both methods are required. So as I unfold these new values, examine carefully your own relationship to them:

• Let us teach the value of fear. What an extraordinary human ability is this ability to be afraid. It is fear that brings right into our faces whatever is actually going on around us. When people say to me, and I come across them from time to time, that they are not afraid, truly I tremble. At this particular point in time, if we were truly more afraid, there would a better chance that a lot more of what needs to be done would in fact be done.

• Let us teach the value of anger. Anger is emotional pain. There is not one person on this planet who can make you angry. They simply do not exist. But what they can do is take a finger and plunge it deep into a sore spot of your own that has never been healed, and anger is our reaction to this. This makes our anger very valuable because it indicates to us what needs to be healed.

• Let us teach the value of pain. This is anger's first cousin. Pain, any kind of pain, tells us that something is wrong and needs to be fixed. It is part of our modern culture that pain is bad and is to be avoided at almost any cost. We have therefore cut ourselves off from our own innate ability to first be aware that something needs to be put right and second and more important, the ability to heal ourselves at all levels.

• Let us teach the value and the power of the mistake. This is an extraordinary ability that sets us apart from virtually every other life form on the planet. What more marvelous opportunity for us to grow can there be than to do something, realize it is not going to produce the hoped-for result, and then go and do it differently? We teach our children that to make mistakes is not a terribly clever thing to do. I say that it is the very essence of our humanity.

All those things that I have mentioned—our fear, anger, pain, and ability to make a mistake—are seen as weaknesses of the human condition. The reality is that it is in these areas that our greatest potential for growth exists. Each, when worked with, has the potential to be our driving force. They are part of the human condition and to fight them is a futile exercise. What we need to do is learn how to work with them and assimilate them. We cannot afford to deny them.

- Let us also teach the value of difference. Much has been written in recent years about gender equality. How sad. Men are not equal to women. Equally neither are women equal to men. Long may it remain so! There is the business of equal pay. Any business that hides behind that ridiculousness deserves to have its doors closed and quickly!
- Let us teach celebrating the differences. Our differences are the source of our power as a species. These days when I look at business with its essentially male domination, then it is small wonder that business is not well. Anything that is that far out of energy balance is going to be in trouble. When I look at our personal relationships, small wonder that they too are ill. For all sorts of reasons that go beyond the scope of this chapter, men have abdicated their responsibility and withdrawn from the realm of personal relationships into the world of business. This has resulted in our personal relationships as characterized by the family unit becoming essentially female in character. These relationships are as ill as our business ones.
- Let us teach about relationships. All relationships, in the bedroom and in the boardroom, are subject to the same rules and skill set. The differences are only superficial and largely a matter of degree and location.

Let us teach how to be aware of the other person's state of being. Perhaps then we can look at somebody who is different to us, and say: "Yes it is okay for you to be like that because I respect who you are. Equally it is okay for me to be me."

- Let us teach the value of work. I do not mean a job in the sense that we talk about work. Life is work. Relationships are work. It was Marcus Aurelius, the great Roman emperor philosopher, who said, and I paraphrase him, "I rise each day to do the work of being a man." Work is a glorious thing. So let us teach that to rise each day and celebrate your existence is an act of work. Business has a huge responsibility to create the environment where this can become a reality.
- Let us teach the reality of the quantum world in which we live. This is the ever-changing world where nothing is certain except uncertainty. In this world, it is we who create the reality we each experience. That is a huge statement. As soon as we come to the realization that it is we who create our reality, then there is truly nothing out there that is beyond our capacity to handle. However, we have been taught, and we are busy teaching our children, that the world is larger than we are and that there are things out there that are beyond our capacity to handle. It is a belief system, and in that sense I acknowledge it. However, that is all it is: a belief system. It is most certainly not somewhere chipped

in stone as some great truth. I have little time for it. If that is truly what you believe, then I must ask you to reexamine the relationship between you and your God—whatever that means for you. Because if you truly believe that your God, if you believe that life, will give you something that is beyond your capacity to handle, then you make that God small-minded, vicious, and quite irresponsible. You have in that moment made life a pointless process. I have great difficulty with that. This is the reality of the quantum world.

- Let us teach that we are physical and also spirit. There are two sides to our nature. We are human beings, and the spirit of humankind must also be catered for in all our dealings, both personal and business.

- Let us teach the concept of integrity. When we say something, we better mean it. Our word is our bond. The only reason that we bring in the lawyers to prepare a five-hundred-page contract document is that we know perfectly well that the handshake as we finalized the deal meant nothing.

- Let us teach impeccability. This means that the very best you can do is all you can do. If you can live by that, if you can live with the impeccability of that statement, then there is nothing more that you can do at that point in time. Can you imagine a world like that: where everybody was simply striving to do their very best simply because they said they would?

- Let us teach that we have, as human beings, an extraordinary ability. We can change our minds. We can set out to do things in one particular way and within a very short period of time can simply decide to do it another way. Let us teach this. If others are not getting the results that they want in their lives and in their businesses, they can change their mind. It is the one thing over which you have absolute control. As certainly as night follows day, if you change your mind, you are going to change your results.

- Let us teach about love. This is almost the last of the new values. First, let us teach that the most valuable person within our immediate environment is the one we call the enemy. It is our enemies who have the greatest capacity to show us our own shortcomings. If we do not listen to our enemies with great attention, we hasten our own demise.

Second, let us teach others that they are worthy of love. When they learn that, perhaps they can learn that the rest too are worthy of being loved.

Finally, let us teach others to constantly have this question on their lips in all their dealings at every level with each other: "How can I serve you?" If we can make that the watchword phrase that guides all our actions and for all our communications with one another in both in our personal and business relationships, then truly we can change the world—you and I.

CHAPTER THIRTY-EIGHT

The Future of Integrated Communication

Jane Sparrow

The first communication book I ever read contained a chapter for each of the different disciplines: investor relations, public relations/press, marketing communication, distributor communication, and internal communication. When I started my first communication role, the structure within that multinational organization was the same. There was a marketing communication department containing advertising, exhibitions, and events. A press office handled public relations. An investor relations groups worked fairly independently from the press office and a dealer/partner communication team. Internal communication was not a formal discipline at that time.

Many organizations have realized that these different communication functions are not independent of each other. Communication disciplines are part of the same function in many organizations today. This is resulting in a recognition that integrated communication is the only way of working in the future, as many small organizations have known for years.

However, although there is an increasing recognition that communication needs to be integrated, an International Association of Business Communicators (IABC) study among 375 senior professionals across the globe in May 2005 showed that only 15 percent of companies currently integrate their communication activity. Although only 22 percent of respondents believed their organizations had definite room for improvement, 87 percent believed communication would become more integrated in the future.

This chapter explores why we are seeing a move toward more integrated communication and how this is likely to continue in the future.

THE DRIVERS TOWARD INTEGRATED COMMUNICATION

Many factors are driving more integrated approaches to communication.

Technology

The world economy has changed significantly in the past decade. Technology has enabled a 24/7 world where stories and messages can be heard instantly across the world. If a story breaks on a news channel in one country, the news wires report it across all continents within seconds. No longer is there a time delay as faxes are transmitted or telephone calls made.

This creates two dimensions of integrated communication (see Figure 38.1). The communication professionals themselves have to integrate across geographies. Organizations that trade across multiple geographical regions will increasingly need to ensure they collaborate on press announcements so that everyone understands the messages, timings, and possible reactions and impact of the communication in their local market.

The second dimension is a need for external and internal professionals to work together in an integrated way. The 24/7 world presents huge challenges for internal communicators because they have to coordinate and act

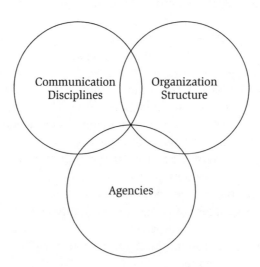

Figure 38.1. Levels of Integration

to ensure employees are informed before, or at the same time as, external stakeholders.

New Competitors

Another key driver of integrated communication is the new competitive threats facing many Western organizations. New entrants such as China and India are forcing Western organizations to review their position and define strategies to ensure they have competitive advantage. This will have an impact on communication professionals because marketing and brand image will be a critical way of gaining competitive advantage for many organizations.

Advertising, public relations, electronic communication, and internal communication professionals will need to work together to ensure that differentiation and brand proposition are powerfully reflected in all media. The agencies and consultancies will need to respond by coordinating and integrating their efforts. Some will choose to do this by continuing to expand into other disciplines. Others will partner with other specialist agencies on specific projects.

Need for Increased Efficiency

An increasingly competitive environment means organizations are focusing on differentiation but also efficiency. New entrants often have leaner businesses, and we are already seeing large multinationals focus on becoming more efficient and cost conscious. The impact on communication is a need for communication professionals to do more with less: less budget, fewer people, and less time. The result will be communication professionals who look for ways to act smarter. One key outcome will be integrating other communication disciplines and departments in other geographies to maximize all the resources available.

Engaging Employees and Creating Ambassadors

Employee engagement is the buzzword of the moment because many organizations see this as another way of gaining competitive advantage. Increasingly companies are seeing a need to engage their people, to unlock discretionary effort, and ensure all their employees are working toward a common goal. Why will this influence the level to which communication is integrated? The human resource group is involved because this is fundamentally about people. The internal communication function sees this as a core part of its role. As more companies see employees as potential brand ambassadors, the marketing teams see a need to communicate and engage employees. In the future, we may also see an increasing need from finance and strategy groups to be involved in planning communication. For example, they will increasingly want to ensure that all employees are working toward a common goal through clear communication of strategy, progress, and direction.

BARRIERS TO INTEGRATING COMMUNICATION

If these drivers are creating a shift toward more integrated communication, why do only 15 percent (International Association of Business Communicators, 2005) of communication professionals integrate their communication approaches today? There are some clear barriers and reasons that the rate of integration is not happening more quickly (see Figure 38.2).

• Leadership support. Many communication professionals perceive their leadership as seeing communication as operational, not strategic. This means that gaining their support to the extra effort needed to integrate communication is difficult in many cases.

• Hierarchy, power bases, and silos. It is not just large organizations that see a barrier created from silos and hierarchy. In the IABC integrated communication survey (2005), respondents from colleges, universities, and small nonprofit organizations cited silos as being a key barrier to integrating communication. The hierarchy and power bases also cause issues. For example, human resources may want to "own" internal communication in some organizations, and marketing may want to "own" external messaging.

• Resistance to changing the status quo. Communication has often been operated in the same way for many years. In periods of organization growth, in particular, why would the organization want to change the status quo?

• Lengthy approval flows that dilute messages. Communication professionals complain that there are "too many chiefs" who want to approve communication messages. Many business units, operations heads, and vice presidents often want

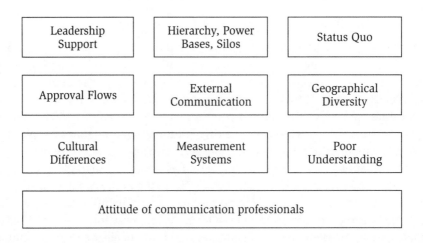

Figure 38.2. Barriers to Integrating Communication

to approve designs and words. This can often dilute the message and make it bland because so many people have an opinion about what can be said and what should not. If the communication becomes more integrated across geographies, it may mean more approvers are needed, and this compounds the time it takes to gain approvals.

• External communication is king. In many organizations, external communication is still seen as the priority, and so it has the budgets, focus, power, and decision making. It becomes more of a challenge to integrate employee communication to the mix without it becoming diluted and forgotten.

• Geographical diversity. Communication groups are often situated in different buildings, countries, or continents. They speak different languages and are often on different time zones. Even with advances in technology, it is challenging to collaborate across such proximity and often involves communicators' changing their work patterns accordingly.

• Cultural differences. Integrated communication can sometimes be inappropriate. An example is cultural differences among audiences such as the difference in press expectations between the United States and Europe.

• Measurement systems that do not support integration. A key barrier noted by respondents to the IABC Integrated Communication study (2005) was that bonus systems often reward groups for their individual or immediate business area performance and not that of the total organization. This does not encourage integration of any function within the business.

• Lack of understanding about the benefits integration brings. People are often so busy working on daily tasks that they do not take time to consider the benefits of working together and integrating their communication approach, or, in fact, to consider the implications of not integrating their communication.

• A change of attitude among communication professionals themselves. Much of the change toward integrated communication involves a change in attitude and ultimately behavior by the communication professionals themselves. Making this change is often challenging and time-consuming and involves one person taking leadership to make it happen. Ideas are often challenged by other communicators, causing frustration and resentment. It can be all too easy to give up at the first meeting.

OVERCOMING THE BARRIER OF ORGANIZATION STRUCTURE

In the 1980s, we saw communication disciplines that were independent of each other. They planned and implemented activities in isolation from the other groups. The late 1980s and 1990s saw those functions being brought together

Figure 38.3. The Evolving Integration of the Communication Function

into corporate communication departments. This meant managers from all disciplines began working together. Indeed, 31 percent of communication professionals still report to the corporate communication function (IABC, 2005; see Figure 38.3).

As we entered the twenty-first century, the internal communication area became increasingly owned by HR. A recent Melcrum survey about how to structure internal communication (2005) found that 19 percent of internal communication professionals report to human resources. This is the second most common reporting line according to Melcrum's findings. This move is coming from the recognition that employee communication is not just about internal news and information, but about involving employees and creating an atmosphere and momentum for change too. However, this structural shift could fragment communication and create misalignment of internal and external messages.

The future will therefore see more virtual teams that comprise members from across the business to plan communication at a corporate and project level.

The IABC *Complete Guide to Integrated Change Communication* (2000) report suggests that communication team members can be from a variety of business areas: for example, communication advisers, human resource members, business unit members, customer and marketing communication representatives, legal representatives, investor relations members, media relations, employee training and development, regional communication representatives, external partners, and, in some cases, consultants.

The organization structure and reporting line is therefore less relevant (see Figure 38.4). In some organizations, we may continue to see internal communication reporting to human resources and external relations accountable to corporate communication. In others, we may see internal communication reporting to a transformation or change office or direct to the CEO. The critical success factor will be for the different communication parties to work together on integrated communication messaging and approaches for all audiences.

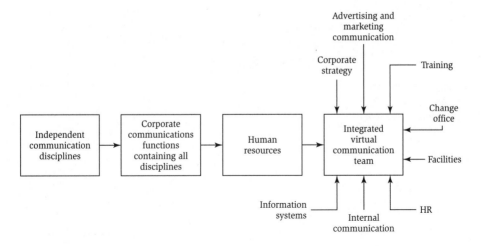

Figure 38.4. The Organization Structure of the Integrated Virtual Communication Team

THE EVIDENCE FROM EARLY INTEGRATORS

In researching for this contribution, I studied many organizations to find examples of early adopters of fully integrated communication. The Royal Bank of Canada works in an integrated way to plan and deliver messages to all audiences.

Another example of a company integrating its organization structure is Sony Europe. I believe the model we use in Sony will become one we will see in many organizations in the future.

THE BENEFITS OF INTEGRATED COMMUNICATION APPROACHES IN THE FUTURE

Communication teams that can break through the barriers and organization structures to truly integrate messages, teams, and geographical timings will see a plethora of benefits in the future (see Figure 38.5):

- Improved customer experience. Integrated communication can mean that messages are clearer to internal and external stakeholders. This means customer-facing staff are often better equipped to answer customer questions and even up-sell. The result is an improved customer experience.
- Greater customer insight. Integrated communication approaches are often two-way and thus give a greater opportunity to improve customer knowledge

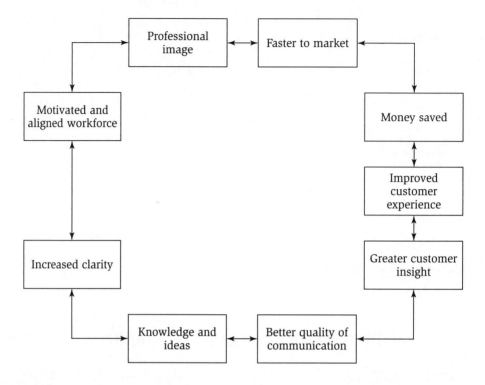

Figure 38.5. Benefits of Integration

and insight. If all communication disciplines and the information systems groups are working together, processes and systems can be created to capture customer feedback through communication and turned into improved products and services.

• Better quality of communication. Quality of communication can improve because all potential audiences and areas are covered. This reduces the risk of misinterpretation or incorrect assumptions being made.

• Capitalizing on knowledge and generating more ideas. An organization that integrates communication will collaborate more, capitalize on each others' strengths, and build on stories, messages, and ideas. This means better quality of communication, but just as important, it can create a more fulfilling working environment for communicators. Working in a more diverse environment and learning from colleagues from the other business disciplines results in a more enriching job for those who want to take the opportunity.

• Increased clarity and message retention. Where communication is integrated, an employee will hear a consistent message from the press, employer, and union or works council. This means the message can be clearer, and it does not feel so much like information overload, because the core message is crystal clear from any angle. It also gives greater opportunity for messages to be retained.

- All audiences are included. When approaches are integrated, all audiences are considered, and there is less risk that one group will be left out.

- Motivated and aligned workforce. Better alignment of corporate messaging to internal and external stakeholders can create a more educated and motivated workforce. Common complaints in attitude surveys among staff are related to lack of clarity of direction and priorities. Aligned messaging can overcome this issue and help employees feel empowered to take action within a framework of priorities so that they feel they are able to make a real difference. Motivated, empowered, and aligned employees are often brand ambassadors who have a direct impact on the employer brand and on sales.

- Professional image. The communication team will look more professional when audiences see that messages are not being duplicated. Reduced overlap and coordinated timing can improve the credibility of the combined communication function or virtual team.

- Faster to market with messages. One respondent to the IABC integrated communication survey (2005) expressed benefits from communication teams having a single point of contact. This has enabled faster message approval and publication. This means there is an opportunity to benefit from faster messages to market, potentially having an impact on an organization's competitive advantage.

- Dollars saved! Increased efficiencies come from messages being communicated consistently and sometimes just once rather than with several people duplicating the effort. Budgets can also be used more effectively by combining resources for maximum gain or by repurposing advertising creative for internal use. Buying power can improve if all communicators are working together to negotiate advertising space. All of this helps the communicator do more with less and show it is efficient and effective.

Case Study: Sony Europe

Sony Europe saw a new focus on communication in 2004. There were many factors driving such change. A combination of a new president in Sony Europe, changes to the European board, and results of an employee climate survey all resulted in a higher priority on external and internal communication. A new senior vice president was appointed from Sony Playstation, and a variety of professionals were placed in senior communication positions to revitalize the Sony brand and inspire consumers, employees, and other stakeholders.

In the employee communication area, the first general manager joined with a mandate to work across the organization to improve the communication foundations and processes and ensure all staff understood the strategic direction, brand values, and what it meant for them. In an environment where the organization was experiencing the most fundamental transformational change in its history, the role of communication was critical.

A key challenge was that internal communication was managed and executed by different roles and parts of the organization within each operating unit and sales company in Europe. In one country there was an internal communication manager within the human resource function; in another it was handled by public relations. In one country, the transformation office held responsibility, and in smaller locations it was a part of the personal assistant role. A decision had to be taken about how to structure and operate employee communication from then on.

As general manager of employee communication, I had seen many examples of internal communication professionals that were expected to communicate on behalf of others. I believe that every individual in an organization has a role to play in communication—whether as a line manager engaging a team or an individual sharing knowledge with a colleague—so I decided not to create a formal structure with a new reporting line. Instead, we created an integrated communication structure that combines all relevant parties in each operating unit or country. The teams share responsibility, plan communication, and execute the plan together on a European and local level.

In practice, this is a team that works on three levels: a core European employee communication team, European virtual employee communication team, and then local cross-functional teams that implement.

European Employee Communication Team

The European Employee Communication team is a core group that operates across Sony Europe to advise, plan, and implement communication on a pan-European basis. They work with business unit heads, functional heads, and members of the European board to create messages about organization strategy, change projects, general direction, and performance. The team also takes responsibility for developing templates and tool kits and transferring skills to managers and professionals outside communication within Sony Europe. They are actively involved in brand ambassador programs, improving management communication skills, and change management.

The approach to communication is totally integrated with their Japanese corporate colleagues, European public relations team, and marketing groups. They meet monthly with each European communication manager and associated public relations member to plan the internal communication activity each quarter and have a calendar that combines all external launches with internal messaging.

I am a member of the European Change team and work with project managers of change projects to identify stakeholders and plan communication with them throughout the project. The result is projects that are implemented successfully with minimal resistance to change.

European Virtual Employee Communication Team

The European virtual employee communication team comprises one person from each Sony country operation. That member comes from human resources, public relations, or the transformation office, depending on the country. The individual is nominated by the country managing director. That group meets twice a year to plan European programs and develop skills. They also meet once a month using virtual meeting tools to share ideas, collectively solve problems, and brainstorm new communication ideas to meet changing business needs. I lead this virtual team.

Country-Based Teams

Each country has a local team comprising a representative from human resources, public relations, marketing communication, marketing, transformation/change office (where applicable), facilities management, and information systems. The aim is to have a team containing all parties who regularly communicate within and from a site. This group works together to plan and implement local and operational communication and works with local project teams. They pull in experts from the European team or other country teams as needed.

The result is that all communication is planned and delivered in an integrated way. Customers, press, community, and employee communication happen in a coordinated manner, with clear messages and calls to action. The virtual nature of both the European virtual employee communication team and the local teams means we avoid power struggles, politics, and message overlap. Integrated communication considers all stakeholders so that our customers and internal messaging are completely aligned.

THE FUTURE AND WHAT IT MEANS FOR COMMUNICATION PROFESSIONALS

The IABC integrated communication study (2005) shows that although many organizations see a future of more integrated communication, there are many barriers to this potential reality. Nevertheless, the opportunities are clear for organizations that have already taken the step to become more integrated in their approach.

This means the future is in the hands of communication professionals who can see an opportunity for integration, either geographically or cross-functionally. Patience, an ability to take the lead, taking steps one at a time, and realizing the process will not happen overnight will all be needed by communicators who want to see the benefits from becoming more integrated in their approach. Starting with one or two specific activities or project areas may be the most effective way to begin, or gaining agreement from colleagues to the creation of a single calendar of messages and events.

The biggest shift needed may not be in the organization structure, reporting lines, or hierarchy, but in attitudes from communication professionals. We need to broaden our horizons and start to better use other knowledge around our organizations. It is up to us to take the lead if we want to see integration become a daily reality embedded in everything we do.

The future will also see the process of communication planning widening to include partner companies, suppliers, and customers. This will help organizations gain advantage in an increasingly competitive world. Only organizations that do this will see communication add value to help them grow and prosper.

References

International Association of Business Communicators. (2000). *The complete guide to integrated change communication: Best practices for major announcements.* San Francisco: Author.

International Association of Business Communicators. (2005, May). *Integrated communication study.* Unpublished report.

Melcrum Publishing. (2005). *How to structure internal communication.* New York: Melcrum Publishing.

CHAPTER THIRTY-NINE

International Communication

Sylvie Testard-Ramírez

New technologies and the Web, the volatility of the stock market, mergers and acquisitions consolidation, and spin-offs are combining with changing working patterns to transform corporate life as we know it. It is increasingly difficult for business communicators to plan for the long term as day-to-day working life becomes more complex and demanding.

Economic, social, and technological changes and corporate social responsibility (CSR) have introduced a new uncertainty and new demands, particularly on those managing internal and external communications. Within a world of fast-paced and wholesale change, what are the challenges and obstacles to communications facing international organizations? Are global corporations accurately anticipating change? How are they dealing with these new issues? What does the future hold?

CHANGING BUSINESS ENVIRONMENT AND CORPORATE PRIORITIES

Regardless of the size or scope of an organization, commercial or nonprofit, a world of factors affect business decisions every day. Globalization, reputation management, and accountability are among the leading concerns for business communicators.

Globalization

Globalization has become a growing concern for citizens throughout the world. Often simplified by the media and associations, this complex phenomenon, which is in constant evolution, affects a wide range of stakeholders. It continues to generate much research, thinking, and debate. Although international corporations and organizations are fully part of this process, many of them are hardly heard in the public debate, which is mainly led by pressure groups and governments.

From corporations' point of view, globalization has a strong impact on capital and production, client relationships, and employee and environmental policies, as well as on relationships with diverse states (Thoris, 2004). Success relies not only on their capacity to identify national differences and to adapt locally, but also on their ability to find common ground and share knowledge and expertise. In this process, good communications and responsible behavior play a key role.

Reputation and Stakeholder Relationships

Research undertaken by Fleishman Hillard Public Relations Agency (2004) among CEOs for the World Economic Forum in Davos demonstrated that reputation ranks alongside the quality of products and services as the most significant foundation of corporate success.

Sandra Macleod, CEO of Echo Research Group and an expert in international communications research and reputation analysis, identified two main reasons for this change: "Reputation and the stakeholder relationships that underpin it have moved to the heart of the strategic agenda. First of all because there is a heightened concern about risk and corporate governance compliance in the light of recent corporate scandals, such as Parmalat or Shell; second, because the holy grail of value creation has shifted the focus to intangibles, such as reputation and relationships, because this is where most of the unlocked potential in businesses is seen to reside" (personal communication, June 16, 2005).

Although the importance of reputation has long been recognized, it is now seen to have a clear link with the attainment of organizational objectives. It is viewed as an increasingly precious asset. Its loss can prove fatal or at least enormously damaging.

However, reputation is not an asset in the traditional sense. It cannot be owned or controlled by an organization. It exists in the minds of a myriad of stakeholders and influencers and is based on a summation of influences, including direct customer experiences, employee advocacy, and direct and indirect communication from and about the organization. A strong international reputation can enable organizations to compete more effectively for customers, for employees and for capital.

CSR, Governance, and Accountability

In the past decade CSR, along with governance and accountability, has been pushed to the forefront of corporate challenges. Closely linked to reputation and stakeholder relationships, those challenges have now largely been recognized as new corporate priorities. Increasingly, all stakeholders—shareholders, employees, external suppliers, pressure groups, and financial and local communities—put greater pressure on corporations to be accountable for their activities and strategic decisions and show concern and understanding for each stakeholder's group priorities.

If, at the very beginning of CSR growth, environment was the main aspect that pressure groups and stakeholders were focused on, the phenomenon has now gradually encompassed other business spheres. As a result, social and employee policies—notably, but not exclusively, in relation to managing diversity—as well as management process and governance have now also to be considered. Those issues are more complex at the international level, since the importance and the meaning of CSR and governance vary according to cultures and national values (Echo, 2004, 2005a).

CHALLENGES AND OBSTACLES FOR INTERNATIONAL BUSINESS COMMUNICATORS

Business communicators will continue to see change in their role and responsibilities driven by the necessity to articulate cultural issues and meet the needs of diverse audiences.

The Changing Role of Communication

In this new and increasingly complex business environment, there is no denying the growing influence of communication. Mergers, especially of consumer-employee-citizen opinion groups, the economic crisis, and the aftermath of reorganizations, as well as globalization and offshoring, are largely responsible for this growing interest.

The evolution and the importance of communication, both internally and externally, vary according to sectors, companies, and countries. Beyond the day-to-day constraints and the difficulties encountered in their jobs, business communicators feel the pressure of change. They are facing increasingly complex issues nationally and internationally. They need to reassess their business environment: step back and define precisely which and how many critical strategic messages have to be communicated, taking into account key constraints that might bias or affect their job. Gary F. Grates, vice president communications/North America for General Motors Corporation, compared internal communicators to tour guides: "Like tour guides, our job is to see the big picture in the context of where the business needs to go, and therefore be better equipped to understand what should and should be on our 'tour.' Like tour guides, we must fully appreciate our audience and what they want and need to see and hear, and then respond accordingly" (2005, p. 2). This analogy can be used for external and international communications as it reflects the need to respond to myriad stakeholders' groups and expectations.

Linguistic and Cultural Issues

Among constraints in the international sphere are linguistic and cultural issues. The great majority of international business communicators have for some years chosen to communicate in English. Although this has proved to be the most cost-effective and convenient way to inform a great variety of stakeholders, it is at the same time unsatisfactory. While no doubt expedient, this choice has had the unfortunate impact of excluding groups of employees and external stakeholders from the communication process. Even if they have a good understanding of English, people usually prefer proximity and exchanges in their native tongue.

Beyond languages, cultural issues have proved to be much more complex and difficult to solve, as culture relates to history, education, values, and national experiences, among other things. As a result, international communication calls for an aptitude not only to understand linguistic diversity but also to accept cultural differences in order to find common ground on which to communicate and build support. This is not easily done from a distance.

This was clearly expressed by Sriramesh (2002) in reference to Asia: "The complexities of societal factors such as culture, political systems and media systems make Asia a challenging place to conduct strategic PR. It is time for educators to integrate experiences from other continents into the PR body of knowledge, thereby building PR curricula that contribute to training truly multicultural PR professionals" (p. 54).

Communities of Interest

Beyond the barriers already discussed, international business communicators are also confronted with different stakeholders' expectations and sometimes strong views on how things should be done. In addition, group priorities for corporations often seem to be far removed from those of subsidiaries and local employees or local external stakeholders and the media. Communities' interest can sometimes be stronger than expected and can be a constraint to good communication at the international level. In this context, international business communication appears more than ever before to be a function that is especially challenging and particularly strategic.

While international communication is often seen as mass communication, in daily practice it requires the understanding of local interests and expectations to be efficient. The ability to select the right information to engage and interest as well as to encourage dialogue and debate among internal and external stakeholders is crucial. While welcoming differences and cultural diversity and building support, team spirit, and understanding from external business partners, the media and local communities are essential. Communication professionals need to work closely with all actors, at all levels of the hierarchy, and exhibit strong business skills linked to local cultural knowledge and ability.

Individual Behaviors

Individual behavior is another challenge that corporations and business communicators face. Changing relationships between employees and employers and between corporations and local populations have created a new major issue for companies beyond frontiers and languages. Today it seems that some young people feel betrayed by corporations because of unemployment, working conditions, and the changes in society.

Businesses are no longer the supportive environment they once were. As a result, new generations no longer have the same loyalty toward their employers that previous generations may have felt. Local communities put more and more pressure on corporations, demanding more responsibility and transparency from top management. Research undertaken by Echo Research (2005a) among professionals on international internal communication indicated that this issue was clearly identified as a major one to deal with in the future.

CEOs' and Managers' Roles

CEOs at the international level have a major role in explaining corporate strategies. Some excel at establishing good relationships with the media, the workforce, and a wide range of stakeholders. Others are still reluctant to do so, apart from when they announce annual financial results or a major merger or acquisition. But good communication has to be ongoing. It is not a one-shot event followed by silence, which can be perceived as suspicious.

Overcommunication can be just as bad. It is therefore a question of timing and judgment; weighing what has to be said, when, and to whom. It is a process that requires anticipation from the time of the strategic decision making to maturation at the board level. This implies that business communicators must be informed throughout the process.

Company culture and the origin of communication within the organization play a fundamental role. The legitimacy of the function is closely linked to senior management's willingness to inform and enter into dialogue with internal and external stakeholders. Echo Research's findings showed that if there is reluctance by management to give business communicators a seat on the executive or board level, there is nevertheless an expectation to inform stakeholders—be it employees, external suppliers, the media and local communities, or shareholders. Sadly, this rarely means dialogue.

Another important point is the role played by managers. Research in the United States and in Europe continually underscores that employees prefer to hear about company news and strategy from their immediate supervisors and that they tend to trust them more than senior management. The relationship established by managers with employees is therefore an essential part of the communication process. The so-called cascade measure put into force in many companies was meant to respond to this issue. However, in many instances, managers had little or no experience and training in communication. As a result, the communication process often failed, mostly due to confusion between the meaning of communication and tools used to communicate.

Indeed, the wide range of materials provided to managers by corporate communicators, including PowerPoint presentations, videos, and Web conferences, has shown limitations. Materials and technology can support, but by no means replace, human interaction. The challenge for international business communicators will therefore be not to just provide materials but to actively involve managers. Bearing in mind that successful communication is a two-way process, they need to become internal advisers.

International Media and Internet: Opportunity or Threat?

In the past two decades, the Internet has significantly changed the way business communicators and the traditional media work. The Web has become a preferred source of information for a wide range of stakeholders. It is also a medium where those same stakeholders can communicate among themselves, and usually give a negative opinion, as good news is no news. When a crisis occurs, the Internet is widely used by pressure groups, citizens, and the media and can be a threat for companies facing the crisis. Too many companies have experienced a local crisis turned into an international issue overnight.

The case of the French oil company Total, at the time of the sinking of the oil tanker Erika in 1999, indicated how powerful and damaging the Internet could be (Echo Research, 1999). The analysis of traditional media and Internet contents showed a contrast in the way the information was conveyed to the public. In 24 percent of total coverage analyzed from the French national press, coverage was negative. The traditional French media remained impartial and gave a balanced voice to all stakeholders, including Total when the CEO, Thierry Desmaret, and other delegates, talked to the media (62.5 percent of coverage contained balanced arguments). Conversely, the tone of Internet coverage was far more negative and critical toward the company and the way it managed the crisis (54 percent of Internet extracts)(see Figure 39.1). Emotions—mainly anger,

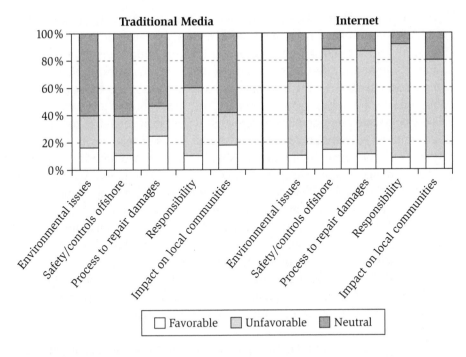

Figure 39.1. Perception of Key Issues, Traditional Media versus the Internet
Source: Echo Research, Dec. 1999–Mar. 2000.

sadness, and desperation—led the Internet debate, which was widely seen and contributed to by analysts, activists, and employees. Total used its Internet site to communicate, but lost the battle against this technology and the use that external stakeholders made of it.

The technology genie is out of its bottle. Employees and local communities often hear about the news before management itself. Therefore, business communicators should pay particular attention to the added value of communication through strategic support at all levels within the organization and a rigorous focus on securing dialogue and building trust.

Relationships with the media at an international level can prove to be a complex exercise. With globalization and greater access to information thanks to the Web, corporate communication has to be even more relevant to all media. In order to ensure qualitative and higher media visibility, groups have to adapt their strategies to readers' interests. There should be access to CEOs and board members to represent the global company policy. Communications should be delegated to local representatives for relationships with national, regional, and trade press.

Why is this strategic? First, companies will more efficiently provide information relevant to key financial partners, potential clients, or local communities with similar reading interests. Second, international media are often a source of information for national and regional ones. As a result, this strategy is more cost-effective for international communicators to reach and support local communicators.

This two-scale approach has become essential because global communication cannot be efficient on its own. The media are as diverse as the world, and Europe is a good example of this diversity. In the past two decades, the continent has changed significantly and shown day-by-day change. With the new freedom for eastern European countries, Europe is now made up of more countries, more languages, and more institutions. The media reflect these new linguistic and geographical differences. Nothing links the sensationalism of Albanian media with a British or a French broadsheet. Nothing alters the reality that Russians can afford to buy only one paper a week or, by contrast, that 80 percent of Swedes read a daily newspaper. Nothing can change the fact that in Italy, the media are linked to politics. In this diverse world, international communication needs to have its own scope but also a close relationship with national communication.

If this complementary relationship is well managed, the media and Internet can be strong allies for business communicators. But in the case of badly managed relationships, the damage to reputation can be irreversible or hard to recover.

WHAT THE FUTURE HOLDS

Changes in technology and business priorities will only continue to increase the importance of international communication. Keeping pace with these changes and being prepared for future concerns through proactive research and evaluation are imperative for continued success.

Training and Skills in International Communication

Faced with current and future complex issues, international business communicators will require a broad range of skills. First, they will have to consider communications as a human science, simply because it is about humans and not about well-packaged messages. Second, they will need to have full understanding of business in order to fully comprehend the economic environment in which corporations operate and to be influential at the board level.

Finally, business communicators will need to receive training in global communications. In spite of the many courses in internal and external communications and public relations, few, if any, however, directly tackle the questions and major changes in international communications. There are no books and no university programs dedicated to international communication. Sriramesh (2002, p. 54) called for a need in international communication training: "In order to prepare PR students in various parts of the world to become effective multicultural professionals it is essential for experiences and perspectives from other continents to be integrated into PR education."

Similarly, more CEOs and executives need to be trained in communication, alongside ethics, CSR, and diversity, to manage effectively in this global village. There is a growing need to educate our leaders, major influencers internally and externally, in the provision of the most appropriate communication response to a given situation.

Measurement, Anticipation, and Integration

Many traditional management tools are not particularly effective in helping businesses understand how they should approach the issue of reputation and stakeholders' perceptions. Those tools were designed for a different age in which corporate assets were tangible and relatively straightforward in terms of understanding and measurement.

In order to find their rightful place in the company and act appropriately among internal and external stakeholders, international business communicators require reliable measurement guides. Those should evaluate the quality of the various tools used (journals, newsletters, intranet, Internet). They must check whether they have reached their target audience. They should also monitor how end users perceive their communication and corporate strategy as well as the degree of satisfaction achieved. Measures must be in place to help provide a clear picture of the organization, linking the findings to corporate objectives.

Business Objectives: The Checklist

- Identify stakeholders' groups and expectations (Figure 39.2).
- Identify communication issues versus each stakeholder's group.
- Define the source of information.
- Measure message impact and accuracy.
- Define channels of effectiveness.
- Identify perception of company values.
- Define commitment to those values.
- Measure employee morale and related issues.
- Assess engagement.
- Link findings to corporate objectives.
- Create dashboards (Figure 39.3).

The apostles	**The good soldiers**
• Commitment	• Commitment
• Advocacy	• Advocacy
• Proactive	• Lack of communication
The spectators	**The anarchists**
• Lack of involvement	• Critical
• Lack of motivation	• Lack of recognition
• Lack of communication	• Rejection of the organization

Figure 39.2. Mapping Stakeholders by Level of Engagement

Source: Echo Research.

Some CEOs still believe that measuring is not necessary because they believe they know all about their business, their employees, and their media profile. But do they really? How can they possibly have a full picture of the international media's perceptions or opinions? Can CEOs or managers trust what an employee tells them? Would this not be biased by saying what their management wants to hear or by the fear of jeopardizing their own futures?

In this complex environment, measurement should aim at anticipating risks to reputation and linking communication to the business strategy. Research should provide business intelligence to help executives and managers master external and internal communication, ensuring a sustainable global future.

International Business Communicators Skills

There are a number of skills for international business communicators to master:

- Manage different cultures and languages to create a truly international culture.
- Ensure all stakeholders understand the strategy.
- Coach and facilitate managers, supervisors, and CEOs to become better communicators.
- Promote the benefits of good communication.

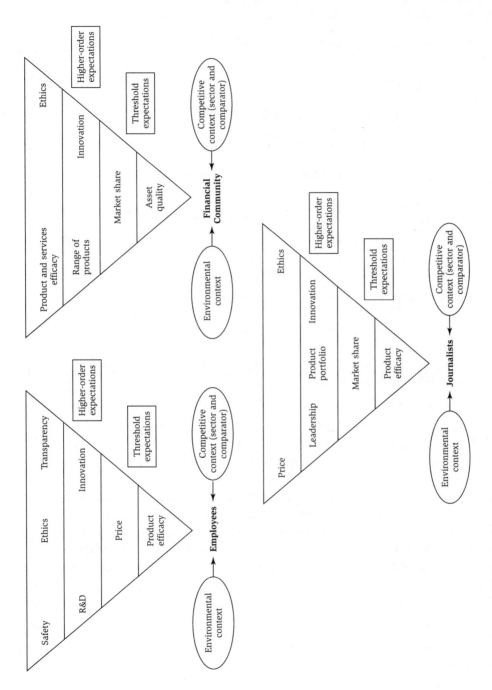

Figure 39.3. Building Dashboards

Source: Echo Research.

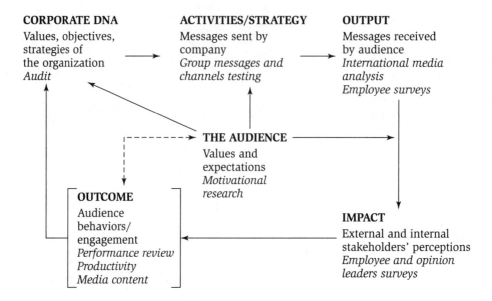

Figure 39.4. Framework for International Communications

- Give all stakeholders the means to be the organization's internal and external ambassadors.
- Recognize and celebrate success!

Clearly, international communication is undergoing major radical changes, and there is no denying the strategic role it plays within organizations. Nevertheless, the function still has to gain credibility among CEOs and executives.

Good international communications unify and integrate cultural differences to get men and women around the world to share and build together (see Figure 39.4). It relies on trust. Business communicators will have to fight to secure their deserved support from CEOs in order to help create a united international culture, as those most responsive to these challenges will be tomorrow's true leaders.

References

Echo Research. (1999). *The Erika Report: A case study for crisis management.* Paris: Author.

Echo Research. (2004). *CSR report.* Paris: Author.

Echo Research. (2005a). *CSR report.* Paris: Author.

Echo Research. (2005b). *International internal communication report.* New York: Author.

Fleishman Hillard. (2004). Research for the World Economic Forum. St. Louis.

Grates, G. F. (2005, May 12) *Perspective: Strategic internal communications. The next level—Employees opt for guided tour.* Gainesville: Institute for Public Relations, University of Florida.

Sriramesh, K. (2002). The dire need for multiculturalism in public relations education: An Asian perspective. *Journal of Communication Management, 7*(1), 54–70.

Thoris, G. (2004). *Les pratiques de la mondialisation: vingt études de cas* [Globalization in practice: Twenty case studies]. Paris, Les Notes de l'Institut, Institut de l'entreprise.

CHAPTER FORTY

The Impact of Technology on Corporate Communication

Shel Holtz

Predicting the future of technology is a fool's game. The most tech savvy among us will admit that we did not see desktop publishing coming or e-mail. It even took a while for businesses to recognize the value of fax machines. Why would anybody buy a machine the utility of which depended on somebody else having the same machine when *nobody* had one?

When it comes to hardware trends, such predictions are not so difficult. For example, it is easy to suggest that the world is going increasingly wireless, or that we will see greater convergence of devices. Consider the cell phone that already takes pictures, browses the Web, and retrieves e-mail. It will probably also become a digital media player, replacing the need for a separate device like the iPod. What is more challenging is predicting new applications.

Predicting the future impact of technology, however, is simpler because we can base our predictions on trends emerging today. This chapter explores the consequences of today's technology on tomorrow's communication environment, the challenges professional communicators will face, and the approaches that will be required to address those challenges.

THE TECHNOLOGIES IN QUESTION

Any technology that simplifies or enhances a professional communicator's ability to communicate also puts the same capabilities into the hands of noncommunicators. This aphorism was not always so. The development of offset printing, for example, benefited communicators but was available to only a tiny fraction of the audience of information consumers. Cost presented a barrier to anybody with a message from using the newest printing technology in order to deliver that message. The same applies to early video production and high-end face-to-face engagements like press conferences or staged promotional events.

The development of the microprocessor—the computer chip—changed all that. By way of example, let us look at the first computer technology to alter the communication landscape: desktop publishing.

Desktop publishing removed the paste-up stage from the production process. Fewer and fewer communicators today remember what it was like to produce galleys of text that had to be waxed and carefully pressed onto a board that was then photographed so it could be turned into a negative that was used as the basis of a metal printing plate. Desktop publishing, introduced in the mid-1980s, opened a number of doors for communicators who could now produce content more frequently at less cost.

But if communicators could do it, so could everybody else. Desktop-published newsletters proliferated through organizations. It was not unusual to see departments producing newsletters boasting fourteen fonts in eight columns on a single sheet of paper. The publishers of these travesties believed desktop publishing put the power to communicate in their hands, obviating the need to work with a professional communicator.

Instead, communication problems arose. There were so many newsletters flying around some organizations that information overload became an issue. Several of these newsletters conveyed conflicting information. Many were difficult to read. Many more were poorly written. Ultimately communication departments were tasked with getting their arms around the problem. Policies were crafted to do away with what we might call "departmental journalism," bringing the organizational communication process back under one roof.

The communication technologies introduced since then have provided communicators with intriguing channels featuring useful capabilities. More important, these are not tools restricted to communicators. Anybody can post a comment to a message board, build a Web site, start a blog, record a podcast. While employee communicators may be able to control much of this inside their companies, any hope of controlling the message with external audiences has been lost.

It is important, before we proceed too much further, to understand the difference between whiz-bang technology and transformational technology. Social software, the category of technology with which we are concerning ourselves here, is transformational in that it puts the ability to communicate in the hands of the audience in a simple and unthreatening way, and it connects all the members of the audience together. They fulfill the initial promise of the Internet.

THE PROMISE OF THE INTERNET

Most communicators ignored the earliest online communication tools. Bulletin board systems (BBSs) allowed people to use a local telephone number to connect to a local service that offered e-mail, file retrieval, and bulletin boards. Several BBS system operators, known as sysops, incorporated feeds from FidoNet (aggregated messages from local BBS message boards) into their systems, letting their local users engage in discussions with people from far-flung corners of the world. Hot on the heels of BBSs came larger commercial online services, such as CompuServe, which was home to the Public Relations and Marketing Forum (also called the PRSIG), the first online destination for communicators. Given the lack of anything else like it anywhere, the PRSIG flourished, attracting over forty thousand participants.

The most significant technology to affect communication was the Internet. Originally a tool for computer scientists and academics, the Internet became generally available to the public, at least those in the public who were aware of it and inclined to figure it out, in the late 1980s. It consisted then mainly of the following services:

- E-mail
- File transfer capabilities, which let individuals upload and download material
- Telnet, which allowed individuals in one location to access material stored on a server in another location
- Usenet, a bulletin board network

The World Wide Web, in its text-only iteration, was added to the mix in 1990.

These services were generally difficult to use, requiring people to learn arcane command prompts in order to issue commands to a server. In fact, an individual's computer essentially connected to the server and provided the user with an interface to the server. The term assigned to the computer at that point was "dumb terminal."

Yet the Internet, even at this early stage, caused an eruption of excited hyperbole based on the notion that it would become a great democratizing force, giving the little guy a voice equal to that of giant corporations. The Internet, pundits everywhere proclaimed, changed everything.

A couple of principles drove the most enthusiastic evangelists to proclaim the Internet would level the communications playing field. First was removal of barriers to publishing. Before the Internet came along, getting the word out required production and distribution of thousands of copies of a printed document or broadcast of a video or audio message. Any way you looked at it, this cost more than the average person could afford. In fact, only institutions (and a few ultrarich individuals) had the wherewithal to buy the delivery of a message or content to large audiences of people.

Second was the connectedness of the Web environment, the characteristic that led its inventor, Tim Berners-Lee, to call it a "web." The Web even became the interface to all those other services. No longer did people need news reader software to access Usenet newsgroups; they could simply go to a Web front end that provided access to those hundreds of thousands of posts and enabled even easier contributions to the mix.

The technologically adept took to the medium like pigeons to telephone wire. Web sites created by enthusiastic individuals and groups proliferated, designed to express a point of view. The fact that your organization monitors the Net for references to the company name is testament to the audience's ability to communicate online, as is the number of "sucks" Web sites (for example, "yourcompanysucks.com").

Some decry this ability to publish, claiming it is a recipe for overload. How can anybody possibly get through all this information? Of course, nobody has an interest in getting through it all. Besides the everybody-is-a-publisher model, the Web has also introduced the receiver-driven model. That is, people pull the information they need when they need it rather than awaiting its delivery.

The real consequence of the ability to publish and the interconnectedness of the Web was the transformation of the notion of publishing, traditionally a one-way, top-down process, into a conversation. The authors of *The Cluetrain Manifesto* (2001) captured the essence of this change in the primary tenet of their declaration: markets are conversations.

Tales of the power of this conversation abound both internally and externally. *Time* magazine once retracted a story based on a campaign orchestrated online to disprove the article's assertions. Still, it was only a small community of people who took advantage of the Net's ability to publish. The average person did not want to take the trouble to learn the ins and outs of software to develop sites. They did not want to figure out where the site would reside. They did not want to learn to navigate the inconsistent and often complex paths that allowed them to contribute their thoughts to online discussions.

So while the Net represented a revolution, the redistribution of the power to publish from an elite few to The People, its application as more than a new tool for getting information and entertainment languished.

A CONFLUENCE OF EVENTS

The first major shift to occur since the introduction of the Web to the broad population is actually a consequence of several changes that occurred simultaneously—sort of an online "perfect storm":

- Audience frustration
- Broad adoption of broadband connectivity

- The development of RSS an online content syndication scheme
- The rapid introduction of social software

Audience Frustration

None of the other elements of this historic confluence would matter if there were no audiences primed to take advantage of them. However, people are ready for a change to their relationships with institutions.

There are several catalysts for this desire to redefine the relationship between organizations and their constituencies, ranging from the distrust that has grown in the wake of corporate scandals (of which Enron is the poster child) to the growing remoteness (or detachment) of the customer from the people in large organizations that can help solve their problems or address their issues.

The existing relationship between audiences and producers of goods and services is actually rather new in the scope of human history. We began movement toward the current relationship with the beginning of the industrial revolution. Consider how people did business before the industrial revolution. Put yourself in the role of a consumer in, say, the 1500s, who needs a pair of shoes. First, you visit the marketplace and talk to others you trust about which cobbler offers the best service, price, and quality. Once you know the cobbler you want to use, you visit his shop. He explains what kind of shoes he makes and you counter with the features you want built into your shoes. He takes measurements of your feet to ensure your shoes fit you. You might even come back while the cobbler is working on your shoes to make sure he had listened and was making the shoes you want.

Now consider the shoe-buying experience today. You visit a store that most likely offers shoes from dozens of manufacturers. The styles, sizes, and colors were determined long before you entered the store. Not only do you have no direct contact with the shoemaker, it is unlikely that you will ever interact with anybody at the manufacturing company. Your contact is with a salesperson at the shoe store or department store. The salesperson has some knowledge of the shoes the store carries but no power to customize the shoes to meet your needs.

Even when customers do deal directly with the company that made the product they bought, their connection is with a customer service representative, usually a telephone operator responding to queries from a database of canned answers. Technical support works the same way. What kind of influence do you have on the features of products in development? Unless you have been invited to participate in a survey or focus group, you have virtually no influence. You are several steps removed from the people in the organization you really want to talk to: the people who design and make the products.

Rather than engage customers in a conversation, organizations have found newer and more intrusive ways to send messages to their audiences. Marketing has become the pervasive communication model, even for nonconsumer audiences such as investors and employees; most communication is delivered from the organization to the audience with no feedback loop (or one that is so formal and limited, like focus groups, that it does nothing to satisfy the customer's desire for engagement).

As this isolation from the organization—this wall that separates customers from the decision makers in the organization—continues to grow and the ability to engage the company and its leaders diminishes, customers are becoming increasingly fed up; they have had enough. Any organization that can find a way to treat customers as partners and engage them in a dialogue that involves as much listening as talking is likely to build the kind of loyalty that has been deteriorating over the last several decades.

Broad Adoption of Broadband Connectivity

When the Internet evolved from an academic tool to a consumer resource, the only way for individuals to access the network from home was by dialing in over a telephone line. Retrieving e-mail, visiting Web pages, and performing other online tasks were time-consuming activities. This low-speed connection inhibited optimal use of the resource. A 1 megabyte file attachment could take half an hour to download. Retrieval of multimedia files was out of the question unless you did not plan to do anything else online—or use your telephone—for hours at a stretch. Even more noteworthy is the fact that users were online only when they needed to be online; when they were finished doing whatever it was they dialed in to do, they disconnected.

The introduction of broadband connectivity has altered the way people can use the Internet. Initially broadband connectivity was expensive and complex, but plummeting prices and ease of setup have led to rapid adoption. Consequently people are able to accomplish a lot more online and, importantly, they are connected all the time. A pervasive connection means users can schedule large downloads in the wee hours of the morning when users are sleeping and nobody is using the computer. The importance of this will become evident shortly.

Recent developments have taken the Net to the next level, a place where the average person can participate. As use of these newest tools proliferates, the dynamics of communication have begun to undergo an irrevocable change based on the fulfillment of the Internet's promise to democratize message creation and delivery.

The Development of RSS

How many Web sites do you read that contain information about which you would like to remain updated? You can visit each site, one at a time, a tedious process of invoking your bookmarks or entering URLs and then waiting for sites to load. Or you can subscribe to e-mail newsletters, assuming the authors of the site make such newsletters available. E-mail newsletters have numerous drawbacks:

- You have to wait for the site authors to assemble and distribute the newsletter, which may not occur until well after the content was first posted to the Web site.

- When the e-mail newsletter arrives, you need to be able to distinguish it from the dozens (or more) of other messages that have flooded your in-box, including unsolicited marketing materials that have managed to sneak in through your spam filter.

- The e-mail newsletter to which you subscribed might get caught up in a spam filter. Would you know that newsletters you wanted had never arrived?

As valuable as the Internet and intranets have become, the volume of information and the difficulty most users experience finding the information they want, and then absorbing the information after they have found it, continues to frustrate most people. All of these issues are addressed with the most important technology to be developed for the Internet since the hypertext transfer protocol (HTTP) was introduced, enabling the World Wide Web: RSS.

RSS stands for "really simple syndication," an apt description of what this simple scripting tool does. At its core, RSS allows individuals to subscribe to Web content on which they would like to stay current. In order to subscribe to content, a user needs an RSS aggregator, also known as a news reader. Readers can be installed on computers as software applications; alternatively, users can establish accounts on Web-based aggregators. A user visiting a Web page would determine that the page includes an RSS feed because there is a link to the feed on the page. This link can be a text-based hyperlink that says something like "RSS 2.0" or "Syndicate." It could also feature a small orange graphic containing the letters "XML" or "RSS."

The link leads to the actual feed, an XML (eXtensible Markup Language) file. The file's URL is copied into the reader in order to create the subscription. The reader will "ping" the site on a schedule as often as every five minutes or as infrequently as once a day. If the feed has changed since the last time it was pinged, the reader displays the new text.

The advantages of RSS are many. Users never see anything they did not subscribe to; there is no such thing as RSS spam. Similarly RSS feeds are never inadvertently caught up in a spam filter. Users learn about new information as it becomes available, not when the author gets around to sending it. And because all the content is displayed within the reader, users can monitor many sites in a short period of time without having to visit the site. Some people are able to keep track of hundreds of sites, a feat that would be impossible if they had to go to each site one at a time.

By itself, RSS presents opportunities and challenges to communicators. The day is coming when e-mail newsletters will be obsolete, driven from the Web by spam and spam filters, replaced by RSS. A feed on a Web page allows any user to stay current on changes, meaning that messages are more likely to be delivered to target audiences. But if users gather all their content from their readers, they never see the branding and other Web design elements on which companies work so hard. But RSS does not exist in a vacuum.

Social Software

The final cornerstone of the transformation leading to the new communication reality is social software. This label applies to the broad range of Internet-based applications designed to enable conversation among people: blogs, wikis, social networking applications, social tagging (or "folksonomies"), and podcasting.

The notion of the "conversation" perplexes many communicators accustomed to delivering messages designed to influence audience opinion and behavior. The concept addresses more than just a dialogue, although it is certainly that. It also incorporates the ability for people to find conversations aligned with their interests, track them, elevate their visibility through search tools, and leverage the shared knowledge that results from these conversations. Taken together, these applications enable true collaboration among the audience formerly relegated to simple receipt of messages.

Blogs. Blogs are personal journals created using a lightweight content management system. Absolutely no technical knowledge is required to set up and maintain a blog, which accounts for the fact that (as of this writing) some 14 million blogs have been introduced. Some estimates suggest that forty thousand blogs are launched each day. With RSS enabling individuals to subscribe to dozens or even hundreds of blogs and stay current without visiting each blog site, readership of blogs has paralleled their growth, with millions of people reading blogs each day.

Blogs, a word formed from the term *web log*, are characterized by a number of features—for example, comments, which allow readers to voice their opinions about what they have read; trackbacks, which let blog authors ("bloggers") to write their own posts and reference the original post that inspired them; and blogrolls, lists of links to other blogs that readers may find relevant and interesting.

While individuals have used blogs to find a voice online, fulfilling that initial promise of the Internet to turn everybody into a publisher, businesses have also begun tapping into the power of blogging. General Motors, for example, maintains a blog called "FastLane," with vice chairman Bob Lutz serving as the primary author. The blog, which focuses on product, has emerged as a discussion between company decision makers and car buyers about the direction of auto development. The customers are enthusiastic that the company is listening to their ideas and issues, and the company is delighted with the candid, valuable feedback that surpasses that obtained through focus groups or surveys.

Other companies have employed blogs to keep audiences up to date on service and support issues. Many, from Microsoft and Sun Microsystems to Thomas Nelson Publishers, have encouraged their employees to blog about work, establishing an authentic human voice for the company that is far more appealing to audiences than the sterile, overreviewed official communications to which they have become accustomed.

Wikis. Wikis are collaborative Web sites, that is, Web sites anybody can edit. Used mostly on intranets for team collaboration, they have also found favor on the World Wide Web. The Wikipedia is an open-source encyclopedia boasting more than 1 million articles in one hundred languages (compared to Encarta's forty-two thousand articles). There is even a public relations wiki (www.thenewpr.com) and an employee communications wiki (www.employeecommunicationsmanifesto.com). The term derives from the wiki wiki buses that run in Hawaii; *wiki* is the Hawaiian word for "quick."

Social Networking. Social networking allows subscribers to these services to make contact with others through the online application of the "six degrees of separation" concept. A network of thirty or forty direct connections can result in access to as many as half a million people.

Social Tagging. The newest of the social software tools, social tagging refers to online bookmarking services that let each individual apply a key-word tag to content on the World Wide Web so that others can find the content using the same key word. People can also view the bookmarks of various individuals. The uses to which social tagging has been put grow increasingly intriguing. For example, project teams are selecting a unique tag, like ProjectXTag, and using it for content they have uncovered that will be useful as the project progresses. All team members can access the tags by simply searching the ProjectXTag. The most popular current social tagging site is at http://del.icio.us.

Podcasting. Podcasting lets anybody produce a radio-like show distributed over the Internet via RSS. Users move the MP3 files from their computers to digital media devices like the iPod so they can listen in the car or while taking a walk, for example. Most podcasts are tied to a blog, where production notes (links to items discussed on the show) and downloadable versions of the shows are posted. As of this writing, there are some six thousand podcasts available, with most listed on any number of podcast directors, such as Podcast Alley (www.podcastalley.com).

WHAT DOES IT ALL MEAN?

Many of the communicators who have embraced social software insist that it is bound to replace existing communication channels. Historically, however, new media have not killed old media; they simply forced old media to adapt.

Traditional mainstream media will not vanish. Instead, they will be influenced tremendously by the collaborative web where the customer and other audiences are evolving from passive recipients of information to active, engaged participants in the conversation.

Communicators will need to continue managing communication as they have but also incorporate a new role: facilitating the free and open conversation between the institutions they represent and their various audiences. This will include active communication through such tools as blogs, monitoring the blogosphere to assess the impact of conversations on the organization, and enabling tools and processes for the organization's representatives, from leaders to employees, to participate in a manner that supports the organization's bottom-line goals and objectives.

It is ultimately a brave new world that will require vigilant monitoring to ensure the organizations we represent are able to benefit from this transformation rather than being steamrolled by it.

Reference

Locke, C., Levine, R., Searls, D., & Weinberger, D. (2000). *The cluetrain manifesto: The end of business as usual.* Cambridge, MA: Perseus.

CHAPTER FORTY-ONE

The Future of Business Communication

Katherine Woodall

For many years communication professionals have talked about the importance of influencing business strategy. They have sought the opportunity to drive business decisions and change within their organizations.

During the past few years, the communication profession seems to have achieved the goal of previous generations: it has a seat at the table and now needs to ensure that its observations, advice, and support can contribute to business success. The future of organizational communication will rest on greater levels of alignment with business goals and measurement to demonstrate tangible results.

This chapter focuses on trends revealed by several major organizational communication studies. An IABC Research Foundation "Future Trends" study (Woodall & Smith, 2003) revealed that communicators were absorbed with changes in their organizations, ranging from major restructuring and layoffs to elimination of product lines, mergers, and divestitures. In short, the priority became survival and keeping pace with change.

From that study, we learned a number of things that are going well for communication professionals:

- Communication professionals are gaining credibility with their organizations (corporations, agencies, clientele and nonprofit entities).

- Communication and organizational priorities are usually aligned.

- Communication functions help managers and leaders communicate more effectively.

- Technology has become more aligned with the communication function and is helping to improve productivity of employees when they have the right information, speeds the sharing of information, and saves costs in certain cases (for example, Webcasts and videoconferencing are replacing travel required for meetings).

- Participants often use Web to provide human resource–related information.

This landmark study also identified shortfalls and areas for improvement. Among the observations, the more than one thousand participants in the study indicated that:

- Communication professionals were too immersed in the tactics of their work and simply trying to keep up with ever-changing business priorities.

- Between 2002 and 2003, businesses represented in the study were actively downsizing, restructuring, replacing leadership, and focusing on survival.

- The impact on the communication function was pressure to keep up with and supporting all that change (including downsizing of staff and budgets within communications).

- The tumultuous nature of their changing business environments left little time for other strategic issues.

The IABC Research Foundation Future Trends study revealed the following key issues that need immediate attention:

- Setting priorities that address immediate business issues

- Demonstrating the value that communication adds to the organization

- Measuring value and results formally—few professionals had formal measures of their value or impact in place, and to the extent that they were conducting any form of measurement, those measures rarely focus on behavioral change

As the IABC Research Foundation study revealed and as communication practitioners know, there is a growing desire to improve the ways to measure communication effectiveness in our companies and increase the value of the function to our organizations and our clients.

To that end, in 2003, Towers Perrin, in collaboration with several leading employers, launched the Communications Effectiveness Consortium (CEC). The CEC's annual study goes directly to employees within organizations, as opposed to the more common practice of going to the communication professionals and leaders, to ask their opinion or what employees think.

The focus of the 2003 CEC study was to:

- Assess performance of employee communication, including major tools and topics, alignment with employee preferences, and overall impact and effectiveness

- Create a benchmark for comparison among leading firms

- Provide an annual mechanism for evaluating and assessing progress

- Provide an opportunity for the study participants to network with peers in the industry and gain deeper understanding behind why some organizations outperform and others fall short in certain areas of communications effectiveness and to learn from those practices

STATE OF THE ART: CONTEMPORARY BUSINESS COMMUNICATION PRACTICES

By early 2004, the CEC had created a standardized communications survey to assess the overall effectiveness of communication. Part of that process included seeking a common definition of what we mean by *effective communication,* as defined from the employee point of view. More than twenty-five thousand employees surveyed during 2004 reported that their definition of effective communication within their organization includes:

- Open and honest exchanges of good and bad news within the organization

- Clear and understandable communication or information

- Timely dissemination of key information (for example, about the organization's performance, external events affecting the business, and internal changes and updates)

- Trusting the source of information

- Reciprocal flow of feedback and information to and from senior leadership

- Senior leaders' demonstration of a sincere interest in employees

- Consistency of internal messages across sources

- Where to find the key information and knowledge one needs to do one's job well

- Senior leaders' communicating the long-term vision for the success and progress of the organization (including course corrections and reasons for change)

- The company or the organization is highly ethical in business dealings

In addition to this fundamental definition of effective communication, in 2004 the CEC study demonstrated that employees expect to hear or learn about the following five primary topic areas or themes from their organizations: supervisory effectiveness, basic tools, the deal, market understanding, and business understanding.

Supervisory Effectiveness

Supervisory effectiveness refers to a supervisor's ability to manage effectively and communicate effectively in that process, which includes setting performance goals, providing context about what is expected of the individual and the team, how performance will be measured, providing timely feedback, discussing individual career development, and creating linkage to other parts of the organization.

It is not a surprise to many in the field of communications or human resource management that the effectiveness of supervisors has a major affect on employees' overall perceptions. One of our findings validated that investments in leadership and supervisory communication are the two areas that will likely make the most difference in employees' experience with their employer.

Consistent with Towers Perrin's 2003 Talent Management Study and two other studies (2002, 2004), the most powerful driver of employee engagement is senior leaders' ability to demonstrate sincere interest in their employees' wellbeing, as perceived by employees. Organizations whose executives are effective in demonstrating interest in their people also are better able to attract, retain, and engage those employees in helping to achieve the organization's goals.

Basic Tools

Basic tools refers to the fundamental information employees have at their fingertips to do their work effectively, ranging from organization handbooks, to policies and procedures, to all types of organizational communication in electronic, print, or face-to-face forms.

Employees' access to basic communication tools has a major impact on their ability to work effectively and how they perceive their employers.

The Deal

The deal is the expectation the organization sets with its employees about the employment experience, overall work environment, culture, and the expectations it has of its people.

Employees expressed interest in understanding the fundamental deal or value proposition of their employment, that is, the fundamental relationship between them and their employers. Employees who participated in the 2004 and 2005 CEC surveys indicate they want clear expectations about what is expected of them by their employers and what they can reasonably expect in return from employers for their dedicated performance, contributions, and results.

Market Understanding

Market understanding refers to understanding the external market in which the organization competes, provides its products or services, and operates from a business point of view.

Employees expect their employers to help interpret changes in the external business climate, particularly as related to their organization's ability to compete and opportunities for the future. While employees have access to news through a variety of media, they still value their employer's ability to provide context and help them understand how well their firm is performing, how well the competition is doing, and what they need to do to improve the organization's overall performance.

Business Understanding of the Organization

Business understanding refers to creating a "line of sight" or direct connection between individual employees, their organizations, and how they contribute to overall performance.

Employees also feel that they need a stronger sense of context for how their work contributes to their organization's success. They want more information that helps them align with the goals of their work groups and a sense of how their work groups fit into the whole. Many organizations that scored well in this area have developed extensive line-of-sight-related communication and education programs. Employees who have been through these programs seemed to be happier or more satisfied with communication overall.

2005 Consortium Findings

The results during the second year of our benchmarking validated what we learned in the first year and also revealed some differences. The most significant gains were in the following key areas of employee communications:

• Effectiveness of senior leaders as communicators within their organization. This could be related to consortium members' redoubled efforts in this area or changes in the external environment with Sarbanes-Oxley and other developments that are requiring greater levels of transparency in communication from executives.

• Communication credibility. Compared to the first year, the 2005 respondents believe messages from their organizations are more consistent than in previous years and employees also have more trust in communications from their companies. This could be related to process and program improvements by consortium members or a factor of changes in the external environment. In sharing this finding at an annual Council of Communication Management Conference, one audience member commented, "Employees have more trust now because the other leaders who were problematic in the past are gone now."

- Work group communication tools are perceived as improving, with a focus on increased group meetings and voice mail within specific teams or business units. Many organizations have invested in improvements at business-unit-level or location-specific communication.
- Understanding the factors that make their company successful and the employee's role in helping to achieve that success.

In contrast, the declines in the 2005 CEC study scores appear to relate more broadly to the management of the business and what employees think about business operations:

- How organizations ensure quality (of products, services, customer relations)
- Supervisors' ability to explain employees' roles in the organization's success
- Effective communication of company strategy, vision, and overall performance by senior leaders.

There have been some shifts in media preferences. In 2004 we saw a strong preference for communicating with print material, especially when it comes to a company's financial results. In 2005, we find less interest in print materials. Instead, we see a strong preference for live meetings and town halls, plus information through the Internet.

In terms of overall declines in study scores, our analysis suggests that to maintain or improve employee opinions around communication effectiveness, organizations should focus on delivering high-quality communication from leadership—communication of core values, strategy, and vision using quality live meetings.

To maintain or improve employee opinions around supervisor effectiveness in communication, organizations should focus on feedback and one-on-one communications skills and on improving supervisors' ability to communicate around issues affecting the business or organization's success, that is, what employees should focus on doing to improve both their performance and their organization's ability to win.

Based on the results, it appears that to maintain or improve employee opinions around market understanding, organizations should focus on the way the business "protects" its product or service (quality) and creating an understanding of how the business is really performing (from senior leadership).

To maintain or improve employee understanding of business fundamentals (how the organization increases sales, if it is in the for-profit category, how it increases donations for the nonprofit category, how it builds constituencies and support within universities and other governmental agencies), organizations should focus on the following:

- The role that the supervisor plays in helping employees understand the importance of their role and impact of their performance (or lack of performance)
- Clarifying the implications for their pay and careers based on performance expectations (short and longer term)
- Information access (where people need to go to get the information they need to do their jobs effectively)

We also learned the following from the 2005 study when it comes to the quality, content, and preferences for communication. Fewer study participants in 2005 believe communications are effective around overall company performance and strategy and vision. However, we saw a slight improvement on effectiveness of communication about competitors.

In terms of aligning the message with the approach, we learned the following from the 2005 analysis (Table 41.1):

- There is a strong preference for live meetings and intranet.
- Print communication (company newsletters and magazines) appears to be losing perceived preference or popularity to electronic forms of communication.
- Voice mail and video/Webcast are strikingly not preferred.

BEST PRACTICES IN EMPLOYEE COMMUNICATIONS

Based on several best practices studies conducted during the past ten years, we have found the following communication trends and practices. First, organizations must craft their communication strategies based on company vision and business priorities (usually an annual process). Second, by focusing on a small number of priorities first and aligning all communication activities with those priorities, communications departments or functions are most likely to be successful. Third, developing and using a thoughtful, well-defined set of guiding principles or mission statement to help make decisions (and adjusting as business evolves) can help crystallize matters of policy and philosophy for communications leaders and their staffs. Fourth, it is critical to have a CEO and other executive leaders who are strong communication advocates and seek counsel from their communications staff.

Finally, in terms of managing change, the following are critical:

- Communicating context (the "why's" and "what's") to employees on an ongoing basis.

Table 41.1. Preferences for Communication Approach by Business Issue

	E-Newsletters	E-mail	Company Intranet	Voice Mail	Live Presentations/ Town Halls	Presentations via Video or Web Cast	One-on-One with Your Direct Supervisor	Printed Material	Coworkers Who Are Peers	
Company strategy and vision	9%	21%	17%	1%	25%	8%	19%	9%	1%	100%
The company's overall performance	10	25	19	1	21	8	7	9	1	100
Business unit strategy and vision	7	18	11	1	32	5	18	7	2	100
Information on business unit performance	7	24	11	1	26	4	19	7	2	100
The role I play in helping my company reach its goals	13	4	0	9	1	63	3	3	4	100
Information on compensation and benefits programs	6	15	34	0	12	3	10	18	1	100
Information on customers (for example, satisfaction with products/services)	13	22	23	1	13	3	10	13	2	100
Information on competitors	16	21	29	0	12	3	5	13	2	100
Information on learning and development opportunities	8	26	30	0	5	2	19	8	1	100

Source: Towers Perrin (2004).

The highlighted items direct the reader to the greatest preferences indicated by the responses.

- Focusing on managers and supervisors as one of the most critical communication channels
- Using storytelling as a way to deliver key organizational messages and reinforce desired behaviors
- Leveraging the intranet for measurement, feedback, branding, and line of sight
- Knowing your audience (what they need, what they understand, and what messages will reach them) so communications can be tailored to meet their needs and have an impact on specific behavior
- Budgeting the majority of dollars for salaries with a third to a fourth of the total budget consisting of program dollars, and other funding coming from other internal sources sponsoring activities and vehicles

CEC participants shared the following ways for coordinating the flow of information:

- Mapping out the "ideal" process for cascading information to each target employee population (managers, front-line employees, and others)
- Focusing on including information in regular, systematic vehicles
- Holding regular meetings to ensure all internal and external communications are aligned and delivered in a manner consistent with the overall strategy
- Using a formal review process (often a council or sounding board) to review employee communication plans and materials
- Researching existing communication methods before launching new channels or practices and testing new methods during pilot or trial periods before expanding companywide
- Establishing objectives (key performance indicators) that communication vehicles need to hit in order to survive on an ongoing basis

TOOLS FOR MANAGERS AS CHANGE AGENTS

Many best practices organizations focus on providing targeted messages and tools to help managers and other change agents communicate both the why, or business rationale for change, and the how, or impact of planned change on people. It is common for these organizations to offer a weekly or monthly online update or frequent face-to-face presentations aimed at managers and supervisors. Managers are equipped with information and tool kits (including CD-ROMs, meetings-in-a-box, video programs, and letters and messages from leadership).

Supporting the Brand

Organizations can support their employment brand by:

- Establishing brand standards and guidelines companywide for more consistency and greater efficiency in delivering communications.
- Developing an internal branding strategy, heavily grounded in the external brand but focused on the employee experience
- Focusing on delivering brand communications through the Web
- Continuing a "constant conversation" between communications and public relations and the external communications group to ensure consistency in clearly defining the brand value proposition
- Encouraging employees to put a face on the brand
- Training employees on how to be ambassadors for the brand
- Ensuring all recruitment-related materials track with the external brand

Creating Linkage with Business Performance

To create a connection between employees' daily activities and how they can affect business performance, many organizations are expert at the following activities:

- Translating messages into stories to motivate behavior, reinforce strategy, and shape culture
- Communicating vision for success in terms of operational objectives (for example, customer acquisition, retention, satisfaction, and revenue and overall performance) and how people in each business unit drive performance
- Focusing on how to free up more of employees' time for value-added activities

Contemporary Communication Measurement Practices

Here are a few effective practices that have emerged from recent polls of communication leaders:

- Measuring communications effectiveness through quarterly feedback from communication councils (made up of representatives from all divisions)
- Measuring return on investment through various types of employee surveys by incorporating questions related to communication initiatives and then tracking improvements in those scores as they relate to specific communication initiatives

- Measuring managers' communication effectiveness frequently against a leadership model (for example, how well they use communication to drive organizational alignment, motivate others, support high-performing teams) to which incentives are tied

- Conducting annual audits

- Looking for best practices through ongoing benchmarking efforts

- Conducting mini or spot surveys frequently used to learn about employees' perceptions about current and specific issues

INNOVATIVE PRACTICES: NEW MEDIA ARE CHANGING THE WAY WE WORK

As shown in Figure 41.1, new media are making contributions to improved communications in our organizations. Adoption and innovative applications of new media are contributing to business communication successes.

Forms of Interactive Communications

- One-on-one conversation with direct supervisor

- One-on-one conversation with others in the company

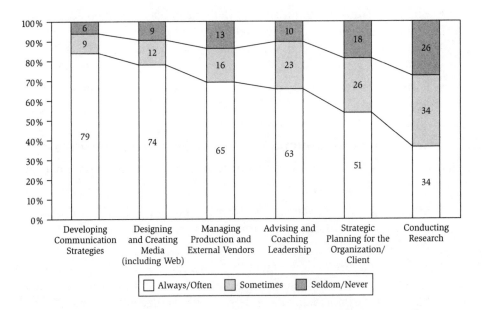

Figure 41.1. Study Respondents' Use of New Technology

Source: Tower Perrin.

- One-on-one telephone conversations
- Intranet link for questions and answers
- E-mail questions and answers link
- Audio conferences
- Videoconferences
- Online "pulse" testing system to poll a cross-section of employees (feedback becomes an early warning for CEO and other leaders); employees can also submit questions or ideas
- Online games to test knowledge of content
- Online communications forums

Examples of Interactive Communications Best Practices
- Fast-breaking and emergency news or information, such as an acquisition, merger, reorganization, or spin-off
- Initial announcement on the intranet, Internet, and e-mail from the CEO
- Intranet link to questions and answers (with timely postings and updates)
- Live meeting with audio and Webcast questions and answers
- Presentation and question-and-answer tools provided to managers and supervisors (usually through a manager newsletter or Web site)
- Strategic business updates (for example, new initiatives such as a new benefits program)
- Initial announcement via e-mail blast
- Live meeting by initiative leader, supplemented with audio or Webcast questions and answers
- Presentation and question-and-answer tools provided to initiative team members
- Initiative details on intranet
- Telephone-based question-and-answer hot line (for example, a benefits vendor customer service number)
- Online game with prizes after the meetings to test knowledge

CHALLENGES FOR THE FUTURE

Communications professionals identified a number of the priorities addressed by in the IABC Research Foundation "Future Trends" Study (see Figure 41.2).

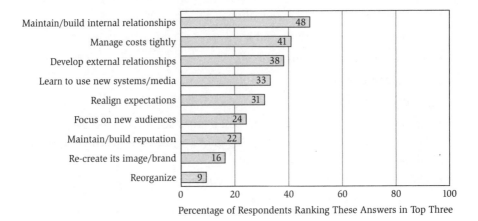

Figure 41.2. Top Priorities for Communication Professionals
Source: Tower Perrin (2003).

Recent studies suggest that communication professionals need to focus on the total communication environment, as opposed to programs and vehicles, to be effective. Figure 41.3, depicts some necessary areas of focus:

• The employee experience: The focus has shifted to how supervisors can contribute to creating the "right" employee experience. *Employee experience* refers to an employee's collective experience with an organization, which drives employee perceptions, behavior, and performance.

• Frontline supervisors, managers, and opinion leaders: This includes giving employees the resources they need; providing guidance and philosophy to help employees make informed business decisions; clarifying what employees can expect in terms of their jobs, career opportunities, pay, and benefits; and equipping managers with tools so they can effectively cascade consistent messages to employees.

• Environmental factors: These include enabling employees to voice their opinions, make suggestions, flag problems, and suggest process improvements; providing two-way dialogue and feedback opportunities; and creating a culture that invites healthy and open communication and a sincere expression of opinions.

• Networking, dialogue, and the grapevine: This includes using informal influencers; participating in hallway conversations; using informal channels within the organization (networking, dialogue, the grapevine); providing informal networking opportunities; conducting regular informal communication activities; and providing opportunities for informal exchange of ideas.

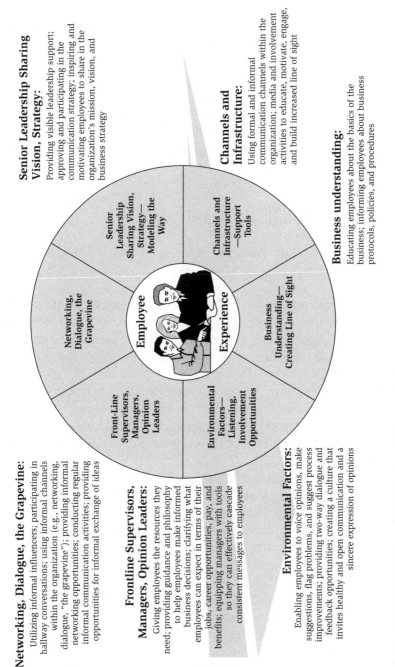

Senior Leadership Sharing Vision, Strategy:
Providing visible leadership support; approving and participating in the communication strategy; inspiring and motivating employees to share in the organization's mission, vision, and business strategy

Channels and Infrastructure:
Using formal and informal communication channels within the organization; media and involvement activities to educate, motivate, engage, and build increased line of sight

Business understanding:
Educating employees about the basics of the business; informing employees about business protocols, policies, and procedures

Networking, Dialogue, the Grapevine:
Utilizing informal influencers; participating in hallway conversations; using informal channels within the organization (e.g., networking, dialogue, "the grapevine"); providing informal networking opportunities; conducting regular informal communication activities; providing opportunities for informal exchange of ideas

Frontline Supervisors, Managers, Opinion Leaders:
Giving employees the resources they need; providing guidance and philosophy to help employees make informed business decisions; clarifying what employees can expect in terms of their jobs, career opportunities, pay, and benefits; equipping managers with tools so they can effectively cascade consistent messages to employees

Environmental Factors:
Enabling employees to voice opinions, make suggestions, flag problems, and suggest process improvements; providing two-way dialogue and feedback opportunities; creating a culture that invites healthy and open communication and a sincere expression of opinions

Figure 41.3. Components of Organizational Communication

Source: Tower Perrin (2004).

- Senior leadership sharing vision and strategy: This includes providing visible leadership support; approving and participating in the communication strategy; and inspiring and motivating employees to share in the organization's mission, vision, and business strategy.
- Channels and infrastructure: These include using formal and informal communication channels within the organization; and media and involvement activities to educate, motive, engage, and build increased line of sight.
- Business understanding: This includes educating employees about the basics of the business and informing employees about business protocols, policies, and procedures.

PREDICTIONS AND ADVICE

In summarizing the research reviewed for this chapter, here are the issues raised most often and some advice for handling them.

1. *Chief communication officer.* Communication professionals need to become gurus of technology themselves or at minimum form effective alliances with their information technology organizations. A trend seems to be emerging of blending communication, marketing, organizational development, and information technology.

2. *New media—Blogs, instantaneous messaging, direct to consumer.* Every new technology presents added complexity of the media we must master and maintain. The emergence of blogs suggests another avenue for employees, customers, and various segments of your organization and its many constituencies to communicate.

3. *Measurement/ROI.* There is an increased focus on and acceptance of the importance of measurement for the function. I predict and hope that the next phase of measurement will provide even more concrete connections to business results. If communication professionals want to be in the executive sessions, then they will need to justify their budgets as rigorously as any line leaders and as effectively as any CFO.

4. *Call to action: Think like a CEO, know the numbers like a CFO, be as informed about new technology as the CIO.* I predict that the renaissance of the past will reemerge for communications professionals and that there will be a demand for leaders in communication who can think even more broadly about their roles and their work.

5. *Add value: Know your audiences, and do not be afraid to tell leaders what employees and other constituencies are really thinking, feeling, saying, and predicting how they may act (on such matters as turnover, strikes, and brand*

ambassadors). Part of the advisory nature of our roles will require us to deliver good and bad news effectively and on a regular basis to our peers in leadership. With the blurring of the lines of our work with that of other functions and internal communication overlapping increasingly external information, we will need to be able to use measurement and other trend data at our disposal to predict behavior of all constituencies.

6. *Shake it up.* Do not be afraid of change. This includes embracing and learning new skills ourselves and being willing and able to rotate our own teams to build their skills, knowledge, ability, experience, expertise, and capability for growth.

7. *Know yourself and your organization.* This is a good time to assess ourselves, our communications programs, and our organizations and to be willing to recommend bold new changes if what we find does not serve us well. This may include retooling ourselves.

8. *Listen and keep listening.* Communication professionals must listen effectively to the organization to anticipate employee opinions, reactions, and challenges on the horizon. In effect, we are the eyes and ears of our organizations and may be in the rare positions of sharing information with other executives that they cannot or do not receive candidly from other sources but which they need to lead effectively. Major studies predict there will be gaps in skilled knowledge workers in the future. Employees will remember how they were treated when times were tough as they consider where they wish to work during other phases of their careers.

9. *Teach your staff; transfer those skills.* We will all be more successful by devoting portions of our time to teaching the skills we learn. This includes internal development of our own staff and running effective communication training sessions for our organizations.

10. *A brave new world.* No one really knows what the future holds. I am optimistic that times will be positive for those who are broad-minded about change, are willing to change and learn new skills themselves, and can teach others.

References

Towers Perrin. (2002, October 21). *Talent report: How leading organizations manage talent.* Stamford, CT: Towers Perrin.

Towers Perrin. (2003). *Working today: Understanding what drives employee engagement.* Stamford, CT: Towers Perrin.

Towers Perrin. (2004, July 13). *2004 European talent survey.* Stamford, CT: Towers Perrin.

Woodall, K., & Smith, S. (2003). What will the future hold? *Communications World, 20*(2), 18–20.

INDEX

About the International Association of Business Communicators

The International Association of Business Communicators (IABC) is a global network of over thirteen thousand communication professionals in sixty-seven countries, one hundred chapters, and ten thousand organizations. Established in 1970, IABC ensures that its members have the skills and resources to progress in their careers, develop and share best practices, set standards of excellence, build credibility and respect for the profession, and unite as a community. IABC members practice the disciplines of corporate communication, public relations, employee communication, marketing communication, media relations, community relations, public affairs, investor relations, and government relations.

Programs

IABC sponsors several conferences throughout the year in addition to its annual international conference. To further the education of communication professionals, IABC offers monthly teleseminars and Web seminars. IABC honors the best in the profession with the Gold Quill Awards program and the accreditation program. IABC also maintains an online job board.

Publications

The publishing division of IABC offers books, manuals, and communication templates on a number of organizational communication topics. IABC also publishes the award-winning, bimonthly magazine, *Communication World,* and a monthly online newsletter, *CW Bulletin.*

Research

The IABC Research Foundation is a nonprofit corporation dedicated to the support and advancement of organizational communication by delivering research findings vital to the profession. The Foundation translates leading-edge communication theory into real-world practice, helping communicators be effective and visionary in their work. Founded in 1970, the Foundation is building a research portfolio aligned with a new research agenda. The Foundation offers grants for communication research in support of this agenda. Learn more about the International Association of Business Communicators at *www.iabc.com*